Financial Planning: Process and Environment

Individual Medical Expense Insurance
Thomas P. O'Hare

Meeting the Financial Need of Long-Term Care
Burton T. Beam, Jr., and Thomas P. O'Hare

Financial Planning: Process and Environment
Don A. Taylor and C. Bruce Worsham (eds.)

Fundamentals of Insurance Planning
Burton T. Beam, Jr., and Eric A. Wiening

Fundamentals of Income Taxation
James F. Ivers III (ed.)

McGill's Life Insurance
Edward E. Graves (ed.)

McGill's Legal Aspects of Life Insurance
Edward E. Graves and Burke A. Christensen (eds.)

Group Benefits: Basic Concepts and Alternatives
Burton T. Beam, Jr.

Planning for Retirement Needs
David A. Littell and Kenn Beam Tacchino

Fundamentals of Investments for Financial Planning
Walt J. Woerheide and David M. Cordell

Fundamentals of Estate Planning
Constance J. Fontaine

Estate Planning Applications
Ted Kurlowicz

Planning for Business Owners and Professionals
Ted Kurlowicz, James F. Ivers III, and John J. McFadden

Financial Planning Applications
Thomas P. Langdon and William J. Ruckstuhl

Advanced Topics in Group Benefits
Burton T. Beam, Jr., and Thomas P. O'Hare (eds.)

Executive Compensation
John J. McFadden

Health and Long-Term Care Financing for Seniors
Burton T. Beam, Jr., and Thomas P. O'Hare

Financial Decisions for Retirement
David A. Littell and Kenn Beam Tacchino

Huebner School Series

Financial Planning: Process and Environment
Second Edition

Don A. Taylor, Editor
C. Bruce Worsham, Editor

The American College Press/*Bryn Mawr, Pennsylvania*

This publication is designed to provide accurate and authoritative information about the subject covered. While every precaution has been taken in the preparation of this material, the editors and The American College® assume no liability for damages resulting from the use of the information contained in this publication. The American College is not engaged in rendering legal, accounting, or other professional advice. If legal or other expert advice is required, the services of an appropriate professional should be sought.

Contents

Preface

In the not too distant past those who provided professional education for financial planning practitioners had difficulty finding relevant literature on the subject. While in recent years great strides have been made in filling this literature gap, much remains to be done. This textbook attempts to fill that gap beginning with chapter one, which introduces the six-step financial planning process. This process is the foundation on which the financial planning profession is built, and it provides a framework around which financial planning practitioners develop comprehensive plans for their clients.

After a thorough discussion in chapter one about what the financial planning process is and how to use it to solve the client's financial problems, the 10 chapters that follow explore the basic tools and techniques used in support of the financial planning process as well as the ethical, regulatory, and economic environment in which financial planning practitioners operate. Briefly, chapter two focuses on how to communicate effectively with the client; chapter three explains the role of ethics and professionalism in dealing with the client; chapter four analyzes the concept of risk tolerance and explains its role in shaping client attitudes toward risk; chapter five explains the importance of fact finders in gathering information about the client and also shows the critical role played by personal financial statements in analyzing the client's financial situation; chapters six and seven explain how to use the HP-10BII financial calculator to solve time-value-of-money problems; chapter eight applies the financial planning process to several common financial problems including that of education funding; chapters nine and ten discuss the regulatory and economic environment within which financial planning is conducted.

New to this edition is chapter 11, which discusses financial planning for special circumstances.

While it is entirely up to you, the reader, to decide if our effort to help fill the financial planning literature gap with suitable materials is a success, we hope at the very least that we have helped to shape your understanding of the financial planning process and its environment.

Don A. Taylor
C. Bruce Worsham

Acknowledgments

The publication of this textbook involved the contributions of many individuals. We are especially grateful to the following individuals for their work in authoring and/or editing materials used in this textbook:

- Thomas M. Brinker, Jr., LLM, CPA, professor and Accounting Program Coordinator at Arcadia University for his editing of and contributions to chapter 11
- Ronald F. Duska, the Charles Lamont Post Chair of Ethics and the Professions and Professor of Ethics at The American College, for his contributions to chapter 3
- Robert W. Cooper, the Employers Mutual Distinguished Professor of Insurance at Drake University and a former faculty member of The American College, for his contributions to chapters 1, 5, 6, 7, and 8
- David M. Cordell, Associate Professor of Personal Financial Planning at Texas Tech University and a former faculty member of The American College, for his contributions to chapters 1, 5, 6, 7, 8, and 9
- the late Robert M. Crowe, a former faculty member of The American College, for his contributions to chapters 1, 5, 6, and 7
- Dale S. Johnson, a former faculty member of The American College, for his contributions to chapters 2 and 5
- Jeffrey Kelvin, a former faculty member of The American College, for his contributions to chapter 9
- Lewis B. Morgan, Professor of Counseling and Human Services at Villanova University, for his contributions to chapter 2
- Michael J. Roszkowski, Director of Institutional Research at LaSalle University, for his contributions to chapter 4

We would also like to thank the following individuals from The American College for their contributions:

- Joe Brennan (cover design)
- Patricia Cheers (permissions and proofreading)
- Susan Doherty (proofreading)
- Jane Hassinger (graphics)
- Lynn Hayes (page layout)
- Evelyn Rice (production assistance)

- Very special thanks to Maria Marlowe who spent countless hours poring over the entire manuscript trying to decipher our esoteric gibberish. Her outstanding editing skills and unwavering commitment to excellence made an unmistakable imprint on the textbook. It is no exaggeration to say that this textbook could not have been done without her; such is our appreciation to Maria.
- Very special thanks to Charlene McNulty who typed the brunt of the manuscript. Typically she typed, retyped, and retyped each chapter again and again as we changed, rechanged, and rechanged the wording again and again. Her patience in following our arrows and reading our scribbles was commendable, as was her grace under pressure in learning a new computer technique just days before this textbook went to print; such is our appreciation to Charlene.

Finally, we would like to thank H. King McGlaughon, Jr., former executive vice president at The American College and editor of the Huebner School Series, for providing the support and encouragement necessary to complete this project and to keep the Series, of which this textbook is a part, at the highest standards.

All of these individuals made this a better textbook, and we are grateful. However, in spite of the help of all these fine folks, some errors have undoubtedly been successful in eluding our eyes. For these we are solely responsible. At the same time, however, we accept full credit for giving those readers who find these errors the exhilarating intellectual experience produced by such discovery. Nevertheless, each of the editors acknowledges that any errors discovered are the fault of the other editor.

Don A. Taylor
C. Bruce Worsham

About the Editors

Don A. Taylor, CFA, is associate professor of finance at The American College. Dr. Taylor received his undergraduate degree in finance from The Pennsylvania State University. He earned his master's degree at the Rochester Institute of Technology and his PhD at Florida Atlantic University. He has taught personal finance, investments, financial institutions, corporate finance, and advanced managerial finance classes at Florida Atlantic University and at the University of Wisconsin-Platteville. Apart from teaching, Dr. Taylor has been the treasurer of a county-wide school district in Florida and a debt management analyst for the fiscal agent of the Federal Home Loan Banks.

He also writes a daily advice column on personal finance topics and consults on financial planning and investments for corporate and individual clients.

Dr. Taylor is a member of the Academy of Financial Services, the Financial Management Association, and the CFA Institute.

C. Bruce Worsham, CLU, is an associate professor at The American College. He has been with The College since 1969, and his current responsibilities include the development of course materials for The College's LUTCF and FSS programs.

Mr. Worsham is author of *Foundations of Investment Planning*, co-author of *Essentials of Long-Term Care Insurance* and *Foundations of Financial Planning: The Process*, and editor of *Foundations of Financial Planning*, all published by The American College.

Mr. Worsham earned his BS from The University of California at Berkeley and an MA from the Wharton School at the University of Pennsylvania. He received his JD from Widener University School of Law and an LLM in taxation from Villanova University School of Law.

Special Notes to Advisors

Textbook Materials Disclaimer

This publication is designed to provide accurate and authoritative information about the subjects covered. While every precaution has been taken in the preparation of this material to ensure that it is both accurate and up-to-date, it is still possible that some errors eluded detection. Moreover, some material may become inaccurate and/or outdated either because it is time sensitive or because new legislation will make it so. Still other material may be viewed as inaccurate because your company's products and procedures are different from those described in this textbook. Therefore, the editors, authors, and The American College assume no liability for damages resulting from the use of the information contained in this textbook.

Caution Regarding Use of Textbook Materials

Any illustrations, fact finders, techniques, and/or approaches contained in this textbook are not to be used with the public unless you have obtained approval from your company. Your company's general support of The American College's educational programs and publications does not constitute blanket approval of any illustrations, fact finders, techniques, and/or approaches presented in this textbook, unless so communicated in writing by your company.

Use of the Term Financial Advisor or Advisor

Use of the term "financial advisor" as it appears in this textbook is intended as the generic reference to professional members of our reading audience. It is used interchangeably with the term "advisor" so as to avoid unnecessary redundancy. Financial advisor takes the place of the following terms:

Account Executive	Financial Planning	Producer
Agent	Professional	Property & Casualty
Associate	Financial Services	Agent
Broker (stock or	Professional	Registered Investment
insurance)	Health Underwriter	Adviser
Employee Benefit	Insurance Professional	Registered Representative
Specialist	Life Insurance Agent	Retirement Planner
Estate Planner	Life Underwriter	Senior Advisor
Financial Consultant	Planner	Tax Advisor
Financial Planner	Practitioner	

Financial Planning: Process and Environment

The Financial Planning Process

Special Note to Readers Enrolled in American College Courses

Many readers of this book are using it as part of their work for courses in designation programs of The American College (TAC). If you are one of these students, you need to be aware that the book is used in conjunction with materials that are found on The American College Online. It is important that you use this site for additional study materials and instructions on how to prepare for your course. If you have not received instructions on how to access The American College Online, contact the Office of Student Services at 1-888-AMERCOL (263-7265).

Learning Objectives

An understanding of the material in this chapter should enable the student to

1-1. Explain the six steps in the financial planning process.

1-2. Describe three different approaches to financial planning, and identify several areas of specialization in which advisors concentrate their activities.

1-3. Identify the subjects that should be included in a comprehensive financial plan.

1-4. Describe what is meant by a person's financial life cycle, and explain how it relates to life-cycle financial planning.

1-5. Explain how a financial plan can be developed around the steps in the financial planning process.

1-6. Explain how a financial plan can be developed using the financial planning pyramid.

1-7. Explain the trends that are creating opportunities in the financial planning marketplace.

1-8. Identify the principal financial goals/concerns of most consumers, and describe three major obstacles that prevent them from achieving these goals.

Chapter Outline

The primary goal of this chapter is to introduce the six-step financial planning process. This process is the foundation on which the financial planning profession is built; it provides a framework around which financial planning practitioners develop comprehensive plans for their clients. The nine chapters that follow this one explore the basic tools and techniques used in financial planning as well as the environment in which financial planning practitioners operate.

WHAT IS FINANCIAL PLANNING?

financial planning   One factor that has hampered the development of *financial planning* as a discipline and as a profession is the fact that there has been very little agreement among advisors as to what exactly it is. Indeed, it sometimes seems that there are as many definitions of financial planning as there are people who believe they are engaged in it. This debate, which continues among financial advisors even now,[1] is not merely an exercise in semantics. It becomes intensely practical when questions are raised about such issues as who shall regulate those advisors engaged in financial planning, who shall set standards for the financial planning profession, what sort of education these advisors should have, or which advisors may hold themselves out to the public as practicing financial planning.

Financial Planning Is a Process

Despite this ongoing controversy among advisors, financial planning can be defined conceptually as a process that accomplishes both of the following:

- ascertaining the client's financial goals
- developing a plan for achieving the client's goals

financial planning process

Whether a single financial problem is being addressed or a comprehensive financial plan is being developed, the *financial planning process* has six steps: (1) establish and define the advisor-client relationship, (2) determine goals and gather data, (3) analyze and evaluate the data, (4) develop and present a plan, (5) implement the plan, and (6) monitor the plan. Advisors who primarily sell financial products generally view the financial planning process as a selling/planning process that has eight steps, that is, the six steps of the financial planning process identified above preceded by two additional steps: (1) identify the prospect, and (2) approach the prospect. See appendix A in the back of the textbook for an outline of the eight-step selling/planning process as compared with the six-step financial planning process.

Steps in the Financial Planning Process

For advisors, this process for helping clients achieve their financial goals can be applied to the full range of client goals on a comprehensive basis. The process can also be applied on a narrower basis to only a subset of those goals or even to only a single financial goal of a client. It is not the range of client goals addressed that determines whether an advisor is engaged in financial planning. Rather, it is the process used by the advisor in addressing client goals that is the determining factor. The following pages present a brief discussion of the six steps in the financial planning process.

Steps in the Financial Planning Process

- Establish and define the advisor-client relationship.
- Determine goals and gather data.
- Analyze and evaluate the data.
- Develop and present a plan.
- Implement the plan.
- Monitor the plan.

Step 1: Establish and Define the Advisor-Client Relationship

The first step in the financial planning process is to establish and define the advisor-client relationship. This normally begins at the first client meeting, although it can start prior to this meeting through telephone interactions and/or disclosure documents sent to the client. In any event, the first client meeting is essential for establishing the framework for a successful advisor-client relationship. This meeting is where the advisor begins building trust with the client, ensuring client satisfaction, and creating a relationship with the client that it is hoped will span the client's entire financial life.

Establishing the advisor-client relationship when the client is a couple is a more complex challenge because the advisor needs to build trust and rapport with both parties. Covering the goals of both parties in one financial plan requires the advisor to be aware of the goals that both have in common and how their needs may differ. Chapters 2 and 5 both discuss this aspect of financial planning in greater depth.

In any kind of planned and purposeful communication setting, the first element that needs attention is structuring. Structuring serves to determine both the format and the subject matter of the interaction that is to follow. The financial advisor's task in structuring is to make the purpose of the initial meeting and those that follow clear to the client at the outset. This would include the inevitable introductions, an explanation of the financial planning process, a discussion of forms that are used (for example, a fact-finder form and a disclosure form) and the amount of time that will be required to complete them, a discussion of the confidential nature of the relationship, and some prediction of what kinds of outcomes the client might reasonably expect. This structuring need not be lengthy and cumbersome; in fact, it is far better to structure communication in a clear, straightforward, and succinct fashion.

More specifically, structuring for the financial planning process requires the advisor to explain how he or she works and the types of products and/or services that he or she is able to provide. It requires the advisor to explain the financial planning process and how that process is used to develop financial plans for clients. It may even require the advisor to give examples of how some of his or her products and/or services can be utilized to help clients meet their financial goals and objectives.

At the first meeting, the financial advisor also needs to disclose his or her background, philosophy, and method of compensation, whether that be fee-only, commission, or a fee and commission. The CFP Board's Code of Ethics and Professional Responsibility (covered in chapter 3) requires CFP designees to provide written disclosure to clients (prior to the engagement) of the method and source of their compensation, as well as information on their educational background, experience, conflicts of interest, and practice philosophy. Appendix B is a sample of the type of disclosure document that can be given to clients at the beginning of the initial meeting (or sent to them prior to the meeting) to satisfy this requirement.

Step 2: Determine Goals and Gather Data

Once having established and defined the advisor-client relationship, the advisor is ready to move on to step 2 of the financial planning process. Time permitting, this step can begin during the initial meeting with the client and may even be completed during this session if the client's goals are few in number and relatively straightforward, and the data is easy to gather. This, however, is rarely the situation.

While it is true that few people begin a vacation without a specific destination in mind, it is also true that millions of people make significant financial decisions without a specific financial destination in mind. Determining a specific financial destination, that is, goal setting, is critical to creating a successful financial plan. However, few people actually set clearly defined goals. By leading the client through the goal-setting exercise, the financial advisor helps establish reasonable, achievable goals, and also sets the tone for the entire financial planning engagement.

Clients typically express concern about a whole host of topics including retirement income, education funding, premature death, disability, taxation, and qualified plan distribution. Sometimes clients enumerate specific, prioritized goals, but they are more likely to present a vague list of worries that suggest anxiety and frustration rather than direction. The advisor's responsibility is to help the client transform these feelings into goals.

Advisors should question clients to learn what they are trying to accomplish. Usually the response is couched in general terms such as, "Well, we want to have a comfortable standard of living when we retire." At first glance this seems to be a reasonable goal, but a closer evaluation reveals that it is far too vague. When do they want to retire? What is meant by "comfortable"? Do they want to consider inflation? Do they want to retire on "interest only" or draw down their accumulated portfolio over their expected lives?

Skillful questioning may reveal a more precise goal such as, "We want to retire in 20 years with an after-tax income of $60,000 per year in current dollars, and we want the income to continue as long as we live without depleting the principal." Helping the client quantify specific goals is one of the most valuable services a financial advisor can provide.

Another important service the advisor provides is goal prioritization. Clients usually mention competing goals such as saving for retirement and saving for education. Advisors help clients rank these competing goals.

After a client expresses goals, objectives, and concerns, the advisor must then gather all the information about the client that is relevant to the problem(s) to be solved and/or the type of plan to be prepared. The more complex the client's situation and the more varied the number of goals, the greater the information-gathering task.

Two broad types of information will need to be gathered: objective and subjective. A few examples of objective (factual) information that might be needed from the client include a list of securities holdings, inventory of assets and liabilities, a description of the present arrangement for distribution of the client's (and spouse's) assets at death, a list of annual income and expenditures, and a summary of present insurance coverages. Of at least equal importance is the subjective information about the client. The financial advisor often will need to gather information about the hopes, fears, values, preferences, attitudes, and nonfinancial goals of the client (and the client's spouse).

One piece of information worthy of special attention is the client's *financial risk tolerance* (see chapter 4). Advisors must determine the client's (and spouse's) attitude toward risk before making recommendations, preferably with the help of a scientific risk tolerance questionnaire developed by a third party. The American College's *Survey of Financial Risk Tolerance* (see appendix D) is just such a questionnaire. It provides the type of analysis that helps the advisor suggest financial strategies and investment alternatives that are truly appropriate for the client. Such information offers the additional benefit of helping avoid (or at least defend) lawsuits from a dissatisfied client.

Before the financial advisor begins the information-gathering process, he or she should discuss a couple of concerns with the client. First, the client should be made aware that he or she will have to invest time, perhaps a significant amount of time, in the information-gathering stage of financial planning. Even though part of the financial advisor's responsibility is to avoid consuming the client's time unnecessarily, this commitment of the client's time is essential. The magnitude of the needed time commitment will depend on the scope and complexity of the client's goals and circumstances, but the proper development of even a narrowly focused and fairly uncomplicated plan requires information that only the client can furnish.

Second, the client should be made aware that he or she probably will have to provide the advisor with some information that is highly confidential, perhaps even sensitive or painful, for the client to reveal. Again, the scope and complexity of the client's goals will influence this matter. The creation of even straightforward plans, however, may require clients to disclose such things as their income and spending patterns, their attitudes toward other family members, or their opinions as to the extent of their own financial responsibilities to others. Another prerequisite for the effective gathering of client information is a systematic approach to the task. Although there are many possible ways to systematize the gathering of information, one way that has proven helpful is using a structured *fact-finder form*. (See chapter 5.) Some fact finders are only a few pages long and ask for basic information, while others are thick booklets that seek very detailed data on each asset and

financial risk tolerance

fact-finder form

amount. Most fact finders are designed for specific financial planning software to simplify data entry. For many client situations, a formal fact finder elicits considerably more information than needed. The sections that should be completed depend on the particular areas of concern to be addressed in each client's financial plan.

Obviously, information gathering is far more than asking the client a series of questions during an interview in order to fill out a fact-finder form. Certainly that is required, but usually information gathering also requires examination and analysis of documents—such as wills, tax returns, employee benefit plan coverage, and insurance policies—supplied by the client or the client's other financial advisors. It also requires counseling, advising, and listening during face-to-face meetings with the client (and spouse). These skills are especially important because the advisor needs to help the client (and spouse) identify and articulate clearly what he or she really wants to accomplish and what risks he or she is willing to take in order to do so. Moreover, no matter how the information is gathered, it must be accurate, complete, up-to-date, relevant to the client's goals, and well organized. Otherwise, financial plans based on the information will be deficient—perhaps erroneous, inappropriate, and inconsistent with the client's other goals, or even dangerous to the client's financial well-being.

Before leaving the step 2 discussion, it is important to point out that while many advisors focus their efforts on goal determination first before shifting their attention to data gathering, many advisors reverse this order and gather information first. The choice of whether to first focus on goal determination or data gathering is really up to each individual advisor and/or the specifics of the particular engagement. In fact, goal determination and data gathering are both frequently done simultaneously by advisors.

Step 3: Analyze and Evaluate the Data

Once the client's goals have been determined and data has been gathered, organized, and checked for accuracy, consistency, and completeness, the financial advisor's next task is to analyze and evaluate the data in order to determine the client's present financial status. The objective here is to determine where the client is now in relationship to the client's goals that were established in step 2.

This analysis may reveal certain strengths in the client's present position relative to those goals. For example, the client may be living well within his or her means, and thus resources are available with which to meet some wealth accumulation goals within a reasonable time period. Maybe the client has a liberal set of health insurance coverages through his or her employer, thereby adequately covering the risks associated with serious disability.

Perhaps the client's will has been reviewed recently by his or her attorney and brought up-to-date to reflect the client's desired estate plan.

More than likely, however, the financial advisor's analysis of the client's present financial position will disclose a number of weaknesses or conditions that are hindering achievement of the client's goals. For example, the client may be paying unnecessarily high federal income taxes or using debt unwisely. The client's portfolio of investments may be inconsistent with his or her financial risk tolerance. Maybe the client's business interest is not being used efficiently to achieve his or her personal insurance protection goals, or important loss-causing possibilities have been overlooked, such as the client's exposure to huge lawsuits arising out of the possible negligent use of an automobile by someone other than the client.

One conclusion from the advisor's analysis may be that the client cannot attain the goals established in step 2. For example, the client's resources and investment returns may preclude reaching a specified retirement income goal. In this case, the advisor helps the client to lower the goal or shows what changes the client must make to achieve the goal. Postponing retirement, saving more money, seeking higher returns, and deciding to deplete principal during retirement are four ways to help achieve the goal. Presented with alternatives, the client can restate the original goal by either lowering it or revising restrictive criteria to make it achievable.

Step 4: Develop and Present a Plan

financial plan

After the information about the client has been analyzed and, if necessary, the goals to be achieved have been refined, the advisor's next job is to devise a realistic *financial plan* for bringing the client from his or her present financial position to the attainment of those goals. Since no two clients are alike, a well-drawn financial plan must be tailored to the individual with all the advisor's recommended strategies designed for each particular client's concerns, abilities, and goals. The plan must be the client's plan, not the advisor's plan.

It is unlikely that any individual advisor can maintain an up-to-date familiarity with all the strategies that might be appropriate for his or her clients. Based on his or her education and professional specialization, the advisor is likely to rely on a limited number of "tried and true" strategies for treating the most frequently encountered planning problems. When additional expertise is needed, the advisor should always consult with a specialist in the field in question to help him or her design the client's overall plan.

Also there is usually more than one way for a client's financial goals to be achieved. When this is the case, the advisor should present alternative strategies for the client to consider and should explain the advantages and disadvantages of each strategy. Strategies that will help achieve multiple goals should be highlighted.

The financial plan that is developed should be specific. It should detail who is to do what, when, and with what resources.

Implicit in plan development is the importance of obtaining client approval. It follows that the plan must not only be reasonable, it must also be acceptable to the client. Usually interaction between advisor and client continues during plan development, providing constant feedback to increase the likelihood that the client will approve the plan.

Normally, the report containing the plan should be in writing (although plans developed for achieving single goals are often not expressed in a formal written report). Since the objective of the financial planning report is to communicate, its format should be such that the client can easily understand and evaluate what is being proposed. Some financial advisors take pride in the length of their reports, although lengthy reports are often made up primarily of standardized or "boilerplate" passages. In general, the simpler the report, the easier it will be for the client to understand and possibly adopt. Careful use of graphs, diagrams, and other visual aids in the report can also help in this regard.

After the plan has been presented and reviewed with the client, the moment of truth arrives. At this time, the advisor must ask the client to approve the plan (or some variation thereof). As part of this request, the advisor must ask the client to allocate money for the plan's implementation. While there are those who frown at the mere mention of selling in connection with financial planning, the fact is that financial planning does involve selling. Even financial advisors who are compensated entirely on a fee-for-service basis must sell the client on the need to work with the advisor to develop and implement a plan.

Step 5: Implement the Plan

The mere giving of financial advice, no matter how solid the foundation on which it is based, does not constitute financial planning. A financial plan is useful to the client only if it is put into action. Therefore, part of the advisor's responsibility is to see that plan implementation is carried out properly according to the schedule agreed on with the client.

Financial plans that are of limited scope and limited complexity may be implemented for the client entirely by the advisor. For other plans, however, additional specialized professional expertise will be needed. For example, such legal instruments as wills and trust documents may have to be drawn up, insurance policies may have to be purchased, or investment securities may have to be acquired. Part of the advisor's responsibility is to motivate and assist the client in completing each of the steps necessary for full plan implementation.

Step 6: Monitor the Plan

The relationship between the financial advisor and the client should be an ongoing one that hopefully will span the client's entire financial life. Therefore, the sixth and final step in the financial planning process is to monitor the client's plan. Normally the advisor meets with the client at least once each year (more frequently if changing circumstances warrant it) to review the plan. The first part of this review process should involve measuring the performance of the implementation vehicles. Second, updates should be obtained concerning changes in the client's personal and financial situation. Third, changes that have occurred in the economic, tax, or financial environment should be reviewed with the client.

If this periodic review of the plan indicates satisfactory performance in light of the client's current financial goals and circumstances, no action needs to be taken. However, if performance is not acceptable or if there is a significant change in the client's personal or financial circumstances or goals or in the economic, tax, or financial environment, the advisor and client should revise the plan to fit the new situation. This revision process should follow the same six steps used to develop the original plan, though the time and effort needed to complete many of the steps (for example, step 1) will probably be less than in the original process.

Summary Figure

The financial planning process described above is depicted schematically in figure 1-1. The blocks on the left represent the six steps in the process, while the blocks on the right indicate the main activities that should occur in each step. The phrase, "*Egad, I'm* a financial planner," is a good way to remember these six steps: *E*stablish, *G*ather, *A*nalyze, *D*evelop, *I*mplement and *M*onitor.

HOW IS FINANCIAL PLANNING CONDUCTED?

The ongoing debate over what financial planning is and, thus, who is engaged in financial planning has often centered on the breadth of services provided to clients. Some have contended that the financial advisor who focuses on solving a single type of financial problem with a single financial product or service is engaged in financial planning. Others have argued that true financial planning involves consideration of all of the client's financial goals and all the products and services available to achieve these goals. What if the advisor's focus is somewhere between these two extremes?

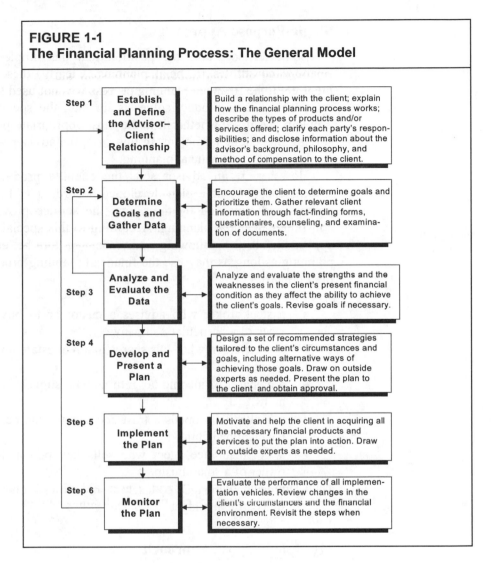

FIGURE 1-1
The Financial Planning Process: The General Model

Step 1 — **Establish and Define the Advisor–Client Relationship**
Build a relationship with the client; explain how the financial planning process works; describe the types of products and/or services offered; clarify each party's responsibilities; and disclose information about the advisor's background, philosophy, and method of compensation to the client.

Step 2 — **Determine Goals and Gather Data**
Encourage the client to determine goals and prioritize them. Gather relevant client information through fact-finding forms, questionnaires, counseling, and examination of documents.

Step 3 — **Analyze and Evaluate the Data**
Analyze and evaluate the strengths and the weaknesses in the client's present financial condition as they affect the ability to achieve the client's goals. Revise goals if necessary.

Step 4 — **Develop and Present a Plan**
Design a set of recommended strategies tailored to the client's circumstances and goals, including alternative ways of achieving those goals. Draw on outside experts as needed. Present the plan to the client and obtain approval.

Step 5 — **Implement the Plan**
Motivate and help the client in acquiring all the necessary financial products and services to put the plan into action. Draw on outside experts as needed.

Step 6 — **Monitor the Plan**
Evaluate the performance of all implementation vehicles. Review changes in the client's circumstances and the financial environment. Revisit the steps when necessary.

Once financial planning is recognized as being a process, the traditional debate is relatively easy to resolve. Regardless of the breadth of services provided, an advisor is engaged in financial planning if he or she uses the six-step financial planning process in working with a client to develop a plan for achieving that client's financial goals. Thus, true financial planning can involve a single-purpose, multiple-purpose, or comprehensive approach to meeting a client's financial goals as long as the six-step financial planning process is utilized in doing so.

Single-Purpose Approach

Some advisors take the position that the simple selling of a single financial constitutes financial planning. Clearly, these advisors would be incorrect if the financial planning process was not used to determine whether the problem their product solves is, in fact, the specific client's financial problem and if so, whether it is the most appropriate product or service for solving that client's problem. In this case, the advisor would be involved in product sales, not financial planning.

However, if an advisor sells the client a product to implement the recommendations of a plan developed according to the financial planning process and approved by the client, the service provided by the advisor constitutes financial planning. According to this specialist or *single-purpose approach*, all the following individuals would be engaged in financial planning as long as they use the financial planning process in working with their clients:

- a stockbroker who advises a customer to buy shares of common stock of a particular company
- a salesperson who sells shares in a real estate limited partnership to a client
- a preparer of income tax returns who suggests that a client establish an IRA
- a banker who opens a trust account for the benefit of a customer's handicapped child
- a life insurance agent who sells key person life insurance to the owner of a small business
- a personal finance counselor who shows a client how to set up and live within a budget

Multiple-Purpose Approach

Client financial concerns and financial products and/or services are often seen as falling into one of the major planning areas: insurance planning and risk management, employee benefits planning, investment planning, income tax planning, retirement planning, and estate planning. Rather than taking a single-purpose approach of just solving a single financial problem with a single financial product or service, many financial advisors take a *multiple-purpose approach* by dealing with at least a large part of one of these planning areas, and perhaps some aspects of a second planning area. According to the multiple-purpose approach, the following individuals would be engaged in financial planning as long as they use the financial planning process in working with their clients:

- a multi-line insurance agent who sells all lines of life, health, and property and liability insurance
- a tax attorney who assists clients with their income, estate, and gift tax planning
- an investment advisor who is registered as such with the Securities and Exchange Commission
- a life insurance agent who also sells a family of mutual funds to meet both the protection and wealth accumulation needs of clients

Comprehensive Approach

comprehensive approach

Still other advisors take a *comprehensive approach* to providing financial planning services. Comprehensive financial planning considers all aspects of a client's financial position, which includes the client's financial goals and objectives, and utilizes several integrated and coordinated planning strategies for fulfilling those goals and objectives. The two key characteristics of comprehensive financial planning are

- that it encompasses all the personal and financial situations of clients to the extent that these can be uncovered, clarified, and addressed through information gathering and counseling
- that it integrates into its methodology all the techniques and expertise utilized in more narrowly focused approaches to solving client financial problems

Because of the wide range of expertise required to engage in comprehensive financial planning, effective performance commonly requires a team of specialists. The tasks of the advisor managing the team are to coordinate the efforts of the team and to contribute expertise in his or her own field of specialization.

In its purest form, comprehensive financial planning is a service provided by the managing advisor on a fee-only basis. No part of the managing advisor's compensation comes from the sale of financial products, thus helping to ensure complete objectivity in all aspects of the plan. Some team specialists also are compensated through fees, while others might receive commissions from the sale of products, while still others might receive both fees and commissions. In its less pure but often more practical form, comprehensive financial planning provides the managing advisor with compensation consisting of some combination of fees for service and commissions from the sale of some of the financial products. Again, other members of the team might receive fees, commissions, or both.

Furthermore, in its purest form, comprehensive financial planning is performed for a client all at once, meaning in a single engagement—not a single meeting. A single planning engagement conducted by the managing advisor and his or her team of specialists creates the one plan that addresses all the client's financial concerns and utilizes several planning strategies. This plan is then updated with the client periodically and modified as appropriate. In its less pure form, comprehensive financial planning is performed incrementally during the course of several engagements with the client. For example, the advisor in one year might prepare a plan to treat some of the client's income tax concerns and estate and insurance planning problems. In another year, the advisor might focus on the client's retirement concerns and investment planning problems and then dovetail the strategies for dealing with them with the previously developed income tax, estate, and insurance strategies. In a third engagement, the advisor might address the remaining issues in the income tax, estate, insurance, retirement, and investment planning areas and coordinate all the recommended strategies and previously developed plans. Again, each incremental part, as well as the overall plan, is reviewed periodically and revised as appropriate.

FINANCIAL PLANNING AREAS OF SPECIALIZATION

Regardless of the breadth of the approach to financial planning—single-purpose, multiple-purpose, or comprehensive—employed by a particular advisor in working with clients, financial advisors tend to have areas of specialization in which they concentrate their activities. A survey conducted by the CFP Board of Standards in 1999 identified the following areas of specialization which, in turn, give an indication of the types of services provided by advisors to clients:[2]

- investment planning/advice—90 percent (of those surveyed)
- pension/retirement planning—87 percent
- comprehensive planning—73 percent
- estate planning—73 percent
- portfolio management—67 percent
- income tax planning—60 percent
- insurance planning—59 percent
- education planning—55 percent
- elder/long-term care planning—46 percent
- closely-held business planning—37 percent
- financial planning employee education—31 percent
- income tax preparation—25 percent
- divorce planning—19 percent

CONTENT OF A COMPREHENSIVE FINANCIAL PLAN

As indicated in the previous section, many financial advisors see comprehensive financial planning as being one of their areas of specialization. In practice, however, it is the least frequently encountered type of financial planning engagement for most advisors for several reasons. First, not many clients are willing to invest the amount of time that comprehensive financial planning requires. Second, it is usually affluent clients only who are able to afford to have a comprehensive financial plan developed. Third, not many clients can easily deal with the totality of their financial goals, capabilities, and difficulties all at one time. Instead, most prefer to concentrate on only a few related issues at once. As has been mentioned, however, even clients in the last group can have a comprehensive plan developed and implemented in incremental stages.

FOCUS ON ETHICS
Beginning a Dialogue on Ethics

Every chapter in this book contains an ethics dialogue box similar to this one. Ethics is a topic that should be implicit in any discussion of financial planning and the role of the financial advisor. This first box addresses a question that many advisors have asked: Is the highly ethical advisor financially rewarded for being ethical? The answer is maybe, but there is no guarantee. There are certainly some illustrations of the shady advisor reaping significant financial gains. Disciplined ethical conduct by itself does not guarantee financial success.

Perhaps the question should be addressed from a different perspective. Do clients want to do business with someone who really understands financial planning but who has questionable morals? Do clients want to do business with someone whose integrity is unassailable but whose financial planning skills are marginal? The answer to both questions is no.

The skilled financial advisor who is client focused and ethically well disciplined clearly has the attributes that clients desire and deserve. Again, the practice of ethics provides no guarantees of financial success. It is clear, however, that clients want to do business with financial advisors who have both earned their trust and are technically competent.

When the advisor prepares a comprehensive financial plan for a client, whether entirely in one engagement or incrementally over a period of time, what should the plan contain? Clearly, comprehensive financial planning is such an ambitious and complex undertaking that it must cover numerous subjects. At a minimum, these subjects should include the major planning areas identified by the Certified Financial Planner Board of Standards in its Topic List for CFP® Certification Examinations (see appendix C). These areas are

- general principles of financial planning (for example, personal financial statements, client attitudes and behavioral characteristics, and so forth)
- insurance planning and risk management
- employee benefits planning
- investment planning
- income tax planning
- retirement planning
- estate planning

A comprehensive financial plan should address all of these major planning areas as they relate to the client. If the financial advisor does not have the expertise to personally address each of the major planning areas in the development of the plan, he or she should form a team of specialists and serve as its manager. The advisor's role would then be to coordinate the efforts of the team and to contribute expertise in his or her own field of specialization. If, for some reason, one of the major planning areas does not apply to the client, the plan should spell out this fact. This will indicate that an important planning area was not overlooked in the development of the plan but was investigated and found not to apply to the client at this time.

In addition to the major planning areas that pertain to almost every client, there are a number of more specialized areas that are relevant to many. These specialized areas are for the most part subsets of, and typically involve several of, the major planning areas. However, because all of these specialized areas are unique, they merit separate treatment. They should be part of a client's comprehensive financial plan only if he or she is affected by them. Typically, a single-purpose or multiple-purpose financial plan that is focused on the particular planning need deals with these specialized areas.

The most important of these specialized areas in terms of the number of people it affects is education funding, a topic covered in greater depth in chapter 8. Most clients understand the need to save for college and are aware that college costs have risen at a faster pace than the *consumer price index (CPI)*. Still, the vast majority of families accumulate far too little money for college by the matriculation date. They usually have to cut back on living expenses, borrow money, tap into retirement assets, or seek additional employment to meet the funding need. Often they lower their sights and target a school that is less expensive rather than the one best suited to their children's needs. Consequently planning to meet the costs of higher education has become a necessity for most parents.

The other specialized areas worthy of mention are those that can be categorized as financial planning for special circumstances. These areas typically include planning for

consumer price index (CPI)

- divorce
- disability
- terminal illness
- nontraditional families
- job change and job loss
- dependents with special needs
- monetary windfalls

As previously mentioned, all of these specialized planning areas are subsets of one or more of the major planning areas. For example, divorce planning could affect every single one of the major planning areas but, nevertheless, should not be part of a comprehensive financial plan unless the client is contemplating divorce. Even then, divorce planning would be better handled under a single-purpose or multiple-purpose financial plan because of its unique aspects and shorter planning horizon than the major planning areas.

Life-Cycle Financial Planning

financial life cycle   There are five distinct phases in an individual's *financial life cycle*. Starting at a relatively young age (age 25 or younger), a career-minded person typically will pass through four phases en route to phase five, retirement. These five phases and their corresponding age ranges are

1. early career (age 25 or younger to age 35)
2. career development (age 35 to age 50)
3. peak accumulation (age 50 to ages 58–62)
4. preretirement (3 to 6 years prior to planned retirement)
5. retirement (ages 62–66 and older)

Together these five phases span a person's entire financial life. Although some people will not experience all of the phases or will spend more or less time in any one phase, the vast majority of career-minded people will go through all five.

As previously discussed, the first step in creating a comprehensive financial plan is for the advisor to establish and define the advisor-client relationship. Once the ground rules for the financial planning engagement have been set, the advisor's next task is to lead the client through the goal-setting process. Goal setting requires clients to recognize that there are several phases in their financial life; for young clients, the early career phase is the beginning of that life. The goals that young clients who are in this phase typically set reflect this fact. For example, a client who is in the early career phase often is newly married and has young children, and the client and/or his or her spouse are establishing employment patterns. The client probably is concerned about accumulating funds for a home purchase if he or she has not already done so. As the children grow older, the client begins to think about saving for college. Protecting his or her family from a potential financial disaster due to death or disability is also important, as is building a cash reserve or emergency fund to meet unexpected contingencies. However, the client's goals that pertain to retirement and estate planning generally will not have a very high priority in the first few years of the early career phase, but they still need to be considered if the financial plan is to be a truly comprehensive one.

Once the client has a comprehensive financial plan, it is incumbent on the advisor to monitor the plan. As the client moves into the career development phase of his or her financial life cycle, some goals may need revision. This phase is often a time of career enhancement, upward mobility, and rapid growth in income. The phase usually includes additional accumulation and then expenditure of funds for children's college educations. Moreover, the advisor should recommend coordinating the employee benefits of the client and his or her spouse and integrating them with insurance and investment planning goals.

As the client moves into the peak accumulation phase, the ever-vigilant advisor should be monitoring the plan for any needed changes. In this phase, the client is usually moving toward maximum earnings and has the greatest opportunity for wealth accumulation. The phase may include accumulating funds for special purposes, but it is usually a continuation of trying to meet the goals set for the major planning areas.

The preretirement phase often involves winding down both the career and income potential, restructuring investment assets to reduce risk and enhance income, and a further emphasis on tax planning and evaluating retirement plan distribution options relative to income needs and tax consequences. Throughout this phase, the financial advisor should be actively involved in keeping his or her client's financial plan on target to meet all the client's goals.

The final phase in the client's financial life cycle is retirement. If the advisor has kept the client's financial plan fine-tuned, then this phase should be a time of enjoyment with a comfortable retirement income and sufficient assets to preserve purchasing power. While all of the major planning areas should have been receiving attention throughout the client's financial life cycle, now is the time for the advisor to make certain that his or her client's estate plan is in order.

life-cycle financial planning

The advisor who monitors a client's financial plan throughout the client's financial life cycle is practicing *life-cycle financial planning*. A comprehensive financial plan that is developed for a relatively young client needs to be reviewed and revised periodically as the client ages and passes through the phases of the financial life cycle. Many of the client's financial goals will need adjusting as life's circumstances change; having the right goals is critical to creating a successful financial plan. The advisor's role in setting goals is to help the client establish reasonable, achievable goals and to set a positive tone for the entire financial planning process. The entire process encompasses not only the development of the client's first financial plan but also any future revisions and/or modifications to that plan.

The content of a comprehensive financial plan should, as already mentioned, include a discussion of each of the major planning areas. Financial planning is a process that should be ongoing throughout the client's financial life. That is why financial planning over the client's financial life is called life-cycle financial planning. Whichever phase of the financial life cycle the client is currently in strongly influences the priority given to the goals for each of the planning areas.

Format of a Comprehensive Financial Plan

A financial plan, whether comprehensive or not, is essentially a report to the client regarding the advisor's findings and recommendations. This report results from the application of the financial planning process to the client's present situation in an effort to assist the client in meeting his or her financial goals. Although there are as many different formats for a comprehensive financial plan as there are financial advisors, it is easy to agree that every comprehensive financial plan should include certain types of information. For example, every comprehensive plan should cover all of the major planning areas. Every plan should be based on reasonable, achievable goals set by the client. And every plan should be structured around strategies for achieving the client's goals. In addition, in the process of formulating strategies, assumptions have to be made and should be spelled out in the plan documents. Typical assumptions include the interest rate, the rate of inflation, and the client's financial risk tolerance, to name but a few. Finally, every plan is developed around information gathered during a fact-finding process. Much of this information, such as financial statements, should also be included in the plan.

Recognizing that there are many possible variations for organizing all of this information into a cohesive plan, one possible approach is to structure the plan to parallel the steps in the financial planning process. This type of plan typically is developed for the client all at once. A single planning engagement with the advisor, generally with a team of specialists, utilizes several planning strategies and creates the one plan that addresses all the client's financial concerns.

A comprehensive financial plan organized to follow the financial planning process should start (paralleling step 1, establishing and defining the advisor-client relationship) by specifying the responsibilities of each party for implementing the plan and carrying it through to completion. Along with specifying responsibilities, the plan also needs to clarify how the advisor is to be compensated for his or her work in developing, implementing, and monitoring the plan. Covering these all-important ground rules at the beginning of the plan helps not only to define the advisor-client relationship but to set the tone for that relationship as well.

Next (paralleling step 2, determining goals and gathering data), the comprehensive plan should specify the client's stated goals indicating the priority of each one and the time frame for achieving it. Each goal, as indicated earlier in this chapter, should be stated as specifically as possible. Because there are likely to be a number of goals included in a comprehensive financial plan, it may be helpful for the client to list them in relevant categories, such as protection, accumulation, liquidation, and so forth. Keep in mind that the best solution for a specific goal may involve a combination of the major planning areas; whatever approach is adopted for categorizing the goals, the plan should be designed to avoid confusing the client.

In addition to specifying the client's goals, the plan should also describe the client's present situation based on both the personal and financial data gathered from the client. In terms of the personal situation, this should include not only basic information about the client and his or her family, such as names, addresses, phone numbers, dates of birth, Social Security numbers, and so on, but also other relevant personal information that helps define the client's present situation and consequently will affect the financial plan. This other relevant information could include such topics as a child's serious health problem, a feeling of personal obligation to support aging parents, a desire to treat adopted or stepchildren differently from natural children, previous marriages and alimony or child-support obligations, and gifts or inheritances pending or anticipated.

Besides defining the client's present personal situation, the plan should include a description of the client's present financial situation. This is most commonly done by including a copy of the client's financial position statement on the plan date, listing his or her assets and liabilities and showing net worth; a cash-flow statement that identifies all the client's income and expenses and indicates his or her net cash flow for the latest period; and a copy of the client's most recent federal income tax return and an analysis thereof. The information presented should also include pro forma statements, that is, projections of future financial position relevant to understanding the client's current position. The client's current investment portfolio should also be presented with an indication of, among other things, its liquidity, diversification, and risk characteristics.

Next, for each goal at least three critical areas of information should be presented

- (paralleling step 3, analyzing and evaluating the data) the problem(s) identified by the advisor that the client would encounter in attempting to accomplish the goal
- (paralleling step 4, developing and presenting a plan) the recommended financial and tax services, products, and strategies for overcoming the identified problem(s) (including any underlying assumptions the advisor made in formulating the recommendation) so that the client can achieve the goal
- (paralleling step 5, implementing the plan), recommendations for implementing the proposed solution for achieving the goal

A second possible approach for structuring a comprehensive financial plan is to build the plan from the ground up in three stages. This type of plan typically requires several meetings with the client over a period of years. At the first stage of plan development, the advisor should concentrate his or her efforts on protecting the client against unexpected occurrences that could cause financial hardship. At the second stage, the advisor should focus on the client's wealth accumulation objectives. At the third and final stage, the advisor should address retirement and estate concerns. To help in understanding how these stages fit together in a comprehensive plan, one needs to look at the *financial planning pyramid* in figure 1-2.

financial planning pyramid

The financial planning pyramid is a common approach to prioritizing a comprehensive financial plan over a period of time. The pyramid illustrates how developing a plan begins with a sound foundation and proceeds in an orderly fashion. Stage 1, the foundation of the pyramid, in its simplest form protects the client against life's financial uncertainties. It is built with emergency savings, insurance coverages, and a properly drawn will.

Stage 2, the middle part of the pyramid, is the wealth accumulation component of the financial plan. As the client moves up the pyramid (that is, as the client's financial well-being improves), the focus of the plan shifts from income protection needs to wealth accumulation goals. This typically involves growing money through various types of investments.

Stage 3, the top part of the pyramid, becomes important once the client has achieved most of his or her accumulation goals. This last component of the financial plan addresses both the management of retirement assets and the conservation and distribution of the estate. This part of the financial plan typically is carried out by an estate plan and other advanced planning strategies including trusts and an updated will.

Regardless of the format a financial advisor adopts to organize a comprehensive financial plan, the important point to remember is that the plan should be communicated to the client in the form of a written report. The format of this financial planning report should make it easy for the client to understand and evaluate what is being proposed. In general, the simpler the report, the easier it will be for the client to understand and adopt. Careful organization, as well as the use of graphs, diagrams, and other visual aids, can help in this regard.

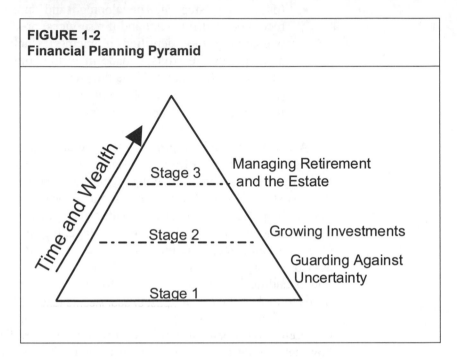

FIGURE 1-2
Financial Planning Pyramid

TRENDS CREATING OPPORTUNITIES FOR FINANCIAL PLANNING ADVISORS

A number of trends having important implications for advisors engaged in financial planning have emerged in the United States in recent years. They all point to enormous opportunities for these advisors to render valuable service to clients.

One of the most important trends is that the population is growing older. The median age of Americans has risen more than 7 years in the past 3 decades, meaning that a larger proportion of the population has moved into the period of highest earnings. Also, as people get older they tend to devote a smaller share of their income to current consumption and a larger share to savings and investments.

baby-boom generation

One of the causes of the rising median age of Americans is that the members of the *baby-boom generation* are no longer babies. The children born from 1946 to 1964 now range in age from their mid 40s to their early 60s and constitute about 30 percent of the U.S. population. Another cause of the rising median age is that Americans are living longer. Approximately

12.4 percent of them are now age 65 or over as compared to 9.2 percent in 1960, and this percentage will continue to rise. Government statistics indicate that the average life expectancy for 65-year-old males is now over 16 years and for 65-year-old females is now over 19 years.

The aging of the American population means that more consumers need retirement planning assistance during both their remaining years of active work and their retirement years. An increasing proportion of the population also needs assistance in planning for the cost of their children's college educations.

A second important trend in the financial planning marketplace is that dual-income families are increasingly common. This trend results from an increasing percentage of women entering (and reentering) the labor force, even during the years when they have young children. Dual-income families typically have higher total incomes, pay higher income and Social Security taxes, and have less time to manage their finances. The opportunities for financial planning advisors to assist people in this situation are obvious.

Trends Creating Opportunities for Financial Planning Advisors

- rising median age
- increased impact of dual-income families
- volatility of financial conditions
- technological change

A third broad trend is the increasing volatility of financial conditions in the American economy. Three indicators of this volatility that have confronted and confused Americans for the past 40 years are the changes that have occurred in inflation rates, in the level of interest rates, and in common stock prices. For example, during the first half of the 1960s, annual increases in the CPI averaged only 1.3 percent; the *prime interest rate* charged by banks on short-term business loans averaged only about 4.68 percent, and the *Standard & Poor's 500 Index* of common stock prices averaged around 72.0. Consider the dynamic patterns of these indicators since then, as shown in table 1-1.

Inflation and interest rates rose steadily in the late 1960s, and they were undoubtedly a motivating factor behind the growth in the number of advisors engaged in financial planning. Inflation and interest rates then cooled but bounced up again sharply in the mid-1970s. After a 3-year respite, they rose very sharply in the late 1970s and into the 1980s. Throughout this entire period, stock prices rose only modestly.

prime interest rate

Standard & Poor's 500 Index

TABLE 1-1
Consumer Price Index Changes (Urban Consumers), the Prime Rate, and Standard & Poor's 500 Stock Index: 1965–2003

Year	Percentage Change in CPI	Average Prime Rate %	Average S&P 500 Index
1965	1.6	4.54	88.47
1966	2.9	5.63	84.46
1967	3.1	5.63	92.18
1968	4.2	6.31	98.54
1969	5.5	7.96	97.58
1970	5.7	7.91	83.45
1971	4.4	5.72	98.21
1972	3.2	5.25	109.82
1973	6.2	8.03	106.51
1974	11.0	10.81	81.48
1975	9.1	7.86	87.13
1976	5.8	6.84	102.79
1977	6.5	6.82	97.48
1978	7.6	9.06	95.46
1979	11.3	12.67	103.33
1980	13.5	15.27	119.58
1981	10.3	18.87	127.84
1982	6.2	14.86	120.28
1983	3.2	10.79	160.72
1984	4.3	12.04	160.32
1985	3.6	9.93	188.97
1986	1.9	8.33	238.92
1987	3.6	8.21	285.99
1988	4.1	9.32	267.72
1989	4.8	10.87	326.31
1990	5.4	10.01	332.68
1991	4.2	8.46	381.53
1992	3.0	6.25	417.12
1993	3.0	6.00	453.45
1994	2.6	7.15	460.66
1995	2.8	8.83	546.88
1996	3.0	8.27	674.85
1997	2.3	8.44	875.86
1998	1.6	8.35	1,087.86
1999	2.2	8.00	1,330.60
2000	3.4	9.23	1,419.73
2001	2.8	6.91	1,186.00
2002	1.6	4.67	989.38
2003	2.3	4.12	967.93
2004	2.7	4.34	1132.60
2005	3.4	6.19	1207.75
2006	3.2	7.96	1318.31

Percentage change in CPI calculated from data provided by the U.S. Department of Labor, Bureau of Labor Statistics and available at: *www.bls.gov/cpi/home.htm*. The source for Average Prime Rate is: "H.15 Selected Interest Rates: Historical Data" (updated weekly), the Federal Reserve Board available at: *www.federalreserve. gov/releases/h15/data.htm*. Average S&P 500 Index is based on monthly data provided by The Financial Forecast Center™ and available at: *www.forecasts.org, except for 2006 data, which is provided by Standard & Poor's.*

Inflation rates slowed again during the mid-1980s, as did the prime interest rate. Meanwhile the stock market rose dramatically but erratically. As the 1980s came to a close, inflation and interest rates were creeping up again and average common stock prices were gyrating sharply from day to day. Then in the early 1990s, inflation started cooling again, stock prices rose dramatically, and interest rates plummeted. The mid-1990s saw continued moderation of inflation, yet interest rates crept upward while the stock market set record highs. Inflation in 1998 dropped to 1.6 percent, its lowest level in 3 decades. From 1997 to early 2000 the stock market soared to unprecedented highs but also displayed unsettling volatility. In mid 2000, the stock market turned downward and continued to drop in 2001, 2002, and early 2003. From a high near 1500 in the summer of 2000, the S&P 500 Index average of daily closing prices fell below 1000 by the middle of 2002, quite close to where it was in the beginning of 1998. Meanwhile, in response to actions of the Federal Reserve, interest rates dropped to their lowest levels in decades, declining from 9.50 percent during December 2000 to 4.00 percent in July 2003. Then rates increased as the Federal Reserve raised its target for the Federal Funds rate by ¼ percent 17 times in 17 consecutive meetings of the Fed Open Market Committee starting in June 2004.

In addition to the volatility of inflation rates, interest rates, and stock market prices, another destabilizing factor faced by American consumers has been important U.S. income tax laws—from the 1986 Tax Reform Act to the Economic Growth and Tax Reform Reconciliation Act of 2001, the Jobs Creation and Workers Assistance Act of 2002, the Jobs and Growth Tax Relief and Reconciliation Act of 2003, the Working Families Tax Relief Act of 2004, the American Jobs Creation Act of 2004, and the Pension Protection Act of 2006—tax laws that affect all aspects of financial planning. With these tax acts, the landscape for personal and estate taxes changed dramatically and these changes increased the need for financial advisors.

With the possible exception of the bull market of the late 1990s where many investors felt they could "do it themselves" without either professional advice or paying much attention to risk,[3] volatile economic conditions generally create greater demand for financial planning services. They also emphasize the need for financial advisors to continuously monitor their clients' financial circumstances and to adjust the plans as circumstances dictate. These volatile financial conditions make it doubly important that advisors thoroughly understand and abide by their clients' risk tolerances. With the 3-year decline in the stock market that began in 2000 and its major impact on the value of invested assets, investors are again recognizing the value of financial planning services and the need to consider risk as well as return in attempting to achieve their financial goals.

A fourth major trend in the financial planning market is the technological revolution that has occurred in the financial services industry. This revolution has made possible the creation of many new financial products and has made it easier to tailor these products to individual client needs. Also the technology has made possible the improved analysis of the performance of these products by advisors with the skills to do so.

CONSUMER NEEDS FOR FINANCIAL PLANNING

A basic and inescapable principle of economics is the law of scarcity—in every society—human wants are unlimited whereas the resources available to fill those wants are limited. The available resources must be somehow rationed among the wants. This rationing problem creates the need for financial planning even in affluent societies, such as the United States, and even among the most affluent members of such societies. To put it colloquially, there is just never enough money to go around.

What are the main financial concerns of American consumers? Are they able to handle those concerns on their own or do they need professional help? In short, do American consumers have a significant need and effective demand for professional financial planning services in the early years of the new millennium?

A national consumer survey conducted by the CFP Board of Standards in 2004 identified the following top 10 reasons people begin financial planning[4] (shown in reverse order for effect):

- generating current income (25 percent of those surveyed)
- sheltering income from taxes (26 percent)
- providing insurance protection (29 percent)
- accumulating capital (31 percent)
- building a college fund (32 percent)
- traveling/vacation (34 percent)
- managing/reducing current debt (34 percent)
- building an emergency fund (40 percent)
- purchasing/renovating a home (41 percent)
- building a retirement fund (82 percent)

In reporting the results of its 2004 Consumer Survey, the CFP Board of Standards also broke the findings down according to three key groups of respondents—"up and coming," "mid-life," and "retirement cusp." Table 1-2 shows the financial planning focus of each of the groups and highlights the relative importance of retirement planning to all three consumer groups.

The annual update of the Retirement Confidence Survey conducted by the Employment Benefit Research Institute (EBRI)[5] emphasizes that in many cases there is a strong need for professional help in planning effectively for retirement.

- Long retirements are expected.
  - EBRI survey: The average number of working respondents expects to retire at age 65 and spend 20 years in retirement.

TABLE 1-2
Financial Planning Needs

Consumer Group	Who Are They?	Financial Planning Focus
Up and Coming • 39% of respondents	• Ages: 20–39 • 28% have a written financial plan • 52% completed plan within the last 3 years • Most tolerant of risk • Most likely to use the Internet for financial purposes • Most likely to have financial software	• Prepare for retirement • Manage/reduce debt • Build an emergency fund • Build a college fund • Save for a home purchase/renovation
Mid-Life • 36% of respondents	• Ages: 40–54 • 39% have a written financial plan • 56% completed plan at least 4 years ago • More likely to use a financial professional to develop a plan • Highest amount of household income • Have low to moderate risk tolerance	• Prepare for retirement (strongest focus of all three consumer groups) • Build an emergency fund • Vacation/travel • Finance college education • Manage/reduce debt • Shelter income from taxes
Retirement Cusp • 25% of respondents	• Ages: 55–69 • 47% have a written financial plan • 62% completed plan at least 5 years ago • Higher net worth and lower risk tolerance • Most likely to have a financial professional as a primary advisor	• Prepare for retirement • Vacation/travel • Accumulate capital • Generate income • Shelter income from taxes • Provide for future medical needs • Build an emergency fund

Source: *2004 Consumer Survey*, Copyright © 2004, Certified Financial Planner Board of Standards, Inc. All rights reserved. Used with permission.

- Retirement income needs are underestimated. (Retirement planning professionals typically recommend 75 to 90 percent of preretirement income to live comfortably in retirement.)
    - EBRI survey: Fourteen percent of working respondents expect to need less than 50 percent of their preretirement income in retirement; 36 percent indicate 50 to 70 percent; and 28 percent indicate 70 to 85 percent. Thirteen percent of workers estimate they will need 85 to 105 percent of their preretirement income in retirement.
- Retirement savings are insufficient.
    - EBRI survey: Twenty-four percent of nonretired workers indicate they are *very confident* in having enough money to live comfortably throughout their retirement years; 44 percent indicate that they are *somewhat confident*. Twenty-two percent of the very confident workers are not currently saving for retirement.
- Planning has been inadequate.
    - EBRI survey: Forty-two percent of the nonretired respondents indicate that they have tried to calculate how much money they will need to have saved by the time they retire so that they can live comfortably in retirement.

As previously stated, baby boomers, Americans born between 1946 and 1964, are now in midlife. A study conducted by the American Association of Retired Persons (AARP) in 2004 found that while baby boomers appear to be quite optimistic about their retirement years, their optimism is moderated somewhat by concerns about finances.[6] Another study conducted by the AARP in 2004 found that the personal finances of baby boomers is one area of their lives with which they are least satisfied, along with their work.[7] About one-third of the survey respondents indicated that they are worse off financially than they thought they would be at this point in their lives. Many baby boomers feel financially strapped, especially when it comes time to pay college tuition. While 29 percent of those surveyed have made "improving their personal finances" their top goal over the next 5 years, nearly half do not believe they are likely to achieve their goal due, among other things, to their own inability to handle credit cards and debt, the volatile stock market, the cost of living, and economic uncertainty in the workplace.

Another study of baby boomers conducted by The Allstate Corporation in 2001 suggests that many baby boomers are likely to encounter a retirement that is quite different in financial terms from the past.[8] Among other things, the survey revealed that during retirement, more than one in three baby boomers will be financially responsible for parents or children, 7 percent will be financially responsible for both parents and children, one in five will pay college tuition for one or more children, and more than 70 percent will continue to work. The survey also suggests that baby boomers appear to be poorly prepared for these financial burdens in retirement. Survey respondents saved only an average of 12 percent of the total they will need to meet even basic living expenses in retirement. Furthermore, they have grossly underestimated the predicted increase in the cost of living over the next 20 years.

sandwiched generation

The baby-boom generation is also known as the *sandwiched generation* because many members are faced with financing their children's educations and aiding their aging parents at the same time when they themselves should be saving for their own retirements. Retirement, college funding, and long-term care are important to many clients but especially to sandwiched boomers. Boomers Envision Retirement II (an AARP study) reports that 35 percent of boomers have been or are responsible for the care of elderly parents; 18 percent expect to provide financially for an aging parent or in-law during retirement; and 19 percent expect to have an aging parent or in-law living with them during retirement.[9]

Obstacles Confronting Consumers

The results of the surveys discussed above and similar studies make it clear that many American households still have not gained control of their financial destinies. Certainly, there are many reasons why they have not developed financial plans that will enable them to do so. Three of the strongest obstacles they face are the following:

- the natural human tendency to procrastinate—Delaying the task of establishing a financial plan may result from a hectic lifestyle, the seeming enormity of the task of getting one's finances under control, and the belief that there is still plenty of time to prepare for achieving financial goals.
- living up to or beyond current income—This is a very common tendency among Americans. The pressure in households to overspend for current consumption is enormous, and many families have no funds left with which to implement plans for the achievement of future goals.
- the lack of financial knowledge among consumers—Although in recent years there has undoubtedly been some growth in the financial sophistication of Americans, there is still widespread ignorance about how to formulate financial objectives and how to identify and properly evaluate all the strategies that might be used to achieve them.

Role of Financial Planning Advisors

A basic inference that can be drawn from the results of consumer surveys is that Americans need help in managing their personal finances to achieve their financial goals. Moreover, many Americans seem to realize that they would benefit from professional help, and with better education many others would reach the same conclusion. A major part of the challenge facing financial planning advisors is to help clients overcome these obstacles by educating them and motivating them to gain control of their own finances.

CHAPTER ONE REVIEW

Key Terms and Concepts
Key Terms and Concepts are explained in the glossary.

financial planning	consumer price index (CPI)
financial planning process	financial life cycle
financial risk tolerance	life-cycle financial planning
fact-finder form	financial planning pyramid
financial plan	baby-boom generation
single-purpose approach	prime interest rate
multiple-purpose approach	Standard & Poor's 500 Index
comprehensive approach	sandwiched generation

Review Questions
The answers to the review questions are in the supplement. Self-test questions and the answers to them are also in the supplement and on The American College Online.

1-1. Identify the six steps in the financial planning process and briefly indicate the kinds of activities involved in each step. [1-1]

1-2. Describe each of the following approaches to financial planning:

   a. single-purpose approach [1-2]
   b. multiple-purpose approach [1-2]
   c. comprehensive approach [1-2]

1-3. At a minimum, what subjects should be included in a comprehensive financial plan? [1-3]

1-4. Explain what is meant by life-cycle financial planning. [1-4]

1-5. Explain the financial planning pyramid. [1-6]

1-6. Describe the opportunities in the financial planning marketplace resulting from each of the following trends:

  a. rising median age [1-7]
  b. increasing number of dual-income families [1-7]
  c. volatility of financial conditions [1-7]
  d. increasing use of sophisticated technology by the financial services industry [1-7]

1-7. What are the top 10 reasons why people begin financial planning? [1-8]

1-8. Describe three of the strongest obstacles preventing Americans from gaining control of their own financial destinies. [1-8]

NOTES

1. Shelley A. Lee, "What Is Financial Planning, Anyway?" *Journal of Financial Planning,* December 2001, pp. 36–46.
2. *First Annual CFP® Practitioner Survey: Executive Summary of Findings,* Certified Financial Planner Board of Standards, Denver, CO, Summer 1999, p. 7. The telephone survey of 661 CFP® practitioners was conducted by Market Facts, Inc.
3. Nancy Opiela, "The State of Financial Planning: A Grassroots Perspective," *Journal of Financial Planning,* December 2002, pp. 8–16.
4. *2004 Consumer Survey,* Certified Financial Planner Board of Standards, Denver, CO. This was a survey of 1,122 upper-quartile households of all ages (incomes ranged from $60,000+ to $100,000+ depending on the householders' ages).
5. *The 2006 Retirement Confidence Survey,* EBRI Issue Brief No. 292, April 2006, Employee Benefit Research Institute, Washington, DC.
6. *Baby Boomers Envision Their Retirement II—Key Findings: Survey of Baby Boomer' Expectations for Retirement,* AARP, Washington, DC, May 2004. Prepared by RoperASW for AARP. A telephone survey of 1,200 Americans ages 38 to 57.
7. *Boomers at Mid-Life 2004: The AARP Life Stage Study,* AARP, Washington, DC 2004. A telephone survey of 3,850 adults 18 and older (including 2,266 boomers) was conducted by Princeton Survey Research Associates for AARP.
8. *Retirement Reality Check,* The Allstate Corporation, Northbrook, IL, December 2001. Harris Interactive polled 1,004 people born between 1946 and 1961 with household incomes ranging from $35,000 to $100,000. An update of this survey has been released annually since the original survey in 2006.
9. *Baby Boomers Envision Their Retirement II,* op. cit., p. 8.

Communicating Effectively With Clients

Learning Objectives

An understanding of the material in this chapter should enable the student to

---

2-1. Explain the importance of communicating effectively with clients throughout the financial planning process.

2-2. Explain the three main types of structured communication used in financial planning.

2-3. Explain the importance of structuring communications, building rapport, and handling resistance in communicating with clients.

2-4. Explain the attributes of an advisor that facilitate communicating with clients.

2-5. Describe several basic communication principles.

2-6. Explain the importance of attending and listening skills to communicating effectively with clients.

2-7. Describe several types of leading responses.

2-8. Compare the advantages and disadvantages of several types of questions used in financial planning.

Chapter Outline

The focus of chapter 1 is the financial planning process. The focus of this chapter is on learning how to communicate effectively with clients throughout that process. In step 1 of the process, the advisor's objective is to establish a relationship with clients that are conducive to planning. To achieve this objective, the advisor must be able to communicate effectively with clients.

Effective Client Communications and the CFP® Exam

The principles of communication and counseling presented in this chapter are now part of the addendum to the Topic List for the CFP® Certification Examination. The CFP® Certification Examination no longer directly tests these topics, but the CFP Board strongly encourages CFP Board-Registered Programs to continue teaching these principles in their curricula.

IMPORTANCE OF COMMUNICATING EFFECTIVELY WITH CLIENTS[1]

Many people take communication for granted. After all, it is an activity that most of us have engaged in since our childhood years, so why not take it for granted? The sad truth is that many of us are ineffective communicators simply because we make that very assumption.

Communication is far too important a skill to treat lightly. This is especially true in the field of financial planning. It is the single most critical skill that an advisor brings to a financial planning session. Ineffective communication is an obstacle to a strong advisor-client relationship. The failure of clients and advisors to communicate fully and clearly with each other can result in improperly identified financial goals and the formulation of inappropriate planning strategies. The result for the client is not being able to achieve his or her financial goals. The communication process is the starting point from which the advisor helps the client to establish financial goals and then designs a plan to achieve those goals. Simply put, effective communication between the advisor and client is crucial to the financial planning process.

The purpose of this chapter is to examine the communication process as it typically exists in an advisor-client relationship. Our goal is to help financial advisors become better communicators. Perhaps you already consider yourself an effective communicator; however, there are probably aspects of the communication process in which you can improve. This chapter will attempt to bring these aspects into sharper focus and provide you with techniques for becoming the very best communicator/advisor that you are able to be.

TYPES OF STRUCTURED COMMUNICATION USED IN FINANCIAL PLANNING

Laypeople often use the terms interviewing, counseling, and advising interchangeably. Yet each of these forms of structured communication has characteristics that are uniquely its own and that differentiate it from the other two. We will describe these three forms of structured communication and discuss how advisors use them in the financial planning process.

Interviewing

interviewing

Interviewing is one of the most common forms of structured communication. Interviewing can be defined as a process of communication, most often between two people, with a predetermined and specific purpose, usually involving the asking and answering of questions designed to gather meaningful information. For example, a critical step in the financial planning process (step 2 of the process depicted in figure 1-1) requires the advisor to gather complete data and information about a client relevant to the client's personal and financial situation. To gather this information, the financial advisor frequently mails the client a fact-finder form to fill out. When the form is returned, the advisor typically schedules a fact-finder session in which he or she interviews the client by asking a series of questions designed to help in reviewing the answers, clarifying any confusion, and filling in the blank spaces. (See chapter 5.) There is a specific purpose to the interview: to gather relevant information through a question-and-answer dialogue.

Stewart and Cash in their book, *Interviewing: Principles and Practices*, refer to two basic types of interviews: directive and nondirective.[2] In a *directive*

directive interview

interview, the financial advisor directs and controls both the pace and the content to be covered. This is a formal and structured style of interaction. The advisor completes a fact-finder form as the client answers pointed questions. Many of the questions are asked and answered rapidly in an almost staccato fashion. What is your date of birth? Where do you live? What is your occupation? What is the highest level of education you completed? The advantages of the directive interview are its brevity and its organized collection of data. Its disadvantages are its inflexibility and the limited opportunity for the client to expound on any of the questions being asked.

nondirective interview

In a *nondirective interview*, both the financial advisor and the client can discuss a wider range of subject areas, and the client usually controls the pacing of the interview through the depth of his or her responses. Thus, the advantages of the nondirective interview include greater flexibility, more in-depth analysis, and the potential for a closer relationship between the advisor and client. Its disadvantages are that it consumes more time and often generates data that are subjective in nature.

Both types of interviews are commonly used in the financial planning process. In fact, both types often take place in the same fact-finding session. Moreover, all interviews, whether directive or nondirective, share common characteristics. They typically take place in a formal and structured setting. The question-and-answer format is the primary method of communication. The subject matter discussed is specific to the overall purpose of the interview, and digressions from the subject are usually not encouraged. Finally, the interview by itself usually requires only a relatively short meeting of the parties. However, as used in the financial planning process, the initial interview typically starts the beginning of what is expected to be a lasting advisor-client relationship.

Counseling

counseling

The second term, *counseling*, connotes an offer of help. A financial advisor's job is to provide assistance to clients as they explore their present financial situations, begin to understand where they are in relation to where they would like to be, and then act to get from where they are to where they want to be. Even though this may sound like a simple process, it is not. Counseling, as used in financial planning, usually takes time and is typified by discussion, reflection, and eventually insights that help the client select a financial plan from among the suggested or recommended alternatives.

While the financial advisor's role as a counselor takes place over a period of time, the interview, as a form of structured communication, is usually of relatively short duration. In counseling, the advisor and client develop an interpersonal relationship, something that generally does not occur in a solitary interview. When we discussed interviewing, we stated that the question-and-answer format was the primary method of communication. While the advisor also asks questions in counseling, they are not his or her primary method of communication. In counseling, the advisor may paraphrase what the client has said, reflect a feeling, share feedback or perceptions, clarify, summarize, interpret, provide information, and confront. In short, counseling is not as stylized as interviewing because it is less formal and less structured. The humanness of both the advisor and the client comes into focus, all with the purpose of providing help to the client.

Advising

advising

The third type of structured communication is *advising*, which involves giving specific guidance or suggestions to clients. Advising is often confused with counseling. In fact, many clients who are unfamiliar with counseling think that what they will receive is advice. Perhaps one reason for this misconception stems from the journalistic proliferation of advice such as is offered in the "Dear Abby" type of newspaper columns. This is not to say that advice is never offered by financial advisors who are counseling their clients because it is; but most financial advisors believe that the very best kind of advice for their clients is self-advice rather than advice from an expert.

Several situations might require that financial advisors give advice. For example, a tax advisor might provide advice on tax shelters, capital gains, tax deferral, and so on. Or an investment advisor might recommend a particular stock or mutual fund because he or she believes that it is consistent with both the client's risk tolerance level and financial ability to handle risk. In each of these instances, the advisor knows much more about his or her field of expertise than do the clients, and the clients use this knowledge to help them make their decisions.

To reiterate, there are several occasions when financial advisors are called on to give advice. After all, financial advisors are the experts and thus their advice has value. However, there is a danger for advisors in offering advice too soon in the advisor-client relationship. This danger is that the client's ability to make decisions becomes discounted in favor of the expert's opinion. In fact, offering advice has been criticized by some counseling experts who maintain that it fosters dependency and robs clients of the right to make decisions for themselves. Moreover, they believe that advisors who provide quick answers to somewhat complex financial problems are often guilty of projecting their own needs, problems, and/or values into the advice. So how do financial advisors give advice to clients without assuming responsibility for their clients' financial lives?

FOCUS ON ETHICS
How Ethical Behavior Improves Communication

Many clients misunderstand the specifics of the plans suggested or recommended by their financial advisors. This problem is compounded when complex financial instruments are required to implement the plans. It is much like drivers and automobiles. Most drivers really need transportation, and cars solve this problem. However, that does not mean that drivers understand how their cars operate.

A financial advisor once stated that there are two essential rules for effectively dealing with clients. The first is to earn their trust because trust breaks down communication barriers. Different advisors may accomplish this in different ways, but the goal is for advisors to feel free to ask challenging questions and continue probing until a satisfactory level of understanding is achieved. When there are limits to what clients can understand, earned trust is essential.

The second rule is to maintain trust, a critical factor in the advisor-client relationship. Although clients may not fully understand, they should not fail to act. Indeed, if clients understood every aspect of financial planning, they would not need their advisors. Clients often make decisions based solely on their trust in their advisors.

There is no better way to earn and maintain trust than to develop an unassailable reputation for ethical and professional behavior. A valuable side benefit is improved communication.

Perhaps the best way for financial advisors to give advice to clients is by using the six-step financial planning process (discussed in chapter 1 and depicted in figure 1-1) to address client concerns. Advisors who adhere to the financial planning process systematically analyze their client's financial situations. They work alongside their clients as partners to help them take control of their financial lives. While the role of advisors in the financial planning process is geared more toward counseling clients than advising them, advising is still an important form of structured communication. The inherent danger of advising clients is minimized when the advice is given within the confines of the financial planning process. In that case, any advice given to a client is the result of a thorough analysis of the client's financial situation. Advisors generally give advice to clients in the form of suggestions or recommendations, but the clients are encouraged to make decisions for themselves and assume responsibility for their own financial lives.

Because there is frequent interaction between advisors and clients in the financial planning process, the distinction between interviewing, counseling, and advising is often blurred. As the discussion about the three types of structured communication indicates, financial advisors use all three types in the financial planning process, and those advisors who routinely use the financial planning process are performing their jobs in a wholly professional and ethical manner.

Types of Structured Communication

- interviewing
- counseling
- advising

CONSIDERATIONS IN COMMUNICATING WITH CLIENTS

In the preceding section, we differentiated the three types of planned and purposeful communication: interviewing, counseling, and advising. Each one is used in the financial planning process. For instance, step 2 of the financial planning process utilizes interviewing to facilitate the completion of fact-finder forms. Counseling occurs in several steps of the financial planning process including step 2 where clients set their financial goals. Advising frequently takes place in step 4 of the process where advisors recommend or suggest several alternative strategies for their clients to consider. In other words, financial advisors generally rely on all three types of structured communication with each type being more or less appropriate for particular tasks. Let us now examine some specific communication issues that advisors confront in their everyday practices.

Structuring Communications With Clients

In any kind of planned and purposeful communication setting, the first element that needs to be attended to is structuring. Structuring serves to determine both the format and the subject matter of the interaction that is to follow. The financial advisor's task is to make the purpose of the sessions clear to the client at the outset. This would include introductions, an explanation of the process involved, a discussion of forms that are used and the amount of time that will be required to complete them, a discussion of the confidential nature of the relationship, and some prediction of what kinds of outcomes the client might reasonably expect. This structuring need not be lengthy and cumbersome; in fact, it is far better to structure in a clear, straightforward, and succinct fashion.

Consider the following example of structuring in which the advisor's approach is friendly and promises cooperation. The client is made to feel important, that he or she is the focal point of the sessions. The statement offers hope to the client that the results of the financial planning process will help him or her achieve the desired goals.

Example: Advisor: "In order for me to provide the best possible service for you, we'll probably need to see each other on three or four separate occasions, although I want you to know that I'm available to meet with you as often as you need me. Today, I thought we'd start by discussing the financial planning process. To put this in proper perspective, I'll explain the products and services that we provide and how they might help you. In the next session, we'll gather some information about your financial situation. To do this, I'll fill out a fact-finder form, which will remain confidential between the two of us. As we go about our business together, I will develop and present to you some alternatives that will be sensible and help you meet your goals. Do you have any questions?"

In step 1 of the financial planning process, the client may be apprehensive or uncertain about how to begin. A good guide for the advisor to follow is to begin where the client is. If the client is, in fact, anxious at the outset, the advisor should take the time to discuss the difficulty of merely getting started. Talking about this will not only alleviate most of the client's anxieties, it will also help to build rapport with the client. It is important to keep in mind that whenever feelings emerge, it is best to focus on those feelings rather than ignore them. If, for example, in the middle of a session a client appears distressed over some aspect of his or her financial situation (for example, an impending divorce), some time should be spent discussing these feelings. Until feelings are addressed and dealt with, a further discussion of content is unproductive and meaningless.

Developing Rapport With Clients

rapport

Financial advisors should seek to develop *rapport* with their clients. Rapport, another way of describing a comfortable and harmonious relationship, is best developed through actions initiated by the financial advisor. The most important step in developing rapport is the advisor's acceptance of the client and the client's awareness of this acceptance. This attitude stems from a sincere desire on the advisor's part to respect the uniqueness of each client and a genuine wish to help. Clients want to work with professionals who build meaningful relationships with them and listen to what they want to accomplish. If rapport and credibility are developed in step 1 of the financial planning process, the products and/or services the advisor recommends will more likely be reflective of the clients' real needs and values. In order for clients to buy products and/or services from an advisor, they must first trust the advisor. Trust is the intangible aspect of selling that must be gradually cultivated and earned. The advisor must prove that he or she is there to help clients, not simply to sell them something. To do this, the advisor must create an environment that promotes openness by

- alleviating the concerns of clients
- responding to the social style of clients
- communicating effectively with clients
- structuring communications with clients (as previously discussed)

Alleviating the Concerns of Clients

Various barriers that can create tension between the advisor and his or her clients during an initial session as well as throughout the financial planning process must be removed if rapport is to be developed. These barriers can be divided into four categories:

- Distrust of Salespeople—Many people have a negative image of people who sell products and/or services and avoid meeting with them for fear of being talked into buying something they do not want or need.
- Fear of Making a Decision—Decisions involve risk, and many people avoid risk especially when money is involved. Also, fear of making the wrong purchase decision (that is, buyer's remorse) can cause avoidance of stressful decision-making situations.
- Need for Stability—Many people are complacent and resist change because they prefer familiarity.
- Time Constraints—At today's increasingly hectic pace of life, busy people are reluctant to commit their time.

Being aware of client stress can help the advisor identify opportunities to alleviate it and build rapport. Here are some tips.

- The advisor should not impose on clients. He or she should schedule the initial session (as well as future ones) at times that are convenient for clients.
- The advisor should watch his or her verbal pace. He or she should talk in an unhurried, businesslike manner and should never interrupt when clients are speaking. He or she should listen carefully to what clients are saying because listening is a necessary component in good communication.
- The advisor should remember nonverbal behaviors. He or she might be surprised to learn that as little as 7 percent of a first impression is based on what is actually said. The remaining 93 percent is based on nonverbal behaviors, such as body positions, gestures, eye contact, and voice tone.[3]
- The advisor should encourage clients to talk. Having clients talk is not only a great tool for getting feedback, it is also a common way to relieve stress. Encourage clients to do most of the talking.
- The advisor should control his or her anxiety. Several studies have shown that a person who is already anxious becomes even more so when talking with someone who displays nervousness or anxiety.

Responding to the Social Style of Clients

Building rapport is the advisor's responsibility. This means that the advisor should be able to detect what each client wants from an advisor-client relationship, and to use his or her communication skills to shape the discussion in order to satisfy those wants. Identifying the client's needs in the relationship is easier if the advisor can identify the client's social style.

social styles

Psychologist David W. Merrill described the following four *social styles:*

- driver
- expressive
- amiable
- analytical

The American population is evenly divided among the four social styles. Each person has a dominant social style that influences the way he or she works. According to David W. Merrill and Roger H. Reid, "We all say and do things as a result of certain habit patterns, and people make predictions about us because they come to expect us to behave in a particular way—the fact is that even though each of us is unique, we tend to act in fairly consistent, describable ways. All of us use habits that have worked well for us, habits that make us comfortable, and these habits become the social style that others can observe."[4]

People are like thermostats; they are constantly seeking to reach a state of equilibrium or comfort. They seek out social situations that reinforce their behavior and avoid situations that cause discomfort. As soon as another person enters the picture, tension is produced, and each one must reestablish his or her balance and comfort zone. The challenge for each of us is to determine the proper amount of tension and stress that will provide the proper balance.

Better communication can be achieved when the advisor understands the client and treats the client the way the client wants to be treated. More effective communications and a better advisor-client relationship can be established by adapting to the client's social style in order to make him or her feel at home and less threatened. By listening to and observing the client during step 1 of the financial planning process, the advisor can learn how to communicate with the client. Table 2-1, Responding to Social Styles, summarizes the characteristics of each social style and how best to respond to a person who engages that style. By communicating with the client in a manner appropriate for the client's social style, the advisor is able to build rapport with the client more quickly and thus facilitate the financial planning process.

Communicating Effectively With Clients

Financial advisors must build rapport with clients in order to help them solve their problems. One aspect of rapport building is communicating effectively, the focus of this chapter. Some advisors, however, think effective communication only means they have to explain their products and/or services to clients. In fact, effective communication involves much more. At a minimum, it requires the advisor to learn how to listen. Failing to hear what the client is really saying can cost the advisor dearly. Developing good listening skills will result not only in increased sales and the sense of a job well done, but clients are more likely to accept the advisor's suggestions or recommendations if he or she demonstrates an interest in the clients by listening to what they have to say. Basic communication principles are discussed more fully later in this chapter.

Dealing With Client Resistance

resistance

Resistance often occurs in even the best advisor-client relationships. Resistance can be expressed as either overt or covert hostility toward the advisor. Overt hostility generally is easier to recognize and handle than covert hostility. In addition, there are several other types of resistance behaviors that advisors might encounter during the financial planning process.

TABLE 2-1
Responding to Social Styles

Social Style	Style Characteristics	How to Respond
Driver	• Forceful, direct • Will not waste time on small talk • Wants power • Is controlling	• Be efficient • Move right along • Support their conclusions and actions • To encourage decisions, provide options and probabilities
Expressive	• Outgoing, enthusiastic • Enjoys telling about personal projects and dreams • Wants recognition • Is energizing	• Be interesting • Take time to listen • Support their visions and intuitions • To encourage decisions, provide testimony and incentives
Amiable	• Easy-going, dependent • Enjoys telling about personal relationships • Wants approval • Is supportive	• Be cooperative • Find areas of common involvement • Support their relationships and feelings • To encourage decisions, provide assurances and guarantees
Analytical	• Logical, quiet • Is uncomfortable with small talk • Wants respect • Is systematic	• Be accurate • Stick to an agenda • Support their principles and thinking • To encourage decisions, provide evidence and service

Recognizing Client Resistance

Open or overt hostility is the easiest type of resistance to recognize and, in most cases, to handle. We all know what angry people look and sound like: their faces become flushed; their jaws tighten; they clench their fists; their voices rise; their language becomes more expressively angry. The only effective thing to do at this point is to reflect this anger by saying, "I can sense your anger. You don't like what I've just said, do you?" This allows clients to vent whatever pent-up feelings of anger they have; the anger slowly begins to dissipate, and the behavior then becomes more rational.

Covert hostility is more difficult to recognize and can be more difficult to deal with because clients themselves may not even be aware of their anger. Some indications of covert hostility are missed appointments; being late for appointments; being sarcastic or cynical; being overly genteel or polite; and not getting down to business. Whatever way covert hostility is demonstrated, the best approach is not to interpret the behavior for the client as latent hostility or passive-aggressiveness but simply to focus on the behavior itself and let the client analyze or interpret it. For instance, the advisor might say, "I've noticed that whenever we talk about your spouse's handling of the family budget, you become sarcastic. What do you think might be going on?" This recognition of client resistance by the advisor helps the client focus on his or her behavior and allows angry feelings to be vented. Resistance must be addressed as directly as possible if any successful planning is to come out of the advisor-client relationship.

Other types of resistance behaviors that advisors might encounter during the financial planning process would include withdrawal or passivity; dwelling in fantasy or nonreality; ambivalence or vacillation; and the use of inappropriate humor, to name a few. As mentioned, the advisor should not analyze or interpret a client's resistance behavior because analysis tends only to make the client defensive. Instead, the advisor should be aware of what is occurring, note whether it is a recurrent pattern, and at an appropriate point share such observations in a nonjudgmental manner with the client.

Sources of Client Resistance

Client resistance is almost a given in the financial planning environment probably because clients, when they enter into an advisor-client relationship, yield a certain amount of their privacy and personal power over the situation to the advisor. Resistance is a way of defending or restoring some of the balance of power. Certain topics, because of their sensitive nature, seem to be particularly vulnerable to client resistance.

One such sensitive topic is death and dying. Because of its uncertainty, death is extremely anxiety producing to most people. Dr. Elisabeth Kubler-Ross, an eminent authority on death and dying, postulated that there are five stages that a person facing death passes through: denial, anger, bargaining, depression, and acceptance.[5] The first four of these stages are different forms of resistance that the person uses for self-protection. Financial advisors, when discussing future plans with older people, need to be particularly sensitive to the feelings of their clients. Advisors must listen and observe very closely what clients communicate when discussing death and dying. Advisors must be empathetic to feelings and communicate accurately what is heard and observed. A genuine concern for the feelings and attitudes of clients must be manifested. Advisors must also be aware of and have control over their own feelings about death, so that they do not impose on what clients are feeling and attempting to communicate.

During the financial planning process, advisors can help to restore some control over the future by involving clients fully in decision making and planning for contingencies. This allows clients to feel useful, worthwhile, and somewhat in control of their situation.

Another area where resistance may be encountered involves marital tensions, such as separation/divorce, parent-child disputes, the empty-nest syndrome, and mid-life crises. While financial advisors are not expected to be highly qualified marriage or family counselors, they should be astute enough to recognize when a married couple is resisting because of an underlying, unexpressed marital problem. And once it is recognized, advisors should be willing and able to focus with the couple on the problem area. Otherwise, if the problem is ignored, whatever decisions are reached will be less valid than those that would be reached after a full airing of the problem. Besides providing a possibly welcome catharsis for the couple, focusing on the problem can enable them to muster their forces in order to arrive at a mutually satisfactory solution. In planning sessions with couples who are in disagreement on a crucial subject, the advisor needs to listen closely to what both partners have to say. Letting the more dominant partner do most of the talking and deciding is far too common, unfortunately. Because the outcome of the decision affects both partners, both should be involved in the discussion. To do any less almost guarantees an unsatisfactory conclusion.

Another sensitive area involves executive clients who have failed to attain the degree of success they had dreamed of in their professions. Their dreams shattered and unfulfilled, they may resort to cynicism, biting sarcasm, or empty humor in an attempt to endure it. Rather than laugh along with them, the effective advisor reflects the underlying feelings to let the clients know that he or she understands their disappointment. A simple statement like, "I suppose it's a bitter pill to swallow when you've worked so hard to see your personal hopes go unfulfilled," allows your clients to feel understood and appreciated. More often than not, the clients will begin to discuss more openly how they feel. And once people are able to express their feelings, they are well on the way to addressing their problems in an effective manner.

Resistance behaviors, in any case, are a certain tip-off that clients are having difficulty subscribing to the advisor's line of reasoning. It does no good for the advisor to proceed with business as usual, ignoring the obvious resistance; nothing can be accomplished as long as the resistance continues. The resistance must be dealt with openly and objectively if there is any chance that it will diminish, allowing the participants to get on with the business at hand.

ATTRIBUTES OF AN EFFECTIVE ADVISOR

The main component that a financial advisor brings to a session with a client is himself or herself. Financial advisors, first and foremost, must be themselves in their relation to and interaction with clients. Each advisor is a human being, complete with strengths and weaknesses. The effective advisor is also sincere and genuine in attempting to help others learn how to help themselves.

Carl Rogers, in his classic book, *Client-Centered Therapy: Its Current Practice, Implications and Theory*, postulated that there are three conditions necessary to bring about constructive client change: (1) unconditional positive regard, (2) accurate empathy, and (3) genuineness.[6] Most experts on the subject agree that if an effective advisor-client relationship is to exist, the advisor must value the client as a unique individual (unconditional positive regard), must be able to perceive and understand what the client is experiencing (accurate empathy), and must be open and spontaneous (genuine).

A constructive advisor-client relationship serves not only to increase the opportunity for clients to attain the goals that are important to them, it also serves as a model of a good interpersonal relationship. Some questions that all financial advisors ought to ask themselves from time to time are the following:

- Knowing myself, do I think it will be possible to value my clients, especially those who think, feel, and act differently than I do?
- How easy or difficult will it be for me to view the world from another's perspective without imposing my own standards, beliefs, and attitudes on that person? Will my own values, ideas, and feelings hinder my understanding of another person?
- How open do I care, or dare, to be with a client? Will I be able to be myself and still adapt to the client's social style?

These are important questions for advisors to consider before engaging in the dynamics of an advisor-client relationship. Far too many financial advisors assume that they have the right kind of personality to counsel others without ever scrutinizing themselves in the same way.

Let us examine the three core conditions to which Rogers refers and a fourth condition, self-awareness.

Attributes of an Effective Advisor

- unconditional positive regard
- accurate empathy
- genuineness
- self-awareness

Unconditional Positive Regard

unconditional positive regard

Unconditional positive regard is an attitude of valuing the client, or being able to express appreciation of the client as a unique and worthwhile person. Liking and respecting another person have a circular effect. When advisors value clients, their sense of liking will be communicated to the clients; this by itself will enhance the clients' self-esteem and add to their appreciation of themselves as worthwhile human beings.

Accurate Empathy

accurate empathy

Accurate empathy means that the advisor's sense of the client's world fits the client's self-image. This gives clients the feeling that advisors are in touch with them. When clients say something like, "Yes, that's it," or "That's exactly right," it indicates that advisors are right on target, and that client's feel they are closely following and understanding them.

Learning to understand clients, however, is not an easy process. It involves the advisor's capacity to put aside his or her own set of experiences in favor of those of the client; the advisor must be able to see the client's problems through the client's eyes instead of his or her own. It requires skillful listening so the advisor can hear not only the obvious but also the subtleties of which even the client may be unaware.

Developing accurate empathy also requires the advisor to identify and resolve his or her own needs so they do not interfere with understanding the client's feelings and concerns. However, the advisor must be careful not to identify strongly with the client because this may impede rather than facilitate the counseling objective.

Genuineness

genuineness

Genuineness means simply that the advisor is a "real" person—there is no facade, no stereotypical role-playing of what a professional advisor is considered to be. Professional advisors who are genuine are wholly aware of themselves and their feelings, thoughts, values, and attitudes. They are not afraid to express themselves openly and honestly at all times. They communicate in an expressive manner and do not conceal anything. They are open and willing to listen to whatever the clients want to discuss. In other words, being genuine means that advisors are able to be themselves without having to sacrifice their integrity or compromise their principles.

And yet, in order for advisor-client relationships to work, advisors must learn how to accommodate client personalities by adapting to each client's social style. As discussed earlier in this chapter, this typically takes place in step 1 of the financial planning process when advisors are busy establishing and defining their relationships with clients. Adapting to a client's social style is an important component in building rapport with the client, and an advisor-client relationship built on rapport is much more likely to be a productive and ongoing relationship than one missing this ingredient.

Self-Awareness

self-awareness

There is general consensus among counselor-educators that advisors should possess *self-awareness*, especially with regard to their attitudes and values. Advisors who are aware of their own value systems have a better chance of avoiding the imposition of their values on their clients. This quality is of vital importance since advisors want to help clients make decisions that stem from the clients' own value systems rather than from the advisors. The more advisors know about themselves, the better they can understand, interpret, evaluate, and control their behavior and the less likely they are to attribute aspects of themselves to clients, a rather common defense mechanism known as projection. Before advisors can be aware of others, it is essential that they be solidly grounded in self-awareness.

In her book, *Effective Helping: Interviewing and Counseling Techniques*, Barbara Okun suggests that an advisor should continually try to determine his or her own needs, feelings, and values by answering the following questions:[7]

- Am I aware when I find myself feeling uncomfortable with a client or with a particular subject area?
- Am I aware of my avoidance strategies?
- Can I really be honest with the client?
- Do I always feel the need to be in control of situations?
- Do I often feel as if I must be omnipotent in that I must do something to make the client "get better" so that I can be successful?
- Am I so problem-oriented that I'm always looking for the negative, for a problem, and never responding to the positive, to the good?
- Am I able to be as open with clients as I want them to be with me?

The adage "know thyself" should apply to financial advisors and other helping professionals even more than it does to the population at large. A very large part of the responsibility of an advisor is to know himself or herself as thoroughly as possible, so he or she is able to provide the very best kind of objective, informed counseling for clients. An advisor who has many blind spots about himself or herself will surely be less effective in a helping situation than an advisor who is comfortably self-aware. This is not to say that an advisor must be a problem-free, completely self-actualized individual; rather, it means that the advisor is a human being with a multitude of strengths and some weaknesses—but weaknesses that are known and will not interfere with the dynamics of counseling another person.

Orientation to Values

People have value systems that are the result of years of living on this planet. Many of these values are inculcated in them by their parents, their schools, their religions, their peers, and society. However these values came to them, they are as much a part of them as their physical and psychological characteristics. This is not to say that they are a permanent, static part of their being because values can, and do, change.

A vivid example of this type of change came during the 1960s and early 1970s when a whole society's value system was rocked to the core by momentous events such as the assassinations of the Kennedys and Martin Luther King, Jr., the civil rights movement, the war in Vietnam, the women's rights movement, and the Kent State killings. This truly was a time when an entire nation's value system was challenged and as a result, certain long-cherished values were thrust into a state of flux and some ultimately changed. And what happened to the nation as a whole was likewise happening to individuals. A sizable number of the people who at first believed the Vietnam War was justified slowly changed their feelings not only about that war but about armed conflict in general. And virtually the same transformation happened on other controversial issues.

The point is that values, while deeply internalized, are not immutable. Advisors need to remind themselves of this as they work with clients who are confused and afraid in approaching important decisions. While people are in many ways a reflection of their past history, they are—or can be—much more than that. There is no need to be shackled to the past. People can, if they choose, overcome their past and live new lives based on who they are in the present and what they believe in and hold to be valuable both now and in the future. This is a liberating concept that frees people to think, feel, and behave in ways that are compatible with their present being, rather than dooming themselves to repeat the past and live in ways that are no longer meaningful.

The financial advisor's role in this situation is to act as a catalyst rather than as a maintainer of the status quo. The implied danger, of course, is that advisors might try to force change in their clients' values and attitudes where none is desired or sought, or that advisors might subtly or not so subtly try to impose their values on clients. Both of these dangers must be consciously guarded against. What advisors must do is listen carefully to clients as they sift through the various value choices faced so when clients finally make the choice, it can be done freely without encumbrances from the past. Clients must actually be opened up to the freedom of making choices that are relevant and meaningful to their very existence. Good advisors have a knack for being able to do this.

Differences in Values

Each person has a hierarchy of values that makes order of his or her life. An older client facing retirement might, for example, rank security above risk taking when deciding how to invest money. On the other hand, a younger financial advisor might rank risk taking above security in the hierarchy of values. What happens, then, when the risk-taking advisor sits down to counsel his or her security-minded client? If the advisor is sensitive and understanding, he or she will listen to the client and try to get a sense of what is important to the client, what the client is willing and unwilling to do. The effective financial advisor does not try to sell the client a product and/or service that the advisor believes is right for the client but that the client believes is wrong, unsafe, or risky.

Counseling is caring, and caring means that the advisor cares enough—has enough faith in the client's worth as a unique human being—to permit the client to make value choices that fit the client's value system. The financial advisor can and should provide information that will help the client make the choice, but the choice ultimately belongs with the client, not the advisor. Only in this way is the advisor truly counseling the client.

In addition to differences in values, which often are reflective of the differences in age between advisors and clients, we should also consider several other "isms"—sexism and racism—and how they impinge on the advisor-client relationship. Let us look first at sex differences.

Sexist counseling occurs when the advisor uses his or her own sex ideology as a framework for counseling. In the field of financial planning, this might take place when a male advisor discourages a female client from doing something that has traditionally been thought by many men to be inappropriate, such as returning to work when there is an infant at home to be cared for. This kind of subtle advice giving, besides reflecting the obvious sex-role bias of the advisor, is not in keeping with what is happening in many households today. More importantly, it is intrusive in that the responsibility for making the decision is clearly the client's and not the advisor's. Advisors must learn to recognize their own biases and sex-role stereotypes and not inflict them on people whom they are trying to help.

In the case of married couples, financial advisors typically counsel both husband and wife. It is important to understand what both spouses have to say. In the past it was far too common to defer to the husband, the perceived "breadwinner," without taking into consideration what the wife had to contribute. Today that is not the case. When both husband and wife are in complete agreement, no problem exists. But when they disagree—and this is often communicated through nonverbal signals like a sigh, a frown, or an angry glance—it is important to make a point of bringing the subject up for a full discussion. It is far better to spend whatever time and energy it takes to bring both spouses to a mutually acceptable decision than to proceed with one spouse's plan of action knowing that it does not satisfy the other one.

Regarding racism in the financial planning profession, advisors should not limit their choice of clients based on race or make assumptions about their client's needs based on race.

The issue of whether white advisors can be effective in a relationship with African American or Hispanic clients has been the subject of much research though no conclusive findings exist. An effective advisor should be able to work with clients of all races because all people have the same basic psychological needs and problems. Advisors need to be conscious of their own biases regarding race and to guard against allowing biases to adversely affect the quality of the advisor-client relationship. The counseling strategies employed should not differ with regard to the race of the client any more than they should differ with regard to the sex, age, or religion of the client.

BASIC COMMUNICATION PRINCIPLES

In the previous section we discussed the attributes of an effective advisor. In this section we will explore communication as a process and attempt to relate fundamental principles of communication to effective counseling in the financial planning process. An effective advisor is also an effective communicator.

Communication is often thought of as one person sending a message through both verbal and nonverbal channels to another person or persons with the intention of evoking a response. A speaker asks, "How are you?" and the listener (or receiver of the communication) answers, "Just fine—except for my back." Effective communication takes place when the receiver interprets the sender's message in precisely the same fashion in which the sender intended it. Difficulties in communication arise when the receiver misunderstands and/or misinterprets the sender's message. Since any individual's intentions are private and rarely clearly stated, the receiver of the message has the difficult job of decoding the message without knowing for a fact what the sender's intentions are.

In addition, communication failures can also be attributed to the wide variety of stimuli with which individuals are bombarded during the course of a conversation. People try to communicate while watching television or listening to the radio, or they attempt to conduct two conversations simultaneously. But all noise is not auditory; some is emotional in nature. For example, labor-management negotiations are often fraught with suspicion and mistrust. Prejudices and biases, then, are emotionally built-in stimuli that interfere with objective listening and effective communication.

Related to this communication failure is the sad but simple truth that individuals listen in order to evaluate and render judgment about the speaker, which, in turn, makes the speaker guarded and defensive about what he or she is attempting to communicate. Perhaps the best example of this type of ineffective communication is a city council meeting where one side advocates raising taxes while the other side interrupts, casts aspersions, and generally fights mightily against the tax hike. Whenever there are two people or two groups, each with a strong vested interest in an emotional issue, the likelihood of there being clear communication is virtually nil.

Even in the best of circumstances communication should not be taken for granted. Let us look now at some basic principles of communication.

- Communication is learned through experience, but experience itself does not necessarily make one an effective communicator. As children, we learn how to communicate by imitating our models—parents, siblings, neighbors, playmates, and babysitters. Unfortunately, not all of our models are effective communicators. Thus, we acquire poor habits of communication early, and those habits, like all habits, are difficult to break. A child reared in a home where everyone talks at the same time and no one listens carries this model when leaving the home.

- The meaning of words is illusory. Words do not mean—people do. Words are merely symbols. Consider, for example, a simple word like rock. The teenager immediately thinks of loud music; the geologist thinks of a hard object created millions of years ago; the burglar thinks of a diamond ring; the old person thinks of a favorite chair, and so on. The point is that a word can have almost as many meanings as there are people who use it.

- Language is learned. Thus, in a sense we are programmed, and the meaning of words stays within us for future reference. This programming is extremely helpful since, once we learn a word, it usually remains ours for a lifetime. However, this programming can also serve as an impediment to open communication with others in that we often refer to our original conceptions of words without thinking how others might interpret them. For example, the word girls, once used to refer to any female, is now clearly inappropriate in referring to an adult woman in this age of women's rights.

- No two people are programmed alike. Therefore, no symbol can always be interpreted the same way. We differ in the nature and degree of our understanding. We perceive our environment differently according to our own frame of reference, so consequently meanings differ.

- It is impossible for any individual to encode or process all parts of a message. Besides the fact that words are often inadequate in describing accurately what we are feeling or thinking, there is also the problem of distortion, that is, altering the event to suit our own purposes. But even if we have the precise word and communicate it without distortion, we still are faced with the problem of the receiver's receiving it in the same way in which it was intended.

- Some experts claim that the single greatest problem with communication is the assumption of it. We assume that our messages are clearly understood. We also sometimes assume that our perceptions are more accurate than the perceptions of another. Where human communication is concerned, no assumptions can or should be made.

- We are constantly communicating. Anything we say or do can be interpreted in a meaningful way as a message. Even during periods of silence, communication takes place. Nonverbal behaviors (which will be discussed in some detail shortly) such as eye contact, facial expressions, gestures, body posture, voice inflections, hesitations, and the like, all speak volumes. In fact, most sociological research claims that approximately two-thirds of the total message is communicated via nonverbal channels, especially where human emotions are concerned.

- Listening is communication too. Unfortunately, not everyone is a good listener. However, that should not be too surprising since listening as a communication skill is rarely, if ever, formally taught. To speak precisely and to listen carefully present a real challenge to all of us. The way in which we listen and respond to another person is crucial for building a fulfilling relationship. When we listen carefully—with understanding and without evaluation—and when we respond relevantly, we implicitly communicate to the speaker, "I care about what you are saying, and I'd like to understand it."

- The most effective communication occurs when the receiver of a message gives understanding responses, sometimes called paraphrases. A client might say, "I don't know. . . . I doubt that we can afford to send both of our kids to college." A financial advisor using an understanding response would reply, "So you're just not sure you have the resources for college educations right now." While it might be tempting to try to convince the clients at this juncture that there is a way to finance their children's college educations, the understanding response communicates a desire to understand the clients without evaluating these statements as right or wrong. It also helps the advisor to see the expressed ideas and feelings of clients from their point of view.

- Personalizing messages enhances the communication process and the advisor-client relationship. The hallmark of personal statements is the use of the personal pronouns, I, me, and my. Using generalized pronouns such as everyone, anyone, or somebody to refer to our own ideas only tends to confuse clients and hence results in ambiguity and faulty understanding. Personal statements like, "I can appreciate your concern over not having adequate resources," reveals your own feelings to clients and builds rapport by increasing the personal quality of the relationship.

Elements of Nonverbal Behaviors

nonverbal behaviors

As mentioned above, clients communicate many feelings and attitudes to their advisors through nonverbal behaviors including (but not limited to) fear, anxiety, sincerity, confusion, anger, aggression, happiness, hostility, interest, boredom, and concern. In the counseling context, *nonverbal behaviors* refer to those aspects of communication other than the words themselves. The two main sources of nonverbal behaviors are the body and the voice. From these two sources come seven types of nonverbal signs of meaning: body positions, body movements, gestures, facial expressions, eye contact, voice tone, and voice pitch. Each of these types of nonlinguistic signs conveys a wealth of information to the observant financial advisor. It should be noted that the advisor's first impressions of the meaning or significance of any body language must be checked out against other clues given by the client.

The Body

When learning to improve one's ability to observe the nonverbal behaviors of clients, it is important to notice the various ways by which the body actually communicates, either in agreement or in disagreement with what is actually said. In particular, the advisor should notice and learn to interpret the communications that are transmitted by the client's body positions and movements.

Body Positions—Overall body posture is often the first thing the observant advisor notices. Clients who sit erectly and comfortably are usually relaxed. Leaning slightly forward is usually a sign of interest and involvement in the planning session. Slouching or seeming to draw away from the advisor may indicate no interest or trust in the advisor—or boredom. Good client posture may indicate self-assurance and high self-esteem. Poor posture may signal a lack of self-assurance and low self-esteem.

The advisor should also notice the position of the client's arms and legs. When the legs are uncrossed and the arms are positioned comfortably at the sides, the client is usually relaxed and open. Tightly crossed arms and legs, on the other hand, may indicate distrust or unreceptiveness. The facial position of the client should also be noticed. Most people's faces are expressive of a wide range of ever-changing feelings. The client whose face appears frozen in one position may be signaling fear, anxiety, anger, or another emotion that could become an obstacle to open communication with the advisor.

Body Movements—The client who frequently changes body positions may be indicating physical or emotional discomfort or a lack of interest. The advisor should take note of such movements and try to relate them to information gleaned later.

There is reason to believe that body language may be more honest or pure than verbal communication. In certain positive, straightforward human experiences we know that it is. The impulsive hug or kiss of greeting for people we care for is the most obvious example. But we also communicate through body language what we do not want to communicate, or when we are in denial or contradicting ourselves. For example, a client may say, "No, I'm not nervous about investing in a tax shelter," while biting his nails, pulling his hair, or fidgeting distractedly. We often say what we think we may be expected to say in a given situation or context and not realize what we may truly be communicating through body language.

Gestures—Hand and arm gestures are usually used to illustrate or accent verbal statements. Hands clasped so tightly that the knuckles are whitened and taut certainly signify something, perhaps fear or anxiety. While jerky hand and arm gestures may indicate anxiety, smooth and flowing gestures usually mean that the client is relaxed and interested in the planning session. Frequent crossing and uncrossing of the legs or bouncing a leg may indicate nervousness, boredom, or lack of interest.

Facial Expressions—The financial advisor can learn much from a client's facial expressions. Look for frowns, smiles, or nervous habits such as biting the lips. Look especially to see if the client's facial expressions change as topics change, and note whether the expression is appropriate or incongruent. For example, if a client talks about anger, does he or she appear angry? If the client expresses disgust about his or her spouse's extravagant spending, do the client's intentions in his or her last will and testament reflect that feeling by providing for the children through a trust, rather than leaving everything outright to the spouse?

Eye Contact—Eye contact or the lack of it can indicate what the client is feeling. If the client's eyes are downcast and rarely meet the gaze of the advisor, the client could be shy, anxious, or fearful (though not necessarily toward the advisor). On the other hand, if the client stares or glares constantly at the advisor, anger or hostility could be indicated. If the client's eyes rove all around the room, looking at the walls and ceiling while the advisor is filling out the fact-finder form, there could be a serious lack of interest in the relevance of data gathering. A client who is open and interested in the fact-finding session will usually meet the gaze of the advisor. This eye contact usually indicates a positive and concerned attitude toward and interest in the fact-finding session. Likewise, the client is inclined to perceive and interpret the advisor's eye contact in the same way.

The Voice

Nonverbal voice clues can be observed in the tone and pitch of the client's voice. Tone and pitch are qualities of the voice that may indicate the speaker's feelings, quite apart from what is actually said. They should be observed closely.

Voice Tone—Voice tone is loudness or softness. The client who talks very loudly or shouts may be indicating anger or hostility. The client who talks very softly may be exhibiting fear or shyness.

Voice Pitch—Voice pitch is the quality of a voice that indicates how high or low the voice is on a musical scale. A high-pitched voice may indicate anxiety, fear, or anger. A low-pitched voice may indicate either comfort or control of strong emotions.

Obviously, some people's voices are naturally louder than others. The natural pitch of different voices also varies greatly. The point is not to type these differences but to observe and determine which vocal qualities are natural to a particular client so as to recognize variations. If these vocal qualities do vary during planning sessions in relation to personal and financial details, they can be important clues to the strong emotions that often affect a client's motivations, needs, and goals. The planning sessions themselves are often an inducement to clients to open up and vent their feelings about their financial situations. Thus, voice tone and pitch are important factors for the advisor to observe and consider in relation to all other clues that characterize the client and reveal his or her self-image.

Elements of Nonverbal Behaviors

- The body
  - Body positions
  - Body movements
  - Gestures
  - Facial expressions
  - Eye contact
- The voice
  - Voice tone
  - Voice pitch

Interpreting the Meaning of Nonverbal Behaviors

Financial advisors should note that in all the descriptions above of nonverbal behaviors, of body language, we have stated that a behavior may or usually does indicate one or more feelings. Nonverbal behaviors are clues that must be clearly observed and compared with what the client says in order to determine whether they are appropriate or compatible with their actions. For example, if a client blurts out, "I am furious with the broker who sold me that bunch of junk last year!" and strikes the desk, the gesture is compatible with the verbal message—it agrees with what the client says. If the client makes the same statement and sits calmly smiling, however, there is incompatible behavior—the body language does not jibe with the verbal message. When the financial advisor observes incompatible behavior of this sort in a client, it should be mentioned to the client in order to clarify the element of the communication that is correct.

Nonverbal behaviors are clues or indicators. While they signify something, their meanings can be clouded by incompatibility, distortion, or vagueness. Premature assumptions about what they really mean would be as unprofessional as failing to notice them altogether. For example, a client's palsied hands might be due to one or more of the following causes: nervousness, fear, Parkinson's disease, too much coffee, chemical poisoning, and/or alcoholism. The client who always talks loudly may be either angry or hearing impaired or merely an overbearing individual. The client who shows no interest in a financial planning session may be worn out with worrying whether his or her recent commodities futures trading is going to wipe him or her out with margin calls, or whether he or she should buy term or whole life for estate liquidity, or whether he or she will have an estate. The client may be on tranquilizers over worry about a son and heir who abuses drugs. For any number of reasons, the client may need psychological counseling or therapy before he or she can undertake financial planning. In short, not all the problems that clients may bring to financial planning sessions are financial in origin or nature. When present, these nonfinancial problems will distort client messages and add to the difficulties of clarifying them.

Observant advisors need to be astute enough to discern from among all the verbal and nonverbal clues presented by the client and be aware that in most cases there will be a mixture of compatible and incompatible clues. Advisors thus understand who clients are, where they are, where they want to go, and can then suggest the optimal ways to help each one get there. The advisor should not assume that he or she knows what a given behavior means. The advisor should check it out and clarify his or her perceptions with each client.

And the advisor should not forget that he or she communicates in both verbal and nonverbal ways too, just as the client does, and that his or her communication behaviors very much affect the client. This is particularly true of nonverbal messages. Therefore, any of the communication and psychological considerations that apply to the client also apply to the advisor. As a financial planning professional, the advisor will want to remove from his or her own behaviors those elements that present obstacles to successful communication with the client and with other professionals. The client is then more likely to accept the advisor's role as a financial planning professional and, ultimately, the financial plan that the advisor develops for meeting the client's financial needs and goals. Similarly, other professionals whose expertise the advisor may need in developing and implementing the client's financial plan will respect the advisor's role as a financial planning professional.

ATTENDING AND LISTENING SKILLS

Paying attention to clients is the first necessary component in good communication. No matter how expert an advisor's other communication skills are, if he or she is inattentive to clients' verbal and nonverbal behaviors, the advisor is apt to lose the clients at the very outset. How often have you been in the company of another person who shies away from looking at you, who glances nervously at his or her wristwatch, who interrupts you, and who, literally and figuratively, turns his or her back to you? Surely, if you had this kind of experience you would recall just how uncomfortable and ill at ease you were with this inattentive behavior.

If an advisor's goal is to understand clients, the advisor must first pay close attention to or focus on their verbal and nonverbal messages. Poor attending and poor listening lead to poor understanding.

Physical Attending

Gerard Egan, a renowned counselor-educator, categorizes attending behavior into (1) *physical attending*, or using the body to communicate, and (2) psychological attending, or listening actively. He identifies five basic attributes associated with physical attending.[8] These attributes are

- face the other person squarely—When there is face-to-face, direct contact, the communication process is enhanced. You communicate nonverbally to the other person, "I'm here with you; I'm tuned in and ready to face the issues with you head-on." Turning your body away lessens your involvement with the other person.
- adopt an open posture—There is something to be said about receiving a person with open arms. Crossed arms and crossed legs can inadvertently communicate a holding-off of the other person. An open posture—open arms and uncrossed legs with a big smile—communicates receptiveness to the other person and, hence, increases good communication and decreases defensiveness.
- lean toward the other person—This is another physical signal of interest, involvement, and caring. Two people who care about what the other is saying almost always lean toward each other. On the other hand, two people who lean away from one another or sit rigidly straight in their chairs seem to be either bored or disinterested, or extremely cautious and defensive about getting involved with each other.
- maintain good eye contact—Good eye contact consists of looking at another individual when you are in conversation. Poor eye contact consists of rarely looking at the other person, or looking away when he or she looks at you, or staring constantly with a blank expression on your face. The eye contact should be natural and spontaneous. Since you are interested in your client, you will want to use your eyes as a vehicle of communication.
- be relaxed while attending—It is possible to focus intently on the client and be relaxed at the same time. A nervous, fidgety, or rigid advisor communicates these feelings to the client. An advisor who sits in a casual fashion, who speaks naturally and spontaneously, and who uses natural gestures has the advantage of being free to focus intently on the client and on his or her communication, as well as helping to facilitate naturalness and spontaneity in the client.

As has been mentioned previously, communication is constantly taking place, so an advisor should use his or her body—gestures, posture, eyes—to communicate whatever message he or she wishes to communicate. Otherwise, the body may communicate something the advisor does not wish to communicate. In other words, the advisor should try to make his or her body work in behalf of the advisor-client relationship.

Attributes Associated With Physical Attending

- Face the other person squarely.
- Adopt an open posture.
- Lean toward the other person.
- Maintain good eye contact.
- Be relaxed while attending.

Active Listening

active listening

So far, attending has been described as a physical activity; *active listening* brings in the psychological activity involved in attending. Many advisors take listening for granted, but there is a distinct difference between simply hearing and actively listening. Hearing means the receiving of auditory signals. A person says, "I have a bad headache," and we hear that message and respond, "That's too bad," or "Here, have a couple of aspirin." An active listener, on the other hand, might respond, "You look as though it's really getting you down." In short, the active listener responds not only to the verbal message received through the auditory channel, but also to the unspoken, or nonverbal message, communicated by the sender's body, facial expression, and/or tone of voice.

Active listening, then, means putting the nonverbal behavior, the voice, and words together—all the cues sent out by the other person—to get the essence of the communication being sent. An active listener is an understanding listener, one who attempts to see the world from the other's frame of reference. If an advisor can state in his or her own words what a client said, and the client accepts the advisor's statement as an accurate reflection of what the client said, then it is safe to say that the advisor listened actively and understood with accuracy.

Active listening is not merely parroting another's words—a toy can be programmed to do that. Active listening means involving yourself in the inner world of another person while, at the same time, maintaining your own identity and being able to respond with meaningfulness to the messages of that other person.

Understanding Responses

As indicated above, active listening is hard work and requires intense focusing and concentration. Years of not listening have made most of us poor listeners. We are distracted easily. We tend to evaluate and judge what is being said while it is being said, so that we are framing our own responses to the speaker's statement before the speaker is finished talking. Thus, we miss the message.

There are several simple ways of responding to people so that they feel accepted and understood. Let us look at some of these understanding responses.

continuing response

Perhaps the simplest type of understanding response is what Allen Ivey refers to as a *continuing response*.[9] Nonverbally, if an advisor wants a client to continue talking, he or she might smile or nod his or her head to communicate agreement and/or understanding. Equally as effective in communicating understanding is a minimal encourager like "uh-huh," "mmmm," "then?" "and . . .?" These relatively unobtrusive responses encourage the speaker to continue talking. They communicate to the speaker, "Go on, I'm with you."

restatement-of-content response

Another type of understanding response that enhances communication is the *restatement-of-content response*. The rationale for restatement is to let speakers hear what they have said on the assumption that this may encourage them to go on speaking, examining, and looking deeper. Restatement communicates to a client, "I am listening to you very carefully, so much so that I can repeat what you have said."

The most effective restatements are those that are phrased in your own words, a paraphrase of what the speaker has stated. To do this effectively, we must temporarily suspend our own frame of reference and attempt to view the world from the other person's perspective. Suppose a client says to an advisor, "I'm really in a financial bind, what with taxes, inflation, and fuel bills. I don't know how we make it from one month to the next." An accurate restatement might be expressed, "So things are tough for you financially. It seems like you can't make ends meet." The client, hearing this understanding response, is encouraged to delve more deeply into the situation, feeling that the advisor has indeed heard the message on the same wavelength on which it was transmitted. Consequently the bond between client and advisor is strengthened, and greater opportunities for creative problem solving are opened up.

Just as the advisor manifests understanding for his or her client by responding to the content of the client's message, so may the advisor also show understanding of the client's experience by responding in a way that reflects the feelings expressed. Sometimes feelings are expressed directly, and at other times they are implied or stated indirectly. In order to respond to a person's feelings, we must observe the behavioral cues like tone of voice, body posture, gestures, and facial expression, as well as listen to the speaker's words.

reflection-of-feeling response

Consider this client statement: "Within the next few months, we need to buy a new refrigerator and another car. [Sighs] I just don't know where the money is going to come from." A *reflection-of-feeling response* might be, "You sound pretty hopeless about your financial state. It sure is hard to break even, let alone get ahead, these days." Again, by responding in an empathic way to the client's statement, the advisor communicates a deep understanding of the client's experience; in addition, the advisor progresses one step further by addressing the nonverbalized feelings. This illustrates to the client that the advisor understands so well what the client is stating that he or she can paraphrase both words and feelings.

It is helpful to both the client and the advisor to struggle to capture in words the uniqueness of the client's experience. The most effective types of understanding responses capsulize both the feeling and the content of the client's message. The basic format for this type of response is "You feel _____ [feeling] because _____ [content]." This response enables the client to get in closer touch with the feelings that are an outgrowth of his or her situation. And that, in turn, facilitates the working through of the problem, because the advisor involves the client in exploring himself or herself in the problem. Because the advisor has accurately understood and responded to the client, the client will go on to share other personal experiences that bear upon the presented problem.

A word might be added here about the difficulties that some people have in dealing with feelings, either their own or others or both. Problems often arise in interpersonal relationships because one or more of the involved persons choose to repress, distort, or disguise their feelings rather than confront them and discuss them openly. This is particularly true of so-called negative feelings like anger, sadness, anxiety, frustration, discomfort, and confusion. In actuality, no feelings are negative since they all are part of being human. In any case, advisors who wish to communicate effectively need to address their own feelings as well as those of their clients. The mutual expression of feelings is an integral part of building a close, trusting, caring relationship.

Two other types of understanding responses should be mentioned. Each is related to the restatement-of-content and the reflection-of-feeling responses. Yet there is a subtle shade of difference. The first is the *clarifying response;* it tends to amplify the speaker's statement. The clarifying response does not add anything new to what the speaker has said; it simply expands what has already been stated. The advisor attempts to restate or clarify for the client what the client has had some difficulty in expressing clearly. It is akin to a translation of the client's words into language that is more familiar and understandable to both client and advisor. Suppose a client says, "I'm not sure. Nothing makes sense anymore. Things get more confusing the more I think about them. It's a real puzzle to me." The advisor, by way of clarification, might say, "I can sense your bewilderment. Let me see if I can help out. From what you've said previously, I get the impression that you want to get your mortgage straightened out before you increase your monthly savings. Is that it?" If the advisor has, indeed, been following the flow of the client's experience, this statement will help to clarify the client's confusion

clarifying response

over the situation. To the extent that the advisor's response is on target, the puzzle becomes suddenly clear and more readily solved.

Clarifying responses by the advisor are helpful for the client because they

- facilitate client self-understanding
- attend especially to the client's feelings
- communicate the advisor's understanding to the client
- move the client toward a clearer definition of the problem

Another side to the clarifying response concerns the advisor's need to have communication clarified. When the advisor is puzzled, then it is certainly legitimate to ask for clarification as, "I'm sorry. I don't follow what you're saying. Can you make that clearer for me?"

summarization response

The second is the *summarization response*. Summaries are especially helpful toward the end of a session, since they focus and capsulize a series of scattered ideas to present a clear perspective. The summary has the effect of reassuring clients that the advisor has been tuned in to their many messages. For the advisor, it serves as a check on the accuracy with which the various messages have been received.

It is sometimes better to have the client do the summarizing. In this way, the client maintains the responsibility for bringing the messages together into a meaningful conclusion. As in clarifying, themes and emotional overtones should be summarized, and the key ideas should be synthesized into broad statements reflecting basic meanings. An example of an effective summary by the advisor might be: "So today you described your overall financial situation as bleak, although you think you might be able to increase your savings if you could refinance your mortgage. I know you're rightly concerned about that." If the advisor has accurately summarized the essence of the session, the client will have a better handle on the intricacies of the situation and a resolution will be closer at hand.

In the last section we covered some basic principles of communication with the focus on nonverbal behaviors. In this section, our attention was directed to the skills of physical attending and active listening plus five types of understanding responses associated with active listening (that is, continuing, restatement of content, reflection of feeling, clarifying, and summarization). The element common to all five of these understanding responses is that the advisor follows, or tracks, the client's lead. These types of responses communicate a high level of understanding that enable the client not only to experience what it feels like to be understood, but also to progress further toward an ultimate resolution of the situation.

Types of Understanding Responses Associated With Active Listening

- continuing
- restatement of content
- reflection of feeling
- clarifying
- summarization

LEADING RESPONSES

leading response

    Now the focus turns to a *leading response* in which the advisor, to a certain extent, takes the lead and deviates somewhat from the client's preceding responses. When the financial advisor decides to make a leading response, it is the advisor's frame of reference that comes into focus. Up to this point, the advisor's responses have followed from the client's statements, but here the emphasis shifts. An obvious danger of this shift is that the advisor may move in a direction in which the client is not yet ready or willing to move. Despite this danger, if the advisor has followed the client closely so far, and if a good relationship has been established, then this different kind of response should not threaten the client as long as it is used carefully and tentatively.

explanatory response

    The first type of leading response is the *explanatory response*. An explanation is a relatively neutral description of the way things are. It deals in logical, practical, and factual information. It is often offered at the client's request, although there are instances when the advisor will offer an explanation without it being requested. A client may be confused by some terminology that the advisor has used and ask, for example, "Exactly what is an annuity?" The advisor's explanation should be simple, concise, and comprehensible. Long-winded explanations tend to become vague and hard to follow. The advisor should also guard against a condescending, patronizing, or pedantic tone. The best explanations are those that are exchanged between equal partners (not superior-subordinates) in a relationship.

interpretive response

    Another type of leading response is the *interpretive response*. Interpretations can be particularly risky when the advisor goes too deep too soon, or when the interpretation is off base. Interpretations often come across as sounding overly clinical, diagnostic, and authoritarian. Despite these drawbacks, interpretations can be extremely effective responses because they often cut to the heart of the matter. When the interpretation makes sense to the client, it definitely accelerates the session. We should keep in mind that the goal of all interpretive efforts is self-interpretation by the client in order to increase the client's ability to act effectively. The following is an example of a facilitative interpretation:

Client:	"I'm not sure whether I want to retire early. I like to keep busy, and I don't know what I'd do with all that free time."
Advisor:	"So the prospect of an early retirement is a bit frightening. Maybe you're afraid that you'd just waste your time away?"

Notice that the financial advisor's interpretation did not stray too far from what the client had said. The advisor used the words "frightening" and "afraid," but probably did so on the basis of some fear or trepidation detected in the client's voice. Further, the advisor responded tentatively, using qualifiers like "a bit" and "maybe," and converted the second statement into a question by a raised voice at the end of the sentence. This enables the client to assimilate the advisor's response without feeling as though it has been offered as a fiat from above. The client, thus, is free to accept, modify, or deny the advisor's interpretation, and this is very important. If the advisor's interpretation is inaccurate, it is far better to discover that early than to proceed indefinitely along the wrong path.

reassuring response

A third type of leading response frequently employed by advisors is reassurance, or encouragement. A *reassuring response* is designed with the intention of making the client feel better, to bolster his or her spirits, and to offer support in a time of need. It communicates clearly to the client that "I am here ready to help you in any way that I can." As a means of helping, however, the reassuring response tends to be merely a temporary measure. It is akin to offering a tissue to someone who is crying; the crying may stop temporarily, but the underlying causes have been left untouched. For this reason the advisor must be careful not to use reassurance indiscriminately. The reflection-of-feeling type of understanding response discussed in the previous section on active listening is far more effective when emotions surface. The reflecting-of-feeling response communicates accurate empathy. The reassuring response offers only sympathy, and very few people like to feel pitied. Contrast the effect of these two different kinds of responses on our hypothetical client:

Client:	"I get so furious whenever my broker ignores me! It's almost as though I don't exist!"
Advisor:	(using a reassuring response): "Well, don't feel so bad. It doesn't do much good to get so worked up. Try not to worry about it, and you'll feel better."
Advisor:	(using a reflection-of-feeling response): "I can feel the rage as you speak. You feel like a nonperson around your broker, that you are not getting adequate service for the money you are paying, and this infuriates you."

The first advisor response patches a Band-Aid on a deep wound and is, therefore, ineffectual. The second response reflects the deeply felt anger and, in so doing, helps the client work through the anger. Reassurance, while not a harmful response, promises pie in the sky and delivers nothing.

suggestive response

The final type of leading response involves giving advice and is called a *suggestive response*. Many people actively seek the advice of others, possibly hoping that the advice giver will make the difficult decisions for them or solve their problems for them. And, as chance or human nature would have it, there is certainly no dearth of people in this world willing to dole out free advice. In an advisor-client relationship, however, the best kind of advice is self-advice. Advisors who have been responding in an understanding fashion are already well on their way toward helping clients discover, in their own way and in their own time, what advice is best for them. There are times in an advisor-client relationship when proffering advice is acceptable, but these times are few. When advice is given, it should be offered tentatively in the form of a suggestion or recommendation about which the client has the final decision. Otherwise, the advisor not only leads, he or she takes over the ultimate responsibility for the client's financial plan. Each person has the right to form his or her own plan. Advice giving robs the client of this right.

The next section looks at another type of communication technique —perhaps the most commonly used communication technique—the question. Questions come in many varieties, some much more effective in communication than others.

Types of Leading Responses

- explanatory
- interpretive
- reassuring
- suggestive

THE QUESTION

The question is surely one of the most timeworn communication techniques. The question is appropriate when used sparingly by the advisor to gather information from the client in order to develop a plan or devise strategies. Unfortunately, the question is not always used in this fashion because many advisors see their main role, however inappropriate, as an interviewer or even an interrogator. Moreover, a lengthy question-answer dialogue sets up a pattern of communication that is difficult for the participants to break: the client waits for the inevitable question; the question comes, followed by the answer (and not much more); and then comes the wait for the next question. Questioning almost always casts the advisor in the role of authority figure and the client in the role of a somewhat passive subordinate—certainly not the type of interpersonal, advisor-client relationship conducive to effective financial counseling.

Despite the disadvantages of using questions, there are times when only a well-phrased question will suffice, particularly when an advisor is seeking data from the client (step 2 of the financial planning process). Even here, though, there is a qualitative difference between the various types of questions that might be asked. With this in mind, several categories of questions are discussed in this final section of the chapter.

Open-Ended Versus Closed-Ended Questions

open-ended question
closed-ended question

Ideally, questions posed by the advisor should be open-ended and should require more than just a yes or no response; otherwise, they tend to stifle interaction. The *open-ended question* allows the client to select a response from a full repertory. The *closed-ended question* limits the client to a specific, narrow response, often either a yes or a no. The open-ended question solicits opinions, thoughts, ideas, values, and feelings. The closed-ended question typically solicits singular facts or one-word replies.

Contrast the differences in the following sets of questions. The first question in each set is closed-ended; the second question in each set is open-ended.

1. a. Are you ready to start an investment program?
    b. How do you feel about starting an investment program?
2. a. Have you given any thought to retirement?
    b. What thoughts do you have about retirement?
3. a. Are you afraid to start saving something now?
    b. Why have you decided to wait to start saving?

As can be readily seen from the above examples, the open-ended questions ask for more complete, comprehensive information. In a way, they force the client to formulate thoughts, ideas, and feelings into fully rounded responses. On the other hand, the closed-ended questions solicit only a one-word or short-answer response, requiring little thought, offering virtually no feedback, and preventing the client from exploring thoughts, ideas, and feelings. However, despite the drawbacks of closed-ended questions, there are times when they can be effectively used to gather certain types of information.

Leading Questions

leading question

A type of closed-ended question that is not only ineffective but also manipulative is a *leading question*. A leading question usually begins with, "Don't you think . . . ," or "Do you really feel . . . ." More often than not it leads the client toward a conclusion that the advisor (not the client) has already formulated, so that there is an element of dishonesty in even asking the question. It is far more effective and honest to rephrase the leading question into a declarative statement that shares a perception or opinion. Consider the following leading questions:

Don't you think you should start an investment program now?
Do you really feel that $100 a month will be enough?
Are you sure you've considered all possibilities?

With just a bit of reflection, we can see that the advisor is actually saying:

I think you ought to start an investment program now.
I don't feel that $100 a month will be enough.
I'm sure there are other possibilities you haven't considered.

The latter statements are much more honest and to the point than the questions from which they stem. Generally speaking, declarative statements communicate far more clearly and are more respectful than the manipulative leading questions. A good rule to follow in everyday intercourse is to make as many statements as possible and save the questions for honest information seeking.

Either/Or or True/False Questions

either/or question
true/false question

Another type of relatively ineffective question is the *either/or question* or the *true/false question*. While this type of question is not quite as closed-ended as the leading question, it is only slightly less closed, since it limits the client to only two options. For example:

Do you plan to stay in this house or move to an apartment?
Are you more apt to take a risk or play it safe?

The client might consider both options or neither or a third or fourth option. But when put this way the client is forced to choose from the two options offered. The world is not simply black or white; there are various shades of gray. Yet when the advisor phrases questions so that the client is forced to choose from one of two options, the client's responses are restricted. The advisor can improve on the preceding examples by asking:

What are your plans after retirement regarding housing?
How do you usually make your decisions?

Again, by opening up the questions, the advisor allows the client to respond freely from the client's own frame of reference and not from the advisor's. And for most purposes, this is what information gathering in the financial planning process requires.

Why Questions

why question

Even though a *why question* can be classified as an open-ended question and thus theoretically appear sound, this is not the case. On the surface, questions beginning with why appear to be legitimate enough, signifying the inquiry of casual relationships as in, "Why are you planning to retire at age 62?" Unfortunately, why questions when asked by the advisor carry with them a connotation of implied disapproval, thus forcing the client to justify or defend his or her thoughts, ideas, or actions. Even when that is not the meaning the advisor intends, that is generally how why questions are received. The why question tends to question the client's motivation (or lack of motivation) and thus creates a certain defensiveness.

Perhaps the chief reason that why questions are received so poorly is related to the manner in which some parents question children: "Why didn't you clean up your room?" "Why don't you have your shoes on?" "Why can't you be more careful?" Some teachers also use this line of inquiry with students: "Why don't you have your homework?" "Why didn't you study for this test?" In short, as children we learned that when an adult asked us a question beginning with why, it meant, "Change your behavior; think as I think; behave the way adults do." And we carry that pattern with us throughout life, usually responding to why questions in a defensive, negative manner.

Consequently it is generally better to avoid why questions unless there is a valid reason for asking one and no other type of question will suffice.

Question Bombardment

question bombardment

Still another kind of faulty questioning technique, called *question bombardment*, occurs when we ask double, triple, or even quadruple questions without waiting for a response. This is frequently referred to as question bombardment. As absurd as this type of questioning may sound, it occurs far too frequently in interviews and planning sessions. For example: "What type of investment program appeals to you most—stock, municipal bonds? Or would you rather look into annuities? When do you think you'd be ready to begin?"

The first question in the series is open-ended in nature and can stand by itself quite well. Yet the advisor is not content to let well enough alone, but instead tacks on other, more restricting closed-ended questions. As a result, the client is caught in a hailstorm of questions all at one time and, more often than not, gets the opportunity to respond to only one of the several questions asked. If more than one question is needed, it is better to form separate questions, waiting for a full response to each question before going on to the next one.

Categories of Questions

- open-ended questions
- closed-ended questions
- leading questions
- either/or and true/false questions
- why questions
- question bombardment

Concluding Remarks

Questioning is a technique in the communications repertory of most financial advisors. However, if advisors wish to become better communicators, they need to convert some of their questions (especially closed-ended, leading, either/or, and why questions) into declarative statements. By using statements, advisors assume responsibility for what they say. By asking questions, advisors shift the responsibility to their clients; this may sometimes be necessary. Nonetheless, far too often advisors simply shirk their responsibility for and involvement in the interaction with clients when they revert to questioning. As stated earlier in this chapter, counseling is not the same as interviewing. If advisors hope to make counseling their primary means of structured communication in the financial planning process, they need to do far more than simply ask one question after another.

CHAPTER TWO REVIEW

Key Terms and Concepts
Key Terms and Concepts are explained in the glossary.

interviewing	social styles
directive interview	resistance
nondirective interview	unconditional positive regard
counseling	accurate empathy
advising	genuineness
rapport	self-awareness

nonverbal behaviors	interpretive response
physical attending	reassuring response
active listening	suggestive response
continuing response	open-ended question
restatement-of-content response	closed-ended question
reflection-of-feeling response	leading question
clarifying response	either/or question
summarization response	true/false question
leading response	why question
explanatory response	question bombardment

Review Questions

The answers to the review questions are in the supplement. Self-test questions and the answers to them are also in the supplement and on The American College Online.

2-1. Describe the three types of structured communication used in the financial planning process. [2-2]

2-2. Describe the importance of structuring communication with clients. [2-3]

2-3. Identify the four social styles and explain the characteristics of each. [2-3]

2-4. Identify several sources of client resistance behavior in the financial planning process. [2-3]

2-5. Identify the attributes of an effective advisor. [2-4]

2-6. What is the importance of self-awareness in the advisor-client relationship especially as it relates to value orientations and differences? [2-4]

2-7. Describe several basic principles of communication. [2-5]

2-8. Identify and briefly describe the ways in which nonverbal behaviors are communicated by the body and the voice. [2-6]

2-9. Why is it important to assess the meaning of both verbal and nonverbal behaviors? [2-6]

2-10. Identify the five basic attributes associated with physical attending. [2-6]

2-11. What type of understanding response made during active listening is illustrated in each of the following examples?

a. "Well, let's see what we've concluded then. You want to set aside about $3,000 per year to save for a down payment on a vacation house at the shore, and safety is your prime consideration in the investment of that money." [2-6]

b. "I'm not sure I'm following you. Tell me again what your plan is for disposing of your interest in the partnership." [2-6]

c. "From what you just told me, then, I gather that you want to stay away from the limited partnership and put the money into the stock market instead." [2-6]

2-12. Describe four types of leading responses. [2-7]

2-13. What type of question or questioning technique is illustrated in each of the following examples? (More than one type of question or questioning technique may be illustrated in each example.)

a. "Why haven't you started converting some of that term insurance to whole life?" [2-8]

b. "Don't you think your present portfolio of investments is pretty illiquid?" [2-8]

c. "What goals do you have with respect to the education of your children?" [2-8]

d. "Do you plan to hold on to your mutual fund?" [2-8]

e. "Don't you think you should put $4,000 into an IRA this year? That isn't much money for you, is it? After all, don't you have at least that much in your passbook savings account right now? Or am I mistaken on that point?" [2-8]

f. "You were born in 1946, right?" [2-8]

NOTES

1. Portions of this chapter have been drawn from chapters 2 and 3 of the third edition of *Readings in Financial Services: Environment and Professions*, edited by Dale S. Johnson (Bryn Mawr, PA: The American College, 1984). Chapter 2 is titled *Effective Communication in Financial Counseling* and was authored by Lewis B. Morgan. Chapter 3 is titled *Practical Communications Skills and Techniques in Financial Counseling* and was authored by Dale S. Johnson. Chapter 3 was also published with the permission of The American College as a two-part article in *The Financial Planner,* vol. 11, no. 6 (June 1982): pp. 98–105, and vol. 11, no. 7 (July 1982): pp. 62–71.
2. Charles J. Stewart and William B. Cash, *Interviewing: Principles and Practices,* seventh edition. (Dubuque, IA: Brown & Benchmark, 1993).
3. Mehrabian, Albert, and Ferris, Susan R. "Inference of Attitudes From Nonverbal Communication in Two Channels," *Journal of Consulting Psychology,* Vol. 31, No. 3, June 1967, pp. 248–258.
4. David W. Merrill and Roger H. Reid, *Personal Styles and Effective Performance* (CRC Press LLC, 1999).
5. Elisabeth Kubler-Ross, *Death and Dying* (New York: Macmillan, 1968).
6. Carl R. Rogers, *Client-Centered Therapy: Its Current Practice, Implications and Theory* (Boston, MA: Houghton Mifflin, 1951).
7. Barbara F. Okun, *Effective Helping: Interviewing and Counseling Techniques,* fourth edition (Pacific Grove, CA: Brooks-Cole Publishing Co., Division of Wadsworth, Inc., 1992).

8. Gerard Egan, *The Skilled Helper: A Model for Systematic Helping and Interpersonal Relating* (Monterey, CA: Brooks/Cole, 1975): chapter 3, pp. 64–70.

9. Allen Ivey and M. Ivey, *Intentional Interviewing and Counseling* (Pacific Grove, CA: Brooks/Cole, 2003).

3

Ethics, Professionalism, and Practice Standards

Learning Objectives

An understanding of the material in this chapter should enable the student to

3-1. Describe the role of ethics in society.

3-2. Explain the relationship between law and ethics.

3-3. Identify the common themes and sentiments found in almost all ethics codes applicable to financial advisors.

3-4. Summarize the content of the codes of ethics of the Certified Financial Planner Board of Standards, Inc. and The American College.

3-5. Explain what these codes mean in terms of daily professional practice.

3-6. Describe the qualities that define a professional.

3-7. Identify the hallmarks of professional behavior for financial advisors.

3-8. Explain why financial planning professionals are subject to an increased risk of legal liability in their business dealings with clients.

3-9. Explain the nature and significance of the Certified Financial Planner Board's practice standards for financial planning practitioners.

Chapter Outline

Financial professionals have frequently made the news with stories about their breaches of ethical behavior, which has resulted in the public losing confidence in the financial services industry. Ethical expectations and trust hold business, the economy, and society together and, to the extent that people act unethically, these systems falter. With this in mind, this chapter provides insight into the related concepts of ethics, professionalism, and practice standards as they pertain to the relatively new and still emerging financial planning profession.

THE ROLE OF ETHICS

There was a time when the search for a practical way to describe applied ethics seemed analogous to the familiar story of the three blind men's attempt to describe an elephant. There are still many views on what the "ethics elephant" looks like.

Most of our conscious encounters with ethics occur as a result of negative media headlines: a public official is caught accepting a bribe; physicians are accused of performing unnecessary surgery; and salespeople intentionally mislead the public to increase sales. The media's emphasis on unethical behavior paints a grim picture: Some (most?) people are indeed behaving badly. This makes the value of ethics all the more compelling. Ethical behavior can and should be viewed as a worthwhile goal that is essential to the success and well being of every individual and society as a whole.

In its most abstract form, ethics is just one of several branches of philosophy. It is that part concerned with moral behavior—the product of moral standards and moral judgment. As Socrates said, "We are discussing no small matter, but how we ought to live."[1]

Deciding "how we ought to live" is the foundation of ethics. If we approach it conscientiously, the results will appear in daily conduct. Each person takes his or her morality to work each day. Regardless of how clear our own personal standards may be, on the job we soon discover that colleagues, competitors, and clients are governed by what appears to be a different vision of "how we ought to live." Sometimes the vision is considerably different. In the midst of all these differences, ethics forms the common bond that drives our efforts. It is the glue that holds our entire economic and free enterprise system together.

Without ethical behavior business deals would collapse, working conditions would be intolerable, and trust would be nonexistent. In business activities, people act based on the trust that their associates will behave ethically. In financial planning, ethics is the foundation for mutual trust in the advisor-client relationship. Consequently ethics must be understood as a powerful element in the financial planning environment.

Example:	A financial advisor and a client make a verbal agreement to meet again after the advisor has had a chance to analyze the client's needs. The advisor trusts that the client will come to the meeting and listen to his or her recommendations, while the client trusts that the advisor will keep personal information confidential.

People act in ways that demonstrate a trust in the fundamental assumptions of fair treatment, honest communication, accurate representation of intentions, and the avoidance of deception. Certainly there are unethical people whom we have learned not to trust and many situations in which it is wise to be cautious. But in situations where there is little trust, it is more difficult to negotiate contracts and to conduct business. Business diminishes and disintegrates without trust. The behavior of untrustworthy individuals and organizations is too unpredictable to risk involvement. When a person lies (deceives, cheats, or steals), it is difficult to restore trust in that individual. If a business develops a reputation for fraud and deception, it is extremely challenging for that business to overcome that reputation. When confidence erodes, customers, suppliers, stockholders, and even potential employees will take their resources elsewhere.

Ethics is not public relations. It is not about creating a good image, nor is it a luxury that a company may indulge in after it meets the critical bottom line. Ethics is about how people conduct business every hour of every day. It is about prompt response to client complaints and honest feedback to subordinates, peers, and superiors. Ethical behavior is being honest with ourselves and others. It involves the quality of work to which individuals put their names. It is giving clients all the information they need to make decisions that are in their own best interests.

The concept of ethics represents a set of fundamental assumptions that underlie nearly all relationships and transactions within society. These are assumptions about the way we treat people: what our rights and the rights of others are, where our individual rights end and the rights of others begin, how individual and public property ought to be treated, and what constitutes fair and equitable treatment of all people.

Discussing ethical conflicts is one important way that people can express their moral values to those with whom they live and work. If trust in ethical behavior facilitates and underlies all economic transactions, then people must be sure to build ethical behavior into their business decisions and operations. Only if they integrate an awareness of ethics into their daily work routines will they create a working environment that is founded on strong ethical principles.

What about competitive business practices? Is not business fundamentally about trying to gain the advantage over competitors? Does ethical behavior put an advisor at a competitive disadvantage?

A financial advisor can be ethical, competitive, and tough about goals all at the same time. Business is not just about competition. It is also about cooperation. It is about meeting the needs of customers. It is about making deals that work for the good of as many people as possible. If a business focused entirely on competing with rivals and neglected its customers, the business would quickly fail.

Honest competition is healthy, contributing to a stronger economy, higher quality service, and a better selection of products. However, competition is not the fundamental purpose of business, and some of its aspects are destructive.

Ethical behavior implies doing what is right, and that is sufficient justification to behave ethically. Furthermore, in business there are two pragmatic reasons that also justify ethical behavior. The first reason is that ethical expectations and trust serve to hold business, the economy, and society together. To the extent that people act unethically, these systems fail. The outcome may be that our own business systems falter as a result of distrust, deception, or a lack of client confidence. Adherence to ethical business practices adds a cornerstone to the foundation of any business organization.

The second reason that warrants ethical behavior in business practices is that individual actions create the work environment in which people spend most of their waking hours. People are constantly creating their own working environment by how they treat others, by statements they make, by attitudes they hold, and by the practices they condone. Ethical behavior in business profoundly improves the quality of life at work.

THE RELATIONSHIP BETWEEN LAW AND ETHICS

Each person is the major contributor in shaping his or her environment. A person's initiation of or reactions to ethical challenges determine the character of all of his or her relationships. If people lie, cheat, and steal, they are then living in a lying, cheating, and stealing environment of their own creation. An ethical environment is the only possible one in which society can progress economically, physically, morally, and spiritually. This is the ethical responsibility: to actively create an environment in which everyone can survive. The fulfillment of this responsibility requires people to assess the ethical implications of all their actions, the long-term costs, and the alternatives as well as to listen to others who are affected by those actions.

The practical result of this process is the development of frames of reference that we use to make decisions. Societal units such as nations develop laws that represent a framework based on what the governing unit considers to be minimal standards of conduct. Penalties are established, often severe, to discourage people from violating laws. Frequently, industries and/or specific business organizations develop their own standards of behavior that are more demanding than the law. These standards, known as codes of ethical conduct, statements of values, rules of conduct, and so on, become the benchmark against which the organization's ethical conduct is measured. It follows that we as individuals often have our own codes of ethical conduct. One of the early studies on business ethics done by Raymond Baumhart found that the number one influence on a business executive's ethical decision making was a personal code of behavior.[2]

Law and ethics are both standards of conduct that govern a nation, the morality of an organization, and the moral actions of individuals. Those desiring to be a part of society have more or less voluntarily accepted those standards.

There are other ways to examine the relationship between law and ethics. Figure 3-1 shows that law and ethics overlap, but each has its own domain as well. The dotted lines at the intersection of law and ethics represent their mutable boundaries. Laws are largely ethical standards that society has codified in order to insist on and enforce certain behaviors. They are the minimum moral requirements that we have agreed to demand for society as a whole. Ethical issues that are deemed sufficiently important may become laws. On the other hand, laws considered to be excessive or intrusive may be either ignored or struck down in court proceedings.

Figure 3-1 helps us focus on a common misunderstanding. The term compliance is often used as if it were synonymous with ethics. Compliance means obedience to the law. A "compliance" emphasis may even undermine ethics because it is targeted only at meeting legal requirements rather than addressing the causes of ethical misconduct.

Lynn Sharp Paine states that "legal compliance is unlikely to unleash moral imagination or commitment. The law does not generally seek to inspire human excellence or distinction. Those managers who define ethics as legal compliance are implicitly endorsing a code of moral mediocrity for their organizations."[3] This is because the law simply sets <u>minimum</u> requirements for behavior; it does not set <u>optimum</u> standards for professional behavior. Nevertheless, because what is legal is usually an expression of the ethical, no matter how minimal, one needs to follow the law to be ethical.

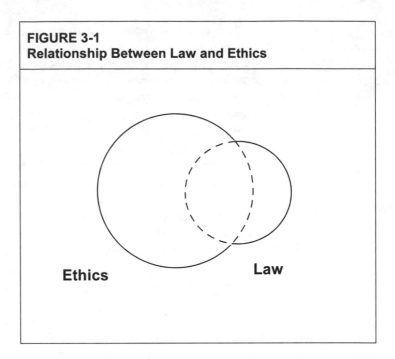

FIGURE 3-1
Relationship Between Law and Ethics

Ethics

Law

"You cannot legislate morality" is a popular saying. But morality, or the definition of right and wrong behavior, is precisely the focus of the American legal system. Laws regarding stealing, killing, invading another's privacy, defrauding, and misrepresenting intentions all reflect ethical rules. If these are violated, a penalty is imposed on the violator. So society does, in fact and out of necessity, legislate the most important aspects of morality.

It is true, however, that society cannot legislate all morality. Laws cannot be made to cover every situation that arises. Laws cannot mandate decent treatment and concern for other human beings, although that is certainly an ethical issue. If an attempt were made to define and mandate all moral behavior, it would be impossible to enforce. Furthermore, citizens in democratic countries generally prefer fewer laws and greater personal freedom. With a significant increase in laws governing individual behavior, courts and prisons would be even more crowded. We want a certain amount of personal independence to resolve our ethical dilemmas. But we also need to adhere to some common moral standards since our decisions about such dilemmas inevitably affect others. We are all expected to adhere to a shared morality.

The law is relatively clear-cut. Lawyers, police officers, and court officials are all employed to provide guidance on how to follow the law. Although lawyers do not always agree and the body of law is always evolving, there is a concrete and accessible legal system. Ethical rules, however, are not as clear-cut. An ethical problem is not as easily defined as a legal problem.

There is no concrete body of ethical standards that serves as recourse in ethical dilemmas. Nonetheless, there are commonly accepted rules and standards of behavior regarding the basic norms that govern moral life. These include such rules as

- Do not kill.
- Do not cause pain.
- Do not disable.
- Do not cheat.
- Do not deceive.
- Keep your promises.

Some of these are laws, while others are not. They are all commonly held expectations about life in our society, reflecting our values of individual rights and obligations to others. These values and the resulting moral rules extend into the realm of business because business operates within the larger realm of society as a whole. With this in mind, let us discuss several codes of ethics that have been written specifically for advisors in the financial services industry.

ETHICS CODES FOR FINANCIAL ADVISORS

Financial advisors take the law as a starting point in guiding their actions. Because law is primarily a codification of ethical principles, ethical issues that are deemed sufficiently important become laws. It is not only governments, however, that pass laws to regulate behavior. Industries and/or specific professions develop their own codes of ethical conduct because there are areas of behavior that the law does not address. In the financial services industry, several codes of ethics have been developed to provide financial advisors with ethical rules and working guidelines that go beyond the law. Because these codes are more demanding than the law, they have become the benchmark against which an advisor's ethical conduct is measured. Ethics, via the law and these codes, gives us rules and standards of conduct that govern us as citizens of a nation, members of a profession, or simply as individuals living in everyday society.

Financial advisors are fortunate in that they have a variety of organizations dedicated to their professional needs. These organizations are aware of the increasing ethical pressures on their members. In response, they have drafted professional pledges and codes of conduct. Among the pledges and codes applicable to financial advisors are the following:

- The American College Code of Ethics
- CFP Board's Code of Ethics and Professional Responsibility

- Society of Financial Service Professionals' Code of Ethics
- The Financial Planning Association Code of Ethics
- LUTCF Pledge
- NAIFA Code of Ethics
- The Million Dollar Round Table Code of Ethics

Copies of these pledges and/or codes are available from the respective organizations. Some of them can even be obtained from Internet websites.

In addition to the pledges and/or codes listed above, the Securities and Exchange Commission (SEC) adopted a new rule under the Investment Advisers Act of 1940 that requires registered investment advisers to adopt codes of ethics. The rule requires an adviser's code of ethics to set forth standards of conduct and to demand compliance with federal securities laws. While the codes adopted by each adviser must contain certain minimum standards, advisers are left with substantial flexibility to design individualized codes that would best fit the structure, size, and nature of their advisory businesses. (See chapter 9 for more discussion of the SEC's new rule 204A-1.)

There is no need for financial advisors to feel overwhelmed by the number of pledges and ethical codes that apply to them. They should be thought of only as reference points. Most codes applicable to financial advisors share seven common themes and sentiments:

- They call on advisors to look out for the best interests of clients.
- They ask advisors to conduct themselves with fairness, objectivity, honesty, and integrity.
- They require advisors to protect the confidential information of clients.
- They require advisors to present enough information to clients to allow them to make informed decisions.
- They require advisors to continue the learning process throughout their careers.
- They ask advisors to conduct themselves in such a way as to bring honor to themselves and to their profession.
- They specify that advisors should comply with the law.

These common themes and sentiments should strike the advisor as ethical common sense. The advisor is urged to study these codes and take them seriously. They will serve as strong guideposts to his or her professional development and achievement.

Knowledge of the codes and their common themes can enable the advisor to better deal with the complexities of today's marketplace. They can provide a barometer of what is expected of the advisor by his or her profession and by the public. They are not a substitute for the law. They are meant to act as a supplement. Besides, they often go beyond the law in providing guidelines for ethical behavior, guidelines that, in turn, translate into sound business practices.

The American College Code of Ethics

A holder of an American College designation must comply with The American College's Code of Ethics. This code was adopted in June 1984 and consists of two parts: a professional pledge and eight canons. The pledge reads as follows:

> In all my professional relationships, I pledge myself to the following rule of ethical conduct: I shall, in light of all conditions surrounding those I serve, which I shall make every conscientious effort to ascertain and understand, render that service which, in the same circumstances, I would apply to myself.

The eight canons are

I.   Conduct yourself at all times with honor and dignity.
II.   Avoid practices that would bring dishonor upon your profession or The American College.
III. Publicize your achievement in ways that enhance the integrity of your profession.
IV.   Continue your studies throughout your working life so as to maintain a high level of professional competence.
V.   Do your utmost to attain a distinguished record of professional service.
VI.   Support the established institutions and organizations concerned with the integrity of your profession.
VII. Participate in building your profession by encouraging and providing appropriate assistance to qualified persons pursuing professional studies.
VIII. Comply with all laws and regulations, particularly as they relate to professional and business activities.

Violations of the code are subject to disciplinary sanctions that include the temporary or permanent suspension of the designation. Enforcement of the code is through specified procedures.

> The Certified Financial Planner Board of Standards, Inc., has revised its *Code of Ethics and Professional Responsibility (Code of Ethics).*The revised Code of Ethics was passed by the board in May 2007 and will become effective July 1, 2008. The following section presents the Code of Ethics as revised. Candidates planning on sitting for the CFP® exam prior to the July 2008 date will be tested on the earlier code and should obtain a copy of that code from the CFP Board's website.

CFP Board's Code of Ethics and Professional Responsibility[4*]

As part of the CFP® certification process and the terms and conditions imposed upon certificants and registrants, CFP Board maintains professional standards necessary for competency in the financial planning profession. Through its *Code of Ethics and Professional Responsibility* (*Code of Ethics*), CFP Board identifies the ethical principles certificants and registrants should meet in all of their professional activities. Through its *Rules of Conduct,* CFP Board establishes binding professional norms that protect the public and advance professionalism. CFP Board's *Financial Planning Practice Standards (Practice Standards)* describe the best practices expected of certificants engaged in financial planning and refer to those sections of the *Rules of Conduct* that provide ethical guidance. Through its *Disciplinary Rules and Procedures* (*Disciplinary Rules*), CFP Board enforces its *Rules of Conduct* and establishes a process for applying the Principles of the *Code of Ethics* to actual professional activities.

Code of Ethics. CFP Board adopted the Code of Ethics to establish the highest principles and standards. These Principles are general statements expressing the ethical and professional ideals certificants and registrants are expected to display in their professional activities. As such, the Principles are aspirational in character and provide a source of guidance for certificants and registrants. The Principles form the basis of CFP Board's *Rules of Conduct*, *Practice Standards* and *Disciplinary Rules*, and these documents together reflect CFP Board's recognition of certificants' and registrants' responsibilities to the public, clients, colleagues and employers.

Rules of Conduct. The *Rules of Conduct* establish the high standards expected of certificants and describe the level of professionalism required of certificants. The *Rules of Conduct* are binding on all certificants, regardless of their title, position, type of employment or method of compensation, and they govern all those who have the right to use the CFP® marks, whether or not those

---

* This section is taken from the CFP Board's website at *www.CFP.net* and preserves the original language as much as possible. For complete coverage of the CFP Board's Code of Ethics and Professional Responsibility, go online to the CFP Board's website. Used with the permission of the CFP Board. All rights reserved.

marks are actually used. The universe of activities engaged in by a certificant is diverse, and a certificant may perform all, some or none of the typical services provided by financial planning professionals. Some Rules may not be applicable to a certificant's specific activity. As a result, when considering the *Rules of Conduct*, the certificant must determine whether a specific Rule is applicable to those services. A certificant will be deemed to be in compliance with these Rules if that certificant can demonstrate that his or her employer completed the required action.

Violations of the *Rules of Conduct* may subject a certificant or registrant to discipline. Because CFP Board is a certifying and standards-setting body for those individuals who have met and continue to meet CFP Board's initial and ongoing certification requirements, discipline extends to the rights of registrants and certificants to use the CFP® marks. Thus, the Rules are not designed to be a basis for legal liability to any third party.

Practice Standards. The *Practice Standards* describe best practices of financial planning professionals providing professional services related to the six elements of the financial planning process. Each Standard is a statement relating to an element of the financial planning process, followed by an explanation of the Standard and its relationship to the *Code of Ethics* and *Rules of Conduct*. CFP Board developed the *Practice Standards* to advance professionalism in financial planning and enhance the value of the financial planning process, for the ultimate benefit of consumers of financial planning services.

Disciplinary Rules. The *Disciplinary Rules* describe the procedures followed by CFP Board in enforcing the *Rules of Conduct*. The *Disciplinary Rules* provide a fair process pursuant to which certificants are given notice of potential violations and an opportunity to be heard by a panel of other professionals.

Part I—Principles

These Code of Ethics' Principles express the profession's recognition of its responsibilities to the public, to clients, to colleagues, and to employers.

CFP Board designees They apply to all *CFP Board designees* and provide guidance to them in the performance of their professional services. (CFP Board designees denotes current certificants, candidates for certification, and individuals who have any entitlement, direct or indirect, to the CFP certification marks.)

Principle 1—Integrity.
Provide professional services with integrity.
Integrity demands honesty and candor which must not be subordinated to personal gain and advantage. Certificants are placed in positions of trust by clients, and the ultimate source of that trust is the certificant's personal

integrity. Allowance can be made for innocent error and legitimate differences of opinion, but integrity cannot co-exist with deceit or subordination of one's principles.

Principle 2—Objectivity.
Provide professional services objectively.
Objectivity requires intellectual honesty and impartiality. Regardless of the particular service rendered or the capacity in which a certificant functions, certificants should protect the integrity of their work, maintain objectivity and avoid subordination of their judgment.

Principle 3—Competence.
Maintain the knowledge and skill necessary to provide professional services competently.
Competence means attaining and maintaining an adequate level of knowledge and skill, and application of that knowledge and skill in providing services to clients. Competence also includes the wisdom to recognize the limitations of that knowledge and when consultation with other professionals is appropriate or referral to other professionals necessary. Certificants make a continuing commitment to learning and professional improvement.

Principle 4—Fairness.
Be fair and reasonable in all professional relationships. Disclose conflicts of interest.
Fairness requires impartiality, intellectual honesty and disclosure of material conflicts of interest. It involves a subordination of one's own feelings, prejudices and desires so as to achieve a proper balance of conflicting interests. Fairness is treating others in the same fashion that you would want to be treated.

Principle 5—Confidentiality.
Protect the confidentiality of all client information.
Confidentiality means ensuring that information is accessible only to those authorized to have access. A relationship of trust and confidence with the client can only be built upon the understanding that the client's information will remain confidential.

Principle 6—Professionalism.
Act in a manner that demonstrates exemplary professional conduct.
Professionalism requires behaving with dignity and courtesy to clients, fellow professionals, and others in business-related activities. Certificants cooperate with fellow certificants to enhance and maintain the profession's public image and improve the quality of services.

Principle 7—Diligence.
Provide professional services diligently.
Diligence is the provision of services in a reasonably prompt and thorough manner, including the proper planning for, and supervision of, the rendering of professional services.

Part II—Rules of Conduct

1. Defining the Relationship With the Prospective Client or Client

1.1   The certificant and the prospective client or client shall mutually agree upon the services to be provided by the certificant.

1.2   If the certificant's services include financial planning or material elements of the financial planning process, prior to entering into an agreement, the certificant shall provide written information and/or discuss with the prospective client or client the following:

    a. The obligations and responsibilities of each party under the agreement with respect to:

        i.   Defining goals, needs and objectives,
        ii. Gathering and providing appropriate data,
        iii. Examining the result of the current course of action without changes,
        iv. The formulation of any recommended actions,
        v.   Implementation responsibilities, and
        vi. Monitoring responsibilities.

    b. Compensation that any party to the agreement or any legal affiliate to a party to the agreement will or could receive under the terms of the agreement; and factors or terms that determine costs, how decisions benefit the certificant and the relative benefit to the certificant.

    c. Terms under which the agreement permits the certificant to offer proprietary products.

    d. Terms under which the certificant will use other entities to meet any of the agreement's obligations.

If the certificant provides the above information in writing, the certificant shall encourage the prospective client or client to review the information and offer to answer any questions that the prospective client or client may have.

1.3   If the services include financial planning or material elements of the financial planning process, the certificant or the certificant's employer shall enter into a written agreement governing the financial planning services ("Agreement"). The Agreement shall specify:

    a. The parties to the Agreement,
    b. The date of the Agreement and its duration,
    c. How and on what terms each party can terminate the Agreement, and
    d. The services to be provided as part of the Agreement.

    The Agreement may consist of multiple written documents. Written documentation that includes the elements above and is used by a certificant or certificant's employer in compliance with state and/or federal law, or the rules or regulations of any applicable self-regulatory organization, such as a Form ADV or other disclosure, shall satisfy the requirements of this Rule.

1.4   A certificant shall at all times place the interest of the client ahead of his or her own. When the certificant provides financial planning or material elements of the financial planning process, the certificant owes to the client the duty of care of a fiduciary as defined by CFP Board.

2. Information Disclosed to Prospective Clients and Clients

2.1   A certificant shall not communicate, directly or indirectly, to clients or prospective clients any false or misleading information directly or indirectly related to the certificant's professional qualifications or services. A certificant shall not mislead any parties about the potential benefits of the certificant's service. A certificant shall not fail to disclose or otherwise omit facts where that disclosure is necessary to avoid misleading clients.

2.2   A certificant shall disclose to a prospective client or client the following information:

    a. An accurate and understandable description of the compensation arrangements being offered. This description must include:

        i. Information related to costs and compensation to the certificant and/or the certificant's employer, and
       ii. Terms under which the certificant and/or the certificant's employer may receive any other sources of compensation, and if so, what the sources of these payments are and on what they are based.

b. A general summary of likely conflicts of interest between the client and the certificant, the certificant's employer or any affiliates or third parties, including, but not limited to, information about any familial, contractual or agency relationship of the certificant or the certificant's employer that has a potential to materially affect the relationship.

c. Any information about the certificant or the certificant's employer that could reasonably be expected to materially affect the client's decision to engage the certificant that the client might reasonably want to know in establishing the scope and nature of the relationship, including but not limited to information about the certificant's areas of expertise.

d. Contact information for the certificant and, if applicable, the certificant's employer.

e. If the services include financial planning or material elements of the financial planning process, these disclosures must be in writing. The written disclosures may consist of multiple written documents. Written disclosures used by a certificant or certificant's employer that includes the elements listed above, and are used in compliance with state or federal laws, or the rules or requirements of any applicable self-regulatory organization, such as a Form ADV or other disclosure documents, shall satisfy the requirements of this Rule.

The certificant shall timely disclose to the client any material changes to the above information.

3. Prospective Client and Client Information and Property

3.1   A certificant shall treat information as confidential except as required in response to proper legal process; as necessitated by obligations to a certificant's employer or partners; to defend against charges of wrongdoing; in connection with a civil dispute; or as needed to perform the services.

3.2   A certificant shall take prudent steps to protect the security of information and property, including the security of stored information, whether physically or electronically, that is within the certificant's control.

3.3   A certificant shall obtain the information necessary to fulfill his or her obligations. If a certificant cannot obtain the necessary information, the certificant shall inform the prospective client or client of any and all material deficiencies.

3.4   A certificant shall clearly identify the assets, if any, over which the certificant will take custody, exercise investment discretion, or exercise supervision.

3.5   A certificant shall identify and keep complete records of all funds or other property of a client in the custody, or under the discretionary authority, of the certificant.

3.6   A certificant shall not borrow money from a client. Exceptions to this Rule include:

a. The client is a member of the certificant's immediate family, or
b. The client is an institution in the business of lending money and the borrowing is unrelated to the professional services performed by the certificant.

3.7   A certificant shall not lend money to a client. Exceptions to this Rule include:

a. The client is a member of the certificant's immediate family, or
b. The certificant is an employee of an institution in the business of lending money and the money lent is that of the institution, not the certificant.

3.8   A certificant shall not commingle a client's property with the property of the certificant or the certificant's employer, unless the commingling is permitted by law or is explicitly authorized and defined in a written agreement between the parties.

3.9   A certificant shall not commingle a client's property with other clients' property unless the commingling is permitted by law or the certificant has both explicit written authorization to do so from each client involved and sufficient record-keeping to track each client's assets accurately.

3.10   A certificant shall return a client's property to the client upon request as soon as practicable or consistent with a time frame specified in an agreement with the client.

4. Obligations to Prospective Clients and Clients

4.1   A certificant shall treat prospective clients and clients fairly and provide professional services with integrity and objectivity.

4.2   A certificant shall offer advice only in those areas in which he or she is competent to do so and shall maintain competence in all areas in which he or she is engaged to provide professional services.

4.3   A certificant shall be in compliance with applicable regulatory requirements governing professional services provided to the client.

4.4   A certificant shall exercise reasonable and prudent professional judgment in providing professional services to clients.

4.5   In addition to the requirements of Rule 1.4, a certificant shall make and/or implement only recommendations that are suitable for the client.

4.6   A certificant shall provide reasonable and prudent professional supervision or direction to any subordinate or third party to whom the certificant assigns responsibility for any client services.

4.7   A certificant shall advise his or her current clients of any certification suspension or revocation he or she receives from CFP Board.

5. Obligations to Employers

5.1   A certificant who is an employee/agent shall perform professional services with dedication to the lawful objectives of the employer/principal and in accordance with CFP Board's *Code of Ethics*.

5.2   A certificant who is an employee/agent shall advise his or her current employer/principal of any certification suspension or revocation he or she receives from CFP Board.

6. Obligations to CFP Board

6.1   A certificant shall abide by the terms of all agreements with CFP Board, including, but not limited to, using the CFP® marks properly and cooperating fully with CFP Board's trademark and professional review operations and requirements.

6.2   A certificant shall meet all CFP Board requirements, including continuing education requirements, to retain the right to use the CFP® marks.

6.3   A certificant shall notify CFP Board of changes to contact information, including, but not limited to, e-mail address, telephone number(s) and physical address, within forty-five (45) days.

6.4   A certificant shall notify CFP Board in writing of any conviction of a crime, except misdemeanor traffic offenses or traffic ordinance violations unless such offense involves the use of alcohol or drugs, or of any professional suspension or bar within ten (10) calendar days after the date on which the certificant is notified of the conviction, suspension or bar.

6.5 A certificant shall not engage in conduct which reflects adversely on his or her integrity or fitness as a certificant, upon the CFP® marks, or upon the profession.

CFP Board's Financial Planning Practice Standards

Statement of Purpose for *Financial Planning Practice Standards*

Financial Planning Practice Standards are developed and promulgated by Certified Financial Planner Board of Standards Inc. (CFP Board) for the ultimate benefit of consumers of financial planning services. These *Practice Standards* are intended to:

1. Assure that the practice of financial planning by CERTIFIED FINANCIAL PLANNER™ professionals is based on established norms of practice;
2. Advance professionalism in financial planning; and
3. Enhance the value of the financial planning process.

Description of Practice Standards

A *Practice Standard* establishes the level of professional practice that is expected of certificants engaged in financial planning.

The *Practice Standards* apply to certificants in performing the tasks of financial planning regardless of the person's title, job position, type of employment or method of compensation. Compliance with the *Practice Standards* is mandatory for certificants whose services include financial planning or material elements of the financial planning process, but all financial planning professionals are encouraged to use the *Practice Standards* when performing financial planning tasks or activities addressed by a *Practice Standard*.

The *Practice Standards* are designed to provide certificants with a framework for the professional practice of financial planning. Similar to the *Rules of Conduct*, the *Practice Standards* are not designed to be a basis for legal liability to any third party.

Format of the *Practice Standards*

Each *Practice Standard* is a statement regarding an element of the financial planning process. It is followed by an explanation of the Standard, its relationship to the *Code of Ethics* and *Rules of Conduct*, and its expected impact on the public, the profession and the practitioner.

The Explanation accompanying each *Practice Standard* explains and illustrates the meaning and purpose of the *Practice Standard*. The text of each *Practice Standard* is authoritative and directive. The related Explanation is a guide to interpretation and application of the *Practice Standard* based, where indicated, on a standard of reasonableness, a recurring theme throughout the *Practice Standards*. The Explanation is not intended to establish a professional standard or duty beyond what is contained in the *Practice Standard* itself.

Compliance With the *Practice Standards*

The practice of financial planning consistent with these *Practice Standards* is required for certificants who are financial planning practitioners. The *Practice Standards* are used by CFP Board's Disciplinary and Ethics Commission and Appeals Committee in evaluating the certificant's conduct to determine if the *Rules of Conduct* have been violated, based on the *Disciplinary Rules* established by CFP Board.

100-1: Defining the Scope of the Engagement

The financial planning practitioner and the client shall mutually define the scope of the engagement before any financial planning service is provided.

Explanation of This *Practice Standard*

Prior to providing any financial planning service, the financial planning practitioner and the client shall mutually define the scope of the engagement. The process of "mutually-defining" is essential in determining what activities may be necessary to proceed with the engagement.

This process is accomplished in financial planning engagements by:

1. Identifying the service(s) to be provided;
2. Disclosing the practitioner's material conflict(s) of interest;
3. Disclosing the practitioner's compensation arrangement(s);
4. Determining the client's and the practitioner's responsibilities;
5. Establishing the duration of the engagement; and
6. Providing any additional information necessary to define or limit the scope.

The scope of the engagement may include one or more financial planning subject areas. It is acceptable to mutually define engagements in which the scope is limited to specific activities. Mutually defining the scope of the engagement serves to establish realistic expectations for both the client and the practitioner.

As the relationship proceeds, the scope may change by mutual agreement. This *Practice Standard* shall not be considered alone, but in conjunction with all other *Practice Standards*.

Relationship of This *Practice Standard* to CFP Board's *Code of Ethics* and *Rules of Conduct.*

This *Practice Standard* relates to CFP Board's *Code of Ethics* and *Rules of Conduct* through Principle 4—Fairness, Principle 7—Diligence and Rules 1.1, 1.2, 1.3 and 2.2.

Anticipated Impact of This *Practice Standard*
Upon the Public

The public is served when the relationship is based upon a mutual understanding of the engagement. Clarity of the scope of the engagement enhances the likelihood of achieving client expectations.

Upon the Financial Planning Profession

The profession benefits when clients are satisfied. This is more likely to take place when clients have expectations of the process, which are both realistic and clear, before services are provided.

Upon the Financial Planning Practitioner

A mutually defined scope of the engagement provides a framework for the financial planning process by focusing both the client and the practitioner on the agreed upon tasks. This *Practice Standard* enhances the potential for positive results.

Gathering Client Data
200-1: Determining a Client's Personal and Financial Goals, Needs and Priorities

The financial planning practitioner and the client shall mutually define the client's personal and financial goals, needs and priorities that are relevant to the scope of the engagement before any recommendation is made and/or implemented.

Explanation of This *Practice Standard*

Prior to making recommendations to the client, the financial planning practitioner and the client shall mutually define the client's personal and financial goals, needs and priorities. In order to arrive at such a definition, the practitioner will need to explore the client's values, attitudes, expectations, and time horizons as they affect the client's goals, needs and priorities. The process of "mutually-defining" is essential in determining what activities may be necessary to proceed with the client engagement. Personal values and attitudes shape the client's goals and objectives and the priority placed on them. Accordingly, these goals and objectives must be consistent with the client's values and attitudes in order for the client to make the commitment necessary to accomplish them.

Goals and objectives provide focus, purpose, vision and direction for the financial planning process. It is important to determine clear and measurable objectives that are relevant to the scope of the engagement. The role of the practitioner is to facilitate the goal-setting process in order to clarify, with the client, goals and objectives. When appropriate, the practitioner shall try to assist clients in recognizing the implications of unrealistic goals and objectives.

This *Practice Standard* addresses only the tasks of determining the client's personal and financial goals, needs and priorities; assessing the client's values, attitudes and expectations; and determining the client's time horizons. These areas are subjective and the practitioner's interpretation is limited by what the client reveals.

This *Practice Standard* shall not be considered alone, but in conjunction with all other *Practice Standards*.

Relationship of This *Practice Standard* to CFP Board's *Code of Ethics* and *Rules of Conduct.*

This *Practice Standard* relates to CFP Board's *Code of Ethics* and *Rules of Conduct* through Principle 7—Diligence and Rules 3.3, 4.4 and 4.5.

Anticipated Impact of This *Practice Standard*
Upon the Public

The public is served when the relationship is based upon mutually defined goals, needs and priorities. This *Practice Standard* reinforces the practice of putting the client's interests first which is intended to increase the likelihood of achieving the client's goals and objectives.

Upon the Financial Planning Profession

Compliance with this *Practice Standard* emphasizes to the public that the client's goals, needs and priorities are the focus of the financial planning process. This encourages the public to seek out the services of a financial planning practitioner who uses such an approach.

Upon the Financial Planning Practitioner

The client's goals, needs and priorities help determine the direction of the financial planning process. This focuses the practitioner on the specific tasks that need to be accomplished. Ultimately, this will facilitate the development of appropriate recommendations.

200-2: Obtaining Quantitative Information and Documents

The financial planning practitioner shall obtain sufficient quantitative information and documents about a client relevant to the scope of the engagement before any recommendation is made and/or implemented.

Explanation of This *Practice Standard*

Prior to making recommendations to the client and depending on the scope of the engagement, the financial planning practitioner shall determine what quantitative information and documents are sufficient and relevant.

The practitioner shall obtain sufficient and relevant quantitative information and documents pertaining to the client's financial resources, obligations and personal situation. This information may be obtained directly from the client or other sources such as interview(s), questionnaire(s), client records and documents.

The practitioner shall communicate to the client a reliance on the completeness and accuracy of the information provided and that incomplete or inaccurate information will impact conclusions and recommendations.

If the practitioner is unable to obtain sufficient and relevant quantitative information and documents to form a basis for recommendations, the practitioner shall either:

A. Restrict the scope of the engagement to those matters for which sufficient and relevant information is available; or
B. Terminate the engagement.

The practitioner shall communicate to the client any limitations on the scope of the engagement, as well as the fact that this limitation could affect the conclusions and recommendations.

This *Practice Standard* shall not be considered alone, but in conjunction with all other *Practice Standards*.

Relationship of This *Practice Standard* to CFP Board's *Code of Ethics* and *Rules of Conduct.*

This *Practice Standard* relates to *CFP Board's Code of Ethics* and *Rules of Conduct* through Principle 7—Diligence and Rules 3.3, 4.4 and 4.5.

Anticipated Impact of This *Practice Standard*
Upon the Public

The public is served when financial planning recommendations are based upon sufficient and relevant quantitative information and documents. This *Practice Standard* is intended to increase the likelihood of achieving the client's goals and objectives.

Upon the Financial Planning Profession

The financial planning process requires that recommendations be made based on sufficient and relevant quantitative data. Therefore, compliance with this *Practice Standard* encourages the public to seek financial planning practitioners who use the financial planning process.

Upon the Financial Planning Practitioner

Sufficient and relevant quantitative information and documents provide the foundation for analysis. Ultimately, this will facilitate the development of appropriate recommendations.

300-1: Analyzing and Evaluating the Client's Information

A financial planning practitioner shall analyze the information to gain an understanding of the client's financial situation and then evaluate to what extent the client's goals, needs and priorities can be met by the client's resources and current course of action.

Explanation of This *Practice Standard*

Prior to making recommendations to a client, it is necessary for the financial planning practitioner to assess the client's financial situation and to determine the likelihood of reaching the stated objectives by continuing present activities.

The practitioner will utilize client-specified, mutually agreed upon, and/or other reasonable assumptions. Both personal and economic assumptions must be considered in this step of the process. These assumptions may include, but are not limited to, the following:

- Personal assumptions, such as: retirement age(s), life expectancy(ies), income needs, risk factors, time horizon and special needs; and
- Economic assumptions, such as: inflation rates, tax rates and investment returns.

Analysis and evaluation are critical to the financial planning process. These activities form the foundation for determining strengths and weaknesses of the client's financial situation and current course of action. These activities may also identify other issues that should be addressed. As a result, it may be appropriate to amend the scope of the engagement and/or to obtain additional information.

Relationship of This *Practice Standard* to CFP Board's *Code of Ethics* and *Rules of Conduct.*

This *Practice Standard* relates to *CFP Board's Code of Ethics* and *Rules of Conduct* through Principle 2—Objectivity, Principle 3—Competence, Principle 7—Diligence and Rules 1.4, 4.1, 4.4 and 4.5.

Anticipated Impact of This *Practice Standard*
Upon the Public

The public is served when objective analysis and evaluation by a financial planning practitioner results in the client's heightened awareness of specific financial planning issues. This *Practice Standard* is intended to increase the likelihood of achieving the client's goals and objectives.

Upon the Financial Planning Profession

Objective analysis and evaluation enhances the public's recognition of and appreciation for the financial planning process and increases the confidence in financial planning practitioners who provide this service.

Upon the Financial Planning Practitioner

Analysis and evaluation helps the practitioner establish the foundation from which recommendations can be made that are specific to the client's financial planning goals, needs and priorities.

Preface to the 400 Series

The 400 Series, "Developing and Presenting the Financial Planning Recommendation(s)," represents the very heart of the financial planning process. It is at this point that the financial planning practitioner, using both science and art, formulates the recommendations designed to achieve the client's goals, needs and priorities. Experienced financial planning practitioners may view this process as one action or task. However, in reality, it is a series of distinct but interrelated tasks.

These three *Practice Standards* emphasize the distinction among the several tasks which are part of this process. These *Practice Standards* can be described as, "What is Possible?," "What is Recommended?" and "How is it Presented?" The first two *Practice Standards* involve the creative thought, the analysis, and the professional judgment of the practitioner, which are often performed outside the presence of the client. First, the practitioner identifies and considers the various alternatives, including continuing the present course of action (*Practice Standard* 400-1). Second, the practitioner develops the recommendation(s) from among the selected alternatives (*Practice Standard* 400-2). Once the practitioner has determined what to recommend, the final task is to communicate the recommendation(s) to the client (*Practice Standard* 400-3).

The three *Practice Standards* that comprise the 400 series should not be considered alone, but in conjunction with all other *Practice Standards*.

400-1: Identifying and Evaluating Financial Planning Alternative(s)

The financial planning practitioner shall consider sufficient and relevant alternatives to the client's current course of action in an effort to reasonably meet the client's goals, needs and priorities.

Explanation of This *Practice Standard*

After analyzing the client's current situation (*Practice Standard* 300-1) and prior to developing and presenting the recommendation(s) (*Practice Standards* 400-2 and 400-3) the financial planning practitioner shall identify alternative actions. The practitioner shall evaluate the effectiveness of such actions in reasonably meeting the client's goals, needs and priorities.

This evaluation may involve, but is not limited to, considering multiple assumptions, conducting research or consulting with other professionals. This process may result in a single alternative, multiple alternatives or no alternative to the client's current course of action.

In considering alternative actions, the practitioner shall recognize and, as appropriate, take into account his or her legal and/or regulatory limitations and level of competency in properly addressing each of the client's financial planning issues.

More than one alternative may reasonably meet the client's goals, needs and priorities. Alternatives identified by the practitioner may differ from those of other practitioners or advisers, illustrating the subjective nature of exercising professional judgment.

Relationship of This *Practice Standard* to CFP Board's *Code of Ethics* and *Rules of Conduct*

This *Practice Standard* relates to CFP Board's *Code of Ethics* and *Rules of Conduct* through Principle 2—Objectivity, Principle 3—Competence,

Principle 6—Professionalism, Principle 7—Diligence and Rules 1.4, 4.1 and 4.5.

400-2: Developing the Financial Planning Recommendation(s)

The financial planning practitioner shall develop the recommendation(s) based on the selected alternative(s) and the current course of action in an effort to reasonably meet the client's goals, needs and priorities.

Explanation of This *Practice Standard*

After identifying and evaluating the alternative(s) and the client's current course of action, the practitioner shall develop the recommendation(s) expected to reasonably meet the client's goals, needs and priorities. A recommendation may be an independent action or a combination of actions which may need to be implemented collectively.

The recommendation(s) shall be consistent with and will be directly affected by the following:

- Mutually defined scope of the engagement;
- Mutually defined client goals, needs and priorities;
- Quantitative data provided by the client;
- Personal and economic assumptions;
- Practitioner's analysis and evaluation of client's current situation; and
- Alternative(s) selected by the practitioner.

A recommendation may be to continue the current course of action. If a change is recommended, it may be specific and/or detailed or provide a general direction. In some instances, it may be necessary for the practitioner to recommend that the client modify a goal.

The recommendations developed by the practitioner may differ from those of other practitioners or advisers, yet each may reasonably meet the client's goals, needs and priorities.

Relationship of This *Practice Standard* to CFP Board's *Code of Ethics* and *Rules of Conduct.*

This *Practice Standard* relates to *CFP Board's Code of Ethics* and *Rules of Conduct* through Principle 2—Objectivity, Principle 3—Competence, Principle 6—Professionalism, Principle 7—Diligence and Rules 1.4, 4.1 and 4.5.

400-3: Presenting the Financial Planning Recommendation(s)

The financial planning practitioner shall communicate the recommendation(s) in a manner and to an extent reasonably necessary to assist the client in making an informed decision.

Explanation of This *Practice Standard*

When presenting a recommendation, the practitioner shall make a reasonable effort to assist the client in understanding the client's current situation, the recommendation itself, and its impact on the ability to meet the client's goals, needs and priorities. In doing so, the practitioner shall avoid presenting the practitioner's opinion as fact.

The practitioner shall communicate the factors critical to the client's understanding of the recommendations. These factors may include but are not limited to material:

- Personal and economic assumptions;
- Interdependence of recommendations;
- Advantages and disadvantages;
- Risks; and/or
- Time sensitivity.

The practitioner should indicate that even though the recommendations may meet the client's goals, needs and priorities, changes in personal and economic conditions could alter the intended outcome. Changes may include, but are not limited to: legislative, family status, career, investment performance and/or health. If there are conflicts of interest that have not been previously disclosed, such conflicts and how they may impact the recommendations should be addressed at this time.

Presenting recommendations provides the practitioner an opportunity to further assess whether the recommendations meet client expectations, whether the client is willing to act on the recommendations, and whether modifications are necessary.

Relationship of This *Practice Standard* to CFP Board's *Code of Ethics* and *Rules of Conduct.*

This *Practice Standard* relates to *CFP Board's Code of Ethics* and *Rules of Conduct* through Principle 1—Integrity, Principle 2—Objectivity, Principle 6—Professionalism and Rules 2.1, 4.1, 4.4 and 4.5.

Anticipated Impact of These *Practice Standards* Upon the Public

The public is served when strategies and objective recommendations are developed and are communicated clearly to specifically meet each client's individual financial planning goals, needs and priorities.

Upon the Financial Planning Profession

A commitment to a systematic process for the development and presentation of the financial planning recommendations advances the financial planning profession. Development of customized strategies and recommendations enhances the public's perception of the objectivity and value of the financial planning process. The public will seek out those professionals who embrace these *Practice Standards*.

Upon the Financial Planning Practitioner

Customizing strategies and recommendations forms a foundation to communicate meaningful and responsive solutions. This increases the likelihood that a client will accept the recommendations and act upon them. These actions will contribute to client satisfaction.

500-1: Agreeing on Implementation Responsibilities

The financial planning practitioner and the client shall mutually agree on the implementation responsibilities consistent with the scope of the engagement.

Explanation of This *Practice Standard*

The client is responsible for accepting or rejecting recommendations and for retaining and/or delegating implementation responsibilities. The financial planning practitioner and the client shall mutually agree on the services, if any, to be provided by the practitioner. The scope of the engagement, as originally defined, may need to be modified.

The practitioner's responsibilities may include, but are not limited to the following:

- Identifying activities necessary for implementation;
- Determining division of activities between the practitioner and the client;
- Referring to other professionals;
- Coordinating with other professionals;
- Sharing of information as authorized; and
- Selecting and securing products and/or services.

If there are conflicts of interest, sources of compensation or material relationships with other professionals or advisers that have not been previously disclosed, such conflicts, sources or relationships shall be disclosed at this time.

When referring the client to other professionals or advisers, the financial planning practitioner shall indicate the basis on which the practitioner believes the other professional or adviser may be qualified. If the practitioner is engaged by the client to provide only implementation activities, the scope of the engagement shall be mutually defined in accordance with *Practice Standard* 100-1. This scope may include such matters as the extent to which the practitioner will rely on information, analysis or recommendations provided by others.

Relationship of This *Practice Standard* to CFP Board's *Code of Ethics* and *Rules of Conduct.*

This *Practice Standard* relates to *CFP Board's Code of Ethics* and *Rules of Conduct* through Principle 3—Competence, Principle 4—Fairness, Principle 6—Professionalism, Principle 7—Diligence and Rules 1.2, 2.2, 4.1 and 4.4.

500-2: Selecting Products and Services for Implementation

The financial planning practitioner shall select appropriate products and services that are consistent with the client's goals, needs and priorities.

Explanation of This *Practice Standard*

The financial planning practitioner shall investigate products or services that reasonably address the client's needs. The products or services selected to implement the recommendation(s) must be suitable to the client's financial situation and consistent with the client's goals, needs and priorities.

The financial planning practitioner uses professional judgment in selecting the products and services that are in the client's interest. Professional judgment incorporates both qualitative and quantitative information.

Products and services selected by the practitioner may differ from those of other practitioners or advisers. More than one product or service may exist that can reasonably meet the client's goals, needs and priorities.

The practitioner shall make all disclosures required by applicable regulations.

Relationship of This *Practice Standard* to CFP Board's *Code of Ethics* and *Rules of Conduct*

This *Practice Standard* relates to *CFP Board's Code of Ethics* and *Rules of Conduct* through Principle 2—Objectivity, Principle 4—Fairness, Principle 6—Professionalism, Principle 7—Diligence and Rules 1.2, 1.4, 2.2, 4.1, 4.4 and 4.5.

Anticipated Impact of These *Practice Standards*
Upon the Public

The public is served when the appropriate products and services are used to implement recommendations; thus increasing the likelihood that the client's goals will be achieved.

Upon the Financial Planning Profession

Over time, implementing recommendations using appropriate products and services for the client increases the credibility of the profession in the eyes of the public.

Upon the Financial Planning Practitioner

In the selection of products and services, putting the interest of the client first benefits the practitioner over the long-term.

600-1: Defining Monitoring Responsibilities

The financial planning practitioner and client shall mutually define monitoring responsibilities.

Explanation of This *Practice Standard*

The purpose of this *Practice Standard* is to clarify the role, if any, of the practitioner in the monitoring process. By clarifying this responsibility, the client's expectations are more likely to be in alignment with the level of monitoring services which the practitioner intends to provide.

If engaged for monitoring services, the practitioner shall make a reasonable effort to define and communicate to the client those monitoring activities the practitioner is able and willing to provide. By explaining what is to be monitored, the frequency of monitoring and the communication method, the client is more likely to understand the monitoring service to be provided by the practitioner.

The monitoring process may reveal the need to reinitiate steps of the financial planning process. The current scope of the engagement may need to be modified.

Relationship of This *Practice Standard* to CFP Board's *Code of Ethics* and *Rules of Conduct.*

This *Practice Standard* relates to *CFP Board's Code of Ethics* and *Rules of Conduct* through Principle 7—Diligence and Rules 1.2, 3.3, 3.4 and 4.1.

Anticipated Impact of This *Practice Standard*
Upon the Public

The public is served when the practitioner and client have similar perceptions and a mutual understanding about the responsibilities for monitoring the recommendation(s).

Upon the Financial Planning Profession

The profession benefits when clients are satisfied. Clients are more likely to be satisfied when expectations of the monitoring process are both realistic and clear. This *Practice Standard* promotes awareness that financial planning is a dynamic process rather than a single action.

Upon the Financial Planning Practitioner

A mutually defined agreement of the monitoring responsibilities increases the potential for client satisfaction and clarifies the practitioner's responsibilities.

Relationship of the CFP Practice Standards to the CFP Code of Ethics

Financial Planning Process	Related Practice Standards	Related Code of Ethics	
		Principle	*Rule*
Step 1: Establishing and defining the advisor-client relationship	**100-1**: Defining the scope of the engagement	4 – Fairness 7 – Diligence	1.1, 1.2, 1.3, and 2.2
Step 2: Determining goals and gathering data	**200-1**: Determining a client's personal and financial goals, needs, and priorities	7 – Diligence	3.3, 4.4, and 4.5
	200-2: Obtaining quantitative information and documents	7 – Diligence	3.3, 4.4, and 4.5
Step 3: Analyzing and evaluating the data	**300-1**: Analyzing and evaluating the client's information	2 – Objectivity 3 – Competence 7 – Diligence	1.4, 4.1, 4.4, and 4.5
Step 4: Developing and presenting a plan	**400-1**: Identifying and evaluating financial planning alternative(s)	2 – Objectivity 3 – Competence 6 – Professionalism 7 – Diligence	1.4, 4.1, and 4.5
	400-2: Developing the financial planning recommendation(s)	2 – Objectivity 3 – Competence 6 – Professionalism 7 – Diligence	1.4, 4.1, and 4.5
	400-3: Presenting the financial planning recommendation(s)	1 – Integrity 2 – Objectivity 6 – Professionalism	2.1, 4.1, 4.4, and 4.5
Step 5: Implementing the plan	**500-1**: Agreeing on implementation responsibilities	3 – Competence 4 – Fairness 6 – Professionalism 7 – Diligence	1.2, 2.2, 4.1, and 4.4
	500-2: Selecting products and services for implementation	2 – Objectivity 4 – Fairness 6 – Professionalism 7 – Diligence	1.2, 1.4, 2.2, 4.1, 4.4, and 4.5
Step 6: Monitoring the plan	**600-1**: Defining monitoring responsibilities	7 – Diligence	1.2, 3.3, 3.4, and 4.1
Source: Jeffery V. Hicks, an American College student, contributed an earlier version of this table.			

PRACTICAL APPLICATION OF ETHICS CODES

What do ethics codes mean in terms of daily professional practice? The American College pledge says, "I shall . . . render that service which I would apply to myself." The CFP code calls for the practitioner to act "in the interest of the client." Though not identical, each code mandates a variation of the Golden Rule: "Do unto others as you would have them do unto you."

To offer a client the same thorough attention to detail that a financial advisor would apply to himself or herself is no small requirement. Think about the kind of service an advisor would give to himself or herself and to close relatives or friends. The advisor would make absolutely certain to understand all the apparent and hidden costs. The advisor would want to know how much it would cost now and whether the cost over the life of the product or service would be fixed or variable. The advisor would want to know the potential risks of the product or service. The advisor would want to know the potential benefits of the product or service in the short term as well as in the long term. And finally, the advisor would want to know exactly how to maximize those benefits or what actions to take to reduce the potential harms. In other words, the advisor would not purchase a product or service without making use of as much information about the product or service as he or she was able to responsibly acquire.

One of the benefits of being in the financial services business is having access to information that the general public does not have. Some clients have a particularly strong interest in knowing all the details about a product and/or service while others are not interested in details. Nevertheless, the advisor-client relationship requires the advisor to make this information available to clients to help them make better-informed decisions.

The American College's professional pledge says that financial advisors shall render that service to clients which in the same circumstances, they would expect to receive themselves. In keeping with this charge, it is the advisor's responsibility to present the information to clients in a way that allows them to understand it and use it in their decision making. Of course, a financial advisor cannot force a client to listen, but it is definitely the advisor's responsibility to provide the client with the needed information and to present it in a manner that he or she can understand. However, the advisor may first have to explain to the client why he or she needs the information to make a decision.

The American College's pledge also stipulates that the financial advisor shall take into account the conditions surrounding the client and that the advisor "shall make every conscientious effort to ascertain and understand" such conditions. This means that the financial advisor cannot simply sell a product or service and be a professional. To be a professional, the financial advisor must use the financial planning process to determine whether the problem his or her product or service solves is, in fact, the client's problem and if so, whether it is the most appropriate product or service for solving the client's problem. Such an approach requires the advisor to gather as much information as possible from the client about his or her financial goals and current financial situation in order to put together a plan to solve the client's problem and best meet his or her goals.

The sale of financial products or services by advisors who consider themselves professionals is client-focused. *Client-focused selling* is a sales philosophy that rejects high pressure, hard sell methods and supports the counselor model of an advisor, which is deeply embedded within the financial planning process. Client-focused selling emphasizes helping clients by providing solutions to their financial problems and helping them achieve their goals. Advisors who embrace the financial planning process are, in reality, practicing client-focused selling. They approach clients with a willingness to listen carefully because clients can best provide the information regarding their own financial goals. Since clients often believe they know which products or services best fit those goals, advisors should keep clients focused on articulating their goals so they can assist them in finding the best products and/or services for achieving them.

Because client-focused selling is a major component of the financial planning process, the financial planning process is a sound approach for building good advisor-client relationships and selling financial products and services. It is also an ethical requirement because of the nature of the advisor-client relationship. Many financial advisors perform a dual role that can lead to conflicts of interest if they are not careful. This dual role finds them as agents for their financial services companies while they are simultaneously serving their clients in an agent-like capacity. As agents for their companies, financial advisors must accurately represent their companies' products and/or services to clients. Most advisors deal primarily with one company and feel that their obligation to that company is to look to its products and/or services first to meet their clients' needs. They will only approach another company if appropriate products and/or services are not available from their company.

This traditional approach benefits clients in several ways. First, the advisor is able to gain in-depth knowledge of the products and/or services of one company, which would be nearly impossible if he or she tried to cover all the products and services on the market. This knowledge enables the advisor to serve his or her clients better. Second, it saves the advisor extensive research time to be able to work from a body of familiar products and/or services. Of course, in some instances this could be detrimental to clients who need more extensive research to find just the right product or service. Therefore, it is important that the advisor honestly inform clients of his or her primary relationship with a particular company. Clients should understand that the particular company's products and/or services are the ones that the advisor will

client-focused selling

research and present in most cases. It is deceptive and clearly unethical for the advisor to fail to disclose his or her primary company relationship.

The financial advisor's role in serving clients often requires him or her to act like an agent. Clients typically trust their advisor with confidential information. Consequently courts have held that when an advisor induces reliance on his or her professional expertise, he or she incurs liability for decisions made on the basis of that professional expertise. When the advisor's actions in effect say to clients, "I am your agent," the advisor takes on certain responsibilities and liabilities associated with being an agent for those clients.

Many financial services educators and experts stress the importance of selling financial products and/or services solely on the basis of client need. Selling on any other basis, such as the needs and interests of the financial advisor or the company, makes no sense in the long term and is contrary to client-focused selling. The advisor may be persuasive enough to sell a product or service fairly quickly in order to meet a bonus deadline, or the company may promote a particular product by paying higher commission rates. However, unless a product or service really meets the needs of a client over the long term, the client will not continue to financially support the product or service, which ends up being costly for the company. Clients who feel they were sold products and/or services that did not meet their needs are unlikely to remain as clients in the long term. A client will not refer friends and/or relatives to an advisor if the client does not believe in the advisor's ability to listen carefully and respond. So while the short-term sales of a product or service may look good, the long-term financial position of the advisor and the company are hurt when a client ends up with a product or service that does not meet his or her needs.

In summary, it is both ethically required and financially wise for the advisor to thoroughly understand his or her clients' needs and act to fulfill those needs. The financial planning process provides the best methodology for the advisor to do this. The codes of both The American College and the Certified Financial Planner Board of Standards reinforce using this methodology.

To take actions that would enhance public regard for the profession is to act in ways that are commonly regarded as highly professional. As shown in the next section, being a professional requires adherence to a code of ethics. However, there is more to being a professional than just adherence to an ethics code. Just what makes a professional is the next topic for discussion.

CHARACTERISTICS OF A PROFESSIONAL

The adjective "professional" is loosely attached to many careers and is used in significantly different ways. An example would be the professional athlete who is highly skilled; but what makes the athlete a professional is the fact that he or she gets paid. Amateur athletes, regardless of how talented they are, are not professional because they are not compensated.

Today, there is much discussion about the professional politician. This is a person who has chosen politics as a career. Frequently, the term is used in a derisive way to describe a politician who is more interested in manipulating the system for personal gain than developing public policy.

There are a few occupations that are widely viewed as professions. Included on most lists are doctors, lawyers, and clergy. Similar status is often given to pharmacists, engineers, and architects. Still others could be added to the list.

What do people mean when they say, "She is a real professional" or "His behavior was completely unprofessional"? What is commonly understood as professional conduct?

In the first example, the positive connotation includes such characteristics as job proficiency, reliability, dedication, thoroughness, dependability, a commitment to providing good service, and an awareness that one's quality of performance affects the reputations of others.

In contrast, the term unprofessional suggests shoddy or careless performance; a lack of concern for customers or clients; disregard for the reputation of a larger group of people; and a narrow, selfish concern for one's own well-being.

professional   Burke A. Christensen, former general counsel and vice president of the Society of Financial Service Professionals, suggests that "a *professional* is a person engaged in a field that requires (1) specialized knowledge not generally understood by the public, (2) a threshold entrance requirement, (3) a sense of altruism, and (4) a code of ethics.[5]

Of these requirements, numbers one and four are immediately evident in the financial planning field. Certainly financial advisors doing financial planning have a specialized knowledge not generally understood by their clients. Moreover, if they have earned one or more of the professional designations available to practitioners in the field and have joined one or more of the membership organizations for financial planning practitioners, they must adhere to one or more of the codes of ethics that were discussed previously in this chapter.

The earning of a professional designation or a degree in an appropriate subject matter represents a kind of threshold entrance requirement even though there are many successful people working in the field who have not earned either. In addition to a professional designation or degree, continuing education in the major planning areas that make up the financial planning profession is an important aspect of meeting clients' needs. These areas are increasingly competitive and complex. Federal and state regulations are constantly evolving. Understanding these changes is essential to providing sound advice to clients. The truly professional financial advisor must in some way meet both an entrance requirement of foundational education and a requirement of continuous professional education. Another type of threshold entrance requirement is a licensing examination. To provide some types of financial planning services, the advisor must be licensed by the state.

altruism

Requirement number three, a sense of *altruism*, is a characteristic that facilitates adherence to the code of ethics. Altruism is defined as an unselfish regard for the welfare of others and thus requires the professional to adhere to ethical standards unselfishly and to take others' needs and views into account. It facilitates the achievement of the characteristics commonly expected of a professional: competence, reliability, and high ethical standards.

At first glance altruism seems to contradict the underlying premise of a free enterprise economy in which individuals are allowed to operate their businesses in a competitive environment where success is measured by the financial rewards they receive. However, altruism does not require the professional to act entirely without self-regard. Altruism does not supplant the professional's own welfare—it balances it. It requires the professional to recognize that the well being of others is equally as important as his or her own in contributing to success. While receiving the financial rewards of success requires hard work, it cannot be achieved at the expense or exclusion of others. An unselfish regard for the welfare of others contributes to the professional's success. Demonstration of concern for others often wins great trust and confidence in the professional, which will translate into more business and greater success.

However, the worst kind of hypocrisy is to feign altruism in order to create the image of trustworthiness and reliability. The image of altruism is quite different from deeply felt altruism, and the false image will inevitably be uncovered to reveal the underlying motivations. Such deception is not worth the personal and professional cost.

Characteristics Defining a Professional

- specialized knowledge not generally understood by the public
- threshold entrance requirement
- sense of altruism
- code of ethics

One important question facing professionals is: What environment do we want to create and work in? This is quite different from the question, How do we want to be perceived? The former question is about daily choices and our expectations of others. The latter question is about image.

Financial planning professionals are understandably concerned about their image in American society. But working merely to improve their image is the wrong approach to changing it. The critical issues are how these professionals are conducting themselves and how they are behaving toward their clients, not how members of the public think they are doing. Professional respect and credibility will follow professional behavior. Adherence to the highest ethical standards as elaborated here will contribute significantly to the achievement of professional behavior and, subsequently, to respect.

FOCUS ON ETHICS
Professionalism Begins With Ethics

Writing with the financial services industry in mind, Dr. Ronald C. Horn, CPCU, CLU, Williams Professor of Insurance Studies at Baylor University, developed a list of seven characteristics that he considered necessary for a particular occupation to be considered a profession.[6] First on Horn's list was a commitment to high ethical standards. The complete list follows:

- a commitment to high ethical standards
- a prevailing attitude of altruism
- mandatory educational preparation and training
- mandatory continuing education
- a formal association or society
- independence
- public recognition as a profession

Compare this list with Christensen's four characteristics of a professional discussed previously. Both lists emphasize that ethical standards are a critical component of a professional.

Behaving Professionally

Clients may or may not be familiar with the aforementioned characteristics of being a professional. Nevertheless, they typically do have an idea of whether their financial advisors are behaving professionally. To make this determination, they implicitly evaluate their advisors according to how well they stack up against the hallmarks of professional behavior. These hallmarks applied to a financial advisor are embodied in the following 10 questions.

1. Does the advisor listen to the client? Good fact finding depends on getting the client to reveal both financial and personal information. The advisor should not do all the talking. He or she must stop and listen in order to get to know the client's needs and aspirations. Obtaining this information permits the advisor to custom design a financial plan geared to the client's specific needs.
2. Does the advisor answer the client's questions? Sometimes a client will ask a question to which the answer is not immediately clear. The advisor should not ignore the question or gloss over it. If the advisor

needs to research an answer, he or she should say so. The client will respect the advisor for being honest.

Sometimes clients should ask obvious questions but frequently they do not. In this case, the advisor should probe clients for information and, if necessary, the advisor should ask them if they have any questions. This will provide the advisor with feedback on whether or not the clients understand their needs and the role of the advisor's products and/or services in fulfilling those needs.

3. Is the advisor gathering information sufficient to provide good advice? The answer will be "yes" if the advisor is conducting a thorough fact-find. The point is the advisor should be sure that he or she has enough facts before making any recommendations.

4. Has the advisor educated the client about the advisor's products and/or services? Some clients understand the intricacies of financial products and/or services, but many do not. The advisor should take the time to educate clients on basics and the range of available products and/or services. This way, clients will understand what they purchased and why they purchased it.

5. Has the advisor taken the client's ability to deal with risk into consideration in making recommendations? We know that different clients regard risk differently. Many clients will reject a proposal that makes them feel uneasy because it is outside their financial comfort zone. It is good ethics and good business for the advisor to find out where clients stand in this regard before making recommendations. (Financial risk tolerance will be discussed more thoroughly in chapter 4.)

6. Has the advisor told the client about the advisor's educational background and affiliations in financial planning so the client can determine whether the advisor is knowledgeable? Many clients are individuals whom the advisor has known for only a short time. Many are unfamiliar with the advisor's background but will want to know more before entrusting him or her with financial or other highly confidential information. Some clients will ask questions in this regard while others will not and instead move on to another topic. To avoid this possibility, the advisor should provide clients with appropriate information regarding his or her background.

7. Does the advisor provide the client with a sense of a continuing advisory relationship or is the advisor seeking a one-time sale? Both during and after the planning process, the advisor should maintain contact with the client. He or she should explain the role of the financial planning process and its reliance on monitoring in the form of periodic reviews. If the advisor periodically reviews the client's

situation, the client will view the advisor as a professional with whom a business relationship has been established.

8. Does the advisor handle money matters properly? The advisor should never ask the client to make a check payable to anyone other than the specific financial services company. In simpler terms, the advisor should never ask the client to make out a check to the advisor for financial products and/or services. This invites commingling of funds and represents a violation of most state laws. The advisor should keep records of what monies he or she has collected from the client, and he or she should provide the client with proper receipts. Also, the advisor should not leave client checks in his or her briefcase for very long just because the necessary paperwork is a hassle.

9. Does the advisor refer to other experts or is the advisor intimidated by them? Financial advisors are not accountants, attorneys, or trust officers. Nor is every financial advisor an expert in all the major planning areas. Clients understand this. If necessary, the advisor should refer the client to a specialist. Better yet, the advisor should become part of a team of specialists. If the advisor manages the team, the advisor will be responsible for coordinating the efforts of the team and for contributing expertise in his or her own field of specialization.

10. Does the advisor seem up-to-date? Many clients can sense when an advisor seems out-of-touch with current issues. It is all well and good, for example, to obtain a professional designation or a specialized degree, but these credentials are meaningless if the advisor's knowledge becomes outdated and irrelevant.

The Hallmarks of Professional Behavior

- Does the advisor listen to the client?
- Does the advisor answer client questions?
- Is the advisor gathering information sufficient to provide good advice?
- Has the advisor educated the client about the advisor's products and/or services?
- Has the advisor taken the client's ability to deal with risk into consideration in making recommendations?
- Has the advisor told the client about the advisor's educational background and affiliations in financial planning so the client can determine whether the advisor is knowledgeable?
- Does the advisor provide the client with a sense of steady service or is the advisor meeting with the client seeking a one-time sale?
- Does the advisor handle money matters properly?
- Does the advisor refer to other experts or is the advisor intimidated by them?
- Does the advisor seem up-to-date?

Many designation or certification programs require financial advisors to complete a specified number of continuing education (CE) hours in order to maintain their status. CE should not be viewed as a burden. Advisors should look at CE requirements as an opportunity to maintain and enhance their skills. The more an advisor knows, the better able he or she will be to provide clients with timely and up-to-date financial advice.

Increased Risk of Legal Liability

Professional status confers additional responsibility in the eyes of the law. Professionals are held to higher standards in the execution of their business duties. They are expected to have expertise and to act responsibly with it. They are expected to have knowledge of the law and to comply with its dictates. They are expected to place the interests of clients above their own. Under the law of torts, professionals have historically been held by the courts to higher standards of expertise and behavior than nonprofessionals.

This high expectation places many financial advisors in situations of greater legal liability than previously. Lawsuits can damage their reputations, not to mention the considerable time and emotional energy spent defending them. If an advisor is accused of unethical and/or illegal behavior and cannot adequately support his or her innocence, then no matter how innocent the advisor is, the court may find in favor of the disgruntled client.

CHAPTER THREE REVIEW

Key Terms and Concepts
Key terms and concepts are explained in the glossary.

CFP Board designees   professional
client-focused selling   altruism

Review Questions

The answers to the review questions are in the supplement. Self-test questions and the answers to them are also in the supplement and on The American College Online.

3-1. Explain why "ethics is the glue that holds an entire economic and free enterprise system together." [3-1]

3-2. Describe a number of similarities and differences between law and ethics. [3-2]

3-3. Describe seven common themes and sentiments that are found in most codes of ethics applicable to financial advisors. [3-3]

3-4.   Identify the seven Principles in the Code of Ethics and Professional Responsibility of the Certified Financial Planner Board of Standards. [3-4]

3-5.   What famous rule does The American College's professional pledge require its designation holders to follow? [3-4]

3-6.   What are the characteristics that define a professional? [3-6]

3-7.   Identify the hallmarks of professional behavior. [3-7]

3-8.   Why are professionals subject to a higher risk of legal liability than nonprofessionals? [3-8]

3-9.   What is the intended outcome of the CFP Board's Financial Planning Practice Standards? [3-9]

NOTES

1. James A. Rachels, *The Elements of Moral Philosophy* (New York: McGraw-Hill, 1986), p. 1.
2. Raymond Baumhart, *"How Ethical Are Businessmen?"* Harvard Business Review, July–August 1961, p. 7.
3. Lynn Sharp Paine, *"Managing for Organizational Integrity,"* Harvard Business Review, March–April 1994, p. 111.
4. *CFP Board's Standards of Professional Conduct: Code of Ethics and Professional Responsibility*, downloaded from the Certified Financial Planner Board of Standards website at *http://www.cfp.net/Downloads/2008Standards.pdf, July 2007.*
5. Burke A. Christensen, *Journal of the American Society of CLU & ChFC*, January 1990, p. 21.
6. Ronald C. Horn, *On Professions, Professionals, and Professional Ethics* (Malvern, PA: American Institute for Property and Liability Underwriters, Inc., 1978), p. 40.

Client Attitudes Toward Risk

Learning Objectives

An understanding of the material in this chapter should enable the student to

4-1. Distinguish between people who are risk seekers, risk averters, and risk indifferent, and compare people's subjective perceptions of risk with the objective definition of financial risk.

4-2. Describe several tendencies or characteristics of people that limit their ability to rationally assess risk.

4-3. Compare the four major categories of life situations that involve risk taking.

4-4. Summarize the differences in the characteristics of risk takers versus risk averters.

4-5. Describe and evaluate several techniques for assessing the risk tolerance of clients.

4-6. Identify some guidelines that a financial advisor should follow when assessing the risk tolerance of clients.

Chapter Outline

Investments are characterized by different levels of risk and potential return. Both ethical and regulatory principles require that the financial advisor recommend only those products and investment strategies that are suitable given the client's investment objectives, financial capacity to absorb a loss, and psychological propensity for risk taking. The goal is to deliver the most return for the amount of tolerable risk. Proper asset allocation requires a determination of the client's risk tolerance.

Financial advisors of all types need to understand risk tolerance and convey to their clients its significance in reaching proper investment decisions. Determining a client's level of risk tolerance, while extremely important, is also one of the most difficult tasks facing the financial advisor. Done properly, however, it will improve relationships with clients and lessen the possibility of litigation by those who have invested beyond their comfort level.

Although it may appear to be a rather simple topic, risk tolerance is an extremely complex phenomenon. It is an area of interest for many academic disciplines—notably economics, psychology, finance, and management science. Each field has a different tradition and approaches risk tolerance from a different perspective. This chapter integrates the relevant research from all these disciplines and thereby reveals areas of professional disagreement.

Specifically, this chapter examines how people view risk and how they process information about risk factors. It explores the reasons people either minimize or maximize the objective level of risk in a situation. It also identifies demographic and personality characteristics that have been linked to risk tolerance. Finally, it considers various approaches to assessing a client's risk-taking propensity and notes their relative merits and drawbacks.

After reading this chapter, financial advisors should better understand why clients accept or refuse risk, and they will be able to use this understanding to serve their clients more effectively.

RISK AVERSION, RISK SEEKING, AND RISK INDIFFERENCE

risk seekers (risk-tolerant individuals) risk averters (risk rejecters) risk indifferent

Individuals react differently to risk. Some are always willing to accept it; others are always ready to reject it. Think of reactions to risk as a continuum, with *risk seekers* (or *risk-tolerant individuals*), at one end and *risk averters* (or *risk rejecters*) at the opposite end. People in the middle are referred to as *risk indifferent*. Risk indifferent individuals are willing to take on risk when they expect that it will make them better off, or at least no worse off, than if they did not assume that risk in the first place. Frequently, the terms aggressive and conservative are used to describe investors who are, respectively, risk seeking and risk averse. According to conventional wisdom, investment decisions involve a trade-off between risk and expected return. Risk-averse investors prefer low risks and are, therefore, willing to sacrifice some expected return in order to reduce the variation in possible outcomes.

The majority of the population is thought to be closer to the risk-averter end of the continuum. The generally negative view people hold about exposing themselves to the risk of a loss is, in fact, the basis for many consumer warranties. Is it any wonder that advertisements allowing for a "risk-free examination period" are so appealing for all products, including many life insurance (for 10 days) and long-term care insurance (for 30 days) policies?

Why are some people more willing than others to take risks? Various factors contribute to the attitude of risk acceptance. They include biological makeup, upbringing, and other life experiences.

People's unwillingness to accept losses is a fundamental part of their attitude toward risk. Although it is typically stated that most people are risk averse, it is really more appropriate to say that they are loss averse.

In finance and related disciplines, risk aversion means the preference for certain outcomes over uncertain outcomes. Conversely, risk seeking refers to a preference for uncertain outcomes over certain outcomes. Studies have demonstrated conclusively that people are indeed cautious when faced with a choice between certain and uncertain gains. That is, they most often select the certain gain, even if it is smaller. However, when the two alternatives are a choice between a relatively small but certain loss and a relatively larger but only probable loss, most people are risk takers. In other words, they are willing to risk a large loss rather than accept a smaller but certain loss. These choices indicate *loss aversion* rather than risk aversion.

loss aversion

FORMAL CONCEPT OF RISK AND PEOPLE'S INTUITIVE PERCEPTION

The term risk has many definitions. Psychologists and other scientists have compared these definitions to people's intuitive understanding of the concept of risk. There are some striking differences.

In the field of finance, the conventional measures of investment risk are statistical concepts of variability such as standard deviation. This approach holds that any potential deviation from the expected return, whether positive or negative, contributes to the investment's riskiness. High variability in past, and expected future, returns is equated with risk.

To the average person who is unsophisticated about investment matters, however, the most important factor in evaluating the riskiness of an investment is the historical trend line in the return generated by the investment. If the trend is upward, the investment is perceived as less risky than if the trend is downward. Fluctuations in the return are only a secondary consideration.

Intuitively, then, people do accept variability of investment returns as a measure of risk, but the evidence shows that many do not treat uncertainty about positive outcomes as an aspect of risk. Rather, most people focus on the probability of negative returns in defining a risk. Generally, people regard the word risk to mean danger or possible loss.

With respect to investments, the danger lies in either getting less than the expected return or sustaining a loss of the principal. Surveys have demonstrated that portfolio managers and professionals who must routinely deal with capital budgeting tend to incorporate the probability of not achieving an expected, or target, return on an investment into their personal definition of a risky investment. However, in most other people's minds, the loss of principal is closest to their intuitive understanding of the word risk.

Any investment product promising no loss of principal will appear safe to most consumers. Some individuals tend to draw a distinction between investing and speculating. According to this view, investments assure the safety of principal whereas speculations do not. It is no accident that mutual funds guaranteeing the return of the principal appeared after the October 1987 stock market crash.

Risk and Uncertainty

risk

uncertainty

Another difference between people's intuitive understanding of the word risk and some formal definitions of this term involves the distinction between risk and uncertainty. Many people associate risk with the word uncertainty. However, in the decision sciences, risk and uncertainty are not considered the same. *Risk* in decision sciences refers to situations in which (1) the various consequences of each alternative are known and (2) their exact probabilities can be specified. *Uncertainty* in decision sciences, in contrast, is said to exist when the possible alternatives and their associated probabilities of occurrence are unknown.

Example: There are only two possible outcomes that students face when they take a pass-fail examination—pass or fail. Assume for a moment that someone is asked to estimate his or her chances of passing the course. If he or she can assign a probability to this event (for example, 60 percent chance of passing/40 percent chance of failing), then the exam represents a risk. If, however, the person has no way of assigning probabilities (being unfamiliar with the instructor's grading policies), then the exam represents an uncertainty.

Perceived Versus Objective Risk

In essence, there are four dimensions to a choice involving risk: (1) the potential gain, (2) the probability of achieving this gain, (3) the amount of potential loss, and (4) the probability of this loss occurring. Whether a person accepts or rejects a risk depends on his or her analysis of these four elements. In analyzing the risk, people tend to focus more on some of these dimensions than on others. Some people look most closely at the probability of winning, while others focus on the probability of losing. Still others are mainly concerned with the amounts involved.

perceived risk

Objective riskiness of a situation and one's interpretation of it, called *perceived risk,* are not necessarily the same. Different people exposed to the same information interpret it differently. The objective odds are either lowered or heightened depending on the person's experiences, inclinations toward risk taking, and the particular circumstances surrounding a given situation.

LIMITATIONS IN RATIONAL THINKING

bounded rationality

Debates abound regarding the extent of rationality shown in individual financial behavior. While some continue to view financial actions as always totally rational, recent evidence suggests less than totally rational behavior. At best, human beings act within what the Nobel prize-winning economist and psychologist Herbert Simon calls *bounded rationality.* That is, there are bounds or limits to how rational people can be. Their choices in financial matters are shaped not only by knowledge and rational thinking but also by their values and emotions.

Challenges to rationality are often reported in the behavior of the stock market. Certain research suggests that volatility in the stock market is due to fads and mass psychology (that is, people doing something because others are doing it) as well as changes in the economy and the fundamental soundness of the companies issuing the stocks. Attitudes about the economy change faster than the economy itself. Some have likened the spread of enthusiasm and disenchantment about a given stock to the spread of an epidemic. The technology boom of the late 1990s is an example of the spread of enthusiasm for a particular market segment.

Psychologists have conducted studies on how people perceive and process information about uncertain events. Most studies have found that people tend to violate rationality to some degree. Flaws in judgment are due in part to people's limited abilities to process information and in part to the interference of their emotions.

With respect to risky decisions, many people do not understand the laws of probability, and their ability to combine two or more probabilities is especially flawed. For example, in one study many people preferred a lottery in which they were allowed one draw out of 10 tickets to another lottery in which they were allowed 20 draws out of 100 tickets. (The 20-draw lottery is, of course, a better deal.) Individuals tend to process information about probability in an intuitive, rather than mathematical, manner. Few people know how to make optimal decisions using mathematical decision rules.

Overconfidence in Intuitive Judgments

Most people, laymen and professionals alike, tend to be overconfident in their judgment, as shown in studies that ask people to make a choice and then estimate their probability of being right. These research findings indicate that if a person believes he or she has an 80 percent chance of being right, in reality this probability is only 70 percent. In other words, people are right in their judgment 7 out of 10 times rather than 8 out of 10. Errors are frequent even when one is totally certain about something. In one study, when people said something always happened, it actually occurred only 80 percent of the time. Likewise, when these individuals indicated that something never happened, it occurred about 20 percent of the time.

Typically, people use fewer clues to make a decision than they claim. The importance of minor clues is overestimated in most instances. Presenting people with more facts seems to make people feel more confident about their decisions, but generally the accuracy of their decisions is not greatly enhanced.

Nonrepresentative Quality of Short-Run Trends

Most people disregard "the Law of Large Numbers." They are willing to make their risk assessments on the basis of very small samples, not realizing that long-run performance may not occur in the short run. Most analysts believe that investors overvalue short-run economic developments. Recent events get undue emphasis in people's decision making.

Example: In an experiment designed to illustrate people's failure to appreciate the significance of small versus large samples, people were asked to indicate which of the following is more likely to be an honest coin—coin A or coin B. Remember, in a single flip of an honest coin there is a 50-50 chance of the coin falling on its head or tail.

Coin A: 8 heads in 10 flips
Coin B: 70 heads in 100 flips

The honest coin is more likely to be A, but many people say B because the distribution of heads and tails is closer to 50-50 for coin B. These individuals are in error, however, because they fail to appreciate the small number of flips that took place with coin A. In the short run, an outcome that defies what one would expect in the long run is quite possible.

Likewise, people tend to perceive patterns in totally random events. Which of the following sequences is more likely to occur by chance on six tosses of an honest coin?

Coin 1: HHHTTT
Coin 2: HTHTTH

Most people erroneously believe that the coin 2 sequence is more likely because it appears random, whereas the sequence of coin 1 seems less likely because it looks more systematic. In reality, the sequences are equally likely to occur by chance (that is, $\frac{1}{2}$ x $\frac{1}{2}$ x $\frac{1}{2}$ x $\frac{1}{2}$ x $\frac{1}{2}$ x $\frac{1}{2}$). This tendency to see a pattern where none exists is sometimes called the "hot hand" fallacy because of the almost universal belief among both players and fans that basketball players have "hot" and "cold" shooting streaks, despite statistical evidence that fails to show any marked deviations from a player's long-term shooting percentage.

Daniel Kahneman and Mark Riepe (1998) contended that the "hot hand" fallacy could be observed in the "unfounded credibility" achieved by some fund managers who were able to beat the market for only a few short years.[1] Their skill could simply be chance.

Failure to Correctly Evaluate Exposure Time

Most people have a particularly hard time evaluating the true magnitude of a risk that is not constant. In one study, the participants were asked to estimate the magnitude of risks that varied by both the extent of exposure time and the potential harm (that is, long-duration high risk; long-duration low risk; short-duration high risk; short-duration low risk). The study found that individuals fail to factor exposure time correctly into their estimates of risk. They tend to overestimate the impact of short-duration high-risk events. Being in danger for a very short time is seen as much more dangerous than it really is.

Denial of Risk

denial of risk

High risk taking could be due to either a failure to assess the level of danger or simply a willingness or desire to engage in the activity regardless of the level of danger. The evidence suggests that people engaging in risky behaviors on a voluntary basis often fail to appreciate the true level of danger in the situation. They may know the statistical odds but they refuse to believe that these odds apply to them personally. This concept is called *denial of risk*.

Example: In a study sponsored by the Insurance Information Institute, it was discovered that only 58 percent of people who smoke in bed consider it to be a very risky activity, whereas 92 percent of those who do not smoke in bed find it to be so. Similar patterns were identified for activities such as gambling (35 versus 63 percent), driving a car (27 versus 39 percent), skiing (13 versus 33 percent), and investing in the stock market (26 versus 39 percent).

People frequently claim that there is less risk in their own personal case because their skills reduce the risky aspects of the situation. For instance, many skydivers deny that their sport is risky. To them, it is risky only if one "does not know what he or she is doing." Similar attitudes exist among people who speculate in the stock market and real estate. A sharp distinction is drawn by such individuals between taking risks and being foolhardy. In many cases, people have unwarranted confidence in their skill levels.

Other people deny the risk because they feel especially lucky. They believe they can beat the odds. Even if the odds of success are only 10 in 100, these individuals are apt to think, Somebody has to be in that 10 percent, so why shouldn't it be me? When the objective probability of an event is unknown, people tend to overestimate the probability of a desired outcome and underestimate the probability of an undesired outcome. Many an individual who felt that the odds could be beaten has traveled to Las Vegas in a $15,000 car and, indeed, has come home in a $100,000 vehicle. Unfortunately, in a majority of such cases the $100,000 vehicle was not a new car but a bus.

People's reluctance to buy insurance stems in part from this type of unrealistic optimism. Some agents present actuarial data to their prospects regarding the probability of death, disability, and hospitalization, but most prospects believe that these statistics do not really apply to them personally. Most people believe that they are less likely than average to die prematurely, be hospitalized, or become disabled. In a recent study, people were presented with the statistic that during a given year approximately 19 out of every 1,000 persons would sustain a disability lasting over 3 months. (In other words, the odds of disability were 19 in 1,000.) The group was then asked to estimate their personal odds of sustaining a disability. On average, the subjects felt their personal odds to be much lower—only 6 in 1,000.

Findings indicate that people tend to especially discount very small negative probabilities, treating them as if they were nonexistent. Due to this bias in the processing of risk information, many people are reluctant to insure against low-probability events even if a catastrophic loss potential exists and the insurance is underpriced (in relation to the actuarial risk). For example, flood insurance, despite being federally subsidized, is not easy to sell. Sales do increase after a flood occurs, but only for a few months. Psychologists have examined the style of thinking that supports this undue optimism. It has been found that people tend to overgeneralize from their previous experiences. The person's thinking is, It hasn't happened to me yet, so it probably never will.

Two techniques might encourage the purchase of insurance coverage for underestimated perils. One, the insurance should be sold as part of a comprehensive package rather than as a separate policy. Two, a partial refund can be offered to the policyholder during years in which no claims occur.

Complete Elimination Versus Reduction in Risk

Research comparing how people react to a reduction in risk relative to its complete elimination suggests that most people place a disproportionately high value on the latter.

Example: You are facing a chance for a gain of $20,000. You do not know the exact probability. Consider these three pairs of outcomes (as cited in Kahneman and Riepe, 1998):[2]

A. The probability is either   0% or   1%
B. The probability is either 41% or 42%
C. The probability is either 99% or 100%

How much are you willing to pay to increase your probability from 0 percent to one percent, from 41 percent to 42 percent, and from 99 percent to 100 percent? Research shows that people will pay more to raise the probability of a desirable event from 0 percent to one percent or from 99 percent to 100 percent than from 41 percent to 42 percent, even though the increase amounts to one percent in all three cases.

This mindset may have implications for marketing insurance products. The high value placed on the elimination of risk may explain why many people select low deductibles on property and casualty coverages, despite the relatively high premiums. Furthermore, this bias implies that the way a particular coverage's degree of protection is described to a client is very important. For instance, an insurance policy guarding against a particular peril, like fire, may be viewed as either full protection against the specific risk or a reduction in the overall probability of property loss. Based on the observed preference for the elimination of a risk compared with its reduction, there is a distinct marketing advantage in focusing on the coverage's full protection aspect. Telling a prospective client that buying the policy will lower his or her chances of suffering property damage will have a lower inducement value than will stressing to the client that he or she has full protection against fire.

Availability Bias

availability bias

Availability bias alters individuals' estimates of risk when events that are easy to imagine or recall are judged as more probable than they actually are. Events that are dramatic and vivid or that receive heavy media attention are easily available to one's mind and are, therefore, overestimated. In contrast, events that are dull or abstract are underestimated. A few examples should help explain this particular bias.

- After the September 11, 2001, airline hijackings, many people were especially reluctant to fly, even though the probability of dying in an airliner is significantly lower than the probability of dying in an automobile accident.
- People overestimate the probability of dying from accidents in comparison to dying from illnesses. Again, this is because the media devotes more coverage to deaths resulting from events like airplane crashes than to deaths resulting from heart attacks.
- Which is more frequent, homicide or suicide? Most people believe that homicide is five times more frequent. Yet suicides are 30 percent more common. People tend to believe that the opposite is true because homicides are reported in the news, while suicides generally go unreported, unless the suicide involves a well-known personality.
- People tend to be more influenced by personal experiences because they are more vivid. Thus, research shows that people overestimate the probability of death from diseases that have killed people they knew personally. Individuals also tend to be influenced more by anecdotal evidence from their friends than by more representative and trustworthy information in statistical reports. Consequently, many individuals who normally did not wear a seat belt, despite repeated warnings from various governmental agencies, start to wear one after a friend's or neighbor's failure to use a seat belt results in injury or death.

Familiarity Bias

familiarity bias

Most people dread the unknown. Risks that are familiar are feared less than risks that are unfamiliar. This tendency is called *familiarity bias*. For example, investors see greater risk in foreign equities than warranted based on historical returns. This fear occurs because they know less about other countries than their own country. In other words, people tend to perceive less risk in things they know. The more a person knows about a country, company, product, or situation, the lower will be his or her perception of risk. For instance, sophisticated investors tend to be more risk tolerant than naive investors. Educating clients about unfamiliar investments may lower their inherent fears.

Typically, people overreact to unexpected news. Studies show that both securities analysts and the lay public overreact to recent information, giving the new (that is, unfamiliar) information more importance than it really deserves.

Illusion of Control Bias

Illusion of control bias refers to the tendency of people to underestimate the risk involved in activities under their control, like driving a car, relative to activities in which the control is given over to someone else, like being a passenger in an airplane. Ironically, the chance of being involved in a car accident driving to the airport to catch a flight is greater than the chance of the airplane crashing.

Time Horizon

For most decisions involving an element of risk, the length of the time elapsing between making the decision and the knowledge of the eventual outcome is very crucial. If the time span between these two events is long, the person is more likely to accept the risk than if the time span is relatively short. In other words, if something is imminent, there is an increased sense of danger.

People tend to psychologically overemphasize short-term risks. Some authorities have suggested that people start smoking because the threat of cancer is so far in the future. The long-term risk, although quite threatening, does not seem real to them. (This refusal to consider future risks seriously can be seen in Mark Twain's reaction to being told that, by giving up smoking and drinking, he could add another 5 years to his life. Twain's reaction was that without smoking and drinking another 5 years of living would not be worth it.)

Fortunately, there may be some synergy between people's willingness to bear risk under a broad time horizon and the performance of the riskier investment products. Analysis of historical data has shown that, although these products show great volatility in the short run, they are less volatile in the long run. In other words, they are safer when viewed in a broad investment time horizon. Unfortunately for their financial well-being, people typically have a short-range rather than long-range planning horizon.

Example: The tendency to be myopic about one's investment planning horizon is well illustrated in a study conducted by psychologist R. J. Herrnstein.[3] Herrnstein presented participants with the following situation: Let's suppose that you win a lottery that gives you two alternative ways, A and B, of collecting your winnings.

Situation 1

Choice A: You can collect $100 tomorrow.
Choice B: You can collect $115 a week from tomorrow.

Most of the group selected option A, even though by waiting only one more week they would have earned 15 percent. (There are few investments that would pay 15 percent interest per week.)

Next, the people who selected choice A were presented with another hypothetical lottery in which the two payment schedules were C and D.

Situation 2

Choice C: You can collect $100 52 weeks from today.
Choice D: You can collect $115 53 weeks from today.

Almost all of those who selected payment schedule A now selected payment schedule D. If they were consistent in their behavior, they would have chosen C. There was the same one-week difference between A and B as between C and D. However, the one-week difference meant much more in the present than it did in the future.

Research shows that 10 to 15 years is the longest time horizon that most people consider practical for planning purposes. Surveys of the general public continue to find that people do recognize that upon retirement they may not have enough income to live in their present style, yet they fail to do anything to remedy the situation. The reason typically offered as justification is that they have a more pressing immediate crisis or concern. Many people who purchase term insurance instead of permanent insurance intend to invest the premium difference in securities, but do not because more immediate concerns arise.

Mood

Psychologists have studied the impact of a person's mood on his or her willingness to undertake risk. The relationship between mood and risk tolerance is quite complex, given the results of various studies. The research shows that a good mood leads to more positive expectations and lower perceived risk. Conversely, a bad mood leads to increased estimates of risk. However, when it comes to actual behavior, a good mood does not necessarily effect greater risk taking. While it does increase willingness to take relatively low risks, it decreases the person's willingness to accept high risks. Perhaps this is because the person does not want to jeopardize his or her good mood.

Some theoreticians attribute the generally lower stock prices on Monday as compared with Friday (known as the weekend effect) to differences in people's moods on Mondays as opposed to Fridays. Monday is said to be an unpleasant day for most people because it is the start of a workweek. On Friday, though, most people are in a pleasant mood because they are anticipating the weekend. These differences in mood are believed to be reflected in stock prices. The same explanation can be extended to the observation that stock returns are generally high in January (the January effect). Because January marks the beginning of a new year, people are generally optimistic, which again shows up in higher prices. However, there are other competing explanations for both the weekend and January effects.

Effects of Alcohol on Risk Taking

Studies have shown that alcohol consumption causes people to become reckless and take greater risks than they would ordinarily. In some cases people thought they were drinking alcoholic beverages when in reality they were not. An intriguing result is that even these people increased their risk-taking behaviors.

Parties Bearing the Consequences of a Decision

The answer to the question, Who will be affected by the consequences of my actions? is a strong determinant of whether a risk will be acceptable or unacceptable. Individuals tend to be more risk averse if the decision's outcome will have consequences for both the individual making the decision and those the individual cares about. Decision makers are somewhat less risk averse if only the individual decision maker is affected. The most risk-prone decisions are made if only others will bear the consequences of the decision.

Example: Managers take more risks when they invest their company's money than when they invest their own personal funds. Studies of stock market trading reveal a similar pattern. If the money invested is his or her own, the investor requires more information before making a transaction and makes significantly fewer trades.

Group Dynamics of Risk Taking

choice shift

A phenomenon studied for about 30 years concerns the difference between individual and group reactions to risk. This phenomenon, known as the *choice shift,* refers to the finding that a group decision is usually more extreme than a decision favored by most members of the group when polled individually (before the discussion). Generally, the shift is toward more risky action, although in some instances the shift is toward a more cautious attitude.

Several studies on the choice shift phenomenon bear directly on financial planning. In one study, people were asked to identify the investment products they would be willing to buy. The investments available ranged from low risk with no variability in their historical return patterns, to very variable high risk with low returns in certain years and high returns in other years. First, each person made his or her selection individually. Next, participants met in a group to reach a consensus regarding their choices. While on an individual basis most members of the group wanted the less risky products, the group decision was in favor of the riskier products. There were similar results in another study where the group's task was the selection of automobile physical damage coverage. When polled individually, the participants were willing to pay, on average, about another $48 in premiums in order to get collision coverage. As a result of the group discussion, however, the consensus was that they would be willing to pay less—only $31—for this particular coverage. In other words, the group was willing to bear more risk.

Possible explanations for the shift in the risky direction include:

- The responsibility for a decision is shared by the group, so no one person feels totally responsible if it turns out to be the wrong one.
- The risk-tolerant members in the group are influential.
- As a result of the group discussion, the members become more familiar with the situation, and this lessens their inherent fears.

Mental Accounts

Various psychological experiments have been conducted to illustrate how mental accounts operate in people's evaluation of monetary gains and losses. One such study shows that the opportunity to save a given amount of money will be viewed quite differently, depending on what mental account a person uses to evaluate the psychological value of this money.

Example: Psychologists Daniel Kahneman and Amos Tversky asked people what they would do if they went out to buy a $125 jacket and a $15 calculator and, upon arrival at the main store, the sales clerk informed them that the calculator was on sale for $10 at a branch store 20 minutes away.[4] Under these circumstances, 68 percent of people were willing to drive 20 minutes to save $5.

In a second version of this same story, the $5 in savings was on the jacket rather than the calculator. (That is, the price of the jacket was $120 at the branch store and $125 at the main store. The price of the calculator was $15 at both stores.) The percentage of people willing to drive 20 minutes to save $5 under the second set of circumstances was only 29 percent.

Five dollars would be saved either way, yet the number of people willing to save this amount of money was substantially different. Why? The simple reason is that people maintain different mental accounts for the prices of jackets and calculators. Money to be gained or lost is not evaluated in a vacuum. Rather, there is always some subjective standard employed as a yardstick to gauge the value.

The concept of mental accounts has many implications for financial advisors. The amount of pleasure or displeasure that the appreciation or depreciation in the value of a certain asset will bring to a client is not necessarily determined by the simple dollar amounts gained or lost. Other factors will influence the client's assessment of the event. For example, did the client's neighbor (or family member) do better or worse? How did a different security that the client considered purchasing fare?

Financial advisors must recognize that because of mental accounts their clients may have different risk-tolerance levels for different funds, depending on how they acquired the money and what they intend to do with it. Inherited versus earned money is one factor that may account for different risk-tolerance levels. Some people who inherit hard-earned money from a loved relative may refuse to risk losing the principal. With money they earned personally, however, they may have less fear of potential loss. For others, the reverse may be true.

People's mental accounting for posting gains and losses does not treat money earned and money lost as equal units. Money lost carries a much heavier psychological value. For instance, making $5,000 on an investment, provided that this return is equal to what was expected, will make a client happy. Conversely, losing $5,000 on an investment will make a client unhappy. Research shows, however, that the unhappiness experienced at losing the $5,000 is greater than the happiness felt at earning $5,000. Therefore, clients are apt to be more upset about a given loss than pleased about an equivalent gain. Similarly, most investors feel worse if they sell a security that shortly thereafter increases in value than if they failed to buy the security in the first place.

Mental accounting may also be the underlying cause for the finding that most investors prefer cash dividends over capital gains. Dividends and capital gains are placed into separate mental accounts according to some theorists.

RISK TAKING:
SITUATION-SPECIFIC OR GENERAL PERSONALITY TRAIT?

Some financial advisors tend to describe people as risk takers or risk averters, without considering the type of behaviors on which they base such classifications. It is as if they expect people to act in a similar manner in all aspects of life. Yet psychologists are still debating whether most people have a consistent pattern of risk taking in all realms of their lives or whether the degree of risk they are willing to assume depends on the nature of the situation. Although some evidence suggests that there is a slight predisposition to act in either a risk-taking or risk-averse manner in different situations, this predisposition is weak for most persons. Only those with the personality type that psychologists call the "thrill seeker" (also known as the "sensation" or "arousal" seeker) seem to be relatively consistent.

In general, the more similar any two situations are, the greater is the consistency in risk-taking behavior in these two situations. Research has shown that essentially four major types of life situations involve risk taking:

- Monetary situations: They involve such risks as investments, gambling, or job changes.
- Physical situations: They involve risks that could result in bodily harm, such as mountain climbing or skydiving.
- Social situations: They involve risks that could lead to loss of self-esteem or another person's respect.
- Ethical situations: They involve risks in which one is faced with the prospect of compromising one's moral or religious standards or society's legal standards. (For example, trading on insider information involves an ethical risk.)

Cases in which the level of risk taking is quite different across different contexts are not hard to find, as many people change their behavior from situation to situation. One such case involved a Navy pilot who had been decorated for heroism during the Vietnam War. After his discharge from the service, this individual was encouraged to begin a career in life insurance sales. His new career proved to be both financially and emotionally unrewarding, however, because he was uncomfortable with prospecting. This came as a surprise to the person's manager because there was clear-cut evidence of fearlessness and risk taking in the person's war record. The former pilot and his manager had a discussion about his fear of prospecting. During the course of the conversation, it became evident to the manager that it was actually a low level of social risk tolerance that accounted for this person's high physical risk tolerance during the war. The individual related that what kept him flying was the fear of disapproval by others. As he put it, whenever he got jittery about a mission and thought of turning back, all he had to do was picture the look of disapproval from his commander and fellow pilots. In this case, low tolerance for social risk was, in part, responsible for high physical risk tolerance.

Four Major Types of Life Situations That Involve Risk Taking

Risk Contexts	Perceived Consequences
monetary risk	potential loss of capital
physical risk	potential loss of life
social risk	potential loss of "face"
ethical risk	potential loss of freedom

One should be careful in using a client's attitude toward risk in nonfinancial matters to infer a level of risk tolerance for investments. Knowing that someone is a risk taker in a certain physical activity provides clues about how the individual will react in other situations that involve potential bodily harm. However, this information provides little insight as to whether this person will be willing to invest in a financially risky venture. The latter information is best determined from a knowledge of the person's typical behavior in monetary risk-taking situations. Therefore, a financial advisor who promotes an "aggressive" mutual fund to a skydiving club should not be surprised if the responses to the ad are not dramatically greater than responses from the general public. The best predictor of an investor's risk tolerance in a financial matter is his or her risk preference in other financial matters, rather than how the person reacts to risk in sports, social situations, and so on.

The client's risk tolerance in financial matters should be of primary concern to the financial advisor, since this is the aspect of the client's situation that is within the advisor's purview. However, there may be some value in looking at the client's total risk-taking disposition. First, the client could learn that he or she may not necessarily have the same propensity for risk in money matters as in physical activities or social activities. Often clients assume (falsely) that they have a general predisposition to take on the same level of risk in all spheres of life. Second, consistency across different contexts may alert the financial advisor to whether the individual is someone who is a thrill seeker (discussed later in this chapter).

Physical risk taking could be a relevant issue when determining a client's insurance needs. It has been shown that risk taking in the physical realm is a major factor in various types of accidents. Therefore, people who have high levels of physical risk tolerance are more apt to die from accidental causes or to suffer disabling injuries from an accident. According to the *Statistical Bulletin* published by the Metropolitan Life Insurance Company, accidents are the leading cause of death among children and young adults. When the U.S. population is considered as a whole, accidental death is third in line after death due to cardiovascular diseases or cancer. Deaths from motor vehicle accidents account for approximately half of the accidental deaths reported in this country. Accidental death riders and disability income insurance may be of interest to the physical risk taker, especially if the individual has, at the same time, a low level of monetary risk tolerance.

Physical risk taking is also a contributing factor in death from nonaccidental causes. Consequently risk taking in health-related matters increasingly concerns insurance companies. It is now standard for insurance carriers to charge lower premiums for nonsmokers, and an emergent trend may be to extend similar premium reductions to people who avoid other health risks as well. Because of the AIDS epidemic, a growing area of research—some sponsored by the insurance industry—is concerned with risk taking in sexual behaviors (a form of physical risk taking).

LIFESTYLE OF THE RISK TAKER

Most of the early studies on the personality of the typical risk taker assumed that risk taking was a general personality trait rather than being specific to a particular context. Therefore, the measures of risk taking used in these studies did not differentiate between attitudes toward physical, social, ethical, and monetary risk taking. Consequently one needs to exercise caution in utilizing these findings in financial planning because they may apply more to one of the other categories of risk taking than to monetary risk taking in particular.

For example, the following life experiences that some researchers identify as typical of the risk taker probably apply more to physical risk takers than monetary risk takers:

- took dares as a child
- drank and smoked at an early age
- was sexually active at a young age
- enjoys dangerous leisure activities, such as mountain climbing, surfing, hang gliding, scuba diving, racing a car, motorcycling, or skydiving
- is likely to hold a job as a pilot, soldier, firefighter, or police officer

Likewise, the following characteristics of risk takers may be related mostly to social risk taking:

- has a social presence
- is self-accepting
- is self-confident
- is aggressive
- is independent
- is irresponsible
- is status-seeking
- has strong leadership abilities
- is not governed by other people's opinions

Similarly, the finding that risk takers feel low levels of guilt for wrongdoing probably applies more to the ethical risk taker than to the physical, monetary, or social risk taker.

Other characteristics identified in this type of research may, however, also apply to monetary risk takers. Among these are the following:

- emphasizes merit rather than seniority in job promotions
- enjoys work that involves decision making
- requires little time to make a major decision
- completes tests that have a time limit very quickly, attempting to compensate for more mistakes by answering more questions
- takes a chance and guesses on tests that impose a penalty for guessing (such as the Scholastic Aptitude Test)
- is optimistic, seeing mistakes as setbacks, not personal failures
- has a low need for an ordered environment
- is able to handle stress
- is persistent

Some studies have focused on the biographical and psychological characteristics of monetary risk takers per se. Psychologist Frank Farley found that monetary risk takers are good money managers who spend considerable time reading about investments and related financial matters and express confidence in their money-making abilities. In contrast to the monetary risk averters, who stated that their long-term goal was happiness, the monetary risk takers listed success as their primary goal. Farley also found that monetary risk takers tend to possess leadership skills and good sales skills. For many monetary risk takers, money is the center of their lives.

Distinguishing Characteristics Between Monetary Risk Averters and Risk Takers in Life Outlook

<u>Risk Averter</u>	<u>Risk Taker</u>
• sees risk as danger	• sees risk as challenge or opportunity
• overestimates risk	• underestimates risk
• prefers low variability	• prefers high variability
• adopts the worst-case scenario (emphasizes the probability of a loss)	• adopts the best-case scenario (emphasizes the probability of a win)
• is pessimistic	• is optimistic
• likes structure	• likes ambiguity
• dislikes change	• enjoys change
• prefers certainty to uncertainty	• prefers uncertainty to certainty

---

A study of mutual fund shareholders sponsored by the mutual fund industry trade association[5] indicates that investors with high-risk tolerance have clear financial goals. They were also more likely to be raised in homes that had an interest in investing, discussed such matters, and actually invested. In describing the outcomes of their families' investments, the high risk takers were more likely to indicate that it was successful. High-risk-tolerant mutual fund owners made their own first investment at an earlier age than their low-risk-tolerant counterparts, and their first investment was more likely to be an individual stock. The first investment for low-risk-tolerant mutual fund owners was more likely to be real estate.

Compared with low and moderate risk takers, high-risk-tolerant shareholders in this study were more apt to have confidence in their ability to make their own investment decisions, rather than relying on the advice of professionals. They used magazines and newspapers as their primary source of investment information to make these decisions. High-risk-tolerant shareholders were also more likely to read the mutual funds prospectus for investing information (that is, 38 percent of the high risk takers versus 25 percent of the moderate risk takers and 13 percent of the low risk takers). The same pattern was found in the readership of investment newsletters (26 percent, 19 percent, and 15 percent for high, moderate, and low risk takers, respectively). Low risk takers, in contrast, indicated that they were confused by the multitude of investment choices, and therefore relied on others for advice; their most frequent sources of information were friends, family, and business associates. The high-risk-tolerant investors were more likely to actually adapt a long-term view of their investments even though the low and moderate risk takers agree just as strongly that a long-term strategy leads to the best results. Low risk takers seem overly concerned about short-term fluctuations. (See figure 4-1.)

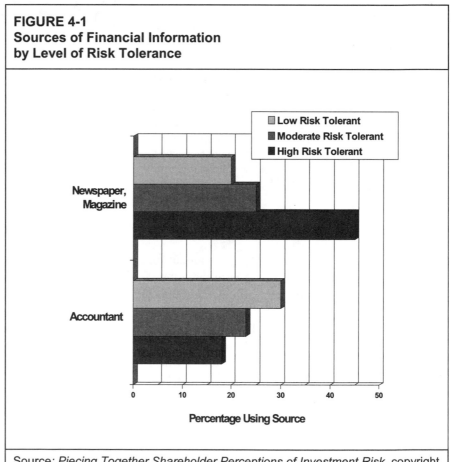

FIGURE 4-1
Sources of Financial Information
by Level of Risk Tolerance

Source*: Piecing Together Shareholder Perceptions of Investment Risk*, copyright © 1993, Investment Company Institute (*www.ici.org*). Reprinted with permission.

The groups were also compared on their knowledge of investment principles, and as one might expect, the high-risk-tolerant group showed the best understanding of the subject.

Another significant survey comparing the investment attitudes of risk-tolerant and risk-intolerant investors concerns their satisfaction with the returns they previously received on their investments. Whereas risk-averse investors are generally satisfied, those who are risk tolerant tend to feel that they were not adequately compensated.

Research has found differences in the type of regret experienced by risk-taking and risk-averting investors. Wealthy investors were asked to think of a bad financial decision that they now regretted, and to indicate if the regret was over one investment they made (regret of commission) or over an investment that they failed to make (regret of omission). Most of these investors reported regrets of commission, that is, about investments that they actually made. A minority, however, reported their greatest regret was about missed opportunities to make an investment. This minority constituted the risk takers in this group.

The risk takers also had another characteristic in common. Asked whether they attributed investment outcomes to luck or skill, the risk takers attributed skill to all outcomes, even the ones they regretted.

THE THRILL SEEKER

thrill seeker

The *thrill seeker* is the personality type most likely to be consistently risk seeking across all dimensions of life including financial matters. Sometimes a distinction is made between physical thrill seekers and mental thrill seekers. However, all thrill seekers abhor routine, be it mental or physical. These individuals are always on the lookout for experiences that offer novelty, ambiguity, complexity, and intensity. If a thrill seeker cannot find excitement, he or she will create it. "In-and-out" trading in the stock market, for instance, provides many such quick thrills. For the thrill seeker, the uncertainty of an investment decision may hold as much enticement, perhaps even more, than the anticipated payoff. To the thrill seeker, money made from a safe investment does not hold as much value as the same amount of money made from a risky one. There is some research showing that thrill seekers have a biologically based need for greater than normal levels of arousal.

Thrill seeking can have either very constructive or very destructive outlets. For example, constructive mental outlets are available in the arts or sciences, fields that reward the creative thinking characteristic of the thrill seeker. Crime, on the other hand, provides a common destructive outlet for both mental and physical thrill seeking. Even in prison, thrill seekers are a problem because they continually try to escape.

Not everyone who takes many risks is necessarily a thrill seeker, although by definition, every thrill seeker must be considered a risk taker. How can a financial advisor spot the thrill seeker? To a certain extent, the thrill seeker is a caricature of a risk taker, showing many of the same basic characteristics but in a markedly exaggerated form. In addition to the characteristics already mentioned in defining the thrill-seeking personality, the financial advisor should be alert to those that follow.

Thrill seeking is more common among men than women. Thrill seekers enjoy loud parties. They tend to be outgoing, spontaneous, and fast decision makers. In looking for a history of sensation seeking, the advisor needs to check to see if the person participates in risky sports and likes to gamble, especially at blackjack. A history of traffic violations is common. Thrill seekers may associate with unconventional persons and have an intense dislike for people they perceive as boring. The thrill seeker looks for variety in his or her sex life. If the thrill seeker uses recreational drugs, a variety of drugs rather than just one drug are taken.

Thrill seekers may appear to be perfect candidates for risky investments, given their obviously high tolerance for risk. But this very desire for novel, intense, and varied experiences may lead the thrill seeker to pursue legal action against the advisor for suggesting an overly risky product if the investment does not produce the expected returns. With this type of client, the advisor must take particular care in documenting due diligence.

DEMOGRAPHIC CHARACTERISTICS

Numerous studies have been conducted over the years in which risk tolerance was related to such factors as wealth, education, age, gender, birth order, marital status, and occupation. The results of this research are discussed below.

Wealth

absolute risk tolerance
relative risk tolerance

Do wealthy individuals take more risks with their money? First, a distinction must be drawn between absolute and relative risk tolerance. *Absolute risk tolerance* is gauged by the amount of wealth one allocates to risky assets. *Relative risk tolerance,* in contrast, is measured by the proportion of one's wealth allocated to risky assets. It is generally accepted that absolute risk tolerance increases with wealth since the wealthy have more money to spend on everything. There is some disagreement, though, about whether relative risk tolerance increases with wealth. Several studies have addressed this question by examining people's investment portfolios.

Some researchers have been unable to find such relationships. One reason for the discrepancy is attributable to differences in the type of assets considered and how these assets were classified (safe versus risky). The way the primary residence is treated seems to be especially critical. Relative risk tolerance goes up with increasing wealth if housing is either excluded from the definition of wealth or classified as a riskless asset.

Example: A study conducted by R. A. Cohn and his colleagues found that relative risk tolerance increases with wealth—the wealthier a participant was, the greater the proportion of total wealth that person put in risky assets.[6] For instance, if the individual's assets were above $175,000, on average 62 percent of his or her investments were risky. If the total value of assets was below $175,000, only 42 percent of the investments were of the risky type. This pattern held even after sex, age, and marital status were taken into account. However, this relationship between wealth and risk tolerance was strongest among male investors and married investors.

There is further support for a positive relationship between relative risk tolerance and wealth in studies using questionnaires as the basis for determining the degree of risk tolerance. In the survey sponsored by the Insurance Information Institute, the wealthy were more likely to associate the word risk with the word opportunity than the other respondents. Similarly, a study of the upper affluent sponsored by the CIGNA Corporation found that the risk takers in this group were more likely to have higher incomes and were much more likely to be millionaires. The "chicken and egg" question still remains: Did the wealthy become so because of their greater willingness to assume risk, or is it that they are more risk taking now that they are wealthy? That is, does having money make one more risk seeking?

How money was acquired may also be a factor in the risk-taking propensity characteristic of the wealthy. Differences in risk tolerance have been reported between those who made their fortune themselves over time and those who did not make it themselves and acquired it relatively quickly. For instance, people who acquired their wealth through a windfall (such as winning a lottery) are more apt to expose it to risk than those who acquired their money through hard labor. Yet, people who earned their own wealth tend to be more risk tolerant than those who inherited their wealth from beloved relatives.

Education

Numerous studies have found that financial risk tolerance increases with the degree of formal education. Riley and Chow, for instance, looked at the percentage of total wealth held in risky assets by individuals with differing levels of education and made the observations as reflected below in table 4-1.[7]

TABLE 4-1	
Risk Tolerance and Degree of Formal Education	
Education	Percentage of Wealth in Risky Assets
Less than high school	2.0%
High school diploma	3.4%
Some college	5.2%
College degree	7.9%
Post graduate	8.0%

Among the mutual fund shareholders studied by the Investment Company Institute, the percentage of investors with at least a 4-year college degree increases with risk tolerance (39 percent among the low risk tolerant, 57 percent among the moderate risk tolerant, and 66 percent among the high risk tolerant).[8] The reason for this relationship is not entirely clear, however. Because education is correlated with income and wealth, it could be that it is the latter two variables that account for the greater risk tolerance among the better educated, rather than education per se. It is also possible that people with higher levels of education become familiar with the range of investment options available to them.

Age

In general, financial risk tolerance is negatively correlated with age. One study of mutual fund investors asked whether they agreed or disagreed with the statement, The older people get, the less willing they are to take investment risk. Ratings were on a scale from 0 to 10, with 0 indicating no agreement and 10 indicating strong agreement. In general respondents agreed with this statement, since the average rating was 7.6. Low-risk-tolerant, moderate-risk-tolerant, and high-risk-tolerant shareholders were compared on their opinions about this issue, and surprising differences were noted. The low-risk-tolerant investors were most likely to agree with this statement (average rating = 8.6), while the high-risk-tolerant investors were least likely to agree with it (average rating = 6.7). The moderate risk takers fell in the middle (average rating = 7.5).

A substantial body of research exists on the relationship between age and risk taking in all sorts of activities, financial as well as nonfinancial. The bulk of this research points to an inverse relationship between age and willingness to take risks. That is, as one gets older, one becomes more cautious. For instance, the Investment Company Institute Study of Risk Tolerance (cited previously) found that the average ages of their low-, moderate-, and high-risk tolerant investors were 60, 51, and 42 years, respectively.[9]

Some qualifiers are in order, however. This relationship between more advanced age and increased caution may not be as strong for monetary risks as it is for physical risks. Moreover, the relationship between monetary risk tolerance and age may be weaker among the wealthy, according to some studies. When looking at the impact of age on risk taking, the advisor also should consider the client's particular circumstances. For instance, some financial advisors report that they have encountered middle-aged couples who were previously very conservative investors but who now take an interest in aggressive investing because their obligations to raise and educate their children are at an end.

Gender

The study of psychological differences between men and women has a long history. Almost all research prior to the women's movement indicates that men were more risk tolerant than women in most aspects of life. Both biologically based and psychologically based explanations have been offered. One psychological explanation is that women had been socialized to be more dependent and risk averse.

The results of more recent studies are mixed. Some newer studies encourage consideration of age and income when looking at sex differences in monetary risk taking. While older married women are less likely to accept financial risks than their husbands, the differences in financial risk taking between younger men and women with comparable incomes are either small or nonexistent.

Birth Order

Although there is only limited research on the topic, it appears that birth order is related to risk taking. Namely, the firstborn child tends to be less willing to take risks than the later-born children in the same family. The favored explanation is that parents exert greater control over the early life of the firstborn child and instill in him or her the need to be dependable and act responsibly. To the child, this means not taking unnecessary chances.

Marital Status

Single individuals appear more risk tolerant than married individuals in some studies, and more risk averse in other studies. The reason for the conflicting results is a failure to consider whether both spouses are employed. The key is the presence of dependents, rather than marital status per se. If the individual feels that his or her actions might have negative consequences for dependents, then he or she is likely to be more cautious. In dual-income families, the spouse's level of risk tolerance may be no less than that of a single person, because neither party is the dependent under these circumstances. In fact, a dual income may increase the level of risk tolerance.

Example:	A study of mutual fund shareholders found that among married low-risk-tolerant investors, 61 percent of the spouses worked, compared with 73 percent of the high-risk-tolerant married households.

Other research indicates that widowed and separated people are more risk averse than either never-married persons or persons who are currently married.

Occupation

Most people spend much of their adult life working. Certainly the types of jobs they hold in some way relate to risk tolerance. Several aspects related to occupation and risk tolerance have been studied and are discussed below.

Public-Sector Versus Private-Sector Employment

One important manifestation of financial risk-taking propensity is the need for job security—the greater the probability of becoming unemployed, the greater the financial riskiness in that occupation. Thus, one would expect monetarily risk-averse individuals to gravitate toward jobs that offer security, even if the pay is lower. It is generally accepted that the public sector offers greater job security. A number of studies have compared the monetary risk-taking propensities of private-sector and public-sector employees. This research points to greater risk aversion among public-sector employees.

Professionals Versus Nonprofessionals

According to the results of some studies, professionals (physicians, lawyers, managers, and so on) tend to take on more risk in investment decisions than nonprofessionals (farmers, unskilled and skilled laborers, clerical workers, and so on). This disparity is perhaps due to differences in the level of sophistication about investment matters. As mentioned earlier, risk tolerance tends to increase with increased knowledge and familiarity.

Risk tolerance differences within a given profession cannot be explained in these terms, however. Certain reports indicate that professionals in private practice or professionals working for small firms are more risk tolerant than individuals in the same profession who are employed by large firms. Among physicians, differences have also been observed between surgeons and physicians in other specialties (internists, for example). Specifically, surgeons reportedly are more likely to be risk tolerant than other physicians.

Length of Job Tenure

Chances of advancement decrease the longer a person remains in one position with the same company. Again, many financially risk-averse people remain in positions that offer few possibilities for upward mobility because of financial security needs. Financial risk takers, in contrast, change jobs quite frequently (that is, they are job hoppers).

Management Level

Studies comparing the risk-tolerance levels of managers at different levels within an organization usually find that risk takers hold more senior level positions, earn higher incomes, and have greater authority. Risk takers are also more likely to work as managers in small rather than large firms.

Salary Versus Commission

Monetary risk takers are well represented in occupations in which all or a substantial portion of the earnings depends on commissions. Moreover, the more successful performers in such jobs generally take higher risks.

Example 1:	It has been found that the risk-taking individual is more likely to pursue one or two large accounts instead of a large number of small accounts.
Example 2:	A recent study examined the personality character-istics of job seekers and how these characteristics re-lated to the compensation system preferred by the job seeker. It was determined that risk-averse individuals were more attracted to positions and organizations that offered a fixed rather than a contingent (upon performance) pay system. Moreover, risk-averse

individuals did not consider pay level to be as important a criterion in the job they were seeking.

Entrepreneurship

According to the Small Business Administration, about 75 percent of new business ventures fail within 5 years. Given the financial risks involved, one would naturally expect people who are successful entrepreneurs to be high-risk takers. Surprisingly, however, research points to only a moderate propensity for taking risks among entrepreneurs. In other words, risk taking is not the characteristic that differentiates entrepreneurs from nonentrepreneurs. Rather, it seems to be the need for independence—to be one's own boss—and a need to achieve. This pattern of motivation may explain the preference for moderate levels of risk over low and high levels of risk. People with a strong need to achieve prefer moderate levels of risk where skill can have a marked influence on the outcome. In low-risk situations, everyone can achieve the desired outcome, whereas in high-risk situations, it becomes more a matter of luck than skill.

COMMUNICATING PROBABILITY STATEMENTS VERBALLY

Poor communication between client and advisor is responsible for many of the allegations of investment unsuitability filed against financial advisors. Typically, the client claims that the risks of the investment were not conveyed adequately. This brings us to the issue of communicating probabilities of success and failure to one's clients.

Research indicates that people prefer to obtain information about the probability of an event in numerical form. However, they are generally more comfortable describing the probability of an event to others in words rather than in numbers. Perhaps it is because in everyday situations it is not always possible to assign an exact probability to outcomes. But what does it mean to clients if their financial advisor tells them that a certain investment will probably double their money in 6 years, while another investment offers only a low chance of producing this rate of appreciation?

At least 282 words and phrases can be used to report the likelihood of something happening. Researchers have attempted to quantify these expressions by asking people questions like: If you were told that an outcome was _____ [the blank being filled in by a word or phrase such as "very improbable" or "likely"], what percentage would best represent the probability of that outcome occurring? The intent is to provide the financial advisor with a basis for determining how these terms would be understood by

clients if he or she were to use them in communicating estimates of the
probabilities of various investment opportunities.

Example:	On average, "almost impossible" is understood as having a 2 percent (2/100) chance of occurring. "Medium chance" and "even chance" are understood to represent about a 50 percent chance of occurring.

Research conducted by the Investment Company Institute dealt with how
much risk certain investment terms connoted for mutual fund shareholders.[10]
Participants in this study were asked to indicate, on a scale of 0 (no risk) to
10 (great risk), how much risk they associated with an investment described
by the particular term. The mean ratings for the terms can be found in figure
4-2. These ratings ranged from 7.2 to 3.2, with "high yield" conveying the
greatest risk and "guaranteed investment" connoting the lowest risk. Other
terms suggesting high risk were "emerging growth" (6.9), "maximum return"
(6.7), and "international" (6.6). Other terms suggesting low risk were "fixed-
rate" (3.5) and "tax-free" (3.7).

It was reported that low, moderate, and high risk-taking shareholders did
not vary much in their assessment, other than for the term "maximum return"
and "international." "Maximum return" implied less risk for low risk-tolerant
investors than for moderate or high risk-tolerant investors, whereas
"international" connoted more risk for the low risk-tolerant investors relative to
the other two groups.

When communicating with clients, advisors need to be aware of
differences in linguistic style between men and women. In the *Harvard
Business Review,* Deborah Tannen reported that women tend to downplay
their certainty about situations whereas men tend to minimize their doubts.[11]

ASSESSMENT OF THE CLIENT'S RISK TOLERANCE

Purpose of Assessment

So far, some of the factors that exert an influence of one sort or another
on a person's willingness to undertake a risky course of action have been
examined. Now comes the issue of assessment. How does one measure a
client's typical level of risk tolerance? By typical, we mean the level at
which the aforementioned distortions do not cause the client to make
decisions that are either riskier or safer than would generally be characteristic
of that individual.

One way would be to observe the client repeatedly over an extended time period in situations that are likely to reveal his or her characteristic risk-

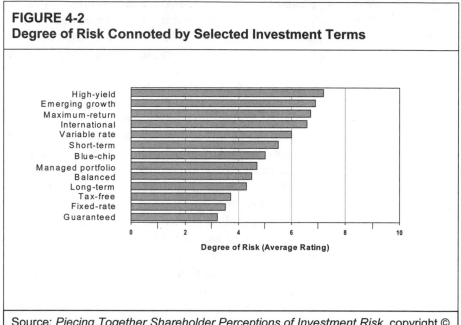

FIGURE 4-2
Degree of Risk Connoted by Selected Investment Terms

Source: *Piecing Together Shareholder Perceptions of Investment Risk*, copyright © 1993, Investment Company Institute (www.ici.org). Reprinted with permission.

tolerance level. Of course, this approach is not really feasible since it would be unreasonably time-consuming for the financial advisor and would constitute an unwarranted intrusion for the client. Some observations may even be misleading since the individual may not even be aware of the risks he or she is incurring. Consequently, there is a need to estimate the client's risk tolerance within a relatively short time period.

The sections that follow review some of the available options for estimating the client's risk tolerance within a relatively short time period. All of these options call for sensitivity to appropriate cues and an ability to integrate them into a total impression of the client.

Whatever method is used, one should realize that the assessment process is meant to help clients understand their own level of risk tolerance. Quite frequently, clients are not aware of how risk-tolerant or risk-averse they are. To them risk tolerance is a vague concept that requires both explanation and exploration. The purpose of assessment is not to enable the advisor to impose his or her perceptions on the client. For example, it is inappropriate to advise the client that the choice is between "eating" (risky investments) and "sleeping" (nonrisky investments). In the end, it is the client who must decide what constitutes an acceptable level of risk. The advisor's role is to help the client learn enough about himself or herself to be able to make an informed decision.

Assessment Methods

Many financial advisors fail to appreciate the complexity of the task facing them in trying to determine a client's risk tolerance accurately. Considerable time and effort are required to do it correctly. The primary problem is that frequently the various techniques do not give the same picture of a particular person's level of risk tolerance. All too often the individual may appear to be a risk taker when assessed with one technique and a risk averter when assessed with another.

Example: In one study employing 16 different assessment procedures, the percentage of people who could be classified as risk takers ranged from 0 percent to 94 percent, depending on the technique used. Practically, this means that more than one approach should be employed for an accurate assessment of a client's risk-taking propensity.

Contrasts Between Qualitative and Quantitative Assessment

The assessment process can be either qualitative or quantitative in its orientation. When one relies on a qualitative approach, one typically collects the necessary information primarily through conversations with the client, without assigning numbers to the information gathered. The information is collected in an unstructured format and is evaluated on an intuitive or impressionistic basis, based on the advisor's training and experience. A quantitative approach, in contrast, relies on the use of a structured format—questionnaires, for example—that allows one to translate observations into some type of numerical score. These scores are then used to interpret the client's risk-taking propensities.

Most advisors do not rely on one approach to the exclusion of the other. For example, few quantitatively oriented advisors are willing to surrender their professional judgment to the results of a questionnaire. It is really a matter of degree of how qualitative or quantitative one advisor is compared with another. One can use a primarily qualitative approach and still not forfeit some of the advantages of quantifiable information. Questionnaires and other quantitative devices can be valuable tools in the hands of any skilled financial advisor.

Often a questionnaire or similar device used to assess a client's risk tolerance can facilitate the beginning of a dialogue between the advisor and the client. The content of the questionnaire highlights issues that the client may not have thought about. Another advantage is that a quantitative approach allows one to standardize the assessment process.

A number of limitations are inherent in a strictly qualitative approach— one in which the financial advisor relies solely on the verbal comments made by a client and interprets their significance on an intuitive basis. One study found that financial advisors (like all people) are overconfident about their ability to make intuitive judgments. The advisors, presented with various statements that clients could make, were asked to evaluate the level of risk tolerance these statements implied on a 10-point scale, where one indicated low risk tolerance and 10 indicated high risk tolerance.

It is understandable that an ambiguous statement such as "Taking calculated risks is different from being rash" would receive ratings as low as 4 and as high as 8. (The average was 6.7.) However, even on more straightforward statements there was also a lack of consensus. The statement, I like to speculate on my investments, if made by a client was interpreted on average as an 8.5. However, again there was diversity of opinion about its meaning. Some financial advisors saw the statement as meriting only a rating of 5 whereas others assigned it a rating of 10. "Rubber yardsticks" of this type can be minimized in a quantitative-assessment approach.

When using a qualitative orientation to the assessment of risk tolerance, the advisor should be familiar with good interviewing skills, as discussed in chapter 2. There are standards for quantitative assessment procedures as well, most of which are beyond the scope of this chapter. Suffice it to say that a quantitative measurement device, such as a test or even a questionnaire, needs to be constructed very carefully. The questions should be written in such a way that they do not lead or bias the individual to answer them in a certain way. Moreover, evidence must be provided to demonstrate that the test or questionnaire does, in fact, assess the attributes it is meant to measure and that it measures them accurately on a consistent basis.

norms

Provided that they are accurate, the best quantitative measurement devices have *norms*, standards of measurement such as averages that allow the advisor to compare the standing of a particular individual with a representative group. Through the use of such norms, one can compare the individual to the public at large or to some subgroup. For instance, using a normed measure of risk tolerance, it is possible to see whether the client is more or less risk tolerant than people in general or to compare the client with other people of the same age and sex.

Unfortunately, most assessment devices now employed by financial advisors to measure client risk tolerance have not been developed under such strict standards. A majority was created for in-house use by individual advisors, brokerage houses, or mutual funds. Many of the developers of these devices are probably unaware of such requirements. There is a critical need for well-constructed questionnaires that provide some evidence to support their use as measures of risk tolerance.

Most of the available assessment devices suffer from the same problems. In some, the wrong questions are asked or they are presented in an incorrect format. Many devices are too short, thereby failing to contain an adequate representation of questions. It has been demonstrated repeatedly that answers to similar questions about risk tolerance may not concur. In order to avoid being misled by the answer to any one question, the financial advisor needs to ask a series of questions. Some answers may underestimate the client's true level of risk tolerance, whereas others may overestimate it. Other things being equal, the more questions that are used to measure a psychological characteristic, the more precise are the results.

Some questionnaires do not separate the different contexts of risk taking, so a high score on such a questionnaire is probably better at identifying tendencies toward thrill seeking rather than high risk tolerance for investment or financial matters. For all these reasons, one must exercise caution. It is strongly recommended that the financial advisor examine the content of the questionnaire. A questionnaire or checklist or inventory purporting to assess risk tolerance may, in fact, be measuring some other attribute.

Many techniques can be used to assess a client's risk tolerance. Some lend themselves more to a qualitative approach, whereas others call for a more quantitative approach. In the section that follows, a brief overview of the most common approaches is provided.

Aspects Considered in the Most Common Approaches Used to Measure Client Risk Tolerance

- investment objectives
- preferences for various investment vehicles
- real-life choices involving risk
- attitudes toward risk
- preferences for different probabilities and payoff levels

Examination of Client Investment Objectives

Frequently, clients are asked to identify their financial objectives. For example, the client may be asked to indicate how important the following are to him or her: liquidity, safety of principal, appreciation, protection from inflation, current income, and tax reduction.

The client's level of risk tolerance is inferred from the answers. If the client's primary concerns are safety of principal and/or liquidity, then risk aversion is assumed. If, however, the main objectives are protection from inflation or tax relief, then the inference is that the client is risk tolerant.

Objectives, however, must not be confused with risk tolerance. There are many individuals who desire tax relief yet are quite risk averse. One's stated objectives may, in fact, be quite incompatible with one's level of risk tolerance. In many cases, the client may be unaware of this incongruity. In a sense, the client's level of risk tolerance should be the basis for evaluating how reasonable the client's objectives are. However, using objectives for the purpose of gauging risk tolerance, without any further attempts to assess actual risk tolerance, is a mistake. To do so is to have "the tail wag the dog."

Example of Examination of Client Investment Objectives:	Rank the following investment objectives from 1–6, with 1 being the most important. _____ liquidity _____ safety of principal _____ protection from inflation _____ growth _____ current income _____ reduced taxation

Preferences for Various Investment Products

This is the most direct approach to measuring a client's risk tolerance. With this method, the client indicates the products that he or she prefers as investments. Several variations of this procedure exist. In its simplest form, the client is presented with the available alternatives and is then asked how he or she wishes to distribute available assets among these options. The products are usually presented in some rank order, ranging from very safe investments to very risky investments. Either actual (real) or imaginary funds can be used.

For the latter variation of this task, the client is asked something like, What would you do if you got a windfall? Naturally, people tend to be more daring with imaginary money than with actual money. A third variation of this approach is to ask the client to rank the products from most preferred to least preferred or to assign to each product some rating that represents the client's level of preference (for example, low, medium, or high).

The accuracy of this procedure (in all its variants) rests on the client's knowledge of the actual risk-return potential of the various investments. Preferably these differences are explained and specified to the client, since many clients may lack even basic knowledge. One should never assume that clients are highly knowledgeable about financial matters. Surveys of the general public, including the wealthy, reveal a startling level of financial ignorance.

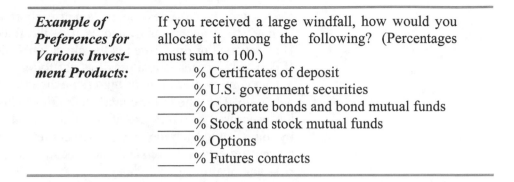

Example of Preferences for Various Investment Products: If you received a large windfall, how would you allocate it among the following? (Percentages must sum to 100.)

_____% Certificates of deposit

_____% U.S. government securities

_____% Corporate bonds and bond mutual funds

_____% Stock and stock mutual funds

_____% Options

_____% Futures contracts

FOCUS ON ETHICS
When Risk Attitude and Risk Capacity Collide

Consider the case of client John Doe who views himself to be highly risk tolerant in monetary matters. His existing portfolio consists of common stock investments in small, highly risky companies. A third-party evaluation of this client's risk tolerance confirms that he is among the top 5 percent in terms of his attitude toward risk. The client asks about specific, aggressive stocks. Should the advisor feel free to recommend or sell high-risk investments to this client?

Now consider some additional information. The client is a 30-year-old widower with three small children. He is an aeronautical engineer employed by a defense contractor that relies entirely on the government for revenues. His total savings including his investment portfolio are less than one month's earnings, and he is not vested in his pension plan. He has no life or disability insurance. Both his father and grandfather died of heart attacks in their mid-forties.

Ask the question again: Should the advisor feel free to recommend or sell high-risk investments to this client?

Clearly this client has an attitude toward risk tolerance that is at odds with his economic and family situation. Selling the client what he wants will generate a commission—but is it ethical?

Real-Life Choices Involving Risks

As with investment products, a person's past performance is no guarantee of future performance. But it has been observed that the best predictor of future behavior is typically past behavior. This notion underlies the real-life choices approach to risk-tolerance assessment. That is, factual information about the client's life is gathered and evaluated. The following lifestyle characteristics can be used to gauge a client's disposition toward monetary risk:

- composition of present investment portfolio. How risky is it? What percentage of total assets are in passbook savings accounts, Treasury notes, mutual funds, stocks, options and commodities, and so on? If stocks are owned, does the person use short selling and margin buying? If an annuity is owned, is it of the fixed or variable type? How satisfied or dissatisfied is the client with this type of portfolio? If changes were made to a previous portfolio, were these changes in a more conservative or more aggressive direction?

- debt ratio. The ratio of the client's liabilities to his or her gross assets has been used as a measure of risk tolerance. It has been suggested by some that a debt ratio over 23 percent reflects risk taking, under 8 percent reflects risk aversion, and 8 percent to 23 percent reflects a risk-neutral attitude.

- ratio of life insurance to annual salary. The assumption is that the larger the resulting ratio, the higher the client's level of risk aversion.

- size of deductibles on property-liability coverage. It has been observed that as the amount of wealth allocated to risky securities rises, so does the size of the deductible on the client's insurance coverages. Risk-tolerant individuals elect larger deductibles.

- percentage of net wealth used for recreational gambling. The larger the ratio, the more risk-seeking the individual is considered to be.

- job tenure. The willingness to make a voluntary job change is considered an indicator of a willingness to take financial risks. Therefore, clients can be asked how many job changes they have made during the last 15 years. Over three changes is considered by some as a sign of a risk-taking attitude. Quitting a job before one has found a replacement is particularly significant. Job changes at middle age may also be especially noteworthy.

- variations in income. Risk-taking individuals may show greater variations in their annual income from year to year, and not always in an upward direction. The financial advisor should also look at the duration of unemployment if the client was ever unemployed. Did the individual take the first job offer he or she received during this period of unemployment or did he or she wait until a job to his or her liking was found? What was the salary of the new job the client took after the period of unemployment? If it was lower than that of the previous job, it could indicate risk aversion.

- type of mortgage. A willingness to undertake a variable rather than a fixed mortgage could be a sign of monetary risk taking. If the client has chosen a fixed mortgage, did he or she lock in on a guaranteed rate before settlement? Locking in is a sign of risk aversion.

Attitudes Toward Risk

A method frequently used to obtain information about a client's degree of risk tolerance involves eliciting his or her attitude toward risk. Attitudes toward risk can be ascertained by using either a quantitative or a qualitative approach. Questions can take many different forms. First, clients can be asked global questions such as whether they view themselves as risk averters or risk takers. For example, On a 10-point scale, where one is an ultimate risk averter and 10 is an ultimate risk taker, where would you place yourself?

Second, clients can be asked about their specific reactions to risk. For example, does the client experience the following:

- is unable to sleep after making a risky investment
- has persisting second thoughts about the investment
- views risk as an opportunity rather than a danger
- gets more pleasure from making $3,000 on a risky investment than $3,000 on a safe investment
- is afraid of losing what he or she has
- is willing to borrow money to make a good investment
- believes that it is impossible to get ahead without taking chances
- agrees with the saying, "Better safe than sorry"

Example: Do you experience anxiety or thrill when awaiting the outcome of an important investment decision?

_____ always experience anxiety
_____ most frequently experience anxiety
_____ experience neither anxiety nor thrill
_____ most frequently experience thrill
_____ always experience thrill

Earlier it was noted that many questions must be asked in order to assess risk tolerance accurately. This is especially true in the case of the attitude approach to measurement. It has been found that the reason why many attitudes, as measured by questionnaires or other scales of that type, fail to predict actual behavior is because not enough questions were asked. When the number of questions was increased, there was a much clearer connection between attitude and behavior.

A major problem with the attitude approach to risk-tolerance assessment is that people want to present themselves to others in the best possible light. Any characteristic that is valued is likely to be overstated. In America it is considered more desirable to be risk taking than risk averting. Clients are, therefore, likely to exaggerate their willingness to take risks. Consequently, discrepancies between verbally expressed attitudes and actual behavior are frequent, even if numerous questions are asked. When using this approach, one needs to ascertain how well the expressed attitudes agree with other evidence, such as factual information about the person's risk-taking proclivities.

Probability and Payoff Preferences

A variety of assessment techniques fall under this classification. Three types will be considered:

- preferences for certain versus probable gambles
- minimum required probability of success
- minimum required return

All of these methods rely on a manipulation of at least one of the four elements found in any gamble: probability of loss, probability of gain, amount to be lost, and amount to be gained. Consequently, the techniques falling under this classification are best used in a quantitative approach to assessment.

framing

Anyone using the probability and payoff-preferences approach to measuring a client's risk tolerance needs to be aware of how framing a question affects the answer, lest he or she be misled by the results. *Framing* refers to the way in which a question is structured with regard to the issue being evaluated. For example, the same objective facts can be described either in terms of the probability of gaining or the probability of losing. Although it may not seem that—to use an analogy—describing a bottle as half empty or half full should have any marked consequences on one's choices in a risky situation, the evidence shows otherwise. To illustrate, consider research in which one group of people is informed that there is a 50 percent chance of success in a particular venture. Another group is told that this same venture has a 50 percent chance of failure. Logically, the same proportion of people in each group should be willing to take this risk. Yet this was not the case. When the risk was described (framed) in terms of the probability of success, more people were willing to take it than when this same risk was described in terms of the chances of failure. Other related research has shown that describing ground meat in terms of how lean versus how fat the product was made a big difference. To shoppers, ground meat described as 90 percent lean was seen as a better buy than the same ground meat described as 10 percent fat.

unpacking effect

Another consideration is the *unpacking effect*. This principle refers to the finding that the perceived likelihood of an event is influenced by how specifically it is described. The more specific the description becomes, the more the situation is judged as likely to occur.

| *Example:* | Stanford University undergraduate students were asked to estimate the probability of different causes |

of death. When asked to estimate the probability of death from a natural cause, on average, the answer was 58 percent. However, when they were requested to estimate the probability of death from a list of three possible natural causes—cancer, heart disease, and other natural causes—the probabilities assigned to these respective events were 22 percent, 18 percent, and 33 percent. Together, they sum up to 73 percent (22% + 18% + 33%), which is higher than the first estimate, 58 percent. In other words, the sum of the components was greater than the whole. This type of effect has been observed among both novices and experts and in different professions including professional options traders estimating the closing price of Microsoft stock.

Preferences for Certain Versus Probable Gambles. Gambles are abstract representations of real-life situations. One very common technique is to present the client with two alternatives. One choice is a certain win, whereas the other choice offers only some probability of winning.

Example 1:   A person is asked to indicate whether he or she would choose

> A: a sure gain of $1,000
> B: a 50 percent chance of gaining $2,000

Persons who are risk averse chose options similar to A, whereas risk-taking individuals chose options similar to B.

Example 2:   On some questionnaires, these choices are woven around a story line. An item of this type may be to imagine you are a winning contestant on a game show. Which of the following actions would you take?

> A: Stop playing with a certain cash prize of $8,000.
> B: Go another round with a 50 percent chance of winning $16,000 and a 50 percent chance of winning nothing

Minimum Probability of Success Required Before Undertaking a Risky Action. A good example of a procedure relying on this approach is the "choice dilemma" questionnaire, often used to study the risky shift phenomenon discussed earlier. This questionnaire presents 12 situations. For each situation, two alternatives are described. One choice is risky and the other is safe. In every case, the risky course of action offers a larger potential payoff. Five odds are given for the chance of success for the risky course of action, namely 1 in 10, 3 in 10, 5 in 10, 7 in 10, and 9 in 10. The person answering the questionnaire is asked to select the odds that would make it worthwhile to take the risky alternative instead of the safe one. The situations involve a broad range of dilemmas, such as job change, heart operation, football game, marriage decision, and so on. One such question involves a business investment decision.

Example: Mr. E is president of a light metals corporation in the United States. The corporation is quite prosperous and has strongly considered the possibilities of business expansion by building an additional plant in a new location. The choice is between building another plant in the United States, where there would be a moderate return on the initial investment, or building a plant in a foreign country. Lower labor costs and easy access to raw materials in that country would mean a much higher return on the initial investment. On the other hand, there is a history of political instability and revolution in the foreign country under consideration. In fact, the leader of a small minority party is committed to nationalizing, that is, taking over all foreign investments.

Imagine that you are advising Mr. E. Listed below are several probabilities or odds of continued political stability in the foreign country under consideration. Please check the lowest probability that you would consider acceptable for Mr. E's corporation to build a plant in that country.

The chances that the country will remain politically stable are

____ 1 in 10
____ 3 in 10
____ 5 in 10
____ 7 in 10

___ 9 in 10

___ Place a check here if you think Mr. E's corporation should not build a plant in the foreign country no matter what the probabilities.

The higher the odds of success the person requires, the greater the level of risk aversion. The choice dilemma questionnaire is a research instrument with well-known measurement properties. However, its appropriateness for assessing monetary risk taking is questionable because it looks at risk taking in all contexts (for example, it looks at risk taking as if it were an invariable trait—which it is not, as noted in the earlier discussion of the subject). Only a few of the 12 situations are concerned with financial risk taking. Furthermore, some of the items are quite dated. Nonetheless, some researchers have found this questionnaire useful in differentiating investors who are risk taking from those who are risk averting.

Minimum Return Required Before Undertaking a Risky Action. An example of a question that requires an answer in terms of amount to be gained rather than in terms of probability (as was the case in the choice dilemma task) is: You are faced with an investment opportunity in which you stand a 50 percent chance of losing half of your personal net wealth and a 50 percent chance of making a certain amount of money. How much of a return would you require in order to take this risk? (The answers are evaluated in relation to the person's net wealth.)

Figure 4-3 provides a sample question for each of the risk-tolerance estimation approaches discussed above. (Appendix D presents The American College's Survey of Financial Risk Tolerance, which is a 40-item questionnaire that also utilizes each of the risk-tolerance estimation approaches discussed above.)

Guidelines on Assessment

The following guidelines are based on the preceding discussion of assessment, taking into consideration the information presented about risk and situational influences on risk-taking propensity:

- Focus on monetary risk taking.
- Assume the client is risk averse, unless evidence to the contrary can be obtained.
- Remember that people are more likely to overstate than understate their risk-taking propensity.
- Keep in mind that even risk-averse individuals may be risk seeking in situations where the choices are between losses. People are reluctant to cut their losses.

FIGURE 4-3
Sample Questions for Estimating Risk Tolerance

---

1. Examination of Client Investment Objectives
   Rank the following investment objectives from 1 to 6, with 1 being the most important.

   ___liquidity   ___growth
   ___safety of principal   ___current income
   ___protection from inflation   ___reduced taxation

2. Preferences for Various Investment Products
   If you received a large windfall, how would you allocate it among the following (percentages must sum to 100)?

   ___% Certificates of deposit   ___% Stock and stock mutual funds
   ___% U.S. government securities   ___% Options
   ___% Corporate bonds and bond mutual ___% Futures contracts
        funds
                    Total   100%

3. Real-Life Choices Involving Risks
   How often have you used "short selling" or "margin buying" in stock market investments?

   ___ Never   ___ Seldom   ___ Frequently   ___ Very Frequently

4. Attitudes toward Risk
   Do you experience anxiety or thrill when awaiting the outcome of an important investment decision?

   ___Always experience anxiety
   ___Most frequently experience anxiety
   ___Experience neither anxiety nor thrill
   ___Most frequently experience thrill
   ___Always experience thrill

5. Probability/Payoff Preferences: Certain versus Probable Gambles
   In some instances you are faced with a choice between (a) earning a certain amount of money for sure and (b) taking a risk and earning either a larger amount of money or nothing at all.

   For example, consider an investment choice between a certain gain of $50 and an 80 percent chance of earning $100. If you take the certain choice, you will get $50 for sure (no more, no less). On the other hand, if you take the 80 percent probability of earning $100, you also stand a 20 percent chance of earning nothing at all.

   For the choices shown below, please indicate whether you would take the sure gain or some probability of earning twice as much (or nothing at all). Be sure to select one option for each pair, A through F.

   Pair A: 1. A certain gain of $10,000
              2. 80 percent probability of gaining $20,000 (with a corresponding 20 percent chance of earning nothing)
   Pair B: 1. A certain gain of $10,000
              2. 50 percent probability of gaining $20,000 (with a corresponding 50 percent chance of earning nothing)
   Pair C: 1. A certain gain of $30,000
              2. 80 percent probability of gaining $60,000 (with a corresponding 20 percent chance of earning nothing)
   Pair D: 1. A certain gain of $30,000
              2. 50 percent probability of gaining $60,000 (with a corresponding 50 percent chance of earning nothing)
   Pair E: 1. A certain gain of $50,000
              2. 80 percent probability of gaining $100,000 (with a corresponding 50 percent chance of earning nothing)

FIGURE 4-3 (continued)
Sample Questions for Estimating Risk Tolerance

Pair F: 1. A certain gain of $50,000
2. 50 percent probability of gaining $100,000 (with a corresponding 50 percent chance of earning nothing)

6. Probability/Payoff Preferences: Required Probability of Success
Assume you are a contestant on a TV game show. After winning a prize that is equivalent to one year's salary, you are offered the option of walking away with this prize money or taking a chance on either doubling it or losing it all. What are the odds of success that you would require before agreeing to accept this gamble?

    1.   Would not take the bet no matter what the odds
    2.   9 in 10
    3.   8 in 10
    4.   7 in 10
    5.   6 in 10
    6.   5 in 10
    7.   4 in 10
    8.   3 in 10
    9.   2 in 10
    10.   1 in 10

7. Probability/Payoff Preferences: Minimum Required Return
You are faced with an investment opportunity in which you have a 50 percent chance of losing half of your personal net worth and a 50 percent chance of making a certain amount of money. What percentage of expected return would you require in order to take this risk? _____ %

- Start your assessment by looking at the client's demographic characteristics and personality makeup. However, remember you are dealing with an individual rather than a group. Just because a person belongs to a group that is more risk tolerant or risk averse than average, it does not mean that the client facing you today will necessarily follow the group pattern. The differences in risk tolerance between demographic groups are usually small, so there will be many people who do not fit the stereotype. Do not judge the individual merely by the group to which he or she belongs. Group differences simply provide you with some hunches that can be explored through the assessment process; you still need to assess the individual client.

- Look for quantitative-assessment devices that are accurate and allow you to compare the client's performance with a norm group.

- Consider the results from a questionnaire or other measurement device as only an approximation of the client's actual risk tolerance. No assessment procedure is perfect; they are all susceptible to some error.

- Diversify your methods of assessment. This will allow you to draw on the strengths of the various techniques.

- Use the information you collect to start a dialogue with the client about risk tolerance. Be sure to remember that assessing the client's risk tolerance is a cooperative venture. When an agreement is reached, ask the client to provide a written confirmation of the results of this assessment.
- Realize that biases may be operating on the client's risk perceptions (for example, familiarity, availability, and so on), which may be inflating or deflating the client's true level of risk tolerance.
- Remember that a client's propensity for risk taking does not necessarily remain constant throughout his or her lifetime. As noted throughout this chapter, changes in personal circumstances such as age, wealth, and number of dependents can produce shifts. Likewise, world events can either increase or decrease a person's level of risk tolerance. Therefore, it is prudent to periodically reassess the client's risk tolerance.

EPILOGUE

To manage risk in the client's portfolio and in his or her daily life, the advisor needs to understand the client's risk tolerance. Risk tolerance is still an evolving field. However, what is known is that developing a relationship with the client gives the advisor a starting point in handling manageable risks. It is also important to monitor client attitudes toward risk as these attitudes can change over time. The field of behavioral finance has taken on the challenge of trying to explain why investors act the way they do.

Loren Dunton, one of the early leaders in the development of the financial planning profession, wrote that the media frequently asked him to describe the difference between the approach used by financial planning advisors and the one used by other financial services practitioners. In his reply, Dunton made the following comment about financial planning advisors: "Most of them, and all the good ones, will first find out the risk tolerance of the individual or couple they might be going to counsel."

CHAPTER FOUR REVIEW

Key Terms and Concepts

Key Terms and Concepts are explained in the glossary.

risk seekers (risk-tolerant individuals)	loss aversion
risk averters (risk rejecters)	risk
risk indifferent	uncertainty

perceived risk   thrill seeker
bounded rationality   absolute risk tolerance
denial of risk   relative risk tolerance
availability bias   norms
familiarity bias   framing
illusion of control bias   unpacking effect
choice shift

Review Questions

The answers to the review questions are in the supplement. Self-test questions and the answers to them are also in the supplement and on The American College Online.

4-1. Compare the conventional measure of the riskiness of an investment in the field of finance with most people's intuitive evaluation of the riskiness of the same investment. [4-1]

4-2. Explain briefly how each of the following tendencies of individuals may limit how rationally they can act in financial matters:
a.   placing too much confidence in intuitive judgments [4-2]
b.   making risk assessments on the basis of small samples [4-2]
c.   failing to correctly evaluate exposure time [4-2]
d.   denying risk [4-2]

4-3. Explain how each of the following factors can influence people's estimates of risk:
a.   availability bias [4-2]
b.   familiarity bias [4-2]
c.   illusion of control bias [4-2]

4-4. Explain how the time horizon associated with decisions involving an element of risk may affect people's willingness to accept the risk. [4-2]

4-5. Summarize the relationships that research suggests exist between a person's mood and his or her willingness to take on risk. [4-2]

4-6. How does the answer to the question, Who will be affected by the consequences of this decision?, tend to influence whether a risk is acceptable or unacceptable to the decision maker? [4-2]

4-7. For what reasons may group dynamics lead to more risky decisions than if the members of the group were to make entirely individual decisions? [4-2]

4-8. a.   Identify the four major types of life situations that involve risk taking. [4-3]
b.   To what extent can the financial advisor assume that a person who is a risk taker in one of these life situations will also be a risk taker in his or her investment decisions? [4-3]

4-9. Identify several characteristics that differentiate risk averters from risk takers. [4-4]

4-10. Explain how high risk-tolerant mutual fund investors differ from moderate and low risk-tolerant investors in the type of investment advice they use. [4-4]

4-11. Summarize the results of the research on the relationship between people's risk-taking propensities and each of the following characteristics:
   a. wealth [4-4]
   b. education [4-4]
   c. age [4-4]
   d. gender [4-4]
   e. birth order [4-4]
   f. marital status [4-4]

4-12. Describe the relationship that research suggests exists between a person's risk tolerance and each of the following occupational characteristics:
   a. whether the person works in the public sector [4-4]
   b. whether the person works in a professional occupation [4-4]
   c. whether the person has been in a given job for a long time [4-4]
   d. whether the person works in a position of upper management [4-4]
   e. whether the person works in a commission-based job [4-4]
   f. whether the person is an entrepreneur [4-4]

4-13. a. Describe the characteristics of the typical thrill seeker. [4-5]
   b. Why might thrill seekers pose a serious potential threat to a financial advisor? [4-5]

4-14. Identify some investment terms that suggest "high risk" to clients. [4-5]

4-15. Identify the major problems associated with quantitative approaches to the assessment of clients' risk tolerances. [4-5]

4-16. Briefly describe each of the following techniques for assessing a client's risk tolerance:
   a. examining investment objectives [4-5]
   b. identifying preferences for different investment products [4-5]
   c. reviewing past real-life choices involving risk [4-5]
   d. eliciting attitudes toward risk [4-5]
   e. assessing preferences for different probabilities and payoffs [4-5]

4-17. Describe several guidelines that the financial advisor should observe when attempting to assess the risk tolerance of clients. [4-6]

NOTES

1. Daniel Kahneman and Mark W. Riepe, "Aspects of Investor Psychology," *The Journal of Portfolio Management*, Summer 1998, pp. 52–65.

2. *Ibid.*, pp. 52–65.

3. R.J. Herrnstein, "Rational Choice Theory: Necessary but Not Sufficient," *American Psychologist*, 1990, vol. 45, pp. 356–367.

4. Daniel Kahneman and Amos Tversky, "Choices, Values and Frames," *American Psychologist*," 1984, vol. 39, pp. 341–350.

5. Investment Company Institute, "Piecing Together Shareholder Perceptions of Investment Risk," Spring 1993.

6. R.A. Cohn, W.G. Lewellen, R.C. Lease, and G.G. Schlarbaum, "Individual Investor Risk Aversion and Investment Portfolio Composition," *Journal of Finance*, 1975, vol. 30, pp. 605–620.

7. W.B. Riley and K.V. Chow, "Asset Allocation and Individual Risk Aversion," *Financial Analysts Journal*, Nov./Dec. 1992, pp. 32–37.

8. Investment Company Institute, "Piecing Together Shareholder Perceptions of Investment Risk," Spring 1993.

9. *Ibid.*

10. Investment Company Institute, "Piecing Together Shareholder Perceptions of Investment Risk," Spring 1993.

11. Deborah Tannen, "The Power of Talk: Who Gets Heard and Why," Harvard Business Review, September–October 1995, pp. 138–148.

5

Gathering Data and Preparing Financial Statements

Learning Objectives

An understanding of the material in this chapter should enable the student to

5-1. Describe the initial financial planning session, and explain the importance of fact finders.

5-2. Describe the types of information contained in comprehensive fact finders, and explain why it is important to review this information periodically and keep it up to date.

5-3. Explain the importance of personal financial statements in financial planning.

5-4. Explain what a financial position statement indicates to a financial advisor, and describe its key components.

5-5. Explain the steps involved in the preparation of a financial position statement.

5-6. Explain how financial position statements are used in the financial planning process.

5-7. Explain what a cash flow statement indicates to a financial advisor, and describe its key components.

5-8. Explain the purpose of cash flow management, and describe its key components.

5-9. Explain the steps involved in the preparation of a cash flow statement.

5-10. Explain how cash flow statements are used in the financial planning process.

5-11. Define, be able to calculate, and explain the importance of consumer financial ratios such as a solvency ratio, a debt service ratio, and a liquidity ratio in financial planning.

5-12. Discuss the importance of monitoring the client's financial position and the use of pro forma forecasts as evaluation tools in the monitoring process.

Chapter Outline

The development of a comprehensive financial plan covering all the major planning areas is neither a quick nor an easy task. The diversity and complexity of needed information require a systematic method for gathering, organizing, and processing that information. Although there are many possible ways to systematize the gathering of information, almost all financial advisors prefer to use a structured fact-finder form.

With the financial information gathered by a fact finder, an advisor is able to determine a client's current financial position and cash flow status. Without this type of financial information about the client, it would be difficult, if not impossible, for the advisor to develop a financial plan and/or formulate strategies for achieving the client's financial goals.

THE INITIAL SESSION

To ensure that fact-finding and planning sessions with the client will be both productive and efficient, the financial planning process usually begins with an initial session to determine whether the client is interested in the financial advisor's services. While this session will generally involve a single prospective client, the advisor may wish to conduct a seminar for a group of prospective clients, such as the executives of a business firm or the members of the local community. In either case, the advisor will describe the nature and scope of the services to be provided (including referral to other specialists), the modes of operation, the structure of compensation for services, and the form of the financial plan to be developed for the client. In addition, the advisor will give the client a disclosure form that describes his or her philosophy in working with clients; his or her educational background and employment history; professional certifications and licenses; and sources of compensation. (A sample disclosure form is located in appendix B at the end of this textbook.)

If the advisor and the prospective client hope to establish an advisor-client relationship (step 1 of the financial planning process), ground rules must be clarified. Foremost among them should be the understanding that comprehensive financial planning for the client can be done only if complete information about the client's personal and financial situation is revealed. The client should understand the need to furnish financial records and documents and to participate in fact-finding and planning sessions with the advisor, during which time his or her financial situation, problems, and goals will be thoroughly discussed.

THE IMPORTANCE OF FACT FINDERS

If an advisor-client relationship begins to evolve at the initial session, the advisor may want to follow up by sending the client a letter summarizing the session and offering his or her financial planning services. In addition, the advisor may also want to send a fact-finder form along with the letter so the client can begin to gather and organize his or her personal and financial information. Assembling complete, accurate, and up-to-date information about the client is the single most important task in financial planning. Some fact-finder forms, however, are only thin pamphlets that ask for basic information; the forms most useful for financial planning purposes generally are thick booklets that seek very detailed information. It is therefore imperative that the fact finder used to gather information for financial planning purposes be sufficiently comprehensive to enable the advisor to (1) evaluate the client's total financial condition, (2) identify what type of person the client really is, (3) determine where the client wants to be, and (4) formulate the most appropriate strategies for getting there.

If the client is married, his or her spouse should be fully involved in providing information and both the client and spouse should be present during fact-finding and planning sessions with the advisor, unless there are compelling personal reasons to the contrary (such as an impending divorce). Indeed, in households in which both spouses have income and assets, the financial advisor should counsel both spouses and develop a plan that reflects their mutual as well as their individual concerns and goals. In such cases, appropriate sections of the fact finder should be duplicated and filled out by both the client and spouse.

Because every financial advisor operates in a complex marketplace of varying services, products, and clients, no single fact-finder form can serve the needs of everyone. If the advisor is not required to use his or her company's designated fact finder, the experienced advisor typically will modify an existing fact finder or develop a new one that can be used to meet the needs of his or her practice. The type of information requested by comprehensive financial planning fact finders includes not only quantitative data about the client's current financial position but qualitative information about the client's personal circumstances. Armed with complete information about the client, the advisor is then able to analyze and evaluate the client's financial condition and make appropriate recommendations in the form of a multiple-purpose or comprehensive plan tailored exclusively for the client.

In cases where the financial advisor is hired to provide solutions for a single planning objective and does not need all the information elicited by a comprehensive fact finder, the client only needs to fill out those sections of the fact finder that are relevant to analyzing and evaluating the single objective. To help determine exactly what information is needed in each case, the advisor must ask himself or herself the following questions:

- What information do I need from the client for a particular area (or areas) of planning?
- How do I evaluate this information and discuss it with the client?
- What information on products, services, and taxes do I need in order to address this area (or areas) of planning? (That is, what information do I need from the marketplace?)
- How do I apply this information to my client's planning objective(s) in order to develop recommendations that the client will adopt and implement?

Because many clients do not understand how comprehensive financial planning can benefit them, they seek help only in a planning area (or areas) in which they have a financial problem or goal that needs immediate attention. In order for these clients to understand and embrace comprehensive financial planning, they must be exposed to its principles and procedures through the financial planning process. This is done when the advisor presents his or her recommendations for the planning area (or areas) in which the clients are seeking help. At this time, the advisor must show these clients how his or her recommendations affect other planning areas and explain to them how a comprehensive financial plan could thoroughly integrate and coordinate all the planning areas. One of the tools that makes the integration and coordination of all the planning areas possible is a comprehensive fact finder.

COMPREHENSIVE FINANCIAL PLANNING FACT FINDER

The variety of clients and potential planning areas requires a fact finder that is both flexible and adaptable. It should be divided into several sections and subsections that can be used individually or in various combinations. The American College's Comprehensive Financial Planning Fact Finder (hereinafter referred to simply as Fact Finder), reproduced in appendix E, was designed with these requirements in mind.

Together all sections of The College's Fact Finder elicit the information necessary to design and implement a comprehensive financial plan tailored exclusively for the client. In cases where the whole Fact Finder elicits more information than is needed, the advisor can select the relevant sections for the client to fill out. In those rare cases where the advisor needs more extensive and detailed information than the whole Fact Finder can provide, the advisor can supplement the Fact Finder with special analysis forms and computer software programs specifically designed for more complex planning situations.

Although The College's Fact Finder is the "real thing" and can be used by financial advisors, its purpose in being included in this book is to demonstrate how important a comprehensive fact finder is to financial planning. Most advisors choose fact finders that are designed to be used with specific financial planning software to simplify data entry. Moreover, many large financial services companies have developed their own fact-finder forms to satisfy their compliance departments, and they fully expect their advisor-representatives to use them. Therefore, even though The College's Fact Finder will probably not be adopted for use by many advisors, its real value lies in providing an example of the types of client information needed by financial advisors who engage in comprehensive financial planning. To this end, a fairly brief section-by-section discussion follows that describes the Fact Finder and how the information it gathers relates to comprehensive financial planning.

Personal Data

In order to involve clients in the planning process and diminish the time spent in fact-finding sessions, many advisors send their clients the whole Fact Finder form after the initial session. The client is instructed to fill out as much of the Fact Finder as possible. The Fact Finder begins the accumulation of client information with the Personal Data section. The information requested by this section is of the type that clients typically can provide without the assistance of the advisor.

The content of the Personal Data section includes information about the client and his or her family. It begins on page 3 by requesting the street addresses, phone numbers, and e-mail addresses of the client (and spouse if the client is married). The unmarried client should ignore Fact Finder spaces requesting information about a spouse unless he or she has a domestic partner, in which case these spaces could be adopted to accommodate this type of arrangement.

Also on page 3, this section asks for the names, addresses, and phone numbers of the client's other advisors. One of them may be a resource for clarifying the client's financial history and may even provide important expertise that could help in implementing a financial plan. Moreover, it is important for the advisor to know who holds the client's confidence and trust and who (if anyone) is already considered the client's primary financial advisor. Knowing who the client's other advisors are helps to avoid alienating them, infringing on their territory, or giving them cause to thwart the planning process.

On page 4 of the Fact Finder, the Personal Data section requests information about the client's whole family including their dates of birth, Social Security numbers, occupations (if applicable), and whether the client (and/or spouse) provides any support for them. Support obligations are vital in determining the client's income needs while working, in retirement, and in the event of disability; they also help determine the income needs of survivors in the event of the client's (or spouse's) death. In addition, the section requests information about any health problems and/or special needs of family members including the client (and spouse).

The information sought on page 5 of the Fact Finder is designed to uncover potential complications in the client's (or spouse's) situation, such as previous marriages and alimony or child-support obligations; the existence (or lack) of current wills and prenuptial or postnuptial agreements; the existence of trusts or custodial accounts for children or others; guardian nominations for the children; trusts in which the client (or spouse) is the beneficiary; gifts or inheritances pending or anticipated; education background; and any benefits resulting from military or government service. Not only are these items important for subsequent financial planning, but they also provide insight into what kind of person the client is and the level of sophistication and complexity of the client's current financial program. In spite of their importance, however, the Fact Finder does not attempt to gather detailed information about existing wills, trusts, nuptial agreements, or guardianships. What the financial advisor needs to know at this point in time is whether these items exist and if they do, will he or she be able to examine them at a future time to determine if they are in line with the client's expressed wishes and overall financial plan. The client's perception of problems in these personal affairs should also be explored at this time so the advisor will have the benefit of the client's current thoughts and feelings about these sensitive matters.

Financial Objectives

The Financial Objectives section on page 6 of the Fact Finder asks the client to rank his or her financial objectives. However, both the rankings and the objectives are subject to change. Subsequent analysis of the client's actual financial position and prospects may compel radical revisions of both the priorities and objectives or, at least, deferment of the target dates for achieving some of the objectives. Often the client will establish different priorities and objectives as a result of going through the planning process. Nevertheless, these preliminary rankings of objectives will give the advisor a perception of the client's concerns, which can be explored in planning sessions and evaluated in light of the client's current financial position, risk tolerance level, and projections for the future. Knowing what the client believes his or her priorities and objectives are will help the advisor establish a track for the client to run on.

This section of the Fact Finder also contains questions about the client's current monthly budget and annual savings/investments. Information provided here will be important for the projections into future years that will be made in the Cash Flow Statement and the Financial Position Statement (pages 9 and 37–38 of the Fact Finder).

Factors Affecting Your Financial Plan

In this section, which is on page 6 of the Fact Finder, there are several questions that are of particular importance to the financial advisor's perception of the client's personality and willingness to implement subsequent recommendations. The first two questions ask whether the client or spouse has made gifts or is willing to consider making gifts. Although positive responses to these two questions exhibit an openness to gift giving as a strategy, negative responses do not necessarily indicate the opposite.

The next two questions ask whether the client is dissatisfied with the results of previous savings/investments or feels committed to them. If the answers are yes, the client's thoughts should be explored. The Risk/Return Profile on page 23 of the Fact Finder may provide some insight into the source of the client's dissatisfaction or commitment.

The next four questions in this section probe the nature of the client's family relationships. These questions about the client's spouse (if married), desired age of retirement, and how the estate is to be distributed are helpful in discovering the client's (and the spouse's) underlying attitudes and motives for a whole range of financial objectives.

The final question in this section—"What do you think financial planning should do for you?"—may bring to a head a whole range of client concerns. Certainly the client's response to this question will have an impact on what direction the financial planning process should take.

One final comment is necessary. It concerns the relevance of the types of personal information sought on pages 3 through 6 of the Fact Finder. It is in these areas that the client's most sensitive feelings and thoughts are likely to emerge and that profound human and relational concerns are likely to be discovered. Therefore, these areas demand the most sensitive employment of the advisor's communications skills and techniques. Even though the client may provide extensive and accurate data and facts before and during the planning sessions, responses should be thoroughly evaluated for clues to personal, family, and economic problem areas. The advisor should ask appropriate clarifying questions in a nonjudgmental way. The client's responses should be compared with information and facts provided in other sections of the Fact Finder to ascertain consistency.

Objectives Requiring Additional Income/Capital

The section titled Objectives Requiring Additional Income/Capital is on page 7 of the Fact Finder; it gathers details about specific client financial objectives that may require income and/or capital beyond what is needed for retirement and estate planning purposes. The most common objective typically is the client's desire to send his or her children to college. Because of its importance to a large number of people, the topic of education funding is covered in greater depth in chapter 8.

Besides education funding, the client may have other objectives that require either long- or short-term planning, and allocation. These objectives could include a desire to take care of a handicapped child, to provide support for a parent or other relative, or to accumulate funds for a future charitable bequest. The advisor should thoroughly explore the client's situation and uncover all funding objectives beyond the need to provide for personal economic well-being. The advisor can then lead the client to a full determination of all other resources (including the resources of the proposed beneficiary) that may be available to help fund these needs, such as Social Security benefits, private pensions, part-time work, life insurance proceeds, and income from the proposed beneficiary's own earlier investments.

A major consideration in financial planning is the comprehensive and efficient use of both financial resources and tax advantages to achieve the client's objectives. Therefore, all of the client's specific objectives requiring additional income and/or capital should be considered in relation to the client's total financial condition and funded with the most appropriate tax-advantaged investment media available.

Sources of Income

Page 8 of the Fact Finder is a survey of the client's income from all sources including the income of spouse and dependents, if any; income tax obligations; estimated income 1, 3, and 5 years in the future; and anticipated salary increases and bonuses.

After the client has provided all of the income information, the financial advisor should check tax returns to verify the amounts reported. It is crucial that all of this information be correct and complete, as many recommendations the advisor may make for family budgeting, savings, investment, funding for specific objectives, additional insurance coverage, tax planning, retirement planning, and estate planning will be related to the current and continuing income sources inventoried on page 8. Using this information, the advisor may project the probable growth rate of the client's financial position for years into the future. But planning is only as good as the information on which it is based.

The sources and amounts of the client's income will be transferred to the Cash Flow Statement on page 9 of the Fact Finder where it will be evaluated in relation to the client's annual expenses.

Cash Flow Statement

The most important point to be made about the Cash Flow Statement on page 9 is that the figures for all items should be complete and correct. Most individuals and families do not follow a realistic and exacting budget; indeed, many are averse to doing so. For these individuals and families the completion of the Cash Flow Statement, detailing all items of income and expense, will be an uncomfortable task for which most will not have kept adequate records. Nevertheless, completing this statement, analyzing and evaluating total income and expenses, and seeing their relationship to both short- and long-term financial objectives are extremely important in the financial planning process. Clients must have a positive net cash flow in the long run if they want the flexibility to fund additional financial objectives that may arise. Clients who experience a negative net cash flow will either have to borrow or liquidate assets in order to balance income and expenses. No financial plan can work, let alone be formulated, if net cash flow is consistently negative.

Because of their importance to financial planning, cash flow statements (along with financial position statements) are discussed and analyzed in greater depth later in this chapter.

Inventory of Assets and Liabilities

Three Fact Finder sections, Inventory of Assets, Business Interest, and Inventory of Liabilities, are pivotal in financial planning. When information about a client's assets and liabilities is transferred to the first column of the Financial Position Statement (pages 37–38 of the Fact Finder), the client's total financial position and net worth will be reflected. Moreover, this inventory of assets and liabilities will enable the financial advisor to understand how the client uses financial resources and debt, what the client's preferences and aversions are, what the client's liquidity position is, what problems exist, whether all assets (including any business interest) are being used efficiently to meet financial objectives, how diversified the assets are, whether the client is aware of his or her total financial condition (or even wants to be), and how the client thinks and feels about his or her present assets and financial resources.

Many clients have an inexact and often sketchy idea of what their total assets are. Even more have a poor grasp of whether their assets are working efficiently toward their objectives or whether their investment risk exposures are really consistent with their temperaments. No other area of the client's financial posture is more crucial for achieving realistic financial objectives than his or her total asset and liability positions and their tax implications, particularly if the client's business interest represents a substantial portion of his or her total assets.

Financial Position Statement

Pages 37 and 38 of the Fact Finder should be used to bring together information on the client's assets and liabilities in a Financial Position

Statement, both current and projected for one or more years into the future. This statement is in effect a balance sheet that uses fair market value for asset items instead of historical cost.

All items in the statement have been transferred from the Inventory of Assets, the Business Interest, and the Inventory of Liabilities sections of the Fact Finder but have been somewhat rearranged here. Client assets are classified in three broad groups: (1) cash and near-cash equivalents, (2) other financial assets, and (3) personal assets. These broad groups contain the subsections from the Inventory of Assets on pages 10–13 of the Fact Finder in addition to a value of business interest item derived from the valuation of business interest subsection on page 15.

The client's total liabilities are subtracted from his or her total assets to determine net worth. To increase this bottom-line figure is, of course, one of the primary objectives of financial planning.

The Financial Position Statement, in conjunction with the Cash Flow Statement on page 9, provides a profile of the client's total financial position as of a particular date. It also provides projections of the client's asset, liability, and net worth positions for one or more years into the future, which makes it possible to establish some working objectives. It goes without saying that these working objectives should be consistent with the client's wishes, what his or her resources can realistically support, and the various methods and vehicles used to implement his or her comprehensive financial plan.

The projections are based on certain assumptions about the future (such as the inflation rate and the rates of anticipated return on investment). The fact, however, that the projections are based on assumptions needs to be clarified for the client; otherwise they might be misleading, especially since they are likely to give the illusory impression of certainty. Only by periodically reviewing and adjusting a client's plan can there be any assurance that it will achieve the client's objectives.

Because of their importance to financial planning, financial position statements (along with cash flow statements) are discussed and analyzed in greater depth later in this chapter.

Individually Owned Insurance

Pages 18–20 of the Fact Finder ask for information on the life, long-term care, medical/dental, disability income, and property/liability insurance policies currently held by the client. Complete information about these coverages is crucial for developing a comprehensive financial plan. For example, the coverage amounts provided by the client's personal life and disability income policies should also be listed on page 39 of the Fact Finder, where they will constitute one element of the client's current resources available for death, disability, and retirement needs. Personal life insurance coverage amounts will also be a factor in the value of the client's estate and its liquidity position. Moreover, personal property and liability insurance coverages should be analyzed to see if they give adequate protection against potential property and liability losses.

People typically do not know how to read and interpret the provisions of their insurance policies, so this type of information probably cannot be provided by the client. It most likely will have to be recorded directly from the client's insurance policies.

Once the advisor has reviewed the policies and filled out the appropriate spaces of the Fact Finder, the amounts, types of coverages, and other relevant policy provisions should be reviewed with the client and analyzed in light of areas of risk in the client's personal and financial situation. By the end of the data-gathering phase (step 2, determine goals and gather data) of the financial planning process, the advisor should have enough information about the client and his or her family to determine whether the client's current insurance coverages provide adequate protection relative to his or her overall financial position and degree of exposure to risk.

Pages 14–15 of the Fact Finder, pertaining to the client's business interest, should also be reviewed with the client during the discussions about insurance protection. This information relates directly to the possible need or desire to fund buy-sell or other business-continuation agreements through disability income and life insurance and to cover various liability risks in the client's particular business or professional practice.

The financial advisor who is not an insurance specialist should include appropriate specialists on the financial planning team who can thoroughly analyze all of the client's business and personal risk exposures and recommend appropriate coverages if needed.

Employment-Related Benefits

The Employment-Related Benefits Checklist on page 21 and the Employment-Related Retirement Benefits/Deferred Compensation section on page 22 of the Fact Finder have several important uses in financial planning. If a client or spouse owns a controlling interest in a business, these sections provide a convenient place for not only recording existing employee benefits but also identifying additional benefits that might be implemented in order to put the business ownership to more effective use (and to greater tax advantage) in planning for personal financial objectives. The financial advisor should analyze the advantages of possible additional benefits in relation to the client's or spouse's particular form and degree of business ownership. This type of planning will almost always involve bringing other specialists (an attorney for drafting legal instruments, a CPA, an employee benefits specialist, and so on) onto the financial planning team at both the development (step 4, develop and present a plan) and the implementation (step 5, implement the plan) stages of the financial planning process.

If a client and spouse have no business ownership interest, or have no control over the kinds of benefits their business interest can provide, then pages 21–22 should be used as a checklist for the benefits they actually derive from their employment. The client and spouse should each furnish the name and title of the person in their company who can provide detailed information and documents they may not have in their own possession. The documents relating to these benefits are listed on Fact Finder page 27, Receipt for Documents, which is also a checklist of information and documents that the client and spouse, or their companies, will need to make available for the financial advisor's use.

The column titled information/comments on the Employment-Related Benefits Checklist on page 21 can be used either to describe a benefit or to indicate the advisor's or the client's feelings about the benefit. Besides being listed on page 21, the amounts of benefits should also be listed on page 39 of the Fact Finder, Income and Lump-Sum Resources for Disability, Retirement and Death.

Risk/Return Profile

The Risk/Return Profile on page 23 of the Fact Finder is designed to provide a quick assessment of the client's psychological propensity for risk taking, that is, his or her financial risk tolerance. (A much more detailed and exhaustive treatment of financial risk tolerance is presented in chapter 4.) Risk tolerance, however, is difficult to measure in clients. No matter what method of measurement is used, the result will be misleading unless it is related to the rate of return the client expects on invested money. It is equally difficult, however, to measure the risk characteristics of investment media themselves especially in an environment of fluctuating interest rates, an uncertain economy, an unpredictable stock market, and a financial marketplace of evolving concepts and many new and unseasoned investment media. Because nothing in the financial markets stays the same for very long, even the most sophisticated portfolio-management strategies are little more than rules of thumb that require periodic adjustment for changing circumstances. Therefore, the investment strategies developed for an individual client should reflect the client's current risk-taking propensities, the rate of return required to achieve agreed-on financial objectives, and the client's understanding that both personal circumstances and the financial environment will change over time, thus altering his or her Risk/Return Profile and requiring modification of the financial plan.

Risk/Return Investment Pyramid

What the Risk/Return Profile intends to measure is dramatically illustrated by the *Risk/Return Investment Pyramid* shown in figure 5-1. Typical investment media are arranged in a pyramid with the most conservative, least risky, and (generally) lowest-yielding media at the broad base of the pyramid. The investment media become progressively riskier as they approach the apex where speculative investments are located. Toward the apex there is typically a corresponding and commensurate potential for higher return.

FIGURE 5-1
Risk/Return Investment Pyramid

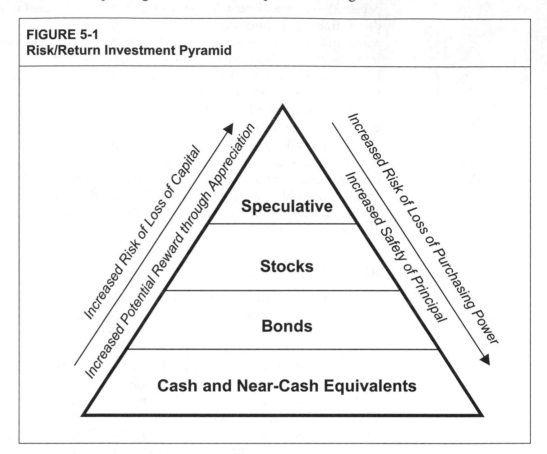

The arrows along the sides of the pyramid demonstrate the relationship between risk and return as one ascends or descends through this pyramid of investment possibilities. Figure 5-1 illustrates that all investments bear an element of risk and that the rate of return is inextricably related to a corresponding degree of risk of loss. There is no way out of this risk/return trade-off; even investment in the most conservative media risks erosion of capital if the rate of return is less than the rate of inflation. In other words, all efforts to manage money involve a trade-off of risk against return. Clients must choose the investment media most closely suited to both their financial objectives and their range of psychological comfort as represented by their risk tolerance levels.

A note about how the Risk-Return Profile on page 23 is used. On the top part of the page the client is asked to evaluate, on a scale of 0 to 5, his or her preference for a range of savings and investment media, from a savings account (conservative, virtually no risk) to commodities (speculative, extremely high risk). In the middle part of the page the client is asked to rate personal financial priorities, also on a scale of 0 to 5. The results of the two rankings should correlate with each other, giving an indication of the client's financial risk tolerance.

However, if the rankings are inconsistent and do not correlate well with each other, the advisor should question the client about the inconsistencies and, if necessary, make the required changes. When both the advisor and client are satisfied with the rankings, the advisor should note the results on the bottom part of the page and indicate the types of investment media most likely to achieve the client's expectations and objectives.

Income and Lump-Sum Needs for Disability, Retirement, and Death

On page 24 of the Fact Finder the client should record the monthly amounts of income needed if the client or his or her spouse becomes disabled, retires, or dies. These estimates of monthly income needs are expressed in current dollars, that is, in amounts needed now. However, in formulating a retirement plan for the client, the advisor will have to adjust the client's estimate of these monthly needs by an agreed-on inflation factor.

Survivors' monthly income needs in the event of the client's or spouse's death are assessed for three periods: (1) an adjustment period when a continuing and unreduced income flow is needed; (2) a period of reduced income after the adjustment period until the youngest child is self-supporting; and (3) the period after the youngest child is self-supporting.

In addition, the survivors may need certain lump sums—to establish an emergency fund, to pay postmortem expenses, to pay off any outstanding mortgage balance on a personal residence, to pay off the deceased's notes and loans, to pay accrued taxes, and to fund college educations for surviving children. These lump-sum needs can be substantial and very real, but often there is not enough ready cash or other assets to meet them.

Close consultation with the client in establishing both income and lump-sum needs upon disability, retirement, and death is always called for. But there is little purpose in establishing precisely the amounts needed unless there is also a concerted planning effort to assure that the resources are available when needed.

Tax-Planning Checklist

Pages 31–35 of the Fact Finder inquire in some detail into the client's present and possibly advisable tax planning strategies. Since the impact of taxation on nearly all types of income and assets is one of the primary concerns of comprehensive financial planning, this section of the Fact Finder should prove to be especially helpful in evaluating the client's current financial position and for exploring a range of possible strategies for reducing the client's tax burden.

Tax planning involves the analysis, evaluation, and client acceptance of the tax consequences of every capital and financial transaction—before the transaction is made. It is one thing to look up the tax law and determine the consequences of one's economic activity during the past year (or to pay a tax return preparer a fee for doing that onerous task). It is quite another thing to determine in advance what short- and long-term tax liability will result from every transaction and then to conduct one's transactions so as to achieve financial objectives by the most tax-advantaged means. Tax planning, in other words, is a delineation and analysis of primary tax considerations in determining when, whether, and how to conduct various personal and business transactions to affect both the desired economic end and to minimize the tax impact of achieving that end.

In the complicated financial situations of most clients there is almost always at least one alternative (and in most cases several) to the one that may seem most obvious. Financial strategies and products have inherent advantages and disadvantages and therefore are rarely appropriate for every client situation. When tax consequences are considered as well, there is even more divergence—some result in greater, some in lesser, tax liability. But it should be remembered that the most apparent route for an immediate (or even long-term) tax saving may not, in the final analysis, be the most advantageous. Tax and economic advantages and disadvantages must be balanced against the risk tolerance profiles and the objectives of each client. What works well for one client may not work at all for another in virtually the same position. What works well this year may be a disaster next year or several years down the road. As both the client's tax bracket and the level and complexity of his or her financial affairs increase, it becomes ever more urgent that the client seek and that the financial advisor provide sound tax planning as a central part of comprehensive financial planning.

It should be noted that the Tax Planning Checklist on pages 31–35 of the Fact Finder is not intended to be complete or to raise all of the questions that would be relevant to every client. At best the checklist introduces some of the more common considerations, knowledge of which will enable the advisor to take the client's tax temperature and factor the information into the financial planning process.

Personal Assessment of the Client

Before the client's financial plan is formulated, the financial advisor should sum up his or her observations and impressions about the client on page 29 of the Fact Finder in the section titled Observations from Planning Sessions. These observations and impressions are vital to the planning process and to the acceptability and ultimate success of the client's plan, which will incorporate some of the most profound and far-reaching decisions the client will have made about life and relationships. But the plan will not be implemented unless it reflects the kind of person the client is; or, if implemented, it will not be updated. The financial planning process will have been wasted and a client relationship lost.

MONITORING THE CLIENT'S PLAN

When the individually tailored financial plan is developed, fine-tuned, presented to and accepted by the client, and implemented, the first cycle of the financial planning process will have been completed. The process will be renewed periodically, however, (though in a very abbreviated form) in the ongoing monitoring and restructuring of the plan when necessary during the client's subsequent financial life. If the planning process has met the client's needs and directed him or her toward desired goals, and if the plan meets the client's expectations reasonably well, a long-term relationship between the client and the advisor will likely result.

To facilitate this ongoing relationship and to keep in touch with the client's changing circumstances, interests, and needs, the financial advisor must have some method for routinely reviewing the client's situation at specified periodic intervals—usually annually. The Checklist for Financial Planning Review on page 41 of the Fact Finder is a convenient checklist for keeping up with changes in the client's personal and financial circumstances. Mailing this form to the client or simply going through it in a telephone call will enable the advisor to keep up to date with the client.

When significant events have happened in the client's financial life, or are expected to, an appointment should be set up to evaluate the impact of these events on the client's financial plan and to make appropriate adjustments to the plan if necessary. Likewise when the advisor sees or foresees changes taking place in the financial markets, in tax laws, and/or in the general economy that have a significant effect on the client's plan, he or she should inform the client.

The ever-changing nature of economic conditions and of clients' lives makes it almost impossible for a financial plan, no matter how well it was initially conceived and executed, to continue performing indefinitely at maximum efficiency. Unless the plan is periodically reviewed and updated when necessary, the entire planning process may have to be repeated. Both clients and advisors will be well served if they recognize and act on this fundamental fact. Comprehensive financial planning that is monitored conscientiously serves the interests of both client and advisor in an ongoing professional relationship characterized by mutual respect and trust.

An important function of the Fact Finder is to gather enough information about the client so that his or her financial position and cash flow statements can be developed. Together these two statements provide a profile of the client's total financial condition as of a particular date, which is related to what has occurred in the past. However, to facilitate the monitoring of a comprehensive plan, it is useful to prepare projected financial statements for one or more years into the future. These projected statements show what the client's future financial statements are expected to look like if certain strategies are followed under specified assumptions. At some point in the future, the advisor will then be able to compare current financial statements with past projected statements to see if the client's financial plan is on target. Next, let us look more closely at financial position and cash flow statements to see how they are used by advisors to help clients achieve their goals through application of the financial planning process.

PERSONAL FINANCIAL STATEMENTS IN FINANCIAL PLANNING

The preparation of organized financial information is an important but often ignored aspect of personal financial planning. Like businesses, individuals must often prepare financial information for external use. Banks and other lending institutions rarely make loans to individuals without first analyzing their current financial situations and their future ability to repay the loans. However, the primary use of financial information in personal financial planning is for the financial advisor and the client's use.

Financial analysis, planning, and control are important planning techniques, whether conducted by the individual or the individual assisted by a financial advisor. Personal financial statements summarizing a client's current financial situation, as well as those projecting future results, are both useful for internal purposes. It is difficult, if not impossible, to develop a financial plan and/or formulate strategies for achieving a client's financial goals without knowing the client's current financial situation and resources. Moreover, the ongoing analysis of the client's personal financial information is crucial in monitoring whether the client's financial goals are being achieved.

financial position statement (balance sheet) cash flow statement (income statement)

In personal financial planning, the two primary financial statements advisors use are the *financial position statement* (known in business as the *balance sheet*) and the *cash flow statement* (the *income statement*). Before each is discussed in greater detail, a few general comments follow regarding the timing of their preparation and use.

While it is common to see personal financial statements that have been prepared only at the end of a calendar or fiscal year, the timing and frequency of financial statements can vary. When a lending institution needs personal financial information for a lending decision, it usually requires that the information be prepared as of the date of the loan application. Similarly, a financial advisor needs financial information at the time the planning process begins, and at each subsequent review. If reviews take place every 6 months, it is necessary to update the personal financial statements at these same intervals. In other words, personal financial statements are not prepared at arbitrary times but rather when the information is needed for the financial planning process.

FOCUS ON ETHICS
The Role of Ethics in Preparing Financial Statements

Ethics is important in preparing and using personal financial statements because the client places blind faith in the skills, knowledge, and integrity of the advisor who prepares them. Moreover, the information contained in personal financial statements is confidential. The client is entitled to confidentiality, and ethical responsibility demands it. Finally, it is the advisor's responsibility to help the client establish attainable goals, which set the ethical tone for the entire financial planning process. Therefore, the advisor must resist the temptation to push for goals that are unattainable and require that unrealistic projections and/or assumptions be used in pro forma statements.

---

pro forma

A client's current financial position and cash flow statements relate to what has occurred in the past. For purposes of financial planning, however, it is also necessary to prepare *pro forma* (or projected) financial position and cash flow statements. These pro forma statements illustrate what future financial statements are expected to show if certain activities are implemented under specified assumptions. Finally, current financial statements can be compared with past pro forma statements to see if the client's financial plan was realized.

WHAT IS A FINANCIAL POSITION STATEMENT?

The financial position statement shows an individual's (or family's) wealth at a point in time and reflects the results of the individual's past financial activities. It contains three basic classifications—assets, liabilities, and net worth—that make up the basic accounting equation:

$$ASSETS = LIABILITIES + NET\ WORTH$$

Financial advisors can choose from many different formats for the financial position statement since there is no standard. However, statements usually group the items that make up assets and liabilities into sub-classifications that better enable the advisor to analyze the components of the client's total financial situation and to evaluate the mix of assets in relation to the client's objectives. Table 5-1 shows a typical financial position statement.

Obviously, a financial statement should be in a format that is understandable, and uniformity is desirable. However, the actual format is really secondary to the quality of the information. It should be noted that the format of a financial position statement (and a cash flow statement) is often determined by the software system used by the financial advisor for analyzing data and producing reports.

TABLE 5-1					
Financial Position Statement for Jack and Jill Klient—June 30, 2007					
Assets			**Liabilities and Net Worth**		
Cash and Cash Equivalents			Liabilities		
Cash	$	12,000	Credit card balances	$	2,000
Money market fund		50,000	Consumer loans		4,000
Life insurance cash value		18,000	Automobile loans		12,000
	$	80,000	Mortgage loans		220,000
Other Financial Assets					
Stock	$	150,000	**Total Liabilities**		**$ 238,000**
Bonds, taxable		90,000			
Bonds, tax-exempt		80,000			
401(k)		120,000	**Net Worth**		**$ 692,000**
	$	440,000			
Personal Assets					
Residence					
Automobiles	$	300,000			
Household furnishings,		30,000			
possessions, jewelry,					
art					
		80,000			
	$	410,000	**Total Liabilities and**		
			Net Worth		**$ 930,000**
Total Assets	$	**930,000**			

As illustrated in table 5-1, financial position statements have traditionally been presented in two columns—one containing assets, the other containing liabilities and net worth. The term balance sheet is derived from the fact that the two side-by-side columns must balance according to the accounting equation (total assets = total liabilities + net worth). However, it is now more common to present financial position statements in a single-column format as illustrated in table 5-2. As will be shown later, the major advantage of the single-column format is that it facilitates the preparation of pro forma financial position statements and the comparison of consecutive statements over time.

Assets

Assets are items the client owns. It is immaterial whether the items were purchased for cash, financed by borrowing, or received as gifts or inheritances.

TABLE 5-2
Financial Position Statement for Jack and Jill Klient—June 30, 2007

ASSETS

Cash and Cash Equivalents	$ 12,000
Cash	50,000
Money market fund	18,000
Life insurance cash value	$ 80,000
Other Financial Assets	$ 150,000
Stock	90,000
Bonds, taxable	80,000
Bonds, tax-exempt	120,000
401(k)	$ 440,000
Personal Assets	$ 300,000
Residence	30,000
Automobiles	
Household furnishings, possessions,	
jewelry, art	80,000
	$ 410,000
	$ 930,000
TOTAL ASSETS	

LIABILITIES AND NET WORTH

Liabilities	
Credit card balances	$ 2,000
Consumer loans	4,000
Automobile loans	12,000
Mortgage loans	220,000
TOTAL LIABILITIES	**$ 238,000**
NET WORTH	**$ 692,000**
TOTAL LIABILITIES AND NET WORTH	**$ 930,000**

Items that the client possesses but does not own, such as rented apartments or leased automobiles, are not shown as assets.

It is common practice for personal financial position statements to show assets at their current fair market values. These values may vary considerably from the original purchase prices. In contrast, business balance sheets list many assets on the basis of adjusted historical costs, net of depreciation.

At a minimum, assets should be subdivided into two categories: financial assets and nonfinancial (or personal) assets. Many statement formats include other categories such as use assets, nonuse assets, personal assets, investment assets, and retirement assets. The financial position statements in tables 5-1 and 5-2 use three major categories of assets by separating total assets into (1) cash and cash equivalents, (2) other financial assets, and (3) personal assets. Other financial assets are sometimes further subdivided according to their relative liquidity, income characteristics, tax status, or growth characteristics.

Liabilities

Liabilities are the debts of the client. While the financial position statement in table 5-1 does not separate liabilities into major subcategories, it is not unusual to see liabilities grouped by the time period in which they must be repaid. For example, the statement might show subtotals for short-term liabilities (due in one year or less), intermediate-term liabilities (due in more than one year but no more than 5 years), and long-term liabilities (due in more than 5 years).

In theory, the liabilities section of the financial position statement should show all liabilities as of the date of the statement—even if the client has not received a formal bill. This process may require the client to make estimates for such items as taxes due, utility charges owed, and credit card obligations. In practice, clients and advisors often ignore relatively small accruals for unaudited statements.

Net Worth

Net worth measures the client's wealth or equity at the date of the financial position statement. It is calculated by restating the basic accounting equation as follows:

$$\text{NET WORTH} = \text{TOTAL ASSETS} - \text{TOTAL LIABILITIES}$$

or

$$\text{Ours} = \text{Own} - \text{Owe}$$

In other words, net worth is what remains if all the client's assets are sold at their fair market values and all debts are paid. If a client has a negative net worth, the client is considered to be bankrupt. However, such clients can avoid formal bankruptcy proceedings if cash flow is sufficient to service all financial obligations.

By itself, net worth reveals little about the nature of the assets or liabilities. A client with considerable net worth may have all his or her assets tied up in non-income-producing assets, such as homes, automobiles, and other personal possessions. Conversely, a client with a modest net worth may hold most assets in the form of financial assets that may be generating income, capital appreciation, or both. Further, it is possible for a client to have a positive cash balance with a negative net worth or to have a zero cash balance with a very high net worth. The key to understanding net worth is to recognize that it is simply a residual—the difference between total assets and total liabilities.

A client's net worth may increase or decrease during a period of time. Other things being equal, it will increase as a result of any one of the following:

- appreciation in the value of assets
- addition to assets through retaining income
- addition of assets through gifts or inheritances
- decrease in liabilities through forgiveness

The following are examples of actions that have no effect on net worth:

- paying off a debt. The cash account declines by the same amount that the liability declines, leaving the difference between total assets and total liabilities unchanged.
- buying an asset with cash. Total assets remain unchanged because cash declines by the same amount that the other asset category increases. However, commissions and other transaction costs cause net worth to decline because the cash that pays these costs is not reflected in the value of the purchased asset.

PREPARING A FINANCIAL POSITION STATEMENT

Since net worth is determined by subtracting total liabilities from total assets, preparing a client's financial position statement involves

- identifying each of the client's assets and liabilities
- valuing each asset and liability as of the date of the statement
- recording those values in an appropriate format that shows the client's net worth as the difference between total assets and total liabilities

Identifying the Client's Assets and Liabilities

Assets

As mentioned earlier, assets—that is, the items a client owns—can be categorized in a number of ways. One commonly used approach involves first dividing the client's assets into two groups—financial assets and nonfinancial (personal) assets. The results of the Federal Reserve Board's Survey of Consumer Finances[1] conducted in 2004 (hereinafter referred to as the FRB Survey) indicate that 42 percent of the value of all the assets held by the 4,522 families interviewed were financial assets and 64.3 percent were nonfinancial (or personal) assets.[2] Additional findings of the FRB Survey are presented throughout this section. They provide a sense of the relative roles played by various types of assets and liabilities in defining the financial positions of U.S. families.

financial assets

Financial Assets—Financial assets consist of cash and cash equivalents (or liquid assets) and other financial (or investment) assets. Cash and cash equivalents are liquid in the sense that they are either already cash or can be converted into cash relatively quickly with little, if any, loss in value. In addition to cash on hand, cash and cash equivalents also include various transactions accounts such as checking, savings and money market deposit accounts, money market mutual funds, call accounts at brokerages, and certificates of deposit maturing in the near future (generally, within one year). The cash value of life insurance polices can also be considered as cash. Clients require cash and liquid cash equivalents to, among other things,

- pay daily expenses (Transactions)
- provide funds to cover unanticipated emergencies that may arise (Emergency Fund)
- provide funds to take advantage of unforeseen investment opportunities that may arise (Opportunistic)

As illustrated in table 5-3, cash and cash equivalents in the form of transactions accounts made up 11.5 percent of all financial assets held in 2001 by families participating in the FRB Survey. Certificates of deposit (of all maturities, not distinguished as to extent to which they represent money marketer investment assets) accounted for only 3.1 percent of total financial assets, continuing the pattern of decline they have experienced over the past decade.

Assets classified as "investment assets" for financial position statement purposes represent a variety of assets with wide-ranging degrees of risk in which clients may invest in an effort to earn a return. In addition to certificates of deposit that mature more than one year after the date of the financial position statement, investment assets include

- savings bonds
- other bonds—corporate and mortgage-backed bonds; federal, state and local government bonds; and foreign bonds that are more likely to be owned directly by families in the highest income and wealth (net worth) groups

- stocks—although also concentrated among high income and high wealth families, direct ownership of publicly traded stocks is more widespread than it is for bonds

---

TABLE 5-3
Distribution of the Total Value of Financial Assets Held by All Families Participating in the 2001 and 2004 FRB Surveys by Type of Asset

Type of Financial Asset	% of Total Value of Financial Assets Held in 2001	% of Total Value of Financial Assets Held in 2004
Transactions Accounts	11.5	
Certificates of Deposit (all maturities)	3.1	
Savings Bonds	.7	
Bonds	4.6	
Stocks	21.7	
Mutual Funds (except money market funds)	12.2	
Retirement Accounts	28.4	
Cash Value of Life Insurance	5.3	
Other Managed Assets	10.6	
Other	2.0	
Total Financial Assets	100.0*	
Financial assets as a share of total assets	42.0	35.7

* Percentage distribution does not add precisely to 100 because of rounding error.

Source: B.K. Bucks, Arthur B. Kennickell, and Kevin B. Moore, "Recent Changes in U.S. Family Finances: Evidence From the 2001 and 2004 Survey of Consumer Finances," *Federal Reserve Bulletin*, vol. 92 (February 2006), p. Λ10.

- mutual funds (excluding money market funds)—directly held stock funds, taxable funds of government-backed bonds, tax-exempt bond funds, other bond funds and combination funds
- tax-advantaged retirement accounts—IRAs and employer-sponsored accounts such as 401(k) plan accounts, 403(b) plan accounts, profit-sharing plan accounts, stock bonus plan accounts, and ESOP accounts (Note: Undoubtedly, clients view their vested retirement benefits earned under a defined-benefit pension plan as being a valuable asset. However, since the current value of those benefits depends very heavily on a number of critical assumptions about future work-related events and economic conditions [and thus is quite difficult to estimate], the value of defined-benefit plan retirement benefits is generally not listed as an asset on a personal financial position statement.)

- other managed assets—personal annuities, trusts with an equity interest, and managed investment accounts
- other—a heterogeneous category including a variety of other assets generally acquired or held for investment purposes such as futures contracts, stock options, oil and gas leases, commodities, royalties, loans made to others, and proceeds from estates in settlement

Table 5-3 shows each type of financial asset's percentage of the total value of all the financial assets held in 2001 and 2004 by families participating in the FRB Survey. The reduction of stocks held outside of retirement accounts, a resurgence in bonds, the increase in retirement accounts, and the continued decline in cash value life insurance are all noteworthy in this table.

Table 5-4 shows the FRB Survey findings regarding the percentage of families holding each type of financial asset in 2004 for families in various income, age of head of household, and net worth groups. Table 5-5 shows the median value of the holdings of each type of financial asset for families holding that asset in 2004 who are in various income, age of head of household, and net worth groups. The tables provide some answers to the question, Who owns what and how much? For example, table 5-4 indicates that

- certificates of deposit (CDs) are more likely to be held by families headed by persons 65 years and older
- savings bonds tend to be held most frequently by households headed by persons between 35 and 54 years of age, families in the top 40 percent of the distribution income, and families in the top half of the distribution of net worth
- direct ownership of other bonds tends to be more common among families in the top income and net worth groups
- direct ownership of publicly traded stock is more likely in families with relatively high incomes and high net worth, but is not as highly concentrated in the top income and net worth groups as is direct ownership of bonds
- direct ownership of mutual funds (other than money market funds) follows a pattern quite similar to that of direct ownership of publicly traded stocks
- ownership of tax-deferred retirement accounts increases with income and net worth and is more common among families headed by persons between ages 35 and 64
- likelihood of owning cash value life insurance increases with income and net worth as well as for families with heads of household less than age 75

TABLE 5-4
Percentage of FRB Survey Families Holding Each Type of Financial Asset in 2001

Percentile of Income	Before-tax Family Income		Transactions Accounts	CDs	Savings Bonds	Bonds	Stocks	Mutual Funds	Retirement Accounts	Life Insurance	Other Managed Assets	Other
	Median Income	Mean Income										
Less than 20	10,300	10,000	70.9	10.0	3.8	*	3.8	3.6	13.2	13.8	2.2	6.2
20–39.9	24,400	24,100	89.4	14.7	11.0	*	11.2	9.5	33.3	24.7	3.3	9.9
40–59.9	39,900	40,300	96.1	17.4	14.1	1.5	16.4	15.7	52.8	25.6	5.4	9.9
60–79.9	64,800	65,200	98.8	16.0	24.4	3.7	26.2	20.6	75.7	35.7	8.5	9.0
80–89.9	98,700	98,000	99.7	18.3	30.3	3.9	37.0	29.0	83.7	38.6	10.7	10.8
90–100	169,600	302,700	99.2	22.0	29.7	12.7	60.6	48.8	88.3	41.8	16.7	12.5
Age of Head of Household (Years)												
Less than 35			86.0	6.3	12.7	*	17.4	11.5	45.1	15.0	2.1	10.4
35–44			90.7	9.8	22.6	2.1	21.6	17.5	61.4	27.0	3.1	9.5
45–54			92.2	15.2	21.0	2.8	22.0	20.2	63.4	31.1	6.4	8.5
55–64			93.6	14.4	14.3	6.1	26.7	21.3	59.1	35.7	13.0	10.6
65–74			93.8	29.7	11.3	3.9	20.5	19.9	44.0	36.7	11.8	8.5
75 or more			93.7	36.5	12.5	5.7	21.8	19.5	25.7	33.3	11.2	7.3
Percentile of Net Worth	Family Net Worth											
	Median Mean											
Less than 25	0		72.4	1.8	4.3	*	5.0	2.5	18.9	6.9	*	7.9
25–49.9	44,100		93.6	8.8	12.8	*	9.5	7.2	45.3	26.0	1.3	8.6
50–74.5	165,700		98.2	23.2	23.5	*	20.3	17.5	63.2	34.5	6.2	8.7
75–89.9	449,400		99.6	30.1	25.9	5.3	41.2	35.9	77.6	41.7	13.9	9.4
90–100	2,754,900		99.6	26.9	26.3	18.4	64.3	54.8	87.4	48.6	26.4	16.1

Source: Ana M. Aizcorbe, Arthur B. Kennickell and Kevin B. Moore, "Recent Changes in U.S. Family Finances: Evidence From the 1998 and 2001 Survey of Consumer Finances," *Federal Reserve Bulletin*, January 2003, pp. 5, 7, and 13.

- ownership of other managed assets is most likely among families with higher levels of income and net worth and headed by persons aged 55 or older
- ownership of other financial assets is most likely among families in the top 20 percent of the distribution income, and families in the top 10 percent of the distribution of net worth

Table 5-5 provides the median value of the holdings for each type of financial asset.

TABLE 5-5
Median Value of the Holdings of Each Type of Financial Asset for FRB Survey Families Holding That Asset in 2001

Percentile of Income	Before-tax Family Income		Trans actions Accounts	CDs	Savings Bonds	Bonds	Stocks	Mutual Funds	Retirement Accounts	Life Insurance	Other Managed Assets	Other
	Median Income	Income										
Less than 20	10,300	10,000	900	10,000	1,000	*	7,500	21,000	4,500	3,600	24,200	1,700
20–39.9	24,400	24,100	1,900	14,000	600	*	10,000	24,000	8,000	6,200	36,000	3,000
40–59.9	39,900	40,300	2,900	13,000	500	10,000	7,000	24,000	13,600	7,000	70,000	3,000
60–79.9	64,800	65,200	5,300	15,000	1,000	40,000	17,000	30,000	30,000	12,000	60,000	3,000
80–89.9	98,700	98,000	9,500	13,000	1,000	50,000	20,000	28,000	55,000	10,000	70,000	7,000
90–100	169,600	302,700	26,000	25,000	2,000	88,700	50,000	87,500	130,000	24,000	112,000	15,000
Age of Head of House- hold (Years)												
Less than 35			1,800	4,000	300	*	5,700	9,000	6,600	10,000	40,000	1,300
35–44			3,400	6,000	1,000	13,600	15,000	17,500	28,500	9,000	50,000	2,000
45–54			4,600	12,000	1,000	60,000	15,000	38,500	48,000	11,000	60,000	5,000
55–64			5,500	19,000	2,500	60,000	37,500	60,000	55,000	10,000	55,000	10,000
65–74			8,000	20,000	2,000	71,400	85,000	70,000	60,000	8,800	120,000	8,000
75 or more			7,300	25,000	3,000	35,000	60,000	70,000	46,000	7,000	100,000	17,500
Percentile of Net Worth	**Family Net Worth**											
	Median	Mean										
Less than 25	1,100	0	700	1,500	200	*	1,300	2,000	2,000	1,800	*	1,000
25–49.9	40,800	44,100	2,200	5,000	500	*	3,200	5,000	7,500	5,200	10,100	2,300
50–74.5	156,100	165,700	5,500	11,500	1,000	*	8,300	15,000	30,000	9,000	22,000	4,500
75–89.9	430,200	449,400	13,700	20,000	2,000	20,000	25,600	37,500	76,500	12,000	70,000	10,000
90–100	1,301,900	2,754,900	36,000	40,000	2,000	90,000	122,000	140,000	190,000	30,000	200,000	30,000

Source: Ana M. Aizcorbe, Arthur B. Kennickell and Kevin B. Moore, "Recent Changes in U.S. Family Finances: Evidence From the 1998 and 2001 Survey of Consumer Finances," *Federal Reserve Bulletin*, January 2003, pp. 5, 7, and 13.

nonfinancial (personal) assets

Nonfinancial (Personal) Assets—*Nonfinancial (personal) assets* include a client's

- primary residence
- other residential real estate
- net equity in nonresidential real estate such as commercial property, rental property, farm land, and undeveloped land
- net equity in privately held businesses such as sole proprietorships, various types of partnerships, subchapter S corporations, and other types of corporations that are not publicly traded

- vehicles such as cars, vans, sports utility vehicles, trucks, motor homes, recreational vehicles, motorcycles, boats, airplanes, and helicopters
- other tangible personal assets such as clothes, household furnishings, appliances, artwork, jewelry, antiques, hobby equipment, and collectibles

As mentioned earlier, nonfinancial (personal) assets accounted for 64.3 percent of the total value of all the assets held by the families participating in the 2004 FRB Survey. Table 5-6 shows the percentage breakdown for these nonfinancial assets by type of asset. As compared with the findings of the 2001 FRB Survey, equity in residential real estate drove the increase, and the most significant decrease was in the decline in the holding of privately held businesses.

TABLE 5-6
Distribution of the Total Value of Nonfinancial Assets Held by All Families Participating in the 2004 FRB Survey by Type of Asset

Type of Nonfinancial Asset	% of Total Value of Nonfinancial Assets Held in 2001
Vehicles	5.1
Primary residence	50.3
Other residential property	9.9
Net equity in nonresidential property	7.3
Net equity in privately held businesses	25.9
Other (artwork, jewelry, precious metals, antiques, hobby equipment, and collectibles)	1.5
Total Nonfinancial Assets	100.0

Source: Brian K. Bucks, Arthur B. Kennickell, and Kevin B. Moore, "Recent Changes in U.S. Family Finances: Evidence From the 2001 and 2004 Survey of Consumer Finances," *Federal Reserve Bulletin*, vol. 92 (February 2006), p. A16.

Liabilities

Liabilities are debts a client incurs by borrowing. Individuals and families borrow for a variety of reasons. Table 5-7 shows the percentage breakdown of the total amount of debt of all families participating in the 2001 FRB Survey by purpose for borrowing. As indicated, borrowing to purchase a home accounts for the bulk of total family borrowing.

When clients borrow, they incur debts that must be repaid in the future—that is, they incur liabilities. Liabilities are generally identified by the type of debt incurred. The types of liabilities most commonly incurred by clients are

- balances for credit cards and other lines of credit
- mortgages and other loans secured by residential property
- installment loans to finance the purchase of items such as automobiles, furniture, and appliances
- other forms of borrowing such as loans from life insurance policies and retirement accounts

---

TABLE 5-7
Distribution of the Total Amount of Debt of All Families Participating in the 2004 FRB Survey by Purpose for Borrowing

Purpose for Borrowing	% of Total Amount of Debt in 2004
Home purchase	70.2
Home improvement	1.9
Other residential property	9.5
Investments excluding real estate	2.2
Vehicles	6.7
Purchase goods and services	6.0
Education	3.0
Unclassifiable loans against pension accounts	†
Other	.6
Total Debt	100.0

Source: Brian K. Bucks, Arthur B. Kennickell, and Kevin B. Moore, "Recent Changes in U.S. Family Finances: Evidence From the 2001 and 2004 Survey of Consumer Finances," *Federal Reserve Bulletin*, vol. 92 (February 2006), p. A32.

Table 5-8 shows the percentage breakdown by type of debt of the total amount of debt of all families participating in the 2004 FRB Survey. Regardless of the type of debt, debts that are due within one year of the date of the financial position statement are considered short-term (or current) liabilities; those due more than one year from the date of the statement are considered long-term liabilities.

As indicated in table 5-8, three-fourths of the total liabilities of families participating in the 2004 FRB Survey consist of home-secured debt—that is, first and second mortgages, and home equity loans and lines of credit secured by the primary residence. With the exception of the highest income and net worth groups, use of home-secured debt increases with family income and wealth. Use of home-secured debt peaks among families headed by persons aged 45 to 54; following that, it declines. In contrast to the recently growing share of total debt attributable to borrowing secured by the primary residence, the share represented by borrowing on other residential real estate continues to decline as it has over the past decade. Also, as indicated in table 5-8, the use of lines of credit other than home equity lines is not common.

TABLE 5-8
Distribution of the Total Amount of Debt of All Families Participating in the 2004 FRB Survey by Type of Debt

Type of Debt	% of Total Amount of Debt in 2004
Home-secured debt (mortgages and other borrowing secured by the primary residence)	75.2
Borrowing on other residential property	8.5
Lines of credit not secured by residential property	.7
Installment loans	11.0
Credit card balances	3.0
Other	1.6
Total Debt	100.0
Debt as a percentage of total assets	.15

Source: Brian K. Bucks, Arthur B. Kennickell, and Kevin B. Moore, "Recent Changes in U.S. Family Finances: Evidence From the 2001 and 2004 Survey of Consumer Finances," *Federal Reserve Bulletin*, vol. 92 (February 2006), p. A25.

Table 5-8 indicates that the second largest share of the total liabilities of families participating in the 2004 FRB Survey consists of installment borrowing—that is, consumer loans that typically have fixed payments and a fixed term. Examples include automobile loans, student loans, and loans for furniture, appliances, and other durable goods. Use of installment borrowing was widespread in 2004 with the exception of the lowest and highest income groups, the highest net worth group, and families headed by persons aged 65 and older, where the use of installment loans was notably lower.

Another common personal liability arises from the use of credit cards to purchase goods and services. Credit cards consist of bank-type cards such as VISA, MasterCard, Discover, and Optima; travel and entertainment cards such as Diners Club and American Express; gasoline company cards; and store cards or charge accounts. The outstanding credit card balance on the date of the financial position statement is a liability.

Liabilities can also arise from a variety of other types of borrowing. Loans on insurance policies, loans against tax-advantaged retirement accounts, and borrowing on margin accounts should be shown as liabilities on the financial position statement. Also, amounts owed as of the date of the financial position statement for items such as taxes, rent, utility bills, and medical bills should be shown as liabilities on the statement.

Valuing Each Asset and Liability as of the Date of the Statement

Once a client's assets and liabilities have been identified, a value must be determined for each. Unlike business financial position statements (balance sheets) which must list many assets on the basis of historical cost adjusted for depreciation, assets should be listed on a client's personal financial position statement at their fair market value as of the date the statement is being prepared. Values for most financial assets can be determined from checking account, savings account, investment account, and tax-advantaged retirement account statements. For life insurance policies with fixed level premiums and guaranteed cash values such as traditional whole life policies, the amount of a policy's cash value can be determined from a table of lapse (nonforfeiture) option values contained in the policy or from the insurance company for ages not listed in the policy's lapse option table. For other policies whose cash values reflect actual or anticipated investment, mortality, and/or expense experience, statements sent periodically to the policyowner can be used to determine cash value amounts. The fair market value of other financial assets such as oil and gas leases, futures contracts, royalties, and stock options is often difficult to determine, especially when the asset is not traded on an established market.

A variety of techniques may be used in estimating the fair market value of different types of personal assets. For example, the current market value of a client's home can be estimated using information gathered from local newspapers and/or the Internet regarding the prices of similar houses in the area that are being advertised for sale or have recently been sold. On the other hand, the value of quality pieces of art and jewelry may best be estimated by an appraisal. Today the values of many types of personal assets can be estimated using Internet websites – including eBay. For example, values for automobiles can be determined by using a number of websites including *www.edmunds.com*, *www.kbb.com*, and *autos.yahoo.com*. In addition to automobile values, *www.NADAguides.com* provides value estimates for classic cars, motorcycles, boats, and recreational vehicles. Values of many collectibles are available at *www.orionbluebook.com*.

Determination of the fair market value of a client's net equity interest in a closely held corporate business is an especially complex task.[3] The IRS, for example, has identified the following factors to be considered in valuing a corporate business:[4]

- the nature of the business and the history of the enterprise from its inception
- economic outlook in general, and the condition and outlook of the specific industry in particular
- the book value of the stock and the financial condition of the business
- the earning capacity of the company

- the dividend-paying capacity
- determination of whether the enterprise has goodwill or other intangible value
- sales of the stock and the size of the block of stock to be valued
- the market price of actively traded stocks of corporations engaged in the same or a similar line of business

Although all these factors should be considered in determining the fair market value of a client's interest in a closely held corporate business, judgment must be applied in determining the weights that should be accorded to each factor. Moreover, there are a number of different methods, some focusing on assets and others focusing on earning power that can be used in estimating the value of the business. Choice of the most appropriate valuation method or methods is also based heavily on judgment. Finally, the application of discounts for such factors as a minority interest and the lack of marketability of the interest introduce considerable judgment into the valuation process. Given the complexity and subjectivity of this procedure, the valuation of an interest in a closely held corporate business is virtually always handled by a qualified valuation appraiser.

Just as with assets, preparation of a financial position statement also requires that values be determined for each of the client's liabilities. Liabilities are valued by using the amount owed by the client as of the date the financial position statement is prepared. Thus, liabilities arising from the purchase of consumable goods and services are valued at the amount owed on the date of the statement regardless of whether a bill has been received. Likewise, even though a bill has not been received, the value of a liability arising from the use of a credit card is the outstanding balance on the date of the financial position statement. Liabilities resulting from mortgages and other types of loans are valued at the outstanding loan balance—that is, the amount of the unpaid principal—as of the date the financial position statement is prepared.

Recording the Values of the Client's Assets and Liabilities in an Appropriate Format That Shows the Client's Net Worth

The final step in the preparation of a financial position statement involves recording the values of the client's assets and liabilities in an appropriate format that shows the client's net worth as the difference between total assets and total liabilities. As mentioned earlier, although financial position statements have traditionally been presented in a two-column balance sheet format as illustrated in table 5-1, it is now more common in financial planning to present financial position statements in a single-column format. As illustrated in table 5-9, the major advantage of the single-column format is that it facilitates the preparation of pro forma financial position statements and the comparison of consecutive statements

TABLE 5-9
Current and Pro Forma Financial Position Statements for Jack and Jill Klient

Assets	Current on 6/30/07	Pro Forma #1 6/30/08 With Same Asset Allocation	Pro Forma #2 6/30/08 With Planned Asset Reallocation	Current on 6/30/08
Cash and Cash Equivalents				
Cash	$ 12,000	$ 14,000	$ 6,000	$ 6,000
Money market fund	50,000	51,700	20,680	20,510
Life insurance cash value	18,000	19,000	19,000	19,000
	$ 80,000	$ 84,700	$ 45,680	$45,510
Other Financial Assets				
Stock	$ 150,000	$165,000	$ 192,500	$ 187,250
Bonds, taxable	90,000	96,120	101,460	100,653
Bonds, tax-exempt	80,000	84,800	100,700	99,750
401(k)	120,000	139,920	139,920	136,104
	$ 440,000	$ 485,840	$ 534,580	$ 523,757
Personal Assets				
Residence	$ 300,000	$ 330,000	$ 330,000	$ 330,000
Automobiles	30,000	27,000	27,000	27,000
Household furnishings, possessions, jewelry, art	80,000	84,000	84,000	84,000
	$ 410,000	$ 441,000	$ 441,000	$ 441,000
Total Assets	$ 930,000	$1,011,540	$1,021,260	$1,010,267
Liabilities and Net Worth				
Liabilities				
Credit card balances	$ 2,000	$ 1,000	$ 1,000	$ 1,000
Consumer loans	4,000	3,200	3,200	3,200
Automobile loans	12,000	9,600	9,600	600
Mortgage loans	220,000	212,667	212,667	212,667
Total Liabilities	$ 238,000	$ 226,467	$ 226,467	$ 226,467
Net Worth	$ 692,000	$ 785,073	$ 794,793	$ 783,800
Total Liabilities and Net Worth	$ 930,000	$1,011,540	$1,021,260	$1,010,267

over time. The current statement as of June 30, 2007, shows the Klients' actual financial position on that date. Pro Forma #1 projects the Klients' financial position one year if they continue to manage their cash flows, assets, and liabilities in the same manner as at present, and if the underlying assumptions regarding rates of return, asset appreciation and depreciation, debt repayment, and taxes accurately portray conditions occurring during the next year. Based on the same underlying assumptions, Pro Forma #2 reflects improved cash flow management through budgeting and reallocation of some assets as recommended in the Klients' financial plan for the next year; it also projects the impact of those changes on the Klients' financial position as of June 30, 2008. A comparison of the two pro forma statements indicates that if the Klients' follow the recommendations in their financial plan and the underlying assumptions are accurate, their assets and net worth would be $9,720 greater in one year than if they were to continue managing their cash flows, assets, and liabilities in the present manner. Assuming the Klients adopted the cash flow management and asset reallocation recommendations in their financial plan, a comparison of the current statement for June 30, 2007, and Pro Forma #2 indicates that lower than anticipated rates of return resulted in their actual financial position (both assets and net worth) on that date being $10,993 less than projected. However, a comparison of the two current statements indicates that with their assets increasing by $80,267 and their net worth increasing by $91,800, the Klients' financial position did improve between June 30, 2007, and the same date in 2008.

USING A FINANCIAL POSITION STATEMENT

In addition to providing a format for summarizing the asset and liability data gathered in step 2 (determine goals and gather data) of the financial planning process, properly prepared, a client's financial position statement provides an important source of information a financial advisor can use to help the client achieve his or her goals through the application of the financial planning process. The information provided by the statement is especially useful in the following steps of the financial planning process:

- Step 3: Analyze and Evaluate the Data
- Step 4: Develop and Present a Plan
- Step 6: Monitor the Plan

Use in Step 3: Analyze and Evaluate Data

A client's current financial position statement prepared from data gathered in step 2 of the financial planning process provides the financial advisor with a picture of the client's financial position at the beginning of the financial planning engagement. This information regarding the client's present financial position enables the financial advisor to answer a number of key questions including

- What are the types and amounts of the various assets the client currently holds?
- What are the types and amounts of the various liabilities the client incurred?
- What is the amount of the client's wealth—net worth—at the beginning of the financial planning engagement?
- Given this picture of the client's present financial position, will further discussion be required to help the client revise and/or prioritize the goals stated in step 2 of the financial planning process?

While a look at the current financial position statement may be sufficient to answer these questions, further analysis of the data is necessary for the financial advisor to identify the various obstacles that the client's current financial position presents to the achievement of personal goals. For example, obstacles may arise from the current distribution of assets and/or liabilities. Analysis of the distribution of assets in the current financial position statement may reveal that the achievement of the client's goals will be hampered because he or she

- holds too high a percentage of total assets in non-income-producing personal assets rather than in financial assets that provide income and/or appreciation
- holds too high a percentage of financial assets in cash and cash equivalents rather than in other financial assets that provide an opportunity to earn a higher return
- fails to take appropriate advantage of tax-advantaged retirement plans

Comparison of the holdings of various types of assets and liabilities may also reveal possible obstacles to the achievement of the client's goals. For example, comparing the amount of a client's liquid assets with the amount of total current debts by calculating the client's liquidity ratio may indicate either that the client could face serious difficulty in paying current debts if income were unexpectedly reduced or that the client could be holding an excessive amount of funds in liquid assets. The liquidity ratio is calculated as follows:

$$\text{Liquidity Ratio} = \frac{\text{Liquid Assets}}{\text{Total Current Debts}} = \frac{\text{Liquid Assets}}{\text{Current Liabilities} + \text{Annual Loan Payments}}$$

As indicated in table 5-9, Jack and Jill Klients' current financial position statement indicates that on June 30, 2007, their liquid assets consist of $80,000 of cash and cash equivalents and their current liabilities consist of $2,000 of unpaid credit card balances. Assuming the total payments for their consumer, automobile, and mortgage loans will be $25,400 in 2006, the Klients' total current debt is $27,400 ($2,000 + $25,400) and their liquidity ratio is 2.92 ($80,000/$27,400) or 292 percent. This ratio indicates that the Klients hold enough liquid assets to cover nearly three times the amount of their existing total current (one-year) debt. This excessive current debt coverage suggests that the financial advisor recommend some reallocation of the Klients' total assets from cash and low-yielding cash equivalents to other financial assets with higher potential rates of return (as was done and is reflected in Pro Forma #2 and the Current Statement for 6/30/07 in table 5-9). A more appropriate liquidity ratio would be greater than one but less than 2.

In contrast, suppose another client holds $10,000 of liquid assets, has $15,000 of current liabilities (credit card debt), and will need to make various loan payments totaling $40,000 in the coming year. This client's liquidity ratio is .18 ($10,000/[$15,000 + $40,000]) or 18 percent. This ratio indicates that the client can only cover 18 percent of his or her present one-year debt obligations with existing liquid assets. If, for example, the client were to lose his or her job, current liquid assets would cover existing total current debt for only a little over 2 months. In this case, the financial advisor should recommend some reallocation of the client's total assets to build up his or her liquid reserves to provide a longer period of protection. The length of the period of protection and thus the amount of liquid assets required would depend on such factors as the state of the relevant job market, other potential sources of income to help meet current debts, and the period of time with which the client is comfortable.

Another ratio, the solvency ratio, provides an estimate of the extent to which the market value of a client's total assets could decline before wiping out all of the client's wealth as measured by net worth. The solvency ratio is calculated as follows:

$$\text{Solvency Ratio} = \frac{\text{Net Worth}}{\text{Total Assets}}$$

Referring to table 5-1, the Klients' solvency ratio is .74 ($692,000/$930,000), indicating that the market value of the Klients' total assets could decline by approximately 74 percent before wiping out their net worth. As with the high liquidity ratio, this high solvency ratio suggests that the Klients have room to reallocate some of their present financial assets to higher risk assets that also provide the potential to earn a higher rate of return.

As Pro Forma #1 illustrates in table 5-9, another use of the financial position statement in step 3 of the financial planning process is to estimate the client's future wealth position if the client continues to manage cash flows and assets and liabilities in the same manner given realistic assumptions regarding future rates of returns, asset appreciation and depreciation, debt repayment, and taxes. Among other things, this projection of net worth can be used to determine whether or not the client is likely to be able to achieve his or her financial goals at various key points in the future, assuming no changes in cash flow and asset and liability management.

Use in Step 4: Develop and Present a Plan

After the information about the client has been analyzed and, if necessary, the goals have been refined, the advisor's next job is to devise a realistic financial plan for bringing the client from his or her present financial position to the attainment of those goals. The financial position statement can be used by the financial advisor in several ways in step 4 of the financial planning process.

As the financial advisor considers alternative strategies that might be included in a plan to achieve the client's goals, projected financial position statements, each reflecting a particular strategy, can be compared to determine the relative impact of the various strategies on the client's future wealth position under a given set of assumptions. This use is illustrated by comparing Pro Forma #2 with Pro Forma #1 in table 5-9.

Implicit in plan development is the importance of obtaining client approval. In obtaining client approval, the financial advisor can compare a projection of the future financial position statement assuming the recommended plan is adopted (Pro Forma #2 in table 5-9) with

- the projected future financial position statement assuming no change is made in cash flow and asset and liability management (Pro Forma #1 in table 5-9) to illustrate the impact that plan adoption is expected to have on the client's wealth position and thus, achievement of the client's goals
- the current financial position statement (Current on 6/30/07 in table 5-9) to illustrate the extent to which the client's wealth position is expected to change from the present one if the recommended plan is adopted

Use in Step 6: Monitor the Plan

Normally the advisor meets with the client at least once each year to review the plan or more frequently if changing circumstances warrant it. The first part of this review process should involve measuring the performance of the implementation vehicles. One way plan performance can be illustrated is to compare the client's actual financial position statement at the time the plan review is taking place (Current on 6/30/07 in table 5-9) with the projected future financial position statement shown to the client in step 4 of the financial planning process. This projection assumed the plan would be adopted and the assumed rates of return, asset appreciation and depreciation, debt repayment, and taxes underlying the projection would accurately portray conditions that would actually exist in the future (Pro Forma #2 in table 5-9).

WHAT IS A CASH FLOW STATEMENT?

The cash flow statement summarizes a client's financial activities over a specified period of time by comparing cash inflows and cash outflows, and indicating whether the net cash flow for the period is positive or negative. The cash flow statement has three basic components—income, expenses, and net cash flow—that are related as follows:

$$\text{INCOME} - \text{EXPENSES} = \text{NET CASH FLOW}$$

which can also be stated as

Sources of Funds – Uses of Funds = Change in Cash Position

or

Money In – Money Out = Change in Cash

As illustrated in figure 5-2, the cash flow statement for a given year indicates how the client's financial activities changed his or her wealth (net worth) position from that depicted in the financial position statement at the beginning of the year (the end of the previous year) to that depicted in the financial position statement at the end of the year.

When based on a client's past income and expenses, the cash flow statement (or income statement) provides the financial advisor with a summary of the client's financial activities for a specified period (generally one year) prior to the start of the financial planning engagement. This information can be used in analyzing the client's present financial situation. On the other hand, a pro forma cash flow statement based on projections of future income and expenses for a specified planning period provides the financial advisor with a means for assessing the anticipated impact of various alternative planning strategies on the achievement of the client's goals in step 4 (develop and present a plan) of the financial planning process. Moreover, the pro forma cash flow statement (or budget) included in the financial plan adopted by the client provides a basis for implementing and subsequently assessing the performance of the plan. As such, the cash flow statement plays a central role in carrying out the various cash flow management activities involved in providing financial planning services to clients.

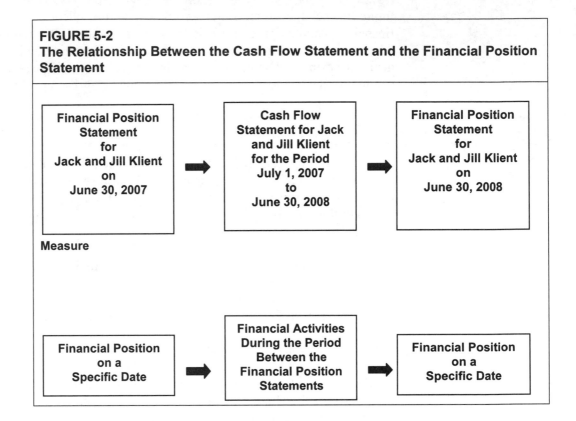

FIGURE 5-2
The Relationship Between the Cash Flow Statement and the Financial Position Statement

What Is Cash Flow Management?

cash flow
management

    Cash flow management is essentially a euphemism for the budgetary planning and control process. Financial advisors adopted the change in terminology partly because cash flow management is more inclusive than budgeting. More importantly, the word budget carries negative connotations for many clients, making them less likely to participate in the process. It may also be referred to as a spending plan, again because the term lacks the negative connotations of budgeting.

    Cash flow management consists of three basic components: cash flow analysis, cash flow planning, and budgeting. In practice, many advisors mix aspects of each of the three and consider them a single process.

Cash Flow Analysis

cash flow analysis

    Cash flow analysis, or income and expense analysis, is the process of gathering data concerning the client's cash flow situation, presenting the data in an organized format (the cash flow statement), and identifying strengths, weaknesses, and important patterns. Cash flow analysis is also a good starting point for the client and the financial advisor to develop goals and objectives in step 2 (determine goals and gather data) of the financial planning process. In addition, it reveals inefficient, ineffective, or unusual utilization of resources, highlights alternative courses of action, motivates the client, and makes family members aware of the need to conserve resources.

Cash Flow Planning

cash flow planning
net cash flow

Cash flow planning involves identifying courses of action that will help optimize *net cash flow*. Net cash flow is defined as the difference between income and expenses. A positive net cash flow is available for any use, whether for consumption, investment, or gifting, although in most financial planning situations, the primary benefit of a positive net cash flow is to provide a source of investable funds.

Note that the goal is to optimize rather than to maximize. Maximizing net cash flow means to make it as large as possible. Pursuit of this goal suggests increasing income in any way possible. Presumably this mandate includes working longer hours, finding a second job, or seeking employment for the nonearning spouse. On the expense side, maximization implies having a less expensive home and automobile, quitting the club, and discontinuing vacations and eating out. Clearly these approaches represent changes in lifestyle and standard of living, not to mention family relationships. In contrast, optimization means seeking the best, not necessarily the largest, net cash flow.

Optimal net cash flow implies a balance between investing for the future and maintaining and/or improving the current lifestyle. While the distinction between maximizing and optimizing may seem arcane, this difference is important not only in substance but also in style. Optimization holds greater appeal to clients because it puts wealth accumulation in perspective. It also gives clients greater control since they ultimately decide their own funds allocation according to their own personal preferences.

Cash flow planning is interwoven through almost all aspects of financial planning. At the extreme, cash flow planning is a factor or a tool in each of the major planning areas:

- insurance planning and risk management
- employee benefits planning
- investment planning
- income tax planning
- retirement planning
- estate planning

Some advisors believe that cash flow planning involves each of the financial planning steps in a sort of microcosm of the larger, overall process. Some even view cash flow management as the framework within which all the major planning areas are analyzed and evaluated.

The more common approach is simply to use cash flow planning as an extension of cash flow analysis in an iterative process that involves the major planning areas. For example, cash flow analysis reveals opportunities for increasing net cash flow by addressing income and expense factors. Cash flow planning then considers what to do with the increase in net cash flow. The result may include an insurance or investment alternative that represents a financial commitment. Typically, the commitment raises expenses, thus lowering cash flow calculated in the cash flow analysis. Based on this new level, the client may consider another alternative for the remaining net cash flow.

Budgeting

budgeting

Budgeting is the process of creating and following an explicit plan for spending and investing the resources available to the client. In simplest terms, the process works via the establishment of a working budget model followed by a comparison of actual and expected results. By constantly monitoring the budget, the advisor and client can recognize problems as they occur and even anticipate them. Budgeting provides both a means of financial self-evaluation and a guideline to measure actual performance.

Budgeting does have some disadvantages, however. For example, many individuals have a psychological aversion to the record keeping required and may not maintain sufficient information for the budget to be useful. Obviously, to the extent the data utilized are inaccurate, the conclusions drawn from the budget may be misleading. For some clients, a rote dependence on budgeting numbers inhibits creativity, stifles risk taking, and encourages mechanical thinking. Such clients may forfeit investment opportunities or fail to minimize losses.

Here are some guidelines for establishing a budget:

- Make the budget flexible enough to deal with emergencies, unexpected opportunities, or other unforeseen circumstances.
- Keep the budget period long enough to utilize an investment strategy and a workable series of investment procedures—typically one calendar year.
- Make the budget simple and brief.
- Follow the form and content of the budget consistently.
- Eliminate extraneous information.
- Estimate especially with insignificant items.

- Tailor the budget to specific goals and objectives.
- Remember that a budget is also a guideline against which actual results are to be measured. Unexpected results should be analyzed: they may be the norm and deserve to be incorporated in a revised budget.
- Pinpoint, in advance, variables that may influence the amounts of income and expenses. Income may vary because of expected annual raises and increases or decreases in interest or dividend rates. Expenses may vary because of fluctuating living costs, changing tastes or preferences, or changing family circumstances.

Role of Cash Flow Management

Cash flow management is one of the most basic tools in financial planning. Ironically, financial advisors often find that clients resist the cash-flow management process more than any other technique even though it is critical to reaching a goal. Communicating the importance of cash flow management and talking the client through the process are among the advisor's greatest services.

The advantages of cash flow management cut across all income levels. Cash flow management is always beneficial and is especially useful when the client needs to accomplish any of the following objectives:

- measure periodic progress toward the achievement of specific goals (a) within a defined time frame and (b) within the confines of limited resources
- monitor especially complex elements of economic activity
- provide guidelines for evaluating the economic performance of elements constituting the client's cash flow
- communicate a planning strategy to those affected by the budget
- provide incentive (goals) for the performance of individuals involved
- control household expenses
- achieve desired wealth accumulation/savings goals, such as retirement or children's educations
- monitor the performance of a specific investment, such as a securities portfolio, rental property, or a closely held business
- reposition assets to improve the likelihood of accomplishing goals

PREPARING A CASH FLOW STATEMENT

While budgeting requires looking to the future, past income and expense data must first be gathered from the client to permit the financial advisor to determine the client's present cash flow situation. It is the client's present cash flow situation depicted in a cash flow statement that provides the starting point for carrying out the three activities of the cash flow management process mentioned earlier—analysis, planning, and budgeting. Financial advisors generally use a cash flow worksheet for gathering the income and expense data and inputting the data into a computer program to create the cash flow statement.

Since net cash flow is determined by subtracting total expenses from total income, preparing a client's cash flow statement involves:

- identifying the sources and amounts of gross income the client receives
- identifying the types and amounts of expenses the client incurs
- recording the amounts of income and expense in an appropriate format that shows the client's net cash flow as the difference between total income and total expenses

Although a cash flow statement can be prepared to reflect a client's income and expenses over any period of time, financial advisors commonly use a 12-month period. This period is comparable in length to the 12-month period most advisors use for budgeting. Regardless of whether a cash flow statement is being prepared in connection with gathering data, analyzing data for planning purposes or budgeting, the one-year period commonly used for a cash flow statement can be broken down on a month-by-month basis not only to show those cash flows that occur only in specific months, but also to permit more frequent monitoring of the performance of the client's cash flow plan.

Constructing a cash flow statement is largely a mechanical process involving very specific steps. Although some clients are in unusual situations, the majority fit into the following framework.

Identifying the Sources and Amounts of Gross Income Received by the Client

Identify the amount of gross (before-tax) income from each of the following:

- salary
- bonus
- commissions
- self-employment
- real estate
- dividends—closely held corporations
- dividends—publicly traded corporations
- interest—savings accounts
- interest—taxable bonds

- interest—tax-free bonds
- trust income
- other fixed-payment income
- variable sources of income

Basic sources of information regarding items of income include, among others, check stubs from work, bank and investment account statements, prior years' income tax returns, and personal financial position statements that show income-generating assets as well as previously owned assets that have been sold. Clients that use Microsoft Money®, Quicken®, or other personal finance software packages have the ability to develop personal financial statements using that software. Even if the client is only using the software to facilitate transactions using the electronic bill payment feature, it still provides a cash flow history that the advisor can use to prepare a cash flow statement. The advisor's ability to use the client's software to generate financial statements could shorten the time spent in the data-gathering phase (step 2, determine goals and gather data) of the financial planning process and improve the accuracy of the statements.

Identifying the Types and Amounts of Expenses Incurred by the Client

Annual expenses can be classified as either fixed or discretionary. Fixed expenses involve payments the client makes for products and services essential to meet basic needs (for example, food and clothing) and/or to meet obligations established by contract or law (for example, mortgage payments or rent and income tax payments). Some fixed expenses involve equal periodic payments over time. Monthly mortgage or rental payments, installment loan payments, contributions to retirement plans, and insurance premiums are examples of this type of fixed expense. Other fixed expenses such as payments for food, clothes, household furnishings, medical needs, and utilities involve payments that vary from one time period to another. However, "fixed" applies only in the short run and can often be changed without imposing a radical shift in the client's lifestyle. Even the most fixed of all expenses, housing, can be changed if necessary.

With discretionary expenses, the client has considerable choice as to whether or not to incur the expense. Examples include payments for, among other things, vacations, other forms of recreation, charitable contributions, and education.

Identify the amount of expense from each of the following:

- fixed expenses
  –housing costs (mortgage or rental payments)
  –utilities

   –food, groceries, and so on
   –clothing and cleaning
   –federal, state, and local income taxes
   –Social Security and Medicare taxes
   –property taxes
   –transportation costs
   –medical and dental expenses
   –debt repayments
   –household supplies and maintenance costs
   –life and disability insurance premiums
   –property and liability insurance premiums
   –current school expenses
- discretionary expenses
   –vacations, travel, and so on
   –gifts and contributions
   –household furnishings
   –education fund
   –savings
   –investments
   –other

Basic sources of information regarding items of expense include, among others, checking account statements, credit card statements, investment account statements, and prior years' income tax returns. Expenses incurred for items purchased with cash must generally be estimated.

Note that a client's expenses can vary generally in the upward direction as a result of increased cost of living, unexpected business expenses, financial catastrophes (such as uninsured theft or fire losses), changes in tastes or preferences, and large-scale expenses (such as college costs).

Recording the Amounts of the Client's Income and Expenses in an Appropriate Format Shows the Client's Net Cash Flow

Table 5-10 illustrates a cash flow statement for Jack and Jill Klient prepared by using items and amounts of income and expense for the year prior to the beginning of the financial planning engagement. Subtracting total expenses from total income reveals the Klients' net cash flow. Table 5-10 indicates that with their present pattern of consumption, investment, and gifting/contribution activities, the Klients' net cash flow is negative—that is, they experienced a cash shortfall of $4,500 during the period of July 1, 2007, to June 30, 2008. This shortfall was met by either reducing the Klients' cash

TABLE 5-10
Cash Flow Statement for Jack and Jill Klient for the Period July 1, 2007, to June 30, 2008

Annual Income	Amount	% of Total Income
Salary/Bonus—Jack	$110,000	71.9%
Salary/Bonus—Jill	30,000	19.6
Self-Employment (Business)	0	0.0
Dividends—Closely Held Corporation Stock	0	0.0
Dividends—Investments	3,000	2.0
Interest on Savings Accounts	2,000	1.3
Interest on Bonds, Taxable	5,000	3.3
Interest on Bonds, Exempt	3,000	2.0
Trust Income	0	0.0
Rental Income	0	0.0
Other	0	0.0
Total Annual Income	**$153,000**	**100.1%***
Fixed Expenses		
Housing (Mortgage/Rent)	$ 15,500	10.1%
Utilities & Telephone	7,000	4.6
Food, Groceries, etc.	10,500	6.9
Clothing and Cleaning	7,000	4.6
Income Taxes	23,500	15.4
Social Security and Medicare Taxes	7,500	4.9
Real Estate Taxes	5,000	3.3
Transportation	8,000	5.2
Medical/Dental Expenses	8,000	5.2
Debt Repayment	5,000	3.3
Housing Supplies/Maintenance	6,000	3.9
Life Insurance	8,000	5.2
Property & Liability Insurance	5,000	3.3
Current School Expenses	4,500	2.9
Total Fixed Expenses	**$ 120,500**	**78.8%**
Discretionary Expenses		
Vacations, Travel, etc.	$ 4,000	2.6%
Recreation/Entertainment	5,000	3.3
Contributions, Gifts	7,500	4.9
Household Furnishings	5,000	3.3
Education Fund	5,000	3.3
Savings	3,000	2.0
Investments	2,500	1.6
Other	5,000	3.3
Total Discretionary Expenses	**$ 37,000**	**24.3%**
Total Annual Expenses	**$ 157,500**	**103.1%**
Net Cash Flow	**$ -4,500**	**–3.0%**

*Discrepancies in totals are due to rounding.

and cash equivalents (a reduction of assets) and/or borrowing (an increase in liabilities). In either case, their net worth was reduced by $4,500.

Suppose another client experienced a positive net cash flow (that is, an excess of income over expenses) for a given year and that, as with the Klients, his or her discretionary expenses included amounts for savings, investments, and an education fund. Since the net cash flow is positive, the client can allocate even more to these categories (although most clients are more adept at finding ways to spend the money to enhance their lifestyles). A positive net cash flow for a given period can be used to increase assets and/or reduce liabilities, the net result of which is an increase in the client's net worth.

Individuals, like businesses, commonly experience some months with positive net cash flows and others with negative. In practice, cash or cash-equivalent balances simply grow in positive months and shrink in negative months. A vacation or holiday spending can reduce cash balances in the months surrounding these events.

USING A CASH FLOW STATEMENT

In addition to providing a format for summarizing the income and expense data gathered in step 2 (determine goals and gather data) of the financial planning process, properly prepared, a client's cash flow statement provides an important source of information for a financial advisor to use in helping the client achieve his or her goals through application of the financial planning process. The information provided by the statement is especially useful in the following steps of the financial planning process:

- Step 3: Analyze and Evaluate the Data
- Step 4: Develop and Present a Plan
- Step 6: Monitor the Plan

Use in Step 3: Analyze and Evaluate Data

A client's cash flow statement for the prior year prepared from data gathered in step 2 of the financial planning process provides the financial advisor with a picture of the client's cash flow situation at the beginning of the financial planning engagement. Analysis of the client's present cash flow situation—referred to earlier as cash flow analysis—enables the financial advisor to identify various opportunities for, as well as potential obstacles to, achieving the client's goals as a result of the way the client currently manages his or her cash flow. Key cash management issues such as these are often identified and discussed with the client before plan development begins:

- Is the client's current rate of saving adequate to enable him or her to achieve the goals stated in step 2 (determine goals and gather data) of the financial planning process and if not,
    - to what level must the rate of saving be increased to achieve those goals?
    - is the client both willing and financially able to make the changes required to achieve this increased rate of saving?
    - is the client willing to modify either the timing of his or her goals and/or the factors influencing the amount of resources required to achieve them?
- If the client's net cash flow is negative, what alternative courses of action are available for either increasing income or reducing expenses? Some possibilities include
    - reallocating some assets from low-yielding cash and cash equivalents to other financial assets with higher potential returns
    - reducing the amount of spending for discretionary expenses
    - reducing the amount of certain fixed expenses to the extent possible
    - refinancing the home mortgage at a lower interest rate
    - reducing income taxes through greater use of tax-advantaged retirement accounts and tax-exempt bonds
    - revising and/or prioritizing the goals stated in step 2 of the financial planning process
    - modifying the timing of some goals requiring the accumulation of savings
- If the client's net cash flow is positive, what opportunities exist for the client to increase savings and investment and/or tax-advantaged gifts and contributions instead of spending the entire amount of the positive net cash flow on nonfinancial assets?

Whether responding to opportunities or obstacles found during cash flow analysis, clients should be realistic in identifying categories for revision—blind optimism is counterproductive. Financial advisors should encourage clients to avoid lowering the savings, investment, and education planning figures unless there is no alternative.

Saving is essential for achieving many, if not most, of a client's goals. Table 5-11 shows the most important motivations for saving indicated by the 4,522 families participating in the 2004 FRB Survey. Regardless of the specific accumulation-type goal that is most important to a particular client, the percentage of after-tax income that is saved by a client is a critical factor in determining if and when that goal will be achieved.

TABLE 5-11
Reasons FRB Survey Participants Gave as Most Important for Their Families' Saving in 2004

Reasons	% of Survey Participants
Education	11.6
For the family	4.7
Buying own home	5.0
Purchases	7.7
Retirement	34.7
Liquidity (emergencies, possibilities of unemployment and health care costs, and having ready money)	30.0
Investments	1.5
No particular reason	.7
When asked for a reason, reported do not save	4.0
Total	100.0*

Source: Brian K. Bucks, Arthur B. Kennickell, and Kevin B. Moore, "Recent Changes in U.S. Family Finances: Evidence From the 2001 and 2004 Survey of Consumer Finances," *Federal Reserve Bulletin*, vol. 92 (February 2006), p. A7.

* Amounts do not sum to 100 percent because of rounding.

The percentage of after-tax income being saved by a client can be computed as follows:

$$\text{Savings Ratio} = \frac{\text{Net Cash Flow} + \text{Amounts Already Being Saved or Invested for Various Purposes}}{\text{Annual After-Tax Income}}$$

Using the data from table 5-10, the Klients' savings ratio is calculated as follows:

$$\text{Savings Ratio} = \frac{-\$4,500 + \$10,500}{\$153,000 - \$23,000 - \$7,500} = \frac{\$6,000}{\$122,000} = .049$$

The numerator of the ratio includes the $4,500 negative net cash flow and the $10,500 currently being saved as indicated by the amounts listed for education fund, savings, and investments in table 5-10. The denominator shows the $23,500 expense for income taxes; it also shows the $7,500 expense for Social Security and Medicare taxes being subtracted from the Klients' total annual income of $153,000.

The savings ratio indicates that the Klients are saving slightly less than 5 percent of their total after-tax income. Although the U.S. personal saving rate (adjusted by adding back capital gains, which were shifted by the government to business savings in 1998)[5] has declined yearly since 1992, on average, the savings ratio is different from the personal saving rate calculated by the government. The government calculates disposable income and subtracts from that number total consumption. The personal savings rate as calculated by the federal government actually turned negative in 2007 and has been in decline over the last two decades. While the Klients' savings ratio is less than the U.S. personal savings rate, it is the client's goals—not a national average—that should, along with other personal considerations, determine the percentage of after-tax income a client is willing to attempt to save. For example, the Klients might want to increase their rate of saving in order to achieve a goal requiring the accumulation of funds at a quicker pace than would be possible with their present 5 percent savings ratio. To both eliminate deficit spending and increase savings levels will require that the Klients make major changes in their spending and/or income if they want to increase their future rate of saving above 5 percent.

While adequate personal saving is important to financial planning, even more important is a client's ability to pay his or her debts promptly. The ability of a client to service his or her debts is a function of the level of the client's debt payments, and the income and assets the client has available to meet those payments. Although assets, especially cash and cash equivalents, can be and often are used to repay debt, personal debt burden has traditionally been measured by a debt service ratio that compares debt payments to net income, but does not include liquid assets in the denominator as a source of debt repayment. A client's debt service ratio is calculated as follows:

$$\text{Debt Service Ratio} = \frac{\text{Total Debt Payments}}{\text{Net Income}}$$

Using the values of Jack and Jill Klients' debt payments and gross income shown in table 5-10, their debt service ratio is calculated as follows:

$$\text{Debt Service Ratio} = \frac{\text{Mortgage Payment} + \text{Debt Repayment}}{\text{Net Income}}$$

$$\text{Debt Service Ratio} = \frac{\$15,500 + \$5,000}{\$120,000} = \frac{\$20,500}{\$120,000} = .171$$

The Klients' debt service ratio indicates that their annual debt payments account for 17.1 percent of their annual income. The Klients should have little, if any, difficulty repaying their current debts with their income.

Use in Step 4: Develop and Present a Plan

Once the information about the client has been analyzed and, if necessary, the goals to be achieved have been refined, the advisor's next job is to devise a realistic financial plan for bringing the client from his or her present financial position to the attainment of those goals. The cash flow statement can be used by the financial advisor to carry out cash flow planning and budgeting in step 4 (develop and present a plan) of the financial planning process.

Given the opportunities and obstacles identified in the analysis of the client's present cash flow situation in step 3 (analyze and evaluate the data) of the financial planning process, cash flow planning involves developing recommendations as to what the client should consider doing about

- the increase in net cash flow that is expected to result from taking advantage of the opportunities
- the obstacles to generating a net cash flow that is adequate to achieve the client's goals

Projected cash flow statements can be prepared to show the expected impact of each of the alternative courses of action available for consideration in developing an effective plan to take advantage of the existing opportunities or to deal with the existing obstacles. This is illustrated by the two pro forma cash flow statements in table 5-12. Pro Forma #1 shows the projected net cash flow for the period July 1, 2007 to June 30, 2008 if no changes are made in the Klients' cash management strategy. In this case, the only factors causing a change in net cash flow are the Klients' higher salaries and the resulting adjustment to income taxes. Pro Forma #2 shows the expected net cash flow for the same period if the Klients were to undertake an alternative strategy including certain changes in asset allocation and cash flow management.

Implicit in plan development is the importance of obtaining client approval. In obtaining client approval, the financial advisor can compare a projection of the future cash flow statement assuming the recommended plan is adopted (Pro Forma #2 in table 5-12) with

- the projected future cash flow statement assuming no change is made in cash flow or asset management (Pro Forma #1 in table 5-12) to illustrate the impact that plan adoption is expected to have on the client's net cash flow and thus, achievement of the client's goals
- the actual cash flow statement (Actual for 7/1/06 to 6/30/07 in table 5-12) to illustrate the extent to which the client's net cash flow position is expected to change from the present one if the recommended plan is adopted

Once the client approves the financial plan, the pro forma cash flow statement included in the plan becomes a budget—that is, an explicit plan for spending and investing the resources available to the client if the financial plan is properly implemented.

TABLE 5-12
Actual and Pro Forma Cash Flow Statements for Jack and Jill Klient

Annual Income	Actual 7/01/06–6/30/07	Pro Forma #1 7/01/07–6/30/08	Pro Forma #2 7/01/07–6/30/08	Actual 7/01/07–6/30/08
Salary/Bonus—Jack	$ 110,000	$115,500	$ 115,500	$ 115,500
Salary/Bonus—Jill	30,000	31,000	31,000	31,000
Self-Employment (Business)	0	0	0	0
Dividends—Closely Held Corporation				
Stock	0	0	0	0
Dividends—Investments	3,000	3,000	5,000	4,500
Interest on Savings Accounts	2,000	2,000	2,600	2,450
Interest on Bonds, Taxable	5,000	5,000	5,600	5,400
Interest on Bonds, Exempt	3,000	3,000	3,600	3,500
Trust Income	0	0	0	0
Rental Income	0	0	0	0
Other	0	0	0	0
Total Annual Income	**$153,000**	**$159,500**	**$ 163,300**	**$162,350**
Fixed Expenses				
Housing (Mortgage/Rent)	$ 15,500	$ 15,500	$ 15,500	$ 15,500
Utilities & Telephone	7,000	7,000	7,000	7,000
Food, Groceries, and so on	10,500	10,500	10,500	10,500
Clothing and Cleaning	7,000	7,000	7,000	7,000
Income Taxes	23,500	25,450	26,410	26,155
Social Security and Medicare Taxes	7,500	7,500	7,500	7,500
Real Estate Taxes	5,000	5,000	5,000	5,000
Transportation	8,000	8,000	8,000	8,000
Medical/Dental Expenses	8,000	8,000	8,000	8,000
Debt Repayment	5,000	5,000	5,000	5,000
Housing Supplies/Maintenance	6,000	6,000	6,000	6,000
Life Insurance	8,000	8,000	8,000	8,000
Property & Liability Insurance	5,000	5,000	5,000	5,000
Current School Expenses	4,500	4,500	4,500	4,500
Total Fixed Expenses	**$120,500**	**$122,450**	**$ 123,410**	**$123,155**
Discretionary Expenses				
Vacations, Travel, and so on	$ 4,000	$ 4,000	$ 4,000	$ 4,000
Recreation/Entertainment	5,000	5,000	4,000	4,000
Contributions, Gifts	7,500	7,500	7,500	7,500
Household Furnishings	5,000	5,000	3,000	3,000
Education Fund	5,000	5,000	5,000	5,000
Savings	3,000	3,000	3,000	3,000
Investments	2,500	2,500	2,500	2,500
Other	5,000	5,000	5,000	5,000
Total Discretionary Expenses	**$ 37,000**	**$ 37,000**	**$ 34,000**	**$ 34,000**
Total Annual Expenses	**$157,500**	**$159,450**	**$157,410**	**$157,155**
Net Cash Flow	**$-4,500**	**$50**	**$5,890**	**$5,195**

*Discrepancies in totals are due to rounding.

Use in Step 6: Monitor the Plan

In addition to providing a plan for spending and investing the client's resources, a budget is a tool for monitoring the performance of the client's cash management plan. In simplest terms, the process works via the comparison of a cash flow statement showing the actual results produced by the client's cash management plan (Actual for 7/1/07 to 6/30/08 in table 5-12) with the expected results reflected in the pro forma cash flow statement (budget) contained in the client's financial plan (Pro Forma #2 in table 5-12). In the situation illustrated in table 5-12, the Klients' actual cash flow in the period July 1, 2007 to June 30, 2008 ($5,195) was somewhat less than the amount projected for the period ($5,890) due to lower rates of return having been realized from the investment of financial assets than those that were assumed in the preparation of Pro Forma #2.

By constantly monitoring the budget, the financial advisor and client can recognize problems as they occur and even anticipate them. Cash flow statements, both actual and pro forma, can be broken down on a month-by-month basis to facilitate more frequent monitoring of the performance of the client's plan for spending and investing available resources. Budgeting provides both a means of financial self-evaluation and a guideline to measure actual performance.

CHAPTER FIVE REVIEW

Key Terms and Concepts

Key Terms and Concepts are explained in the glossary.

Risk/Return Investment Pyramid	nonfinancial (personal) assets
financial position statement	cash flow management
balance sheet	cash flow analysis
cash flow statement	cash flow planning
income statement	net cash flow
pro forma	budgeting
financial assets	

Review Questions

The answers to the review questions are in the supplement. Self-test questions and the answers to them are also in the supplement and on The American College Online.

5-1. Describe the types of information about the advisor that the typical disclosure form provides to the client. [5-1]

5-2. Explain the role of projected financial statements in monitoring a client's financial plan. [5-3]

5-3.   Identify the various ways in which a client's net worth can increase during a period of time. [5-3]

5-4.   Explain why the following actions have no effect on a client's net worth:
a.   paying off a debt [5-3]
b.   buying an asset with cash [5-3]

5-5.   Identify the key components of a financial position statement and briefly explain what each component represents. [5-4]

5-6.   Distinguish financial assets from nonfinancial (personal) assets. [5-4]

5-7.   Explain how each of the following is valued for purposes of a client's personal financial position statement.
a.   assets [5-4]
b.   liabilities [5-4]

5-8.   Briefly describe how a financial position statement is used. [5-6]

5-9.   Briefly describe how a cash flow statement is used, and identify its three basic components. [5-7]

5-10.   Explain the purpose for each of the following components of cash flow management:
a.   cash flow analysis [5-7]
b.   cash flow planning [5-7]
c.   budgeting [5-7]

5-11.   With regard to the preparation of a cash flow statement
a.   describe and give examples of fixed expenses [5-7]
b.   describe and give examples of discretionary expenses [5-7]

5-12.   Explain the impact that a positive net cash flow for a given period has on a client's assets, liabilities, and net worth. [5-7]

5-13.   If a client's net cash flow is negative, what alternative courses of action are available for either increasing income or reducing expenses? [5-7]

5-14.   Describe the disadvantages associated with budgeting. [5-10]

5-15.   With regard to a client's liquidity ratio
a.   explain how it is calculated [5-11]
b.   describe how it is used by the financial advisor [5-11]

5-16.   With regard to a client's solvency ratio
a.   explain how it is calculated [5-11]
b.   describe how it is used by the financial advisor [5-11]

5-17.   With regard to a client's savings ratio
a.   explain how it is calculated [5-11]
b.   describe how it is used by the financial advisor [5-11]

5-18.   With regard to a client's debt service ratio
   a.   explain how it is calculated [5-11]
   b.   describe how it is used by the financial advisor [5-11]

NOTES

1. Brian K. Bucks, Arthur B. Kennickell, and Kevin B. Moore, "Recent Changes in U.S. Family Finances: Evidence From the 2001 and 2004 Survey of Consumer Finances," *Federal Reserve Bulletin,* vol. 92 (February 2006), p. A1–A38.
2. Bucks, p. A19.
3. For an overview of the key factors considered and the variety of valuation methods used in estimating the fair market value of a closely held business, see T. Kurlowicz, J.F. Ivers III, and J.J. McFadden, *Planning for Business Owners and Professionals* (Bryn Mawr, PA: The American College, 2007), pp. 11.2–11.30.
4. Rev. Rul. 59-60, 1959-1 C.B. 237.
5. For an explanation of the modifications made to the definition of personal savings in 1998 by the Bureau of Economic Analysis, its impact on the magnitude of the personal saving rate, and past and projected personal saving rates adjusted to include capital gains, see Satyendra Verma and Jules Lichtenstein, "In Brief—The Declining Personal Saving Rate: Is There Cause for Alarm?" AARP Public Policy Institute, Washington, DC, March 2000. Available at: http://research.aarp.org/econ/inb16_rate.html.

6

Time Value of Money: Basic Concepts and Applications

Learning Objectives

An understanding of the material in this chapter should enable the student to

6-1. Describe several basic concepts underlying the time value of money.

6-2. Calculate the future value of a single sum, and calculate the number of periods or the interest rate in future-value-of-a-single-sum problems.

6-3. Calculate the present value of a single sum, and calculate the number of periods or the interest rate in present-value-of-a-single-sum problems.

6-4. Calculate the future value of an annuity or an annuity due, and solve sinking fund problems.

6-5. Calculate the present value of an annuity or an annuity due, and solve debt service/capital-sum-liquidation problems.

6-6. Create an amortization schedule for a level payment loan, and delineate the level payment into principal and interest components.

6-7. Solve single sum and annuity problems with five values.

Chapter Outline

This chapter discusses several basic concepts that are essential to understanding the concept of money having a time value and its application to financial planning. These concepts can be divided into those involving either present values or future values. The present value concepts are the present value of a single sum (PVSS), the present value of an annuity (PVA), and the present value of an annuity due (PVAD). Future value concepts include the future value of a single sum (FVSS), the future value of an annuity (FVA), and the future value of an annuity due (FVAD). Emphasis is placed on showing how these concepts are used to solve time value of money problems in the broader context of financial planning.

This chapter explains how to solve time-value-of-money problems by using a formula or by using factors in the formula. It then shows you how to solve the problem using a financial calculator. While most financial calculators with time-value capabilities could be used to solve time-value-of-money problems, this book explains how to solve these problems by using only an HP-10BII. If you already own another financial calculator and do not want to acquire an HP-10BII, then make sure you know how to solve the various types of time-value-of-money problems with your calculator. The answers to both the review questions and self-test questions in the supplement to this text show the keystrokes for solving time-value-of-money problems for both the HP-10BII and the HP-12C. Your calculator's instruction booklet or user's guide is a good source of information about how to use it to solve time-value problems.

Although this chapter and the next one present many time-value-of-money concepts mathematically with the aid of factor tables, you should avoid becoming bogged down in the math. Instead, concentrate on recognizing the different types of problems and learning how to use an HP-10BII to solve them. With practice you should be able to roughly estimate answers before solving the problems. Learning to estimate will help you get a feel for time-value-of-money problems, and you will sometimes catch calculation errors when they vary too much from your estimate.

In those instances where the same time-value-of-money problem is solved twice, first by using a formula (with the aid of factor tables) and then by using an HP-10BII, there will be minor differences in the two answers due to rounding and decimal precision. Do not dwell on these differences as they are not important. As mentioned above, what is important in this chapter and the next one is learning how to recognize the different types of time-value-of-money problems and how to solve them with a financial calculator.

THE BASICS OF TIME VALUE

An investment requires capital today and generates the expectation that, at some point in the future, the capital will be returned along with a return on the funds invested. The riskier the investment, the higher the expected return needs to be to entice investors to invest. This risk-return trade-off is a cornerstone of finance and financial planning. Investors expect to be compensated for the risk they assume in an investment. The expected return is not always realized because if expectations are always realized, investing would be a sure thing and a sure thing does not have any risk.

Money now versus money later is an easy choice when it is the same dollar amount. Offer someone a choice between receiving a $1,000 today or a $1,000 a year from now and he or she will invariably take the money today. To get the person to wait for the money there needs to be an incentive to wait. That incentive is the return he or she can expect to receive by waiting. Investors want to be compensated for the use of their money by others over time. If they wait for the money, they incur what economists call an **opportunity cost** *opportunity cost.* The opportunity cost of an activity (in this case waiting to receive the money) is the value of the lost opportunity to engage in the best alternative activity (spending or investing the money now) with the same resource (the specified sum of money). The opportunity cost is typically expressed as a percentage rate of return.

Conversely, most people would intuitively conclude that if they must pay out a specified sum of money, they would prefer to pay it later rather than sooner. Why? Because the longer they can delay the payment, the longer they can use the money either by spending it or investing it for their own benefit. If they pay the money early, they also incur an opportunity cost. **time value of money** These differences in value over time, due to opportunity costs, relate to the **(TVM)** *time value of money (TVM).* The time value of money reflects the idea that a dollar today is worth more than a dollar received in the future.

The Role of Interest

A given sum of money due in different time periods does not have the same values, so a tool is needed in order to make the different values comparable. That tool is *interest.* Interest is a way of quantifying the **interest** opportunity cost incurred by waiting to receive money or by giving up the opportunity to delay payment.

For example, if you deposit $1,000 in a savings account and leave the funds there for one year, you expect to have more than $1,000 in the account at the end of the year. You expect the account to earn interest. By postponing your use of the money and allowing the bank to use it, you incur an opportunity cost. The bank pays interest as compensation for that loss of use.

To reverse the situation, assume a loan you took out at your bank matures in one year, at which time you are obligated to pay $10,000. If you repay the loan today, a year early, you should be required to pay less than the full $10,000. If you forgo the opportunity to delay the repayment, you should be compensated by a reduction in the amount of the repayment due.

risk-free rate The specific interest rate used to quantify opportunity cost consists of **risk premium** two components: a *risk-free rate* and a *risk premium.* At a minimum, the opportunity cost of letting someone use your money is the rate of return you could have earned by investing it in a perfectly safe investment. A reasonable measure of this minimum opportunity cost is the rate of interest available on 3-month U.S. Treasury bills. These bills are always available and, for all practical purposes, risk free.

In contrast, most situations where you allow someone else to use your money entail some risk. For example, the market value of the investment may decline. Inflation may erode the purchasing power of your principal sum. The person or organization using your funds may default on scheduled interest or principal payments. Tax laws may change lowering the after-tax return on your investment. These and other types of risk associated with letting someone else use your funds should be reflected in a risk premium, in addition to the risk-free opportunity cost of money. Theoretically, the higher the degree of risk, the greater the risk premium and, therefore, the higher the interest rate you should require.

Simple Interest Versus Compound Interest

simple interest
compound interest

There are two ways of computing interest. *Simple interest* is computed by applying an interest rate to only the original principal. *Compound interest* is computed by applying an interest rate to the sum of the original principal and the interest credited to it in previous periods. With compound interest, interest earned is added to the principal balance and also earns interest. Interest earning interest is the reason why it is called compounding.

The difference between simple and compound interest can be demonstrated with an example. Assume $1,000 is deposited in an account that earns 6 percent simple interest per year. At the end of each year, the account will be credited with $60 of interest. At the end of 5 years, there will be $1,300 in the account (if no withdrawals have been made), as shown in table 6-1.

If, instead, the account earns 6 percent compound interest per year, the deposit will grow to a larger amount than $1,300, as shown in table 6-1. The account grows to $1,338.23. The extra $38.23 in the account at the end of 5 years is the result of interest earned on previous interest earnings.

Notice the difference in the annual amount by which the account grows when compound rather than simple interest is credited. The balance grows by a constant amount, $60 per year, when simple interest is credited. In the case of compound interest, the account balance grows by an increasing amount each year because the interest is paid on the principal plus interest already earned. However, the rate of growth in the compound interest case remains the same 6 percent as in the simple interest case.

Compound interest can have a powerful impact on future value, especially when a high interest rate or a long period of time is involved. For example, in the year 1980, the consumer price index (CPI), a commonly used measure of the inflation rate, rose by 13.5 percent over the preceding year. If that rate of inflation had continued, the same bag of groceries that cost $100

TABLE 6-1
Accumulation of $1,000 in 5 Years at 6 Percent Simple and Compound Interest per Year

Year	Simple Interest			Compound Interest		
	Principal Sum	Interest	Ending Balance	Principal Sum	Interest	Ending Balance
1	$1,000	$60	$1,060	$1,000.00	$60.00	$1,060.00
2	$1,000	$60	$1,120	$1,060.00	$63.60	$1,123.60
3	$1,000	$60	$1,180	$1,123.60	$67.42	$1,191.02
4	$1,000	$60	$1,240	$1,191.02	$71.46	$1,262.48
5	$1,000	$60	$1,300	$1,262.48	$75.75	$1,338.23

at the beginning of 1980 would have cost about $355 at the beginning of 1990 and would have risen to over $2,370 by the beginning of 2005. Based on actual CPI inflation rates experienced over that time period, the groceries would have cost $158.62 in 1990, $208.83 in 2000, and $250.83 in 2007.

Most of the day-to-day situations requiring time-value-of-money calculations involve compound interest rather than simple interest. That is why this chapter and chapter 7 deal only with compound interest.

Compounding Versus Discounting

compounding

discounting

The process by which a dollar today, a present value, grows over time to a larger amount, a future value, is called *compounding*. The process by which a dollar due in the future, a future value, is reduced over time to a smaller amount today, a present value, is called *discounting*.

Figure 6-1 shows the difference between present and future value with compound interest as the link between the two. Compounding can be viewed as a movement up the curve, while discounting can be viewed as a movement down the curve. Note also that the link between present and future value in figure 6-1 is shown as a curve (and not a straight line) to reflect the application of compound interest rather than simple interest. When compound interest is used, the future value rises each year by an increasing amount as shown by moving up the curve (or the present value declines by a decreasing amount as shown by moving down the curve).

Two major factors influence the shape of the curve in figure 6-1. These are (1) the number of periods over which compounding/discounting occurs and (2) the interest rate used in the compounding/discounting process. Consequently, as the number of periods is increased, the difference between the present value and the future value also increases. Similarly, all other things being equal, the higher the interest rate, the steeper the slope of the curve. Thus, as the interest rate is increased, the difference between the present value and the future value also increases.

FIGURE 6-1
Compound Interest as the Link Between Present Value and Future Value

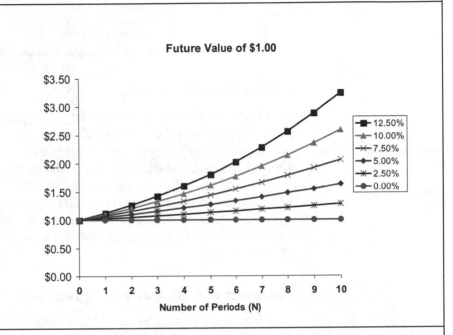

Future Value of $1.00

These lines show how time and interest rates link present and future values. Dollar amounts are reflected by the vertical axis, and the number of periods during which compounding or discounting occurs (N) is reflected on the horizontal axis. As one moves up a curve (compounding), the future value grows by increasing amounts. As one moves down a curve (discounting), the present value declines by decreasing amounts. When the interest rate is 0 percent, money has no time value and the present value is equal to the future value.

These relationships among the number of periods (N), the interest rate (i), the future value of money (FV), and the present value of money (PV) can be summarized as follows: in compounding, FV moves in the same direction as N and i (it increases as they increase); in discounting, PV moves in the opposite direction from N and i (it decreases as they increase).

Note that there are four key values in the most basic problems involving the time value of money. These values are the number of periods (N), the interest rate (i), the present value (PV), and the future value (FV). In these problems, you will be given three of the values and be called on to solve for the fourth. More complex time-value problems may include a fifth value—the value of each payment (PMT) in a series of payments.

Values in Basic TVM Problems

---

1. number of periods (n)
2. interest rate (i)
3. present value (PV)
4. future value (FV)

Effect of Income Taxes

nominal rate of return

Financial advisors must consider the impact of income taxes—federal, state, and local—on their time-value analyses. For example, the *nominal rate of return* realized on most investments should be adjusted downward to an after-tax return. Similarly, a borrower should adjust the nominal payment or interest rate on a loan downward to an effective payment or rate if the payments are deductible for income tax purposes. We have not explicitly factored tax considerations into the problems discussed in this chapter but have instead implicitly assumed that all values in the problems discussed are after-tax values.

Frequency of Compounding or Discounting

There is another factor in addition to the interest rate and the number of periods that affects the size of the present and future values of money. That factor is the frequency with which the interest rate is applied in the compounding or discounting process.

Throughout this chapter our focus will be on applying the interest rate once per year, which is called annual compounding or discounting. You should recognize, however, that in many cases interest rates are applied several times within a year—semiannually, monthly, daily, or even continuously.[1] For example, most coupon-paying bonds pay interest semiannually. Many certificates of deposit pay interest daily. Being able to solve time-value-of-money problems requires an understanding of how interest is paid on an investment.

All other things being equal, the greater the frequency with which compounding or discounting occurs, the greater the effect on the growth in future values or the decline in present values. This is explained in detail in the next chapter. In this chapter, however, assume that compounding or discounting occur on an annual basis.

Measuring the Number of Periods (Years)

Before moving on, you should keep in mind one other factor regarding the compounding or discounting process—the importance of accuracy regarding the timing of payments. Drawing time lines, such as those in figure 6-2, can be very helpful. The timing of known dollar values can be noted on the line with unknown dollar values denoted with question marks. In figure 6-2, the upper time line depicts a case in which you are to calculate the future value as of the beginning of the sixth year (which is the same as the end of the fifth year) of a deposit made at the beginning of the first year. The lower time line depicts a situation in which you are to compute the present value as

FIGURE 6-2
Time Lines as a Help in Counting the Number of Periods (Years) of Compounding or Discounting

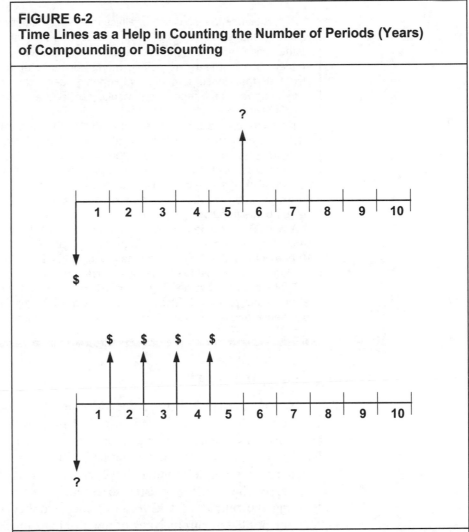

The top time line reflects a problem where a present value is deposited at the beginning of year one and you are asked to solve for the future value at the beginning of year 6, or the end of year 5. The lower time line depicts a problem where a sum of money is paid at the end of each of the next 4 years and you are asked to solve for their present value as of the beginning of year one.

of today (the beginning of year one) of a series of payments that will occur at the end of each of the next 4 years. Time lines can be constructed for all types of time-value-of-money problems, as will be shown frequently throughout this chapter and the next one.

FOCUS ON ETHICS
Ethics and the Time Value of Money

At first glance, a discussion of ethics may seem ill suited to the topic of the time value of money. After all, does not time value of money rely strictly on mathematical formulas without regard to ethical values? While it is true that mathematical formulas are neither moral nor immoral in and of themselves, it is also true that these formulas, improperly used, can lead to some extremely misleading results. These errant results can lead to decisions that are not in the client's best interests.

TVM formulas are dependent on interest-rate assumptions. Higher rates of return provide more optimistic results. In a competitive marketplace, it is not uncommon for projected yields to be a determining factor as the client weighs alternative courses of action. Time-value-of-money formulas do not know one yield from another. If a salesperson offers an exaggerated yield, the formula will provide an exaggerated result. It may be the decisive factor in leading the client into an inappropriate purchase.

A $10,000 tax-deferred investment that earns 8 percent per year will grow to $46,610 in 20 years. What if a financial advisor exaggerates the rate of return to 10 percent per year? The mathematical result is $67,275—a 44 percent increase in future value. Would this projection "close the sale"?

There is an old saying: "Figures don't lie, but liars figure." The ethical financial advisor uses projected rates of return that are fully justified in terms of historical experience and an analysis of future economic conditions.

Using an HP-10BII

To use your HP-10BII to solve TVM problems, turn it on by pressing the ON key in the lower left-hand corner of the keyboard. Many keys on the HP-10BII have more than one function. Keys that have second functions have orange printing on the bottom half of the key, and keys that have third functions have purple printing above the key. Pressing the orange shift key, ▭, causes the next key pressed to assume the function printed in orange. Pressing the purple shift key causes the next key pressed to assume the function printed in purple. None of the problems in chapters 6 or 7, however, require use of the purple shift key. Therefore, everywhere the shift key symbol ▭ appears in this textbook, it refers to the orange shift key, not the purple one.

We need to take care of several housekeeping tasks. Press the 🔲 and C ALL keys to clear any data that may have been stored earlier in your HP-10BII's memory. It is a very good idea to get into the habit of doing this every time you turn on your HP-10BII, as "trash" left over from an earlier problem can cause an incorrect answer to the problem you are now working to solve.

HP-10BII: Clearing Memory

🔲, C ALL

To set the number of decimal places displayed on your HP-10BII, press the 🔲 shift key and the DISP key (which has = printed on the top half). Then press 2, 4, or 5 to specify the number of decimal places to be displayed. All calculations in this chapter will be performed at a precision of two decimal places. Therefore, before continuing, set your HP-10BII for two decimal places.[2]

HP-10BII: Changing the Number of Decimal Places Displayed

🔲, DISP, 2 (for 2 decimal places)

Another very important housekeeping chore is to set your HP-10BII for one payment period and one compounding/discounting period per year. In chapter 7, as previously indicated, we will take up problems in which more than one payment or compounding/discounting period occurs in a year, but for now we need to keep life simple. Press 1, 🔲, and P/YR (which has PMT printed on the top half). Press 🔲 and C ALL to lock this in place. ("1P - Yr" will appear briefly on the display.) Do not change this setting until you are instructed to do so in the next chapter.

HP-10BII: Setting for One Payment Period and One Compounding Period per Year

Keystrokes	*Explanation*
1, 🔲, P/YR	one compounding period per year
🔲, C ALL	displays the number of payment periods per year

Now that the housekeeping chores are done, we will not need to discuss them again (except to remind you to clear your HP-10BII after/before every problem). We are ready to proceed to a discussion of the future value of a single sum.

FUTURE VALUE OF A SINGLE SUM

future value of a single sum (FVSS)

The most frequently encountered and easiest to understand application of the time-value-of-money concept involves the *future value of a single sum (FVSS)*. A single sum is an individual cash flow and not an annuity or series of cash flows. As explained earlier, determining the future value of a sum of money requires compounding, or increasing, the present value at some interest rate for a specified number of years. The most common example is the growth of a sum placed in an interest-bearing savings account. Recall, for example, that in table 6-1 a $1,000 deposit made today (present value) will grow to $1,338.23 (future value) at the end of 5 years at 6 percent compound interest.

Future Value of a Single Sum Formula

The basic formula for computing the future value of a single sum of money, from which all other time-value formulas are derived, is the following:

FVSS formula

$$FVSS = PVSS \times (1 + i)^n$$

where,

$$
\begin{aligned}
FVSS &= \text{the future value of a single sum} \\
PVSS &= \text{the present value of a single sum} \\
i &= \text{the compound annual interest rate expressed as a decimal} \\
n &= \text{the number of years over which compounding occurs} \\
(1 + i)^n &= \textit{FVSS factor}
\end{aligned}
$$

FVSS factor

When expressed in words, the FVSS formula requires you to add the interest rate (expressed as a decimal) to one and raise the sum to a power equal to the number of years over which compounding occurs. Then multiply the result by the present value of the single sum or deposit in question.

For example, assume that $500 is placed on deposit today in an account that will earn 9 percent compound annual interest. To what amount will this sum of money grow by the end of year 7? This problem is depicted on a time line in figure 6-3 and, as shown in the next section, can be solved using the FVSS formula.

FIGURE 6-3
Time Line Depiction of FVSS Problem

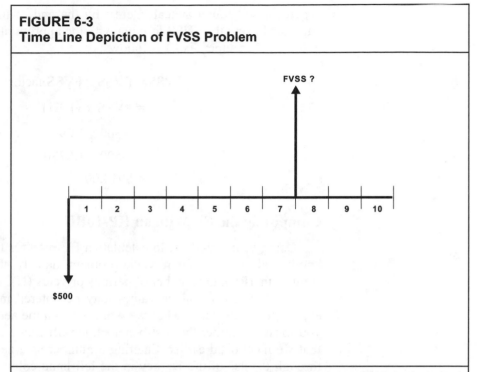

This time line depicts a problem in which a known single sum, $500, is deposited today, at the beginning of year one, and you are to calculate its future value as of the end of year seven. The time line also illustrates the basic trade-off present in all time-value-of-money problems. Here the trade-off is a cash outflow today (the deposit shown below the time line) for a larger cash inflow later (the account balance shown above the time line at the end of the seventh year).

It is important, both conceptually and mathematically, to recognize that in every time-value-of-money problem there is an implicit trade-off over time of a sacrifice for a gain or a cost for a benefit. For instance, you may be willing to loan money to a friend today (a cost or cash outflow in the present) in order to be repaid a larger amount later (a benefit or larger cash inflow in the future). Throughout the time-value-of-money discussions in this chapter and the next, the nature of this trade-off will be pointed out repeatedly. For purposes of consistency when using the time lines to depict various types of TVM problems, future values and periodic cash inflows will be shown above the line, while present values and periodic cash outflows will be shown below the line.

Using the FVSS Formula

Returning to the problem at hand, the $500 placed on deposit today represents a present value. The future value to which it will grow at

9 percent compound annual interest by the end of the seventh year can be computed using the FVSS formula with the appropriate FVSS factor (located in table F.1 in appendix F) as follows:

$$
\begin{aligned}
\text{FVSS} &= \text{PVSS x FVSS factor} \\
&= \text{PVSS x } (1+i)^n \\
&= \$500 \text{ x } 1.09^7 \\
&= \$500 \text{ x } 1.8280 \\
&= \$914.00
\end{aligned}
$$

Computing the FV With an HP-10BII

Using your HP-10BII to calculate a FV requires that you enter the three known values in the future value problem, namely, the present value of the single sum (PV), the number of periods or years (N), and the interest rate per year (I/YR). These known values may be entered in any order, as will be explained momentarily when we work through the above problem. However, you must remember the cost-benefit trade-off found in every TVM problem that we mentioned earlier. Entering a number as a negative is accomplished through the use of the +/− key in the left-hand column of the keyboard. For purposes of consistency, we will enter or display present values as negative numbers. Later we will take up problems involving periodic cash flows in or out. Periodic outflows will also be entered or displayed as negative numbers.

Take a moment to review the top row of the keyboard. The first five keys (N, I/YR, PV, PMT, and FV) as well as the +/− key and, later, the ▭ shift key, will be used to solve various types of TVM problems.

The HP-10BII employs a cash flow sign convention. This convention requires that inflows and outflows have opposite signs. This means that when a present value is entered as a negative number, the future value calculated will be displayed as a positive number. Conversely, when a present value is entered as a positive number, the future value calculated will be displayed as a negative number. To designate a number as negative, simply press the +/− (change sign) key after pressing the key for the final digit. One approach to remembering what sign to use with a cash flow is to think of inflows as being good, so enter them as positive numbers. Outflows can be viewed as bad; consequently, enter them as negative numbers.

Returning to the example we solved using the FVSS formula, assume that you want to know the amount to which a single sum of $500 will grow in 7 years at 9 percent compound annual interest. First, if you have not already done so, set your HP-10BII to display two decimal places. (We will not remind you to do this again.) Then clear its memory by pressing ▭ and C ALL. Since $500 is the sum today, enter 500, +/−, and PV. These three entries (that is, 500, +/–, and PV) are a sequence, the order of which cannot be varied when being entered. Then press 9 and I/YR (because 9 percent is the compound annual interest rate). These two entries (that is, 9 and I/YR) are a sequence, the order of which cannot be varied when being entered. Next, press 7 and N (because 7 is the number of periods or years in the problem). These two entries (that is, 7 and N) are also a sequence, the order of which cannot be varied when being entered. However, the order in which the three sequences (with each sequence representing a known value) are entered can be varied. They can be entered in any order without affecting the answer. Finally, press FV (the unknown value to be calculated) and the answer, $914.02, will appear on the display screen. This answer ($914.02) is slightly different than the answer obtained using the FVSS formula and factor tables ($914.00). However, as noted at the beginning of the chapter, this difference is due to rounding and decimal precision and can be ignored.

HP-10BII: Keystrokes for Computing the FVSS

Keystrokes	Explanation
⬛, C ALL	clearing memory
500, +/–, PV	present value
9, I/YR	interest rate
7, N	number of periods (years)
FV	914.02 displayed as FVSS

If you want to change one of the data items in the problem, you may do so without reentering all the information. For example, if you want to recalculate the same problem with an 8 percent compound annual interest rate, before clearing your HP-10BII, simply enter 8 and I/YR. Then enter FV and the new amount, $856.91, will appear on the screen.

Impact of a Change in the Interest Rate or the Number of Years

To reiterate a point made earlier in this chapter, the higher the interest rate or the greater the number of years, the larger the future value. Conversely, the lower the interest rate or the fewer the number of years, the smaller the future value. So keeping money invested longer increases its future value, as does earning a higher return on the money. Lowering the return or shortening the investment horizon has the opposite effect on money; it decreases its future value.

Rule of 72 Approximation

So far we have calculated the future value of a single sum. Being able to estimate the impact of interest on a single sum can be useful when you do not have a financial calculator handy to figure out the exact dollar value. In this situation, the Rule of 72 can be useful.

Rule of 72

The *Rule of 72* is a quick method of estimating how long it will take for a sum to double at some interest rate. The formula is

$$\frac{72}{i} = n$$

where i = the interest rate expressed as a whole number, that is, 7 percent is
    stated as 7

n = the number of years it will take a single sum earning i to double

For example, at an annual interest rate of 9 percent, a single sum of one dollar will double in value and reach $2 in approximately 8 years (72 ÷ 9). This value will double again and reach $4 in approximately another 8 years and double still again, reaching $8, at the end of approximately 8 more years. On the other hand, at a compound annual interest rate of 4 percent the growth of the single sum will be slower; it will take about 18 years (72 ÷ 4) for each doubling to occur.

A restatement of the formula will approximate the interest rate that will be required to double an amount within a certain time period. We can restate the formula by multiplying both sides of the equation by i/n to result in 72/n = i.

To illustrate, if you want to double an amount in 10 years, then you will need to invest at 7.2 percent (72 ÷ 10 = 7.2).

Remember that the Rule of 72 provides only an approximation and that for most purposes you will want to be more precise. The higher the interest rate used the less precise the result using the Rule of 72. Knowing how to use this rule often gives you a quick and easy way to double check your work when using your HP-10BII.

Solving for the Number of Periods (Years) or the Interest Rate With an HP-10BII

Sometimes both the future value and the present value are known and you need to solve for either the interest rate or the number of periods (years). As long as you know three of the four values you can compute the fourth. For example, if you are depositing $1,000 in an account paying 7.5 percent interest compounded annually and want to determine how long it will take for this account to reach $1,500, you would use the PVSS, FVSS, and i to compute the value of n. In contrast, if you want to determine what compound annual interest rate you must earn on $6,000 that you have available to invest today in order to have $10,000 in 6 years, you would use the PVSS, FVSS, and n to compute the value of i.

Although a formula can be used to solve for the number of periods (years) or the interest rate, using an HP-10BII is faster and easier. Therefore, with the aid of your HP-10BII, determine how long it would take for a $1,000 deposit to reach $1,500 when the account earns 7.5 percent compound annual interest. First, clear the HP-10BII's memory by pressing ⬛ and C ALL. Then press 7.5 and I/YR; 1000, +/–, and PV; 1500 and FV. Finally, press the N key and the answer, 5.61 years, will be displayed.

HP-10BII: Keystrokes for Computing n

Keystrokes	*Explanation*
⬛, C ALL	clearing memory
7.5, I/YR	interest rate
1000, +/–, PV	present value
1500, FV	future value
N	5.61 displayed as years

Note that the PV is entered as a negative number because the $1,000 deposit in the account is a cash outflow. The FV is a positive number because the $1,500 accumulation goal for the account is a cash inflow to the depositor.

In the second problem, you want to know the interest rate you must earn on $6,000 in order to have $10,000 in 6 years. Using your HP 10BII to solve for the unknown value, that is, the interest rate, first enter ⬛ and C ALL to clear the HP-10BII's memory. Then enter 6 and N; 6000, +/–, and PV; 10000 and FV. Finally, press I/YR and the answer will appear as 8.89 percent. (For both problems, you may enter the three known values, each represented by a sequence, in any order.)[*]

HP-10BII: Keystrokes for Computing i

Keystrokes	*Explanation*
⬛, C ALL	clearing memory
6, N	number of periods (years)
6000, +/–, PV	present value
10000, FV	future value
I/YR	8.89 displayed as interest rate

---

[*] The HP-12C will always round up to the nearest whole number in solving for n. In the example above that means that the HP-12C will return a value of 6 instead of 5.61.

Again, the PV is entered as a negative number because investing is a cash outflow.

PRESENT VALUE OF A SINGLE SUM

**present value of
a single sum
(PVSS)**

So far we have discussed compounding, that is, accumulating a known single sum of money at a compound annual interest rate over a specified number of years to determine a future value. Now, rather than moving forward in time and compounding, we will move back in time by discounting a future value to a present value. We will use an interest or discount rate to calculate the *present value of a single sum (PVSS)*. A single sum is an individual cash flow and not an annuity or series of cash flows.

For example, assume that in 4 years you will spend $100,000 to replace a piece of manufacturing equipment. How much should be set aside today to pay for that equipment if the account is expected to earn 10 percent compound annual interest? In a second example, assume that 5 years from now you will receive a $95,000 single-sum distribution from a trust. How much is that distribution worth in today's dollars if the appropriate discount rate is 7 percent per year? Both of these problems are depicted on time lines in figure 6-4.

The bottom of figure 6-4 illustrates the second problem where there is a $95,000 trust fund distribution due in 5 years. If the fund is discounted at a compound annual interest rate of 7 percent, its present value is $67,735. That is, using the PVSS formula with the appropriate PVSS factor (located in table F.2 in appendix F) to solve the problem,

$$PVSS = FVSS \times \left[\frac{1}{(1+i)^n} \right]$$

$$= \$95,000 \times \left[\frac{1}{1.07^5} \right]$$

$$= \$95,000 \times .7130$$

$$= \$67,735.00$$

Present Value of a Single Sum Formula

We learned earlier that the FVSS can be solved using the formula

$$FVSS = PVSS \times (1+i)^n$$

FIGURE 6-4
Time Line Depiction of PVSS Problems

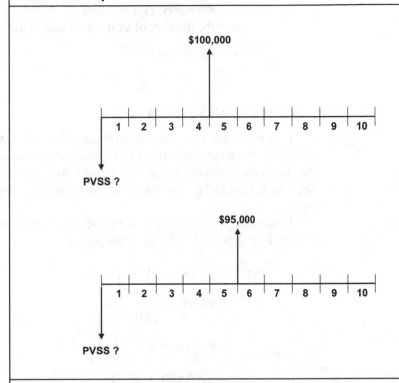

The time line on the top represents a problem in which you are asked to determine the present value of a $100,000 single sum due 4 years hence. In the time line on the bottom, the problem is to compute the PVSS when the FVSS is $95,000 due in 5 years.

By multiplying both sides of this equation by $\dfrac{1}{(1 + i)^n}$, the formula can be written as

$$\text{FVSS} \times \left[\frac{1}{(1 + i)^n}\right] = \text{PVSS}$$

or alternatively

PVSS formula

$$\text{PVSS} = \text{FVSS} \times \left[\frac{1}{(1 + i)^n}\right]$$

where,

PVSS = the present value of a single sum

FVSS = the future value of a single sum
i = the compound annual interest or discount rate
expressed as a decimal
n = the number of years over which discounting occurs

PVSS factor $\dfrac{1}{(1+i)^n} = PVSS\ factor$

Using the PVSS Formula

Using a time line, the top of figure 6-4 illustrates the problem where $100,000 is needed in 4 years to replace some manufacturing equipment. If the funds are expected to earn 10 percent compound annual interest, you will need to set aside $68,300 today in order to have the $100,000 needed in 4 years.

Using the PVSS formula with the appropriate PVSS factor (located in table F.2 in appendix F) to solve the problem,

$$PVSS = FVSS \times PVSS\ factor$$
$$= FVSS \times \left[\frac{1}{(1+i)^n}\right]$$
$$= \$100,000 \times \left[\frac{1}{1.10^4}\right]$$
$$= \$100,000 \times .6830$$
$$= \$68,300.00$$

That is, $68,300.00 accumulating at 10 percent compound annual interest will grow to the $100,000 needed in 4 years.

Computing the PV With an HP-10BII

However, instead of having to memorize the PVSS formula and use the PVSS factors to solve the two problems, use your HP-10BII to compute the present values. You know three of the four values. Have your HP-10BII solve for the fourth. Thus, to solve the first problem, clear your HP-10BII's memory. Then enter the three known values into your HP-10BII in any order (that is, enter the three sequences of 100000 and FV; 4 and N; 10 and I/YR in any order). Finally, press the PV key and the answer, $68,301.35, will appear on the display screen.

HP-10BII: Keystrokes for Computing the PVSS

Keystrokes	Explanation
▭, C ALL	clearing memory
100000, FV	future value
4, N	number of periods (years)
10, I/YR	discount interest rate
PV	−68,301.35 displayed as PVSS

The negative present value on the display screen reflects that the monies are invested today, which is a cash outflow.

To solve the second problem, first clear your HP-10BII's memory and then enter in any order the three known values (that is, enter the three sequences of 95000 and FV; 5 and N; 7 and I/YR in any order). Finally, press the PV key and the answer, $67,733.69, will appear on the display screen.

HP-10BII: Keystrokes for Computing the PVSS

Keystrokes	Explanation
▭, C ALL	clearing memory
95000, FV	future value
5, N	number of periods (years)
7, I/YR	discount interest rate
PV	−67,733.69 displayed as PVSS

Impact of a Change in the Discount (Interest) Rate or the Number of Periods (Years)

You should understand the impact on the PVSS resulting from a change in the discount rate (i) or the number of periods or years (n). The higher the discount rate, the lower the present value. The greater the number of periods or years, the lower the present value. Discounting is the stripping away of interest to arrive at the value in today's dollars. A higher discount rate or a longer investment horizon means there is more interest to be stripped away, which lowers the present value. Conversely, a lower discount rate or a shorter investment horizon means there is less interest to be stripped away, which raises the present value.

FUTURE VALUE OF AN ANNUITY OR AN ANNUITY DUE

Earlier in this chapter we explained how to compute the future value of a single sum credited with compound interest. Now we will build on and expand that case to deal with the calculation of the future value of a series of equal deposits or payments. For example, if $3,000 is deposited or paid into an account each year and is credited with 11 percent compound annual interest, how much will be in the account at the end of 6 years? The income stream is called an annuity. An *annuity* is a finite stream of equal periodic payments. A *perpetuity*, in contrast, is an infinite stream of equal periodic payments. Perpetuities are uncommon enough that they will not be discussed further in this textbook.

annuity
perpetuity

The example describes either a *future value of an annuity (FVA)* or a *future value of an annuity due (FVAD)* problem. An annuity is a series of equal payments made at the end of each period (or year) for a specified number of periods (or years). An *annuity due* is a series of equal payments made at the beginning of each period (or year) for a specified number of periods (or years).[3]

future value of an
annuity (FVA)
future value of an
annuity due (FVAD)
annuity due

There are many personal and business situations where money is invested periodically. Some businesses, for instance, enable their employees to invest deductions from each paycheck in U.S. government savings bonds. Many individuals deposit predetermined amounts each week or month in Christmas club or vacation club accounts at banks or credit unions. Many individuals deposit funds each year in Individual Retirement Accounts (IRAs) at banks, thrift institutions, brokerage firms, insurance companies, or mutual funds. Tax-advantaged employee retirement programs, like 401(k) plans or 403(b) tax-deferred annuity plans, enable employees to make periodic deposits that may also have matching employer contributions. Businesses may contribute sinking fund payments to accumulate money to purchase fixed assets.

Assumptions

To simplify the solution of FVA and FVAD problems, we will assume for now that the deposits or payments are made annually. Also, we will assume that the deposits or payments all earn the same rate of compound annual interest.

It is particularly important in annuity problems to accurately measure the length of time during which each deposit or payment earns compound interest. One possible assumption is that all deposits or payments are made at the beginning of each year (an annuity due); the other is that they are all made at the end of each year (an annuity).

For example, assume that five annual deposits of $1,000 each earn 7 percent compound annual interest. At the end of the fifth year, the future value of these equal annual deposits will be $6,153.29 if they are made at the beginning of each year versus only $5,750.74 if they are made at the end of each year. The $402.55 difference between the two future values occurs because each deposit earns one more year of interest under the FVAD than under the FVA. That is, when deposits are made at the start of each year, the first deposit earns interest for 5 years rather than 4; the second deposit earns interest for 4 years rather than 3, and so on. The last deposit earns interest for one year rather than none. (See figure 6-5 for a time line depiction.)

Using Formulas to Compute the FVA and the FVAD

A problem requiring the calculation of the future value of an annuity or annuity due can be viewed as a collection of FVSS problems. Each annuity deposit or payment can be viewed as a single sum, each of which earns compound annual interest for a different number of years. Hence, the FVA or FVAD is really the sum of a series of FVSS calculations.

To illustrate, assume that $100 is deposited at the end of each of 4 years and earns 5 percent compound annual interest. What is the total future value of these annual $100 deposits at the end of the fourth year? The first $100 deposit earns interest for 3 years (that is, from the end of year one till the end of year 4). The future value of this deposit using the FVSS formula with the appropriate FVSS factor (located in table F.1 in appendix F) is

$$\text{1st FVSS} = \text{PVSS} \times (1+i)^n$$
$$= \$100 \times 1.05^3$$
$$= \$100 \times 1.1576$$
$$= \$115.76$$

The future value of the second $100 deposit, which earns interest for 2 years, is

$$\text{2d FVSS} = \text{PVSS} \times (1+i)^n$$
$$= \$100 \times 1.05^2$$
$$= \$100 \times 1.1025$$
$$= \$110.25$$

The future value of the third $100 deposit, which earns interest for one year, is

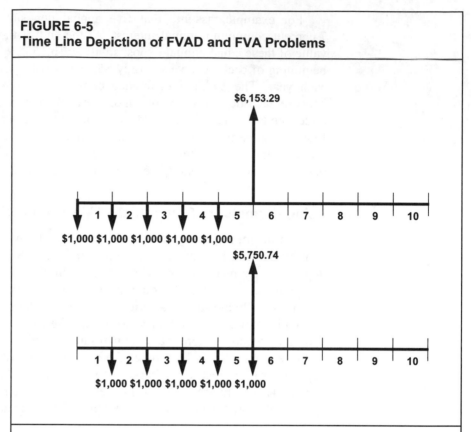

FIGURE 6-5
Time Line Depiction of FVAD and FVA Problems

The top line depicts a problem in which $1,000 deposits are made at the beginning of each of 5 years (an annuity due) and invested at 7 percent compound annual interest. The problem is to determine the future value as of the end of the fifth year. In the lower time line, the problem is the same in all respects except that all deposits are made at the end of each of the 5 years (an annuity).

$$3d \ FVSS = PVSS \times (1 + i)^n$$
$$= \$100 \times 1.05^1$$
$$= \$100 \times 1.0500$$
$$= \$105.00$$

And the future value of the fourth $100 deposit is the same as its present value because it earns no interest. Thus the FVA in this problem is $431.01 (that is, $115.76 + $110.25 + $105.00 + $100.00).

If, on the other hand, the deposits had been made at the beginning of each year, their future values would have been as follows:

$$1st \ FVSS = \$100 \times 1.05^4 = \$100 \times 1.2155 = \$121.55$$
$$2d \ FVSS = \$100 \times 1.05^3 = \$100 \times 1.1576 = \ \ \ 115.76$$

$$3d\ FVSS = \$100 \times 1.05^2 = \$100 \times 1.1025 = \quad 110.25$$
$$4th\ FVSS = \$100 \times 1.05^1 = \$100 \times 1.0500 = \quad \underline{105.00}$$
$$FVAD \qquad\qquad\qquad\qquad\qquad\qquad = \quad \underline{\$452.56}$$

For cases where the deposits are made at the end of each year, there is an alternative to the approach of summing the future values of each of the separate deposits. The same result can be achieved in one step by using the FVA formula with the appropriate FVA factor as follows:

FVA formula

$$FVA = annual\ deposit \times \left[\frac{(1 + i)^n - 1}{i} \right]$$

FVA factor

where the bracketed portion is the *FVA factor*

Because the bracketed portion of the equation is the FVA factor, the FVA formula can be written as follows:

$$FVA = annual\ deposit \times FVA\ factor$$

Using the FVA formula with the appropriate FVA factor (located in table F.3 in appendix F) to determine the future value of the deposits made at the end of each year,

$$FVA = annual\ deposit \times \left[\frac{(1 + i)^n - 1}{i} \right]$$

$$= \$100 \times \left[\frac{(1 + .05)^4 - 1}{.05} \right]$$

$$= \$100 \times 4.3101$$

$$= \$431.01$$

For cases in which the deposits are made at the beginning of each year, a modified version of the FVA formula (that is, a FVAD formula) is used. Because each deposit will be credited with one extra year of interest, it is necessary to multiply the result of the FVA formula by $(1 + i)$. That is, if deposits are made at the beginning of each year, the FVA formula is transformed into

$$FVAD = FVA\ formula \times (1 + i)$$

FVAD formula

$$\text{FVAD} = \text{annual deposit} \times \left[\frac{(1+i)^n - 1}{i}\right] \times (1+i)$$

which is the same as

$$\begin{aligned}
\text{FVAD} &= (\text{annual deposit} \times \text{FVA factor}) \times (1+i) \\
&= \$100 \times \left[\frac{1.05^4 - 1}{.05}\right] \times (1+.05) \\
&= \$100 \times 4.3101 \times 1.0500 \\
&= \$452.56
\end{aligned}$$

In other words, a simple way to calculate the FVAD is to calculate the FVA and then multiply the result by one plus the interest rate $(1+i)$.

Computing the FVA and the FVAD With an HP-10BII

As with the time-value problems discussed earlier in this chapter, an HP-10BII is a very useful tool for solving FVA and FVAD problems. Among its advantages over formulas are speed, reduced likelihood of error, and range of available values for n and i.

To use your HP-10BII to solve FVA or FVAD problems, you will be using a new key in the top row of the calculator keyboard—PMT (payment)—to reflect the fact that a series of deposits is involved rather than a single sum. Also, when solving a problem involving a series of payments or deposits, you must always remember to instruct your HP-10BII whether the payments or deposits will be made at the end of each period (FVA) or at the beginning (FVAD). This is accomplished through the use of the ▭ shift key and the BEG/END key that is in the second row.

So that your HP-10BII reflects when the payments occur in each period, press ▭ and BEG/END. If the screen displays the word BEGIN, it is set for beginning-of-year payments. If after pressing ▭ and BEG/END the screen displays no word, then it is set for end-of-year payments. If the current setting is what you want, proceed with the data entry. If the current setting is not what you want, press ▭ and BEG/END before proceeding with the data entry.

Let us return to the problem involving $100 annual deposits earning 5 percent compound annual interest over a 4-year period. If the deposits are to be made at the end of each year, check your HP-10BII to be sure that BEGIN is <u>not</u> displayed on the screen. If BEGIN is displayed, press ▭ and BEG/END to erase it. Then clear your HP-10BII's memory and enter 100, +/−, and PMT; 4 and N; 5 and I/YR. Finally, press FV and the answer, $431.01, will be displayed.

HP-10BII: Keystrokes for Computing the FVA

Keystrokes	Explanation
▭, C ALL	clearing memory
▭, BEG/END	only if BEGIN displayed
100, +/−, PMT	yearly deposit
4, N	number of payments (deposits)
5, I/YR	interest rate
FV	431.01 displayed as FVA

If the $100 deposits are to be made at the beginning of each year, check your HP-10BII to be sure that BEGIN is displayed on the screen. If BEGIN is <u>not</u> displayed, press ▭ and BEG/END to display it. Then clear your HP-10BII's memory and enter 100, +/−, and PMT; 4 and N; 5 and I/YR. Finally, press FV and the answer, $452.56, will be displayed.

HP-10BII: Keystrokes for Computing the FVAD

Keystrokes	Explanation
▭, C ALL	clearing memory
▭, BEG/END	only if BEGIN not displayed
100, +/−, PMT	yearly deposit
4, N	number of payments (deposits)
5, I/YR	interest rate
FV	452.56 displayed as FVAD

Practice is the key to learning how to use your HP-10BII so let us work through another example. Assume that a married couple deposits $5,000 today and at the start of each of the next 4 years in a savings account to accumulate funds for their young child's college education. If the account is credited with 8 percent compound annual interest, how much of a college fund will there be 5 years from now? (See figure 6-6 for a time line depiction.)

Clear your HP-10BII's memory and set it for beginning-of-year deposits (by pressing ▭ and BEG/END if BEGIN is <u>not</u> already displayed). Next,

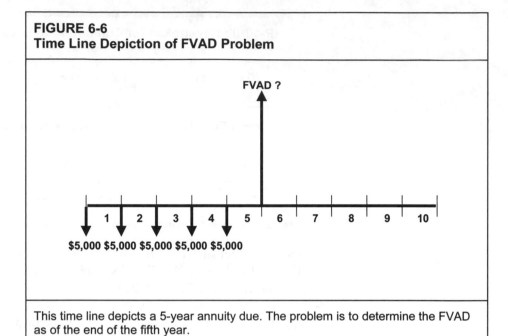

FIGURE 6-6
Time Line Depiction of FVAD Problem

This time line depicts a 5-year annuity due. The problem is to determine the FVAD as of the end of the fifth year.

enter the following information to reflect the known values: 5000, +/– (as noted earlier, deposits that represent cash outflows are treated as negative numbers), and PMT; 5 and N; 8 and I/YR. Finally, press FV and the answer, $31,679.65, should appear on the display screen. However, if the deposits are to be made at the end of each of the 5 years, the keystrokes would be identical except that you would need to set your HP-10BII for end-of-year payments. Under this new assumption, the answer displayed would be $29,333.00. You can produce this solution by pressing ▭, BEG/END and FV, rather than reentering all the information in the problem.

HP-10BII: Keystrokes for Computing the FVAD

Keystrokes	Explanation
▭, C ALL	clearing memory
▭, BEG/END	only if BEGIN not displayed
5000, +/–, PMT	annual deposits
5, N	number of payments (deposits)
8, I/YR	interest rate
FV	31,679.65 displayed as FVAD

Keystrokes for Computing the FVA Without Reentering All the Information

FVAD	31,679.65 currently displayed
Keystrokes	*Explanation*
▭, BEG/END	switches to end of year
FV	29,333.00 displayed as FVA

Alternatively you can start over.

HP-10BII: Keystrokes for Computing the FVA

Keystrokes	*Explanation*
▭, C ALL	clearing memory
▭, BEG/END	only if BEGIN displayed
5000, +/–, PMT	annual deposits
5, N	number of payments (deposits)
8, I/YR	interest rate
FV	29,333.00 displayed as FVA

Keystrokes for Computing the FVAD Without Reentering All the Information

FVA	29,333.00 currently displayed
Keystrokes	*Explanation*
▭, BEG/END	switches to beginning of year
FV	31,679.65 displayed as FVAD

When the Number of Periods (Years) Over Which Compounding Occurs Exceeds the Number of Periods (Years) in Which Deposits Are Made

Sometimes a problem is encountered in which the number of periods (years) during which compounding occurs exceeds the number of periods (years) during which deposits are made. For example, assume that $500 is to be deposited at the end of each of the next 6 years in an account earning 8 percent compound annual interest. How much will be in the account at the end of 10 years? (See figure 6-7 for a time line depiction.)

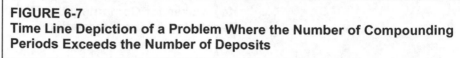

FIGURE 6-7
Time Line Depiction of a Problem Where the Number of Compounding Periods Exceeds the Number of Deposits

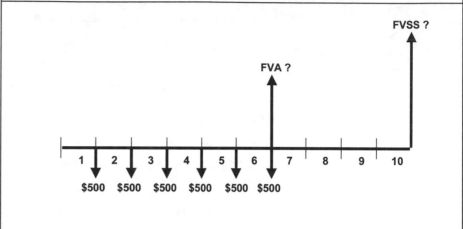

In this time line, level payments are made at the end of each of 6 years. The future value of that annuity as of the end of the sixth year is then left as a single sum to accumulate until the end of the tenth year.

This type of problem can be solved by dividing it into two separate parts and using the answer from solving the first part as an input in solving the second part. The first part of the problem involves computing the FVA; the second part of the problem involves treating the FVA as the PVSS and computing its FVSS. While the procedures for calculating the FVA and the FVSS have already been explained, solving this two-part problem not only provides an example of solving TVM problems by breaking them down into their component parts, it also provides a review of these two important future value concepts.

As previously demonstrated, the FVA can be calculated using either the FVA formula or an HP-10BII. However, because the HP-10BII is much more efficient than using the formula, it will be the only method explained here.

To solve this two-part problem using your HP-10BII, first set it for end-of-year deposits. Then find the FVA of six deposits of $500 each at 8 percent interest, which is $3,667.96. Next, clear your HP-10BII's memory and enter this amount (that is, $3,667.96) as the present value of a single sum deposited for 4 years at 8 percent compound annual interest. Solve for FV, which is $4,990.22. (Note: Chapter 7 presents a more efficient approach to solving this type of problem.)

HP-10BII: Keystrokes for Solving the Two-Part FV Problem

Part 1 Keystrokes	Explanation
⬜, C ALL	clearing memory
⬜, BEG/END	only if BEGIN displayed
500, +/–, PMT	yearly deposits
6, N	number of payments (deposits)
8, I/YR	interest rate
FV	3,667.96 displayed as FVA
Part 2 Keystrokes	**Explanation**
⬜, C ALL	clearing memory
3,667.96, +/–, PV	present value
4, N	number of periods (years)
8, I/YR	interest rate
FV	4,990.22 displayed as FVSS

Since the PV in part two of the problem was input as a negative number, your HP-10BII returns a positive number for the FVSS solution.

Solving Sinking Fund Problems With an HP-10BII

sinking fund

So far in this section we have learned how to compute the future value of a series of annual payments or deposits when the number of payments, the rate of interest, and the amount of each payment are known. Sometimes, however, the amount of the annual payment or deposit is the unknown value. This situation occurs in a *sinking fund* problem. For example, assume that a company wishes to accumulate $10,000,000 by the end of 3 years in order to retire an outstanding mortgage bond issue. The company plans to make three annual deposits into a sinking fund that will earn 9 percent compound annual interest. How large must each of the deposits be in order to reach the target amount in 3 years?

The answer to a sinking fund problem can be found by rearranging the FVA or FVAD formula and solving for the amount of the deposit. However, because the use of an HP-10BII is much more efficient than using formulas, only the HP-10BII method will be explained here.

Returning to the sinking fund problem, it is first necessary to decide whether the deposits should be made at the beginning of each year or at the end of each year. Of the two possibilities, it makes more sense to expect that the sinking fund deposits will be made at the end of each year. If they were made at the beginning of each year, the company would immediately upon receiving the $10 million bond proceeds have to make a deposit into the sinking fund.

To solve for the amount of the sinking fund deposits when they are made at the end of each year, set your HP-10BII accordingly and then clear its memory. Proceed by entering 10000000 and FV; 9 and I/YR; 3 and N. Then solve for the amount of each deposit by pressing PMT and the answer, $3,050,547.57, will be displayed.

HP-10BII: Keystrokes for Computing End-of-Year Sinking Fund Payments or Deposits

Keystrokes	Explanation
▭, C ALL	clearing memory
▭, BEG/END	only if BEGIN displayed
10000000, FV	future value
9, I/YR	interest rate
3, N	number of payments (deposits)
PMT	−3,050,547.57 displayed

Switching from end-of-year payments or deposits (an annuity) to beginning-of-year payments or deposits (an annuity due) does not require that you clear your HP-10BII's memory and input all the known values again. Instead, press ▭ and BEG/END (so that BEGIN is displayed on the screen). Then press PMT to solve for the amount of a beginning-of-year deposit, which is $2,798,667.50.

If you are not able to switch from end-of-year payments or deposits to solve for beginning-of-year payments or deposits, then you must start over and input all the known values. First, however, set your HP-10BII for beginning-of-year payments or deposits and clear its memory. Then proceed by entering 10000000 and FV; 9 and I/YR; 3 and N. Then solve for the amount of each deposit by pressing PMT and the answer, $2,798,667.50, will be displayed.

The HP-10BII solutions for PMT are negative numbers reflecting the fact that the payments or deposits are viewed as cash outflows. These payments or deposits are necessary in order to reach the target $10 million, which is considered a cash inflow, at the end of year 3.

HP-10BII: Keystrokes for Computing Beginning-of-Year Sinking Fund Payments or Deposits

Keystrokes	Explanation
▭, C ALL	clearing memory
▭, BEG/END	only if BEGIN not displayed
10000000, FV	future value
9, I/YR	interest rate
3, N	number of payments (deposits)
PMT	−2,798,667.50 displayed

Variations of the sinking fund problem include those in which the task is to compute n (the number of deposits that will be required) or i (the interest rate that must be earned on the deposits) in order to reach the target amount. Assume, for example, that you need to accumulate $10,000 for a dream vacation to Tahiti and that you can afford to save $1,200 per year beginning a year from now. If your savings earn 10 percent compound annual interest, how long will you have to wait before you can afford the trip? While you can use the annuity formulas to solve for the number of years, the HP-10BII method is a lot less cumbersome.

To use your HP-10BII to solve the problem, first clear its memory and set it for end-of-year payments. Then enter 10000 and FV; 10 and I/YR; 1200, +/ −, and PMT. Solve by pressing N for the number of years, which is 6.36 years. Rounding up, you discover that it will take you 7 years of making annual deposits to save enough money to pay cash for the dream vacation to Tahiti.

HP-10BII: Keystrokes for Computing the Number of Years in End-of-Year Sinking Fund Payment Problems

Keystrokes	Explanation
▭, C ALL	clearing memory
▭, BEG/END	only if BEGIN displayed
10000, FV	future value
10, I/YR	interest rate
1200, +/−, PMT	yearly payments
N	6.36 displayed as years

On the other hand, if you insist on waiting only 5 years before going to Tahiti with your $10,000, what compound annual interest rate must you earn on your yearly deposits? Set your HP-10BII for end-of-year payments. Then enter 10000 and FV; 1200, +/−, and PMT; 5 and N. Finally, press I/YR to obtain the shocking answer of 25.78 percent.

HP-10BII: Keystrokes for Computing the Required Return in End-of-Year Sinking Fund Payment Problems

Keystrokes	Explanation
▭, C ALL	clearing memory
▭, BEG/END	only if BEGIN displayed
10000, FV	future value
1200, +/−, PMT	yearly payments
5, N	number of payments (deposits)
I/YR	25.78 displayed as interest rate

PRESENT VALUE OF AN ANNUITY OR AN ANNUITY DUE

present value of an annuity (PVA)
present value of an annuity due (PVAD)

An earlier section of this chapter contained an explanation of how to calculate the present value of a single sum that is due or needed at some time in the future. This section deals with the question of how to compute the present value of a series of level future payments. This type of problem is a *present value of an annuity (PVA)* problem if the payments are made at the end of each year or a *present value of an annuity due (PVAD)* problem if the payments are made at the beginning of each year.

To illustrate this type of problem, assume that you have lent money to a business associate and expect to be repaid in eight annual payments of $1,000 each starting one year from now. How much would you be willing to sell the promissory note for today if you believe you can earn 6 percent compound annual interest on the money in an alternative investment? What is the present value of this 8-year annuity discounted at 6 percent?

Assumptions

As discussed earlier in the chapter, each payment is assumed to be made annually. This assumption will be dropped in the latter part of the next chapter. In addition, we need to specify whether the annuity payments are to be made at the end or at the beginning of each year. For example, an 8-year, $1,000 annuity discounted at 6 percent has a PVA of $6,209.79 versus a PVAD of $6,582.38. (See the time line depiction of these two types of problems in figure 6-8.)

FIGURE 6-8
Time Line Depiction of PVA and PVAD Problems

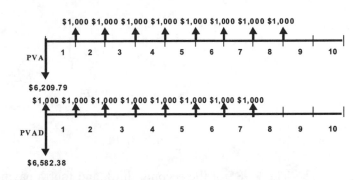

The upper time line depicts a case in which 8 annual payments of $1,000 are to be made beginning in one year, and the problem is to compute the PVA. The lower time line depicts an 8-year annuity due, in which $1,000 payments are to be made at the start of each year, and the problem is to compute the PVAD.

Using Formulas to Compute the PVA and the PVAD

The basic formula for computing the present value of a single sum can also be used to compute the present value of an annuity or an annuity due. All that is needed is to calculate the PVSS for each annuity payment separately and total the results.

For example, assume that as part of a divorce settlement a father has been ordered to deposit a lump sum in a trust account sufficient to provide child support payments for his son. The child support payments are to be $5,000 per year for 4 years, beginning one year from today. If the amount placed in the trust account is assumed to earn 7 percent compound annual interest, how much should the father place in the trust account today?

Using the formula for the PVSS described earlier in the chapter, the present value of each separate payment can be found. Once the present value of each separate payment has been calculated, the present value of the sum of all four payments can easily be determined.

Specifically, the present value of the first payment to be made one year from now can be calculated using the PVSS formula with the appropriate PVSS factor (located in table F.2 in appendix F) as follows:

$$\text{1st PVSS} = \text{FVSS x} \left[\frac{1}{(1+i)^n} \right]$$

$$= \$5{,}000 \text{ x} \left[\frac{1}{1.07^1} \right]$$

$$= \$5{,}000 \text{ x } .9346$$

$$= \$4{,}673.00$$

The PVSS of the second, third, and fourth payments would be calculated as follows:

$$\text{2d PVSS} = \$5{,}000 \text{ x} \left[\frac{1}{1.07^2} \right] = \$5{,}000 \text{ x } .8734 = \$4{,}367.00$$

$$\text{3d PVSS} = \$5{,}000 \text{ x} \left[\frac{1}{1.07^3} \right] = \$5{,}000 \text{ x } .8163 = \$4{,}081.50$$

$$\text{4th PVSS} = \$5{,}000 \text{ x} \left[\frac{1}{1.07^4} \right] = \$5{,}000 \text{ x } .7629 = \$3{,}814.50$$

The sum of these present values, the PVA, is $16,936.00 (that is, $4,673.00 + $4,367.00 + $4,081.50 + $3,814.50). This amount deposited today at 7 percent compound annual interest will be just enough to provide four annual payments of $5,000 each beginning one year from now. To verify this, examine what would happen to the account each year as that year's payment is made.

Year	Beginning Balance	Interest Earnings	Amount Withdrawn	Ending Balance
1	$16,936.00	$1,185.52	$5,000.00	$ 13,121.52
2	$13,121.52	$ 918.51	$5,000.00	$ 9,040.03
3	$ 9,040.03	$ 632.80	$5,000.00	$ 4,672.83
4	$ 4,672.83	$ 327.10	$5,000.00	($ 0.07)*

* The -.07 represents a rounding error. The ending balance must be zero. In practice the last withdrawal is adjusted to make the ending balance $0.00.

If, on the other hand, the four annual payments were to be made at the beginning of each year rather than at the end, the PVAD would be calculated by summing the four separate PVSS.

$$1st\ PVSS\ =\ \$5{,}000 \times \left[\frac{1}{1.07^0}\right]\ =\ \$5{,}000\ \times\ 1.0000\ =\ \$\ 5{,}000.00$$

$$2d\ \ PVSS\ =\ \$5{,}000 \times \left[\frac{1}{1.07^1}\right]\ =\ \$5{,}000\ \times\ .9346\ =\ \$\ 4{,}673.00$$

$$3d\ \ PVSS\ =\ \$5{,}000 \times \left[\frac{1}{1.07^2}\right]\ =\ \$5{,}000\ \times\ .8734\ =\ \$\ 4.367.00$$

$$4th\ PVSS\ =\ \$5{,}000 \times \left[\frac{1}{1.07^3}\right]\ =\ \$5{,}000\ \times\ .8163\ =\ \underline{\$\ 4{,}081.50}$$

$$PVAD\ =\ \underline{\underline{\$18{,}121.50}}$$

Note that a larger amount ($18,121.50 compared with $16,936.00) would have to be deposited in the trust account if the payments were to be made at the beginning of each year rather than at the end. This is because when payments are made at the beginning of each year, total interest earnings are lower. Each withdrawal to make a child support payment occurs a year earlier under a beginning-of-year assumption compared with an end-of-year assumption.

As an alternative to the approach of summing the present values of each of the separate payments, the same result can be achieved in one step by using the PVA formula with the appropriate PVA factor for cases where the payments are made at the end of each year:

PVA formula

$$PVA\ =\ \text{annual payment} \times \left[\frac{1 - \dfrac{1}{(1 + i)^n}}{i}\right]$$

PVA factor

where the bracketed portion is the *PVA factor*.

Because the bracketed portion of the equation is the PVA factor, the PVA formula can be written as follows:

$$PVA\ =\ \text{annual payment} \times PVA\ \text{factor}$$

Using the PVA formula with the appropriate PVA factor (located in table F.4 in appendix F) to determine the amount that needs to be deposited in the trust account in order to make the child support payments at the end of each year,

$$\text{PVA} = \$5,000 \times \left[\frac{1 - \dfrac{1}{(1+i)^n}}{i} \right]$$

$$= \$5,000 \times \left[\frac{1 - \dfrac{1}{1.07^4}}{.07} \right]$$

$$= \$5,000 \times 3.3872$$
$$= \$16,936.00$$

For cases in which the child support payments are made at the beginning of each year, a modified version of the PVA formula (that is, a PVAD formula) is used. To reflect the fact that each child support payment will earn one less year of interest before being distributed, it is necessary to multiply the result of the PVA formula by $(1 + i)$. That is, if the child support payments are made at the beginning of each year, the PVA formula is transformed into

$$\text{PVAD} = \text{PVA formula} \times (1 + i)$$

PVAD formula

$$\text{PVAD} = \text{annual payment} \times \left[\frac{1 - \dfrac{1}{(1+i)^n}}{i} \right] \times (1 + i)$$

which is the same as

$$\text{PVAD} = (\text{annual payment} \times \text{PVA factor}) \times (1 + i)$$

$$= \$5,000 \times \left[\frac{1 - \dfrac{1}{1.07^4}}{.07} \right] \times 1.07$$

$$= \$5,000 \times 3.3872 \times 1.0700$$

$$= \$18,121.52$$

Computing the PVA and the PVAD With an HP-10BII

Instead of using fairly complex formulas to calculate the PVA and the PVAD, it is much easier and quicker to use an HP-10BII. An HP-10BII can simplify the task of calculating the PVA or the PVAD and is less likely to produce mistakes.

In the child support example, set your HP-10BII for end-of-year payments. Then enter 5000, +/–, and PMT; 4 and N; 7 and I/YR. Next, press PV for the answer, which is $16,936.06.

HP-10BII: Keystrokes for Computing the PVA

Keystrokes	*Explanation*
▭, C ALL	clearing memory
▭, BEG/END	only if BEGIN displayed
5000, +/–, PMT	yearly payments
4,N	number of payments
7, I/YR	discount interest rate
PV	16,936.06 displayed as PVA

To compute the amount that needs to be in the trust account for beginning-of-year payments, simply press ▭ and BEG/END (so that BEGIN is displayed on your HP-10BII's screen). Then press PV for the answer, which is $18,121.58. There is no need to input all the known values again since they are still in your HP-10BII's memory. However, if the memory has been cleared, then the known values will have to be entered again.

HP-10BII: Keystrokes for Computing the PVAD

Keystrokes	*Explanation*
▭, C ALL	clearing memory
▭, BEG/END	only if BEGIN not displayed
5000, +/–, PMT	yearly payments
4, N	number of payments
7, I/YR	discount interest rate
PV	18,121.58 displayed as PVAD

To sharpen your skills, work through another example. Therefore, assume that several years ago the owner of a small business borrowed

$10,000 from a relative and agreed to repay the loan in 10 equal annual installments of $1,500. Today, six payments remain, the first of which is due in one year. The business owner now would like to pay off the remainder of the debt. What sum should the business owner propose to the lender as a payoff figure if money is presently earning 7 percent?

First, clear your HP-10BII's memory and set it for end-of-year payments. Then enter the following known values: 1500, +/– (because the payments are cash outflows, they are shown as negative values), and PMT (because the problem involves a series of payments, rather than a single sum); 6 and N; 7 and I/YR. The HP-10BII is now programmed to compute the PVA. Press the PV key and the answer, $7,149.81, will be displayed on the screen.

HP-10BII: Keystrokes for Computing PVA

Keystrokes	Explanation
⬛, C ALL	clearing memory
⬛, BEG/END	only if BEGIN displayed
1500, +/–, PMT	yearly payments
6, N	number of payments
7, I/YR	discount interest rate
PV	7,149.81 displayed as PVA

If the facts of the problem are revised so that the remaining six payments are to be made at the beginning of each year, your HP-10BII first has to be set for beginning-of-year payments. Then press PV and the answer, $7,650.30, will be displayed. Like the previous example, there is no need to input all the known values again because they are still in your HP-10BII's memory. However, if you cleared your HP-10BII's memory, then you will have to re-enter the known values.

HP-10BII: Keystrokes for Computing the PVAD

Keystrokes	Explanation
⬛, C ALL	clearing memory
⬛, BEG/END	only if BEGIN not displayed
1500, +/–, PMT	yearly payments
6,N	number of payments
7, I/YR	discount interest rate
PV	7,650.30 displayed as PVAD

When the Number of Periods (Years) Over Which Discounting Occurs Exceeds the Number of Periods (Years) in Which Payments Are Made

Sometimes a problem is encountered in which the number of periods (years) during which discounting occurs exceeds the number of periods (years) during which annuity payments are to be made. For example, discounting at a 7 percent compound annual interest rate, what is the present value of an income stream consisting of five annual payments of $2,000 each, the first of which will be made 3 years from now? (See the time line depiction of this type of problem in figure 6-9.)

FIGURE 6-9
Time Line Depiction of a Problem Where the Number of Discounting Periods Exceeds the Number of Payments

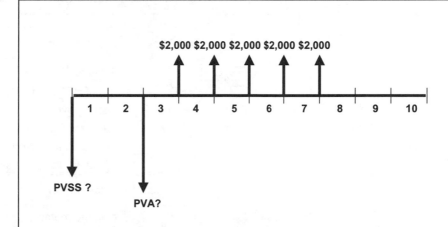

This time line depicts a case in which five annual payments of $2,000 each are to be made beginning in 3 years. The problem, which is to determine the present value of the income stream, can be divided into two parts. First, determine the present value of the annuity as of the start of the annuity period, which is the beginning of year 3. (Note: It is not the beginning of year 4, even though that is when the first payment will be made.) Then compute the present value of that single sum as of today, 2 (not 3) years earlier.

---

deferred annuity

The way to solve this type of problem, called a *deferred annuity* problem, is to divide it into two separate parts and use the answer from solving the first part as an input in solving the second part of the problem. The first part involves computing the PVA; the second part involves treating the PVA as the FVSS and computing its PVSS.

Using an HP-10BII to solve a deferred annuity problem requires that the problem be divided into two separate parts. The first part of the problem requires you to solve for the PVA of five annual payments of $2,000 each using a 7 percent discount rate. First set your HP-10BII to end-of-year payments. Then enter 2000, +/−, and PMT; 5 and N; 7 and I/YR. Then press PV for the answer, $8,200.39, which is the PVA.

The second part of the problem requires you to use the answer, $8,200.39, from the first part (that is, the PVA) as the FVSS 2 years from now and compute its PVSS by discounting it at 7 percent. First be sure to clear your HP-10BII's memory before proceeding. Then enter 8200.39 and FV; 2 and N; 7 and I/YR. Next, press PV to calculate the answer, which is $7,162.54. In other words, $7,162.54 is the present value of an income stream consisting of five annual payments of $2,000 each, the first of which will be made 3 years from now. (Note: Chapter 7 presents a more efficient approach to solving this type of problem.)

HP-10BII: Keystrokes for Solving the Two-Part PV Problem

Part 1 Keystrokes	Explanation
▭, C ALL	clearing memory
▭, BEG/END	only if BEGIN displayed
2000, +/−, PMT	yearly payments
5, N	number of payments
7, I/YR	discount interest rate
PV	8,200.39 displayed as PVA
Part 2 Keystrokes	**Explanation**
▭, C ALL	clearing memory
8200.39, FV	future value
2, N	number of periods (years)
7, I/YR	interest rate
PV	−7,162.54 displayed as PVSS

Note that the same result can also be achieved if the first part of the problem is viewed as calculating the PVAD and the second part as discounting it as a single sum for 3 additional years. (Re-examine figure 6-9 to verify that a 5-year PVA discounted for an additional 2 years is identical to a 5-year PVAD discounted for an additional 3 years.)

Solving Debt Service/Capital-Sum-Liquidation Problems With an HP-10BII

Thus far we have discussed how to compute the present value of a stream of equal annual payments when the number of payments, the discount rate of interest, and the amount of each payment are known. Sometimes, however, the amount of the annual payments (PMT) is the unknown value. A frequently encountered problem of this type involves determining the amount of the annual payments required in order to retire a debt. Likewise, a similar problem involves determining the amount of the annual withdrawals from a pool of capital in order to liquidate it over a given number of years.

In installment loans, like those used to finance the purchase of automobiles, each annual payment, called the debt service consists of some repayment of the principal and some payment of interest on the remaining unpaid principal. (In reality, most installment loans call for monthly payments. However, as indicated earlier in this chapter, we assumed that all periodic payments or deposits are made annually. The method for computing more frequent payments or deposits will be explained in chapter 7.) Given the initial size of the loan, the discount rate of interest, and the number of annual payments to be made, the problem is to compute the amount of each **debt service problem** required payment. A *debt service problem* can be solved in a manner analogous to that used for solving sinking fund problems as explained earlier, though here we are dealing with the PVA or the PVAD rather than the FVA or the FVAD.

For example, assume that in a negligence case a jury awards $125,000 to support a 10-year-old injured child until the child reaches age 21. How much will this capital sum provide for the child each year over the next 11 years if the fund earns 8 percent compound annual interest?

Although the answer can be found by rearranging the PVA formula and solving for the amount of the payment, that procedure is complex and unwieldy when compared with using an HP-10BII. Hence, only the HP-10BII method is explained here.

You can solve the problem with your HP-10BII by setting it for beginning-of-year payments and clearing its memory. Beginning-of-year payments are selected because when a jury awards support for an injured person, that person needs some of the support money immediately. Thus, the first payment will be made now (while the child is age 10) and the last payment will be made when the child is age 20, for a total of 11 payments. The last payment should support the child until he or she reaches age 21. To proceed, enter 125000, +/–, and PV; 11 and N; 8 and I/YR into your HP-10BII. Then press PMT to determine that the amount of each support payment is $16,212.54.

HP-10BII: Keystrokes for Computing Beginning-of-Year Payments in Debt Service and Capital-Liquidation Problems

Keystrokes	Explanation
⬛, C ALL	clearing memory
⬛, BEG/END	only if BEGIN not displayed
125000, +/–, PV	original capital amount
8, I/YR	interest rate
11, N	number of payments
PMT	16,212.54 displayed as payment

Variations of the foregoing problem are problems in which the task is to compute n, the number of years that payments will be made, or i, the interest rate that needs to be charged.

For example, assume that a company plans to borrow $200,000 to expand its fleet of delivery vans. If the financial officer believes the company can afford to make loan payments of $55,000 per year beginning one year from now, and if the lending institution is quoting an interest rate of 10.5 percent, how long will it take the company to repay the loan?

Set your HP-10BII for end-of-year payments and clear its memory. Then enter 200000 and PV; 55000, +/–, and PMT; 10.5 and I/YR. Finally, press N to find out how long it will take the company to repay the loan. The answer

HP-10BII: Keystrokes for Computing the Required Number of End-of-Year Payments in a Debt Service or Capital-Liquidation Problem

Keystrokes	Explanation
⬛, C ALL	clearing memory
⬛, BEG/END	only if BEGIN displayed
200000, PV	original loan amount
55000, +/–, PMT	yearly loan payments
10.5, I/YR	interest rate
N	4.82 displayed as years

displayed is 4.82 years, which assumes that in the final year a fraction of a year's interest is paid as well as a fraction of a full year's loan payment.

However, if the financial officer believes the company must have the loan repaid in 4 years but cannot afford higher annual payments, what interest rate must he or she obtain from the lending institution to accomplish this objective? Set your HP-10BII for end-of-year payments and clear its memory. Then enter 200000 and PV; 55000, +/–, PMT; 4 and N. Finally, press I/YR to find that the interest rate is 3.92 percent.

It is not realistic to think that the company has enough negotiating power with the lending institution to reduce the loan interest rate from 10.5 percent to 3.92 percent. It may have more success in negotiating a lower purchase price for the vans or extending the loan term beyond 4.82 years.

HP-10BII: Keystrokes for Computing the Interest Rate in a Debt Service or Capital-Liquidation Problem With End-of-Year Payments

Keystrokes	Explanation
▭, C ALL	clearing memory
▭, BEG/END	only if BEGIN displayed
200000, PV	original loan amount
55000, +/–, PMT	yearly loan payments
4, N	number of payments
I/YR	3.92 displayed as interest rate

CREATING AN AMORTIZATION SCHEDULE

amortization schedule

Another useful calculation in connection with debt service problems is to generate an *amortization schedule*. In any installment loan, as previously indicated, a portion of each payment is used to pay interest while the rest is applied to reduce the loan principal. Over the term of a loan, the portion of each payment used to pay interest declines while the portion used to reduce loan principal increases. An amortization schedule shows the portion of each payment that is applied toward interest and principal.

For example, assume that a $1,000 loan with a compound annual interest rate of 11 percent is to be repaid in four equal annual installments of $322.33 beginning one year from now. How much of each payment will be applied to interest and how much to principal?[4]

	(1)	(2)	(3)	(4)	(5)
Year	Unpaid Balance, Beg. of Year	Payment, End of Year	Interest Payment i x (1)	Principal Payment (2) – (3)	Unpaid Balance, End of Year (1) – (4)
1	$1,000.00	$322.33	$110.00	$212.33	$787.67
2	787.67	322.33	86.64	235.69	551.98
3	551.98	322.33	60.72	261.61	290.37
4	290.37	322.33	31.94	290.39	(.02)

TABLE 6-2
Loan Amortization Schedule

If you are preparing an amortization schedule manually, you should set up a worksheet with column headings as shown in table 6-2. After inserting the initial loan amount and the first year's payment, calculate the first year's interest by multiplying the 11 percent interest rate by the loan amount. This produces the figure for column (3). The balance of the payment shown in column (4) is principal and is subtracted from the initial loan amount to produce the unpaid balance at the end of the first year in column (5). This amount is also the unpaid balance at the beginning of the second year in column (1). Again, 11 percent of this amount is the second year's interest in column (3). The balance of the payment in column (4) is principal, which is subtracted from the unpaid balance at the beginning of year 2 in column (1) to produce the unpaid balance at the end of year 2 in column (5). This process is repeated through the end of the fourth and final year of the loan.

Rather than doing it manually, however, it is easier and quicker to set up an amortization schedule with your HP-10BII. Using the $1,000 loan example to demonstrate how, first set your HP-10BII for end-of-year payments and clear its memory. Then enter the loan specifics: 4 and N; 11 and I/YR; 1000 and PV. Next press PMT to obtain the yearly payment amount of $322.33. This figure is displayed as a negative number because it is a cash outflow. Then press ▭ and AMORT (located on the bottom half of the FV key) and the screen will display 1–1, indicating that the first year's payment will be broken down into its components. Next press = to display the first year's principal payment. Press = again to display the first year's interest payment. Again press = and this time the end of the first year's balance will be displayed. This process is repeated for the second-, third-, and fourth-year column breakdowns. That is, press ▭ and AMORT and then press = three times, making sure you read the screen display each time = is pressed.

HP-10BII: Calculating All Values in an Amortization Schedule

Keystrokes	Explanation
▭, C ALL	clearing memory
▭, BEG/END	only if BEGIN displayed
4, N	number of payments
11, I/YR	interest rate
1000, PV	original loan amount
PMT	–322.33 displayed as payment
▭, AMORT	1–1 displayed
=	–212.33 first-year principal payment
=	–110.00 first-year interest payment
=	787.67 end-of-first-year balance
▭, AMORT	2–2 displayed
=	–235.69 second-year principal payment
=	–86.64 second-year interest payment
=	551.98 end-of-second-year balance
▭, AMORT	3–3 displayed
=	–261.61 third-year principal payment
=	–60.72 third-year interest payment
=	290.37 end-of-third-year balance
▭, AMORT	4–4 displayed
=	–290.39 fourth-year principal payment
=	–31.94 fourth-year interest payment
=	–.02 ending balance

Note: The final year principal payment usually differs from the previous year's ending balance because of a rounding error in calculating payments. Typically, the last payment is reduced so that the ending balance is zero.

An alternative approach to setting up an amortization schedule is similar to the one just described. It provides flexibility for looking at individual years without having to look at all the years that precede it. As before, the keystrokes for the $1,000 loan example begin with setting your HP-10BII for end-of-year payments and clearing its memory. Then, as before, enter the loan specifics: 4 and N; 11 and I/YR; 1000 and PV. Next, as before, press PMT to obtain the yearly payment amount of $322.33. Then enter the number for the amortization year you want to view (such as 3), INPUT, ▭, and AMORT and 3–3 will be displayed. Next press = three times, each time displaying a different set of information.

HP-10BII: Calculating Specific Values in an Amortization Schedule

Keystrokes	Explanation
▭, C ALL	clearing memory
▭, BEG/END	only if BEGIN displayed
4, N	number of payments
11, I/YR	interest rate
1000, PV	original loan amount
PMT	–322.33 displayed as payment
3, INPUT, ▭, AMORT	3–3 displayed
=	–261.61 third-year principal payment
=	–60.72 third-year interest payment
=	290.37 end-of-third-year balance

Your HP-10BII can easily calculate the total principal paid and total interest paid for a user-specified interval in an amortized loan. In the case of the $1,000 loan, simply enter 1000 and PV; 4 and N; 11 and I/YR. Then press PMT to calculate the yearly payment, which is displayed as –322.33 because it is a cash outflow. Next, enter the number representing the first year of the time frame being evaluated (such as 1), INPUT, the number representing the last year of the time frame (such as 4), ▭, and AMORT. Then press = and the display will show the total principal paid during the specified time frame, which is $1,000.02 for this example. Finally, press = again and the display will show the total interest paid during the specified time frame, which in the example is $289.30.

HP-10BII: Calculating Principal Paid and Interest Paid for a User-Specified Time Interval in an Amortized Loan

Keystrokes	Explanation
⬜, C ALL	clearing memory
⬜, BEG/END	only if BEGIN displayed
1000, PV	original loan amount
4, N	number of payments
11, I/YR	interest rate
PMT	−322.33 displayed as payment
1, INPUT, 4,⬜, AMORT	1–4 displayed
=	−1,000.02 total principal paid
=	−289.30 total interest paid

As an exercise, compute the total principal and total interest paid at the end of the third year for the 4-year loan. Your answer should be $709.63 for total principal paid and $257.36 for total interest paid.

SOLVING OTHER SINGLE SUM AND ANNUITY PROBLEMS WITH AN HP-10BII

Earlier in this chapter we noted that most TVM problems involve four values, although sometimes they involve five. In any event, the task is to solve for the unknown value whether the total number of values is four or five. For example, a problem might involve an initial deposit of $1,000 into a savings account, annual deposits of $300 at the end of years one, 2, and 3, and compound annual interest earnings of 7 percent on all the deposits. The task might be to compute the account balance at the end of the third year. Problems such as these are simply combinations of the types of problems we have already been solving. To illustrate, the preceding problem is made up of a FVSS problem ($1,000 for 3 years at 7 percent) and a FVA problem ($300 at the end of each year for 3 years at 7 percent).

To solve this problem with your HP-10BII, clear its memory and set it for end-of-year payments. Then enter 1000, +/−, and PV; 300, +/−, and PMT; 3 and N; 7 and I/YR. Then solve for FV, which should be $2,189.51.

HP-10BII: Keystrokes for Solving a FV Problem

Keystrokes	Explanation
🔲, C ALL	clearing memory
🔲, BEG/END	only if BEGIN displayed
1000, +/–, PV	present value
300, +/–, PMT	yearly deposits
3, N	number of payments (deposits)
7, I/YR	interest rate
FV	2,189.51 displayed

A frequent situation calling for the calculation of an unknown fifth value when there are four known values is the computation of a bond's yield to maturity. For example, what is the yield to maturity of a $1,000 face amount bond, currently selling for $920, that will mature in 6 years and, in the meantime, will pay $80 of interest at the end of each year? Using your HP-10BII, first clear its memory and then set it for end-of-year payments. Then enter 1000 and FV; 920, +/–, and PV; 6 and N; 80 and PMT. Finally, press I/YR to solve for the bond's yield to maturity, which is 9.83 percent.

HP-10BII: Keystrokes for Computing Yield to Maturity of a Bond

Keystrokes	Explanation
🔲, C ALL	clearing memory
🔲, BEG/END	only if BEGIN displayed
1000, FV	bond face amount
920, +/–, PV	current bond price
6, N	number of years (payments) to maturity
80, PMT	yearly interest payments
I/YR	9.83 displayed as yield to maturity

TIME VALUE OF MONEY APPENDIXES

This chapter has three appendixes to assist you in understanding the time value of money. Appendix F, referred to several times in the chapter, is composed of four TVM factor tables (that is, one table each for the FVSS, the PVSS, the FVA, and the PVA) that are designed to help you solve TVM problems using mathematical formulas.

A second appendix, appendix G, is designed to help you recognize various TVM problems you may encounter. Recognizing the structure of a TVM problem helps the experienced advisor "guesstimate" an answer. However, even a novice can detect an error in calculations by understanding basic concepts. This appendix is valuable for solving TVM problems using either the math formulas or an HP-10BII.

Appendix H is even more relevant in learning how to use an HP-10BII financial calculator to solve TVM problems. It shows keystrokes for solving selected TVM problems. Reviewing the keystrokes for each type of problem will help you learn how to translate a TVM problem into a problem that you can easily solve with your HP-10BII.

CHAPTER SIX REVIEW

Key Terms and Concepts
Key Terms and Concepts are explained in the glossary.

opportunity cost	perpetuity
time value of money (TVM)	future value of an annuity (FVA)
interest	future value of an annuity
risk-free rate	due (FVAD)
risk premium	annuity due
simple interest	FVA formula
compound interest	FVA factor
compounding	FVAD formula
discounting	sinking fund
nominal rate of return	present value of an annuity (PVA)
future value of a single sum (FVSS)	present value of an annuity
FVSS formula	due (PVAD)
FVSS factor	PVA formula
Rule of 72	PVA factor
present value of a single	PVAD formula
sum (PVSS)	deferred annuity
PVSS formula	debt service problem
PVSS factor	amortization schedule
annuity	

Review Questions

The answers to the review questions are in the supplement. Self-test questions and the answers to them are also in the supplement and on The American College Online.

6-1.   You have received a bill for services rendered, and the invoice requests that you pay within 30 days. Should you pay the bill immediately on receipt or wait until the end of the 30 days? [6-1]

6-2.   To what amount would $1,000 grow by the end of 3 years if it earned
a.   10 percent simple interest? [6-2]
b.   10 percent compound interest? [6-2]

6-3.   Draw a time line depicting each of the following problems:
a.   What amount will a deposit of $X made at the end of year one grow to by the beginning of year 7? [6-2]
b.   What is the present value at the beginning of year one of a sum of $Y due to be received at the end of year 4? [6-2]

6-4.   The FVSS formula for calculating the future value of a $5,000 single sum for a particular number of years and a particular interest rate can be represented as $5,000 x 1.07^6. What compound annual interest rate is being used, and how many years of compounding are involved? [6-2]

6-5.   How is the future value of a single sum (FVSS) affected by
a.   the interest rate used in the calculation? [6-2]
b.   the number of years used in the calculation? [6-2]

6-6.   Frank received $7,020 from his grandmother on his 10th birthday. The money was invested and has been earning 10 percent interest for the last 8 years.
a.   How much money should be in Frank's account? [6-2]
b.   How much interest did Frank earn from his 10 percent investment over the 8 years? [6-2]
c.   How much money would be in Frank's account if the money had been deposited in a 5 percent savings account? [6-2]
d.   How much interest would have been earned at the 5 percent interest rate? [6-2]
e.   Was the amount of interest earned exactly twice as much when the interest rate was 10 percent rather than 5 percent? [6-2]

6-7.   Lyle has an opportunity to work overseas for 5 years. He is trying to decide whether to keep his house or sell it and invest the money. If he sells the house, he will have the net sales proceeds of $100,000 to invest after paying $10,000 in selling expenses on the sale.
a.   The current market value of the house is $110,000 and its value is expected to increase 4 percent each year over the next 5 years. What will the house sell for after 5 years if 4 percent growth is correct? [6-2]

      b. How much will the $100,000 net sale proceeds be worth after 5 years if they are invested at 9 percent compound interest? [6-2]

6-8. At a 5 percent compound annual interest rate, approximately how long will it take for a $1,000 single sum to grow to $2,000 according to the Rule of 72? [6-2]

6-9. Approximately what rate of compound annual interest must be earned in order for a $100 single sum to grow to $300 in 10 years? [6-2]

6-10. Your personal net worth has risen in the past 4 years from $110,000 to $260,000 due to your shrewd investing. What has been the compound annual rate of growth of your net worth during this period? [6-2]

6-11. A real estate appraiser has advised you that the value of the homes in your neighborhood has been rising at a compound annual rate of about 6 percent in recent years. On the basis of this information, what is the value today of the home you bought 7 years ago for $119,500? [6-3]

6-12. According to the Rule of 72, approximately how long will it take for a sum of money to double in value if it earns a compound annual interest rate of 4 percent? [6-3]

6-13. Although you have made no deposits or withdrawals from your emergency fund savings account at the bank, the account balance has risen during the past 3 years from $15,000 to $17,613.62.
      a. What has been the compound annual interest rate that the bank has been crediting to your account? [6-3]
      b. At that rate, how many more years will be needed until your account balance reaches $20,000? [6-3]

6-14. The factor for calculating the present value of a single sum for a particular number of years and discount rate can be represented as

$$\frac{1}{1.11^7}$$

What discount rate is being used, and how many years of discounting are involved? [6-3]

6-15. How is the present value of a single sum (PVSS) affected by
      a. the discount rate used in the calculation? [6-3]
      b. the number of years used in the calculation? [6-3]

6-16. Steve invested the proceeds from the sale of his business in an investment that pays no current income to him. This investment will provide him with $60,000 when it matures in 9 years.
      a. What is the present value of $60,000 when discounted at 8 percent for the 9 years? [6-3]

b. Immediately after making the investment, Steve decided to purchase another business. However, he needs the funds he just invested. His friend Paul will buy the investment at a price that yields 10 percent on his investment. How much will Paul pay for the investment? [6-3]

6-17. Assume that you owe $10,000 and that it is to be repaid in a lump sum at the end of 5 years. If the lender is willing to accept $6,000 today in full settlement of the loan, what annual rate of return (discount) is the lender effectively offering you? [6-3]

6-18. How many years will it take $10,000 to grow to $25,000 at a rate of 9 percent? [6-3]

6-19. There is an attractive piece of undeveloped land that you are considering purchasing. You think that in 5 years it will sell for $30,000. What would you pay for it today if you want to earn a compound annual rate of return of 12 percent on your investment? [6-3]

6-20. You hope to accumulate $45,000 as a down payment on a vacation home in the near future.
a. If you can set aside $38,000 now in an account that will be credited with 8 percent compound annual interest, how long will it take until you have the needed down payment? [6-3]
b. What if you can get 9 percent per year on your money? [6-3]

6-21. Draw a time line depicting a problem in which you are to calculate the future value of
a. an annuity of $100 per year for 5 years [6-4]
b. an annuity due of $200 per year for 4 years [6-4]

6-22. Using a compound annual interest rate of 12 percent, calculate the future value of
a. an annuity of $100 per year for 5 years [6-4]
b. an annuity due of $100 per year for 4 years [6-4]

6-23. Sally is contributing $2,000 each year to her individual retirement account (IRA). She makes her deposits at the end of the year. How much will she have in the IRA after
a. 10 years, if the account earns 8 percent compound interest every year? [6-4]
b. 8 years, if the account earns 7 percent compound interest every year? [6-4]

6-24. What is the future value of an annuity due of $1,500 per year for 17 years at 11.5 percent interest? [6-4]

6-25. Tracy wants to buy a house for her grandson when he finishes college 10 years from now. In the following situations, calculate how much money

Tracy will have to set aside each year, beginning one year from now, in order to have $30,000 for a down payment when her grandson graduates.
   a.   The annual contributions earn 8 percent interest each year. [6-4]
   b.   Tracy assumes a 5 percent interest rate. [6-4]

6-26.   You have decided that, beginning one year from now, you are going to deposit your $1,200 annual dividend check in a savings account at the credit union to build up a retirement fund. The account will be credited with 6 percent compound annual interest.
   a.   If you plan to retire 18 years from now, how much will be in the account at that time? [6-4]
   b.   If you should decide to retire 3 years earlier than that, how much will be in the account? [6-4]
   c.   How much would be in the account if you contributed at the beginning of each year instead of waiting a year to start contributing to the account and still retired 3 years earlier? [6-4]

6-27.   The round-the-world trip you and your spouse intend to take on your 25th wedding anniversary, 6 years from now, will cost $22,000.
   a.   How much should you set aside each year, beginning today, to reach that objective if you can earn 9 percent compound annual interest on your money? [6-4]
   b.   How will the size of the annual deposit be affected if you can earn only 8 percent compound annual interest? [6-4]

6-28.   You have just started a program of depositing $2,000 at the beginning of each year in an education fund account for your newborn son. How much will be in the account
   a.   after 11 years, if it earns 8.5 percent compound annual interest? [6-4]
   b.   after 13 years, if it earns 8.5 percent compound annual interest? [6-4]

6-29.   Mary receives $5,000 each year from a trust. She is interested in obtaining a cash sum for the down payment on a house. Mary's cousin is willing to pay Mary the present value of the next seven trust payments (the next payment will occur one year from now) discounted at 9 percent interest if Mary will pay her the seven trust payments.
   a.   How much can Mary receive from her cousin for the down payment? [6-5]
   b.   How much can Mary receive if she convinces her cousin to discount the seven trust payments at 7 percent interest? [6-5]

6-30.   A bank is willing to lend $20,000 for a home improvement loan to be repaid annually over 5 years based on 7 percent interest. What is the amount of each level payment required to repay the loan? [6-5]

6-31. A company leases an office building you own for $25,000 each year. The next rental payment is due in one year.
  a. For what lump-sum amount would you today sell the next three payments if you could invest the proceeds at a 12.5 percent compound annual rate of return? [6-5]
  b. If the next rental payment is due later today, what amount would you sell the payments for? [6-5]

6-32. Which would you prefer to have: $10,000 today in a lump sum or $1,000 per year for 13 years, beginning one year from now, if your opportunity cost is
  a. 4 percent? [6-5]
  b. 6 percent? [6-5]

6-33. The account in which you deposited your inheritance has a present balance of $48,000. If the account is credited with 10 percent compound annual interest and if you plan to withdraw $7,500 from it per year beginning one year from now, how long will it be before the balance is zero? [6-5]

6-34. Suppose that a bank will lend you $10,000 if you agree to repay $4,000 at the end of each of the next 3 years. What compound annual interest rate is the bank charging you? [6-5]

6-35. A bank is willing to lend you $15,000 to make some home improvements. The loan is to be repaid in five equal annual installments, beginning one year from now. If the interest rate on the loan is 8 percent,
  a. what will be the size of the annual payment? [6-6]
  b. how much of the second payment will be interest? [6-6]
  c. how much of the final payment will be principal? [6-6]

6-36. If you deposit $1,100 in your bank account today, and add deposits of $600 to it at the end of each of the next 9 years, and if all your deposits earn 6 percent compound annual interest, how much will be in your account immediately after you make the last deposit? [6-7]

6-37. A bond with a $1,000 face value matures in 15 years and pays $80 in annual interest. If the bond's yield to maturity (discount rate) is 9 percent, what is the current value of the bond? what will be the size of the annual payment? [6-7]

NOTES

1. Practical applications of continuous compounding are so infrequent that the topic is not discussed further in this textbook.
2. A note about precision in calculations—when the answer is a dollar value, then rounding to the nearest penny (that is, two decimal places) is appropriate. However, calculations using interest rates or solving for an interest rate may require greater precision than two decimal places. The common unit of measure for interest rates is a basis point, which is 1/100th of a

percentage point. One basis point is represented in decimal form as .0001. Twenty basis points is expressed as .0020 or 20 bps. To be able to round to the nearest basis point requires that your HP-10BII be set for five decimal precision. Therefore, there will be instances in chapter 7 when we will have you adjust your HP-10BII to four or five decimal precision.

3. In some fields, such as insurance, the terms *annuity* and *annuity due* are used to refer to a series of payments, the value of which includes both compound interest and mortality factors. Such annuities are more accurately referred to as life annuities or life annuities due.

4. The procedure for creating an amortization schedule where the loan is repaid through monthly installment payments is the same as described in this chapter except that (a) the figure used as the periodic payment should be the monthly payment, (b) the figure used as the interest rate should be the annual rate divided by 12, and (c) the number used as the N should be the total number of monthly payments to be made. Payments more frequent than annual payments will be introduced in chapter 7.

7

Time Value of Money:
Advanced Concepts and Applications

Learning Objectives

An understanding of the material in this chapter should enable the student to

---

7-1. Calculate the present value of a series of uneven cash flows.

7-2. Calculate the present value of a series of cash flows that grow by a constant percentage.

7-3. Calculate the future value of a series of uneven cash flows.

7-4. Calculate the future value of a series of cash flows that grow by a constant percentage.

7-5. Compute the net present value (NPV) of an investment project.

7-6. Compute the internal rate of return (IRR) on an investment project.

7-7. Solve several types of time-value problems when compounding or discounting occurs more frequently than annually.

Chapter Outline

After a thorough grounding in the basics of time value of money in chapter 6, you should be ready for more advanced concepts and applications. These include understanding uneven cash flows; evaluating investments using discounted cash flow analysis; and increasing the compounding, discounting, or payment frequency. While the mechanics of using your HP-10BII to solve these advanced problems are more complex than those described in chapter 6, the general strategy remains the same. You enter the known values of a problem and solve for the unknown value.

DEALING WITH UNEVEN CASH FLOWS

Chapter 6 described calculations for the present value and future value of a single sum and for the present value and future value of an annuity or an annuity due. The annuity discussion in that chapter dealt only with equal, regular payments on an annual basis. This chapter describes calculations for the present value and future value of a stream of uneven or irregular payments on an annual basis. (Uneven cash flows that occur other than annually are not dealt with in this textbook.) You will see that these calculations are useful for problems that financial advisors frequently encounter, such as college funding or evaluating investments.

Present Value of Uneven Cash Flows

Assume, for example, that a young man will be entering college in one year. The estimated tuition is $6,000 to be paid at the start of the freshman year, $6,700 at the start of the sophomore year, $7,300 at the start of the junior year, and $8,200 at the start of the senior year. How much would a client need to set aside today in an account earning 8.5 percent compound interest in order to pay the four tuition payments as they come due? In other words, what is the present value of this series of uneven cash flows at an 8.5 percent discount rate?

Using the PVSS and the PVA Formulas to Compute the Present Value of Uneven Cash Flows

As described in the previous chapter, the formula for calculating the present value of each of the future tuition payments is the present value of a single sum (PVSS) formula with the appropriate PVSS factor (located in table F.2 in appendix F). The PVSS formula is

$$PVSS = FVSS \times \left[\frac{1}{(1+i)^n} \right]$$

where the bracketed portion of the equation is the PVSS factor.

Because the bracketed portion is the PVSS factor, the PVSS formula can be written as

$$PVSS = FVSS \times PVSS\ factor$$

The solution to the tuition problem using the PVSS formula with the appropriate PVSS factor is actually a five-step process. The first four steps involve finding the present value of each year's tuition payment. Step five, which provides the answer, requires you to sum the present values computed in the first four steps.

Step 1 (1st year tuition): $\$6,000 \times \left[\dfrac{1}{(1+.085)^1} \right] = \$6,000 \times .9217 = \$ 5,530.20$

Step 2 (2d year tuition): $\$6,700 \times \left[\dfrac{1}{(1+.085)^2} \right] = \$6,700 \times .8495 = \$ 5,691.65$

Step 3 (3d year tuition): $\$7,300 \times \left[\dfrac{1}{(1+.085)^3} \right] = \$7,300 \times .7829 = \$ 5,715.17$

Step 4 (4th year tuition): $\$8,200 \times \left[\dfrac{1}{(1+.085)^4} \right] = \$8,200 \times .7216 = \underline{\$ 5,917.12}$

Step 5 (add years 1 through 4):   Total $22,854.14

If $22,854.14 is deposited today at 8.5 percent compound interest, the account will be sufficient to pay each of the estimated tuition payments as it falls due over the next 4 years. At the end of the 4-year period, the account will be depleted, as illustrated in table 7-1.

TABLE 7-1
Liquidation of a Capital Sum Compounding at 8.5 Percent Interest Through Uneven Cash Withdrawals

Year	Beginning Balance	Interest Earnings	Cash Withdrawal	Ending Balance
1	$22,854.14	$1,942.60	$6,000	$18,796.74
2	18,796.74	1,597.72	6,700	13,694.46
3	13,694.46	1,164.03	7,300	7,558.49
4	7,558.49	642.47	8,200	0.96

ungrouped cash flows

This example involving tuition payments illustrates *ungrouped cash flows,* which are a series of cash flows where there are no consecutive payments of the same amount and direction, that is, the cash flow can be either positive (inflow) or negative (outflow). In ungrouped cash flows, each payment must be discounted separately. In situations with *grouped cash flows,* where some of the consecutive payments are of the same amount and flow in the same direction (that is, either as cash inflows or outflows), a shortcut can be used to find the present value.

grouped cash flows

A corporate bond provides a good illustration of an uneven cash flow where some cash flows are grouped. For example, consider a bond that will pay you interest of $80 per year at the end of each of the next 6 years, as well as the $1,000 face amount at the end of the sixth year.[1] If you want to earn a 13 percent rate of return on this investment, how much would you be willing to pay for the bond? That is, determine the present value, discounted at 13 percent, of the bond's cash flows as depicted in figure 7-1.

This series of cash flows actually consists of two separate parts. Part one is an annuity of $80 per year for 5 years (or an annuity of $80 per year for 6 years), and part two is a single sum of $1,080 at the end of the sixth year (or a single sum of $1,000 at the end of the sixth year). To compute the present value of the entire series of cash flows, first calculate the present value of the annuity (PVA). Next calculate the PVSS. Finally add the results of the two parts.

The solution for part one can be calculated using the PVA formula. This formula, as described in the previous chapter, is

$$PVA = \text{annual payment} \times \left[\frac{1 - \dfrac{1}{(1 + i)^n}}{i} \right]$$

where the bracketed portion of the equation is the PVA factor.

FIGURE 7-1
Time Line Depiction of a Bond Value

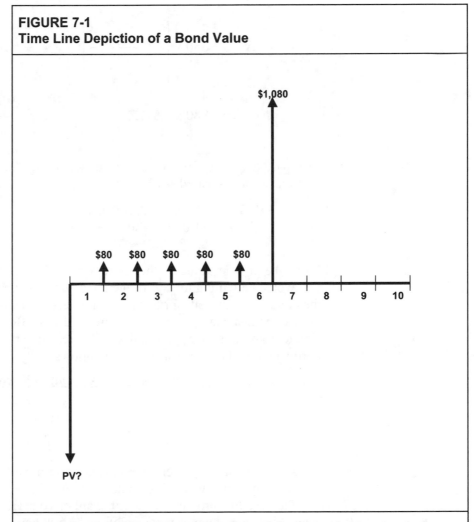

This time line depicts the uneven stream of cash flows provided by a bond—five annual payments of $80 each and a sixth of $1,080. The problem is to compute the present value of the stream of cash flows.

Because the bracketed portion is the PVA factor, the PVA formula can be written as

PVA = annual payment x PVA factor

The use of the PVA formula with the appropriate PVA factor (located in table F.4 in appendix F) to find the present value of the series of $80 interest payments is as follows:

$$PVA \; = \; \$80 \times \left[\frac{1 - \dfrac{1}{(1.13)^5}}{.13} \right]$$

$$= \; \$80 \times 3.5172$$
$$= \; \$281.38$$

The part two solution can be calculated using the PVSS formula. This formula, as previously described, is

PVSS = FVSS x PVSS factor
     = $1,080 x .4803
     = $518.72

Thus, the present value of the entire series of cash flows, that is, the price you would be willing to pay for the bond, is $800.10 ($281.38 + $518.72). If the bond currently sells for this amount or less, you would buy the bond.

In another example involving grouped cash flows, assume you loan a simple sum to a borrower today. The repayment schedule calls for the borrower to make payments to you as follows:

End of Year	Amount of Payment
1	$ 0
2	2,500
3–9	3,000
10	5,500

Assuming an 11 percent interest rate, determine the present value of this series of payments, which is depicted in figure 7-2.

To solve this problem without the aid of your HP-10BII requires several steps. First, find the present value of the $2,500 payment at the end of year 2. Second, calculate the present value of a 7-year, $3,000 annuity. Third, discount the present value of that annuity as a single sum to its present value today, rather than its value 2 years from now when the annuity begins. Refer to the figure 7-2 time line depiction and note that this regular annuity begins

FIGURE 7-2
Time Line Depiction of the Present Value of Uneven Cash Flows

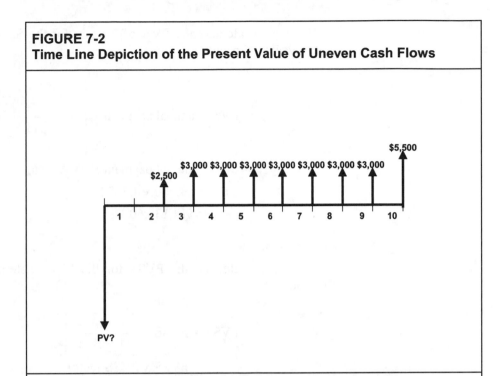

This time line depicts a problem in which the task is to compute the present value of a stream of cash flows consisting of zero at the end of year 1, $2,500 at the end of year 2, $3,000 at the end of years 3–9, and $5,500 at the end of year 10.

at the start of the third year (the end of the second year) with the first $3,000 payment to be made at the end of the third year. Fourth, find the present value of the $5,500 payment at the end of year 10. Finally, sum the PVSS of the first payment, the twice-discounted value of the PVA of the next seven payments, and the PVSS of the ninth payment to obtain the present value of the entire series of cash flows.

Using the PVSS and the PVA formulas with the appropriate factor tables to explain each of the steps and calculate all the values, the problem is solved as follows:

In step 1, calculate the PVSS for the $2,500 payment at the end of year 2.

$$\text{PVSS} = \text{FVSS} \times \left[\frac{1}{(1 + .11)^2} \right]$$
$$= \text{FVSS} \times \text{PVSS factor}$$
$$= \$2,500 \times .8116$$
$$= \$2,029.00$$

In step 2, calculate the PVA of 7 years for the $3,000 payments at the end of years 3 through 9.

$$PVA = \text{annual payment} \times \left[\frac{1 - \frac{1}{(1 + .11)^7}}{.11} \right]$$

$= \text{annual payment} \times \text{PVA factor}$

$= \$3,000 \times 4.7122$

$= \$14,136.60$

In step 3, calculate the PVSS for the PVA (determined in step 2) of $14,136.60.

$$PVSS = FVSS \times \left[\frac{1}{(1 + .11)^2} \right]$$

$= FVSS \times \text{PVSS factor}$

$= \$14,136.60 \times .8116$

$= \$11,473.26$

In step 4, calculate the PVSS for the $5,500 payment at the end of year 10.

$$PVSS = FVSS \times \left[\frac{1}{(1 + .11)^{10}} \right]$$

$= FVSS \times \text{PVSS factor}$

$= \$5,500 \times .3522$

$= \$1,937.10$

In step 5, total the present values of the cash flows from steps 1, 3, and 4.

$ 2,029.00   (PVSS from step 1)
11,473.26   (PVSS from step 3)
 1,937.10   (PVSS from step 4)
$15,439.36

So far, all of the cash flows in the previous problems have been inflows and thus positive. In some problems, however, one or more of the cash flow amounts may be an outflow and thus negative. For example, assume you own rental property that is expected to generate net income of $15,000 per year at the end of each of the next 15 years, except for year 10. In year 10 you anticipate replacing the roof and making various other repairs, resulting in a net cash outflow for the year of $10,000. What is the present value of this stream of cash flows discounted at 9 percent? To solve this problem, like the last problem, requires several steps.

The solution to the problem can be found using the PVA and the PVSS formulas with the appropriate factor tables to explain each of the steps and calculate all the values. Note that in step 2 a negative sign representing the cash outflow must be used.

In step 1, calculate the PVA of 9 years for the $15,000 cash inflows that begin at the end of year 1 and continue to the end of year 9.

$$PVA = \text{annual payment} \times \left[\frac{1 - \dfrac{1}{(1 + .09)^9}}{.09} \right]$$

$$= \text{annual payment} \times PVA \text{ factor}$$
$$= \$15,000 \times 5.9952$$
$$= \$89,928.00$$

In step 2, calculate the PVSS of the $10,000 cash outflow at the end of year 10.

$$PVSS = FVSS \times \left[\frac{1}{(1 + .09)^{10}} \right]$$

$$= FVSS \times PVSS \text{ factor}$$
$$= -\$10,000 \times .4224$$
$$= -\$4,224.00$$

In step 3, calculate the PVA of 5 years for the $15,000 cash inflows that begin at the end of year 11 and continue to the end of year 15.

$$PVA = \text{annual payment} \times \left[\frac{1 - \dfrac{1}{(1 + .09)^5}}{.09} \right]$$

$$= \text{annual payment} \times PVA \text{ factor}$$

$$= \$15,000 \times 3.8897$$
$$= \$58,345.50$$

In step 4, calculate the PVSS of the PVA (determined in step 3) of $58,345.50.

$$PVSS = FVSS \times \left[\frac{1}{(1 + .09)^{10}} \right]$$

$$= FVSS \times PVSS \text{ factor}$$
$$= \$58,345.50 \times .4224$$
$$= \$24,645.14$$

In step 5, total the present values of the cash flows from steps 1, 2, and 4.

$$
\begin{array}{ll}
\$ \ \ 89,928.00 & \text{(PVA from step 1)} \\
-4,224.00 & \text{(PVSS from step 2)} \\
\underline{24,645.14} & \text{(PVSS from step 4)} \\
\underline{\$110,349.14} &
\end{array}
$$

This problem could be solved in several other ways. One approach, for instance, is to calculate the PVA of 15 years for the $15,000 cash inflows. Then you could subtract the PVSS of the outflow of $25,000 at the end of year 10 from the PVA. Remember you received a $15,000 cash inflow as rental income at the end of year 10, which was offset by the $25,000 cash outflow for repairs at the end of year 10, leaving a $10,000 net cash outflow for year 10.

Using an HP-10BII to Solve Present Value Problems With Uneven Cash Flows

The preceding problems illustrated simple patterns of payment and were solved using time-value formulas. Although not technically difficult, the process of solving these problems using time-value formulas is tedious and cumbersome, even with the aid of factor tables. To speed up the process, you could use an HP-10BII to calculate the present value of each cash flow or group of cash flows. However, even with the aid of your HP-10BII, the process is still rather tedious and cumbersome unless you learn how to use some new keys that can speed up the procedure. With the knowledge of these new keys, your HP-10BII can be especially helpful when there is a lengthy series of cash flows with many different payment amounts, including positive (inflow), zero, and negative (outflow) amounts. If a problem exceeds the capacity of your HP-10BII, you can use a computer to solve it.

Speaking of the HP-10BII's capacity, it has the capability to solve problems with up to 14 end-of-year or 15 beginning-of-year cash flows when there are no consecutive equal cash flows. When there are consecutive equal cash flows that can be grouped, the HP-10BII's capacity is expanded.

As suggested above, to efficiently solve uneven cash flow problems with your HP-10BII, you must learn how to use several new keys. First is the CFj key in the third row of the keyboard. This key is used to record the items in a series of uneven cash flows, starting at the beginning of the time horizon. The j in CFj refers to the timing of the cash flow. The cash flow at the start of year one is CF_o, and the subsequent cash flows (or groups of cash flows) are numbered consecutively from Cf_1 through as many as Cf_{14}.

To compute the present value of a series of uneven cash flows, start by entering all of the cash flows in sequence. Then enter the discount rate using the I/YR key as usual. Next, take notice of the NPV (net present value) key in the second row of the keyboard. Together the ▭ and NPV keys are used to produce the solution. Also, as noted above, the CF_j key assumes that payments begin immediately, so it makes no difference whether your HP-10BII is set for beginning-of-year or end-of-year payments. If the first payment in the problem begins at the end of the year, you must enter 0 as the first cash flow to tell your HP-10BII that there is no cash flow at the beginning of the time horizon.

To illustrate the process, assume that you have a deferred compensation agreement with your employer. Under the agreement the employer is obligated to pay you the following amounts:

End of Year	Amount of Payment
1	$ 0
2	70,000
3	80,000
4	85,000
5	95,000

Using a 12.5 percent discount rate, determine the present value of this income stream. After clearing your HP-10BII's memory (▭, C ALL), press the following keys: 0 and CFj (because there is no immediate cash flow at the start of year one); 0 and CFj (because there is no immediate cash flow at the end of year one); 70000 and CFj (to enter the cash flow at the end of year two); 80000 and CFj (to enter the cash flow at the end of year three); 85000 and CFj (to enter the cash flow at the end of year four); 95000 and CFj (to enter the cash flow at the end of year five). Next press 12.5 and I/YR (to enter the discount rate). Finally, to solve the problem, press ▭ and NPV, which provides the answer of $217,278.53.

HP-10BII: Keystrokes for Computing the Present Value of a Series of Uneven (End-of-Year) Cash Flows

Keystrokes	Explanation
▭, C ALL	clearing memory
0, CFj	no payment at beginning of first year
0, CFj	no payment at end of first year
70000,CFj	end of second year payment
80000, CFj	end of third year payment
85000, CFj	end of fourth year payment
95000, CFj	end of fifth year payment
12.5, I/YR	discount interest rate
▭, NPV	217,278.53 displayed

Solving Problems That Include Grouped Cash Flows. Your HP-10BII can solve present value problems with more than 14 end-of-year or 15 beginning-of-year cash flows if the series includes some grouped data. Grouped data counts as only one cash flow amount. To illustrate, a cash flow of $50,000 followed by 40 annual cash flows of $1,000 involves 41 cash flows but only two cash flow entries for the HP-10BII. For problems that include grouped data, enter the cash flow amount, CFj, the number of times the cash flow occurs in succession (including the first time), ▭, and N_J (the secondary function on the CF_J key in the third row).

For example, consider an investment that generates a cash inflow of $6,000 per year for 5 years, starting at the end of year one, followed by $4,000 per year for 10 years, followed by $1,000 per year for 15 years, followed by a lump-sum payment of $20,000. Determine the present value of this income stream discounted at 8 percent.

Using your HP-10BII, press ▭ and C ALL to clear its memory. Then press 0 and CFj (because there is no cash flow at the start of year one). Then press 6000, CFj, 5 (because $6,000 will be paid 5 consecutive years), ▭, and Nj. Next enter 4000, CFj, 10 (because $4,000 will be paid 10 consecutive years), ▭, and Nj. Then enter 1000, CFj, 15 (because $1,000 will be paid 15 consecutive years), ▭, and Nj. Next enter 20000 and CFj (for the final one year cash flow). Then enter 8 and I/YR (for the discount rate). Finally, press ▭ and NPV to compute the answer, which is $46,761.96. If you would like to discount this same cash flow again, but at a different rate, simply enter the new rate and I/YR. Then press ▭ and NPV to compute the answer at the new discount rate.

HP-10BII: Keystrokes for Computing the Present Value of Grouped Cash Flows

Keystrokes	Explanation
▭, C ALL	clearing memory
0, CFj	no payment at the beginning of year one
6000, CFj, 5, ▭, Nj	5 consecutive $5,000 cash flows
4000,CFj, 10, ▭, Nj	10 consecutive $4,000 cash flows
1000, CFj, 15, ▭, Nj	15 consecutive $1,000 cash flows
20000, CFj	one $20,000 cash flow
8, I/YR	discount interest rate
▭, NPV	46,761.96 displayed

Cash Flows at Beginning of Year. In the preceding example, cash flows began at the end of the first year. If a cash flow occurs at the beginning of the first year, only a slight change in procedure is needed to find the present value of the cash flows. Enter the amount of the initial cash flow (if it occurs only once as ungrouped data) and CFj. Then proceed in the usual manner to enter the size and number of each of the remaining cash flows. However, if the first cash flow consists of grouped data—for example, $1,000 at the beginning of years 1, 2, 3, and 4—the data must be treated as two separate cash flows, $1,000 occurring at the start of the first year followed by a group of three additional cash flows of $1,000 each.

For example, at a discount rate of 12 percent, what is the present value of the following series of cash flows?

Beginning of Year	Amount of Cash Flow
1–5	$3,500
6–10	2,500
11	1,500
12	1,000

First clear the HP-10BII's memory (▭, C ALL) and then enter the first five cash flows by pressing 3500 and CFj (for the first cash flow); 3500, CFj, 4, ▭, and Nj (for the remaining four $3,500 cash flows). Next enter the next five cash flows (for years 6 through 10) by pressing 2500, CFj, 5, ▭, and Nj. Then enter the last two cash flows by pressing 1500 and CFj (for year 11); 1000 and CFj (for year 12). Next enter the discount rate by pressing 12 and I/YR. Finally enter ▭ and NPV to compute the answer, which is $20,628.41.

HP-10BII: Keystrokes for Computing Present Value If There Is a Cash Flow at the Beginning of the First Period

Keystrokes	Explanation
▭, C ALL	clearing memory
3500, CFj	cash flow at beginning of first year
3500, CFj, 4, ▭, Nj	4 consecutive cash flows for years 2 through 5
2500, CFj, 5, ▭, Nj	5 consecutive cash flows for years 6 through 10
1500,CFj	the cash flow for year 11
1000, CFj	the final cash flow for year 12
12, I/YR	discount interest rate
▭, NPV	20,628.41 displayed

Payments or Deposits Growing by a Constant Percentage. In many cases, financial advisors need to discount a stream of payments that increase each year by a constant percentage. Educational funding is a frequent application, when an assumed education inflation rate is applied to the tuition payments.

To illustrate this concept in another application, assume that you wish to have an income stream of $30,000 per year in constant purchasing power for the next 10 years, with the first payment occurring immediately. In other words, you wish to receive a total of 10 payments in the form of an annuity due. To fund this annuity, how much would you have to set aside today if the annual inflation rate is expected to be 5 percent and the deposit will earn a compound annual interest rate of 8 percent per year? To answer this question, you need to determine the present value, discounted at 8 percent, of a 10-year stream of payments beginning with $30,000 and increasing by 5 percent per year.

One approach to solving this type of problem is to use a formula that takes inflation into consideration. However, rather than attempting to solve this problem by using a formula, it is much easier and quicker to use your HP-10BII. First set it for beginning-of-year payments and clear its memory. Then enter 30000 and PMT (for the first payment due immediately). Next enter 1.08, ÷, 1.05, −, 1, x, 100, =, and I/YR (for the inflation-adjusted interest rate). Then enter 10 and N (for the number of payments). Finally press PV to compute the answer, which is $265,147.15.

If you want to see the answer under an end-of-year assumption without reentering all the information, divide the beginning-of-year answer by 1.08. In other words, enter PV on your HP-10BII and the beginning-of-year answer, $265,147.15, reappears. Then enter ÷, 1.08, and = to compute the end-of-year answer, which is $245,506.62.

HP-10BII: Keystrokes for Computing the Present Value of Payments or Deposits That Grow at a Constant Rate If the First Payment Is Due Immediately

Keystrokes	*Explanation*
⊟, C ALL	clearing memory
⊟, BEG/END	only if BEGIN not displayed
30000, PMT	first payment
1.08, ÷, 1.05, −, 1, x, 100, =, I/YR	adjusts the discount rate (8%) by the inflation rate (5%) for an adjusted rate of 2.86
10, N	number of payments
PV	−265,147.15 displayed

Without Reentering All the Information If the First Payment Is Due One Year From Now

Keystrokes	*Explanation*
PV	−265,147.15 displayed
÷, 1.08, =	−245.506.62 displayed

Alternatively you can start over.

To obtain the adjusted discount rate, you may be tempted to simply subtract the inflation rate of 5 percent from the discount rate of 8 percent. Unfortunately, this simple approach is incorrect. To understand why, assume that the inflation rate, as before, is expected to be 5 percent during the year and that you want to earn an inflation-adjusted rate of 8 percent on a $100 investment in order to have $108 of purchasing power ($100 x 1.08) in today's dollars one year from now. If inflation is 5 percent during the year, how much will you need at the end of one year to have the equivalent of $108 in today's dollars? The answer is $113.40, which is $108 x 1.05, where1.05 is the adjustment factor for inflation. In other words, you must earn a nominal rate of 13.4 percent [($113.40 − 100) ÷ $100] to earn a real(inflation-adjusted) rate of 8 percent if inflation is 5 percent. (To obtain 13.4 percent instead of just 13 percent on the display screen, you need to change the decimal precision on your HP-10BII from two to four. As explained in chapter 6, this is done by entering ⊟, DISP, and 4 for the number of decimal places to be displayed.)

HP-10BII: Keystrokes for Computing the Present Value of Payments or Deposits That Grow at a Constant Rate If the First Payment Is Due One Year From Now

Keystrokes	Explanation
▭, C ALL	clearing memory
▭, BEG/END	only if BEGIN displayed
30000, ÷, 1.05, =, PMT	28,571.43 displayed as the adjusted first payment
1.08, ÷, 1.05, –, 1, x, 100, =, I/YR	adjusts the discount rate (8%) by the inflation rate (5%) for an adjusted rate of 2.86
10, N	number of payments
PV	–245,506.62 displayed

Fisher Effect

This concept, called the *Fisher Effect*, can be expressed in equation form as follows:

nominal rate of return = [(1 + real rate) x (1 + inflation rate)] –1

where all rates are expressed as decimals.

Inserting the data from the example:

nominal rate of return = (1.08 x 1.05) –1 = 0.134

That is, 13.4 percent is the nominal rate required to earn a real rate of 8 percent if the inflation rate is 5 percent.

In order to solve these problems as an annuity, you have to modify the interest rate to reflect both the investment returns and the growth or inflation rate. Every cash flow has to be subject to both rates in order for the modified interest rate to solve the problem. If the first cash flow is not subject to the growth/inflation rate, then you need to adjust it by that rate to solve the problem. That is what was done in the text box above. When the first cash flow takes place today (annuity due), then no adjustment is necessary. An alternate adjustment is shown in the example on page 7-15. There, instead of adjusting the first cash flow, the present value is adjusted to reflect the timing of cash flows. In other words, the problem is solved as an annuity due and then is converted to an ordinary annuity.

Future Value of Uneven Cash Flows

Compounding a series of uneven cash flows to a future value utilizes our usual approach to calculating FVSS problems.

For example, assume that a business plans to make a deposit each year to fund certain pension obligations as follows:

End of Year	Amount of Deposit
1	$60,000
2	40,000
3–5	50,000
6–10	60,000

If these deposits earn 10 percent compound annual interest, how much will be in the account after 10 years? In other words, what is the future value of this series of uneven cash flows?

The solution to this problem requires compounding each individual deposit from the time it is made until the end of the 10th year, then totaling the individual FVSS to obtain the answer. Thus, the first $60,000 deposit should be compounded for 9 years at 10 percent to produce its FVSS. The second deposit should be compounded for 8 years, the third for 7 years, and so on. The final $60,000 deposit, of course, earns no interest because it is made at the end of the 10th year.

Using the FVSS and the FVA Formulas to Compute the Future Value of Uneven Cash Flows

Continuing with the pension funding example, the FVSS and the FVA formulas can be used to compute the future value of the series of pension funding deposits (a series of uneven cash flows) earning 10 percent compound annual interest.

As described in chapter 6, the FVSS formula is

$$FVSS = PVSS \times (1 + i)^n$$

where $(1 + i)^n$ is the FVSS factor. Because $(1 + i)^n$ is the FVSS factor, the FVSS formula can be written as

$$FVSS = PVSS \times FVSS \text{ factor}$$

Also described in chapter 6, the FVA formula is

$$FVA = \text{annual deposit} \times \left[\frac{(1 + i)^n - 1}{i} \right]$$

where the bracketed portion of the equation is the FVA factor. Because the bracketed portion is the FVA factor, the FVA formula can be written as

$$\text{FVA} = \text{annual deposit} \ \text{x} \ \text{FVA factor}$$

Using the FVSS and the FVA formulas with the appropriate factor tables (located in appendix F), the solution to the pension funding problem requires the following six steps:

In step 1, calculate the FVSS for the $60,000 deposit at the end of year 1.

$$
\begin{aligned}
\text{FVSS} &= \text{PVSS} \ \text{x} \ (1+.10)^9 \\
&= \text{PVSS} \ \text{x} \ \text{FVSS factor} \\
&= \$60,000 \ \text{x} \ 2.3579 \\
&= \$141,474.00
\end{aligned}
$$

In step 2, calculate the FVSS for the $40,000 deposit at the end of year 2.

$$
\begin{aligned}
\text{FVSS} &= \text{PVSS} \ \text{x} \ (1+.10)^8 \\
&= \text{PVSS} \ \text{x} \ \text{FVSS factor} \\
&= \$40,000 \ \text{x} \ 2.1436 \\
&= \$85,744.00
\end{aligned}
$$

In step 3, calculate the FVA of 3 years for the $50,000 deposits at the end of years 3 through 5.

$$
\begin{aligned}
\text{FVA} &= \text{annual deposit} \ \text{x} \ \left[\frac{(1+.10)^3 - 1}{.10}\right] \\
&= \text{annual deposit} \ \text{x} \ \text{FVA factor} \\
&= \$50,000 \ \text{x} \ 3.3100 \\
&= \$165,500.00
\end{aligned}
$$

In step 4, calculate the FVSS for the FVA (determined in step 3) of $165,500.00.

$$
\begin{aligned}
\text{FVSS} &= \text{PVSS} \ \text{x} \ (1+.10)^5 \\
&= \text{PVSS} \ \text{x} \ \text{FVSS factor} \\
&= \$165,500 \ \text{x} \ 1.6105 \\
&= \$266,537.75
\end{aligned}
$$

In step 5, calculate the FVA of 5 years for the $60,000 deposits at the end of years 6 through 10.

$$FVA = \text{annual deposit} \times \left[\frac{(1 + .10)^5 - 1}{.10} \right]$$

$$= \text{annual deposit} \times \text{FVA factor}$$

$$= \$60,000 \times 6.1051$$

$$= \$366,306.00$$

In step 6, total the future values of the deposits from steps 1, 2, 4, and 5.

$141,474.00	(FVSS from step 1)
85,744.00	(FVSS from step 2)
266,537.75	(FVSS from step 4)
366,306.00	(FVA from step 5)
$860,061.75	

Using an HP-10BII to Solve Future Value Problems With Uneven Cash Flows

The HP-10BII is unable to directly compute the future value of a series of uneven cash flows. Therefore, the way to solve this type of problem with an HP-10BII is to divide it into two separate parts. The first part requires you to compute the present value of a series of uneven cash flows; the second part requires you to compute the future value of the present value determined in part one.

For example, assume the following deposits to a savings account:

End of Year	Amount of Deposit
1	$500
2–5	600
6–8	700
9	200

If these deposits earn 7 percent compound annual interest, how much will be in the account after 9 years?

To solve the first part of the problem you have to compute the present value of the deposits. First clear your HP-10BII's memory. (Remember, as previously noted, the CFj key assumes that deposits are made immediately. Therefore, it makes no difference whether your HP-10BII is set for beginning-of-year or end-of-year deposits. Either way the answer will be the same.) Then enter 0 and CFj (because there is no deposit at the start of year one); 500 and CFj (for the first deposit at the end of year 1); 600, CFj, 4, ⬛, and Nj (for the next four deposits for years 2 through 5); 700, CFj, 3, ⬛, and Nj (for the next three deposits for years 6 through 8); 200 and CFj (for the final deposit for year 9). Next enter 7 and I/YR (for the interest rate). Finally enter ▭ and NPV to find the present value of this series of uneven cash flows or deposits, which is $3,785.22.

To solve the second part of the problem you need to compute the future value of the present value determined in part one. This requires you to carry the present value from part one forward as a single sum to the end of year 9 using the same 7 percent compound annual interest rate. Thus, enter +/−, PV; 9 and N. Then enter FV to find the future value of this set of uneven cash flows or deposits, which is $6,958.97.

HP-10BII: Keystrokes for Computing the Future Value of a Series of Uneven (End-of-Year) Cash Flows

Part 1 Keystrokes	Explanation
▭, C ALL	clearing memory
0, CFj	no deposit at beginning of first year
500, CFj	deposit at end of first year
600, CFj, 4, ▭, Nj	4 consecutive deposits for years 2 through 5
700, CFj, 3, ▭, Nj	3 consecutive deposits for years 6 through 8
200, CFj	final deposit for year 9
7, I/YR	discount interest year
▭, NPV	3,785.22 displayed as the present value
Part 2 Keystrokes	**Explanation**
+/−, PV	−3,785.22 displayed as the present value from Part 1
9, N	number of payments
FV	6,958.97 displayed as future value

Payments or Deposits Growing by a Constant Percentage. Now we will move from uneven irregular cash flows to those that increase each year by a constant percentage. This type of problem frequently arises when a client sets up a savings plan and the annual contribution to the plan increases each year at some assumed rate.

For example, assume that you plan to begin a program of annual saving, beginning with a $5,000 deposit now. Assume also that you expect your income and therefore the amount you plan to save to increase at an annual rate of 10 percent. If your savings earn a 7 percent compound annual rate of interest, how much will be in your account after 5 years? What is the future value, compounded at 7 percent interest, of this 5-year stream of deposits that increase at an annual rate of 10 percent?

HP-10BII: Keystrokes for Computing the Future Value of a Series of Beginning-of-Year Deposits That Increase at a Constant Rate

Part 1 Keystrokes	Explanation (Finding the PV)
⬛, C ALL	clearing memory
⬛, BEG/END	only if BEGIN not displayed
5000, PMT	first deposit
1.07, ÷, 1.10, −, 1, x, 100, =, I/YR	adjusts the discount rate (7%) by the growth rate (10%) for an adjusted rate of -2.73
5, N	number of payments
PV	−26,441.73 displayed as the present value of the deposits

Part 2 Keystrokes	Explanation (Finding the FV of the PV in Part I)
PV	−26,441.73 displayed as the present value from Part 1
7, I/YR	restores original interest rate
0, PMT	no additional deposits
FV	37,085.89 displayed as the future value of the deposits

Without Reentering All the Information If the Deposits Occur at the End of Each Year

FV	37,085.89 displayed
÷, 1.07, =	34,659.71 displayed as the future value of the deposits

---

One approach to solving this type of problem is to use a formula first that takes growth into consideration. However, rather than attempting to solve this problem by using a formula, it is much easier and quicker to use your HP-10BII. The procedure is similar to that used in calculating the future value of a series of uneven cash flows, which requires that the problem be divided into two parts. In part one of the problem, compute the present value of the series of increasing cash flows. In part two compute the future value of the present value determined in part one.

Begin by setting your HP-10BII for beginning-of-year payments or deposits. (Since the problem does not involve the CFj key, it is necessary to set your HP-10BII to reflect the proper payment mode.) Next clear its memory. Then for part one of the problem enter 5000 and PMT (for the first deposit); 1.07, ÷, 1.10, –, 1, x, 100, =, and I/YR (for the inflation-adjusted interest rate of -2.73); 5 and N (for the number of payments). Then solve part one by entering PV (for the present value of the series of increasing deposits), and $26,441.73 will appear on the screen.

For part two enter 7 and I/YR (to restore the original compounding rate); 0 and PMT (to clear out extraneous data). Then to solve the problem and find the future value of the series of beginning-of-year increasing deposits enter FV and the answer, $37,085.89, will be displayed on the screen. However, before clearing your HP-10BII's memory, the future value of end-of-year increasing deposits can be found by first entering FV and then entering ÷, 1.07, and =. The answer displayed on the screen will be $34,659.71.

EVALUATING INVESTMENTS WITH DISCOUNTED CASH FLOW ANALYSIS

One of the most common personal and business applications of time-value-of-money principles and techniques is the evaluation of a proposed investment. For example, assume that you are considering the purchase of a bond that involves a cash outflow now (the purchase price) and a series of cash inflows over several time periods in the future (the interest payments and the face amount). Or perhaps you are considering construction of an apartment building that involves a cash outflow now and perhaps again next year (the construction costs), after which you anticipate a series of cash inflows for a period of years (the rental payments). Or perhaps the investment under consideration is the purchase (cash outflow) of a piece of equipment that reduces expenses (cash inflow) over some future period.

In all of these situations there is a trade-off: one or more cash outflows in return for one or more cash inflows. Are the inflows expected worth the outflows expended? Is the investment a good one? These questions cannot be answered adequately without taking the time value of money into account. Discounted cash flow analysis can be used to assist you in evaluating an investment by making the time value of cash outflows and inflows comparable. It can help you decide (1) whether a proposed investment opportunity is an acceptable one and (2) how to rank several competing investment opportunities in terms of their relative acceptability.

There is more, however, to evaluating an investment opportunity than simply crunching some numbers through various time-value-of-money formulas or calculator functions. The degree of certainty in amount, timing, and duration associated with various cash outflows and inflows, as well as the tax aspects, must also be considered. Evaluation of tax aspects is beyond the scope of this chapter. Risk considerations, however, are incorporated in the interest rate that is used in discounted cash flow analysis.

As you will see, the mechanics of discounted cash flow analysis are quite straightforward when the pattern of the cash outflows and inflows is simple. Calculations become more complex when the amounts vary from year to year, and still more complex when the amounts are positive in some years and negative in others. The remainder of this chapter deals with discounted cash flow analysis situations, first showing simple applications then gradually demonstrating more complex ones.

Discounted Cash Flow Techniques Defined

There are two commonly used techniques for discounted cash flow analysis: (1) calculation of an investment's net present value (NPV) and (2) calculation of its internal rate of return (IRR).

Net Present Value

net present value (NPV)

The *net present value (NPV)* of an investment is the present value of the stream of cash inflows minus the present value of the stream of cash outflows. The interest rate selected by the investor for discounting the two cash flow streams is either the minimum rate of return acceptable to the investor in light of his or her assessment of the investment's risk, the investor's cost of capital to fund the investment, or the rate available on alternative investment opportunities with a similar degree of risk.

If the result of the NPV calculation is positive, that is, if the present value of the cash inflow stream exceeds the present value of the cash outflow stream, the investment is a good one and the investor's wealth will increase (in a time value sense) by the amount of the positive NPV. A positive NPV means that the rate of return provided by the investment (whatever that rate is) exceeds the interest rate selected by the investor as the discount rate. If the NPV is negative, the reverse is true and the investor's wealth will decrease (in a time value sense) by the amount of the negative NPV. And if the NPV of the investment is zero, the investor's wealth will neither increase nor decrease (in a time value sense), leaving him or her indifferent as to whether the investment should be made.

Internal Rate of Return

internal rate of return (IRR)

The *internal rate of return (IRR)* on an investment is the discount rate at which the present value of the stream of cash inflows (investment returns) equals the present value of the stream of cash outflows (investment costs). This is to say that the IRR on an investment is the discount rate at which the

NPV of the investment is zero. If the investment's IRR is larger than the minimum rate acceptable by the investor, the investment is a good one and should be undertaken. If not, it should be rejected. The investor's choices for determining an acceptable minimum rate of return are the same as those described in selecting a discount rate for a net present value calculation.

    Similarity of the NPV and IRR Techniques. Note that the NPV and IRR methods of evaluating an investment are very similar. In computing NPV, the investor specifies the minimum acceptable interest rate and determines whether at that rate the present value of the inflows exceeds the present value of the outflows. In computing IRR, the investor ascertains the interest rate that makes the present value of the inflows equal to the present value of the outflows; that is, the investor ascertains the interest rate that produces an NPV of zero.

    As a general rule, when used to evaluate a particular investment, the two techniques will lead the investor to the same conclusion. If the NPV is positive, the IRR normally is acceptable and the investment is an attractive one. Conversely, if the NPV is negative, the IRR normally is unacceptable and the investment should be rejected. When used to rank several investments as to their relative acceptability, however, there are situations in which the NPV and IRR techniques produce different results using the same data. In most cases, the NPV method is more reliable for ranking several competing investment possibilities. The project with the largest NPV should be ranked first, the one with the next largest NPV should be second, and so on.

Solving Simple NPV Problems With Formulas

    Assume that you are evaluating a project that requires purchasing a piece of equipment that costs $100,000. The project is expected to provide a positive net cash flow of $40,000 per year at the end of each of the next 4 years, after which it will have no value. If your cost of capital is 10 percent per year, should you invest in this project?

    The cash flows associated with this project are illustrated in the time line in the upper half of figure 7-3. The sole cash outflow, $100,000, occurs immediately, so its present value is $100,000. The four cash inflows of $40,000, totaling $160,000, are a regular annuity for 4 years, and should be discounted at the 10 percent cost of funds. Using the PVA formula with the appropriate PVA factor (located in table F.4 in appendix F), you can find the present value of the cash inflows as follows:

$$PVA = \text{annual payment} \times \left[\frac{1 - \frac{1}{(1 + i)^n}}{i} \right]$$

FIGURE 7-3
Time Line Depiction of NPV Problem: Level and Uneven Inflows

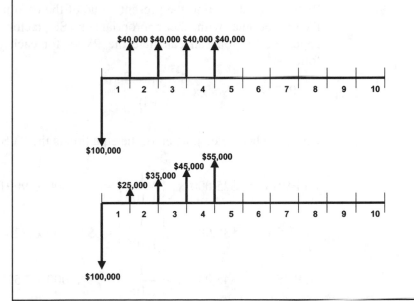

The upper time line depicts an investment that entails an initial cash outflow of $100,000 and a level stream of four $40,000 cash inflows. In the lower time line, the initial cash outflow is also $100,000, but the four cash inflows increase over time.

where the bracketed portion of the equation is the PVA factor.

$$PVA = \$40,000 \times \left[\frac{1 - \frac{1}{(1.10)^4}}{.10} \right]$$

$$= \$40,000 \times 3.1699$$
$$= \$126,796.00$$

Subtracting the present value of the cash outflow from the present value of the stream of cash inflows ($126,796.00 – $100,000.00 = $26,796.00) results in a positive NPV of $26,796.00. This positive NPV indicates that your wealth will increase by $26,796 (in today's dollars) if you invest in the project.

Even when a problem involves uneven cash flows, the approach to solving for NPV remains the same. For example, assume that another project with the same $100,000 initial cost will create increasing cash inflows that total $160,000, as shown on the bottom half of figure 7-3. In this situation, you can calculate the PVSS for each cash inflow and then total the four PVSS amounts to find the present value of the cash inflows. Thus, using the PVSS formula with the appropriate PVSS factor (located in table F.2 appendix F), you can calculate the PVSS for each of the cash inflows as follows:

$$\text{PVSS} = \text{FVSS} \times \left[\frac{1}{(1+i)^n} \right]$$

where the bracketed portion of the equation is the PVSS factor.

$$\text{1st PVSS} = \$25,000 \times \left[\frac{1}{1.10^1} \right] = \$25,000 \times .9091 = \$22,727.50$$

$$\text{2d PVSS} = \$35,000 \times \left[\frac{1}{1.10^2} \right] = \$35,000 \times .8264 = \$28,924.00$$

$$\text{3d PVSS} = \$45,000 \times \left[\frac{1}{1.10^3} \right] = \$45,000 \times .7513 = \$33,808.50$$

$$\text{4th PVSS} = \$55,000 \times \left[\frac{1}{1.10^4} \right] = \$55,000 \times .6830 = \underline{\$37,565.00}$$

Sum of the PVSS inflows from each year $\underline{\$123,025.00}$

The sum of the four PVSS is $123,025.00, which is the present value of the stream of increasing cash inflows. Subtracting the present value of the cash outflow from the present value of the stream of cash inflows ($123,025.00 – $100,000.00 = $23,025.00) results in a positive NPV of $23,025.00. Notice that although both projects generate the same total undiscounted cash inflow of $160,000, the project with the increasing pattern of cash inflows has a lower NPV because its higher cash inflows occur further in the future.

The entire costs of the projects in the two problems depicted in figure 7-3 were incurred at their inceptions. Cash outflows, however, may occur at

FIGURE 7-4
Time Line Depiction of NPV Problems: A Series of Cash Outflows and Cash Inflows and Years of Zero Outflows or Inflows

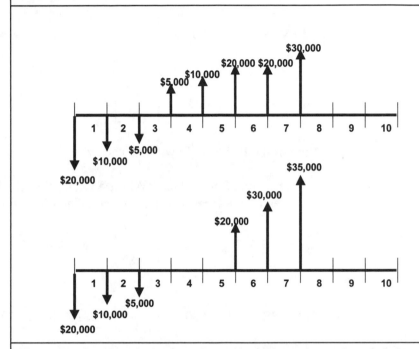

The upper time line depicts a project with a decreasing series of cash outflows followed by an increasing series of cash inflows. The lower time line depicts a similar project with a 3-year gap between the last cash outflow and the first cash inflow. Already you should expect that the NPV of the upper time line project would exceed that of the lower time line project because the same dollar amount of undiscounted cash inflows occurs earlier in the upper project.

any time during the lifetime of a project. For example, the top half of figure 7-4 depicts a project in which there are 3 years of uneven cash outflows ($20,000, $10,000, and $5,000) followed by 5 years of uneven cash inflows ($5,000, $10,000, $20,000, $20,000, and $30,000). As in the earlier calculations, to compute the NPV for this project, you need to subtract the present value of the series of cash outflows from the present value of the series of cash inflows. Note also from the figure 7-4 upper time line that the cash outflows occur at the beginning of years 1, 2, and 3, while the cash inflows occur at the end of years 3, 4, 5, 6, and 7.

If you determine that the minimum acceptable rate of return is 8 percent, you can use the PVSS formula with the appropriate PVSS factor (located in table F.2 appendix F) to calculate the PVSS for each of the cash outflows and inflows. Thus the PVSS for each cash outflow is

$$\text{1st PVSS} = \$20,000 \times \left[\frac{1}{1.08^0}\right] = \$20,000 \times 1.0000 = \$20,000.00$$

$$\text{2d PVSS} = \$10,000 \times \left[\frac{1}{1.08^1}\right] = \$10,000 \times .9259 = \$9,259.00$$

$$\text{3d PVSS} = \$5,000 \times \left[\frac{1}{1.08^2}\right] = \$5,000 \times .7513 = \underline{\$4,286.50}$$

Sum of the PVSS outflows from each year   <u>$33,545.50</u>

The sum of these three PVSS is $33,545.50, which is the present value of the stream of decreasing cash outflows. The PVSS for each cash inflow is

$$\text{1st PVSS} = \$5,000 \times \left[\frac{1}{1.08^3}\right] = \$5,000 \times .7938 = \$3,969.00$$

$$\text{2d PVSS} = \$10,000 \times \left[\frac{1}{1.08^4}\right] = \$10,000 \times .7350 = \$7,350.00$$

$$\text{3d PVSS} = \$20,000 \times \left[\frac{1}{1.08^5}\right] = \$20,000 \times .6806 = \$13,612.00$$

$$\text{4th PVSS} = \$20,000 \times \left[\frac{1}{1.08^6}\right] = \$20,000 \times .6302 = \$12,604.00$$

$$\text{5th PVSS} = \$30,000 \times \left[\frac{1}{1.08^7}\right] = \$30,000 \times .5835 = \underline{\$17,505.00}$$

Sum of the PVSS inflows from each year   <u>$55,040.00</u>

The sum of these five PVSS is $55,040.00, which is the present value of the stream of increasing cash inflows. Subtracting the present value of the stream of cash outflows from the present value of the stream of cash inflows ($55,040.00 – $33,545.50 = $21,494.50) results in a positive NPV of $21,494.50.

This approach isolated the cash inflows from the cash outflows. However, isolating the cash flows by direction (in or out) is not necessary as long as you remember to use a negative sign for each outflow. Then, when you sum the PVSS amounts, you will be combining both positive (adding) and negative (subtracting) numbers.

There may be one or more years in which there is neither a cash outflow nor a cash inflow. The procedure for solving these problems remains the same. A time line will be helpful for confirming that inflows and outflows are discounted for the correct number of years. For example, if the previous problem (depicted on the top time line of figure 7-4) is changed so that there is no cash inflow at the end of years 3 and 4 even though there is still the same dollar amount of undiscounted cash inflows in the problem (compare the bottom time line in figure 7-4 with the top time line), then the present value of the stream of cash flows (that is, both inflows and outflows) becomes:

$$\text{1st PVSS} = -\$20,000 \times \left[\frac{1}{1.08^0}\right] = -\$20,000 \times 1.0000 = -\$20,000.00$$

$$\text{2d PVSS} = -\$10,000 \times \left[\frac{1}{1.08^1}\right] = -\$10,000 \times .9259 = -\$9,259.00$$

$$\text{3d PVSS} = -\$5,000 \times \left[\frac{1}{1.08^2}\right] = -\$5,000 \times .8573 = -\$4,286.50$$

$$\text{4th PVSS} = \$20,000 \times \left[\frac{1}{1.08^5}\right] = \$20,000 \times .6806 = \$13,612.00$$

$$\text{5th PVSS} = \$30,000 \times \left[\frac{1}{1.08^6}\right] = \$30,000 \times .6302 = \$18,906.00$$

$$\text{6th PVSS} = \$35,000 \times \left[\frac{1}{1.08^7}\right] = \$35,000 \times .5835 = \underline{\$20,422.50}$$

Sum of the PVSS flows from each year $\underline{\$19,395.00}$

Thus, combining both the PVSS cash outflows (negative amounts) and the PVSS cash inflows (positive amounts) results in a positive NPV of $19,395.00. As suggested in figure 7-4, you would expect a lower NPV in the bottom time line ($19,395.00) compared with the top time line ($21,494.50) because even though the dollar amount of the undiscounted cash inflows is the same in both time lines, the cash inflows occur earlier in the upper time line.

Finally, in some situations there may be both cash inflows and cash outflows in the same year. In these cases, first subtract the year's outflows from its inflows. Next, determine the PVSS of the year's net cash flows, whether they be positive (inflows) or negative (outflows). Then, as before, sum the PVSS from each year with a net cash flow whether that flow is positive or negative. The result is the NPV. If positive, the project should be undertaken because it will increase your wealth (in today's dollars). If negative, the project is a bad investment and should be rejected.

As net present value problems become more involved, formula solutions become cumbersome and time consuming. At this juncture, it is necessary to pick up your HP-10BII.

Solving Complex NPV Problems With an HP-10BII

Ungrouped Cash Flows

Now we will take up somewhat more complicated problems, starting with NPV problems in which there are no consecutive cash flows of the same amount and sign. To solve this type of problem with your HP-10BII, you must use the CFj (cash flow) key (explained earlier in this chapter). In addition, you must also use the +/– key to enter outflows as negative numbers. Finally, you need to enter the discount rate, as before, and use the NPV key to produce the answer.

To illustrate the process, assume you have been asked to make a $75,000 loan. The borrower agrees to the following repayment schedule:

End of Year	Amount of Payment
1	$ 0
2	15,000
3	20,000
4	25,000
5	30,000

Should you make the loan if you insist on a rate of return of at least 11 percent on your investment?

Using your HP-10BII, first clear its memory. Then enter 75000, +/–, and CFj. The loan (an outflow at the start of the first year) has now been entered as a negative amount. Next enter 0 and CFj (because there is no net cash inflow or outflow at the end of the first year). Then enter (the remaining cash inflows) 15000 and CFj; 20000 and CFj; 25000 and CFj; 30000 and CFj. Now enter 11 and I/YR (the minimum acceptable rate of return). Finally, press 🔲 and NPV to produce the answer of –$13,930.02.

Obviously, the loan has a negative NPV and should not be made since, in light of the time value of money, it would cost you almost $14,000. This loan would be unacceptable even if you were willing to settle for a 5 percent rate of return. To check this (without clearing your HP-10BII's memory and starting over) enter 5 and I/YR. Then enter 🔲 and NPV and you will display a negative NPV of –$44.46.

HP-10BII: Keystrokes for Computing the Net Present Value (NPV)

Keystrokes	Explanation
⬛, C ALL	clearing memory
75000, +/–, CFj	to enter the amount of the loan as an outflow
0, CFj	no cash flow at the end of year 1
15000, CFj	end of year 2 cash flow
20000, CFj	end of year 3 cash flow
25000, CFj	end of year 4 cash flow
30000, CFj	end of year 5 cash flow
11, I/YR	the required rate of return
⬛, NPV	–13,930.02 displayed as the NPV

Grouped Cash Flows

Your HP-10BII can solve NPV problems involving more cash flows if there is grouped data. As explained earlier in this chapter, for such problems you should enter, along with the amount of each cash flow, the total number of times it occurs in succession including the first time.

To illustrate the process, assume you plan to invest in an oil exploration limited partnership that entails the following cash flows:

Timing of Flow	Amount of Cash Flow
Immediately	$50,000 outflow
Years 1 through 5	0
End of years 6 through 9	6,000 inflow
End of year 10	60,000 inflow

Is this investment acceptable if you insist on a rate of return of at least 12 percent per year?

First clear your HP-10BII's memory and then enter 50000, +/–, and CFj (for the initial cash outflow). Next enter 0, CFj, 5, ⬛, and Nj (for the years 1 through 5 with no cash flows). Then enter 6000, CFj, 4, ⬛, and Nj (for the inflows at the end of years 6 through 9). Then enter 60000 and CFj (for the last inflow at the end of year 10). Next enter 12 and I/YR (for the required interest rate). Finally enter ⬛ and NPV to compute the answer, which is – $20,340.76.

HP-10BII: Keystrokes for Computing the NPV of a Project With Grouped Cash Flows

Keystrokes	Explanation
▭, C ALL	clearing memory
50000, +/–, CFj	the investment as a cash outflow
0, CFj, 5, ▭, Nj	no cash flows for years 1 through 5
6000, CFj, 4, ▭, Nj	4 consecutive cash inflows for years 6 through 9
60000, CFj	the final cash inflow for year 10
12, I/YR	the required rate of return
▭, NPV	–20,340.76 displayed as the NPV

Solving IRR Problems With an HP-10BII

Recall that the internal rate of return is the discount rate that equates the present value of cash inflows and outflows, producing an NPV of zero. If the IRR exceeds the investor's minimum desired rate of return, the investment is an attractive one. If it equals the minimum desired rate, the investor should be neutral toward the project. If the IRR is below the minimum desired rate, the investment is unattractive.

The computation of the IRR of an investment is an extremely complex process that can be conducted manually using a trial and error method. Beginning with an estimate of the IRR, such as 10 or 15 percent, discount the cash inflows and outflows to their present values. If the present value of the inflows exceeds the present value of the outflows, so that NPV is positive at the selected rate, choose a higher rate and repeat the calculations. You are choosing a higher rate because you need a higher rate to reduce the NPV to (or close to) zero. On the other hand, if the discounted cash outflows exceed the discounted cash inflows resulting in a negative NPV, choose a lower interest rate and repeat the calculations. Continue this trial-and-error process, adjusting the discount rate until the resulting NPV is equal to (or close to) zero. The discount rate that produces an NPV of zero is the IRR, an average rate of return over the time horizon weighted to reflect the amount and timing of the various cash flows.

When using your HP-10BII to solve for the IRR, do not enter a discount (interest) rate because it is the unknown value that you are solving for. Begin by clearing the HP-10BII's memory and then proceed by entering all the cash flows. After the cash flows have been entered, press ▭ and IRR/YR for the answer. The IRR/YR key is to the left of the NPV key.

For example, to solve a simple IRR problem involving a single cash outflow of $10,000 followed by five cash inflows of $2,300 each, first set your HP-10BII to display four decimal places by entering ▭, DISP and 4. (Remember 4 decimal precision is desired in some interest rate calculations.)[*] Then clear your HP-10BII's memory and enter 10000, +/– and CFj (for the cash outflow). Next enter 2300, CFj, 5, ▭, and Nj (for the five cash inflows). Finally enter ▭ and IRR/YR to compute the answer, which is 4.8472.

HP-10BII: Keystrokes for Solving a Simple IRR Problem

Keystrokes	Explanation
▭, C ALL	clearing memory
▭, DISP, 4	set at 4 decimal precision
10000, +/–, CFj	the initial cash outflow
2300, CFj, 5, ▭, Nj	5 consecutive cash inflows
▭, IRR/YR	4.8472 displayed as the IRR

To take a more complex IRR example, assume the investment you are considering involves an immediate $6,000 cash outflow followed by a series of cash flows:

Timing of Flow	Amount of Cash Flow
Immediately	$6,000 outflow
End of year 1	200 inflow
End of years 2 through 5	900 inflow
End of year 6	1,000 outflow
End of year 7	1,100 inflow
Year 8	0
End of year 9	1,200 inflow
End of year 10	3,000 inflow

To solve for the IRR of this investment, first make sure that your HP-10BII is set for 4 decimal precision (if you have not already done so) and then clear its memory. Then enter 6000, +/–, and CFj (for the immediate cash outflow). Next enter 200 and CFj (for the cash inflow at the end of year 1); 900, CFj, 4, ▭, and Nj (for the cash inflows at the end of years 2 through 5); 1000, +/–, and CFj (for the cash outflow at the end of year 6); 1100 and CFj (for the cash inflow at the end of year 7); 0 and CFj (because there are no cash flows in year 8); 1200 and CFj (for the cash inflow at the end of year 9); 3000 and CFj (for the cash inflow at the end of year 10). Finally enter ▭

---

[*] Four decimal precision is useful in time-value-of-money problems because the calculator will round to the nearest basis point. A basis point is 1/100 of a percentage point. A basis point, expressed as a decimal, is .0001.

and IRR/YR to compute the IRR, which is 4.6664. After solving for the IRR and without reentering the cash flows, you can choose a discount (interest) rate, such as 10 percent (enter 10 and I/YR), and solve for the NPV (enter ▭ and NPV).

HP-10BII: Keystrokes for Solving a Complex IRR Problem

Keystrokes	Explanation
▭, C ALL	clearing memory
6000, +/–, CFj	immediate cash outflow
200, CFj	end of year 1 cash inflow
900, CFj, 4, ▭, Nj	end of years 2 through 5 cash inflow
1000, +/–, CFj	end of year 6 cash outflow
1100, CFj	end of year 7 cash inflow
0, CFj	no cash flows in year 8
1200, CFj	end of year 9 cash inflow
3000, CFj	end of year 10 cash inflow
▭, IRR/YR	4.6664 displayed as the IRR

Keystrokes for Computing the NPV Without Reentering All the Information

10, I/YR	discount interest rate
▭, NPV	–1,559.1085 displayed as the NPV

Problems in Using IRR as a Decision Rule

As previously indicated, the IRR provided by potential investments must be used with caution in decision making. This is especially true when the IRR is used as a means for ranking competing investment opportunities.

One situation in which an evaluation based solely on comparative IRRs may lead to an incorrect decision is the case of mutually exclusive investment projects that are of substantially different magnitudes. For example, assume you can invest in either of two pieces of equipment for your business, but the investment in one eliminates the possibility of investing in the other. (These are called mutually exclusive investments.) Also assume you can borrow enough money to make the investment in either piece of equipment, neither of which has any salvage value. The total cash flows from the two projects, A and B, are shown below:

Beginning of Year	Cash Flows (A)	Cash Flows (B)
1	$5,000 outflow	$50,000 outflow
2	3,000 inflow	25,000 inflow
3	4,000 inflow	35,000 inflow
4	5,000 inflow	45,000 inflow

The IRR from project A is 54.0603 percent, while the IRR from project B is only 42.9811 percent. (You should confirm these results on your own HP-10BII.) Does this mean that project A is preferable? Not necessarily. For example, if the money to meet the initial outflow is borrowed at a 10 percent rate of interest, it may be preferable to invest in project B. On the basis of a 10 percent discount rate, the NPV of project B is $35,462.06, whereas the NPV of project A is only $4,789.63. In other words, project B increases your wealth (in a time-value sense) by more than seven times the amount of project A. A more modest rate of return on a large project may be preferable to a higher rate of return on a small project. (Note, however, that this illustration deals with mutually exclusive projects. If the projects are not mutually exclusive, then the correct investment decision might be to invest in both projects.)

There are several other situations in which a decision based on the IRR may be incorrect. As in the case of mutually exclusive investment projects with substantially different magnitudes, mutually exclusive investment projects with substantially different cash flow patterns may also lead to an incorrect decision. There is also difficulty in relying solely on IRRs when deciding between investment opportunities that have substantially different durations. Another limitation of the IRR method for comparing investment projects involves the question of financing costs of cash outflows that may be associated with one or both of the projects. A final problem concerning the IRR method is that it is possible for a project to have multiple IRRs, each of which is mathematically correct. It is also possible that an investment may have no IRR within the realm of real numbers. What should you do about these problems of using the IRR as a means of ranking competing investment opportunities? One simple solution is to forget about using the IRR as a method for deciding between investment opportunities and use the NPV method instead.

INCREASING THE COMPOUNDING, DISCOUNTING, OR PAYMENT FREQUENCY

All the explanations and illustrations so far in this and the preceding chapter are based on the assumption that compounding and discounting occur once per year. In reality, however, compounding and discounting often occur more frequently than annually. For example, a certificate of deposit can be credited with compound interest on a monthly basis. A traditional savings account can earn daily compound interest. The present value of the income from a corporate bond typically is computed on a semiannual discounting basis.

In addition, all of the explanations of problems involving periodic payments thus far have been based on the assumption that payments are made annually. Often, however, such payments occur more than once per year. Installment loan payments, for example, are frequently made monthly. Bond interest payments are usually made every 6 months. Deposits into the savings accounts of many people are made weekly.

The remainder of this chapter examines the effect on the interest rate and, therefore, on the time value of money resulting from compounding or discounting more often than annually. It also contains an explanation of how to solve problems involving a series of level payments that occur more often than once per year regardless of how often compounding or discounting takes place.

Nominal Versus Effective Interest Rates

conversion of interest earnings into principal

As you know, compounding results in the *conversion of interest earnings into principal.* For example, if $100 is deposited in an account today and the account is subsequently credited with $7.00 of compound interest, the principal on which future interest is credited rises to $107. The $7.00 of interest, when paid, converts into and becomes principal.

If compounding occurs annually, when does interest convert into principal and begin to earn interest on itself? Obviously, the conversion and thus the capacity for increased interest earnings occur after one year, again after 2 years, and so on. If, on the other hand, compounding occurs on a monthly basis, when does interest convert into principal and thus begin to earn interest on itself? The conversions occur after one month has elapsed, again after 2 months, 3 months, and so on.

Of course, the greater the frequency with which compounding occurs, the smaller the dollar amount of interest earned and converted into principal on the occasion of each compounding. Naturally, the amount of interest a given amount of principal can earn in a week is less than it can earn in a month at any given stated or nominal annual interest rate. Nevertheless, all other things being equal, the more frequent the compounding, the greater the total interest credited to an account for the year. To illustrate, table 7-2 shows the amount of interest credited during one year to a $10,000 deposit at a stated or nominal 9 percent annual interest rate and various compounding frequencies.

Technically, of course, compounding can occur even more frequently than daily—every hour, every minute, every second, or even continuously. As the frequency increases, so does the total interest credited. The upper limit of the total interest credited to a sum of money for a particular stated or nominal annual interest rate occurs in the case of continuous compounding where interest is compounded an infinite number of times per year rather than at discrete time intervals. *Continuous compounding* is a theoretical concept useful principally in the study of advanced financial topics, but it also has some practical applications, since some financial institutions offer a product that credits interest to customer accounts on a continuous basis.

continuous compounding

TABLE 7-2
Total Interest Credited to a $10,000 Deposit During One Year at a 9 Percent Stated Annual Interest Rate and Various Compounding Frequencies

Compounding Frequency	Interest Earnings
Annually	$900.00
Semiannually	920.25
Quarterly	930.83
Monthly	938.07
Weekly	940.89
Daily*	941.62

*Based on 365 days per year[2]

From the figures in table 7-2 it should be obvious that a stated or nominal annual interest rate does not necessarily reflect the true or effective interest rate. You have seen that a 9 percent nominal annual rate produces any one of six separate interest earnings in a year, depending on the frequency of compounding. Hence, it is important to distinguish between the nominal or stated annual rate (9 percent in this illustration) and the true or effective annual rate (EAR).

When compounding occurs once per year, the nominal and effective annual rates are identical. In table 7-2, when annual compounding is applied, the $10,000 deposit earns $900, exactly 9 percent. In all other cases it earns more than $900 (more than 9 percent) because of the more frequent compounding.

effective annual interest rate (EAR)

The *effective annual interest rate (EAR)* is the annual rate that produces in one compounding the same amount of interest as the nominal annual rate with its compounding frequency. For instance, the 9 percent nominal annual rate in table 7-2, when compounded quarterly, produces $930.83 of interest. Thus, the ef th fective annual interest rate is 9.3083 percent ($930.83 ÷ $10,000). Similarly, the 9 percent nominal annual rate compounded daily generates $941.62 in interest. Thus, the effective annual rate is 9.4162 percent ($941.62 ÷ $10,000).

Calculating the EAR

The effective annual interest rate can be computed for any nominal rate and compounding frequency with the following formula:[3]

$$i_{eff} = \left[1 + \frac{i_{nom}}{f}\right]^f - 1$$

where i_{eff} is the effective annual rate in decimal form,
                  i_{nom} is the nominal annual rate in decimal form, and
                  f is the compounding frequency per year

Thus, for example, a 9 percent nominal annual rate compounded monthly represents an effective annual rate of

$$i_{eff} = \left[1 + \frac{.09}{12} \right]^{12} - 1$$

$$= .093807$$

$$= 9.3807\%$$

As an alternative to using this formula, you can calculate the effective annual interest rate for any nominal annual rate and compounding frequency by using your HP-10BII. To illustrate, assume that a 9 percent nominal rate is to be compounded weekly. First, set your HP-10BII to display four decimal places (if you have not already done so) and then clear its memory. Next, in order to convert a nominal rate to an effective rate, use the secondary functions on the lower half of the I/YR, PV, and PMT keys, which are NOM%, EFF%, and P/YR, respectively.

The effective annual rate is 9.4089 percent. Now before you do anything else, restore the calculator's setting to one payment period and one compounding period per year so that subsequent problems you work on will be solved correctly. This is accomplished by pressing 1, ▭, P/YR, and C.

HP-10BII: Keystrokes for Computing the EAR

Keystrokes	Explanation
▭, C ALL	clearing memory
▭, DISP, 4	to set at 4 decimal precision
9, ▭, NOM %	to enter the nominal rate
52, ▭, P/YR	to adjust for weekly compounding
▭, EFF%	to produce the effective rate of 9.4089
1, ▭, P/YR, C	reset for one payment period per year

For those who do not wish to use either a formula or your HP-10BII to determine the effective annual interest rate, appendix I will be of some help. It contains a table showing the effective annual interest rates that correspond to a number of nominal annual rates and commonly used compounding frequencies. The table also includes the effective annual rate for the unusual case of continuous compounding.

To illustrate further the difference between the nominal and effective annual rates of interest, the following list shows the effective annual rate for a nominal annual rate of 7 percent and various compounding frequencies:

7% annually	=	7.0000% effective rate
7% semiannually	=	7.1225% effective rate
7% quarterly	=	7.1859% effective rate
7% monthly	=	7.2290% effective rate
7% weekly	=	7.2458% effective rate
7% daily	=	7.2501% effective rate

Again, it is clear that, for a particular nominal annual interest rate, the true or effective rate rises as the frequency of compounding per year increases. Note, however, that the increase in the effective annual rate becomes smaller and smaller with each increase in compounding frequency. In the above list, for example, the change from annual to semiannual compounding increased the effective rate by .1225 percentage points (7.1225 − 7.0000). The change from semiannual to quarterly compounding changed the effective rate by only .0634 percentage points (7.1859 − 7.1225); and the change from quarterly to monthly compounding increased it by only .0432 percentage points (7.2290 − 7.1859).

Another point worth noting concerning nominal versus effective annual interest rates is that sometimes a nominal rate with a high compounding frequency produces a higher effective rate than a slightly higher nominal rate with a low compounding frequency. For example, assume that you plan to deposit $10,000 in an interest-bearing account for one year. Bank A pays interest of 8 percent compounded semiannually. Bank B pays 7.9 percent compounded daily. Where should you put your money? If you use the formula described earlier or your HP-10BII, you will find that the effective annual rate in Bank A is 8.1600 percent. Bank B, on the other hand, pays an effective annual rate of 8.2195 percent. That is an extra $5.95 credited to your $10,000 deposit if you go to Bank B.

The difference between nominal and effective annual rates inspired the Truth-in-Lending Act (TILA) and the Truth-in-Savings Act (TISA) requiring financial institutions to provide annual percentage rates (APRs) and annual percentage yields (APY). You can use an APR to calculate the EAR. Although APRs are not effective rates, they consider how frequently interest is paid. The TILA is discussed in chapter 10.

Annual Percentage Rates

annual percentage rate (APR)

An *annual percentage rate (APR)* is the periodic rate (that is, the semiannual rate, the quarterly rate, the monthly rate, and so on) multiplied by the number of periods in a year. A daily rate is multiplied by 365, a monthly rate by 12, a quarterly rate by 4, and so on. Credit cards use a daily periodic rate that is multiplied by 365 to produce the APR for the credit card. If a credit card has a daily periodic rate of .00027123 or .027123 percent, then the card's APR is 9.8999 percent (that is, .027123 x 365) or, if rounded, 9.90 percent. It is important to recognize that the periodic rate is not the EAR divided by the number of periods in a year.

If a consumer car loan with monthly payments has an APR of 6 percent, what is its EAR?

$$EAR = (1 + APR/12)^{12} - 1$$
$$EAR = (1 + .06/12)^{12} - 1$$
$$EAR = (1 + .005)^{12} - 1$$
$$EAR = .0617 = 6.17\%$$

Note that the size of the loan, the loan term, and the payment were not needed to calculate the effective annual interest rate on the loan.

Solving for the periodic rate (PER) when you know the EAR requires some algebra skills:

$$PER = (1 + EAR)^{(1/f)} - 1,\ \text{where f is the number of periods in a year;}$$
$$PER = (1.0617)^{(1/12)} - 1 = .005;$$
$$APR = .005 \times 12 = .06 \text{ or 6 percent}$$

As you can see, we are back where we started this exercise.

Impact of Compounding Frequency on Future Values

Because the effective annual interest rate rises as the frequency of compounding increases, so does the future value of a single sum. The same is true of other future values described in this and the previous chapter. For example, the future value of an annual annuity or of a series of annual uneven cash flows rises as compounding frequency increases. Conversely, in sinking fund problems the size of the annual payment needed to reach a targeted future amount diminishes as the frequency of compounding and the effective annual interest rate increase. Finally, the number of years or annual payments needed to reach a particular future value decreases as the frequency of compounding and the effective annual interest rate increase.

Impact of Discounting Frequency on Present Values

You probably have already guessed that increasing the frequency of discounting has the opposite effect on present values than increasing the frequency of compounding has on future values. This again follows from the preceding discussion of nominal versus effective interest rates.

To illustrate, calculate the present value of $100 due in one year at 7 percent. Discounted annually, you know that the effective rate is 7 percent. The present value of $100 discounted for one year at 7 percent is $93.46. Discounted quarterly, however, the effective annual rate is 7.1859 percent. The present value of $100 discounted for one year at 7.1859 percent is $93.30. Discounted monthly, the effective annual rate is 7.229 percent, which produces a present value of $93.26.

Generalizing from these results, you can conclude that, all other things being equal, an increase in the frequency of discounting increases the effective annual interest rate and therefore reduces the present value of a single sum. The same is true of the present value of an annual annuity or of a series of annual uneven cash flows. Conversely, in debt service problems, an increase in the frequency of charging interest per year, all other things being equal, increases the amount of the loan payments per year. Finally, the number of years it takes to pay off a loan or to liquidate a principal sum increases as the frequency of charging or crediting interest per year increases, all other things being equal.

Calculating the FVSS or the PVSS When Compounding or Discounting Occurs More Often Than Once per Year

When you encounter FVSS and PVSS problems in which the interest rate is compounded or discounted more frequently than annually, there are two basic ways of solving them: (1) use the effective annual interest rate or (2) adjust the nominal annual interest rate and number of periods.

Using the Effective Annual Interest Rate

The first basic approach is to solve these problems by computing the effective annual interest rate as explained earlier. Then use the effective rate in the same way you have learned to use the nominal annual interest rate throughout this and the preceding chapter.

To illustrate this approach (that is, using the effective annual interest rate) of solving this type of FVSS problem, what amount will $500 grow to in 3 years at 6 percent interest compounded quarterly? Using your HP-10BII to compute the effective rate, first clear its memory and set it for 4 decimal precision by pressing ⌨, DISP, and 4. Then enter 6, ⌨, and NOM% for the nominal rate; 4, ⌨, and P/YR for the number of compounding periods. Next enter ⌨ and EFF% to find the effective annual rate. The answer, 6.1364 percent, will be displayed on the screen. Then reset your HP-10BII for one payment period per year by entering 1, ⌨, P/YR, and C.

HP-10BII: Keystrokes for Computing the EAR When Compounding Is Quarterly

Keystrokes	Explanation
⬛, C ALL	clearing memory
⬛, DISP, 4	to set at 4 decimal precision
6, ⬛, NOM %	to enter the nominal rate
4, ⬛, P/YR	to adjust for quarterly compounding
⬛, EFF%	6.1364 displayed as the EAR
1, ⬛, P/YR, C	reset for one payment period per year

Once having determined that the effective annual rate is 6.1364 percent (either by using your HP-10BII or appendix I), you can use it in place of the nominal 6 percent rate to solve the problem. First, remember to clear your HP-10BII's memory. Then enter 500, +/−, and PV since $500 is the present value. Next enter 6.1364 and I/YR for the effective annual rate; 3 and N for the number of periods (years). Then solve the problem by entering FV and you will have the answer, $597.81 (rounded).

To illustrate this approach (that is, using the effective annual interest rate) of solving this type of PVSS problem, what is the present value of $3,000 due 6 years hence with a discount rate of 12 percent applied monthly? First determine that the effective annual rate is 12.6825 percent. Then substitute it for the 12 percent nominal rate and solve for PV, which is $1,465.49 (rounded).

Notice that the methodology for computing the FVSS or the PVSS when compounding or discounting is more frequent than annually is the same as when it is annually, except that the effective annual interest rate must be determined and substituted for the nominal rate.

HP-10BII: Keystrokes for Computing the FVSS When Using an EAR

Keystrokes	Explanation
⬛, C ALL	clearing memory
500, +/−, PV	present value
6.1364, I/YR	effective annual rate
3, N	number of periods (years)
FV	597.8098 displayed

HP-10BII: Keystrokes for Computing the EAR When Discounting Is Monthly

Keystrokes	Explanation
▭, C ALL	clearing memory
▭, DISP, 4	to set at 4 decimal precision
12, ▭, NOM%	to enter the nominal rate
12, ▭, P/YR	to adjust for monthly discounting
▭, EFF%	12.6825 displayed as the EAR
1, ▭, P/YR, C	reset for one payment period per year

HP-10BII: Keystrokes for Computing the PVSS When Using an EAR

Keystrokes	Explanation
▭, C ALL	clearing memory
3000, FV	future value
12.6825, I/YR	effective annual rate
6, N	number of periods (years)
PV	−1,465.4885 displayed

Adjusting the Nominal Annual Interest Rate and the Number of Periods

The second basic way of solving FVSS and PVSS problems involves using the nominal annual rate rather than the effective rate. In this approach, two adjustments must be made. First, the problem's nominal annual interest rate must be divided by the number of compounding or discounting periods per year. This reflects the fact that only a fraction of the annual rate will be applied each time compounding or discounting occurs during the year. Second, the number of years in the problem must be multiplied by the number of compounding or discounting periods per year. This reflects the total number of times that compounding or discounting of the fractional annual rate occurs. Note that the number (that is, the number of compounding or discounting periods per year) that is divided into the nominal annual interest rate and the number (that is, the number of compounding or discounting periods per year) that is used to multiply the number of years in the problem are always the same (2 for semiannual compounding or discounting, 4 for quarterly, 12 for monthly, 52 for weekly, and 365 for daily).

To illustrate this approach (that is, adjusting the nominal annual interest rate and the number of periods) of solving this type of FVSS problem, let us return to the problem of determining the amount to which $500 will grow in 3 years at 6 percent interest compounded quarterly. Using your HP-10BII to solve the problem, first clear its memory and enter 500, +/–, and PV for the present value. Next make the first of the two adjustments (that is, divide the nominal interest rate of 6 percent by the compounding frequency of 4) by entering 6, ÷, 4, =, I/YR for the quarterly interest rate. Then make the second adjustment (that is, multiply 3 years by the compounding frequency of 4) by entering 3, x, 4, =, N for the number of compounding periods. Then solve the problem by entering FV. The answer displayed is $597.81 (rounded).

To illustrate this approach (that is, adjusting the nominal annual interest rate and the number of periods) of solving this type of PVSS problem, let us return to the problem of determining the present value of $3,000 due in 6 years hence with a discount rate of 12 percent applied monthly. Using your HP-10BII to solve the problem, first clear its memory and enter 3000 and FV for the future value. Next make the first of the two adjustments (that is, divide the nominal interest rate of 12 percent by the discounting frequency of 12) by entering 12, ÷, 12, =, I/YR for the monthly interest rate. Then make the second adjustment (that is, multiply 6 years by the discount frequency of 12) by entering 6, x, 12, =, N for the number of discounting periods. Then solve the problem by entering PV. The answer displayed is $1,465.49 (rounded).

HP-10BII: Keystrokes for Computing the FVSS When Adjusting the Nominal Rate and the Number of Periods

Keystrokes	Explanation
▭, C ALL	clearing memory
500, +/–, PV	present value
6, ÷, 4, =, I/YR	quarterly interest rate
3, x, 4, =, N	number of compounding periods
FV	597.8091 displayed

When the solution to this type of problem is a value for the interest rate (I/YR) or the number of years (N) (rather than the FVSS or the PVSS), it must be remembered that these are periodic values. In other words, if the compounding or discounting frequency is other than annual, the solution will also be an other-than-annual value. To convert the solution to an annual basis, it must be adjusted by a factor. For example, in the case of monthly compounding, the factor is 12. Therefore, if the number of compounding periods is 24, the number of years (N) during which compounding takes place is 2 (that is, $24 \div 12 = 2$).

HP-10BII: Keystrokes for Computing the PVSS by Adjusting Payments per Year [P/YR]

Keystrokes	Explanation
▭, C ALL	clearing memory
3000, FV	future value
12 ▭ P/YR	Sets P/YR to 12
12 I/YR	Inputs 12% as nominal interest rate
6, ▭ x P/YR	Sets N to 72
PV	−1,465.4883 displayed

Likewise, in the case of quarterly compounding, the factor is 4. Therefore, if the number of compounding periods is 8 and you are solving for the interest rate (I/YR), the result will be a quarterly value that needs to be converted to an annual value. However, in the case of an interest rate, it is insufficient to merely multiply the quarterly rate by the factor of 4, since the result of such a multiplication would be a nominal annual rate. A more accurate result is found by converting the nominal annual rate to an effective annual rate as described earlier.

FOCUS ON ETHICS
The Impact of Inflation

The financial advisor must never lose track of the impact of inflation. If a couple planning to retire in 20 years projects their annual needs at $50,000, that projection is in the current year's dollars. If inflation is estimated at 3 percent per year, at the retirement date the inflation-adjusted needs will be $90,000! Twenty years into retirement (40 years from today), the adjusted income requirement at 3 percent annual inflation would be $163,000! Viewed another way, a $50,000 income in 40 years will have a purchasing power equal to only $15,000 in today's dollars.

Often advisors supply future projections of mutual fund or insurance cash values with specific rate-of-return assumptions. The projected accumulation usually is extremely large, and the client is lulled into a dangerous complacency because inflation is ignored.

Unfortunately, fully informing the client of the perils of inflation often (unintentionally and ironically) results in frightening the client into inaction. Regardless of this possibility, the advisor's ethical responsibility is clear. Inflation is a critical factor that must be addressed in all financial projections. Withholding this information is the same as misinforming the client.

Calculating Annuity Values When Compounding or Discounting Occurs More Often Than Once per Year

Thus far we have examined FVSS and PVSS problems in which compounding or discounting occurs more frequently than annually. A related but separate topic is the question of annuity values when compounding or discounting occurs more frequently than once per year.

Simple Annuities and Simple Annuities Due

simple annuity
simple annuity due

A *simple annuity* or *simple annuity due* is one in which the frequency of payments and the frequency of compounding or discounting are identical. An example of a simple annuity is a series of six quarterly deposits credited with interest quarterly, beginning 3 months from now. Likewise, an example of a simple annuity due is a series of 15 monthly payments discounted on a monthly basis, beginning immediately. All of the annuity topics discussed so far involved simple annuities or simple annuities due because both the payment frequency and the compounding or discounting frequency were identical, once per year.

The calculation of the present or future value of a simple annuity or a simple annuity due when payments are more frequent than annual involves the same tools and procedures you have already learned. The same formulas you used for computing the FVA, the FVAD, the PVA, and the PVAD can be used; you can even enter the same keystrokes on your HP-10BII—except for two adjustments. First, you need to adjust the number of payments per year by entering the number of payments per year, ▭, and P/YR. Second, you need to enter the total number of payments in the problem, not the number of years. This is done by entering the number of years, ▭, and x P/YR. The nominal interest rate is entered as an annual rate and not a periodic rate.

A corporate bond is a frequently encountered security that includes a simple annuity with payments occurring more frequently than annually. For example, assume that a bond provides semiannual interest payments of $40 for 10 years, beginning 6 months from now, as well as payment of the $1,000 principal sum at the end of the 10th year. If bonds with a similar degree of riskiness are yielding 11 percent, what should you pay for this bond? Using your HP-10BII, first clear its memory and set it for end-of-period payments. Next make the two adjustments noted above, namely enter 2, ▭, and P/YR to adjust for two payments per year and semiannual discounting. Then enter 10, ▭, and x P/YR for the total number of payments over the 10-year period. Next enter 40 and PMT for the amount of each interest payment; 1000 and FV for the maturity value of the bond; 11 and I/YR for the interest rate. Then solve for PV to determine the price you should pay for the bond, which is $820.74 (rounded). Finally, enter 1, ▭, P/YR, and C to reset your HP-10BII for one payment period per year.

Now assume that you buy this bond for $820.74 and hold it for 3 years, at which time it is called by the issuing corporation at a call price of $1,040. What has been your annual yield to the call date? To solve this problem on your HP-10BII, first clear its memory and set it for end-of-period payments. Then enter 2, ▭, and P/YR (for the number of payments per year); 3, ▭, and x P/YR (for the total number of payments up to the call); 40 and PMT (for the amount of each payment); 820.74, +/–, and PV (for the purchase price of the bond); 1040 and FV (for the call price of the bond). Then to solve for the nominal annual yield enter I/YR and the answer, 16.94 percent, will appear on the screen. Then without clearing your HP-10BII's memory, you can also solve for the effective annual yield of 17.66 percent by entering ▭ and EFF%. Finally, reset your HP-10BII for one payment period per year by entering 1, ▭, P/YR, and C.

HP-10BII: Keystrokes for Computing the Present Value of a Bond

Keystrokes	Explanation
▭, C ALL	clearing memory
▭, BEG/END	only if BEGIN displayed
2, ▭, P/YR	number of payments per year
10, ▭, x P/YR	total number of payments
40, PMT	amount of each payment
1000, FV	value of bond at maturity
11, I/YR	interest rate
PV	–820.7443 displayed
1, ▭, P/YR, C	reset for one payment period per year

You can also calculate N or PMT in a simple annuity or simple annuity due involving other-than-annual payments. However, the item you compute as N is the total number of payments, not the total number of years. When N is one of the known values, you should enter the keystroke of: number of years, ▭, and xP/YR (as shown in the previous problem), which will provide you with the total number of payments. This keystroke must be entered after the keystroke that enters the number of payments per year: number of payments per year, ▭, and P/YR (as shown in the previous problem). The item you enter or compute as PMT is the single periodic payment, not the sum of the payments per year.

HP-10BII: Keystrokes for Computing the Annual Yield of a Bond

---

Keystrokes	Explanation
⬛, C ALL	clearing memory
⬛, BEG/END	only if BEGIN displayed
2, ⬛, P/YR	number of payments per year
3, ⬛, xP/YR	total number of payments
40, PMT	amount of each payment
820.74, +/–, PV	purchase price of bond
1040, FV	call price of bond
I/YR	16.9444 displayed
⬛, EFF%	17.6622 displayed
1, ⬛, P/YR, C	reset for one payment period per year

Complex Annuities and Complex Annuities Due

complex annuity
complex annuity due

A *complex annuity* or *complex annuity due* is one in which the frequency of payments and the frequency of compounding or discounting are different. For example, a complex annuity due is a series of 14 monthly deposits that are credited with interest daily, beginning immediately. Likewise, a complex annuity is a series of 10 semiannual lease payments that are discounted on a monthly basis, beginning 6 months from now.

HP-10BII: Keystrokes for Computing the EAR When Discounting Is Weekly

---

Keystrokes	Explanation
⬛, C ALL	clearing memory
⬛, DISP, 4	to set at 4 decimal precision
8, ⬛, NOM%	to enter the nominal rate
52, ⬛, P/YR	to adjust for weekly compounding
⬛, EFF%	8.3220 displayed as the EAR
1, ⬛, P/YR, C	reset for one payment period per year

Problems involving complex annuities or complex annuities due are fairly complicated and generally beyond the scope of this textbook. However, it is a relatively easy matter to solve for the present value of a complex annuity or complex annuity due in which the payments are made annually but discounting occurs more frequently. For example, what is the present value of a 5-year annuity of $2000 if it is discounted at 8 percent weekly? Using your HP-10BII, first determine the EAR. Then substitute the EAR for the nominal rate and solve for the PVA, which in the example is $7,918.11 (rounded).

HP-10BII: Keystrokes for Computing the PVA When Using an EAR

Keystrokes	Explanation
▭, C ALL	clearing memory
▭, BEG/END	only if BEGIN displayed
2000, PMT	amount of payments
5, N	number of payments
8.3220, I/YR	effective annual interest
PV	−7,918.1066 displayed as the PVA

CHAPTER SEVEN REVIEW

Key Terms and Concepts
Key Terms and Concepts are explained in the glossary.

ungrouped cash flows
grouped cash flows
Fisher Effect
net present value (NPV)
internal rate of return (IRR)
conversion of interest earnings
   into principal

continuous compounding
effective annual interest rate (EAR)
annual percentage rate (APR)
simple annuity
simple annuity due
complex annuity
complex annuity due

Review Questions
The answers to the review questions are in the supplement. Self-test questions and the answers to them are also in the supplement and on The American College Online.

7-1. Calculate the present value of the following payments based on 8 percent interest: [7-1]

End of Year	Amount of Payment
1	$ 800
2	800
3	800
4	6,000
5	6,000

7-2. Find the present value of Ted's vested renewal commissions discounted at 9 percent interest if he expects $30,000 next year, $20,000 in 2 years, and $10,000 per year in years 3 through 9. [7-1]

7-3. The divorce is final and you have been awarded the following alimony: $5,000 at the end of each of the next 3 years; $6,000 at the end of each of the following 5 years; and $7,000 at the end of each of the following 10 years. If you remarry, however, you receive no further alimony. Measured in terms of present value and at a discount rate of 6.5 percent, how much alimony will you relinquish if you remarry today? [7-1]

7-4. Which of the following income streams would you rather have if interest rates currently are 7 percent? [7-1]

Beginning of Year	Stream A	End of Year	Stream B
1	$2,000	1	$ 0
2	2,500	2	0
3	3,000	3	5,500
4	3,000	4	5,500
5	3,000	5	5,500

7-5. Your racehorse is sure to win $60,000 at the end of each of the next 3 years, after which you believe that the horse will be able to earn about $10,000 per year in stud fees at the end of each of 5 years. If you insist on a compound annual rate of return of at least 20 percent, what is the minimum offer you would accept for the horse today? [7-1]

7-6. Tuition at the university your daughter will be attending next year is expected to be $11,000, which includes an annual inflation assumption of 8 percent per year. You plan to set aside just enough money today that, invested at 6 percent interest, will be sufficient to pay her tuition in full at the start of each of the next 4 years. How large a capital sum is needed to accomplish this objective? [7-2]

7-7. Jerry wants to set aside a sum of money today that, together with the interest earnings, will be just enough to pay his son's four annual college tuition bills. He expects tuition to increase by 8 percent annually and that freshman tuition, due one year from now, will cost $9,000. If the college fund can be expected to earn 11 percent per year, how much money should Jerry set aside today? [7-2]

7-8. Sarah is the recipient of a trust fund that has earned 8 percent interest annually. It was originally funded several years ago with $4,000 deposited at the end of the first year. The only other deposits were $1,000 per year at the end of the 18th, 19th, and 20th years of the trust's life. How much is available in the trust at the end of the 20th year? [7-3]

7-9. To convince yourself of the wisdom of your recent decision to quit smoking (and this time you really mean it), you plan at the end of each of the next 5 years to put into a savings account earning 6 percent compound annual interest the money you would have spent on cigarettes. You anticipate that the amounts of the five deposits will be $400, $450, $500, $550, and $600. If all goes according to plan, how much will be in your account after 5 years? [7-3]

7-10. Rusty just opened an IRA account with a $1,000 deposit. If he increases the size of each annual deposit by 5 percent and if the account earns 7 percent compound annual interest, how much will be in the account at the end of 5 years? [7-4]

7-11. Your goal is to have accumulated a nest egg of $75,000 when you retire 12 years from now. You plan to make an initial deposit of $2,000 today, and on each of the following 11 anniversary dates you will deposit an amount that is 10 percent higher than the previous year's deposit. If your deposits earn 7 percent interest per year, will you reach your goal? [7-4]

7-12. Using a discount rate of 12 percent, compute the net present value of an investment that is expected to produce the following pattern of cash flows: [7-5]

Beginning of Year	Amount of Cash Flow	
1	$10,000	outflow
2	3,000	outflow
3	4,000	inflow
4	5,000	inflow
5	6,000	inflow
6	7,000	inflow

7-13. You have just made a loan of $85,000 to a friend who has agreed to the following repayment schedule:

End of Year	Amount of Payment
1	$ 5,000
2	10,000
3	0
4	0
5	100,000

a.   What is the net present value of this loan if 10 percent is your minimum acceptable compound annual rate of return? [7-5]

b.   What is the internal rate of return of this loan? [7-6]

7-14.   Diane is considering an investment that will involve an initial cash outlay of $1,000 and expected cash inflows of $230 at the end of each of the next 6 years. If the investment performs exactly as expected, what will be its internal rate of return? [7-6]

7-15.   Tax reform legislation notwithstanding, you have located an exotic tax-sheltered investment opportunity. For an initial outlay of $50,000 and an additional $10,000 5 years from now, you will receive the following income stream:

Timing of Flow	Income Stream
End of years 1 through 4	$7,500
End of years 6 through 10	8,000

What is the internal rate of return on this investment? [7-6]

7-16.   You are debating whether to invest $100,000 in a piece of equipment that will produce the following cost savings (after tax) for your business:

Timing of Savings	Amount of Savings
End of years 1 through 3	$30,000
End of year 4	(10,000)
End of years 5 through 7	20,000

a.   What is the internal rate of return on this investment? [7-6]

b.   What is the net present value of this investment at an 8 percent discount rate? [7-5]

7-17.   Calculate the effective annual interest rate if a 12 percent nominal annual rate is compounded
a.   annually [7-7]
b.   quarterly [7-7]
c.   weekly [7-7]

7-18.   Bob purchases a $500 certificate of deposit that pays 6 percent interest compounded semiannually. What will be the value of the CD in 5 years? [7-7]

7-19.   Find the present value of a 2-year annuity based on 8 percent annual interest for
a.   quarterly payments of $300 each [7-7]
b.   semiannual payments of $600 each [7-7]

7-20.   Harold is borrowing $1,000 from his father to repair his car. The loan is to be repaid monthly over one year, beginning one month from now, with monthly compounding based on 12 percent annual interest. Calculate the level monthly payment. [7-7]

7-21. Rita plans to save for a trip that she expects will cost $2,000 when she takes it one year from now. Calculate how much she must save each month, beginning one month from now, to meet her objective if she gets monthly compounding based on a 12 percent nominal annual interest rate. [7-7]

7-22. Calculate the present value of an income stream of $100 per month, beginning one month from now and continuing for 2 1/2 years, discounted at 12 percent compounded monthly. [7-7]

7-23. Compute the effective annual interest rate when a nominal annual rate of 18 percent is compounded
   a. semiannually [7-7]
   b. quarterly [7-7]
   c. monthly [7-7]
   Check your answers by comparing them with table I in appendix I.

7-24. Where should you put your money: in a certificate of deposit that will earn 9.75 percent compounded daily (365 days), or in one that will earn 10 percent compounded semiannually? [7-7]

7-25. a. Show which is the larger amount: the future value of a 10-year, $2,000 annual annuity growing at a nominal annual interest rate of 5 percent compounded weekly or one growing at a nominal annual interest rate of 5 percent compounded monthly. [7-7]
   b. Show which is the larger amount: the present value of a 6-year, $3,000 annual annuity discounted at 11 percent applied quarterly or one discounted at 11 percent applied monthly. [7-7]

7-26. Assume that you plan to save for Junior's college education by depositing $200 per month for the next 12 years in a savings account, beginning immediately. The account is expected to earn a nominal annual rate of 6 percent, compounded monthly. How much will be in the account at the end of the 12th year? [7-7]

NOTES

1. Most corporate bonds pay interest semiannually. For purposes of simplicity, however, annual payments are assumed here. A later section of this chapter deals with compounding and discounting where cash flows occur more frequently than once per year.
2. Financial institutions typically use a 360-day year as the basis for daily compounding calculations. This produces a slightly smaller annual interest, all other things being equal, than if they were to use a 365-day year.
3. The mathematics of calculating the effective rate manually when compounding is continuous is too complex to be dealt with in this textbook.

8

Financial Planning Applications

Learning Objectives
An understanding of the material in this chapter should enable the student to

8-1.   Identify the two funding requirements associated with financing a college education.

8-2.   Describe the process for calculating the resources required to fund a college education including the types of investments typically considered for this purpose.

8-3.   Describe the various tax deductions, tax credits, and penalty waivers that are available to encourage saving for college education.

8-4.   Explain how a college student's financial need is determined for purposes of obtaining federal student aid, and describe the various types of federal student aid available.

8-5.   Explain why emergency fund planning is an indispensable part of financial planning.

8-6.   Explain how an adequate amount of funding for emergencies is estimated and what types of investments are most appropriate for this purpose.

8-7.   Identify the key types of household debt.

8-8.   Explain the difference between secured and unsecured debt.

8-9.   Describe the activities involved in credit and debt management and explain how they relate to the steps in the financial planning process.

8-10. Explain the uses of the financial position statement and the cash flow statement in carrying out credit and debt management activities.

8-11. Explain the ways in which leasing an automobile differs from purchasing it, and identify the key characteristics of people who are particularly suited for leasing rather than buying an automobile.

8-12.   Explain how a lease's monthly payment is calculated.

8-13.   Explain the differences between a home equity loan and a home equity line of credit, and calculate the maximum amount a consumer can borrow under each.

8-14.   Calculate the amount of home equity debt on which interest is deductible for federal income tax purposes.

8-15.   Describe the key features and principal uses of the three types of bankruptcy available to consumers in the United States.

Chapter Outline

INTRODUCTION

This chapter covers three basic financial planning topics—funding a college education, cmergency fund planning, and credit and debt management. In addition to their importance to financial advisors in providing professional financial planning services to clients, these topics were selected because they illustrate various applications of the concepts covered in earlier chapters. For example, helping parents plan the funding of a college education for their children requires estimating future costs that increase with time due to inflation as well as periodic amounts of savings that increase with time due to investment return. Given the influence of time, inflation, and investment return on the college-funding problem, the financial advisor must apply several time-value-of-money concepts presented in chapters 6 and 7—the future value of a single sum, the present value of a single sum, and the present value of an annuity or an annuity due—in determining the amount that must be saved periodically (for example, monthly) to accumulate the funds required to pay for the college education.

The steps in the financial planning process presented in chapter one provide a format for explaining the key activities involved in credit and debt management and how credit and debt management is integrated with other planning techniques in the development of a client's financial plan. Also, the client's financial statements—the financial position statement and the cash flow statement—discussed in chapter 5 are tools that are indispensable for the tasks of gathering client data, analyzing the client's financial status, developing financial planning recommendations and/or alternatives, and monitoring financial planning recommendations in providing emergency fund planning and credit or debt management services to clients.

FUNDING A COLLEGE EDUCATION

Most clients understand the need to save for college and are aware that college costs have risen at a faster pace than the consumer price index (CPI) measure of inflation. Still, the vast majority of families accumulate far too little money for college by the child's matriculation date. This may be due to a variety of factors. The two most common ones are procrastination in establishing and following a savings plan in the case where the client survives until funds are needed for college expenses, and failure to create a fund to pay future college costs when the client dies before an adequate savings plan can be completed. Instead, families cut back on living expenses, borrow money, tap into retirement assets, or seek additional employment to meet the funding need. They often are forced to target a less expensive school rather than choose the school best suited to their child's needs.

Financial advisors who can calculate the college-funding requirements that must be met in the event of either a client's survival or death, who can recommend appropriate investment alternatives for meeting the former and appropriate life insurance products for meeting the latter, and who can explain important aspects of financial aid provide an invaluable service to their clients.

The Cost of a College Education

College education costs vary widely. In addition to factors such as public versus private, in-state versus out-of-state, residential versus commuter, and local versus distant, some schools are simply more expensive to operate while others may be more successful at generating gifts and endowments. Table 8-1 shows the average undergraduate costs for 2006–2007 as calculated by the College Board.

This data provides insight but there are two critical factors to consider. The first one is that a client's expectation or goal may deviate substantially from "average." Perhaps the client anticipates sending his or her child to a premier college with correspondingly high tuition. Conversely, the client may anticipate that the student will attend an in-state public college with particularly low costs. The point is that each case involves estimating a cost that is appropriate for the client rather than one that is an average. The second factor is that the cost for a year of education at some point in the future is difficult to estimate today.

Education Inflation

As table 8-2 shows, in recent years education inflation has exceeded general inflation. During the past 10 years, inflation, as measured by the consumer price index, has averaged 2.5 percent per year. For the same period inflation in tuition and fees for 4-year private colleges has been 6 percent, and for 4-year publicly funded colleges, the rate is 7 percent.

TABLE 8-1
Average College Costs—2006–2007

	Public Colleges*		Private Colleges	
	Resident	Commuter	Resident	Commuter
4-year colleges				
Tuition and fees	$5,836	$5,836	$22,218	$22,218
Books and supplies	942	942	935	935
Room and board	6,960	6,917**	8,149	7,211**
Transportation	880	1,224	722	1,091
Other	1,739	2,048	1,277	1,630
Total	$16,357	$16,967	$33,301	$33,085
2-year colleges				
Tuition and fees	$2,272	$2,272	****	****
Books and supplies	850	850	****	****
Room and board	***	6,299**	****	****
Transportation	***	1,197,	****	****
Other	***	1,676	****	****
Total		$12,294	****	****

Note: The figures are weighted by enrollment to reflect the charges incurred by the average undergraduate enrolled at each type of institution.
   *Public college figures indicate costs for in-state students.
   **Room and board costs for commuter students are average expenses for students living off campus but not with parents.
  ***The sample was too small to provide meaningful information.
 **** Costs were not reported.

Source: *Trends in College Pricing 2006* Copyright © 2006 by the College Board. Reproduced with permission. All rights reserved. www.collegeboard.com.

As indicated in table 8-2, with the exception of 3 years out of 10 for 2-year public institutions, college cost inflation has consistently outpaced the overall inflation rate as measured by the consumer price index (CPI).. While private and public colleges and universities generally encounter essentially the same cost pressures, the relatively large increases for public institutions reflect the sensitivity of their tuition and fee schedules to changes in state government appropriation levels, which have decreased significantly in recent years.

Aside from this influence of fluctuating state government appropriation levels on tuition and fees at public colleges and universities, will both private and public college costs, especially those of 4-year institutions, continue to rise more rapidly than the prices of other goods and services as they have over the past decade? Many people think they will and point to enrollment projections that indicate a continuing growth in demand. For example, Educational Testing Service's analysis of U.S. Census Bureau data and population projections have indicated that undergraduate enrollment will continue to grow annually until at least 2015 (the end of the projection period).

TABLE 8-2 Education Inflation Rates*				
Academic Year	Private 4-Year	Public 4-Year	Public 2-Year	Consumer Price Index Inflation
1997–98	6%	5%	7%	2.3%
1998–99	7%	4%	-1%	1.5%
1999–2000	6%	4%	6%	2.1%
2000–2001	4%	4%	0%	3.5%
2001–2002	8%	7%	-2%	2.8%
2002–2003	4%	9%	4%	1.6%
2003–2004	5%	13%	14%	2.3%
2004–2005	6.%	10%	9%	2.2%
2005–2006	5%	7%	5%	3.6%
2006–2007	6%	6%	4%	3.8%

*Education inflation rates reflect the percentage increase in tuition and fees relative to the prior academic year. Public college figures reflect costs for in-state students. Consumer price index inflation is for the preceding calendar year.

Source: *Trends in College Pricing.* Copyright © 2006 by the College Board. Reproduced with permission. All rights reserved. www.collegeboard.com.

Others, however, think there is reason for optimism. They point out that colleges seem to have realized the importance of efficient management, which may result in future tuition savings. Another perspective is that if education inflation and consumer prices continue at the levels experienced over the past 10 years, the cost of attending a public 4-year college will rise so significantly as compared with prices in general that many potential students would no longer be able to afford a college education. In addition, this dramatic difference between the growth of college costs and prices in general will cause the cost of education to rise significantly relative to the economic benefit unless salaries for college-educated people rise proportionately. Both factors would dampen demand for college education and, presumably, hold down college cost inflation.

Still, no one knows what the education inflation will be in the future. Prudence dictates conservatism in specifying a rate but overestimating the inflation rate, and thus the accumulation needed, can lead to despair-induced inaction. Most advisors use a rate in the (admittedly broad) 3 to 7 percent range.

College cost calculators abound on the web. The best ones allow you to start with current costs at the school(s) you list and input an education inflation percentage that may differ between tuition and cost-of-living inflation rates.[*]

Calculating the Funding Requirement

After this introduction to the college-funding challenge, advisors need to show the client the amounts required to meet the education objective under two possible circumstances—the client's death and the client's survival. These two funding requirements can be stated as follows:

- the lump sum required to fund the college education if the client were to die on the date his or her plan is implemented
- the monthly savings required to fund the college education if the client survives until matriculation begins

The calculation of these two funding requirements lends itself to time-value-of-money concepts discussed in chapter 7. A worksheet that provides a good approximation of the required college funding should contain the following five inputs:

1. current cost of a year of college
2. education inflation rate
3. number of years of college attendance
4. number of years until matriculation
5. investment rate of return

Figure 8-1 shows the steps in calculating the two funding requirements and presents an example. Applying the concept of determining the future value of a single sum (FVSS) discussed in chapter 6, the first step is to calculate the cost of each of the 4 years of the child's college education. Table 8-3 shows the calculator inputs and resulting college costs.

TABLE 8-3				
	Freshman	**Sophomore**	**Junior**	**Senior**
Years until (N)	14	15	16	17
Education inflation (I/YR)	5%	5%	5%	5%
Current college cost (PV)	$ 25,000	$ 25,000	$ 25,000	$ 25,000
Estimated cost (FV)	$ 49,498.29	$ 51,973.20	$ 54,571.86	$ 57,300.46
Note: These are four separate FV calculations.				

---

[*] One example of a web-based college calculator is www.collegeboard.com. Access is free but it does require that you register on the site.

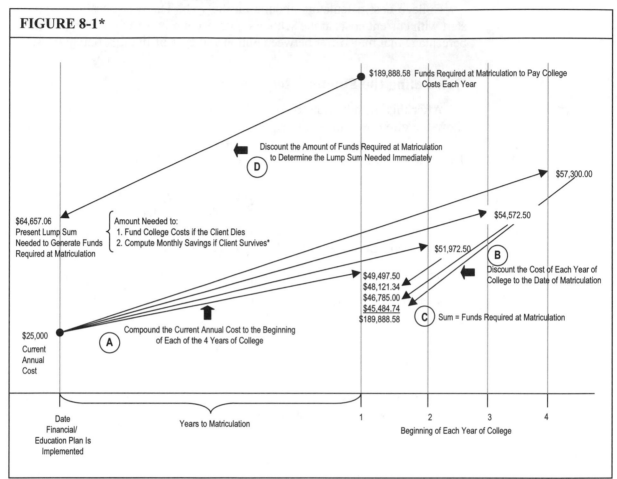

FIGURE 8-1*

* Numbers vary slightly due to rounding.

The second step involves discounting the costs for each of the 4 years of college to determine their present value on the date of matriculation as shown in table 8-4.

TABLE 8-4				
	Freshman	**Sophomore**	**Junior**	**Senior**
Years past matriculation date (N_j)	0	1	2	3
Annual cash flow (CF_j)	$ 49,498.29	$ 51,973.20	$ 54,571.86	$ 57,300.46
Discount rate (I/YR)	8%	8%	8%	8%
Present value at matriculation (Gold) (NPV)	$189,895.15			
Note: On the financial calculator this is one calculation using CF_j, I/YR and computing the NPV.				

Even though the full cost of a college education won't come due all at once, discounting the cash flows to the matriculation date gives the client and the financial advisor a target that is useful for planning purposes. After the target is established the different approaches to reaching that target are evaluated. For example, the client could decide to invest a lump sum today or to make monthly payments over time into an account to meet the $189,895 goal.

Finding the lump-sum cost today (PV) of the discounted costs at matriculation (FV) is a simple matter on the financial calculator as shown in table 8-5. The table looks at funding the account three different ways: as a lump sum today, as monthly payments with the payment being made at the end of each month, and as monthly payments with the payment being made at the beginning of each month.

The differences in the lump sum (PV) amounts are attributable to going from an 8 percent nominal rate discounted on an annual basis for the first scenario and an 8 percent nominal rate discounted on a monthly basis for the second and third scenarios. Making the monthly payments at the beginning of the month rather than at the end shaves about $4.00 off the required monthly investment.

TABLE 8-5			
	Lump Sum (PV)	**Monthly (PMT)* END**	**Monthly (PMT)* BEG**
Lump-sum costs at matriculation (FV)	$189,895.15	$ 189,895.15	$189,895.15
Years (or months) until matriculation (N)	14	168	168
Discount rate (I/YR)	8%	8%	8%
Lump sum today (PV) to fund future college costs (FV)	**$ 64,651.90**	$ 62,189.67	$ 62,189.67
Monthly (PMT) to fund college costs (FV)		$ 616.50	$ 612.41
* P/YR set to 12 for monthly calculations.			

INVESTING FOR COLLEGE

The previous section explained the use of time-value-of-money concepts in calculating the interrelated college-funding requirements in the event of both the client's death and the client's survival. This section focuses on the key considerations involved in designing an appropriate accumulation plan for achieving the college-funding objective in the event the client survives until a specified future date, generally the date of matriculation.

Once the financial goal is established, the client can consider the best methods of accumulation. There are many aspects to investment accumulation for college but two are especially important. The first is selecting a portfolio of assets that is consistent with achieving the funding goal. The second is selecting investment vehicles and techniques. This latter aspect of investing considers both tax effects and financial aid implications.

Selecting a Portfolio for College Funding

At this point our focus shifts to selecting a portfolio for college funding and in order to do this, it is important to understand some basic investment concepts.

asset allocation

The first step in investing funds for college is selection of an asset allocation consistent with the client's risk tolerance and the amount of time until the funds are needed. (*Asset allocation* refers to the proportion of assets invested in broad asset categories, typically stocks, bonds, and money market instruments.) For example, the risk tolerant client saving for a very young child is likely to emphasize stock investments over money market instruments. A client investing the college savings for a high school junior is apt to take the opposite approach.

The second step in investing funds for college is selecting specific investments for the portfolio consistent with the asset allocation decision. Although the portfolio's risk-reward characteristics must be consistent with the client's asset allocation decision, the individual risk-reward characteristics of each investment will not necessarily be uniform. Indeed, standard concepts of diversification dictate that they not be uniform.

The types of investments typically considered for use in funding a college education are

- certificates of deposit (CDs)
- Series EE & Series I U.S. Savings Bonds
- zero coupon bonds
- cash value life insurance
- common stocks
- mutual funds
- CollegeSure CDs
- Sec. 529 plans

Certificates of deposit (CDs) from banks and other financial institutions are a common choice because they are easy to purchase, simple to understand, and can be bought in small denominations. They have a guaranteed rate of return and are federally insured, but they usually carry early withdrawal penalties. Because the income is taxable as it is received, the client has no control over the timing of the income nor does it qualify for lower capital-gains rates. Worst of all, the rate of return is low. The funds are likely to lose ground to education inflation.

Series EE & Series I US savings bonds are considered free from the risk of default. Because the federal income tax can be deferred until redemption, they can be placed in the name of the child and circumvent the so-called kiddie tax, which is discussed later in this chapter. Another benefit is that savings bonds are exempt from state income tax, making them especially appealing to higher-bracket clients. When held in the parents' names, however, the Savings Bonds for Education program may make interest from these bonds either totally or partially exempt from federal income taxation when used for qualified education expenses. This tax-exempt feature phases out for joint filers with modified adjusted gross income of $94,700 to $124,700 and single taxpayers earning between $63,100 and $78,100 for 2006. These AGI limits will adjust upward over time as they are indexed for inflation. The downside for EE bonds, along with CDs and other fixed income investments, is that they are poor hedges against inflation. The Series I savings bonds do offer an inflation hedge with a portion of the bond's return tied to changes in the consumer price index. The Treasury Direct website[1] provides current interest rates, tax information, and details on the Savings Bonds for Education program.

Zero coupon bonds are very popular because they are sold at a substantial discount and pay off the face amount at maturity. This offers the advantage of locking in a return for the life of the bonds, which are usually selected so that their maturity matches the child's college years. Their disadvantages are that their price is more volatile than bonds that make periodic interest payments, the client must report interest income each year even though none is actually received, and they are poor inflation hedges.

Cash value life insurance offers tax deferral on earnings while the policy is in force and allows the client to package education funding with a needed death benefit. Earnings on life insurance policies are competitive with long-term fixed income investments, and variable life insurance policies, whose returns are based on the stock market, provide an excellent inflation hedge. Clients can borrow money from the policy at moderate rates for extended periods, keeping the policy in force. As with many other investments, the premature surrender of a policy will result in a loss to the client.

Common stocks represent an excellent inflation hedge because of their appreciation potential, which also takes advantage of preferential tax treatment of capital gains and dividend income. The trade-off the client makes for the possible growth is a significantly greater risk of losing capital especially if the time period until the funds are needed is short. Additional disadvantages are that many clients are uncomfortable investing in individual stocks and that brokerage fees and commissions reduce the actual investment return.

Mutual funds are often the best choice in financial securities for a child's college education. The client can reduce risk through diversification and can select the type of mutual fund most suitable for his or her risk-taking tolerance. For example, there are money market funds, government bond funds, tax-free bond funds, taxable bond funds, growth funds, balanced funds, and index funds. Clients typically place most of their mutual fund investments with one mutual fund family, and that firm will allow the client to move money from fund to fund. That makes it easier and less expensive to shift investments as their circumstances change.

CollegeSure® *CDs* are federally insured to at least $100,000 per depositor. They pay an interest rate that is linked to the inflation rate in college costs as measured by the College Board's cost index for 500 independent colleges. Introduced by the College Savings Bank two decades ago, they mature on July 31 and offer maturities ranging from one to 22 years. These CDs are purchased in units or parts of units that reflect college costs existing at that time. At maturity, one unit is equal to one full year's *average* tuition, fees, and room and board at a 4-year private college as measured by the Independent College 500 Index. The purchase price per unit exceeds the value of the Independent College 500 Index on the date of deposit. College Savings Bank provided the following example and the illustration in figure 8-2 showing how these CDs work.

Example:	If today's cost for 10 percent of one year of private college is $3,327, you would deposit $4,122 to purchase .10 units of a CollegeSure® CD for your 3-year-old child to guarantee the future cost of college in 15 years. At maturity you'll receive 10 percent of one year of whatever the average private college costs are in 15 years, no matter how high college costs rise. Over the term to maturity of each CollegeSure® CD, the APY is not less than the college inflation rate less 1.50 percent.[2]

The difference between the $4,122 and the $3,327 is explained by this 1.50 percent reduction in return. The future value of $3,327 compounded at 5.74 percent, the 2006 college inflation rate, annually over the next 15 years is $7,685, but the present value of $7,685 discounted at an annual rate of 4.24 percent over 15 years is a present value of $4,122. The depositor pays a 24 percent premium over the current cost for a unit, or fraction of a unit, to allow for the spread between the college inflation rate and the rate earned on the CollegeSure® CD.

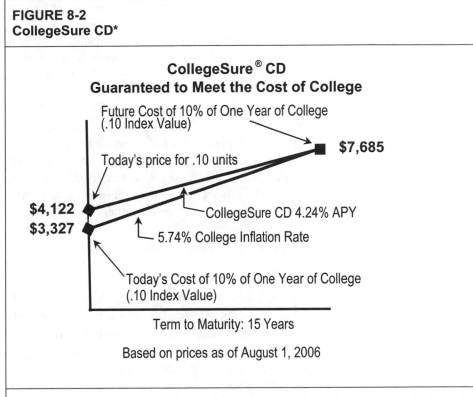

FIGURE 8-2
CollegeSure CD*

CollegeSure® CD
Guaranteed to Meet the Cost of College

Future Cost of 10% of One Year of College
(.10 Index Value)

Today's price for .10 units

$7,685

$4,122
$3,327

CollegeSure CD 4.24% APY

5.74% College Inflation Rate

Today's Cost of 10% of One Year of College
(.10 Index Value)

Term to Maturity: 15 Years

Based on prices as of August 1, 2006

*Source: *About the CollegeSure CD*, College Savings Bank, Princeton, NJ. Retrieved June 11, 2007, from http://www.collegesavings.com/program.html. Reprinted with permission.

Section 529 plans

Section 529 plans, named for the section of the Internal Revenue Code that authorizes them, provide tax-advantaged approaches to saving for college expenses. These programs are sponsored by states or qualified educational institutions and are also called qualified tuition programs (QTPs). Available in almost all states, they can take two forms: prepaid tuition plans and savings plans.

prepaid tuition plans

Plans vary but *prepaid tuition plans* typically allow parents to purchase tuition credits at current prices, thus locking in a child's tuition rate years in advance of enrollment. It should be emphasized, however, that prepaid tuition plans do not guarantee admission to college. The plan beneficiary still has to qualify for admission to the particular college. If the child does not go to college, plans generally offer refunds of the amounts paid without interest. In the event of death, disability or your child receiving a scholarship, most plans not only provide a refund, but also pay interest (generally at a relatively low rate). Although they will not cover the same share of college costs as would be prepaid for a 4-year university or community college or one located in the same state as the plan, plans can often be used for private schools as well as out-of-state schools.

Sec. 529 savings plans

Sec. 529 savings plans typically allow investment in mutual funds. Their returns are not tied directly to tuition inflation at a particular college, but the potential returns can exceed the inflation protection offered by prepaid tuition plans.

Funds from Sec. 529 savings accounts can be applied to qualified higher education expenses, which include tuition, fees, books, supplies, and equipment required for enrollment or attendance at an eligible educational institution, as well as reasonable costs of room and board, specified by the institution, for a beneficiary who is at least a half-time student. The definition of qualified higher education expenses includes expenses of a special-needs beneficiary that are necessary for that person's enrollment or attendance at an eligible institution.

Benefits of Section 529 plans include

- Earnings are tax deferred.
- Qualified withdrawals are free of federal income tax for state-sponsored 529 savings plans and prepaid tuition plans.
- In 2004, qualified withdrawals from prepaid tuition plans of private colleges and universities became free of federal income tax.
- There are no income restrictions.
- State residents who contribute or are the beneficiary of that state's plan may gain state income tax benefits.
- Contribution limits are high.
- Proceeds can be used nationwide.
- There are estate and gift tax benefits.
- Often plans are open to residents of any state.
- Initial minimum investment is low.
- Funds can be transferred from one plan to another once every 12 months.
- Hope or Lifetime Learning credits can be claimed in the same year as a qualified withdrawal from a 529 savings account as long as the same educational expenses are not used to justify both benefits.

SavingforCollege.com provides reviews and rankings of Section 529 offerings by state, discusses other college savings vehicles, and is a ready resource for investment advisors.

FOCUS ON ETHICS
Assets Under Management and Ethics

A potential conflict for the advisor who charges the client based on an assets-under-management model is in providing advice that allows the advisor to retain assets even if that is not in the client's best interests. In this chapter the potential conflict when recommending a Section 529 plan to a client is a good example.

Section 529 college savings plans typically are not closed to nonresidents, but there may be tax or tuition reasons why the client would be better served to invest in his or her home state's offering rather than invest in another state's plan. If an advisor recommends an out-of-state plan for compensation reasons when tax or tuition advantages exist in the home state plan, there's a problem. This has happened often enough that the NASD has issued an Investor Alert[‡] warning investors against investing in out-of-state plans without comparing them with in-state and other college savings alternatives.

Titling Accounts in the Child's Name

Putting money in an account in the child's name is a common practice for saving for college. This helps to segregate the funds and keep track of progress, and it may result in lower taxation. However, there are shortcomings to this approach. First, the so-called kiddie tax reduces the tax advantage for unearned income above the $1,700 threshold of the kiddie tax. Second, the child may elect to forgo college and use the funds for other purposes after reaching majority. Third, financial aid formulas reduce aid availability substantially more for each dollar of the child's assets than for each dollar of the parent's assets. (A subsequent section covers this topic in greater detail.)

Benefits From the Recent Legislation

The Taxpayer Relief Act of 1997 and subsequent legislation contain several provisions beneficial to families saving for post-secondary education. These provisions relate to tax deductions, tax credits, and penalty waivers that were designed specifically to encourage saving.

Changes in Individual Retirement Accounts

Individuals who receive taxable distributions from traditional IRAs before age 59 1/2 no longer pay a 10 percent early withdrawal penalty tax if they use the funds for qualified education expenses. The student on whose behalf the expenses are incurred can be the taxpayer, the taxpayer's spouse, or any child or grandchild of the taxpayer or the taxpayer's spouse.

Qualified education expenses include tuition, fees, books, supplies, and equipment required for enrollment in a post-secondary education institution.

Qualified higher education expenses also include room and board if the student is enrolled at least half time. In determining the amount of the distribution that is not subject to the 10 percent additional tax, total qualified education expenses are reduced by any tax-free educational assistance. This assistance includes payments from a Pell Grant or other tax-free scholarships, a tax-free distribution from a Coverdell education savings account, or tax-free employer-provided educational assistance. However, qualified higher education expenses paid with an individual's earnings, a loan, a gift, an inheritance given to the student or the individual claiming the credit, or personal savings (including savings from a qualified state tuition program) are not deducted from total qualified education expenses in determining the amount not subject to the 10 percent early withdrawal tax.

Roth IRA

The *Roth IRA,* which requires after-tax contributions but allows tax-free withdrawals after age 59 1/2, provides some benefit in college funding. First, as with other IRAs, no early withdrawal tax applies to withdrawals for qualified education expenses. Second, withdrawals may be made up to the amount of the total contribution without taxation. In effect, the client pulls those after-tax contributions back out of the account. The earnings can be left in the Roth IRA to accumulate tax free for retirement, or the earnings can be withdrawn for education purposes, although they will be taxed at the taxpayer's marginal rate. The ability to contribute to a Roth IRA is phased out for individual taxpayers with modified adjusted gross income (modified AGI) between $99,000 and $114,000, and for joint filers with modified AGI between $156,000 and $166,000 for the 2007 tax year. See IRS Publication 590, Individual Retirement Arrangements, for more detail on the taxation of early distributions and modified AGI limits.

A note of caution with using traditional or Roth IRA withdrawals to fund qualified educational expenses. These distributions show up as income when filing the free application for student aid (FAFSA) for the following academic year.

Coverdell Education Savings Accounts (CESAs), formerly known as education IRAs, allow donors (parents, grandparents, or anyone else) to contribute up to $2,000 per child into an education fund. However, the maximum amount that can be contributed on behalf of an individual child from all sources cannot exceed $2,000 per year. Although the contribution is not deductible, earnings are not taxed as long as the funds are used to pay elementary, secondary, or post-secondary education expenses. In the 2006 tax year, the availability of Coverdell education savings accounts is phased out for modified adjusted gross income (MAGI) of $95,000 to $110,000 for individual taxpayers and $190,000 to $220,000 for joint filers. See IRS Publication 970, Tax Benefits for Education, for current MAGI limits.

Despite the tax advantages related to earnings, Coverdell education savings accounts also have potential disadvantages. First, while either the Hope credit or the Lifetime Learning credit can be claimed in the same year the beneficiary takes a tax-free distribution from a Coverdell education savings account, the same expenses cannot be used for both benefits. Second, using this type of account may also limit the amount of financial aid available to a student depending on who is the account holder. Coverdell education savings accounts are considered to be the assets of the account holder, not the beneficiary. Parent-owned accounts would count toward the EFC, while a student-owned account or an account owned by a grandparent would not.

Tax Credits

The Taxpayer Relief Act of 1997 established two tax credits for education—the Hope scholarship credit and the Lifetime Learning credit. Key features of these two tax credits are compared in table 8-6.

Hope Scholarship Tax Credit

The *Hope Scholarship Tax Credit* allows a tax credit of up to $1,650 per student per year for tuition and related expenses incurred during the first 2 years of post-secondary education. The credit equals 100 percent of the first $1,000 of qualified tuition and related expenses, and 50 percent of the next $1,000 of tuition and fees.

Lifetime Learning Tax Credit

The *Lifetime Learning Tax Credit* provides a credit of up to $2,000, calculated as 20 percent of the first $10,000 of tuition and other qualified education expenses.

Claiming the Hope Scholarship Tax Credit and the Lifetime Learning Tax Credit in the same year for the same student is not allowed, but taxpayers paying qualified expenses for more than one student can elect to claim the Hope Scholarship Tax Credit for one student and the Lifetime Learning Tax Credit for the other. In 2006, both credits phase out for modified adjusted gross incomes from $45,000 to $55,000 for single filers and $90,000 to $110,000 for joint filers. See IRS Publication 970, Tax Benefits for Education, to find the MAGI phaseouts for the current tax year.

Tax Deductions

Deductibility of Interest on Education Loans. Another benefit from the Taxpayer Relief Act of 1997 is that some interest on education loans is now deductible even if the taxpayer does not itemize deductions. The available deduction is a maximum of $2,500. It is subject to a phaseout for single filers having between $50,000 and $65,000 of MAGI and for joint filers having between $105,000 and $135,000 of MAGI. Note that borrowing via a home equity loan is a viable alternative since these loans not only tend to carry relatively low interest rates but also because, in most cases, the interest expense is also deductible.

TABLE 8-6 Comparison of Education Tax Credits	
Lifetime Learning Credit	**Hope Credit**
Up to $2,000 credit per return	Up to $1,650 credit per **eligible student**
Available for all years of post-secondary education and for courses to acquire or improve job skills	Available **only** until the first 2 years of post-secondary education are completed
Available for an unlimited number of years	Available **only** for 2 years per eligible student
Student does not need to be pursuing a degree or other recognized education credential	Student must be pursuing an undergraduate degree or other recognized education credential
Available for one or more courses	Student must be enrolled at least half time for at least one academic period beginning during the year
Felony drug conviction rule does not apply	No felony drug conviction on student's record
Source: *Tax Benefits for Education*, Publication 970 (for use in preparing 2006 returns), Internal Revenue Service.	

Deductibility of Higher Education Expenses. Beginning in 2004, taxpayers are able to deduct qualified tuition and related expenses even if they do not itemize deductions. The amount of qualified education expense that can be taken into account in figuring the deduction is $4,000 for individual taxpayers with MAGI not more than $65,000 and joint filers whose MAGI is $130,000 or less. If the MAGI is greater than $65,000 for individual filers ($130,000 for joint filers) but not more than $80,000 for individual taxpayers ($160,000 for joint filers), the maximum deduction is $2,000. No deduction is permitted if the individual taxpayer's MAGI is larger than $80,000 ($160,000 for joint filers). There are also provisions that limit deductibility if a Hope or Lifetime Learning Credit is declared and that require coordination with other education tax benefits including U.S. savings bonds, Coverdell education savings accounts, and distributions for qualified tuition programs.

Interest Exclusion. The Savings Bonds for Education program allows the interest income on savings bonds to be excluded when savings bonds are redeemed for qualified educational expenses. In 2006, the amount of interest exclusion was phased out (gradually reduced) if the taxpayer's filing status was married filing jointly or qualifying widow(er), and MAGI was between $94,700 and $124,700. The taxpayer could not take the deduction if MAGI was $124,700 or more. For single taxpayers, the tax exclusion begins to be reduced with a $63,100 modified adjusted gross income and is eliminated for adjusted gross incomes of $78,100 and above. While other rules and restrictions apply, it is especially important to note that the savings bonds should not be held in the minor child's name. The child can be listed as a beneficiary but not as the owner for the bonds to qualify for the interest exclusion. (The Treasury Direct website has complete information on this program.)[*]

Integrating Education Planning With Retirement Planning

One way that clients can save for a child's education is to increase their 401(k) or 403(b) contribution to the maximum allowable. There are good reasons for taking this approach. First, these balances are not included in the parents' asset base in the financial aid formula, so it is easier to qualify. (However, the contribution does not reduce the parents' income in the formula.) Second, the contributions reduce taxable income, and savings accumulate on a tax-deferred basis. In most plans the client can then borrow part of the account balance to pay for the child's education, and the interest paid will be credited to the 401(k) account.

In general, loans from qualified retirement plans can finance a child's education if the plan permits education loans and the following requirements are met:

- The loan is amortized in substantially level payments over a period no longer than 5 years.
- The loan does not exceed half of the vested amount (with some exceptions).
- The loan does not exceed $50,000 (reduced by amounts outstanding from the prior year).

One drawback to using a 401(k) loan to finance education expenses is that 401(k) loans become immediately due and payable if the employee leaves the company.

Another consideration is that older parents may reach age 59 1/2 while their child is in college. At that point, 401(k) balances can be withdrawn without any penalty even if the client remains with the same employer. Of

---

[*] http://www.treasurydirect.gov/indiv/planning/plan_education.htm

course, income taxes will be due just as if money were withdrawn for retirement.

Clients sometimes find that, by the time their child is in college, they have accumulated enough in their retirement plan to forgo contributions while their child is in college. The budget allocation that was going into the 401(k) could be used to fund some out-of-pocket college expenses.

In the meantime, those already maximizing their 401(k) and Roth IRA contributions can consider a deferred annuity. True, they won't be allowed a deduction and the money won't be accessible. But they can take advantage of the 401(k) as a college-funding vehicle and use the deferred annuity as a retirement supplement. Again, when the child is in college, the client can eliminate the annuity contribution to make room in the budget for tuition payments. A cash value life insurance policy can be used in the same way with increased flexibility. (There will be more on this later.)

Integrating Education Planning With Estate Planning

Clients who have enough assets and for whom estate conservation and distribution is a concern should generally avoid giving education funds directly to their children. For example, they may already be pursuing a "gifting" plan in which the husband and wife each gift $12,000 for a combined gift of $24,000 per year to their child, enough to stay within the annual gift tax exclusion.* Any gift for education funding will count toward the exclusion. However, since expenses paid as parental support obligations are not gifts, a parent typically does not incur gift taxes for the payment of education expenses for their children through the college years. Consequently parents can pay their child's education expenses without diminishing their ability to gift their child up to the $24,000 that is protected by the annual gift exclusion.

A technique especially useful to well-heeled grandparents wishing to help their cash-strapped children by paying their grandchildren's college tuition involves the use of the Sec. 2503(e) exclusion from taxable gifts. This unlimited exclusion provides that gratuitous transfers made directly to the provider of services on behalf of the donee (in this case a grandchild) for certain education or medical expenses are not treated as taxable gifts. In the case of education expenses, the exclusion is limited to tuition payments; payments for books, meals, and lodging may be taxable gifts. The tuition payments must be made directly to educational institutions described in the charitable organization rules—that is, schools that normally have a regular faculty and curriculum and an enrolled student body regularly engaged in educational activities. This exclusion applies independently of and in addition to the annual gift tax exclusion. Thus, by paying for a grandchild's tuition expenses directly, grandparents (or other donors) can pay for a major

---

* Annual gift tax exclusion for the 2007 tax year.

portion of a college education while removing assets from their taxable estates without incurring gift taxation. Moreover, the annual gift tax exclusion is still available to allow an additional $24,000 to be gifted tax free to the grandchild in the same year.

Shifting Wealth and Spreading Income

Shifting wealth and spreading income among members of the family has always been one of the best estate and financial planning techniques. With changes in the tax code made in 2007 to take effect in 2008, shifting wealth from parents to children to reduce taxes has lost its appeal with changes in the kiddie tax rules. Starting with the 2008 tax year, any children who are full-time students are taxed at their parents' income tax rate until they are age 24. Children who are not full-time students are taxed at their parents' rate until they reach age 19.

The rule does not apply until the child has over $1,700 in "unearned income," namely dividends, interest, and capital gains payments. The first $850 of that unearned income is tax free. The second $850 is taxed at the child's income tax rate. Above the $1,700 threshold the parents' rates kick in.

There are at least two caveats in transferring wealth to a child. First, most experts advise against naming the client as the custodian because if he or she dies while the child is a minor, the value of the account can be included in his or her taxable estate. Second, as with any gift, the client runs the risk that the child may decide that the best use of the money is not education. The child could leave the money in the account until the age of majority and then squander it. (Of course, this option may not be as attractive if the child understands that the client's reaction will be to change his or her status in the will!)

Trusts

In general, high taxation makes trusts less beneficial for college funding. However, trusts provide investment expertise, management, flexibility, and unification unequaled by other investment ownership vehicles. A client can plan for a number of beneficiaries with one trust and each of those beneficiaries—and the trust itself—helps to lower the rates at which investment income will be taxed. Alternatively, multiple trusts can be created for each beneficiary to provide even more flexibility and income splitting and shifting potential. Still, advisors must be conscious of the multiplicity of costs incurred in administering and preparing tax returns for multiple trusts. Note also that if the trusts have the same terms, beneficiaries, and grantors, they all will be taxed as if they were one trust.

The 2503(c) trusts are highly useful in taking advantage of the annual gift tax exclusion. A married couple can contribute up to $24,000 gift tax free per year per child to a 2503(c) trust. Since this type of trust can accumulate income, delay payment of principal, and then allow disbursements during the college years, it's an ideal method where larger amounts are involved.

The 2503(b) trusts require that all income be paid at least annually to the beneficiaries. This type of trust is also eligible for the annual gift tax exclusion for the income rights and allows delayed payment of principal until college funding is needed. It differs from the 2503(c) trust in two ways. First, the 2503(b) trust requires that all income be paid out each year, while the trustee of a 2503(c) trust can decide to accumulate it. Second, the 2503(b) trust can retain funds beyond the beneficiary's age of majority while the 2503(c) trust requires that all principal and income be distributed to the minor at age 21. Thus, the 2503(b) trust makes sense if the beneficiary is age 14 or older, or if the amount in the trust is very large and the client wants to be sure payment of the principal can be delayed far longer than when the child reaches age 21.

An alternative to both the 2503(c) and the 2503(b) trusts is the irrevocable trust with a Crummey provision. Under this type of trust, the trustee can choose to accumulate or distribute income and/or principal and the trust can last as long as the income beneficiaries live.

In addition to high taxation and setup and administration costs, the use of trusts also has an unfavorable impact on the determination of a family's expected contribution to college expenses when computing a child's eligibility for financial aid. The value of a trust is treated as an asset of the student, rather than of the parents, for purposes of determining the amount of the family's expected contribution to college expenses and thus the amount of financial aid needed. While only 5.6 percent of the parents' unprotected assets are earmarked for inclusion in the expected family contribution to college costs, 20 percent[*] of the child's unprotected assets are counted in determining the amount the family is expected to contribute to higher education expenses. Thus, in education planning, consideration should be given to the fact that the use of trusts in funding a college education reduces the amount of federal aid the child is eligible to receive.

Family Partnerships as an Education Fund Tool

Many clients who own their own businesses should consider using a family partnership to provide education funding. Transfers of interest in the family partnership to children or grandchildren shift the income into lower tax brackets, allowing it to accumulate faster. The Internal Revenue Service intensely scrutinizes family partnerships since a 2003 Tax Court decision. Sound legal and tax advice is critical in using this structure.

---

[*] Previously 35 percent; it is 20 percent starting with the 2007–2008 tax year.

Key Requirements for a Share of Partnership Income to Be Taxed to the Child as a Partner

---

- Capital must be a material income-producing factor. This means a family partnership income shift typically will not work in a service business such as accounting or law.
- The parent must be receiving reasonable compensation from the business.
- The partnership must have a business purpose and not be created merely to avoid tax.
- The child must have the legal ability to exercise his or her rights as a partner. All transactions should document that the child or his or her legal representative did in fact exercise those rights.

Investing in College Housing

Many parents with ample resources elect to provide college housing by buying a multi-family dwelling near the child's college for investment and/or quality-of-life purposes. By making the college student into a landlord's agent who is hired to manage and care for the property and collect fair rents from other tenants, the parent can deduct reasonable salary payments to the college student son or daughter, depreciation (subject to the passive activity loss rule), as well as travel expenses the parents incur to inspect and maintain their investment property. It is hoped that the property will appreciate over time and either will be sold at a profit after the child graduates or will be the subject of a future deductible gift to the college upon the child's graduation.

OBTAINING FINANCIAL AID

Although this textbook does not go into detailed strategies for obtaining financial aid, financial advisors should have a rudimentary understanding of obtaining financial aid for higher education. Some of the more complex aspects are best left to competent college financial aid counselors. Still, advisors must be aware that qualifying for financial aid is sometimes a function of the structure, rather than the size, of assets and income.

Understanding the Aid Formula

FAFSA

The federal need-analysis formula dictates how much the student and the student's parents are expected to contribute per academic year for higher education. The formula is applied to data requested in the U.S. Department of Education's Free Application for Federal Student Aid *(FAFSA),* which is available from the high school guidance counselor. Information is also available online (http://www.fafsa.ed.gov/).

FIGURE 8-3
Using the Federal Need-Analysis Formula to Determine the Expected Family Contribution to College Expenses and the Student's Financial Need

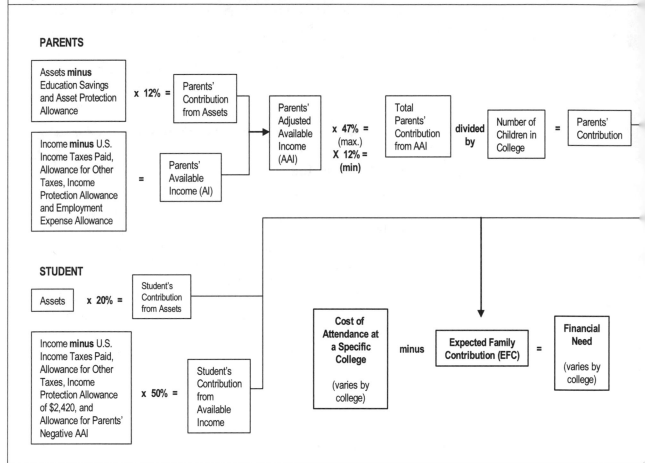

As shown in figure 8-3, the formula calculates the *expected parent contribution* and the *expected student contribution* and combines them to equal the *expected family contribution (EFC)*. Within a month of submitting the FAFSA, the student receives a *student aid report (SAR)* by mail, specifying the EFC. The EFC is subtracted from the *cost of attendance (COA)* to determine financial need. The cost of attendance is specific to each individual college and includes tuition and fees, on-campus room and board, and allowances for books, supplies, transportation, loan fees, and certain other costs.

Deriving Expected Parental Contribution

In the FAFSA formula, income includes wages, interest and investment income, housing and living allowances, tax-exempt interest income, child support received, Social Security benefits, unemployment compensation, and contributions to qualified retirement plans and deductible IRAs. Then it adjusts for federal, state, and Social Security taxes. It also subtracts an income protection allowance ($23,070* for a family of four with one child in college), and an employment expense allowance (the lesser of $3,200 or 35 percent of earned income)* to derive the parents' available income.

The formula considers assets to include all cash, bank accounts, stocks and bonds, mutual funds, commodities, precious metals, real estate, and trust funds. Employer-sponsored retirement plans, IRAs, annuities, life insurance, and primary residence are excluded. Then the formula subtracts an education savings and asset protection allowance. This allowance is based on the age of the older parent. What remains is multiplied by 12 percent to calculate the parents' contribution from assets.

Available income and available assets are now added. Even if the total is negative, the parents may be expected to contribute something. If the total is over $27,100* the expected parent contribution is $7,334* plus 47 percent of the excess over $27,101. If there is more than one family member attending college during the year (other than a parent), the parents' total contribution is divided by the number of attendees to determine the expected parent contribution for each of them.

The good news is that most people can exclude most of their assets through exclusions and allowances, and only 12 percent of the remainder is considered available assets. Even then, the formula only earmarks at most 47 percent of this total for the child's education. This means that, excluding income-based contributions, the parents are expected to kick in an amount equal to no more than 5.6 percent of unprotected assets during each year of school. Think of it this way: 5.6 percent of unprotected assets is probably less than the investment income from the client's investment assets. It's like saying that the clients' sacrifice is to give up their investment income while their child is in college.

Deriving Expected Student Contribution

The child's available income is calculated after subtracting federal, state, and Social Security taxes and an income-protection allowance of $3,000.** The formula dictates that 50 percent of the remainder be contributed to the child's education. Students are also expected to contribute an amount equal to 20 percent of their assets each year. Since the 20 percent is calculated on a

---

* Dollar amounts are for the 2007–2008 award year.
** Dollar amounts are for the 2006–2007 award year.

declining balance, the formula theoretically allows the student to retain almost 41 percent of his or her assets after 4 years.

What Can We Learn From the Formula?

In spite of differential tax rates, shifting assets to the child which is a standard technique of estate planning, may be counterproductive. First, at most 5.6 percent of the parents' unprotected assets are earmarked compared with 20 percent of the child's. Second, rather than shifting assets to the child, clients could move their assets into annuities or cash value life insurance. This removes them from the formula in addition to providing tax deferral. Even so, it might not be worth the effort because, if loans are the only form of aid available, hiding assets may only allow the client to borrow money that he or she does not really need to borrow.

Clients who do qualify for financial aid should spend the child's assets first because they count more heavily in the formula. Eliminating a dollar of the child's assets reduces the formula's required family contribution almost four times as much as eliminating a dollar of the parents' assets. This should help the family qualify for more aid in subsequent years.

Income is the critical variable. The first year of income that figures into the formula is the one that ends in the child's senior year of high school. Clients considering taking capital gains may want to declare them in the year that ends in the child's junior year, before they count in the formula.

Finally, the advisor should be aware that some colleges follow an institutional methodology (IM) that takes a different approach to arriving at an aid package for a student. This is in contrast to the federal methodology (FM) discussed in this section.

Obtaining Government Money

In 2005–2006, undergraduate and graduate students received over $152 billion in financial aid from all sources.[3] As indicated in table 8-7, the relative importance of grants and loans, the two main sources of financial aid, has reversed over the past 10 years with loans now accounting for more than 50 percent of the total.

As shown in table 8-8, the federal government through the Department of Education still plays a significant role in providing funds for college students. Federal student aid includes work-study and other campus-based programs, grants (which do not require repayment), and loans that together account for approximately two-thirds of all student financial aid.[4] In addition to the sources of federal student aid discussed below, many states have their own grant and loan programs that advisors should learn about.

The primary grant program for undergraduate students who qualify under the need-analysis formula is the *Federal Pell Grant*. Pell Grants are available

Federal Pell Grant

in amounts of up to $4,310 per year (2007–2008). The amount students actually receive depends on their financial need, their costs to attend school, their status as full-time or part-time students, and their plans to attend school for a full academic year or less. Pell Grants are viewed as a foundation of federal financial aid to which aid from other federal and nonfederal sources might be added.

TABLE 8-7
Grant, Loan, Work-Study, and Education Tax Benefit Funding in Constant (2005) Dollars (in Millions) and as a Percentage of Total Aid, 1995–96 to 2005–06

	95–96	96–97	97–98	98–99	99–00	00–01	01–02	02–03	03–04	04–05	05–06
Grants	44%	43%	44%	44%	43%	44%	44%	44%	43%	40%	39%
Loans	54%	55%	55%	51%	51%	50%	50%	49%	52%	55%	56%
Work	1%	1%	1%	1%	1%	1%	1%	1%	1%	1%	1%
Tax Credits	–	–	–	4%	5%	5%	4%	6%	4%	4%	4%
Total	100%	100%	100%	100%	100%	100%	100%	100%	100%	100%	100%

Source: *Trends in Student Aid 2006.* Copyright© 2006 by the College Board. Reproduced with permission. All rights reserved. www.collegeboard.com. Components may not sum exactly to totals due to rounding.

TABLE 8-8
Student Aid by Source for Academic Year 2005–2006 in Current Dollars

Sources of Financial Aid	Amount (Billions of Dollars)	Percent of Total Aid
Federal		
Federal Loans	$68.6	51%
Federal Pell Grants	$12.7	9%
Federal Campus Based	$3.1	2%
Other Federal Programs	$5.3	4%
Education Tax Credits	$6.0	4%
Nonfederal		
Institutional Grants	$24.4	18%
State Grants	$6.8	5%
Private and Employer Grants	$9.3	7%
Total Aid	$136.2	100%

Data Source: *Trends in Student Aid 2006.* Copyright © 2006 by the College Board.

Two grants available for the first time for the 2006–2007 school year for first-year students who graduated from high school after January 1, 2006, and for second-year students who graduated from high school after January 1, 2005, are the National SCI Academic Competitiveness Grant and the National Science and Mathematics Access to Retain Talent Grant—also known as the Smart Grant. The Federal Student Aid website[5] has additional information on who can qualify for these grants.

Three additional federal programs—Federal Supplemental Education Opportunity Grants (FSEOGs), Federal Work Study, and Federal Perkins Loans—are referred to as campus-based programs because they are administered directly by the financial aid office at each participating school. *Federal Supplemental Education Opportunity Grants (FSEOG)* are available in amounts of up to $4,000 per year for students who show exceptional need. Most states have similar programs, which use different eligibility formulas. The Federal Work Study Program provides jobs for undergraduate and graduate students with financial need. The program allows students to earn money to help pay their education expenses.

Federal Perkins loans are another source of funds for students who can show exceptional need. A dependent, undergraduate student, for example, can qualify for up to $4,000 per year and $20,000 cumulative. The loan is made with federal government funds although the school also contributes a share. The school is the lender and the student must eventually repay the loan to his or her school. Interest is only 5 percent and in general does not accrue until the student leaves college or drops below half-time status. Payments also begin after the student leaves school and typically can be spread over 10 years.

Stafford loans are the major source of education borrowing from the federal government. They are available through the Direct Loan Program, in which the funds come directly from the federal government, or through the Family Federal Education Loan Program (FFEL), in which participating banks, credit unions, and other lenders serve as intermediaries. For dependent undergraduate students, loans are available in amounts of up to $3,500 for freshman, $4,500 for sophomores, and $5,500 for juniors and seniors. Limits are higher for independent students but not all of the loan is eligible to be subsidized for independent students. The interest rate for all Stafford loans first disbursed on or after July 1, 2006, is fixed at 6.8 percent. This change does not affect variable interest rate loans made before July 1, 2006. Stafford loans are subsidized for students with financial need as determined by subtracting the EFC, Pell Grants, and other aid from the cost of attending the college. This means that interest does not accrue until 6 months after the student leaves college. Unsubsidized Stafford loans are available even if there is no need under the aid formula. (Keep in mind that the formula's determination of need may deviate significantly from reality!) Interest accrues for unsubsidized Stafford loans from the time the funds are disbursed

Federal Supplemental Education Opportunity Grant (FSEOG)

Federal Perkins loans

Stafford loans

and can be paid as incurred or added to the principal of the loan. The loans must be repaid within 10 years.

Parent Loans for Undergraduate Students (PLUS loans)

Parent Loans for Undergraduate Students (PLUS loans) are available through both the Direct and FFEL programs for all family incomes and asset levels (that is, they are not need based), but the borrower cannot have a bad credit history. Applicants can borrow up to the entire cost of the education, less any other financial aid received. The interest rate for PLUS loans (both parent and graduate/professional students) disbursed on or after July 1, 2006, is fixed at 7.90 percent for Direct PLUS loans and 8.50 percent for FFEL PLUS loans). Interest accrues from the time of the first disbursement. Interest is charged on a PLUS loan from the date of the first disbursement until the loan is paid in full.

Effective July 1, 2006, graduate or professional students are eligible to borrow under the PLUS Loan Program up to their cost of attendance minus other estimated financial assistance in both the Federal Family Education Loan Program (FFEL) and the Direct Loan Programs. The terms and conditions applicable to the Parent PLUS Loans also apply to Graduate/Professional PLUS loans.[6]

Federal Loan Consolidation Programs

Federal Loan Consolidation Programs are available under both the Direct and FFEL loan programs mentioned above. Under these programs, a borrower's (a student's or parents') loans are repaid and a new consolidation loan is created. Stafford loans, PLUS loans, and Federal Perkins loans as well as certain Health and Human Services/Health Professionals loans are eligible for consolidation. While loans can be consolidated after the student has left school under both the Direct and FFEL programs, the Direct program also permits students to consolidate their loans while still in school. The consolidated loan has a fixed interest rate equal to the weighted average of the interest rates of the loans at the time of consolidation. Loan consolidation is free—that is, no fees can be charged in connection with the consolidation of eligible student loans.

A client should consider consolidating student loans under one of the federal programs since there are a number of potential benefits that may accrue including

- Lower interest rate: The future fixed interest rate for a consolidated loan may be less than the future variable interest rates for Stafford and PLUS loans if consolidation takes place when interest rates on Stafford and PLUS loans are low and then subsequently are adjusted to higher levels.
- There is only one lender and one monthly bill.
- Lower monthly payments: While Stafford and PLUS loans have maximum repayment terms of 10 years, consolidation loans also offer repayment terms ranging from 12 to 30 years depending on the amount borrowed. Since repayment terms can be extended under

consolidation loans, the monthly payment can be reduced to a more manageable amount. However, there is a cost associated with lowering the monthly payment in this way. Whenever the repayment term on a loan is lengthened at a given interest rate, the total amount of interest paid increases if the loan is not fully paid off until the end of the repayment term.

- Interest rate payment incentives: Lenders under the FFEL program commonly offer repayment incentives such as a discount on the consolidated loan interest rate (for example, a one percent discount) after a stated number of payments (for example, 36 consecutive loan payments) are made on time. Another repayment incentive is a discount on the interest rate (for example, a .25 percent discount) if authorization is given to automatically transfer loan payments from the borrower's checking or savings account.

Tapping the College's Resources

Academic scholarships and grants continue to be available to needy and/or talented students at most institutions. There are literally thousands available, and many can be obtained even by children of upper middle-income families. (Many colleges have their own loan funds also.)

Scholarships and grants are not taxable income to the extent

- The money is for tuition, fees, books, supplies, and equipment.
- The student is a candidate for a degree at a qualified educational institution (an educational institution that maintains a regular faculty and curriculum and normally has a regularly enrolled body of students in attendance at the place where it carries on its educational activities).

To the extent the scholarship is for room and board, payments will be taxable income to the student. Likewise, if the student is not a degree candidate or if payments are for teaching, research, or other services rendered by the student, payments will be taxable.

For those who understand the nuances of financial aid, a private school education often costs no more than that at a state-supported university.

Example: The client plans to spend $10,000 per year at a state university, which happens to coincide with the expected contribution calculated by the need-analysis formula. If the child applies and is accepted to a $25,000 per year private college, financial aid might be available to cover the entire $15,000 difference. However, if the aid takes the form of loans rather than a "free" grant, the client must decide whether the aid is worthwhile.

Life Insurance Policy Loans

Although not a source of financial aid per se, life insurance policies with cash values and low or reasonable interest charges have traditionally been sources of funds for college expenses. The funds are quickly available and require no credit analysis. Furthermore, the transaction is very private and the repayment provisions are typically very flexible. Of course, outstanding loans from a policy reduce the proceeds payable at death.

As noted earlier, interest on loans for higher education is deductible, subject to a phaseout based on adjusted gross income. Loans from life insurance policies are subject to additional rules that severely restrict deductibility.

EMERGENCY FUND PLANNING

The Goal

Planning for emergencies is a critical financial planning activity. Emergencies are unanticipated events that can result in considerable reductions in a client's net cash flow due to either an unexpected decrease in income or an unexpected increase in expenses. If not properly planned for as part of the financial planning process, emergencies can result in a reduction of assets or an increase in liabilities. This can prevent or delay the achievement of the client's goals and objectives, such as accumulating adequate retirement and education funds, or maintaining a credit rating that allows the client to use credit at a favorable cost to take advantage of investment opportunities.

An emergency fund is composed of liquid assets that the client can easily and quickly convert to cash in the event of an unanticipated reduction in net cash flow. Emergency funds neutralize the negative impact on a client's net cash flow resulting from unexpected events such as

- the loss of the client's job
- a car breakdown requiring expensive repairs
- the breakdown of the furnace, hot water heater, and so on

While an emergency fund is appropriate for handling the negative impact of many unexpected events, particularly those that are uninsurable, it is not the best approach for dealing with all emergencies that pose a threat of serious financial loss. Insurance is often a more appropriate technique than an emergency fund for dealing with the financial consequences of some of these situations. For example, a very severe accident or illness could result in medical bills in the hundreds of thousands of dollars (or more). This catastrophe is more appropriately handled with medical expense insurance with high limits than with payments from an emergency fund. Likewise, with the potential loss from legal liability uncapped in most cases, the client would be better off with adequate automobile insurance, homeowners insurance, and umbrella liability insurance than with an emergency fund that is likely to be inadequate for dealing with severe liability losses. Potential loss of a substantial amount of income due to a client's long-term disability or death is best protected against by disability income insurance or life insurance, respectively, just as the destruction of a client's home by a tornado or hurricane is best handled with homeowners insurance. However, in each of these cases except liability, the client should understand that the first few dollars of any loss can be more efficiently handled through retention by the proper use of deductibles and waiting (elimination) periods. If sizeable enough, the retained loss can be paid from an emergency fund, thereby avoiding a reduction in net cash flow that would interfere with the achievement of the client's financial objectives.

WHAT'S ADEQUATE FOR AN EMERGENCY FUND?

In most cases a total loss or substantial reduction of a client's and/or spouse's income for a period of time is likely to cause greater financial difficulty than a one-time unanticipated increase in expense. Consequently financial advisors commonly recommend an emergency fund that equals 3 to 6 months of either the client's take-home pay or at least the total fixed and discretionary expenses that would still have to be paid during that period.

The sample cash flow statement in table 5-10 in chapter 5 lists the various types of fixed and discretionary expenses a household typically faces. Using this list (modified for any special expenses the client incurs), the client should estimate the monthly amount of each type of expense that would be incurred over the likely period of income reduction. Be sure the client considers the month(s) with the highest expenses during the year in making these estimates. Then, should an emergency arise, have the client review the monthly expenses and determine whether any could be eliminated or reduced and by how much. Certain discretionary expenses such as entertainment, club memberships, or magazine subscriptions could probably be reduced temporarily without placing a significant burden on the client's family. While not a popular decision, the client may feel that vacations and other travel could at least be scaled back somewhat in the event of an emergency. The replacement of household furnishings might be delayed at such a time. Also, the client should consider whether it is possible to pay off high interest credit card debt or other high interest loans faster so that the level of monthly debt repayment would be reduced in the future. In identifying the expenses that could be eliminated or reduced in the event of an emergency, the client should be realistic in creating an expense plan that could and thus would be followed during a period of unemployment.

Two other factors should also be considered in estimating the amount of expenses likely to be encountered during a period of unexpected income reduction. First, as the client's income increases over time, expenses, including taxes, will tend to increase also. Second, while some expenses, such as fixed-rate mortgage payments, will remain constant over time, the cost of other items such as food, clothing, and utilities will increase due to inflation.

Not all clients need an emergency fund that will cover essential expenses completely or for the same period of time. The size of a client's emergency fund depends on a number of factors including age, health, job outlook, and personal financial situation. For example, an emergency fund that would cover 3 to 6 months of expenses using liquid assets and credit might be adequate if the client has

- a source of low cost borrowing such as cash value life insurance or considerable home equity
- multiple sources of income such as a spouse's earnings or monthly payments from a trust established by the client's or spouse's parents that could be counted on during an emergency
- stable employment or a skill that is in high demand and thus likely to result in a short period of unemployment

However, an emergency fund that covers 6 months' or even a year's living expenses may be inadequate if the client is self-employed, works in an industry not known for job security, or relies heavily on commissions rather than salary as a primary source of income.

ACCUMULATION AND INVESTMENT OF AN EMERGENCY FUND

Accumulation of an emergency fund involves saving and thus requires an analysis of a client's cash flow statement to determine the amount of net cash flow available for periodically adding to the savings fund. If there is inadequate net cash flow available to build the fund to the desired size in the desired period of time, cash flow planning such as that discussed in chapter 5 and illustrated in table 5-12 must be undertaken to improve the client's monthly net cash flow to the level needed for accumulating an adequate emergency fund. This might involve reallocating some assets to investment vehicles with higher potential returns, reducing the amount of spending for discretionary purposes and possibly also for certain fixed purposes, reducing debt payments through refinancing a mortgage or consolidating high cost credit card debt into a lower cost source of borrowing, and reducing income taxes through greater use of tax-advantaged retirement accounts and tax-exempt bonds. Also, if there is not sufficient time to build the emergency fund to an adequate amount prior to the actual occurrence of an emergency, relatively low cost borrowing such as a home equity line of credit (to be discussed later) or a loan from a life insurance policy may be needed to supplement the cash available from the fund.

Because emergencies are unexpected, emergency fund assets must be able to be quickly converted to cash without loss of value in order to meet the client's needs. Assets meeting this requirement are called liquid assets. It is important to recognize the difference between liquidity and marketability of assets. While *liquidity* is the ability to quickly convert an asset to cash with little or no uncertainty as to value, *marketability* is the ease of (buying or) selling an asset for its market value. While all liquid assets are marketable because marketability is a component of liquidity, not all marketable assets are liquid. For example, while a widely held stock can generally be sold for its current market price and thus is marketable, it is not liquid because its price will vary from day to day.

liquidity
marketability

Emergency funds commonly are invested in a portfolio of liquid assets such as savings accounts, interest-bearing checking accounts, bank money market deposit accounts, very short-term (for example, one-month) CDs, and money market mutual funds. Despite the relatively low rates of interest earned on these liquid assets, the funds will be quickly available in a spendable form at a known value when emergencies occur.

There are, however, some techniques that can enable at least part of the client's emergency funds to be invested in higher yielding assets that may not be available immediately when needed due to withdrawal penalties. For example, if the client has an excellent credit rating and considerable home equity, then temporary, limited, low cost borrowing might be employed to provide cash until the investment can be sold without penalty and used to pay off the home equity loan. Taking out a home equity line of credit when times are good and it is easy to get the loan approved can be a better strategy than applying for a home equity loan or line of credit after the financial emergency arises.

"Laddering" is another technique that provides an opportunity to earn a higher rate of return without jeopardizing the number of months of income protection the client needs to meet expected monthly living expenses following an emergency. For example, suppose a client has a $24,000 emergency fund currently invested in liquid assets and expects to need income protection for at most 6 months following an emergency. Each month the client could invest $4,000 of the liquid assets in a higher yielding

6-month CD. In 6 months, the client will have a series of six 6-month CDs with one CD maturing each month over a period of 6 months. Laddering is more commonly used with a longer investment horizon, but a stepladder can work well in emergency fund investing, meaning you spread your emergency fund over a short-term investment horizon.

As with any component of financial planning, there is no guarantee that either the size or the investment strategy of an emergency fund will precisely meet the client's income replacement needs following a particular emergency. However, it does guarantee that any negative impact on savings and investments earmarked for particular accumulation goals and/or negative impact on the client's creditworthiness will be less than it would have been had no emergency fund planning taken place.

Establishing and funding an emergency account should be a high priority financial goal that overrides retirement savings and college savings. The ability to maintain financial stability in the face of fiscal adversity allows the client greater flexibility in other life choices.

Emergency Fund Problem

Jack and Jill Klient have estimated monthly living expenses of $2,500 and want to establish an emergency fund equal to 6 months' living expenses or $15,000. They currently have $5,000 earmarked for this account. If they can set aside $100/week to continue to fund this account, how long will it take before the emergency fund reaches its target balance, assuming they earn 2 percent interest on the investments? Using the HP-10BII:

HP10BII: Keystrokes for Computing Time Needed to Fund an Emergency Savings Account

Keystrokes	*Explanation*
▭, C ALL	to clear the calculator
52, ▭, (P/YR)	to set payments/year equal to 52
5000, +/–, PV	to enter the initial investment
100, +/-, PMT	to enter the weekly investment
15000, FV	to enter the future value
2, I/YR	to enter the annual interest rate
N	96.32583 is displayed ≈ 2 years

Of course, over the 2-year time period, the Klients' monthly expenses are likely to increase with inflation, so the $15,000 target will not represent

6 months' worth of living expenses. The $100 per week to realize this goal may seem too aggressive. The Klients may want to reevaluate this amount to a more reasonable $50 per week. At this level of savings it would take them 3 1/2 years to reach the $15,000 goal.

CREDIT AND DEBT MANAGEMENT

Mortgage and Consumer Debt

In January 2004, the Federal Reserve reported that America's seasonally adjusted consumer credit outstanding, excluding loans secured by real estate, topped $2 trillion for the first time.[7] At the end of 2006 that number stood at $2.4 trillion. When mortgages are taken into account, U.S. households owed close to $9 trillion in 2005.[8]

About 43 percent of American families spend more than they earn each year. One estimate suggests that on average, Americans spend about $1.22 for each dollar they earn.[9] The Federal Reserve reports that in the third quarter of 2003, U.S. households had a debt service ratio—that is, a ratio of required payments on outstanding mortgage and consumer debt to personal disposable income—equal to 13.1 percent.[10] When automobile lease payments, rental payments on tenant-occupied property, homeowners insurance, and property tax payments were also included to obtain a broader measure of household financial obligations, the ratio increased to 18.3 percent of disposable personal income. As indicated in figure 8-4, both the household debt service and financial obligation ratios have tended to rise over the past decade.

Major Types of Household Debt and Credit

There are two main categories of household debt—mortgage debt and consumer debt. Consumer debt, in turn, is composed of debt arising from the use of nonrevolving and revolving credit.

Mortgage Debt

Having increased approximately 130 percent over the past decade, home mortgage loans outstanding, amounting to nearly $7.3 trillion at the end of 2003, accounted for the largest component of household debt. The recent rapid growth in mortgage debt has resulted from homeowners taking out larger mortgages to take advantage of historically low interest rates. Homeowners are also tapping home equity resulting from rising home values for a variety of purposes including improving the home, consolidating debt, financing a major purchase (a car, a boat, a recreational vehicle, furniture, or an appliance), and paying for a child's education. (The uses and abuses of home equity loans—a form of second mortgage—will be discussed later in the chapter.)

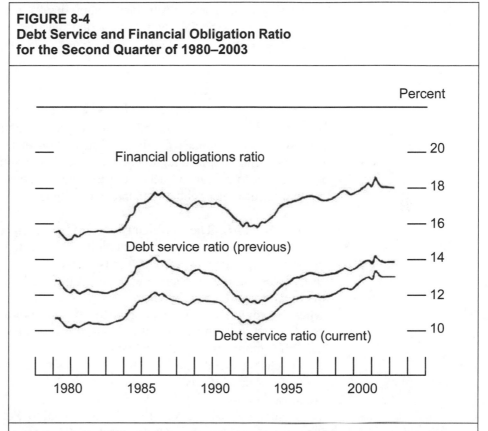

FIGURE 8-4
Debt Service and Financial Obligation Ratio
for the Second Quarter of 1980–2003

Source: Karen Dynan, Kathleen Johnson, and Karen Pence, "Recent Changes to a Measure of U.S. Household Debt Service," *Federal Reserve Bulletin*, October 2003, pp. 417–426.
Note: The "previous" debt service ratio reflects revisions made in 1999. The "current" debt service ratio reflects revisions made in 2002 to account for changes in the structure and sophistication of the financial markets in the past several years. The financial obligations ratio equals the debt service ratio with rent payments, auto lease payments, homeowners' property tax payments, and homeowners' insurance payments also included in the numerator.

Nonrevolving Credit

Nonrevolving credit accounts for 63 percent of the other $2 trillion of household debt outstanding as of January 2004 that is not secured by real estate. Nonrevolving credit includes loans taken out for such things as cars, education, recreational vehicles, home appliances, and vacations. In recent years, much of the increase in the household debt load from nonrevolving credit undoubtedly has come from auto loans stimulated by strong incentives such as low interest financing (in some cases, zero percent), rebates, token down payments, old auto debt rolled into new car financing, and the availability of longer maturity loans (some banks are floating 96-month car loans) as well as by the aggressive extension of credit to consumers with weak credit scores.

Revolving Credit

Revolving credit, also referred to as open account credit, accounts for the remaining 37 percent of the $2 trillion of consumer debt. Revolving credit involves a commitment by a financial institution or another type of business (such as a retailer or airline) to lend a customer an amount up to a stated credit limit subject to repayment according to specific terms. By January 2004, the amount of consumer debt attributable to revolving credit topped $750 billion.

Credit Cards. The two main types of revolving credit are credit cards (and charge accounts) and lines of credit. As indicated in table 5-8 in chapter 5, credit card balances account for the vast majority of the consumer debt from revolving credit. Bank credit cards and retail charge cards account for the biggest portion of this type of revolving credit, which also includes other types of credit cards (for example, travel and entertainment cards, affinity cards issued in conjunction with a nonprofit organization, and prestige cards that offer more features and advantages than other cards), debit cards, and 30-day charge accounts offered by businesses for customer convenience. The average cardholder has 7.6 cards—that is, 2.7 bank credit cards, 3.8 retail credit cards, and 1.1 debit cards.

A summary of the key findings of a Gallup Poll[11] published in April 2004 estimated that all but 21 percent of Americans have at least one credit card. Of the 79 percent of Americans with credit cards, approximately 37 percent pay the full balance owed on their cards each month whereas 63 percent do not pay the full amount owed on a monthly basis. The average outstanding monthly balance for those who do not pay the full amount owed on their credit card(s) each month was $3,815 (or $2,947 per American when both those with and without cards are taken into account). Overall, Americans pay back an average of 14 percent to 16 percent of their credit card balances each month, a range that has remained fairly stable from 2000 through 2003. However, despite this rather steady repayment rate, the credit card delinquency rate, based on the number of accounts 30+ days past due, rose to 4.43 percent of outstanding balances during the fourth quarter of 2003, which surpassed the previous all-time quarterly high of 4.09 percent set a year earlier. Even though the economy was improving at that time, the average duration of joblessness was approaching an all-time high (20.3 weeks in February 2004). Since those looking for employment often rely on credit cards to meet their daily expenses, the record-setting credit card delinquency rate reflects the increased financial strain of lengthening periods of joblessness. At the same time, the delinquency rate on other types of consumer loans, including auto and home equity loans, fell from 2.14 percent to 1.89 percent in the fourth quarter of 2003, which is the lowest rate since the beginning of 1995.

Lines of Credit. In addition to credit cards, revolving credit also includes lines of credit such as overdraft protection, unsecured personal lines of credit, and home equity lines of credit. A line of credit is revolving (or open account) credit when the lender establishes a maximum amount of credit that will be available for the borrower to use at any one point in time. In the case of overdraft protection, it is the maximum amount by which a checking account holder can overdraw his or her account without "bouncing" checks and/or incurring penalty fees. If the account holder writes a check that overdraws his or her account, the bank taps the overdraft protection line of credit, transfers funds to the checking account, and sets up a repayment schedule for the loan plus interest. As an alternative to using a line of credit, the bank linking the account holder's credit card to his or her checking account, and taking a cash advance from the credit card to cover checking account overdrafts, also can provide overdraft protection.

An unsecured personal credit line establishes a line of credit that an individual can use as funds are needed by writing checks against it. Home equity lines of credit operate in much the same way as unsecured personal lines of credit, except that they are secured by a second mortgage on the individual's home. Given their relatively low interest rates and the deductibility of interest charges in computing taxable income by those who itemize, home equity loans have become an extremely popular form of borrowing for a variety of purposes including home improvement, debt consolidation, automobile purchases, furniture or appliance purchases, and education. Table 8-6 shows the average amounts and outstanding balances for home equity lines of credit in the latter part of 2003. (The uses and abuses of home equity lines of credit secured by second mortgages will be discussed later in the chapter.)

Secured Versus Unsecured Debt

secured debt

Mortgage and consumer debt can be either secured or unsecured. *Secured debt* is created when a creditor agrees to sell a client something or extend the client credit in exchange for both a promise to repay and the provision of some type of "collateral" as a guarantee. Collateral can be the client's home, car, furniture, bank account, securities, or any other type of real or personal property. Debt is secured by collateral in order to reduce the risk associated with lending. If the client defaults by violating the terms of

unsecured debt

the contract (for example, fails to make mortgage payments as scheduled), the creditor can take or repossess the collateral.

Unsecured debt is created when a creditor agrees to sell a client something or extend the client credit in exchange for only a promise to repay. The vast majority of credit cards are issued on an unsecured basis. Personal lines of credit and personal loans are also examples of unsecured debt. Since there is no collateral involved, unsecured debt is secured only by the client's creditworthiness. Generally, a higher credit rating is required for unsecured debt than for secured debt. Interest rates for unsecured debt also tend to be higher than those for secured debt. For example, while Bankrate.com's weekly national survey of large banks and thrifts conducted on May 5, 2004, showed secured loan rates of 8.19 percent for home equity lines of credit, 6.84 percent for 30-year fixed rate mortgages, 7.98 percent for home equity loans, and 7.72 percent for 60-month new car loans, rates for standard fixed rate and variable rate credit cards were 13.44 percent and 14.56 percent, respectively.[12]

The Goal

A rather extreme recommendation for personal debt (and investment) management is found in Shakespeare's *Hamlet* where the pompous old windbag Polonius sends his son Laertes off with a speech filled with platitudes including "Neither a borrower nor lender be…." Unfortunately, this recommendation is not very appropriate today since, in most cases, lending and borrowing are essential to the achievement of personal financial objectives. From the standpoint of the financial planning client and financial advisor, borrowing provides a tool for, among other things, making the purchase of expensive assets such as homes, cars, and boats affordable at an earlier point in time, making available part of the funds needed to finance the purchase of various kinds of investment vehicles, and meeting financial emergencies such as covering living expenses during a period of unemployment when savings are not adequate to do so. Although currently viewed as part of investment management rather than credit and debt management for purposes of financial planning, lending accomplished by effectively investing savings in financial assets provides additional income essential to accomplishing a variety of financial accumulation objectives including funding retirement, funding a child's education, and accumulating an estate to pass on to heirs.

While Polonius' recommendation may be too extreme today given the critical roles played by both borrowing and lending in achieving personal financial goals, the reasons he gave his son for his advice—"for loan oft loses both itself and friend, and borrowing dulls the edge of husbandry"—still apply. Failure to borrow and use credit judiciously can lead to a variety of serious personal financial problems including the inability to purchase necessities, failure to create savings essential for meeting accumulation goals, being sued for unpaid debts, damaging a good credit rating, and even having to file for bankruptcy. Just as effective investment planning can lead to lending that produces favorable results in financial planning, effective credit and debt management is essential for ensuring that borrowing produces the desired results for accomplishing a client's financial objectives.

Credit and Debt Management Activities

Gather Client Data

Personal Financial Statements. Effective management of a client's credit and debt involves nearly all the key activities in the financial planning process. Initially, information regarding types and amounts of the client's existing debts and debt payments must be recorded in preparing the client's key personal financial statements as discussed in chapter 5. As shown in table 5-2, the client's debts are recorded as liabilities in the financial position statement, and as shown in table 5-10, mortgage and consumer debt payments are recorded as expenses in the cash flow statement.

Credit Report. In addition, it may be helpful to obtain a copy of the client's credit report, either a bureau credit report containing information from the three national credit bureaus—Equifax, Experian, and TransUnion—or individual reports from the three bureaus. A credit report is a document that contains a record of an individual's credit payment history. In addition to information identifying the person whose credit history is being reported, a credit report contains information about the individual's credit accounts and loans, bankruptcies, tax liens, monetary judgments, and inquiries made to other credit grantors seeking new credit. While credit reporting agencies format and report information differently, figure 8-5 provides additional detail regarding the types of information generally included in an individual's credit report. A consumer is entitled to a free copy of his or her credit report once every 12 months from every consumer reporting agency subject to the Fair Credit Reporting Act (FCRA). As part of client data gathering, the financial advisor should have the client review the information contained in his or her credit report to be certain it is accurate. Credit reports often contain inaccurate information that can negatively affect a client's credit rating and thus should be corrected promptly by using the formal dispute process contained in the FCRA.

Credit Score. The financial advisor should also have the client purchase a copy of his or her credit score, which is a statistical summary of the information contained in the client's credit report. While credit scores measuring a consumer's creditworthiness are calculated by different credit bureaus and lenders using a variety of scoring methods and are used differently by different lenders, obtaining a copy of the client's FICO Score,[13]—the credit score most widely used by lenders—can be useful to the financial advisor in carrying out the credit and debt management process. Considered in more than 75 percent of the credit decisions made in 2003, a FICO Score reflects payment history (accounts for approximately 35 percent of the score), amounts owed (about 30 percent of the score), length of credit history (about 15 percent of the score), inquiries seeking new credit (about 10 percent of the score), and types of credit in use (about 10 percent of the score). Along with the FICO Score, the client receives an explanation of what that score means to him or her, a summary of positive and negative factors affecting the score, a description of how lenders see the client, and a copy of the credit report(s) from which the score was derived.

Analyze and Evaluate the Client's Current Status

Ratio Analysis. As with the financial planning process in general, the next step is to analyze the information gathered regarding the client's current credit and debt position. There are three ratios that can be helpful in assessing the client's current debt and credit status—the liquidity ratio, the debt service ratio, and the debt safety ratio. As discussed in chapter 5, the liquidity ratio is calculated from data contained in the client's financial position statement and cash flow statement by dividing liquid assets by total current (one-year) debts consisting of current liabilities and annual loan payments. The ratio indicates the percentage of the client's current (one-year) debt that can be paid using liquid assets. Since one month is 8.3 percent (1/12) of a year, dividing the liquidity ratio by 8.3 percent equals the number of months the client can pay current debt before liquid assets are exhausted. For example, if the client's liquidity ratio is 22 percent, the client could cover current debts with liquid assets in the case of unemployment for a little over 2.5 months. The length of the period of protection and thus the amount of liquid assets required for an adequate emergency fund in this case would depend on such factors as the state of the relevant job market, other potential sources of income to help meet current debts, and the period of time with which the client is comfortable.

debt service ratio

As discussed in chapter 5, the *debt service ratio* is calculated by dividing total annual loan payments (that is, mortgage and consumer debt payments) by net income. The ratio (which also can be calculated on a monthly basis) indicates the percentage of the client's income required to cover existing loan payments. The lower the debt service ratio, the easier it is for the client to repay his or her current loans with income. Financial advisors commonly recommend striving to keep a client's debt service ratio below 35 percent.

A similar ratio in mortgage lending is called the back end ratio or *back ratio*. This ratio or back ratio is the percentage of gross monthly income allocated to housing expenses plus consumer debt payments. Mortgage lenders typically have an underwriting standard of 36 percent but may be willing to be more flexible on the back ratio than they would be on the front ratio.

FIGURE 8-5
Types of Information Contained in a Credit Report*

CREDIT BUREAU REPORT

IDENTIFYING INFORMATION

I. Wishfor Credit	12 Lost Lane	Sam's Gas & Oil
805 Main Street	Somewhere, USA 66666	Attendant
Anytown, America 77777	Date of Birth: 1-25-50	1980
	SS# 888-88-8888	

TRADE LINE INFORMATION

INDUSTRY	DATE REPORTED	DATE OPENED	HIGH CREDIT	BALANCE	CURRENT RATING	HISTORICAL DELINQUENCY
Bankcard	7-02	3-88	$5,000	$ 0	Current	120+, 6 yrs ago
Auto Loan	7-02	7-97	8,000	1,500	Current	
Retail	5-02	6-91	1,000	0	30 days	
Retail	6-02	11-98	750	300	Current	
Personal Finance	5-02	6-96	2,000	1,400	Current	

INQUIRIES THAT YOU INITIATE

DATE	INDUSTRY	DATE	INDUSTRY	DATE	INDUSTRY
7-01-02	Bank	6-01-02	Auto Finance	10-25-01	Bank
6-15-01	Retail	11-01-01	Retail		

OTHER INQUIRIES

DATE	INDUSTRY	DATE	INDUSTRY	DATE	INDUSTRY
6-15-02	Oil Company	2-07-02	Bank	3-23-01	Bank

PUBLIC RECORD/COLLECTION ITEMS

7-01 Collection $500	9-00 Collection $750
9-99 Judgment $1000 Satisfied 3-00	

* Source: Understanding Your Credit Score, Fair Isaac Corporation, San Rafael, CA, November 2003.

---

debt burden ratio

A client's *debt burden ratio* compares a client's total monthly consumer credit payment with the amount of his or her monthly take-home pay. This ratio differs in two ways from the debt service ratio. Rather than considering total loan payments, the numerator of the consumer debt burden ratio excludes mortgage payments, focusing instead only on consumer (revolving and nonrevolving) credit. The ratio's denominator includes take-home pay rather than gross income. As such, the ratio measures the extent to which the client must use take-home pay to make payments on outstanding consumer credit. For example, if a client who takes home $3,000 per month has balances on several credit cards requiring monthly payments of $200 and an auto loan with monthly payments of $300, the client's consumer debt burden ratio would be .167 [($200 + $300)/$3,000], indicating that monthly consumer credit payments account for 16.7 percent of take-home pay. Financial advisors generally view a consumer debt burden ratio of 20 percent as a maximum, and recommend that clients keep their consumer debt burden ratio in the 10 to 15 percent range. While the client in this example has a consumer debt burden ratio that is likely to be acceptable to lenders, careful consideration should be given to allowing required credit card payments to rise to $500 per month, since this would raise the consumer debt burden ratio to .267. A consumer debt burden of 26.7 percent would likely make it more difficult to convince a lender to extend further credit for other needs. A related ratio in mortgage lending is known as the front-end ratio or *front ratio*, and a lender's loan underwriting standards typically require a front ratio of no more than 28 percent. The front end ratio or front ratio is the percentage of gross monthly income allocated to housing expenses, specifically PITI—principal, interest, taxes, and insurance. Mortgage lenders typically have an underwriting standard of 28 percent or less for the front ratio. Homeowners association dues, if applicable, would also be included in the calculation.

front ratio

Client's Creditworthiness. In addition to ratio analysis based on information from financial statements, information provided by the client's credit report and credit score should be analyzed to further assess the client's future borrowing potential. FICO Scores range from 300 to 850 with higher scores considered better scores. Additional information provided with the client's FICO Score indicates the following:

- where the client's score falls as compared with those of other U.S. consumers
- the relative ease or difficulty an individual with that score should expect to experience in getting credit both in terms of the array of credit products that will be made available and the competitiveness of the rates and terms offered for those products
- the actions the client can take to raise his or her score over time
- delinquency rates for consumers in the client's score range that provide lenders with the probability that borrowers with scores similar to the client's will default on a loan, file for bankruptcy, or fall 90 days past due on at least one credit account in the next 2 years

The purchase of a client's FICO Score makes an online tool, the FICO Score Simulator, available. This simulator can be used to provide answers to a variety of credit-related questions based on the information in the client's credit report and the FICO Score. The FICO Score Simulator can select the action that might result in the best improvement of the client's credit score as well as answer the question, What happens to the client's score if...

- the client pays bills on time for the next (select from one to 24 months)
- the client pays balances down on all credit cards by (enter a monthly amount and select from one to 24 months, or enter the amount of a one-time payment)
- the client pays down delinquent balances first by (enter amount)
- the client seeks new credit (select type of credit card or loan and enter the amount of the credit limit or the loan)
- the client transfers credit card balances to a new credit card (enter amount of credit limit)
- the client misses payments (select from various scenarios)
- the client "maxes out" all his or her credit cards

Thus, the financial advisor can do online much of the analysis of the client's current credit position and its implications for the future availability of credit once the client's FICO Score is known.

Develop a Plan

Once the client's current debt and credit position has been analyzed, the financial advisor must coordinate the use of various possible borrowing strategies with the development and analysis of the alternatives for achieving the client's objectives. While the use of credit and debt might be related to the achievement of any of the client's objectives, it is most directly related to making major purchases and generating adequate savings to meet the client's accumulation objectives such as funding retirement or a child's education. In both of these situations, credit and debt management will have an impact on the client's net cash flow. As shown in table 5-10, mortgage and credit debt repayment is treated as a fixed expense in the client's cash flow statement. As discussed in chapter 5, the expected impact of each alternative course of action available for consideration in developing a plan that will meet the client's objectives should be illustrated through the preparation of a pro forma cash flow statement for that particular alternative.

For example, suppose two alternatives for paying a child's college expenses are for the client to either generate cash by selling some existing investments, or have the child take out a subsidized Stafford loan that the client will ultimately repay. In this case, one set of pro forma cash flow statements should be prepared to show the negative impact of selling the required investments on the client's investment earnings and thus net cash flow in future years. Another set of pro forma cash flow statements should be prepared to show the impact of the child taking out the subsidized Stafford loan. With this alternative, there would be no reduction in net cash flow while the child is in college since no interest accrues on the loan until 6 months after the child leaves college. This alternative would then have a negative impact over the next 10 years or less as the loan is repaid at what in recent years has been a very low variable rate of interest (3.42 percent from July 1, 2003 to June 30, 2004). From a financial standpoint, the preferred alternative would be the one that would have the least negative impact on the client's positive net cash flow (savings) available for new investment or discretionary expenditures. However, both sets of pro forma cash flow statements should be shown to the client along with the financial advisor's recommendation regarding the preferred alternative, since it is the client who must approve the plan.

Implementing and Monitoring the Plan

Once the credit and debt management plan chosen by the client has been implemented either alone or as part of a broader financial plan, its performance should be monitored. As discussed in chapter 5, the plan's performance can be monitored by periodically preparing a net cash flow statement that shows the client's actual net cash flow resulting from the implementation of the credit and debt management plan (as well as other parts of the financial plan).

SELECTED PROBLEMS IN CREDIT AND DEBT MANAGEMENT

Leasing Versus Buying a Car

Car leasing has become increasingly popular for consumers in recent years, now accounting for about one third of all new vehicle deals. As shown in table 8-9, leasing a car differs in a number of ways from buying one.

Automobile leases are particularly suited to people with the following characteristics:

- They do not like to haggle over the prices of cars when buying and selling them.
- They seek to minimize their monthly payments and cash down payments.
- They have a strong preference for driving new cars and plan to keep their cars 3 years or less.

TABLE 8-9
How Leasing Differs From Buying

OWNERSHIP	
LEASING: You do not own the vehicle. You use it but must return it at the end of the lease unless you choose to buy it.	**BUYING:** You own the vehicle and get to keep it at the end of the financing term.

UP-FRONT COSTS	
LEASING: Up-front costs may include the first month's payment, a refundable security deposit, a capitalized cost reduction (like a down payment), taxes, registration and other fees, and other charges.	**BUYING:** Up-front costs include the cash price or a down payment, taxes, registration and other fees, and other charges.

MONTHLY PAYMENTS	
LEASING: Monthly lease payments are usually lower than monthly loan payments because you are paying only for the vehicle's depreciation during the lease term, plus rent charges (like interest), taxes, and fees.	**BUYING:** Monthly loan payments are usually higher than monthly lease payments because you are paying for the entire purchase price of the vehicle, plus interest and other finance charges, taxes, and fees.

EARLY TERMINATION	
LEASING: You are responsible for any early termination charges if you end the lease early.	**BUYING:** You are responsible for any pay-off amount if you end the loan early.

VEHICLE RETURN	
LEASING: You may return the vehicle at lease-end, pay any end-of-lease costs, and "walk away."	**BUYING:** You may have to sell or trade the vehicle when you decide you want a different vehicle.

FUTURE VALUE	
LEASING: You bear the risk of the future market value of the vehicle.	**BUYING:** You bear the risk of the vehicle's market value when you trade or sell it.

MILEAGE	
LEASING: Most leases limit the number of miles you may drive (often 12,000–15,000 per year). You can negotiate a higher mileage limit and pay a higher monthly payment. You will likely have to pay charges for exceeding those limits if you return the vehicle.	**BUYING:** You may drive as many miles as you want, but higher mileage will lower the vehicle's trade-in or resale value.

EXCESSIVE WEAR	
LEASING: Most leases limit wear to the vehicle during the lease term. You will likely have to pay extra charges for exceeding those limits if you return the vehicle.	**BUYING:** There are no limits or charges for excessive wear to the vehicle, but excessive wear will lower the vehicle's trade-in or resale value.

END OF TERM	
LEASING: At the end of the lease (typically 2–4 years), you may have a new payment either to finance the purchase of the existing vehicle or to lease another vehicle.	**BUYING:** At the end of the loan term (typically 4–6 years), you have no further loan payments.

Source: Keys to Vehicle Leasing, Federal Reserve Board, 2004. Retrieved May 15, 2004, from http://www.federalreserve.gov/pubs/leasing/

- They drive less than 12,000 to 15,000 miles per year.
- They keep their cars well maintained.

An important aspect of auto leasing is the estimate of what the market value of the vehicle will be at the end of the lease. The estimated value is referred to as the residual value. Leases may be classified as either a closed-end lease or an open-end lease. With a closed-end lease, if the market value at the end of the lease is less than the projected residual value, the dealer absorbs the loss. With an open-end lease, if the market value is less than the estimated residual value, the consumer is obligated to make up the difference. The majority of consumer leases are closed-end because the consumer is exposed to less risk. Regardless of which type of lease is selected, the individual has the option to buy the car at the residual value.

Monthly lease payments are largely a function of supply and demand, but pricing typically follows the formula shown in figure 8-6. The total monthly lease payment is composed of three monthly costs—the monthly depreciation, the monthly lease rate (the lessor's required monthly return), and the monthly sales tax.

Example:	A consumer wants an automobile with a manufacturer's suggested retail price (MSRP) of $28,000 and is considering a 3-year lease. The gross capitalized cost (negotiated price of the car plus any items paid over the term of the lease such as service contracts, insurance, and any outstanding prior credit or lease balance) of the car is $26,000. While there is no down payment in this case, there is a destination charge of $300, an acquisition fee of $350, and a security deposit of $800. Security deposits should be refunded at the end of the lease. As shown in figure 8-6, any down payment (none in this case), trade-in allowance, and rebates/dealer incentives are typically called a *capitalized cost reduction*.[14] Since the capital cost reduction in this example is $0, the adjusted capitalized cost equals the gross capitalized cost, $26,000.

In addition to the first monthly payment, the total payment due at the lease signing includes the capitalized cost reduction plus the destination charge, the acquisition fee, and the security deposit, or $1,450 in this case. As an alternative, items such as the destination charge and the acquisition fee could be included in the gross capitalized cost if the consumer prefers to have these costs amortized over the term of the lease rather than paid at the time the lease is signed.

The dealer will assume that the residual value will equal a specific percentage of the MSRP, depending on the make and model of the vehicle. If the appropriate residual value is 55 percent of the MSRP for a 3-year lease, the residual value is $15,400. The difference between the adjusted capitalized cost

FIGURE 8-6
Calculating the Monthly Payment on a Lease

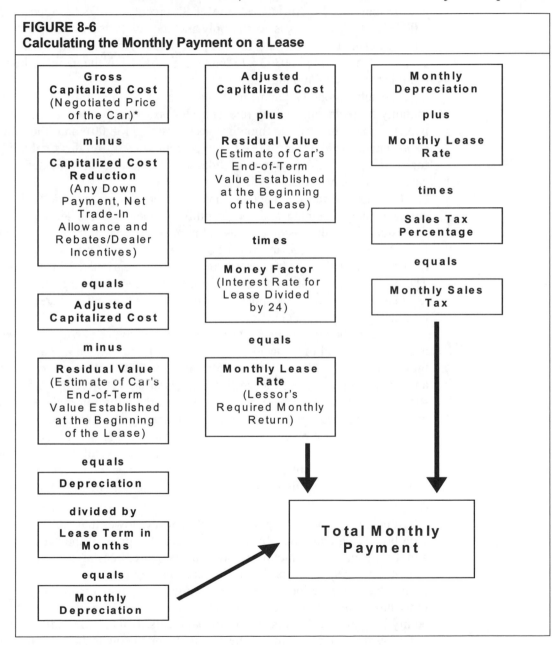

of $26,000 and the residual value of $15,400 is the estimated amount of depreciation over the term of the lease, $10,600. The monthly depreciation is computed by dividing the term depreciation by the term of the lease in months. In our example, the term depreciation is $10,600, so the monthly depreciation is $10,600 divided by the 36-month term of the lease, or $294.44.

Calculation of a money factor involves taking the appropriate interest rate and dividing by 24. An interest rate of 8 percent, or 0.08, divided by 24 is 0.00333. The next step is to multiply the money factor by the sum of the adjusted capitalized cost and the residual value. This product, which in our case equals $138.00 [0.00333 x ($26,000 + $15,400)], is the monthly lease rate but it is not the total monthly payment.

The total monthly payment is the sum of the monthly lease rate, the monthly depreciation, and any relevant sales tax, which we will assume to be 5 percent. The sum of the monthly lease rate ($138.00) and the monthly depreciation ($294.44) is $432.44. A 5 percent sales tax on this total is $21.62 for a total monthly payment of $454.07. Bankrate.com provides a lease calculator on its website.[15]

Leasing contracts generally contain other charges in addition to the payment due at signing and the monthly payments. Some leases include a disposition fee if the customer does not purchase the car at the end of the lease term. Most leases charge an extra 12 or 15 cents for each mile the car is driven over the limit (often 12,000 or 15,000 miles per year) stated in the contract. There are also generally charges for damage in excess of normal wear and tear as well as substantial penalties (up to several thousand dollars) for early termination of the lease contract.

Another potential problem associated with leasing can arise if a leased car is stolen or totaled in an accident. In this case, there may be a "gap" between the lease's early termination payoff amount (not including any past-due amounts) and the amount for which the car is insured (before the deductible is subtracted). Although there is insurance, commonly referred to as GAP coverage, that will protect the individual leasing the car against any gap between the amount owed for early termination of the lease and the amount of auto insurance coverage, the person with the lease may still be responsible for the insurance deductible, for any past-due or other amounts owed under the lease, and for the monthly payments until the lessor receives the insurance proceeds.

With a lease, monthly payments are typically lower than those associated with borrowing and buying a car if the negotiated price of the car is identical and there is no special rate for the loan or the lease. Leasing produces a lower monthly payment because the consumer is paying only for the use of the car during the lease period rather than making full payment for the car. If an individual takes out a 3-year lease, at the end of the 3 years he or she has no equity to show for 3 years' worth of payments. If the same individual takes out a 3-year loan, at the end of the 3 years he or she owns the car outright.

There are advantages to leasing, though. Consumers who lease often have the advantage of driving a car that is always under warranty, and they can easily switch models at the end of the lease to drive the style or type of car that is most suitable at that time. In the case of an underestimate of the residual value, it is possible for the consumer to exercise the option to buy the automobile at a price that is lower than its market value and retain it or resell it at a profit. Leasing also protects the consumer against higher than expected rates of depreciation.

Home Equity Loans and Home Equity Lines of Credit

Home equity loans are usually standard fixed-rate installment loans in which the borrower makes equal, consecutive monthly payments for the life of the loan. What distinguishes them from other loans is that one's home is pledged as collateral. A home equity loan is essentially a second mortgage.

The major advantage of a home equity loan (HELoan) is that, because the loan is a form of a mortgage, the borrower can deduct part or all of the interest payments if the borrower itemizes deductions on his or her tax return. The amount of debt that qualifies as home equity debt for tax purposes, and thus for which interest is deductible, is limited to the lesser of $100,000 ($50,000 if married and filing separately) or the fair market value of the main home (and second home if one exists) reduced (but not below zero) by the amount of the current mortgage indebtedness. For example, if the fair market value of a client's home is $100,000 and the current mortgage debt outstanding is $75,000, interest on an amount of home equity debt up to $25,000 would be deductible. However, if a home equity loan (a second mortgage) is issued for an amount that exceeds the difference between the home's fair market value and the current mortgage balance, the loan amount in excess of this difference is considered to be unsecured (not home equity debt for tax purposes), and thus the interest on that portion of the loan is not deductible. For example, if the client obtains a home equity loan for $45,000 (120 percent of the home's fair market value minus any current mortgage debt outstanding—this type of home equity loan is discussed below) and the current mortgage debt outstanding is $75,000, only $25,000 of the $45,000 home equity loan qualifies as home equity debt for tax purposes. Interest paid on the remaining $20,000 of the home equity loan is not deductible for tax purposes. Figure 8-7 shows how the IRS determines the deductibility of home mortgage interest.

In addition to deductibility of interest for tax purposes, another advantage is that because of the high quality of the collateral, most lenders charge lower rates on these loans than on other loans of comparable maturity without this type of collateral. Furthermore, the monthly payments on home equity loans are usually smaller than those on other consumer loans of the

FIGURE 8-7
Figure A: Is My Home Mortgage Interest Fully Deductible?

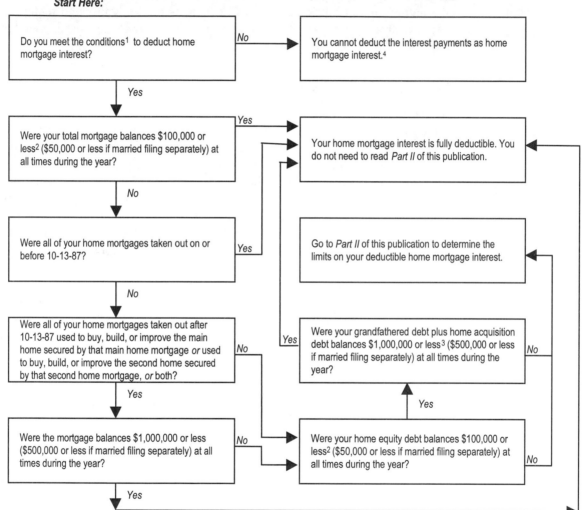

*(Instructions: Include balances of **ALL** mortgages secured by your main home and second home.)*

1. You must itemize deductions on Schedule A (Form 1040) and be legally liable for the loan. The loan must be a secured debt on a qualified home. See *Part I, Home Mortgage Interest.*
2. If all mortgages on your main or second home exceed the home's fair market value, a lower limit may apply. See *Home equity debt limit* under *Home Equity Debt in Part II.*
3. Amounts over the $1,000,000 limit ($500,000 if married filing separately) qualify as home equity debt if they are not more than the total home equity debt limit. See *Part II* of this publication for more information about grandfathered debt, home acquisition debt, and home equity debt.
4. See *Table 2* for where to deduct other types of interest payments.

Source: IRS Publication 936, Home Mortgage Interest Deduction, figure A, for use in preparing 2006 returns. The references in this figure are to that publication, which is available at: http://www.irs.gov/publications/p936/index.html

same size because of their longer maturities and lower interest rates. For example, a $20,000 5-year auto loan at 8 percent will have a substantially larger monthly payment than a $20,000 10-year home equity loan at 7 percent.

A home equity line of credit (HELOC) differs from a home equity loan in that there is more flexibility in the amount borrowed and the repayment process. In a true HELOC, the lender will approve a line of credit up to a specified amount, which the borrower can access for a specified number of years. For example, the lender may approve a $50,000 line of credit that is available for 5 years, and the borrower may borrow from that line for any purpose(s) during the 5-year period. However, the total amount of borrowing that is outstanding cannot exceed $50,000 at any one time.

The minimum monthly payment is usually the interest owed on the amount borrowed. Thus, if the interest rate is 8 percent and the consumer borrows $40,000 on the line of credit, the minimum monthly payment is one-month's interest, or $266.67 ($40,000 x 8% x 1/12). Obviously, this minimum payment will not reduce the amount of the principal of the loan. Beyond the minimum monthly payment, there is no repayment schedule.

Some lenders require the borrower to take out a minimum amount under the line of credit at the time the HELOC is approved and to maintain that loan outstanding for a minimum amount of time. In many cases, lenders offer a "credit card" with a HELOC. Unless a client has a lot of willpower, he or she should not accept the card. Carrying a HELOC-related credit card may make drawing on the home equity line too easy and tempt a client to use it to make everyday purchases like gas, groceries, and clothes or as a source of ready cash without giving thought as to whether that purchase is really an appropriate use of home equity.[16]

HELOCs are variable rate loans that protect the lender in case interest rates rise. While variable interest rates may protect lenders, they can create problems for consumers. Since HELOC rates are priced at a spread to a short-term interest rate, like the prime rate, an increase in the effective Federal Funds rate will lead to an increase in the HELOC's interest rate. For example, suppose a homeowner takes out a $50,000 10-year HELOC with a variable rate initially at 4 percent and borrows the maximum immediately. If the homeowner planned to pay off the $50,000 outstanding in level monthly payments over 10 years, the monthly payments would be $506.23, including both principal and interest. If the prime rate were to increase two percentage points to 6 percent in one year, the monthly payment would grow to $555.10.[17] If the Federal Reserve continued to raise interest rates in succeeding years, the monthly payment would continue to increase and might reach an amount that the homeowner could no longer afford to pay. By law, HELOCs with variable interest rates must have a cap on how much the interest rate can increase over the life of the plan. Some variable rate plans also limit how much the variable rate can increase each time the Federal Reserve raises interest rates and how much it can fall if interest rates drop.

Consumers often seek home equity loans to obtain funds for home improvements or repairs, but they can be used for any purpose. A common use is for debt consolidation. Frequently, consumers will pay off many high-interest credit card balances and even car loans by refinancing at a lower rate over a longer term with tax deductibility using either a home equity loan or more frequently today, a HELOC. There are several potential problems associated with this debt-consolidation strategy, especially when a HELOC is used.[18] First, after consolidating credit card debt with a home equity loan or HELOC, consumers often charge up their credit cards again to their previous balances within 2 or 3 years, and then face not only the home equity debt created to consolidate their old credit card debt, but also the new credit card debt created since then. Moreover, as mentioned above, since HELOCs usually have variable interest rates, an increase in the prime rate can make it more difficult to pay off the outstanding balance. Finally, if home values drop, a HELOC borrower may end up owing more on the house than it is worth.

Like most loans, lenders now use risk models to determine whether they approve the loan and what interest rate they will charge for the loan. A FICO score, income levels, loan-to-values, and debt service ratios all are part of the decision concerning whether to extend credit. Although lenders can establish their own criteria regarding rates and maximum loan size, there are certain guidelines all lenders tend to follow. These guidelines are known as the lender's underwriting standards. Underwriting standards don't vary much among lenders because many originating lenders sell the loan and it becomes part of a pool, or group, of mortgages that is packaged (securitized) and sold to investors.

loan-to-value

If a lender requires that the total *loan-to-value* of all mortgages not exceed 80 percent of the home's appraised value, then the outstanding loan balance of the existing first mortgage limits what the lender will approve for a second (home equity) mortgage.

Example: Gary Stone believes his house would be appraised at $150,000. His first mortgage on his home is down to $99,500, and currently he has no second mortgage. If his lender approves HELOCs up to an 80 percent loan-to-value ratio, what is the maximum HELOC he could take out?

The first step is to compute 80 percent of the appraised value. In this case, 80 percent of $150,000 is $120,000. Thus the sum of Gary's mortgages cannot exceed this figure. Because his total mortgage indebtedness on the home is $99,500, we subtract this amount from the $120,000, which indicates that the maximum HELOC he can obtain is $20,500. Again, the lender must still evaluate Gary's creditworthiness for the line of credit, especially with regard to whether his income is adequate and stable enough to service the debt.

While traditional home equity loans and lines of credit limit the total mortgage borrowing on the home to less than the home's fair market value, "no equity' or "125% LTV" (loan to value) home equity loans and lines of credit have become increasingly popular in recent years, primarily for debt consolidation. In the previous example, with a 125% LTV loan, Gary Stone could obtain a HELOC up to $88,000, the difference between 125 percent of his home's fair market value ($187,500) and his outstanding first mortgage debt ($99,500). Although borrowers need little equity in their homes to qualify, lenders usually require a FICO credit score that is well above the average as well as a good income and a steady job. Thus, "these loans are designed for people who have always had good credit and have used it freely enough to build up considerable debt."[19] In addition to the limited tax deductibility of interest on home equity loans and lines of credit that along with other outstanding mortgages exceed the fair market value of the home, these "no equity" loans and credit lines have relatively high up-front loan fees, and carry interest rates that are considerably higher than those on first mortgages and traditional home equity debt since a portion, usually a major portion, of the amount borrowed with these loans and lines of credit is unsecured.

Lenders advertise the rates they charge on home equity loans and HELOCs just as they advertise any other loan rate. As with other loans, the lower nominal interest rate loan is not always the best deal. Consumers must consider all the fees associated with the loan. For example, the home must be appraised, the lender may require a survey and title search, there may be an origination fee, and there may be a fee to file the loan with the county courthouse. A prepayment fee if the line is closed or paid off in the first few (2–3) years after closing also raises the potential cost of a HELOC. Because these fees can be substantial, borrowers should carefully assess the costs of applying for this type of loan.

BANKRUPTCY

Most financial advisors eventually encounter clients who consider (or should consider) filing for bankruptcy. Although advisors must avoid the illegal practice of law, they must understand the basic tenets of bankruptcy to know when to refer a client to a qualified attorney.

Title 11 of the United States Code governs bankruptcy, and federal bankruptcy law supercedes conflicting state laws. The types of bankruptcy proceedings are known according to chapters in which they are described in the Bankruptcy Code.

There are three primary forms of filing for bankruptcy (each of which is discussed below):

- Chapter 7 Bankruptcy
- Chapter 13 Bankruptcy
- Chapter 11 Bankruptcy

Changes in the bankruptcy laws that went into effect October 17, 2005, made it harder for consumers to file a Chapter 7 bankruptcy. Bankruptcy candidates now face mandatory credit counseling and a means test as part of the process of determining what chapter bankruptcy they are permitted to file. Once filed, bankruptcy petitioners are required to take a course in credit management. According to the U.S. Courts statistical reports, bankruptcy cases begun in 2006 fell by 37.6 percent to 1,112,542 cases.

Most consumers who declare bankruptcy do so under Chapter 7 or Chapter 13. However, the intent under the new bankruptcy law is to have Chapter 13 filings increase and Chapter 7 filings decrease. Table 8-10 shows a decline in total bankruptcy filings after the new law became effective, in large part because so many petitioners tried to file under the old law.

TABLE 8-10
U.S. Bankruptcy Courts
Bankruptcy Cases Commenced During the 12-Month Periods Ended September 30, 2005 and 2006

2005	2006	Percent Change
1,782,643	1,112,542	37.6

Source: U.S. Bankruptcy Court Statistics.
       http://www.uscourts.gov/bnkrpctystats/statistics.htm#fiscal

---

All three types of bankruptcies may eliminate unsecured debts and stop foreclosures, repossessions, garnishment of wages, utility service cancellation, and activities of debt collectors against an individual. However, bankruptcy cannot clean up a bad credit record. Since bankruptcy remains part of a person's credit record for up to 10 years, it makes it difficult to get a mortgage or credit card during that period. Even when a credit card is issued, its interest rate is likely to be higher than normal or it may have to be secured by a deposit with the card issuer.[20] What is typical is that the individual has little to no access to new credit in the first 2 years after filing for bankruptcy and, assuming a clean payment history over that 2-year period, lenders may extend credit but at a high rate of interest. Secured credit cards are often an intermediate step in building that payment history.

The U.S. Court's publication, "Bankruptcy Basics," is available on its website. Revised in 2005 to reflect the changes in the bankruptcy law, this guide provides an overview of the different bankruptcy filings.[21]

Chapter 7 Bankruptcy

Often known as a "straight bankruptcy," Chapter 7 is a liquidation proceeding, which means that the debtor's nonexempt assets are transferred to and sold by a trustee, the proceeds are distributed to creditors according to a Code-specified priority, and the debtor is discharged from specified indebtedness. Creditors cannot target wages that the debtor received subsequent to the filing.

Chapter 7 can be voluntary, meaning that the debtor initiates the proceeding. The debtor can be an individual, married couple, partnership, or corporation (with exceptions). However, a debtor can use Chapter 7 to receive a discharge of debt no more than once every 6 years. Qualifying creditors can also initiate involuntary Chapter 7 proceedings against debtors.

Federal law specifies property that may be exempt from the bankruptcy estate and thus not subject to creditors' claims. Pensions, annuities, life insurance, certain household goods and personal items up to specified limits, the tools of a trade or profession, and various other items are expressly listed in the Code. State laws vary in defining what property may be exempt from the bankruptcy estate, but it can be substantial. For example, some states exempt the debtor's homestead regardless of the debtor's equity in the property. As a practical matter, most individuals filing for Chapter 7 give up no assets to the trustee.

Debts under Chapter 7 are classified as dischargeable or nondischargeable. Nondischargeable debts include recent back taxes, debts incurred due to fraud or other illegal activity, alimony and child support, recent student loans, and several other categories. Recent credit card cash advances and credit-based purchases are typically viewed as having occurred in anticipation of filing and thus are nondischargeable. The court may even issue a denial of discharge for the entire petition if it determines that the debtor is concealing information, transferring assets, filing false oaths, failing to maintain appropriate records, or otherwise behaving in a manner inconsistent with what should be expected of an "honest but unfortunate" debtor.

Individual debtors typically receive a discharge within 4 to 6 months of filing, and notice of the bankruptcy stays on their credit record for 10 years. In a rather perverse twist, many creditors are eager to lend to recently discharged bankruptcy filers because they have minimal debt and can use Chapter 7 to discharge their debt only once every 8 years.

Chapter 13 Bankruptcy

Chapter 13 bankruptcy is a voluntary petition available to natural persons but not to corporations and partnerships. The petitioner must have a regular income that exceeds his or her reasonable living expenses. As of April 1, 2004, the petitioner must have less than $307,675 in unsecured debts and $922,975 in secured debts.

Under Chapter 13, the debtor proposes a repayment plan based on how much income is available after paying current expenses and is then protected from collection actions by creditors. Plans are designed for 3 years and may be extended to 5 years. If the debtor maintains the schedule by forwarding the proscribed payments to the trustee on a timely basis, debts remaining at the end of the period may be discharged with some creditors receiving only pennies on the dollar. Priority claims, such as taxes and child support, must be paid in full, however, and the trustee may also mandate payment in full for the secured indebtedness on an automobile, for example.

Creditors do not vote on whether to accept the plan. Rather, the court must determine that the plan meets the following three tests:

- It must be made in good faith.
- It must be in the best interests of the creditors—that is, unsecured creditors will receive at least as much as they would under Chapter 7.
- It must indicate that the petitioner is making "best efforts," meaning that all disposable income is committed to the plan for at least 3 years.

If creditors object, negotiation usually leads to a compromise. If there are no objections or once a compromise is reached, the debtor and creditors must follow the plan.

Since the debtor retains possession of all his or her property whether it is exempt or nonexempt, Chapter 13 may be the preferred alternative when some of the debtor's property is not exempt for purposes of Chapter 7. Sometimes Chapter 13 is chosen rather than Chapter 7 because certain debts may be dischargeable in the former but not in the latter. Another reason for selecting Chapter 13 is that future potential creditors probably look more kindly on an individual who created a plan for partial repayment under Chapter 13 rather than one who left creditors empty handed under Chapter 7. Also, Chapter 13 can be filed subsequent to Chapter 7, allowing the debtor to deal with some debts that were not dischargeable in Chapter 7. This approach is also used to enable a debtor to first discharge unsecured debt under Chapter 7 and then reorganize secured and nondischargeable debt under Chapter 13. Finally, a Chapter 13 filing can be converted to either a Chapter

7 liquidation or a Chapter 11 reorganization. A debtor is ineligible for discharge under Chapter 13 if he or she received a prior discharge in a Chapter 7, 11, or 12 case filed 4 years before the current case, or in a Chapter 13 case filed 2 years before the current case.

Chapter 11 Bankruptcy

Chapter 11 is a reorganization proceeding that is typically used by corporations and partnerships, but individuals can also use it. As in Chapter 7, the petition can be voluntary or involuntary. As in Chapter 13, the debtor retains possession of his or her assets and continues to operate any business while paying less than the full amount of indebtedness. The plan must be approved by a majority of the creditors in each class and by enough creditors in each class to equal two-thirds of the indebtedness to that class.

Individuals whose debt exceeds the restrictions imposed under Chapter 13 frequently choose Chapter 11, as do debtors who, despite not having a regular income, still want to try to restructure their debt. If necessary, a Chapter 11 filing can be converted to a liquidation, or Chapter 7, proceeding.

Bankruptcy is not merely a legal issue. It is rife with moral and ethical implications for the client as well as the advisor. In some cases, clients attempt to take actions that border on fraud—sometimes crossing the line—and place the advisor in an untenable position. The bankruptcy court can use the discovery of fraud as a reason for dismissal or reversal of a bankruptcy case.

CHAPTER EIGHT REVIEW

Key Terms
Key terms and concepts are explained in the glossary.

asset allocation
Section 529 plans
prepaid tuition plans
Sec. 529 savings plans
Roth IRA
Hope Scholarship Tax Credit
Lifetime Learning Tax Credit
FAFSA
expected parent contribution
expected student contribution
expected family contribution (EFC)
student aid report (SAR)
cost of attendance (COA)
Federal Pell Grant

Federal Supplemental Education
    Opportunity Grant (FSEOG)
Federal Perkins loans
Stafford loans
Parent Loans for Undergraduate
    Students (PLUS loans)
Federal Loan Consolidation
    Programs
liquidity
marketability
secured debt
unsecured debt
debt service ratio
back ratio

debt burden ratio
front ratio
loan-to-value

Review Questions

The answers to the review questions are in the supplement. Self-test questions and the answers to them are also in the supplement and on The American College Online.

8-1. Identify the two funding requirements associated with financing a college education. [8-1]

8-2. Discuss how college costs, inflation, investment returns, and tax considerations shape investing for college. [8-2]

8-3. Compare and contrast the availability of scholarships, grants, and loans for college funding. [8-2]

8-4. Discuss the financial aid process from filling out the FAFSA form to establishing the expected family contribution (EFC). [8-2]

8-5. Your client wants to start a Section 529 College Savings Plan to fund her newborn's undergraduate education. She finds out that tuition and room and board at her alma mater currently cost $20,000 per academic year. Her alma mater's annual college cost inflation has averaged 8 percent, and you expect to be able to direct her investment to earn a 10 percent return. What annual contribution does she need to make if she will make contributions at the beginning of each year, starting today, and she wants to have 4 years worth of college expenses funded when her child starts college 18 years from now? [8-2]

8-6. Discuss how to size a client's emergency fund and how to invest that fund. [8-5]

8-7. What are the key types of household debt? [8-7]

8-8. Explain the difference between secured and unsecured debt. [8-8]

8-9. How does a credit report differ from a credit score? [8-9]

8-10. How do consumer debt ratios influence lending decisions? [8-10]

8-11. How would you help a client decide if leasing an automobile was the right financial decision for him or her? [8-11]

8-12. Compare and contrast a home equity line of credit with a home equity loan. [8-13]

8-13. Calculate the maximum amount a consumer can borrow under a home equity loan or HELOC. [8-13]

8-14. If a lender requires a total loan-to-value of no more than 80 percent, what is the maximum size it will approve for a HELOC given an appraised value of $225,000 and an outstanding balance of $125,000 on the first mortgage? [8-13]

8-15. When is the interest expense on a home equity loan not deductible on a client's federal income tax return? [8-14]

8-16. Differentiate between a Chapter 7, Chapter 13, and Chapter 11 bankruptcy petition. [8-15]

NOTES

1. http://www.treasurydirect.gov.

2. *About the CollegeSure CD*, College Savings Bank, Princeton, NJ. Retrieved June 11, 2007, from http://www.collegesavings.com/program.html.

3. *Trends in Student Aid*, The College Board, Washington, D.C., 2003. Retrieved November 11, 2004, from www.collegeboard.com/prod_downloads/press/cost04/TrendsinStudentAid2004.pdf.

4. *Funding Your Education 2004–2005*, U.S. Department of Education, Washington, D.C., 2004. Retrieved April 28, 2004, from http://studentaid.ed.gov/students/attachments/siteresources/StudentGuideEnglish2004_05.pdf.

5. Federal Student Aid. Retrieved June 14, 2007 from http://studentaid.ed.gov/PORTALSWebApp/students/english/NewPrograms.jsp.

6. Federal Student Aid for Counselors. Retrieved June 14, 2007, from http://www.fsa4counselors.ed.gov/clcf/loans.html.

7. Consumer Credit February 2004, Federal Reserve Statistical Release, April 7, 2004.

8. Federal Reserve Statistical Release Z.1 Retrieved August 21, 2007 from http:www.federalreserve.gov/RELEASES/z1/Current/annuals/a1995–2006.pdf.

9. "How Does Your Debt Compare?"MSN Money. Retrieved May 8, 2004, from http://moneycentral.msn.com/content/SavingandDebt/P70581.asp (link no longer active).

10. Karen Dynan, Kathleen Johnson and Karen Pence, "Recent Changes to a Measure of U.S. Household Debt Service," *Federal Reserve Bulletin*, October 2003, pp. 417–426.

11. David W. Moore, "Average American Owes $2,900 in Credit Card Debt," The Gallup Organization, Princeton, New Jersey, April 16, 2004. Retrieved May 8, 2004, from http://www.gallup.com/content/login.aspx?ci=11377 (link no longer active).

12. Weekly Rate Roundup, June 14, 2007, from http://www.bankrate.com/brm/static/rate-roundup.asp.

13. A client's credit score is based on the information in a credit report. All three nationwide credit bureaus issue scores. Fair Isaac Corporation (FICO) develops the statistical models that compute a credit score, but each of the credit bureaus has a proprietary name for its credit score. Experian calls it the Experian/Fair Isaac Risk score; Equifax calls it a Beacon score; and TransUnion calls it an Empirica score. Credit reports and credit scores for all three of the nationwide credit bureaus can be purchased online from Fair Isaac Corporation at http://www.myfico.com/.

14. For sales/use taxes, states differ in which amounts are taxed, the rate of taxation, and when the taxes are assessed. If taxes are due at lease inception, they are included as part of the capitalized cost reduction and are paid at the time the lease is signed. In most states, sales/use taxes can be paid monthly and are included in the total monthly payment as illustrated in figure 8-6.

15. http://www.bankrate.com/brm/cgi-bin/lease.asp.

16. Jeanne Sahadi, "Eating Your House," CNN/Money, October 7, 2003. Retrieved May 20, 2004, from http://money.cnn.com/2003/10/01/commentary/everyday/sahadi/.

17. Ann Perry, "Don't Bet the House on a Home Equity Loan," TheStreet.com, May 11, 2004. Retrieved May 19, 2004, from http://www.thestreet.com/funds/annperry/10159368.html.

18. Sarah Max, "Don't Blow Your Home Equity," CNN/Money, April 22, 2004. Retrieved May 19, 2004, from http://money.cnn.com/2004/04/19/pf/yourhome/home_equity/.

19. "Borrower Beware: No-Equity Loans May Be Too Good to Be True," Retrieved August 21, 2007, from http://www.creditmatters.com/articles.asp?art=17 (link no longer active).

20. "Bankruptcy Pros and Cons," Practical Law, Public Education, American Bar Association, Chicago, Illinois. Retrieved May 20, 2004, from http://www.abanet.org/publiced/practical/bankruptcypros.html (link no longer active).

21. http://www.uscourts.gov/bankruptcycourts/bankbasics0406.pdf.

9

The Regulation of Financial Advisers

Learning Objectives

An understanding of the material in this chapter should enable the student to

9-1. Describe the tests in the Investment Advisers Act of 1940 that determine whether a financial adviser must register with the SEC as an investment adviser.

9-2. Identify the types of financial advisers who are not required to become registered investment advisers with the SEC.

9-3. Summarize how the Investment Advisers Supervision Coordination Act of 1996 determines whether investment advisers must register at the federal or state level.

9-4. Describe the procedure for becoming a registered investment adviser and the various types of requirements imposed on one who does register.

9-5. Discuss how the role of self-regulatory organizations relates to the SEC's oversight of registered representatives and investment advisers.

9-6. Discuss the responsibility of a fiduciary to his or her client in the area of financial planning.

9-7. Differentiate between the suitability standards of a registered representative and the fiduciary standards of a registered investment adviser.

Chapter Outline

Financial planning as a profession continues to grow and evolve. The proliferation of financial advisers that started in the late 1970s and continues through today[1] makes the regulation of financial advisers an increasingly important topic to investors, consumer advocates, regulatory authorities, elected officials, and even to financial advisers themselves. This chapter reviews federal legislation and regulatory actions that govern the activities of financial planners.

A good example of the rapidly changing regulatory environment is an important piece of legislation that Congress passed and the president signed in October 1996. As explained later in the chapter, the Investment Advisers Supervision Coordination Act of 1996 changed the regulatory environment significantly. As of July 1997, the Securities and Exchange Commission (SEC) no longer requires financial planners with less than $30 million of assets under management to register with the SEC as investment advisers. Exceptions to this exemption include advisers to investment companies and financial planners in states that have no investment adviser laws. In effect, regulation of "small" investment advisers becomes the exclusive purview of the states.

In the current decade, SEC rules have increasingly focused on compliance and ethical standards and established the regulatory requirements of investment advisers practicing predominately on the Internet.

A recent appellate court victory in *Financial Planning Association (FPA) v. the SEC* determined that the SEC's controversial "Merrill Lynch Rule" was in conflict with the Investment Advisers Act of 1940. Registered representatives offering fee-based brokerage accounts will need to change the account relationship or potentially be required to register as investment advisers under the 1940 act. This is a major change in the regulation of financial advisors since registered investment advisers are held to a fiduciary standard in their dealings with clients versus the suitability standard required of registered representatives.

HOW FINANCIAL PLANNERS BECAME INVESTMENT ADVISERS

In the late 1970s and early 1980s when the proliferation of financial planners, plans, and products became evident, Congress grew concerned that, due to this growth in the industry, additional regulation would be necessary. There was talk in Washington at that time of new statutes and regulations to specifically cover the activities of financial planners so consumers could be adequately protected. Much of this talk was precipitated by relatively isolated horror stories involving fraud and abuse.

The SEC became alarmed at the prospect of new legislation in this area since the agency felt that regulation of financial planners was its bailiwick. After expressing this concern to Congress, the SEC was urged to develop a clear and concise position on the subject of what specific activities undertaken by financial advisers would trigger the application of the existing federal securities laws. Congress felt that this approach could remove the need for new legislation.[*]

John R. Macey (2002) describes this approach. Federal or state governments do not regulate financial planners per se. Instead, the activities and conduct of financial planners are subject to government regulation because most of the individual components of the financial planning process are regulated. Thus, federal or state securities regulators oversee financial planners in their capacity as investment advisers; federal or state securities agencies also regulate those financial planners who sell securities. Additionally, those engaged in financial planning may be subject to state regulation of insurance brokers and agents, accountants, or attorneys.[2]

A planner who develops multi-purpose plans for his or her clients may be subject to regulation by multiple regulators (versus a planner who specializes in just one aspect of financial planning) and will need to be aware of and in compliance with the applicable industry regulations. Recommending insurance, selling securities, and providing investment advice are all logical outcomes of

---

[*] It should be noted that both adviser and advisor are acceptable, although the 1940 act is the Investment Advisers Act. This chapter and the next two use adviser but describe the services provided as advisory services.

the financial planning process. Complying with applicable state and federal regulations in doing so may require licensing, registration, and compliance procedures.

For example, "Financial planning often includes an analysis of a client's insurance needs. Financial planners, therefore, may find themselves subject to government regulation of insurance, which primarily means state regulation. In some states, financial planners are even subject to regulation if they recommend a generic insurance product or a specific amount of insurance without referring the client to an insurance agent or acting as insurance agents themselves.... Some states, however, make insurance licensing easier for accredited financial planners by exempting individuals holding the CFP® or other designations from insurance testing requirements."[3]

This chapter cannot provide the depth and scope needed to serve as a definitive guide to federal and state regulation of financial planners. However, it will show how regulation has evolved and provide an overview of the issues in registration, licensing, and compliance.

Speculative excess and self-dealings, combined with the financial hardships of the Great Depression, fostered a legislative environment that produced the current foundation of securities law in the United States. The acts that govern the securities industry, with the exception of the Sarbanes-Oxley Act of 2002, were all enacted from 1933–1940.

The Laws That Govern the Securities Industry

- Securities Act of 1933
- Securities Exchange Act of 1934
- Public Utility Holding Company Act of 1935
- Trust Indenture Act of 1939
- Investment Company Act of 1940
- Investment Advisers Act of 1940
- Sarbanes-Oxley Act of 2002

Source: www.sec.gov/about/laws.shtml

This chapter focuses on the regulation of financial advisers. The Investment Advisers Act of 1940 as amended, along with state oversight of investment advisers, are its major themes.

SEC Release No. IA-770

Investment Advisers Act of 1940

The Securities and Exchange Commission took the position that the *Investment Advisers Act of 1940* was the statutory body of law that should control the area of regulation of financial planners. It is true that this legislation

SEC Release No. IA-770

had been enacted 40 years earlier in a post-Depression era during which a legislative framework to police and control the activities of discretionary money managers was the primary objective. However, the SEC in the early 1980s took the position that this same statute should be applied to the activities of financial planners. In August 1981, the Securities and Exchange Commission adopted *SEC Release No. IA-770.* This rule established three separate tests that were to be applied to the activities of financial planners. In the event that all three tests were answered in the affirmative, the SEC took the position that the Investment Advisers Act of 1940 would apply to the planner's activities. If, however, any one of the three tests could not be answered in the affirmative, the Investment Advisers Act of 1940 would not apply to these professional activities. Let us review these three tests separately.

Advice or Analyses About Securities

security

The first test under IA-770 asked the question of whether the financial adviser provides "advice or analyses" about a security. Since the term *security* is very broadly defined for federal securities law purposes, it can include a great many financial instruments in addition to the best-known securities like common stocks or bonds. For example, the definition includes a certificate of deposit, commercial paper, a limited partnership, or even variable life insurance or variable annuity products. The official definition of the term *security* as set forth by Sec. 80b-2(a)(18) of the Investment Advisers Act of 1940 is as follows:

> "Security" means any note, stock, Treasury stock, security future, bond, debenture, evidence of indebtedness, certificate of interest or participation in any profit-sharing agreement, collateral-trust certificate, preorganization certificate or subscription, transferable share, investment contract, voting-trust certificate, certificate of deposit for a security, fractional undivided interest in oil, gas, or other mineral rights, any put, call, straddle, option, or privilege on any security (including a certificate of deposit) or on any group or index of securities (including any interest therein or based on the value thereof), or any put, call, straddle, option, or privilege entered into on a national securities exchange relating to foreign currency, or, in general, any interest or instrument commonly known as a "security," or any certificate of interest or participation in, temporary or interim certificate for, receipt for, guaranty of, or warrant or right to subscribe to or purchase any of the foregoing.

It is clear, based on the breadth and scope of the definitions under this first test, that financial planners will invariably become involved with providing advice about securities.

The Business Standard

business standard

The second test as set forth by SEC Release IA-770, called the *business standard,* concerns whether the financial planner is presented to the public as being "in the business" of providing advice about securities. This issue is handled by examining how the practitioner's services are communicated to the public. What is printed on the practitioner's business card or on the front door of the office? What does the telephone book advertisement say? How is the telephone answered? What is stated on the business card and letterhead? In short, does the practitioner raise any implication that he or she provides any advice about securities? All of these factors are pertinent in deciding whether the financial adviser is "in the business" of providing advice about securities.

The Compensation Test

compensation test

The last test contained in the SEC release, the *compensation test*, is perhaps the simplest one to apply and yet is the least understood. The issue concerns compensation received by the practitioner, and the test is met regardless of the source of payment. Therefore, although a practitioner who charges a fee to a client for the provision of investment advice will easily meet the third test of IA-770, one who charges no fee but does receive a commission on the sale of a securities product will also meet this test. Actually, in the current environment, it is practically impossible for a financial adviser to fail to meet this third test.

If all three tests are applicable to the specific activities of a financial adviser, the terms and provisions of the Investment Advisers Act of 1940 will apply.

SEC Release No. IA-1092 Reaffirms IA-770

SEC Release No. IA-770 was a landmark ruling from the SEC. As the financial planning profession continued to emerge in the mid to late 1980s, many individuals and groups called on the Securities and Exchange Commission to comment once again on the three tests that had been set forth by IA-770 a few years earlier. Some felt that the original three-test approach might no longer be held applicable by the SEC. In October 1987, in response to multiple requests from various segments of the financial services community, the Securities and Exchange Commission issued *SEC Release No. IA-1092*. This rule is significant since it totally reaffirmed the three-prong approach set forth by IA-770.

SEC Release No. IA-1092

Therefore, the SEC's original application of the three-test approach still applies. As a practical matter, any financial adviser who, by reason of his or her activities, must answer all three tests in the affirmative will have activities subjected to the Investment Advisers Act of 1940 at the federal level.

In addition to total reaffirmation of the three-step test of IA-770, however, IA-1092 devoted renewed attention to the antifraud provisions of the Investment Advisers Act of 1940. These provisions are designed to protect consumers who use the services of investment advisers.

The 1987 release cites *SEC v. Capital Gains Research Bureau*, a Supreme Court case discussing the antifraud provisions. That case held that "an investment adviser is a fiduciary who owes his client an affirmative duty of utmost good faith, and full and fair disclosure of all material facts." As a general matter, the release states that an adviser must disclose to clients all material facts regarding potential conflicts of interest. In this way, the client can make an informed decision about entering into or continuing an advisory relationship with the adviser.

The release includes selected interpretive and no-action letters illustrating the scope of the duty to disclose material information in certain situations involving conflicts of interest. Additional disclosure might be required, depending on the circumstances, if the investment adviser recommends that clients execute securities transactions through the broker/dealer with which the investment adviser is associated. In addition, the investment adviser is required to inform clients that they may execute recommended transactions through other brokers or dealers.

Release IA-1092 goes on to set forth specific examples of situations that require full disclosure on the investment adviser's filing statement with the SEC. Points raised by IA-1092 in the antifraud/full disclosure area include the following:

- An adviser who intends to implement, in whole or in part, the financial plan prepared for clients through the broker/dealer or insurance company with which the adviser is associated, must inform the clients that in implementing the plan the adviser will also act as agent for that firm.

- An investment adviser who is also a registered representative of a broker/dealer and who provides investment advisory services outside the scope of employment with the broker/dealer must disclose to advisory clients that the advisory activities are independent of employment with the broker/dealer. Additional disclosure might be required, depending on the circumstances, if an adviser recommends that a client execute securities transactions through the broker/dealer with which the adviser is associated. For example, an adviser is required to fully disclose the nature and extent of any personal interest in such a recommendation, including any compensation that would be received from the broker/dealer in connection with the transaction. In addition, an adviser is required to inform clients that they may execute recommended transactions with other broker/dealers.

- A financial planner who recommends and uses only the financial products offered by the broker/dealer by which the financial planner is employed should disclose this practice and inform clients that the plan may be limited by such products.

- An investment adviser must not effect transactions in which he or she has a personal interest if this could result in the adviser's preferring his or her own interest to that of the advisory clients.

- An adviser who structures personal securities transactions and then trades on the market result caused by his or her recommendation to clients must disclose this practice.

- An investment adviser must disclose his or her personal securities transactions that are inconsistent with the advice given to clients.

- An investment adviser must disclose compensation received from the issuer of a security that the adviser recommends.

Exceptions and Exemptions From the Investment Advisers Act of 1940

It should be noted that despite the foregoing, there are six areas of activities specifically set forth in Section 202(a)(11) of the Investment Advisers Act of 1940. These exceptions could have the effect of eliminating the need for the financial adviser to be subjected to the mandates of the statute. The six exceptions (A–F in the act) are

(A) a bank, or any bank holding company as defined in the Bank Holding Company Act of 1956, which is not an investment company, except that the term "investment adviser" includes any bank or bank holding company to the extent that such bank or bank holding company serves or acts as an investment adviser to a registered investment company, but if, in the case of a bank, such services or actions are performed through a separately identifiable department or division, the department or division, and not the bank itself, shall be deemed to be the investment adviser;

(B) any lawyer, accountant, engineer, or teacher whose performance of such services is solely incidental to the practice of his profession;

(C) any broker or dealer whose performance of such services is solely incidental to the conduct of his business as a broker or dealer and who receives no special compensation therefore;

(D) the publisher of any bona fide newspaper, news magazine or business or financial publication of general and regular circulation;

(E) any person whose advice, analyses, or reports relate to no securities other than securities which are direct obligations of or obligations guaranteed as to principal or interest by the United States, or securities issued or guaranteed by corporations in which the United States has a direct or indirect interest which shall have been designated by the Secretary of the Treasury, pursuant to section 3(a)(12) of the Securities Exchange Act of 1934, as exempted securities for the purposes of that Act; or

(F) such other persons not within the intent of this paragraph, as the Commission may designate by rules and regulations or order.

There are six other groups that, although they fall within the definition of investment adviser, are nevertheless exempt from registration under Section 203(b) of the Investment Advisers Act of 1940:

(1) any investment adviser all of whose clients are residents of the State within which such investment adviser maintains his or its principal office and place of business, and who does not furnish advice or issue analyses or reports with respect to securities listed or admitted to unlisted trading privileges on any national securities exchange;

(2) any investment adviser whose only clients are insurance companies;

(3) any investment adviser who during the course of the preceding twelve months has had fewer than fifteen clients and who neither holds himself out generally to the public as an investment adviser nor acts as an investment adviser to any investment company registered under Title I of this Act, or a company which has elected to be a business development company pursuant to Section 54 of Title I of this Act and has not withdrawn its election. For purposes of determining the number of clients of an investment adviser under this paragraph, no shareholder, partner, or beneficial owner of a business development company, as defined in this title, shall be deemed to be a client of such investment adviser unless such person is a client of such investment adviser separate and apart from his status as a shareholder, partner, or beneficial owner;

(4) any investment adviser that is a charitable organization, as defined in section 3(c)(10)(D) of the Investment Company Act of 1940, or is a trustee, director, officer, employee, or volunteer of such a charitable organization acting within the scope of such person's employment or duties with such organization, whose advice, analyses, or reports are provided only to one or more of the following:

(A) any such charitable organization;

(B) a fund that is excluded from the definition of aninvestment company under Section 3(c)(10)(B) of the Investment Company Act of 1940; or

(C) a trust or other donative instrument described in Section 3(c)(10)(B) of the Investment Company Act of 1940, or the trustees, administrators, settlors (or potential settlors), or beneficiaries of any such trust or other instrument;

(5) any plan described in Section 414(e) of the Internal Revenue Code of 1986, any person or entity eligible to establish and maintain such a plan under the Internal Revenue Code of 1986, or any trustee, director, officer, or employee of or volunteer for any such plan or person, if such person or entity, acting in such capacity, provides investment advice exclusively to, or with respect to, any plan, person, or entity or any company, account, or fund that is excluded from the definition of an investment company under Section 3(c)(14) of the Investment Company Act of 1940; or

(6) any investment adviser that is registered with the Commodity Futures Trading Commission as a commodity trading advisor whose business does not consist primarily of acting as an investment adviser, as defined in Section 202(a)(11) of this title, and that does not act as an investment adviser to—

(A) an investment company registered under Title I of this act; or

(B) a company which has elected to be a business development company pursuant to Section 54 of Title I of this act and has not withdrawn its election.

In summary, the six groups of individuals discussed in the preceding paragraph are exempt from registration with the Securities and Exchange Commission even though they are considered investment advisers under the act. They must still comply with the act's antifraud provisions. On the other hand, an individual who falls into the first group of exception categories mentioned above will not be covered by the antifraud provisions, and the Investment Advisers Act of 1940 does not apply to any of their activities.

Macey (2002) discusses the attorney and accounting exceptions: "Two very prominent state-licensed professions that were granted a limited exemption from registration as investment advisers in 1940, accountants and attorneys, are beginning to expand their services and products to include financial planning. While only 3 percent of all CFP certificants hold a J.D. degree and one percent of all CFP certificants practice law today, these numbers grossly underestimate the number of attorneys that practice some degree of financial planning. Today, 16 percent of all CFP certificants hold a CPA license and 7 percent practice accounting as a profession. While presently this may not seem like a large number, the AICPA has recognized financial planning as one of five core programs that the accounting industry will focus on in the future."[4]

The "solely incidental" standard for attorneys and CPAs is strict enough that these professionals should look to guidance from their professional organizations in determining when they need to register as advisers either with the SEC or with the states where they conduct business. The next section discusses state versus SEC registration for all investment advisers.

INVESTMENT ADVISERS SUPERVISION COORDINATION ACT OF 1996

Investment Advisers Supervision Coordination Act of 1996

After years of dispute over the direction of regulation of investment advisers, the Congress passed and the president signed the *Investment Advisers Supervision Coordination Act of 1996 (Coordination Act),* which was part of the National Securities Market Improvement Act of 1996 (NSMIA). The Coordination Act, which became effective in July 1997, gives authority to the SEC to deny adviser registration to felons within 10 years of conviction, and mandates a consumer hotline for inquiry concerning disciplinary actions and proceedings against registered investment advisers and associated persons.

SEC Release No. IA-1633

However, the most important aspects of the Coordination Act and *SEC Release No. IA-1633* (which specifies final rules relating to the Coordination Act) concern allocating the regulation of investment advisers between the SEC and state authorities based on the level of assets under an adviser's management. The result is that investment advisers and, thus, financial planners, need to register with either the SEC or state authorities, but not with both.

State Versus SEC Registration

In general, the Investment Advisers Act of 1940, as revised by the Coordination Act, requires investment advisers, and thus financial planners, to register with the SEC if they are

- investment advisers defined under Section 202(a)(11)
- not excluded from the definition of investment adviser by Section 202(a)(11)
- not exempt from SEC registration under Section 203(b)
- not prohibited from SEC registration by new Section 203A

The first three items above were discussed earlier in this chapter. It is the fourth item that the Coordination Act added to the mix. Essentially, new Section 203A of the Advisers Act specifies the following four types of advisers that are *not prohibited* from SEC registration:

- advisers that have "assets under management" of $25 million or more
- advisers to registered investment companies
- advisers that are not "regulated or required to be regulated" as investment advisers in the state where they maintain their "principal office and place of business"
- advisers that are exempted from the prohibition by SEC rule or order

Advisers With $25 Million of Assets Under Management

In general, advisers with less than $30 million of assets under management are regulated by state authorities, unless they operate in 30 or more states or meet other requirements, which are described later. Advisers with more than $30 million in assets under management must register with the SEC. If assets under management are between $25 million and $30 million and they have no other basis for eligibility for SEC registration, they can elect either state or SEC registration. The purpose of this window is to protect advisers from going back and forth between state and SEC registration merely because of volatility in the securities market or changes in the client base.

assets under management

Defining Assets Under Management. Assets under management (AUM) is defined in Section 203A(a)(2) as the "securities portfolios with respect to which an investment adviser provides continuous and regular supervisory or management services." Thus, the following two determinations must be made before the value of an account can be counted toward meeting the $25 million threshold:

- Is the account a securities portfolio?
- Does the account receive continuous and regular supervisory or management services?

Under new SEC rules, securities portfolios include only those accounts of which at least 50 percent of the value consists of securities. Cash or cash equivalents may be treated as securities when making this calculation.

The question concerning continuous and regular supervisory or management services is more complicated. In general, accounts over which advisers have discretionary authority and for which they provide ongoing supervisory or management services are considered to receive continuous and regular supervisory or management services. An adviser will be deemed to provide continuous and regular supervisory or management services to a nondiscretionary account if the adviser has an ongoing responsibility to select or make recommendations—based on the needs of the client—as to specific securities or other investments the account may purchase or sell. If a recommendation is accepted by the client, the adviser is responsible for arranging or effecting the purchase or sale. Other factors that should be considered in deciding whether an account qualifies include

- Terms of the advisory contract. A provision in the contract that the adviser provides ongoing management services suggests that the adviser does provide continuous and regular supervisory or management services. Other provisions in the contract, or the actual management practices of the adviser, may rebut this suggestion.
- Form of compensation. A form of compensation based on the average value of assets under management over a specified period of time would suggest that the adviser provides continuous and regular supervisory or management services. On the other hand, a form of compensation based on the time the adviser spends with a client during a consultation would suggest otherwise.
- The management practice of the adviser. The extent to which the adviser actively manages assets or provides advice bears on whether the services are continuous and regular supervisory or management services. However, infrequent trades (such as those based on a "buy-and-hold" strategy, for example) should not be the sole basis for a determination that the services are not provided on a continuous and regular basis.

Calculation of Assets Under Management. Once a determination is made that an account is a securities portfolio that receives "continuous and regular supervisory or management services," the value of the account may be included in assets under management. If, however, the adviser provides continuous and regular supervisory or management services for only a portion of the account, only the portion of the account that receives such services should be included as assets under management. Current market value of the account should be determined using the same method as that used to determine the account value reported to clients or fees for investment advisory services.

Frequency of Determination. The continuing eligibility of an adviser to remain registered with the SEC must be determined once annually at the time the adviser updates its Form ADV, which is discussed later in this chapter. Thus, the registration status of an adviser whose assets under management falls below $25 million will not be affected unless the assets remained below $25 million after the end of the adviser's fiscal year. To allow an adviser facing potential cancellation of its SEC registration sufficient time to register under applicable state statutes, the SEC has adopted a grace period of 180 days after the date the adviser was required to file its updated Form ADV indicating that it would not be eligible for SEC registration.

Rule 203A-4 provides a safe harbor from the requirement to register with the SEC for state-registered advisers, if the advisers reasonably believe that they are not required to register with the SEC because they have less than $30 million of assets under management. No such similar safe harbor exists for an adviser that registered with the SEC under the mistaken belief that he had greater than $25 million in assets under management.

A state-registered adviser generally is required to register with the SEC promptly when the prohibitions of Section 203A no longer apply (for example, the adviser obtains $30 million of assets under management) unless the adviser is registered in a state that requires the new Schedule I of Form ADV (or a substantially similar form or rule) to be filed and annually updated. Such an adviser may (but is not required to) postpone SEC registration until 90 days after the date the adviser is required to report $30 million or more of assets under management to its state securities authority.

Advisers to Registered Investment Companies

Any adviser that provides advisory services to a registered investment company pursuant to a contract (including a sub-adviser) must register with the SEC regardless of the amount of assets under management. To qualify as an investment company adviser, the adviser must provide advisory services to an investment company that is registered under the Investment Company Act of 1940, and is operational, that is, has assets and shareholders other than organizing shareholders.

Advisers That Are Not Regulated or Required to Be Regulated by a State

Two types of advisers are not regulated or required to be regulated by a state and, thus, must register with the SEC:

- advisers with their principal office in Wyoming (the only state that has not enacted investment adviser statutes as of this writing)
- advisers with their principal office in a foreign country

The SEC's Rule 203A-3(c) defines "principal office" and "place of business" as the "executive office of the investment adviser from which the officers, partners, or managers of the investment adviser direct, control, and coordinate the activities of the investment adviser."

Advisers That Are Exempt From Prohibition on SEC Registration

Section 203A(c) authorizes the SEC to exempt advisers from the prohibition on registration if the prohibition would be "unfair, a burden on interstate commerce, or otherwise inconsistent with the purposes" of that section. The SEC used this authority to exempt, in Rule 203A-2, four categories of investment advisers from the prohibition from registering with the SEC (thereby effectively requiring them to register with the SEC):

- nationally recognized statistical rating organizations—including ratings agencies, such as Moody's and Standard & Poors, that are registered as investment advisers.
- pension consultants—including advisers of government plans and church plans, if the aggregate value of assets of plans receiving such services is at least $50 million. (Note that the exemption is available to advisers to employee benefit plans, not to plan participants.)
- certain affiliates that directly or indirectly control, are controlled by, or are under common control with an investment adviser that is eligible to register (and is, in fact, registered) with the SEC. (The exemption is available only if the adviser's principal office and place of business is the same as that of the affiliated registered adviser. "Control" is defined as the power to direct or cause the direction of the management or policies of the adviser, whether through ownership of securities, by contract, or otherwise.)
- certain start-up investment advisers that have a reasonable expectation of eligibility to register with the SEC within 120 days
- multi-state investment advisers as further described by Rule 203A-2(e)
- Internet investment advisers as further described by Rule 203A-2(f)

Other Aspects of the Coordination Act

Section 203A(b) preempts the application of state laws requiring registration, licensing, or qualification to advisers registered with the SEC. In Release No. IA-1633, the SEC explained that Section 203A(b) "preempts not only a state's specific registration, licensing, or qualification requirements, but all regulatory requirements imposed by state law on SEC-registered advisers relating to their advisory activities or services, except those provisions that are specifically preserved" by the Coordination Act. The Coordination Act preserved three provisions of state investment adviser laws with respect to SEC-registered advisers:

- A state may enforce antifraud prohibitions, thus allowing a state to continue to investigate and bring enforcement actions with respect to fraud or deceit against an investment adviser or a person associated with an investment adviser.

- A state may require the filing of any documents filed with the SEC, solely for notice purposes, and a Form U-2 Uniform Consent to Service of Process.
- A state may require the payment of filing, registration, or licensing fees.

Investment Adviser Representatives of SEC-Registered Advisers

The application of state law has been narrowed, but not eliminated, with respect to investment adviser representatives of SEC-registered advisers. Only representatives who deal directly with individual clients are subject to state registration requirements. In those cases, the representative will have to register only in the state(s) in which he or she has a place of business. If the representative is located only in states that do not register investment adviser representatives, then the representative is not subject to state registration requirements.

supervised person

Supervised Persons. Section 203A(b) preempts state law with respect to supervised persons of SEC-registered advisers, except that a state may continue to license, register, or otherwise qualify any supervised person who is an investment adviser representative and has a place of business located within that state. New Section 202(a)(25) defines *supervised person* to mean a "partner, officer, director (or other person occupying a similar status or performing similar functions), or employee of an investment adviser, or other person who provides investment advice on behalf of the investment adviser and is subject to the supervision and control of the investment adviser."

investment adviser representative

Investment Adviser Representative. Rule 203A-3(a) defines *investment adviser representative* as a supervised person of an investment adviser if clients who are natural persons represent more than 10 percent of the clients of the supervised person. (Rule 203A-3(a)(1)) In 1998, Release No. IA-1733 recognized that advisers with only a few institutional clients were unduly burdened by the 10 percent rule. It specified that supervised persons can have the greater of five natural person clients or the number of natural person clients permitted under the 10 percent allowance, without being subject to state qualification requirements. High net worth individuals (those that may enter into performance fee contracts under Rule 205-3) are excluded from treatment as natural persons. Supervised persons can rely on the definition of "client" in Rule 203(b)(3)-1 to identify clients, except that supervised persons need not count clients that are not United States residents.

The rule contains exceptions: (1) Supervised persons who provide advice to natural persons, but who do not, on a regular basis, solicit, meet with, or otherwise communicate with clients, and (2) supervised persons who provide only impersonal investment advice. The SEC has defined place of business as an office at which the representative regularly provides investment advisory services, solicits, meets with, or otherwise communicates with clients, and any other location that is held out to the general public as a location at which the representative provides investment advisory services, solicits, meets with, or otherwise communicates with clients. (Rule 203A-3(b))

Solicitor. A solicitor who is a partner, officer, director, or employee of an SEC-registered adviser is subject to state qualification requirements only if the solicitor falls within the definition of investment adviser representative under Rule 203A-3(a). A third-party solicitor for the SEC-registered adviser (that is, a solicitor who is not a partner, officer, director, or employee of the adviser) is not an investment adviser representative; he or she is subject to state qualification requirements to the extent state investment adviser statutes apply to solicitors. In some cases, a solicitor may solicit on behalf of both the state-registered adviser and the SEC-registered adviser. The SEC believes that the Coordination Act does not preempt states from subjecting such a solicitor to state qualification requirements.

What Federal Laws and Regulations Apply to State-Registered Advisers?

Although state-registered advisers are no longer subject to many provisions of the Investment Advisers Act or SEC rules, some provisions still apply.

- Section 206 continues to make it unlawful for any investment adviser to engage in fraudulent, deceptive, or manipulative practices.
- State-registered advisers continue to be subject to Section 204A's requirement to establish, maintain, and enforce written procedures reasonably designed to prevent the misuse of material nonpublic information (insider trading).
- State-registered advisers continue to be subject to Section 205, which contains prohibitions on advisory contracts that (1) contain certain performance fee arrangements, (2) permit an assignment of the advisory contract to be made without the consent of the client, and (3) fail to require an adviser that is a partnership to notify clients of a change in the membership of the partnership.
- State-registered advisers continue to be subject to Section 206(3), which makes it unlawful for any investment adviser acting as principal for its own account to knowingly sell any security to, or purchase any security from, a client without disclosing to the client in writing before

the completion of the transaction the capacity in which the adviser is acting and obtaining the client's consent. This limitation also applies if the adviser is acting as a broker for a person other than the client in effecting such a transaction.

Provisions of State Law Modified by the Coordination Act

State securities regulators may not enforce any law or regulation that would require an adviser to maintain books and records in addition to those required by the state in which the adviser has its principal place of business. Neither may state securities regulators enforce any law or regulation that would require an adviser to maintain a higher minimum net capital or to post any bond in addition to any that is required by the state in which the adviser has its principal place of business. These limitations apply only if the adviser is registered or licensed in the state in which it maintains its principal place of business and is in compliance with the appropriate requirements of that state.

national de minimis standard

The Coordination Act also relieves advisers from some regulatory burden by establishing a *national de minimis standard,* which states that investment advisers may not be required to register in any state unless the adviser has a place of business in the state or, during the preceding 12-month period, has had more than five clients who are residents of the state. For purposes of counting clients for the national de minimis standard, the

client

following will be deemed a single *client:* any natural person and

- any minor child of the natural person
- any relative, spouse, or relative of the spouse of the natural person who has the same principal residence
- all accounts of which the natural person and/or the persons referred to above are the only primary beneficiaries
- all trusts of which the natural person and/or the persons referred to above are the only primary beneficiaries

In general, this definition recognizes the family as an economic unit and gives the adviser greater latitude in staying within the de minimis standard. The following will also be considered single clients:

- a corporation, general partnership, limited partnership, limited liability company, trust (other than a trust referred to above) or other legal organization that receives investment advice based on its investment objectives rather than the individual investment objectives of its shareholders, partners, limited partners, members, or beneficiaries
- two or more legal organizations referred to above that have identical owners

The Coordination Act did not affect the application of state law to investment adviser representatives of state-registered advisers. Thus, for example, a state may continue to require representatives of a state-registered adviser to register even if they do not have a place of business in the state, have less than six clients in the state, or do not meet the federal definition of investment adviser representative in Rule 203A-3(a).

The Financial Planning Association notes in a regulatory advisory memorandum[5] that, "Three states do not have a *de minimis* rule for federally registered investment advisers: Texas, New Hampshire, and Nebraska. In addition, Texas does not recognize a *de minimis rule* for state-registered investment advisers. State-registered investment advisers are permitted five clients in New Hampshire and Nebraska, unlike federal RIAs. It is important to note that if a financial planner is an investment adviser representative of an advisory firm, the whole firm is only allowed five clients or less under these *de minimis* rules. *Note:* Wyoming does not have state registration requirements for investment advisers and therefore there is no limit on clients in that state. Advisers with a principal place of business in Wyoming must register with the SEC."

SEC Release No. IA-2091

Investment advisers operating principally on the Internet (mentioned previously in the chapter) was made possible by *SEC Release No. IA-2091, Exemption for Certain Investment Advisers Operating Through the Internet.* The rule amendments (effective in 2003) permit these advisers, whose businesses are not connected to any particular state, to register with the Commission instead of with state securities authorities.

Another change instituted by the Coordination Act relates to advisers to the Employee Retirement Income Security Act of 1974 (ERISA) plans. ERISA permits employee benefit plan trustees to appoint certain entities as investment managers to manage plan assets, and provides that trustees delegating responsibilities to investment managers receive protection from liability with respect to investment decisions made by the investment managers. The Coordination Act amended Section 3(38)(B) of ERISA to include in the definition of investment manager investment advisers registered under the laws of any state, as well as federally registered investment advisers and other types of entities. The definition of investment manager was amended to ensure that small investment advisers not registered with the SEC could serve as investment managers and would not be disadvantaged under ERISA. This amendment contained a sunset provision of 2 years from the date of enactment, which was October 11, 1996, but was made permanent by legislation in 1997. ERISA now requires electronic registration through the Investment Adviser Registration Depository (IARD) for compliance matching IARD requirements by SEC and state regulatory bodies discussed below.[6]

RESPONSIBILITIES OF INVESTMENT ADVISERS WHO MUST REGISTER WITH THE SEC

Each state that regulates investment advisers creates its own set of rules and responsibilities, but states will increasingly adopt standards similar to those required by the SEC. These responsibilities are discussed in the following sections of this chapter.

Registration as a Registered Investment Adviser With the SEC

registered investment adviser (RIA)

Form ADV

Financial advisers who meet the IA-770 and IA-1092 tests and who are not exempt by the Coordination Act must comply with the mandates of the Investment Advisers Act of 1940. The chief requirement is that the practitioner become a *registered investment adviser (RIA)*. This is a somewhat burdensome administrative undertaking and is accomplished by completing what is known as *Form ADV*. The form itself is complicated and will be rejected by the Securities and Exchange Commission's Office of Applications and Reports Services unless completed correctly in each and every regard. In the year 2000, the SEC issued Release No IA-1862, IA-1897, and IA-1916, which specified new rules and rule amendments that (1) require investment advisers to submit their investment adviser filings on an electronic filing system and (2) revise Part 1 of Form ADV to accommodate electronic filing on the Investment Adviser Registration Depository (IARD). IARD permits investment advisers to satisfy filing obligations under state and federal laws by making a single electronic filing. New RIA applicants must submit Form ADV electronically through the IARD website (www.IARD.com), and advisers currently registered with the Commission must also use electronic filing for renewals. The IARD is operated for the Commission and the state securities authorities by NASD Regulation, Inc. (NASDR). The Financial Planning Association provides a *State Summary of IARD Registration Requirements*[7] but up-to-the-minute requirements are available with the securities administrator of each state.[8]

Form ADV itself is divided into two broad parts. The first part of the form asks generalized questions, such as the name, location, and fiscal year of the applicant's business, the form of the business (that is, corporation, partnership, or sole proprietorship), the background of the applicant and any others associated with the applicant, and whether the applicant and the people associated with him or her have ever been convicted of crimes or are subject to certain injunctions. Part I also contains questions relative to the types of clients for which the applicant will provide discretionary or any other account management services.

**Requirement Categories of Responsibility for
Financial Planners Subject to SEC Regulation**

1. registering
2. record keeping
3. charging fees
4. assigning contracts
5. using labels
6. delivering brochures
7. avoiding fraudulent practices

The second part of the form requires more detailed and extensive information. This information includes the specific types of services offered by the applicant, a detailed explanation of the fee structure, the basic method of operation of the applicant's business, and even questions dealing with the kind of direct involvement the applicant has in securities transactions for clients. Part II also asks for the names of business associates of the applicant within the securities industry, additional information on the applicant, and, if certain additional conditions are met, a balance sheet.

If the Securities and Exchange Commission finds that the applicant has satisfactorily met the general standards upon which the registration is normally accepted, it must grant the RIA registration within 45 days of the filing date or, in the alternative, must begin proceedings to determine whether registration should be denied. As a practical matter, registration will be denied if these general standards have not been met or if the Securities and Exchange Commission determines that registration, if granted, would immediately be subject to suspension or revocation. This could be the result if, for example, the SEC discovers that the applicant has failed to disclose a prior securities law conviction. Note, though, that the SEC's acceptance of a registration says nothing about the applicant's competence.

In 2000, the SEC approved Release No. IA-1888, which established the following set of fees for registering as an investment adviser at either the state or federal level. These fees were temporarily waived for IA firms filing electronically.[9]

Assets Under Management	Initial Fee	Annual Updating Fee
More than $100 million	$1,100	$550
$25 million to $100 million	$ 800	$400
Less than $25 million	$ 150	$100

Record-Keeping Responsibilities

Once the application of the registered investment adviser has been approved, the post-registration phase of compliance begins. One of the more significant elements of this post-registration phase is the record-keeping responsibility. It must be noted that there is a 17-step record-keeping requirement with which financial advisers who are registered investment advisers must comply. Included as part of this is compliance with the Insider Trading and Securities Fraud Enforcement Act of 1988.

Specifically, Sec. 204 of the Investment Advisers Act of 1940 provides the following:

> Every investment adviser who makes use of the mails or any means or any instrumentality of interstate commerce in connection with his, her, or its business as an investment adviser shall make and keep for prescribed periods such records, furnish such copies thereof, and make and disseminate such reports as the Securities and Exchange Commission, by rule, may prescribe as necessary or appropriate in the public interest or for the protection of investors. All records of such investors and advisers are subject at any time, or from time to time, to such reasonable periodic, special, or other examinations by representatives of the Securities and Exchange Commission as the Commission deems necessary or appropriate in the public interest or for the protection of investors.

The Securities and Exchange Commission has promulgated a detailed series of record-keeping requirements with which each and every registered investment adviser must comply. Known as Rule 204-2—Books and Records to Be Maintained by Investment Advisers, the requirements have evolved over time.[10] As mentioned above, there are 17 separate steps that must be taken in order for the registered investment adviser to be in compliance in the post-registration phase. The following provides a synopsis of the 17 requirements but should not be relied on as a basis for compliance. For compliance standards the practice should reference the actual rule:

- *Journal requirement:* Keep a journal in accordance with generally accepted accounting principles.
- *Ledger requirement:* Maintain a ledger in accordance with generally accepted accounting principles.
- *Securities purchased record:* Keep a complete record of all securities you have purchased or recommended.
- *Retention of canceled checks:* Save all your canceled checks and bank statements for a 5-year period.

- *Retention of paid and unpaid bills:* Assemble and save all documentation of paid and unpaid bills.
- *Retention of trial balances and financial statements:* Retain all trial balances and financial statements for a 5-year period.
- *Retention of written communication:* Keep records of all written communications you send to advisory clients and those sent to you by advisory clients.
- *Records of discretionary accounts:* Maintain a list of all accounts in which you have discretionary power.
- *Evidence of discretionary authority:* Retain all documents that grant you discretionary authority.
- *Retention of written agreements:* Save all written agreements executed between you and the advisory client.
- *Retention of communications recommending specific securities:* Keep a record of all advertisements, notices, or circulars, sent to 10 or more persons, that recommend specific securities to clients.
- *Code of ethics:* Have available a copy of the investment adviser's code of ethics, adopted and implemented pursuant to Rule 204A-1, that is in effect or was in effect at any time within the past 5 years; maintain a record of any violation of the code of ethics and of any action taken as a result of the violation, and a record of all written acknowledgments as required by Rule 204A-1(a)(5) for each person who is currently, or was within the past 5 years, a supervised person of the investment adviser.
- *Access persons:* Maintain a record of each report made by an access person, a record of the names of persons who are currently, or were within the past 5 years, access persons of the investment adviser; and a record of any decision, and the reasons supporting the decision, to approve the acquisition of securities by access persons under Rule 204A-1(c), for at least 5 years after the end of the fiscal year in which the approval is granted.
- *Retention of written disclosure statements (brochures):* Keep copies of brochures given to clients or prospective clients.
- *Retention of disclosure documents:* Keep signed receipts for the brochures from all advisory clients. Retain copies of all disclosures signed by paid solicitors who refer business to you.
- *Record of rate-of-return calculations:* Retain complete documentation of any calculation of the performance or rate of return of managed accounts and securities recommendations.
- *Development, maintenance, and review of policies and procedures:* Have immediately available current policies and procedures, and

those in effect at any time in the past 5 years. Maintain records of annual review of policies and procedures.

The SEC can mandate ongoing or ad hoc reporting requirements at will. For example, in 1999, SEC chairman Arthur Levitt sent a letter to registered investment advisers indicating that they should disclose to clients their preparedness to deal with the so-called Year 2000 (Y2K) problem. The SEC's Release No. IA-1769 further required planners to report their Y2K readiness to the SEC.

Because each and every practitioner who operates as a registered investment adviser will be subjected to an SEC examination, it is imperative that professional advisers totally comply with these record-keeping mandates. There are both civil and criminal penalties available to the regulators as a method of enforcing these rules. Appendix K includes a brochure written by the Office of Compliance Inspections and Examinations (OCIE) concerning the examination process.

The split between state-registered and SEC-registered investment advisers has given the Commission the ability to improve audit and enforcement actions. This increased probability of a compliance audit is further discussed in Macey (2002):

> As a consequence of the Coordination Act's division of labor with state regulators, however, the rate of SEC inspections is higher today. With only 7,417 registered investment advisers under its watch in 2001, the SEC conducted 1,405 regular inspections, consistent with its goal of inspecting each investment adviser an average of once every five years. This dramatic improvement in the SEC inspection rate led the executive director of the Investment Counsel Association of America (ICAA) to state that the Coordination Act has solved "the only major regulatory problem" of the Advisers Act. Of course, this improved inspection rate presumes that state regulators have increased the number of their inspections to accommodate some of the formerly SEC-registered investment advisers.[11]

Office of Compliance Inspections and Examinations (OCIE)

The *Office of Compliance Inspections and Examinations (OCIE)* and the field offices administer the Compliance Examination Program examinations. According to OCIE, in fiscal year 2002, the Examination staff performed 626 Broker-Dealer (BD), 138 Transfer Agent, 3 Clearing Agency, 32 Self-Regulatory Organization (SRO), 1.50 Investment Adviser (IA), and 278 Investment Company (IC) examinations.[12]

Discouraging Insider Trading: Written Policies and Procedures

insider trading

Insider trading refers generally to buying or selling a security, in breach of a fiduciary duty or other relationship of trust and confidence, while in possession of material, nonpublic information about the security. Insider trading violations may also include tipping such information, securities trading by the person tipped, and securities trading by those who misappropriate such information.

Examples of insider trading cases that have been brought by the SEC are cases against

- corporate officers, directors, and employees who traded the corporation's securities after learning of significant, confidential corporate developments
- employees of law, banking, brokerage, and printing firms who were given such information to provide services to the corporation whose securities they traded
- government employees who learned of such information because of their employment by the government
- other persons who misappropriated, and took advantage of, confidential information from their employers

Many observers consider insider trading to be a direct threat to the continued integrity of securities markets and, by extension, to the entire financial system.

Insider Trading and Securities Fraud Enforcement Act of 1988

The *Insider Trading and Securities Fraud Enforcement Act of 1988* mandates that investment advisers must have written policies and procedures that reduce the likelihood of insider trading. An historical perspective will help explain how this requirement arose.

Legislative history shows that when the Securities Exchange Act of 1934 was being debated, insider trading was one of the major issues even then. However, it was not until 1968 that there was finally a court decision that held that the use of inside information was a violation of federal securities laws (*SEC v. Texas Gulf Sulfur Company*). Since that case was handed down, Sec. 10(b) of the Securities Exchange Act of 1934 (particularly Sec. 10(b)-5) has provided a legal underpinning for the majority of the insider-trading cases brought by the Securities and Exchange Commission.

Insider Trading Sanction Act of 1984

Prior to the 1988 act, Congress enacted the *Insider Trading Sanction Act of 1984* that, among other things, gave the SEC the authority to seek the imposition of civil penalties against insider-trading violations for as much as three times the profit gained (or loss avoided) as a result of the unlawful purchase or sale of securities. The government felt that such a provision would act as a deterrent. Of course, insider-trading problems increased, causing Congress to enact the Insider Trading and Securities Fraud

Enforcement Act of 1988. Because registered investment advisers are viewed as being in a particularly vulnerable position within the insider-trading context, special provisions of the 1988 statute were enacted to deal specifically with the activities of registered investment advisers. Specifically, the 1988 insider-trading statute added Sec. 204A to the Investment Advisers Act of 1940, which provided the following:

> Every investment adviser subject to the Investment Advisers Act shall establish, maintain, and enforce written policies and procedures reasonably designed to prevent the misuse in violation of this act or the Securities Exchange Act of 1934, of material, nonpublic information by such investment adviser or any person associated with the investment adviser. The Securities and Exchange Commission as it deems shall adopt rules or regulations to require specific policies or procedures reasonably designed to prevent misuse in violation of this act or the Securities Exchange Act of 1934 of material, nonpublic information.

It should be noted that there are regulatory, civil, and even criminal penalties under Sec. 204A for failure to comply with this new statute section of the 1940 law. There is even a special bounty provision in Sec. 204A that grants authority to the SEC to award payments to persons who provide information concerning insider-trading violations. At the sole discretion of the SEC, the individual can receive up to 10 percent of the penalty imposed or settlement reached.

As a practical matter, insider-trading legislation imposes liabilities not only on broker/dealers and registered investment advisers, but also on their employees for misuse by such employees of confidential information if the employer has failed to have effectively policed employee activities within the framework of insider trading. The insider-trading statute requires all employers to develop a compliance plan. Every registered investment adviser must have a plan in place.

It is possible to engage in insider trading in many different ways. Examples include conversations with officers of a company with whom the adviser regularly deals or just a normal conversation with clients (for example, "I'm taking my company private in a few months").

It is also possible for employees to receive inside information and act on it without the knowledge of the registered investment adviser. Therefore, the RIA must have a plan. Also, when the RIA firm adopts policies, they must actually be adopted with a view that they will genuinely be enforced. If these policies are adopted pursuant to the statute but are never actually enforced, that can be worse than never having adopted a plan in the first place. An actual policy statement needs to be drafted and enforced. Management of the RIA must provide all employees with copies of the policy statement. This, in effect, is evidence of compliance.

To summarize, there are four basic types of requirements within the context of insider-trading compliance. These are

- development of written policies and procedures setting forth the legal prohibitions against insider trading, explaining key concepts underlying these prohibitions, and including any additional restrictions of the firm on insider trading and related activities
- communication of those policies and procedures to employees and supervisors throughout the firm who may learn material nonpublic information as a result of their positions at the firm
- implementation of those policies and procedures through assignment of specific responsibilities to supervisory personnel
- establishment of monitoring mechanisms to increase the likelihood that the firm will prevent, or at least detect, trading and tipping that is not in compliance with the policies and procedures

Fee Restrictions

performance fees

The Investment Advisers Act of 1940 prohibited an investment adviser from basing fees on any share of the capital appreciation of all or any portion of the client's funds unless the advisory contract related to the investment of assets in excess of $1 million. In 1985, the SEC adopted Rule 205-3, which allowed registered investment advisers to charge *performance fees* (also referred to as incentive fees), under certain circumstances. As modified in 1998 by SEC Release IA-1731, Rule 205-3 allows the RIA to charge performance fees if the RIA is managing $750,000 of the client's assets or if the RIA reasonably believes that the client has a net worth of at least $1.5 million.

Restriction or Assignment of Investment Advisory Agreements

Sec. 205 of the Investment Advisers Act of 1940 prohibits an investment adviser from assigning or transferring an investment advisory contract unless the client expressly consents to such transfer. Congress, in enacting such a provision, wanted to make sure that an adviser would not be able to shift his or her existing responsibilities to some other practitioner or adviser without first obtaining the original client's full consent to the new relationship. Therefore, if an existing registered investment adviser wants, for example, to retire, shut down operations, or move to some other location, such practitioner cannot assign the existing professional relationship to another without first obtaining the existing client's full consent to the assignment.

Prohibition of Labels

Sec. 208(c) of the Investment Advisers Act of 1940 provides that it shall be unlawful for any person registered as an investment adviser to represent that he or she is an "investment counsel" or to use the name "investment counsel" unless (1) his or her principal business consists of acting as an investment adviser and (2) a substantial part of that business consists of rendering investment supervisory services.

Although in the form of a no-action letter and not as an actual provision of the Investment Advisers Act of 1940, the SEC has also taken the position that a practitioner must not use the initials "RIA" after his or her name. The SEC was aware of a growing trend within the financial planning community of practitioners using the "RIA" initials after their names as some form of designation—such as CFP®, CLU or ChFC. Specifically, the SEC stated that, because successful acquisition of professional designations requires the passing of rigorous course examinations, it would be misleading to use the initials "RIA" after a practitioner's name, in light of the fact that no courses or examinations are required (at least at the federal level) in order to obtain this status. However, in a somewhat surprising conclusion, the SEC announced that it would permit use of the complete phrase "registered investment adviser" after a financial planner's name.

Brochure Rule

Since January 30, 1979, when the U.S. Securities and Exchange Commission issued Release No. IA-664, which promulgated Rule 204-3, all registered investment advisers have been required to deliver a written disclosure statement to each and every client. This concept, called the **brochure rule** *brochure rule,* mandates delivery of a disclosure statement not only to existing clients to whom investment advice has been given, but also to prospective clients. This disclosure must be delivered to clients or prospective clients either (1) within 48 hours of entering into an investment advisory agreement or (2) when the contract is entered into if the client can terminate such contract within 5 days.

Compliance with the brochure rule can be accomplished either by providing the client with a copy of Part II of the Form ADV or, in the alternative, by preparing a separate narrative statement containing each and every piece of data that appears as part of Part II of the Form ADV. The SEC seems to prefer the former approach, and most advisers use Part II of Form ADV because of this safe harbor implication.

There are currently 14 basic categories of data that the brochure must communicate to the financial planning client:

- types of clients

- source of information, method of analysis, and investment strategy
- business background and education
- other financial industry activities or affiliations
- conditions for managing accounts
- review procedures
- advisory fee structure
- types of securities about which advice may be provided
- minimum educational standards imposed on associates/employees
- other business activities
- participation or interest in client transactions
- investment or brokerage discretion
- additional compensation (cash or non-cash) received in connection with providing advice to clients or paid for client referrals
- balance sheet in the event that the registered investment adviser maintains custody or possession of the client's funds or securities or requires prepayment of advisory fees 6 months or more in advance, and such fees are in excess of $500 per client

In summary, therefore, the brochure rule requires the registered investment adviser to deliver either Part II of the Form ADV or the substitute brochure to the client or prospective client. It must also be noted, however, that if a continuing relationship exists between the registered investment adviser and the client, the RIA must offer to deliver an updated version of the brochure to the client at the end of each fiscal year. This portion of the brochure rule differs from the initial requirement in that, rather than the registered investment adviser being required to actually deliver the brochure disclosure statement to the client, it is satisfactory to merely offer to deliver such brochure in subsequent years.

Antifraud Provisions

Sec. 206 of the Investment Advisers Act of 1940 has come to be known as the antifraud portion of the act. Specifically, it provides the following:

It shall be unlawful for any investment adviser, by use of the mails or any means or instrumentality of interstate commerce, directly or indirectly:

a. to employ any advice, scheme, or artifice to defraud any client or prospective client
b. to engage in any transaction, practice, or course of business that operates as a fraud or deceit upon any client or prospective client
c. to act as principal for his own account, knowingly to sell any security to or purchase any security from a client, or to act as broker for a person other than such client, knowingly to effect any sale or

purchase of any security for the account of such client, without disclosing to such client in writing before the completion of such transaction the capacity in which he or she is acting and obtaining the consent of the client to such transaction. The prohibitions of this paragraph shall not apply to any transaction with a customer of a broker or dealer if such broker or dealer is not acting as an investment adviser in relation to such transaction.

d. to engage in any act, practice, or course of business that is fraudulent, deceptive, or manipulative. The Securities and Exchange Commission shall, for the purposes of this paragraph (d) by rules and regulations define and prescribe means reasonably designed to prevent such acts, practices, and courses of business as are fraudulent, deceptive, or manipulative.

These antifraud provisions of the Investment Advisers Act of 1940 have been interpreted to mean that the investment adviser becomes a fiduciary who owes the client "an affirmative duty of utmost good faith and full and fair disclosure of all the material facts." The antifraud provisions of the act also deal quite extensively with conflict of interest issues and, in general, hold the investment adviser to an exceedingly high standard of fiduciary responsibility.

The antifraud provisions of the act may even become operative in situations in which a securities transaction per se has not taken place. In essence, the SEC has decided that since Sec. 206 of the act does not refer to dealings in securities as most other general antifraud provisions in the federal securities law do, Sec. 206 is much broader and can be applied to transactions in which fraudulent conduct arose out of the investment advisory relationship between an investment adviser and his, her, or its clients, even if the conduct did not involve a securities transaction. These antifraud provisions apply to all firms and persons meeting the 1940 act's definition of investment adviser whether registered with the SEC, a state regulator, or not at all.

SEC Release No. IA-2204

SEC Release No. IA-2204 Compliance Programs

With *SEC Release No. IA-2204*, the SEC adopted new rules under the Investment Company Act of 1940 and the Investment Advisers Act of 1940 that have several requirements. These requirements include having investment advisers and investment companies register with the SEC to adopt and implement written policies and procedures reasonably designed to prevent violation of the federal securities laws; annually reviewing those policies and procedures for adequacy and effectiveness; and designating a chief compliance officer to administer the policies and procedures. In the case of an investment company, the chief compliance officer will report directly to the fund's board.

SEC Release No. IA-2256 Investment Adviser Codes of Ethics

With *SEC Release No. IA-2256*, the SEC is requiring registered advisers to adopt codes of ethics. The codes of ethics must set forth standards of conduct expected of advisory personnel and address conflicts that arise from personal trading by advisory personnel. Among other things, the rule requires advisers' supervised persons to report their personal securities transactions, including transactions in any mutual fund managed by the adviser. The SEC is also adopting amendments to rule 17j-1 to conform certain provisions to the new rule. The rule and rule amendments are designed to promote compliance with fiduciary standards by advisers and their personnel.

Advisers affiliated with professional organizations, or who have earned professional designations are already bound to uphold a code of ethics. These codes typically do not include provisions for securities reporting or pre-clearance procedures for transactions and as such are less comprehensive than the SEC requirements.

Registered Investment Advisers Versus Registered Representatives

When is a financial adviser not a registered investment adviser? When he or she is a registered representative, and the registered representative earns his or her income from the client account in the form of commissions.

The Finanacial Planning Association (FPA), on appeal in Federal District Court, prevailed in its argument that the SEC overextended its authority in interpreting the 1940 Investment Advisers Act to mean that registered representatives did not have to register as investment advisers when offering clients financial advice in a fee- (versus commission-) based account. This overturned what was known informally as the "Merrill Lynch Rule" that had been in effect since 1999.

The SEC declined the opportunity to file an appeal with the U.S. Supreme Court. At the time this text went to press, the implementation rules had not been formally decided. However, the expectation is that fee-based brokerage accounts must either be converted to commission-only accounts or comply with the requirements of the 1940 Investment Advisers Act.

FOCUS ON ETHICS
Legal Compliance and Ethics

Financial services is a highly regulated industry subjected to intense scrutiny by legislators, regulators, and the media. The media coverage has been relentless, high profile, and negative. A major theme within the industry has been legal compliance. For example, financial planners often feel constrained by home-office demands for prior approval of written sales materials and presentations.

The demand for legal compliance must be maintained. While the public seriously needs the services of financial planners, the industry cannot expect to survive, let alone thrive, if it is losing the struggle of acting legally. Compliance requirements have been re-emphasized with IA-2204, Compliance Programs of Investment Companies and Investment Advisers, discussed in greater depth in this chapter.

Financial planners help clients make their financial dreams become reality. The effective planner must understand a client's financial capability, obligations, and willingness to assume risk. In short, the planner must understand the client's financial aspirations in such depth that they can be converted into achievable goals. To succeed, the financial planner must *earn* the trust and respect of the client. How is this done?

Being in legal compliance is merely the minimum boundary of acceptability. The effective financial planner will strive for a higher standard. It may be to live by The American College's Professional Pledge, The Code of Ethics of the Society of Financial Service Professionals, the Financial Planning Association Code of Ethics, or the Code of Ethics and Professional Responsibility of the CFP Board. On an introspective level, a worthy standard is a personal code of ethics that surpasses what others might impose on themselves. The release of IA-2256, Investment Adviser Codes of Ethics, mandates registered advisers to adopt a code of ethics. It may be true that you cannot legislate ethical behavior, but you can require an adviser to adopt and agree to be bound by a code of ethics.

STATE REGULATION OF FINANCIAL PLANNERS

This chapter has focused on the regulation of financial planners within the framework of the federal securities laws. It must be noted, however, that there is a whole separate series of regulatory responsibilities stemming from the various state securities laws and state securities commissions. At this time 49 states, Wyoming being the lone exception, require the registration of investment advisers. Some states single out the activities of financial planners as part of this requirement, while other jurisdictions merely lump the concept of financial planner and investment adviser together. It should be noted, however, that state registration sometimes involves a series of procedures that is even more difficult than those that exist at the federal level.

For example, many states require a minimum capitalization amount as a prerequisite to granting investment adviser registration approval. Some states require a bond and an audited financial statement to accompany the application as well.

State regulation of investment advisers, however, typically includes important provisions that are not part of the SEC regulatory framework. Most notably, states typically require individual investment adviser representatives—including individuals who are associated with SEC-registered firms and who meet the SEC definition of "investment adviser representative"—to pass examinations designed to test minimum competency. Nearly all of these states have adopted waiver provisions recommended by the North American Securities Administrators Association (NASAA). Thus, most practicing investment adviser representatives who are CFP® certificate holders or CFA® charter holders are exempt from the testing requirements. Effective January 2000, the NASAA Modified Series 65 Exam, or Uniform Investment Adviser Law Examination, replaced a previous Series 65 Exam format. The new Series 65 Exam is more comprehensive than the earlier version, is 3 hours long, and consists of 130 questions covering economics, investment vehicles, investment strategies, and ethics. The previous format included 75 questions focusing mainly on securities law. NASAA designed the format of the Series 65 Exam with the expectation that about 80 percent of those taking it would pass.[13]

Series 63, 65, and 66 are administered by NASAA while the NASD administers other securities exams like the Series 7 General Securities Representative exam.[14]

In addition, the state securities commissions, unlike the SEC, may want to see all contracts, disclosure statements and documents, and literature used by the RIA/financial planner with the client. It is inadequate for the financial adviser to focus only on the federal regulatory implications of providing financial planning advice since the state component of the overall scheme is just as relevant. NASAA maintains a *Find Regulator* channel on its web page that provides the contact information for every state, even Wyoming.[15]

SELF-REGULATORY ORGANIZATION (SRO)

self-regulatory organization (SRO)

A *self-regulatory organization* (*SRO*) is a national securities exchange, registered securities association, or registered clearing agency that is authorized by the Securities Exchange Act of 1934 to regulate the conduct and activities of its members, subject to oversight by a specific government regulatory agency. For example, the National Association of Securities Dealers (NASD) and the New York Stock Exchange (NYSE) are SROs with SEC oversight. The SEC recently approved the merger of the NASD and NYSE into a new SRO, the Financial Industry Regulatory Authority (FINRA) and the bodies are in the process of consolidating their member regulation operations into a new, independent SRO.

Financial planners do not have a separate SRO but registered investment advisers are regulated by the SEC; state-registered advisers are regulated by the states where they do business; registered representatives not registered as RIAs are self-regulated by the NASD; and insurance agents are regulated by their state insurance commissions.

Appointing a separate SRO for financial planners is problematic because of the inherent conflict between the designations in financial planning and the de facto or implied preference of a designation awarded by an SRO over competing designations. Having the Certified Financial Planner Board of Standards, Inc. as the SRO for financial planners, for example, could put other professional adviser designations at a disadvantage to CFP® certificants in marketing their services to clients.

The CFP Board does act as a professional regulatory organization for its members with a Code of Ethics and Practice Standards. The Board will occasionally amplify provisions of the Code and Practice Standards by issuing Advisory Opinions. Appendix J provides two such advisory opinions.

Self-Regulatory Organizations With SEC Oversight

American Stock Exchange (AMEX)
Boston Stock Exchange (BSE)
Chicago Board Options Exchange (CBOE)
Chicago Stock Exchange (CHX)
Depository Trust Company (DTC)
Emerging Markets Clearing Corporation (EMCC)
Fixed Income Clearing Corporation (FICC)
(formerly: Government Securities Clearing Corporation)
Financial Industry Regulatory Authority (FINRA)
International Securities Exchange (ISE)
Municipal Securities Rulemaking Board (MSRB)
National Futures Association (NFA)
National Securities Clearing Corporation (NSCC)
National Stock Exchange (NSX)
(formerly: Cincinnati Stock Exchange)
National Market System (NMS) Plans (NMSP)
NQLX (formerly: Nasdaq Liffe Markets)
One Chicago LLC (OC)
Options Clearing Corporation (OCC)
Pacific Exchange, Inc. (PCX)
Philadelphia Stock Exchange (PHLX)
Stock Clearing Corporation of Philadelphia (SCCP)

Source: http://www.sec.gov/rules/sro.shtml

WHAT IT MEANS TO BE A FIDUCIARY

fiduciary

A *fiduciary* has a duty to the client to behave in a responsible manner when it comes to the financial management of that client's affairs. Registered investment advisers, including state-registered investment advisers, have a fiduciary duty. Registered representatives may not. Insurance agents typically do not but there are exceptions here as well.

According to investor William Scott Simon, there are two definitions of an investment fiduciary: 1) a person who has discretionary control over assets (for example, money managers and custodians) or 2) a professional held in a capacity of trust who renders investment advice (for example, investment consultants). You may be surprised to learn that you do not need to have discretionary control over client assets to be deemed a fiduciary.[16]

When a financial adviser has a fiduciary duty, abrogating that duty can be grounds for civil or criminal proceedings against the adviser. Breach of fiduciary duties can also trigger disciplinary actions by an adviser's professional society or organization. Both a CFP® and a CFA® are fiduciaries when engaged in a financial planning contract with a client. All registered investment advisers are fiduciaries. In some states stockbrokers owe a fiduciary duty to their clients. The revised CFP Board Code of Ethics and Professional Standards, as presented in chapter 3 of this textbook, spells out specifically when a CFP certificant has a fiduciary standard to his or her client.

In addition, as a fiduciary, it is not enough to simply do what is in your client's best interest. You must be able to prove in court that you have done what a "prudent man" (or a prudent person) would have done in that situation.[17]

Under the Employee Retirement Income Security Act (ERISA), whenever an investment professional is deemed to be giving investment "advice" as opposed to providing investment "education," he or she attains fiduciary status.[18]

The Uniform Prudent Investors Act has been enacted in some form by 44 of the 50 states. While the act focuses on the investment management of trusts, the standards of prudence framed in the act are extended to include fiduciaries other than trustees. It speaks to the following issues:

- risk/return objectives emphasized
- unrestricted investment types authorized
- diversification of portfolio as prudent
- trustee/agent liability severed
- notice of delegation required

CONCLUSION

Any argument that the financial planning industry is unregulated is unfounded. However, while regulation exists, it is a patchwork and piecemeal approach to oversight because it regulates advisers differently based on how they are compensated, what they are selling, and whether they are fiduciaries.

This chapter has focused on the registration and regulation of investment advisers by the SEC and the states. Regulation of the insurance and the brokerage industries has only been alluded to in this chapter, in part because the regulation of insurance agents and registered representatives is more firm-led than adviser-led.

The Investment Advisers Act of 1940, securities law, state law, and the various systems are all used to regulate financial planning professionals. Just as the insider trading scandals shaped securities law in the 1980s, and the sandboxes for state and federal regulators were laid out in the 1990s, ethics and compliance now seem to be in the spotlight because of the lack of financial analyst accountability, accounting irregularities, mutual fund market timing scandals, and bid rigging by insurance companies. The SEC is reacting to current market issues, and you can expect to see that manifest itself in new rules and regulations. Insisting on compliance and leaving audit trails to reduce the regulators' burden in enforcing compliance is the logical outcome of policing the securities industry in the aftermath of these market shocks.

There is obviously a highly developed system of regulation involving a variety of legal and regulatory mandates at both the federal and state levels. The financial adviser must become familiar with these responsibilities and accustomed to complying with these mandates on a continuing basis.

CHAPTER NINE REVIEW

Key Terms and Concepts
Key Terms and Concepts are explained in the glossary.

Investment Advisers Act of 1940
SEC Release No. IA-770
security
business standard
compensation test
SEC Release No. IA-1092
Investment Advisers Supervision
   Coordination Act of 1996
SEC Release No. IA-1633
assets under management
supervised person
investment adviser representative
national de minimis standard
client
SEC Release No. IA-2091

registered investment adviser (RIA)
Form ADV
Office of Compliance Inspections
   and Examinations (OCIE)
insider trading
Insider Trading and Securities
   Fraud Enforcement Act of 1988
Insider Trading Sanction Act of
   1984
performance fees
brochure rule
SEC Release No. IA-2204
SEC Release No. IA-2256
self-regulatory organization (SRO)
fiduciary

Review Questions
The answers to the review questions are in the supplement. The self-test questions and the answers to them are also in the supplement and on The American College Online.

9-1. Describe each of the three tests contained in SEC Release IA-770 for determining whether a financial adviser is subject to regulation under the Investment Advisers Act of 1940. [9-1]

9-2. What purposes were served by SEC Release IA-1092 in October 1987? [9-1]

9-3. Under what circumstances is a financial adviser, who otherwise meets the test elements in the definition of an investment adviser, not considered to be one under the Investment Advisers Act of 1940? [9-2]

9-4. What five groups of individuals, who otherwise meet the definition of an investment adviser, are exempt from registration under the Investment Advisers Act of 1940? [9-2]

9-5. Assuming that an individual meets the definition of an investment adviser, what determines whether he or she must register at the state or federal level? [9-3]

9-6. Define *assets under management* as it relates to registering as an investment adviser. [9-3]

9-7. List four types of advisers that are required to register with the SEC despite their status with regard to question 9-5 (above). [9-3]

9-8. List three provisions of state investment adviser laws that still apply to SEC-registered investment advisers. [9-3]

9-9. List four federal securities laws and regulations that still apply to state-registered investment advisers. [9-3]

9-10. What is a *client* for purposes of the national de minimis standard? [9-3]

9-11. Describe the procedure for registering with the SEC as an investment adviser. [9-4]

9-12. What are several types of records that the SEC requires registered investment advisers to maintain? [9-4]

9-13. a. Summarize the provisions dealing with insider trading of section 204A of the Investment Advisers Act of 1940. [9-4]

b. What steps should be taken by a registered investment adviser to meet the requirements of section 204A? [9-4]

9-14. Describe the provisions of SEC Rule 204-3, known as the brochure rule. [9-4]

9-15. Summarize the antifraud provisions of the Investment Advisers Act of 1940, noting to whom these provisions apply. [9-4]

9-16. What are four typical regulatory requirements for state registration as an investment adviser? [9-4]

9-17. If an investment adviser conducts business primarily on the Internet, where should he or she seek registration as an investment adviser? [9-4]

9-18.   What are the responsibilities of a compliance officer for a registered investment adviser? [9-4]

9-19.   Describe the responsibility of a fiduciary to his or her client. [9-6]

9-20.   Compare product suitability standards with fiduciary standards in investing. [9-7]

NOTES

1. The Bureau of Labor Statistics *Occupational Outlook Handbook* had this to say in 2006 about the job growth of personal financial advisers from 2007–2014: "Employment of personal financial advisors is projected to grow faster than the average for all occupations. The rapid expansion of self-directed retirement plans, such as 401(k) plans, is expected to continue. As the number and complexity of investments rise, more individuals will look to financial advisors to help manage their money." www.bls.gov/oco/ocos259.htm

2. John R. Macey, *Regulation of Financial Planners*, White Paper Prepared for the Financial Planning Association, 2002, p. 13.

3. *Ibid.*, pp. 55–56.

4. Macey, *op.cit.,* pp. 50–52.

5. Sujey Kallumadanda, *Client De Minimis Requirements for RIAs*, FPA Regulatory Advisory, April 30, 2004. Available at: www.fpanet.org/member/govt_relation/state/compliance/-loader.cfm?url=/commonspot/security/getfile.cfm&PageID=29239

6. Employee Benefits Security Administration (EBSA) Electronic Registration Requirements for Investment Advisers to Be Investment Managers under Title I of ERISA; Final Rule [8/24/2004]. Available at: www.dol.gov/ebsa/regs/fedreg/final/2004019089.htm

7. www.fpanet.org/member/govt_relation/state/compliance/loader.cfm?url=/commonspot/ security/getfile.cfm&PageID=19043

8. The North American Securities Administrators Association (NASAA) maintains a listing of state regulators and their contact information on its website, http://www.nasaa.org/about_-nasaa/2062.cfm.

9. During the period November 1, 2006–October 31, 2008, SEC registrants will be able to waive this initial set-up fee for Forms ADV filed electronically. SEC registrants will be able to waive this annual system-processing fee for Form ADV Annual Updating Amendments filed electronically.

10. The SEC website provides a link to the University of Cincinnati's online publication of *The Securities Lawyer's Deskbook*, available at: www.law.uc.edu/CCL/InvAdvRls/index.html

11. Macey, *op. cit.,* pp. 36–37.

12. Compliance Examination Deficiency Letter Process, Audit No. 364, available at http://www.-sec.gov/about/oig/audit/364fin.htm

13. Macey, *op. cit.,* pp. 47–48.

14. The NASD website lists the securities exams including the NASAA-administered exams. It is available at: www.nasd.com/RegistrationQualifications/BrokerGuidanceResponsibility/Quali-fications/NASDW_011096

15. www.nasaa.org/Industry___Regulatory_Resources/Directory_of_Securities_ Laws___ Regu-lations/

16. Donald Moine, *Are You a Fiduciary?*, MorningstarAdviser.com, 08-15-03, citing William Scott Simon, *The Prudent Investor Act: A Guide to Understanding*, Namborn Publishing, 2002.

17. Donald Moine, *Are You a Fiduciary? op. cit.*

18. *Ibid.*

10

The Legal and Economic Environment of Financial Institutions

Learning Objectives

An understanding of the material in this chapter should enable the student to

10-1. Learn why financial institutions are so heavily regulated.

10-2. Understand in broad terms the body of laws governing financial institutions and how to research those laws and find guidance in interpreting them.

10-3. Evaluate how deregulation is reshaping the financial services sector.

10-4. Evaluate the trends in regulating the financial services industry.

10-5. Understand in broad terms the body of consumer protection laws and how to research those laws and find assistance in interpreting them.

10-6. Evaluate the trends in regulating consumer protection laws.

10-7. Describe the elements of supply and demand.

Chapter Outline

INTRODUCTION

While chapter 9 focused on the advisor's regulatory responsibility to the client, this chapter looks at the function, purpose, and regulation of the financial services industry and the corresponding consumer protection laws that relate to financial services. It is helpful to take the broader perspective in learning about the regulatory environment rather than getting caught up in the minutia of an individual act. Get a sense of what the regulations are trying to achieve, how regulations are a product of their times, and how the passage of time that shifts the focus of regulation can help you differentiate between what is required as an advisor and how those requirements are changing. This chapter also looks at the body of consumer protection acts, the regulators who uphold these acts, and the trends in consumer protection legislation.

THE REGULATION OF THE FINANCIAL SERVICES INDUSTRY

Defining the financial services industry as banking, securities, insurance, mutual funds, and pensions (this list is not exhaustive; finance companies, for example, won't be discussed) provides a framework for discussing the regulation of the industry. We start with the Bank of the United States receiving its charter in 1796, and the Second National Bank receiving its charter in 1816 and its subsequent demise in 1836. This left the regulation of banks to the states until passage of the National Banking Acts of 1863 and 1864. But this discussion isn't meant to be a history lesson. One nugget that springs from this quick pan of the early banking acts, however, is the differentiation between federally chartered and state chartered banks. (More on that later.)

As pointed out in chapter 9, it is not coincidental that many of the regulations and regulatory bodies sprang from the investment practices in the roaring 20s, the stock market crash of 1929, bank runs in the early 30s, and the ensuing Great Depression. Robert Samuelson pins the Depression's roots even earlier. He states, "The Depression is best understood as the final chapter of the breakdown of the worldwide economic order. The breakdown started with World War I and ended in the 30s with the collapse of the gold standard. As the Depression deepened, governments tried to protect their reserves of gold by keeping interest rates high and credit tight for too long. This had a devastating impact on credit, spending, and prices, and an ordinary business slump became a calamity."[1] Regardless of its roots, the Depression created the opportunity for the government to step in and regulate the financial marketplace. But the need for regulation preceded the Depression.

What Regulation Accomplishes

Regulation first and foremost establishes the regulatory body and legislative intent of the act. It can define acceptable business practices including accounting standards, capitalization requirements, the adequacy of reserves, and a commitment to ethical standards. The financial services industry often seeks to protect and insure depositors or investors against fraud. It imposes barriers to entry that limit the number of providers servicing a locality, state, or region or limit the financial products a financial institution can offer.

Public confidence in financial institutions along with open access to markets for all customers are important regulation goals in the financial services industry. The combination of industry regulation and consumer protection regulation works toward these goals. Consumer protection legislation will be discussed later in the chapter.

Regulation allows the government to manage economic growth and thereby manage inflation and employment by regulations giving it a measure of control over the money supply. Monetary policy and fiscal policy are the two main tools the government has to manage economic growth. Financial services legislation gives the government monetary policy tools.

During the Great Depression public confidence in financial institutions had ebbed. The government had to step in to provide regulations enforced by nascent regulatory bodies to regain public confidence in banks and investments. The Federal Deposit Insurance Corporation (FDIC) was created in 1933; the Securities and Exchange Commission (SEC) was created in 1934. Subsequent legislation amended the Depression era acts to adapt to the changing economic environment. Adaptation can sometimes mean deregulation as well. For example, the Savings & Loan crisis in the 1980s was spawned by bank deregulation. The legislation to correct the problems and restore public trust came about with the passage of the Financial Institutions Reform, Recovery, and Enforcement Act of 1989 (FIRREA) and continued with the Federal Deposit Insurance Corporation Improvement Act of 1991.

The financial services industry focuses on the management of capital. To attract capital to manage, the industry has to provide the investor with a comfort level that proves that the business practices of the industry will not allow a service provider to defraud, embezzle, or abscond with invested funds. Protecting principal from the financial institution's failure or illegal actions is **safety of principal**   one aspect of *safety of principal* when investing. Safety of principal also relates to the probability of suffering a loss or diminished value on an investment.

Safety of principal means different things in the financial services industry, depending on which financial institution has the principal. At commercial banks, savings banks, and thrift institutions, safety of principal means the guarantee that you get your deposit back if the institution should fail. Deposit insurance provides that guarantee for qualified deposits. The FDIC is not the only deposit guarantor, but it does carry the full faith and credit obligation of the United States government behind every insured deposit. The National Credit Union Share Insurance Fund (NCUSIF) provides deposit insurance for credit union accounts and also carries the full faith and credit pledge of the U.S. government. Figure 10-1 shows how FDIC insurance has changed over time.[2] FDIC and NCUSIF insurance limits were increased $250,000 in 2006 for certain retirement accounts, but the basic insurance amount remains at $100,000 per depositor, per insured bank.

FIGURE 10-1
FDIC Insurance Limits*

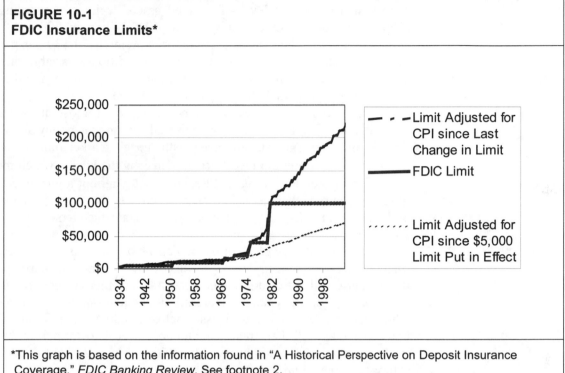

*This graph is based on the information found in "A Historical Perspective on Deposit Insurance Coverage," *FDIC Banking Review*. See footnote 2.

Safety of principal for uninsured deposits rests on the financial institution's capitalization. More equity capital in the financing mix provides a buffer if the financial institution suffers losses. The Basel Accord of 1993 addressed capital adequacy by going beyond a simple equity/total assets approach to two risk-based capital measures for member countries of the *Bank for International Settlements[3] (BIS)*. The next generation of compliance is known as Basel II with a 2007 compliance date.

Bank for International Settlements (BIS)

In the securities arena, the Securities Investor Protection Corporation (SIPC) protects principal to insured limits when a securities firm fails, but it does not protect principal for losses in investment value due to changing securities prices. The SIPC does not cover individuals who are sold worthless stocks and other securities. Rather, it helps individuals whose money, stocks, and other securities are stolen by a broker or put at risk when a securities fails. In insurance the protection of principal and preservation of income come about largely by state regulation of insurance companies for investment policies, capital adequacy, reserves, and premium levels.[4]

For pensions, vested employee pension benefits have a measure of principal protection from the Pension Benefit Guaranty Corporation (PBGC) that was created by the Employee Retirement Income Security Act of 1974. Today, as companies move from defined-benefit plans to defined-contribution plans, the level of covered assets declines. According to the PBGC, "Premium revenue totaled about $1.5 billion in 2006. All single-employer pension plans pay a basic flat-rate premium of $30 per participant per year. Underfunded pension plans pay an additional variable-rate charge of $9 per $1,000 of unfunded vested benefits. The premium for the smaller multiemployer program is $8 per participant per year."[5]

Mutual funds can invest in financial assets of most any stripe with limitations coming from the prospectus and investment policy for the fund. The returns aren't guaranteed. Even with money market mutual funds that invest in short-term liquid investments, protecting the buck—which means the fund keeps its net asset value at $1/share—is a goal, not a guarantee. Mutual funds held in a brokerage account can be covered by SIPC insurance if the brokerage firm fails, but it cannot protect against adverse movements in security prices.

open access

Another regulatory concern is *open access* to markets. Regulation of the financial services industry seeks to ensure that all market participants are treated fairly and not discriminated against. Consumer protection legislation, discussed later in the chapter, addresses both equal opportunity and fairness while defining acceptable business practices. Industry regulation addresses this concern as well. Fair treatment and open access foster public confidence in the financial services industry along with the investor confidence built on safety-of-principal protection.

monetary policy

Financial services regulation also helps implement or manage the government's *monetary policy*. Whether it is by setting the reserve requirements on deposit accounts, setting margin requirements on brokerage accounts, or increasing or decreasing the amount of reserves in the banking system, the government is concerned with managing the level of money in the economy as part of its need to manage economic growth, employment, and inflation. The Federal Reserve Board controls these aspects of monetary policy.

Who Benefits From Regulation?

disintermediation

If we divide the U.S. economy into three sectors—business, government, and consumers—we see that regulation can have different effects on each sector. *Disintermediation* is when depositors stop using financial intermediaries (such as banks), withdraw deposits, and invest in other financial products. Disintermediation in the late 1970s hurt the banking industry. The Federal Reserve's Regulation Q limited the amount of interest paid on deposit accounts, and consequently savers went elsewhere.

Depositors captured higher yields by buying money market instruments, including money market mutual funds, and therefore deposits fell off.

Stigler[6] has suggested that regulated industries prefer a regulated playing field because they benefit from the government controlling markets. Deregulation may bring more competitors into the fray and narrow margins. The movement away from fixed brokerage commissions in the 1970s (May Day 1975) certainly bears that out.

Regulation Fosters Innovation

Kane[7] argues that regulation both increases public confidence in the industry and provides an incentive for regulated industries to innovate around the regulations. Regulatory bodies have to change laws to adjust for the innovations, which forces the industry to continue to innovate. The cat and mouse aspects of this approach keep both sides attentive to opportunities in the marketplace. A current example of innovation around regulation in the marketplace is the development of a deposit-tracking process called the Certificate of Deposit Account Registry Service or CDARS.[8] The FDIC limit for insured deposits is $100,000 per depositor at an FDIC-insured institution. This limit has been in place since 1980. A financial institution that offers CDARS allows the depositor to make a deposit of up to $30 million at a single bank. The deposits are parceled out to other participating financial institutions in less than $100,000 increments. Like-sized deposits at other CDARS banks are routed back to the financial institution that received the $30 million deposit. Consequently the financial institution fully benefits from the large deposit, and the depositor has $30 million dollars fully insured while dealing with just one bank.

Deregulation in Financial Services

May Day 1975

The movement toward deregulation in the financial services industry could arguably have started on *May Day 1975* with the change away from fixed price brokerage commissions. The trend in the industry since has been toward blurring the lines between the players with brokerage firms offering banking services, banks offering brokerage services, and both offering insurance products. When credit unions and commercial banks can compete across virtually all consumer product lines, there is less specialization. From a planning perspective that can be both good and bad depending on whether the advisor has access to a full array of products and services to meet the client's needs without having to outsource the product to other providers. That has created its own controversy in the securities industry with investigations into sales agreements with brokers and firm incentives to sell in-house mutual funds seen as violating the fiduciary standards and duties of a professional advisor.

The Glass-Steagall Act of 1933 stopped commercial banking from participating in investment banking, except for issuing government-backed bonds. An amendment to the Bank Holding Company Act of 1956 stopped bank holding companies from underwriting insurance policies, although they could still sell insurance and insurance products. The Financial Services Modernization Act of 1999 (the Gramm-Leach-Bliley Act or GLB) repealed Glass-Steagall and allowed financial holding companies to compete more fully in the areas of insurance and investment banking. Figure 10-2 shows the inroads financial holding companies have made in these markets in the first years after the passage of GLB. An interesting risk argument is that it was the 30s era regulation that made banking riskier and that GLB, by allowing financial holding companies to diversify, has actually reduced the risk for the holding company. Hindsight in this case may not be 20-20. An argument that both acts are products of their times is the safer statement rather than to ruminate on whether the government took the right course of action over 70 years ago.

The lines between commercial and consumer banking have been dissolving over the past 30 years. The distinction is more by the bank's choice in emphasizing products or markets than by regulatory restrictions keeping these financial institutions from offering a product line. See table 10-1 for a listing of the different types of banking in the United States.

FIGURE 10-2
Financial Holding Companies (FHCs) Engaged in Insurance and Securities Activities, 2000–2003*

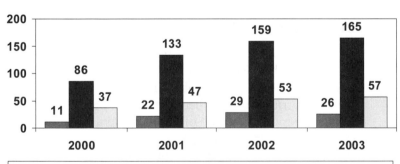

■ **Number of FHCs engaged in insurance underwriting activities**
■ **Number of FHCs engaged in insurance agency activities**
□ **Number of FHCs engaged in securities underwriting and dealing**

* Includes domestic and foreign financial holding companies
  Data Source: Board of Governors of the Federal Reserve System
  Graph Source: Financial Services Fact Book 2004, Insurance Information Institute, NY, NY[9]

TABLE 10-1 Types of Banking	
Commercial Banking	A depository institution that has commercial lending as part of its product line.
Consumer Banking	A depository institution that has consumer lending as part of its product line including first and second mortgages, auto loans, personal loans, and credit cards
Merchant Banking	A bank function where the bank commits its capital as well as arranging to meet the client's borrowing requirements. Merchant banking can also include securities underwriting as an offshoot in providing funding for clients.
Investment Banking	A financial intermediary that underwrites security offerings, advises corporations on mergers and acquisitions, and acts as a broker for institutional accounts
Universal Banking	One-stop shopping for financial services. The bank forms a financial holding company that owns subsidiaries in securities, insurance, investment banking, consulting, and other related businesses. Universal banking is also known as multidimensional banking.

Current Trends in Regulation

In May 2007, the SEC made the decision not to file an appeal to the U.S. Supreme Court over the ruling from the U.S. Court of Appeals for the District of Columbia Circuit that decided in the FPA's favor in *FPA v. SEC*. The ruling from the appeals court, combined with the SEC's decision not to appeal that ruling, means that brokerage firms can no longer use the "Merrill Rule" exemption to avoid complying with the provisions of the Investor Adviser Act of 1940.

Debate over the cost-benefit ratio in compliance with the Sarbanes-Oxley Act, especially for small firms, may point to a modification of that act to provide regulatory relief from full compliance. The compliance discussions also consider whether the act has had a positive or negative effect on the flow of capital to U.S. capital markets, as corporations consider listing their company's stock on foreign exchanges to avoid "Sarbox" requirements.

SELECT LEGISLATIVE ACTS AFFECTING THE FINANCIAL SERVICES INDUSTRY

The following section presents select regulatory acts affecting the financial services industry. While it may appear to be an exhaustive list, it most definitely is not. You are encouraged to use the citations in this section to get a more complete view of the regulations. Again, it is useful to see the trend in industry regulation and to note how innovations caused regulators to go back periodically to update the provisions of an act.

Securities Act of 1933

Securities Act of 1933

Often referred to as the "truth-in-securities" law, the *Securities Act of 1933* has two basic objectives:

- It requires that investors receive financial and other significant information concerning securities being offered for public sale.
- It prohibits deceit, misrepresentations, and other fraud in the sale of securities.[10]

Securities Exchange Act of 1934

Securities Exchange Act of 1934

With the *Securities Exchange Act of 1934*, Congress created the Securities and Exchange Commission. The act empowers the SEC with broad authority over all aspects of the securities industry. This includes the power to register, regulate, and oversee securities firms, transfer agents, and clearing agencies as well as the nation's securities self-regulatory organizations (SROs). The various stock exchanges, such as the New York Stock Exchange and American Stock Exchange, are SROs. The National Association of Securities Dealers, which operates the NASDAQ system, is also an SRO.

The act also identifies and prohibits certain types of conduct in the markets and provides the Commission with disciplinary powers over regulated entities and persons associated with them.

The act empowers the SEC to require periodic reporting of information by companies with publicly traded securities.[11]

Banking Act of 1933 (Glass-Steagall Act)

Banking Act of 1933 (Glass-Steagall Act)

This act created the Federal Deposit Insurance Corporation (FDIC) as a temporary agency to insure deposits and limited the ability for banks to underwrite securities to issuances for governmental bodies. Statewide branching is permitted for national banks if allowed by governing state law.

The FDIC was made a permanent governmental agency by the Banking Act of 1935.[12]

Trust Indenture Act of 1939

This act applies to debt securities such as bonds, debentures, and notes that are offered for public sale. Even though such securities may be registered under the Securities Act, they may not be offered for sale to the public unless a formal agreement between the issuer of bonds and the bondholder, known as the trust indenture, conforms to the standards of this act.[13]

Investment Company Act of 1940

This act regulates the organization of companies, including mutual funds that engage primarily in investing, reinvesting, and trading in securities, and whose own securities are offered to the investing public. The regulation is designed to minimize conflicts of interest that arise in these complex operations. The act requires these companies to disclose their financial condition and investment policies to investors when stock is initially sold and, subsequently, on a regular basis. The focus of this act is on disclosure to the investing public of information about the fund and its investment objectives, as well as on investment company structure and operations. It is important to remember that the act does not permit the SEC to directly supervise the investment decisions or activities of these companies or judge the merits of their investments.[14]

Investment Advisers Act of 1940

This law regulates investment advisers. With certain exceptions, it requires that firms or sole practitioners compensated for advising others about securities investments must register with the SEC and conform to regulations designed to protect investors. Since the act was amended in 1996, generally only advisers who have at least $25 million of assets under management or who advise a registered investment company must register with the Commission.[15]

McCarran-Ferguson Act of 1945

In 1944, the U.S. Supreme Court held that Congress had authority to regulate the insurance industry, overruling past precedent in this area. The McCarran-Ferguson Act of 1945 stated that regulation of insurance would remain with the states provided the states actually regulated it. The National Association of Insurance Commissioners (NAIC) worked with the states to establish regulatory bodies to maintain the primacy of state law in the insurance industry. The federal government can and does influence state laws through the prospect of federal regulation in the absence of adequate state controls. The act has seen extensive legislative scrutiny in recent years with bills promoting both an outright repeal of the act and a national charter for insurance companies.

Bank Holding Company Act of 1956

Bank Holding Company Act of 1956

This act required Federal Reserve Board approval for the establishment of a bank holding company. It also prohibited bank holding companies headquartered in one state from acquiring a bank in another state.

Employee Retirement Income Security Act of 1974

Employee Retirement Income Security Act of 1974

The Employee Retirement Income Security Act of 1974 (ERISA) is a federal law that sets minimum standards for pension plans in private industry.

ERISA also created the Pension Benefit Guaranty Corporation to "encourage the growth of defined benefit pension plans, provide timely and uninterrupted payment of pension benefits, and keep pension insurance premiums at a minimum."[16]

ERISA does not require any employer to establish a pension plan. It only requires that those who establish plans must meet certain minimum standards. The law generally does not specify how much money a participant must be paid as a benefit.[17]

ERISA has been modified by The Retirement Equity Act of 1984, the Omnibus Budget Reconciliation Act of 1986 and 1989, the Consolidated Omnibus Budget Reconciliation Act of 1985 (COBRA), and the Health Insurance Portability and Accountability Act of 1996 (HIPAA). The latter two acts expanded the role of the Employee Benefits Security Administration to include health care.

Depository Institutions Deregulation and Monetary Control Act of 1980

Depository Institutions Deregulation and Monetary Control Act of 1980

This act established "NOW Accounts" and began the phaseout of interest rate ceilings on deposits. It established the Depository Institutions Deregulation Committee, granted new powers to thrift institutions, and raised the deposit insurance ceiling to $100,000.[18]

Depository Institutions Act of 1982 (Garn-St. Germain)

Depository Institutions Act of 1982 (Garn-St. Germain)

This act expanded FDIC powers to assist troubled banks. It established the Net Worth Certificate program and expanded the powers of thrift institutions.[19]

Competitive Equality Banking Act of 1987

This act established new standards for expedited funds availability and recapitalized the Federal Savings & Loan Insurance Company (FSLIC). It expanded FDIC authority for open bank assistance transactions including bridge banks.[20]

Insider Trading and Securities Fraud Enforcement Act of 1988

This legislation was enacted in the wake of insider trading scandals in the 1980s. The act is designed to punish securities fraud and insider trading of financial securities. The SEC was authorized to award bounty to informants with the bounty coming from money paid as penalties under the act.

Financial Institutions Reform, Recovery, and Enforcement Act of 1989

This act is also known as FIRREA. Its purpose was to restore the public's confidence in the savings and loan industry. FIRREA abolished the Federal Savings & Loan Insurance Corporation (FSLIC), and the FDIC was given the responsibility of insuring the deposits of thrift institutions in its place.

The FDIC insurance fund created to cover thrifts was named the Savings Association Insurance Fund, while the fund covering banks was called the Bank Insurance Fund.

FIRREA also abolished the Federal Home Loan Bank Board. Two new agencies, the Federal Housing Finance Board (FHFB) and the Office of Thrift Supervision (OTS), were created to replace it.

Finally, FIRREA created the Resolution Trust Corporation (RTC) as a temporary agency of the government. The RTC was given the responsibility of managing and disposing of the assets of failed institutions. An Oversight Board was created to provide supervisory authority over the policies of the RTC, and the Resolution Funding Corporation (RFC) was created to provide funding for RTC operations.[21]

Federal Deposit Insurance Corporation Improvement Act of 1991

Also known as the FDICIA, this act greatly increased the power and authority of the FDIC. Major provisions recapitalized the Bank Insurance Fund and allowed the FDIC to strengthen the fund by borrowing from the Treasury.

The act mandated a least-cost resolution method and prompt resolution approach to problem and failing banks and ordered the creation of a risk-based deposit insurance assessment scheme. Brokered deposits and the solicitation of deposits were restricted as were the non-bank activities of insured state banks. The FDICIA created new supervisory and regulatory examination standards and new capital requirements for banks. It also expanded prohibitions against insider activities and created new truth-in-savings provisions.[22]

Riegle-Neal Interstate Banking and Branching Efficiency Act of 1994

This act permits adequately capitalized and managed bank holding companies to acquire banks in any state one year after enactment. Concentration limits apply and CRA evaluations by the Federal Reserve are required before acquisitions are approved. Beginning June 1, 1997, the act allowed interstate mergers between adequately capitalized and managed banks subject to concentration limits, state laws, and CRA evaluations. It extended the statute of limitations to permit the FDIC and RTC to revive lawsuits that had expired under state statutes of limitations.[23]

National Securities Market Improvement Act of 1996

This act delineated the requirements for the SEC and state registration of investment advisers based primarily on the level of assets under management. It also established a national de minimis standard for state registration of investment advisers.

Gramm-Leach-Bliley Act of 1999

This act repeals the last vestiges of the Glass-Steagall Act of 1933. It modifies portions of the Bank Holding Company Act to allow affiliations between banks and insurance underwriters. While preserving the authority of states to regulate insurance, the act prohibits state actions that have the effect of preventing bank-affiliated firms from selling insurance on an equal basis with other insurance agents. The law creates a new financial holding company under section 4 of the Bank Holding Company Act that is authorized to engage in underwriting and selling insurance and securities, conducting both commercial and merchant banking and investing in and developing real estate and other "complimentary activities." There are limits on the kinds of nonfinancial activities these new entities may engage in.

Gramm-Leach-Bliley allows national banks to underwrite municipal bonds and restricts the disclosure of nonpublic customer information by financial institutions. All financial institutions must provide customers the opportunity to "opt-out" of the sharing of the customers' nonpublic information with unaffiliated third parties. It imposes criminal penalties on anyone who obtains customer information from a financial institution under false pretenses.

Gramm-Leach-Bliley amends the Community Reinvestment Act to require that financial holding companies cannot be formed before their insured depository institutions receive and maintain a satisfactory CRA rating. It also requires public disclosure of bank-community CRA-related agreements and grants some regulatory relief to small institutions by reducing the frequency of their CRA examinations if they have received outstanding or satisfactory ratings. The act prohibits affiliations and acquisitions between commercial firms and unitary thrift institutions and makes significant changes in the operation of the Federal Home Loan Bank System, consequently easing membership requirements and loosening restrictions on the use of FHLB funds.[24] (*Editor's Note:* Because of its repeal of the Glass-Steagall Act and its financial privacy provisions, Gramm-Leach-Bliley is one of the "big five" financial services regulations. The others are the Securities Act of 1933, the Securities Exchange Act of 1934, the Investment Company Act of 1940, and the Investment Advisers Act of 1940.) Table 10-2 provides the web addresses for most of the regulatory bodies in this chapter. Often the website will provide links to the legislative acts they oversee.

TABLE 10-2
Internet Guide to Regulatory Bodies

Federal Deposit Insurance Corporation (FDIC)	www.fdic.gov/
Federal Reserve Board of Governors (FED)	www.federalreserve.gov/
National Association of Insurance Commissioners (NAIC)	www.naic.org/
National Association of Securities Dealers (NASD)	www.nasd.org/
National Credit Union Administration (NCUA)	www.ncua.gov/
North American Securities Admin. Association (NASAA)	www.nasaa.org/
Office of the Comptroller of the Currency (OCC)	www.occ.gov/
Office of Thrift Supervision (OTS)	www.ots.treas.gov/
Pension Benefit Guaranty Corporation (PBGC)	www.pbgc.gov/
Public Company Accounting Oversight Board (PCAOB)	www.pcaobus.org/
Securities and Exchange Commission (SEC)	www.sec.gov/
Securities Investor Protection Corporation (SIPC)	www.sipc.org/
State Banking Commissions	www.csbs.org/

International Money Laundering Abatement and Financial Anti-Terrorism Act of 2001

International Money Laundering Abatement and Financial Anti-Terrorism Act of 2001

This is legislation designed to prevent terrorists and others from anonymously using the U.S. financial system to move funds obtained from or destined for illegal activity. It authorizes and requires additional record keeping and reporting by financial institutions and greater scrutiny of both accounts held for foreign banks and private banking conducted for foreign persons.

The law requires financial institutions to establish anti-money-laundering programs and imposes various standards on money-transmitting businesses. It amends criminal anti-money-laundering statutes and procedures for forfeitures in such cases and requires further cooperation between financial institutions and government agencies in fighting this practice.[25]

Sarbanes-Oxley Act of 2002

Sarbanes-Oxley Act of 2002

This act mandated a number of reforms to enhance corporate responsibility and financial disclosures and also combat corporate and accounting fraud. It created the Public Company Accounting Oversight Board (PCAOB) to oversee the activities of the auditing profession.[26]

CHARTERING, REGULATION, AND OVERSIGHT OF THE FINANCIAL SERVICES INDUSTRY

Depository Institutions

Depository institutions are banks, savings associations, savings banks, and credit unions. The latter three are often jointly described as thrift institutions or "thrifts." While deregulation has blurred the historical distinctions between these types of depository institutions, differences still remain starting with how they are chartered and regulated.

Nationally chartered banks are chartered and regulated by the federal government through the Office of the Comptroller of the Currency (OCC). Nationally chartered banks are required to become member banks of the Federal Reserve System. State chartered banks are chartered and regulated by their state banking commission and can elect to become members of the Federal Reserve System.

For the Fed, supervising banks generally means carrying out three duties: establishing safe and sound banking practices, protecting consumers in financial transactions, and ensuring the stability of U.S. financial markets by acting as the lender of last resort. The goal of these duties is to minimize risk in the banking system.[27] The Federal Reserve Board also oversees compliance of 31 regulations from Regulation A to Regulation EE. Some of these regulations are well known, like Regulation Z, the Truth-in-Lending Act; others are more obscure.[28]

The Office of Thrift Supervision (OTS) regulates federally chartered savings institutions while state chartered savings institutions are regulated by state banking commissions. Established by FIRREA, the OTS replaced the Federal Home Loan Bank Board.

Savings banks carry FDIC deposit insurance under the Bank Insurance Fund while savings associations carry FDIC deposit insurance under the Savings Association Insurance Fund.

Credit unions are non-profit depository institutions that are owned by their member depositors. They are divided into three tiers: national, corporate, and local, and they can have federal or state charters. The National Credit Union Administration regulates federally chartered credit unions. The National Credit Unions Share Insurance Fund (NCUSIF) provides deposit insurance that matches the FDIC limits per depositor. Federally chartered credit unions must insure deposits through NCUSIF. State chartered credit unions are not required to carry this insurance.

Insurance Companies

The McCarran-Ferguson Act of 1945 provides that regulation of insurance would remain with the states if the states actually regulated the insurance companies operating in their state. The National Association of Insurance Commissioners (NAIC) worked with the states in the 1940s to establish regulatory bodies to maintain the primacy of state law in the insurance industry. The federal government can and does influence state laws through the prospect of federal regulation in the absence of adequate state controls.

Insurance companies typically choose where they are incorporated based on how friendly the state's laws are for insurance companies. Delaware and Arizona are two popular choices.

State regulations focus on insurance premiums, sales practices, commissions, profitability, solvency regulations, and the investment of reserves.

Gramm-Leach-Bliley is expected to be a good law for the insurance industry because it makes banks and investment banks that enter the insurance business subject to insurance regulations.

Mutual Funds

The SEC is the primary regulator of mutual funds. That authority springs from the Securities Act of 1933, the Securities Exchange Act of 1934, and the Investment Company Act of 1940. The 1933 act establishes the parameters for mutual funds in filing a registration statement with the SEC and for sending mutual fund prospectuses to investors.

The 1934 act establishes anti-fraud provisions and financial reporting requirements, and appoints the National Association of Securities Dealers (NASD) to supervise the distribution of mutual fund shares.

The Investment Company Act of 1940 established additional rules to protect against fraud, prevent conflict of interests, and prohibit excessive fees or charges for mutual fund shares.

The 1988 Insider Trading Act, the Market Reform Act of 1990, and the National Securities Market Improvement Act of 1996 all affect mutual funds. The National Securities Markets Improvement Act of 1996 (NSMIA) actually reduced a level of regulation by exempting mutual fund salespeople from state regulatory oversight.

Your Financial Services Practice: Unauthorized Entities

An unauthorized entity is an insurance company that has not gained approval to place insurance business from a department of insurance in the jurisdiction where it or a producer wants to sell insurance. These carriers are unlicensed and prohibited from doing business in that state. It is the responsibility of the agents to do their due diligence to make sure the carriers for which they are selling are approved by the department of insurance in that state.

In most cases, the operators characterized their entities as one of several types to give the appearance of being exempt from state regulation.

Securities Firms

Unlike the insurance industry where the states are the principal regulators of the firm, the NSMIA re-emphasized the primacy of federal regulation for securities firms. This made the SEC the head regulator in the securities industry.

The self-regulatory organizations' (SRO) ability to regulate securities firms in conjunction with the SEC was established in the Securities Exchange Act of 1934. All of the stock exchanges are SROs including the National Association of Securities Dealers (NASD), which monitors trading practices, firm capitalization or solvency, education, and testing. It is a repository for customer complaints against a broker or securities firm. The NASD bills itself as "the world's leading private-sector provider of financial regulatory services...."

When a securities firm fails, the SIPC protects investors against losses of up to $500,000 in securities but only $100,000 in cash. It was established by the Securities Investor Protection Act of 1970.

Pension Companies

The Employee Retirement Income Security Act (ERISA) of 1974 is the major regulatory legislation governing private pension funds. Companies are not forced to offer their employees pensions, but if they do they must follow the provisions of this act.

ERISA requires pension plans to establish a minimum vesting requirement while setting the maximum vesting period of 10 years. It also establishes transferability provisions to transfer pension credits between employers when changing jobs.

Under ERISA the plan sponsor has fiduciary responsibilities along with the plan's trustee(s) and investment managers(s). Beyond the responsibility to invest funds prudently, the plan must meet reporting requirements.

ERISA also established the Pension Benefit Guaranty Corporation. Chronically underfunded since its inception, the Retirement Protection Act of 1994 improved the PBGC's ability to charge higher premiums to underfunded plans. Like the FDIC, the PBGC has moved toward risk-based premiums.

FOCUS ON ETHICS
Staying Current on Regs

It's the compliance department's job to make you aware of changes in regulation. But remember, ethics is more than compliance. Develop a process that keeps you abreast of what's in the regulatory pipeline—what has changed recently, when those changes become effective, and how it influences your practice. It will allow you to be proactive in managing your practice or client relationships.

The CFP® Code of Ethics speaks to competence and professionalism. Staying on top of the regulations in your field helps you better meet those goals.

CONSUMER PROTECTION ACTS

In an effort to protect consumers' rights to obtain, use, and maintain credit, Congress has passed nearly a dozen consumer protection laws dealing with various aspects of the lending-borrowing process including

- prohibition of certain types of discrimination in the lending-borrowing process
- provision of full and accurate information to both lenders and borrowers for use in making their decisions regarding the extension and the acceptance/continuation of credit
- use of acceptable procedures in collecting debt repayment
- protection of consumers harmed by identity theft
- honest treatment of borrowers by credit repair organizations

Prohibition of Discrimination

Equal Credit Opportunity Act

Under the *Equal Credit Opportunity Act*, an individual cannot be denied credit based on his or her race, sex, marital status, religion, age, national origin, or receipt of public assistance. In addition, in applying for credit, individuals have the right to have reliable public assistance payments considered in the same manner as other income. Finally, if credit is denied, the applicant has a legal right to know why.

Provision of Full and Accurate Information

There are several federal laws aimed at ensuring that lenders and borrowers are provided full and accurate information essential to making appropriate decisions regarding the extension and the acceptance/continuation of credit.

Information Provided to the Lender

Fair Credit Reporting Act
Consumer Credit Reporting Reform Act

The *Fair Credit Reporting Act*, passed in 1971 and strengthened significantly by the *Consumer Credit Reporting Reform Act* of 1996, helps to ensure that consumer reporting agencies (credit bureaus) furnish correct and complete information to lenders and other businesses to use when evaluating an individual's credit application. The individual has the following rights under this act:

- the right to receive a copy of the credit report containing all of the information in the file at the time of the request
- the right to know the name of anyone who received the credit report in the last year for most purposes or in the last 2 years for employment purposes
- the right to know the name and address of the credit reporting agency contacted by any company that denies the credit application, provided the denial was based on information given by the credit reporting agency
- the right to a free copy of the credit report when the application is denied because of information supplied by the credit reporting agency, as long as a request is made within 60 days of receiving the denial notice
- the right to file a dispute with the credit reporting agency and with the company that furnished the information to the credit reporting agency to contest the completeness or accuracy of information in the report, in which case both the credit reporting agency and the furnisher of information are legally obligated to reinvestigate the dispute
- the right to add a summary explanation to the credit report if the dispute is not resolved to the individual's satisfaction

Fair and Accurate Credit Transactions Act

In December 2003, Congress passed the *Fair and Accurate Credit Transactions Act* to amend the Fair Credit Reporting Act. This act allows consumers to get one free copy of their credit report annually from any consumer-reporting agency subject to the Fair Credit Reporting Act.

Information Provided to the Borrower/Applicant

Truth-in-Lending Act

The *Truth-in-Lending Act* is designed to protect consumers in credit transactions by requiring clear disclosure of key terms of the lending arrangement and all costs. For closed-end (nonrevolving) credit transactions, the creditor must disclose its identity as well as

- amount financed
- itemization of amount financed
- annual percentage rate (APR) including applicable variable-rate disclosures
- finance charge
- total of payments
- payment schedule
- prepayment/late payment penalties
- if applicable to the transaction: (1) total sales cost, (2) demand feature, (3) security interest, (4) insurance, (5) required deposit, and (6) reference to contract

For open-end (revolving) credit transactions, the creditor must disclose its identity as well as

- annual percentage rate including applicable variable-rate disclosures
- method of determining the finance charge and the balance on which the finance charge is imposed
- amount or method of determining any membership or participation fees
- security interests if applicable to transaction
- statement of billing rights

Home Ownership and Equity Protection Act (HOEPA)

In an effort to curb predatory lending, Congress enacted the *Home Ownership and Equity Protection Act (HOEPA)* to amend the Truth-in-Lending Act and established requirements for certain mortgage loans with high rates and/or high fees. In addition to defining the criteria for identifying loans that are subject to the provisions of the act (which were revised as of October 1, 2002), HOEPA prohibited certain acts and practices in connection with these home-secured loans. Such acts included making loans based on the collateral value of the borrower's property without regard to his or her ability to repay the loan and engaging in repeated refinancings of the creditor's own HOEPA loans over a short time period when the transactions are not in the borrower's best interest. A number of features were banned from high-rate, high-fee loans including nearly all balloon payments, negative amortization, default interest rates higher than pre-default interest rates, and most prepayment penalties. Finally, several disclosures relevant to HOEPA loans were added to those already required by the Truth-in-Lending Act for loans in general.

Consumer Leasing Act

The *Consumer Leasing Act* is designed to protect individuals in consumer leasing transactions by requiring clear disclosure of key terms of the leasing arrangement and all costs. The lessor is required to disclose the following information:

- description of property
- amount due at lease signing or delivery
- payment schedule and total amount of periodic payments
- disclosure of other anticipated charges during normal execution of the lease agreement
- total of payments
- payment calculation
- lease term
- early termination conditions and penalties
- maintenance responsibilities
- purchase option
- statement referencing "nonsegregated" disclosures
- the right of appraisal
- liability at the end of the lease term
- fees and taxes
- insurance and warranties

Fair Credit and Charge Card Disclosure Act

The *Fair Credit and Charge Card Disclosure Act* requires creditors to include certain information in preapproved credit offers and credit card statements including

- annual fee—the yearly charge for having the credit card
- annual percentage rate (APR)—the yearly interest rate charged
- monthly periodic rate—APR divided by 12, or the rate at which monthly interest is calculated
- daily periodic rate—APR divided by 365, or the rate at which daily interest is calculated
- finance charge—the total cost of having the credit card, including interest and fees
- transaction fee—certain charges to use various services, such as receiving a cash advance or using an ATM

- late payment fee—the charge placed on the account when payment is not received by the due date
- over the limit fee—the charge placed on the account when the credit limit has been exceeded
- grace period—the time between the transaction date and the due date where interest charges can be avoided if the card balance is paid in full, usually 20–30 days
- minimum payment—the minimum amount accepted by the creditor for the payment due each month, usually between 2 percent and 3 percent of the balance

Use of Acceptable Procedures in Collecting Debt Repayment

Fair Credit Billing Act

The *Fair Credit Billing Act* establishes acceptable procedures for use when disputes arise in connection with billing errors on open-end (revolving) credit accounts, such as unauthorized charges (consumer's responsibility is limited to $50 per card), charges listing the wrong date or amount, charges for goods and services that either were not accepted or were not delivered as agreed, math errors, failure to post payments or returns, failure to send bills to the purchaser's current address, and charges for which the consumer asks for an explanation or written proof of purchase. The act describes the consumer's and creditor's rights and responsibilities in an effort to resolve these types of problems.

Electronic Fund Transfer Act

The *Electronic Fund Transfer Act* places limits on the extent to which a consumer can be held liable for the unauthorized use of an ATM or debit card. The amount for which the cardholder is liable, if any at all, depends on how quickly the missing card or unauthorized transaction is reported to the card issuer.

Fair Debt Collection Practices Act

The *Fair Debt Collection Practices Act* requires that debt collectors treat debtors fairly and prohibits certain methods of debt collection. The act, which applies to personal, family, and household debts, establishes rules regarding when a debt collector can and cannot contact a debtor. In addition, the act prohibits debt collection practices involving harassment; false statements; threats that the debtor will be arrested if the debt is not paid; threats that the debtor will be sued or have property or wages seized, garnished, attached, or sold unless the creditor intends to do so and it is legal to do so; use of a false name in the process of attempting to collect a debt; use of debtor documents that appear to be from a court or government agency when they are not; and engagement in a variety of unfair practices when attempting to collect a debt.

Protection of Consumers Harmed by Identity Theft

Identity Theft and Assumption Deterrence Act

The *Identity Theft and Assumption Deterrence Act* enacted in 1998 made the theft of identity information a crime and established restitution provisions for individual victims. Prior to passage of this law, the theft of someone's identity was not considered a crime under the law. Instead the crime was the fraud that was committed using the stolen identity. The new law made identity theft a federal crime with penalties of up to 15 years imprisonment and a maximum fine of $250,000. The legislation also enables the Secret Service, the FBI, and other law enforcement agencies to combat this crime.

Prior to passage of this act, only the credit grantors who suffered monetary loss were considered victims under the law. The individual whose identity was actually stolen was not recognized as the victim by the law and thus was left alone to clean up various aspects of his or her life including credit history, traffic and criminal violations on his or her record, and an erroneous record of bankruptcies. The identity theft law established that the person whose identity has been stolen is truly a victim who deserves some assistance in dealing with problems attributable to the identity theft. The law allows the victim to seek restitution if there is a conviction. The Federal Trade Commission was directed to provide a toll-free hotline to report identity theft to specially trained personnel and to act as a clearinghouse for information to aid law enforcement agencies in combating the crime. The Commission can also offer victims information and assistance on the steps to take to resolve the credit problems encountered as a result of this crime as well as information regarding their rights under the Fair Credit Reporting Act, the Fair Credit Billing Act, the Truth-in-Lending Act, and the Fair Debt Collection Practices Act.

Honest Treatment of Borrowers by Credit Repair Organizations

Credit Repair Organizations Act

The *Credit Repair Organizations Act* prohibits a variety of false and misleading statements, as well as fraud by credit repair organizations (CROs). CROs may not receive payment before any promised service is "fully performed." Services must be under written contract that must include a detailed description of the services and contract performance time. CROs must provide the consumer with a separate written disclosure statement describing the consumer's rights before entering into the contract. No services can be performed until the CRO has a signed contract and has completed a 3-day waiting period during which time the contract can be cancelled without paying any fees.

How Consumers Can Use the Acts

Federal consumer protection laws typically encourage consumers to file complaints with the federal agency responsible for enforcing the particular act. If a creditor violates a consumer protection act, the consumer is permitted to sue for actual damages, court costs, and attorney's fees as well as for various penalty assessments (for example, punitive damages or a multiple of finance charges) provided by the particular act. Some of the acts also provide for fines when certain rules are violated.

TRENDS IN CONSUMER PROTECTION LEGISLATION

Privacy and protection are two main trends in consumer protection legislation. Gramm-Leach-Bliley's provisions for the privacy of personal financial information have stretched far beyond the financial services industry.

Technology, with the convenience of buying goods and services over the Internet, has created its own set of problems for regulators, businesses, and consumers. Phishing, the practice of tricking consumers into giving up their financial information to a bogus website, is the new front in identity theft. The word derives from the combination of phony and fishing.

Identity theft will continue to be a thorn in the side of consumers and businesses. Requiring consumer reporting agencies to provide free copies of credit reports once a year, while a helpful step in allowing consumers to monitor their credit and learn of identity theft, will fall short of the actual need for credit monitoring in the economy. Look for more regulation in this area.

FINDING AND INTERPRETING THE LAWS

The Federal Trade Commission's website[29] is very helpful in both providing a consumer fact sheet that explains consumer protection laws and allowing you to access the actual act. The current trend in regulatory websites is to transfer you to the U.S. Code site,[30] maintained by the Legal Information Institute, when you want to access the regulation since it will provide you with the act as currently amended without requiring the regulatory website to periodically update the information.

The SEC provides a synopsis of the securities legislation and a method to link to the actual act. Along with that information is a chronological listing of final rule releases, proposed rules, concept releases, and SRO rule making on its website www.sec.gov.

The Federal Reserve Board maintains a list of Regulation Titles[31] over which it has regulatory oversight. This site is really helpful if you can't remember what Regulation M is in layman's terms. Like the other regulators' sites you can see a synopsis of the act as well as access the full act from the site.

THE ELEMENTS OF SUPPLY AND DEMAND

The economic forces determining the quantity supplied and the quantity demanded for a good or service are so intertwined that it is problematic to consider one element without the other when constructing an economic analysis of the pricing of a good or service.[32] The interdependent nature of supply and demand evolved in large part because they both are expressed as a function of price.

Economics is the study of unlimited wants and scarce resources. The efficient and effective use of resources in an economic system allows the members of that system to, in aggregate, live better lives. The pricing of resources, at least in a capitalistic economy, is the primary method of allocating these scarce resources among competing uses. Price, then, is the driving force in determining both the supply and demand for a good. Demand connotes both the willingness and ability to *buy* a good at its market price. Supply connotes both the willingness and ability to *sell* the good at its market price.

It is both intuitive and correct to note that, other things being equal, the higher the price for a good, the lower the demand for that good. Also intuitive and correct is that at higher prices, more goods become available. On the supply side, the quantity of a good will rise with a price increase and fall with a price decrease. Together these are known as the *laws of supply and demand*. At some point, the higher prices that stimulate increased supply bump up against consumers' unwillingness to pay a higher price for the good. If the quantity demanded, Q_D, equals the quantity supplied, Q_S, the market for the good is in equilibrium. If supply outstrips demand or demand outstrips supply, the market is in disequilibrium. Figure 10-3 shows a simple supply/demand relationship for a product.

Demand, as a single point on the demand curve (or function) represents the quantity of a good required by consumers at a particular price. The function itself represents how quantity demanded changes with changes in price. If the function does not change, then we expect movement along the curve to accurately describe the relationship between price and quantity demanded. A change in the quantity demanded along the existing demand curve is related solely to a price change. Demand can be defined either as the function or a point along that function.

The demand curve does not remain static over time. The forces behind the pricing of a good can change. A simple example is the relationship between weather and crops. Ideal growing conditions, like good weather, increase crop yields. Increased crop yields mean increased supply. The increased supply can drive down prices, thereby increasing demand. A shift in the demand curve results in a new equilibrium price as consumers and producers adjust to the changes in market dynamics for the good.

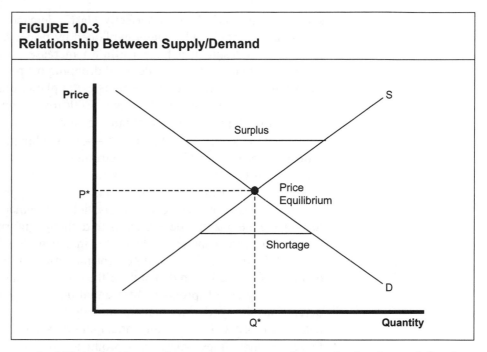

FIGURE 10-3
Relationship Between Supply/Demand

A shift in the demand curve represents a change in the demand for the good and a new demand curve. If the demand curve shifts to the left on the graph, it represents a decrease in demand; a shift to the right represents an increase in demand. Figure 10-4 shows a demand curve shifting to the right for an unnamed good. For the same price, P_0, the quantity demanded increases from Q_0 to Q_1 because of the shift in the demand curve.

Take a can of mixed nuts as an example. What drives the mixture of nuts in the can? Supply and demand is, of course, the right answer, but it is not in-depth enough to demonstrate the issues involved. A bumper crop of almonds would lower the price of almonds. A producer could reduce the cost of a can of mixed nuts by increasing the percentage of almonds in the mix. Put all almonds in the mix, however, and we no longer have a can of mixed nuts. Consequently there are limits to the nut manufacturer's ability to substitute nuts into the mix.

The availability of close substitutes is one factor in the pricing of a good. A good with no close substitutes is said to have an *inelastic demand* since consumers cannot replace the good with an alternative if its price rises too high. Goods that have close substitutes will have a more elastic demand function because consumers can move from the expensive good to the less expensive one if prices get too high.

Figure 10-5 shows two demand functions, D1 and D2. The function represented by line D1 shows a good with a perfectly inelastic demand. Regardless of the price for the good, the quantity demanded remains the same. Function D2 shows a perfectly elastic demand schedule. The quantity demanded cannot be adequately explained by price. A small shift downward in price will result in a huge (infinite) increase in demand; a small shift upward in price will result in demand dropping off precipitously.

In the current market, the precious metal platinum is off its recent high of $936/troy ounce, retreating to about $800/troy ounce. Consumers have the choice of continuing to buy platinum jewelry—with jewelry representing 56 percent of the demand for that metal[33]—or switching to white or yellow gold. Industrial users, like high-tech electronics, may not have the flexibility to substitute platinum for other metals in the manufacturing process. Thus, the elasticity of the demand for platinum is different for jewelry makers than it is for electronics manufacturers. The elasticity of demand is a measure of how responsive the quantity demanded is to a change in price. How, for example, does a 10 percent increase (decrease) in the price of platinum change the demand for the metal? If a 10 percent increase in price has no effect on the quantity demanded, then demand for the good is inelastic.

The degree of product differentiation among producers of a good determines the type of market for the good. A perfectly competitive market has a standardized commodity and numerous buyers and sellers. Products that are commodities—classically products like corn, wheat, pork bellies, and lumber—have minimal product differentiation among producers. Auction markets work well for these goods because the auction process can establish a market clearing price that will match supply with demand. The commoditization of financial securities also allows for a degree of standardization that makes an auction market practical for these goods.

Figure 10-6 shows two supply functions, S1 and S2. The function represented in the graph by line S1 shows a good with a perfectly inelastic supply. Regardless of price, the amount of the good supplied does not change. In contrast, the supply function represented by line S2 shows a good with a perfectly elastic supply. Small changes in price will dramatically affect the amount of the good supplied.

Perfectly elastic (or inelastic) supply or demand functions are rare. Most goods have some substitutes available, and the price relationships between these goods, called cross elasticity, influences the price elasticity of the individual good.

Estimating the supply and demand functions for a good is as much art as it is science. Once the functions have been estimated, though, finding the intersection of the two functions is a fairly straightforward matter. It is this intersection that determines the market equilibrium price where supply equals demand.

Market forces will continually exert pressure on this relationship, causing either a movement along the curve (resulting in price changes), or a change in one or both of the functions (resulting in a shift in the curves). In either case, the market will move toward a new equilibrium price.

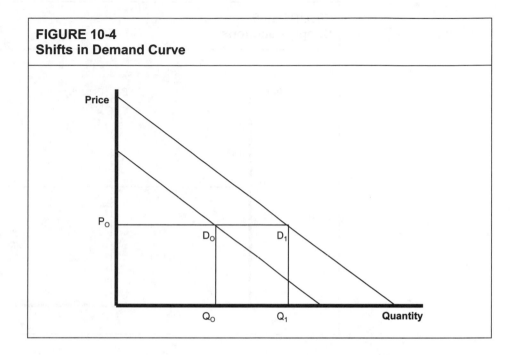

FIGURE 10-4
Shifts in Demand Curve

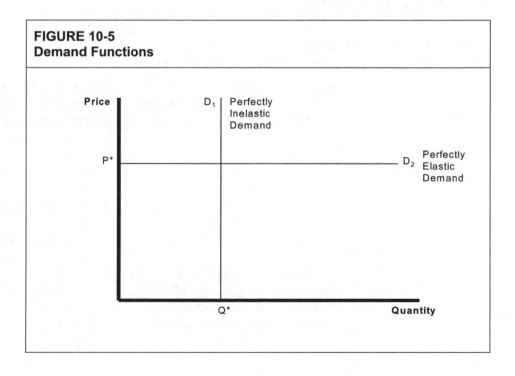

FIGURE 10-5
Demand Functions

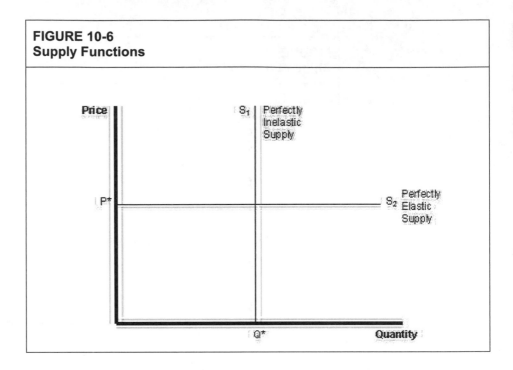

FIGURE 10-6
Supply Functions

CHAPTER TEN REVIEW

Key Terms and Concepts

Key Terms and Concepts are explained in the glossary.

safety of principal
Bank for International Settlements (BIS)
open access
monetary policy
disintermediation
May Day 1975
Securities Act of 1933
Securities Exchange Act of 1934
Banking Act of 1933 (Glass-Steagall Act)
Trust Indenture Act of 1939
Investment Company Act of 1940
McCarran-Ferguson Act of 1945
Bank Holding Company Act of 1956

Employee Retirement Income Security Act of 1974
Depository Institutions Deregulation and Monetary Control Act of 1980
Depository Institutions Act of 1982 (Garn-St. Germain)
Competitive Equality Banking Act of 1987
Financial Institutions Reform, Recovery, and Enforcement Act of 1989
Federal Deposit Insurance Corporation Improvement Act of 1991

Riegle-Neal Interstate Banking and
  Branching Efficiency Act of 1994
National Securities Market
  Improvement Act of 1996
Gramm-Leach-Bliley Act of 1999
International Money Laundering
  Abatement and Financial Anti-
  Terrorism Act of 2001
Sarbanes-Oxley Act of 2002
Equal Credit Opportunity Act
Fair Credit Reporting Act
Consumer Credit Reporting Reform
  Act
Fair and Accurate Credit
  Transactions Act

Truth-in-Lending Act
Home Ownership and Equity
  Protection Act (HOEPA)
Consumer Leasing Act
Fair Credit and Charge Card
  Disclosure Act
Fair Credit Billing Act
Electronic Fund Transfer Act
Fair Debt Collection Practices Act
Identity Theft and Assumption
  Deterrence Act
Credit Repair Organizations Act

Matching Exercises

Match the act with a provision of that act.

1. Depository Institutions
    Deregulation and Monetary
    Control Act of 1980   (   )

    a. Repealed Glass-Steagall

2. National Securities Market
    Improvement Act of 1996   (   )

    b. States regulate insurance

3. McCarran-Ferguson (1945)   (   )

    c. Pension primer for regulators

4. Glass-Steagall (1933)   (   )

    d. Established SEC

5. Financial Institutions Reform,
    Recovery, and Enforcement Act
    of 1989   (   )

    e. Created Public Company Accounting
        Oversight Board

6. ERISA (1974)   (   )

    f. Set FDIC limit at $100,000

7. Securities Exchange Act (1934)   (
)

    g. Limited product lines for banks

8. Investment Company Act (1940)
    (   )

    h. Revamped savings institutions regulation

9. Sarbanes-Oxley Act (2002)   (   )

    i. RIA registration requirements delineated

10. Gramm-Leach-Bliley (1999)
    (   )

    j. Mutual fund disclosure laws established

Match the consumer protection act with a provision of that act.

1. Equal Credit Opportunity Act (   )
2. Fair Credit Reporting Act of 1971 (   )
3. Truth-in-Lending Act (Regulation Z) (   )
4. Home Ownership and Equity Protection Act (   )
5. Consumer Leasing Act (   )
6. Fair Credit and Charge Card Disclosure Act (   )
7. Fair Credit Billing Act (   )
8. Electronic Fund Transfer Act (   )
9. Fair Debt Collection Practices Act (   )
10. Credit Repair Organizations Act (   )

a. Requires contract for credit repair services
b. Establishes dispute procedures of credit cards
c. Establishes required information in credit card offers
d. Advises on how to stop bill collector harassment
e. Limits consumer liability for unauthorized ATM use
f. Forces mandatory cancellation of PMI
g. Requires minimum information in a lease
h. Makes credit markets accessible
i. Regulates consumer reporting organizations
j. Requires APRs in advertising

NOTES

1. Samuelson, Robert J., "Great Depression." *The Concise Encyclopedia of Economics.* Library of Economics and Liberty, accessed August 2007, and available at http://www.econlib.org/library/Enc/GreatDepression.html; Internet.
2. Bradley, Christine M. "A Historical Perspective on Deposit Insurance Coverage." *FDIC Banking Review*, 13, no. 2:1–25, 2000 CPI data provided by the Bureau of Labor Statistics website: http://www.bls.gov/cpi/home.html.
3. The United States is a member of the Bank for International Settlements. Learn more about BIS on its website: www.bis.org.
4. The National Association of Insurance Commissioners (NAIC) maintains a directory of state insurance commissioners on its website: http://www.naic.org.
5. Pension Benefits Guaranty Corporation, *Pension Insurance Premiums Fact Sheet,* accessed August 2007, and available from http://www.pbgc.gov/media/key-resources-for-the-press/content/page13541.html; Internet.
6. Stigler, George J. "The Theory of Oligopoly." *Journal of Political Economy*, February 1965, pp. 44–61.
7. Kane, Edward J. *"Accelerating Inflation, Technological Innovation, and the Decreasing Effectiveness of Banking Regulation." The Journal of Finance*, vol. XXXVI, no. 2, (May 1981), pp. 355–367.
8. You can learn more about the CDARS product by going to its website: http://www.cdars.com/.
9. Available online at: http://www.financialservicesfacts.org/financial2/chartindex/#.
10. U.S. Securities and Exchange Commission, *The Laws That Govern the Securities Industry,* accessed August 2007; available from http://www.sec.gov/about/laws.shtml; Internet.
11. *Ibid.*

12. Federal Deposit Insurance Corporation, *Imported Banking Legislation,* accessed August 2007; available from http://www.fdic.gov/regulations/laws/important/; Internet.

13. U.S. Securities and Exchange Commission, *The Laws That Govern the Securities Industry,* accessed August 2007, and available from http://www.sec.gov/about/laws/shtml; Internet.

14. *Ibid.*

15. *Ibid.*

16. Pension Benefit Guaranty Corporation, *About PBGC,* accessed August 2007, and available from http://www.pbgc.gov/about/default.html.

17. U.S. Department of Labor, Employee Benefits Security Administration. *Compliance Assistance, Synopsis of the Law,* accessed August 2007; available from http://www.dol.gov/ebsa/compliance_assistance.html; Internet.

18. Federal Deposit Insurance Corporation, *Important Banking Legislation,* accessed December 17, 2004; available from http://www.fdic.gov/regulations/laws/important/; Internet.

19. *Ibid.*

20. *Ibid.*

21. *Ibid.*

22. *Ibid.*

23. *Ibid.*

24. U.S. Securities and Exchange Commission, *The Laws That Govern the Securities Industry,* accessed August 2007 and available from http://www.sec.gov/about/laws.shtml; Internet.

25. Federal Deposit Insurance Corporation, *Important Banking Legislation,* accessed August 2007, and available from http://www.fdic,gov/regulations/laws/important/; Internet.

26. U.S. Securities and Exchange Commission, *The Laws That Govern the Securities Industry,* accessed August 2007, and available from http://www.sec.gov/about/laws.shtml; Internet.

27. The Federal Reserve Bank jof St. Louis, *In Plain English: Making Sense of the Federal Reserve: What We Do, Supervising and Regulating Banks,* accessed August 2007; available from http://www.stlouisfed.org/publications/pleng/supervision.html; Internet.

28. The Federal Reserve Board maintains a listing of these regulations on its website. Available at: http://www.federalreserve.gov/regulations/regref.html.

29. You guessed it, www.flc.gov.

30. http://assembler.law.cornell.edu/uscode/. While securities laws are, of course, available here, the SEC transfers you to a different site maintained and published by the University of Cincinnati called The Securities Lawyer's Desk Book at http://www.law.uc.edu/CCL.

31. http:///www.federalreserve.gov/regulations/regref.html.

32. For simplicity during the remainder of this section, the term good is used instead of using the term good or service.

33. New York Mercantile Exchange information. http://www.nymex.com/jsp /markets/ pla_pre_ agree.jsp.

Financial Planning for Special Circumstances

A compilation of selected readings from The American College's Huebner School Series of financial planning textbooks

Thomas M. Brinker, Jr.*

Learning Objectives

An understanding of the material in this chapter should enable the student to

---

11-1. Explain the tax implications for divorcing couples.

11-2. Describe the opportunities, challenges, and strategies for nontraditional families and couples.

11-3. Understand and capitalize on income tax benefits for parents of children and children with special needs.

11-4. Explain the importance and tax implications of having disability, accident, and health insurance benefits.

11-5. Explain the tax implications of gifts, inheritances, and other monetary windfalls.

11-6. Explain how estate planning can be tailored to meet the special needs of elderly and incapacitated individuals.

11-7. Describe some of the basic issues that pertain to estate planning for married couples and single individuals.

11-8. Explain various estate planning arrangements for individuals in nontraditional living arrangements.

---

*Thomas M. Brinker, Jr., CPA, is a professor of accounting at Arcadia University in Glenside, Pennsylvania. He also maintains a private tax practice in Plymouth Meeting, Pennsylvania.

Chapter Outline

UNDERSTANDING THE TAX IMPLICATIONS OF DIVORCE

According to the U.S. Census Bureau, over one-half of the marriages in our country end in divorce. This means there is a good chance that some of your clients will be in that category. In fact, for members of the middle-aged segment, it is statistically more likely that any particular client will get divorced in the next 5 years than that he or she will die. Table 11-1 depicts the relation of age to divorce for one isolated year (1990).

Financial Considerations in Divorce

Marriage typically involves the joining of many financial arrangements. In a divorce, these arrangements must be untangled. A major part of divorce or separation is the transfer of property from one spouse to the other. Short- and long-term finances must be rearranged. Shared and individual properties must be separated according to the laws of the state.

When a divorce is initiated, legal instruments such as wills and trusts must be reviewed and, if necessary, modified based on the changes the divorce effects. The federal estate tax marital deduction will no longer be available to the taxpayer. The divorced persons may need to reconsider choices for estate representatives (administrator or executor) as well as legal guardianship for minor children. Estate planning alternatives for children may need to be reconsidered and the establishment of trusts and other legal instruments executed. Property, such as a home, retirement plans, and other assets may need to be re-titled and beneficiary designations changed. Jointly held property may need to be distributed and/or re-titled. It is also important to consider the consequences of remarriage on the family. This is particularly important where there are children from a prior marriage(s). Parents need to consider children from all marriages in planning for the disposition of their assets.

TABLE 11-1
Age at Time of Divorce

Age	Number of People	Percent of All Divorces
25–29	217,293	19%
30–34	222,713	20%
35–39	181,339	16%
40–44	141,845	13%
45–49	84,657	8%
50–54	45,718	4%
55–59	25,347	2%

Source: National Center for Health Statistics; based on 580,111 divorces or 1,110,222 people in 1990

Divorce may leave one or both parties with little or no accumulation of pension benefits or other private sources of retirement income. If the marriage lasted 10 years or longer, divorced persons are eligible for Social Security based on their former spouse's earnings record. In addition, a spouse may be entitled to a portion of the former spouse's retirement benefits if the divorce decree includes a qualified domestic relations order. Qualified domestic relations orders are judgments, decrees, or orders issued by state courts that allow a participant's plan assets to be used for marital property rights, child support, or alimony payments to a former spouse or dependent.

PAYMENTS IN CONNECTION WITH SEPARATION OR DIVORCE

Alimony or Separate Maintenance Payments

alimony
separate mainten-
ance payments

The basic rule for alimony or separate maintenance payments is that they are includible in the gross income of the payee. Correspondingly, alimony payments includible in the gross income of the payee are deductible for income tax purposes from the gross income of the payer. The term *alimony* or *separate maintenance payments* means payments that are

- received by or on behalf of a spouse under a divorce or separation agreement
- not designated under the divorce or separation agreement as payments for the support of minor children, which are not includible in the gross income of the payee spouse and not deductible by the payer spouse
- not required under the divorce or separation agreement to be made for any period or in any other form after the death of the payee spouse and are not in fact so paid, and
- are made in cash or cash equivalent

In the case of spouses who are legally separated under a legal decree of divorce or of separate maintenance, in order for payments to qualify as alimony the payee spouse and the payer spouse must not be members of the same household at the time the payment is made.

Because of the requirement that alimony payments be made in cash, such benefits as rent-free occupancy of a home by one spouse and the couple's children will not be treated as alimony payments for tax purposes.

Excess "Front-Loading" of Alimony Payments

If a payer makes "excess" alimony payments, a special rule applies to include the excess payment in the gross income of the payer in the third post separation year. At first glance, it seems illogical to include a payment in the income of the taxpayer who made the payment. However, the inclusion of an excess payment in the payer's income eliminates the prior tax benefit of the deduction that was claimed for the payment before it was characterized as an excess payment. Correspondingly, if there is an "excess" alimony payment includible in the payer's income, the payee spouse receives a deduction for such amount that was previously included in his or her gross income to balance the tax treatment of the excess payment. The purpose of these rules is to prevent taxpayers from characterizing property settlements as alimony for tax purposes.

The calculation of an "excess" alimony payment is based on the relative amounts of the payments made during the first three post separation years. In computing the "excess" alimony payment, one starts with the second year payment. To the extent that the second year's payment exceeds the combination of the third post separation year's payment plus $15,000, the excess is classified as an "excess alimony payment" and added to the income of the payer. In addition, for the first post-separation tax year, the "excess" payment is computed by taking the average of the alimony payments in the second and third post-separation year (as adjusted by any recapture from the second year's payment) and adding $15,000 to that figure. Any alimony payment for the first post-separation year that is in excess of that amount is the "excess alimony payment." This combination of the second and first year payment calculations represents the total "excess alimony payment" included in the income of the payer and deductible by the payee in the third post separation year.

Example: Roberta has paid her former husband, Bobby, alimony in each of the 3 years since their divorce settlement. In the first year Roberta paid Bobby $100,000 and deducted that amount on her tax return. Bobby included the $100,000 in his gross income for that year. In the second post separation year, the payment was $50,000. In the third year, it was $25,000. The second year payment exceeds the third year payment plus $15,000 by $10,000. The average of the payments for the second and third post separation years is $32,500 [($50,000 + $25,000 − $10,000) ÷ 2]. To this amount $15,000 is added for a total of $47,500. Any alimony payment in excess of $47,500 for the first year is an excess payment. Therefore Roberta's excess alimony payment for the first post separation year is $52,500

($100,000 − $47,500); for the second post separation year it is $10,000. Roberta will have to include $62,500 in her income in the third post separation year. Bobby will receive a corresponding deduction in that year to equalize the tax treatment of the excess alimony payments.

If either spouse dies before the end of the third post separation year, or if either spouse remarries before the end of that year and payments cease as a result of such event, then the front-loading rules for excess alimony payments do not apply.

Treatment of Child Support Payments

As stated above, payments for support of minor children are not treated as alimony for tax purposes. Such payments are not deductible by the payer spouse and not includible in the gross income of the payee spouse. Payments are treated as child support to the extent that the terms of the applicable divorce or separation agreement fix or designate them as such. For purposes of this rule, a provision in the agreement calling for a reduction in payments based on certain specified contingencies relating to a child is considered to be designating such payments as child support. These contingencies include a reduction in payments happening at the time or associated with the time when a child attains a specified age, marries, leaves school, or dies. The amount of the reduction in the payment that would result from the occurrence of one of these contingencies under the agreement is the amount treated as child support for tax purposes.

The application of the terms of the divorce agreement to fix certain payments as child support provides certainty for planning for the tax consequences of periodic payments. Under these rules, both parties can be confident of the applicable tax treatment. In fact, the divorce or separation agreement may also provide that payments that are not child support under the contingency rules will not be treated as alimony for tax purposes. The tax law respects such a characterization according to the intent of the parties. Therefore spouses can basically choose whether or not they wish to have payments deductible by the payer and taxable to the payee.

Use of Life Insurance Arrangements in Property Settlements

Life insurance contracts will often be involved in property settlement agreements incident to a divorce. The protection afforded by life insurance coverage may be an important component of the settlement. Perhaps the most common arrangement is to transfer the ownership of an existing life policy that insures the life of one spouse to the other spouse. The transfer of the policy itself does not have income tax consequences for either spouse regardless of the policy's cash value. Such a transfer is neither alimony nor child support, but a nontaxable transfer of property incident to a divorce.

However, if the spouse who transferred the policy is obligated to continue to pay premiums on the transferred policy, the payment of such premiums is generally treated as an alimony payment. The same is true for premiums paid on other insurance coverages that benefit the other spouse.

The transfer of a life insurance policy will not cause the subsequent payment of death benefits to be subject to income tax under the "transfer-for-value." Transfers incident to divorce are not subject to the transfer for value rule. Therefore such death benefits retain their income-tax-free character.

Alternatively, the ownership of an existing policy might be retained by the insured spouse, while premium payments continue to be made by the policy owner spouse with the other spouse named as policy beneficiary. In such a case, the payments of the premiums by the policy owner spouse are not alimony payments and are not deductible. Clearly, the ownership rights of the insured spouse may be compromised by a provision in the divorce agreement requiring him or her to pay premiums and/or to maintain the other spouse as the death beneficiary under the policy. Even so, the payment of premiums in such a situation does not constitute alimony payments. As in the case of a transferred policy, a subsequent payment of death benefits from a policy under such an arrangement will not be subject to income tax under the transfer-for-value rule.

A third possible arrangement is to set up a new life insurance policy that insures the life of one spouse and is owned by the other spouse. The policy owner spouse can pay premiums on the new policy and have death benefit protection in the event of the former spouse's death. A portion of alimony payments received from the former spouse could be used to fund the premium obligation.

Other Financial Planning Implications of Divorce

The divorce situation also presents opportunities in regard to retirement planning. When a divorce occurs, spouses may be entitled to pension benefits or other employee benefits provided by the spouse's workplace. When IRAs, 401(k)s, and other individually controlled retirement assets are split, the question frequently arises as to where these sums should be reinvested. Should money remain with the same institution or are better returns or security available elsewhere? An opportunity exists to roll over funds into accumulation vehicles that are part of your portfolio.

Medical coverage should also be discussed. Under the federal COBRA law, a former spouse may continue coverage under a working spouse's plan if the former spouse works for a firm with 20 or more employees. These premiums may be very high. The spouse may also wish to establish a separate identity as soon as possible. Your health portfolio of products may be called into action.

In addition, divorce impacts not only the parties involved but their parents as well, both on emotional and financial planning levels. This could result in the unintended result of inherited property falling into the hands of "hostile" ex-relatives and strangers.

Assets acquired during a marriage including retirement savings, a home and investments are generally considered marital assets subject to more or less equal division. Inheritances are generally excluded from this even split. However, inherited property converted to joint property loses this protection.

For example, during a second marriage, an individual might use inherited money to purchase a house in joint name. Should a divorce occur, a second spouse would have rights in this property. The property could, in fact, pass to a perfect stranger upon the second spouse's remarriage. Parents may wish to protect their children by restricting access to their inheritance. A trust may serve this purpose.

PLANNING FOR NONTRADITIONAL COUPLES AND FAMILIES

Today the traditional family of husband, wife and children, the nuclear family, finds itself surrounded by a variety of other living arrangements. Only 24 percent of the 105 million U.S. households consist of married couples with children. (That figure includes households with remarried parents and blended families; given the country's high divorce rate, the percentage of single-marriage households is even smaller.) In their place is an ever-widening variety of households: divorced parents raising children alone, stepparents sharing blended families, singles, widows and widowers, adoptive parents, same-sex partners with or without children, grandparents caring for grandchildren, adult children caring for aging parents, and so on. As nontraditional living arrangements become commonplace, and with different financial issues emerging, it is important to review the financial aspects of these relationships.

Our Legal System Favors Traditional Families

There are many different aspects of financial planning that are affected by laws largely created with the traditional nuclear family in mind. More than ever, planning methods and software programs modeled on a traditional household do not apply. There are nearly 1,400 rights and benefits of marriage at the federal and state levels, many relating to financial matters, yet these nontraditional individuals cannot currently take advantage of them.

Federal benefits related to income tax, gifting, estate taxes, Social Security benefits, IRAs, and retirement plans governed by ERISA are still out of reach, because under the Federal Defense of Marriage Act nonmarried persons are seen legally as strangers.

Unmarried Couples

Unmarried couples face many legal difficulties, starting with the home in which they live. For example, if one partner owns the home and wants to put his or her partner's name on the title (thereby sharing ownership), the donor is subject to gift taxes. If the house was worth $200,000 and the unmarried partner was to become joint owner, there would be a potential gift tax (on any amount over $12,000). Married couples, on the other hand, are able to transfer property from one partner to the other without being subject to gift taxes. Unmarried couples should consider a domestic partnership agreement, outlining the handling of assets while indicating what assets were acquired both before and subsequent to the relationship. The agreement can also address the issue of household expenses and ownership of real estate. One common way for unmarried couples to own real estate is through "joint tenancy with rights of survivorship," whereby, if one owner dies, 100 percent of the property passes automatically to the other person by operation of law. Another option, "tenants in common," allows each person to own an undivided interest in the property, permitting each party to bequeath his or her share of the property to someone other than the partner (if desired).

Estate tax laws are also more favorable for married couples. First, there is the unlimited marital deduction, which prevents estate as well as gift taxes between spouses. State inheritance taxes on money passed from one unmarried partner to the other may also be imposed. The adviser should be sure that proper legal instruments are executed, because under intestate laws the unmarried partner would be left out. In most states, without a legal spouse or heirs, the state distributes the assets to the closest relative. The partner receives nothing unless the will specifies the distribution of assets to that person. Additionally, the unmarried person should have a durable power of attorney and advanced health care directive. Financial powers of attorney may also be recommended to allow the partner management rights over monetary matters. Life insurance needs would be basically the same and just as important, if not more important, as in traditional relationships. A more comprehensive discussion appears later in the chapter under "Estate Planning Involving Nontraditional Living Arrangements."

Retirement planning should be done separately. In an unmarried relationship, if the relationship ends, one partner may have a retirement plan and the other may not, and there are limitations on what that partner could get, if anything, without going to court. Nontraditional couples also need to consider that they will not benefit from their partner's Social Security and may not benefit from their partner's pension.

Psychological Factors

There are many psychological factors to which the adviser should be sensitive, based on the life situation of these various relationships. For example, there may be other family members who are unhappy with the relationship. In the case of single or widowed persons, there may be feelings of isolation and vulnerability resulting in a lack of trust. They may fear becoming dependent on children or other family members as they age. Divorced persons may have conflicts and other negative emotions in dealing with a former spouse. In unmarried situations, one partner may want the other to show some financial commitment to the relationship, yet the one with more income or assets may be reluctant to do so.

As nontraditional family arrangements continue to proliferate, advisers must become aware of the issues that may impact these relationships.

UNDERSTANDING AND CAPITALIZING ON INCOME TAX BENEFITS FOR PARENTS OF CHILDREN WITH SPECIAL NEEDS[*]

As the number of children diagnosed with autism, Asperger's syndrome, and other neurological disorders skyrockets, the disruption of the lives of all those concerned is unmistakable—as are the costs of providing care for the special needs child. Further complicating the situation, parents with special needs children are often unaware of the substantial tax benefits that are available to them and forgo hundreds, if not thousands, of dollars in potential tax deductions and reductions in their tax liability. Michael A. O'Connor, an attorney who has written extensively on this topic, believes that 15 to 30 percent of families with a disabled child have one or more unclaimed tax benefits (http://www.wrightslaw.com/info/tax.2005.benefits.oconnor.htm). Among these potential tax benefits are deductions or credits for medical expenses, special instruction, child and dependent care, and adoption costs.

[*] A special thank you to Professors W. Richard Sherman of Saint Joseph's University and James F. Ivers III of The American College. Portions of this section were reprinted and updated with permission from *Fundamentals of Income Taxation,* sixth edition, by James F. Ivers III; "Individual Income Tax Credits" pp. 235–242. Copyright 2005, The American College Press, Bryn Mawr, PA. This section appeared as a two-part series article in the November and December 2006 issues of *Exceptional Parent.*

Special Instruction Qualifying as Medical Expense Deductions

In general, costs related to providing a child's traditional education are not considered medical care and, therefore, are not deductible as a medical expense. However, according to Treasury Regulation 1.213-1(e)(1)(v), the unreimbursed cost of attending a special school for the mentally or physically handicapped is deductible as a medical expense if the principal reason for the individual's attendance is to alleviate the handicap through the resources of the school or institution. This deduction may also include amounts paid for lodging, meals, transportation, and the cost of ordinary education incidental to the special services provided by the school. Also, any costs incurred for the supervision, care, treatment, and training of a physically and/or mentally handicapped individual are deductible if provided by the institution.

The Rationale Behind the Special Education and Training Deduction

Under U.S. law, all children are entitled to an equal and appropriate (public) education. However, many public schools do not have special programs and/or facilities to handle the needs of mentally and/or physically handicapped children. As a result, it is sometimes necessary for mentally or physically handicapped children to attend special schools where the focus is not only on education, but also on alleviating the handicap of the child. The cost of these special schools is not always covered by the government or the school district and, therefore, the parents must pay for all or a portion of the tuition. If the school qualifies as a special school, the entire unreimbursed cost (subject to the 7.5 percent adjusted gross income or "AGI" limitation) incurred by the parents is deductible as a medical expense.

However, parents who are eligible to participate in tax-advantaged plans established in their workplace for funding medical expenses, such as flexible spending accounts or health savings accounts, can set aside limited amounts of money to finance medical care expenses on a pretax basis while bypassing the 7.5 percent AGI limitation.

Special Schools

special school

A *special school* is distinguishable from a regular school by the substantive content of its curriculum. A special school may offer ordinary education, but it must be incidental to enabling the student to compensate for or overcome a handicap so that he or she will be prepared for future normal education or normal living. A special school is not determined by the institution as a whole, but by the nature of the services received by the individual for whom a medical care deduction is sought. The IRS considers the medical facilities and therapeutic orientation of a school as critical factors in determining whether a school is a special school for a qualifying medical care deduction. Case law and IRS administrative rulings reveal a litany of examples considered special schools by the IRS:

- schools for teaching Braille to the blind or lip reading to the deaf
- schools for training the mentally retarded
- a military school that accepted a physically and mentally handicapped student (the school gave personal daily attention to the student to improve the student's low attention span)
- a boarding school recommended by a psychiatrist (the school had psychiatrists, psychologists, and social workers who developed a special program for each student)
- schools for average and above average students with learning disabilities that provide an environment in which they can adjust to a normal competitive classroom situation
- a regular school's curriculum that is specially designed to accommodate the needs of handicapped children with IQ scores ranging from 50 to 75

Furthermore, regular schools with special curricula can be classified as a special school for an individual. For example, in one Revenue Ruling, the school in question had a special curriculum for mentally disabled children with the special curriculum representing a separate component of the school's activities. Since the school's special education curriculum was a severable aspect of the school's activities, the IRS ruled that the special curriculum was a special school (Rev. Rul. 70-285, 1970-1 CB 52).

In another case, the IRS specifically ruled in Revenue Ruling 78-340 (1978-2 CB 124) that a taxpayer whose child suffers from severe learning disabilities caused by a neurological disorder (that is, autism spectrum disorder) may deduct as a medical expense amounts paid for tuition and related fees for the child's education at a special school that has a program designed to "mainstream" these children so they can return to a regular school. The Ruling further held that amounts paid for private tutoring (that is, therapeutic and behavioral support services) by a specially trained teacher qualified to deal with severe learning disabilities is also deductible. However, both the special school and tutoring need to be recommended by a physician.

In a Letter Ruling issued in 2005, the IRS expanded the definition of special schooling to include tuition for programs enabling dyslexic children to deal with their condition. The IRS ruled that the children were attending the school for the principal purpose of obtaining medical care in the form of special education. The special education was required for the years in which the children were diagnosed as having a medical condition (including dyslexia) that impaired their ability to learn. As a result, the IRS ruled in favor of a medical expense deduction for the tuition paid to the school (Letter Ruling 200521003).

Medical Expense Deduction for Medical Conferences and Seminars

Parents of special needs children often attend medical conferences and seminars in order to learn more about their child's disability. Using the authority of Revenue Ruling 2000-24 (2000-19 I.R.B. 963), the amounts paid for the registration fees and travel expenses are deductible as medical expenses. However, parents should obtain the recommendation of their child's doctor to insure their medical deduction. In addition, the Ruling did not extend medical care deductibility to any meals and/or lodging costs incurred while attending the conference. Furthermore, the conference or seminar must deal specifically with the medical condition from which the child suffers not just general health and well-being issues. As with the special instruction and other medical expenses, the aggregate amount of all medical expenses incurred must exceed 7.5 percent of the taxpayers' AGI to be deductible.

Deductions for Dependents

In order to claim a dependency exemption ($3,400 for 2007), a taxpayer must satisfy a five-prong test. The taxpayer must provide more than half of the dependent's support (the Support Test). The dependent must be a "qualifying relative" or member of the taxpayer's household for the entire year (the Relationship Test). The dependent's gross income cannot exceed the exemption amount ($3,400 for 2007; the Gross Income Test). If married, the dependent cannot file a joint return for the year (the Joint Return Test). The dependent must be a U.S. citizen or resident, or resident of Canada or Mexico (the Citizenship or Residency Test). With passage of the Working Families Tax Relief Act of 2004 (taking effect for 2005 and years thereafter), the definition of a "qualifying child" or a "qualifying relative" was clarified to provide a uniform definition for purposes of dependency exemptions, child tax, dependent care, and earned income tax credits. Under this definition, in addition to meeting the relationship test (taxpayer's child, stepchild, eligible foster child, or descendent (for example, grandchild) or taxpayer's brother, sister, or descendent (for example, niece, nephew), a "qualifying child" must meet any ONE of the following three requirements:

- The individual must be under the age of 19 at year end; OR
- The individual must be a full-time student under the age of 24 at the end of the year (qualifying "students" must be enrolled as a "full-time" student during any part of 5 calendar months during the year)

- The individual must be totally and permanently disabled at any time during the year.

It is important to note that grandparents, uncles, aunts, brothers, and sisters satisfy this "relationship" test and, therefore, may be allowed to claim the dependency exemption for a "qualifying child" who is totally or permanently disabled, regardless of the age of that child.

Child Tax Credit

In addition to the deductions mentioned above, certain credits may also be available to parents of special needs children. The most common of these credits is the $1,000 credit that is allowed for the taxpayer's "qualifying child" under the age of 17. The definition of a "qualifying child" used for purposes of claiming a dependency exemption under IRC Section 151 is also used for purposes of claiming the child tax credit. Consequently, the taxpayer claiming the dependency exemption for the child is the individual entitled to the credit. This is important to consider in cases involving divorced, separated, or unmarried parents.

Phaseout of the Tax Credit for Children

The credit is phased out for upper-income taxpayers. The phaseout occurs based on the taxpayer's adjusted gross income (AGI) with certain minor modifications ("modified adjusted gross income"). The phaseout begins at the following levels of modified AGI:

Married filing joint return	$110,000
Married filing separately	$ 55,000
Unmarried taxpayers	$ 75,000

The otherwise allowable credit is phased out by $50 for each $1,000 (or fraction thereof) by which modified AGI exceeds the threshold amount. For example, a married couple filing jointly with one child this year would have no child credit if their modified AGI was more than $129,000. This is because their AGI exceeds $110,000 by $19,000 plus a fraction of $1,000. Therefore the credit is phased out by 20 x $50, or $1,000, the total amount of the credit.

The credit is phased out sequentially (rather than simultaneously) per child for taxpayers with more than one child. Therefore, taxpayers with more than one child will have a larger "phaseout range" for the credits. This is different from the phaseout of dependency exemptions for upper-income taxpayers. (Exemptions are phased out simultaneously regardless of the number of exemptions claimed. For example, in 2007, the phaseout of personal exemptions begins at AGI of $234,600 for married couples filing a joint return.)

In addition, the child credit is refundable to the extent of the greater of

- 15 percent of earned income above $11,750 for 2007, or
- for taxpayers with three or more qualifying children, the excess of the taxpayer's Social Security taxes for the tax year over the earned income credit for the year (IRC Section 24(d)).

Tax Credit for Adoption Expenses

An Adoption Credit was signed into law in 2002. This credit of up to $11,390 per eligible child (for 2007) is available for qualified expenses paid in the course of adopting a child. This figure is subject to annual inflation adjustments. The limit on the credit is a cumulative limit per child. In other words, no more than the maximum amount may be claimed for any one child regardless of the number of years for which the credit is claimed for that child. Nevertheless, an additional credit or credits may be claimed for the adoption of more than one child. In addition, the credit has a unique application for adoptions of children with special needs. Similar to other credits, the adoption credit is phased out for upper-income taxpayers. However, the phaseout income level is significantly higher than other credits.

Definition of an "Eligible Child"

eligible child

An *eligible child* is a person who is either under the age of 18 or is physically or mentally incapable of self-care. A child with special needs is defined as a citizen or resident of the United States who is determined by state authorities to be unable to be placed for adoption without adoption assistance. Requirements for such a determination by state authorities include findings that the child should not be returned to his or her biological parents, and that there is a specific factor or condition that makes the child unable to be placed without adoption assistance.

Qualified Adoption Expenses

It is important for individuals considering adoption or in the process of adoption to understand what expenses qualify for the credit. Qualified adoption expenses include legal fees, court costs, attorney's fees, and other related fees and costs associated with a taxpayer's legal adoption of an eligible child or a child with special needs. However, costs associated with the adoption of a child of the taxpayer's spouse or costs for surrogate parenting arrangements are not qualified expenses for purposes of the credit.

Special Rule for Adoptions of Children With Special Needs

The full amount of the adoption credit is allowed to taxpayers adopting a special needs child regardless of the amount of qualified adoption expenses paid by the taxpayer. This means that taxpayers will be eligible for the maximum credit even if they have little or even no actual adoption expenses. Special needs adoptions are typically less expensive than other adoptions. Congress enacted this provision to assist taxpayers who have decided to adopt special needs children and to encourage these adoptions. The credit will not be available, however, until the year in which the adoption becomes final.

For adoptions of children other than special needs children, the amount of the credit will continue to depend on the amount of qualified expenses.

When Is the Credit Claimed?

For tax years in which an adoption becomes final, the taxpayer is allowed to claim the credit for expenses paid during that year. For years in which qualified expenses are paid but in which the adoption does not become final, the taxpayer must claim the credit for those expenses for the tax year following the year in which the expenses are paid. If expenses are paid in a year following the year the adoption becomes final, the expenses may be claimed for the year in which they are made.

Foreign adoptions or adoption of a child with special needs qualify for the credit only if the adoption becomes final and must be claimed in that year even if paid in a prior year.

There is a 5-year carryover period available for taxpayers whose allowable adoption credit exceeds their tax liability for the year the credit is first allowable.

Phaseout of Credit

The adoption credit is phased out for taxpayers with adjusted gross income exceeding $170,820. The credit is completely phased out at $40,000 above the threshold. Adjusted gross income for this purpose is determined with certain minor modifications similar to those used for the tax credit for children.

To calculate the amount of the credit that is phased out, divide the amount of the taxpayer's adjusted gross income in excess of $170,820 by $40,000. Then multiply the resulting percentage by the otherwise allowable amount of the credit.

Related Income Exclusion

In planning for the adoption credit, it is important to note that an income exclusion is available for amounts paid by a taxpayer's employer for qualified adoption expenses on behalf of the taxpayer/employee. Such amounts must be furnished under a nondiscriminatory adoption assistance program. However, the exclusion for adopting a special needs child applies regardless of whether the employee has qualified adoption expenses. The rules defining and limiting this exclusion for adoption assistance payments are similar to the rules just described for application of the adoption credit. For example, the dollar amounts of the available exclusion are the same as the dollar amounts of the credit. Any amounts excluded from gross income under such a program are not eligible to be treated as qualified adoption expenses for purposes of the adoption credit.

Child and Dependent Care Credit

This tax credit applies to expenses paid by individual taxpayers for the care of their dependents if the expenses are necessary to allow them to be gainfully employed. The amount of the credit currently ranges from 20 to 35 percent of qualifying expenses based on the taxpayer's income level. The qualifying expenses on which the credit percentages are based are subject to dollar amount limitations as explained below. The credit was enacted generally for the purpose of providing a tax credit for working parents with children in day-care facilities.

Eligible Expenses for the Credit

As stated above, for the credit to be available, the expenses must be incurred to allow the taxpayer to be gainfully employed. The expenses must be paid by a taxpayer who has a household in which one or more "qualifying individuals" reside for more than half of the taxable year. Expenses must be paid either for household services or specifically for the care of a qualifying individual. A qualifying individual must fall within one of the following definitions:

- the taxpayer's "qualifying child" who is under the age of 13
- an individual who is physically or mentally incapable of caring for himself or herself and is also the taxpayer's dependent for tax purposes
- the taxpayer's spouse who is physically or mentally incapable of caring for himself or herself

As a general rule, the expenses must be paid for services rendered inside the taxpayer's home, unless the services are for the care of either the taxpayer's dependent child who is under the age of 13 (that is, day-care services), or another qualifying individual who regularly spends at least 8 hours per day in the taxpayer's household. As indicated, if the child has a disability and requires supervision, the age limit is waived. For example, an autistic 16-year-old with behavioral disorders who is incapable of self-care and cannot be left unattended would qualify his or her parents for this credit. In no event, however, will expenses paid for an overnight camp be eligible expenses for the credit.

In addition, child-care related expenses are disallowed if paid to certain related individuals. Eligible expenses do not include payments for care provided by a child of the taxpayer who is under the age of 19 (such as a sister or brother of the qualifying individual). Also, eligible expenses do not include those paid for services rendered by any individual who is a dependent of the taxpayer for dependency exemption purposes. The purpose of this rule is to prevent child-care payments made to certain family members from generating a tax credit.

There is a limit on the amount of expenses that can be counted in calculating the allowable credit. For taxpayers caring for one qualifying individual, the maximum amount is $3,000 per year. If there are two or more qualifying individuals, the maximum amount is $6,000. Qualifying expenses may not exceed the amount of the taxpayer's earned income for the year.

Calculation of the Credit

The allowable credit currently ranges from 20 to 35 percent of eligible expenses. The allowable percentage is reduced by one percent for each $2,000 (or fraction thereof) of adjusted gross income in excess of $15,000. The credit is fully reduced to 20 percent once the taxpayer's AGI exceeds $43,000.

Coordination With Dependent-Care Assistance Programs

The same eligible expenses cannot be used for both the dependent-care credit and the income tax exclusion for amounts received from an employer-provided dependent-care assistance program. In addition, if a taxpayer is a participant in such a program, the maximum amount of qualifying expenses for credit purposes is reduced dollar for dollar paid from the employer program and excluded from the taxpayer's gross income. As a result, taxpayers are often forced to choose between the income tax exclusion for such plans and the dependent-care credit. Generally speaking, if a married taxpayer or head of household is in a marginal tax bracket of 25 percent or higher, the exclusion provides a more efficient method of funding dependent-care expenses than the otherwise available credit amount.

Additional Rules for Married Couples

Special rules apply to married couples claiming the dependent-care credit. These rules include:

- Married couples must generally file a joint return to be eligible for the credit. However, if the spouses live apart for the last 6 months of the taxable year, the credit may be available even if separate returns are filed.
- Eligible expenses are limited to the earned income of the spouse with the lower earned income. Therefore, generally speaking, both spouses must be working to claim the credit, although there is no requirement of full-time employment.
- A significant exception to the rule just described involves spouses who either are full-time students for at least 5 calendar months during the year or are incapable of self-care during the year. Such spouses are currently deemed to have a monthly earned income of $250 for each month during which they are either students or incapable of self-care. If there are two or more qualifying individuals in the household, then such spouses are currently deemed to have $500 per month of earned income.

Earned Income Tax Credit

The idea behind the Earned Income Tax Credit (EITC) is to encourage economically disadvantaged individuals to work by partially offsetting the Social Security taxes on wages. Appropriately, the EITC is not available to taxpayers who have unearned income (that is, dividends, interest, gains of sales of securities) above a specified threshold ($2,900 in 2007). Families filing a married joint return with adjusted gross income in 2007 under $39,783 ($2,000 less than taxpayers filing as single or head of household) may qualify for the Earned Income Tax Credit (EITC) based on the presence of two "qualifying children" in the taxpayer's home. For EITC purposes, a "qualifying child" uses the same definition as for the dependency exemption—namely, a biological child, adopted child, stepchild, or foster child who resided with the taxpayer for more than 6 months during the calendar year and is under age 19 at the end of the year, or who is under age 24 and a full-time student. Finally, a severely disabled child is a "qualifying child" regardless of age, even into adulthood, as long as the child continues to live with his or her parent(s). Note that a "qualifying child" for EITC does not have to meet the other requirements (that is, support, gross income, joint return, citizenship) for a dependency exemption. EITC benefits are as high as $4,716 for families with two or more qualifying children for 2007, although the average EITC is generally less.

Concluding Comments in Planning for Special Needs Individuals

The number of individuals with special needs is escalating at unprecedented rates in our society. Just one example of this is the Center for Disease Control's estimate that up to 500,000 individuals under the age of 21 have an Autism Spectrum Disorder (ASD). Recent statistics have indicated that one out of 150 children is born with an autism spectrum disorder. (http://www.cdc.gov/ncbddd/autism/asd_common.htm).This may simply be a matter of better recognition of the special needs. After all, it was not until 1991 that autism was added as a "special education exception" and, therefore, was not included in previously reported statistics. Now autism is one of the most commonly diagnosed disabilities in the United States. Whether or not the increased numbers are due to under-reporting, they are already beginning to impact state and local governmentally funded programs that now face shortfalls, which then forces parents to absorb more of the costs of their children's medical care.

Advisers and parents of these special needs children should be aware that specific rules apply to each of these tax issues. For example, in order to claim the child's educational expenses, parents must carefully examine the facts regarding medical expense deductions in facilities that are primarily educational and not special schools. Similarly, the deductions for medical conference expenses are case specific. Even the generally available credits for dependent care and earned income have multiple requirements and limitations. In the end, it is important to understand the substantial tax benefits that are available to those caring for children with special needs.

DISABILITY, ACCIDENT, AND HEALTH INSURANCE BENEFITS

In this section, we review both the basic classifications of disability insurance and the tax implications in structuring ownership of a disability income policy. In addition, some tax considerations of accident and health plans are reviewed.

Why Do We Need Disability Insurance?

While the need for life insurance receives a great amount of attention, the need for disability insurance is often obscured and rarely discussed. But studies show that

- A 30-year-old has a 24 percent chance of being disabled for at least 90 days before reaching age 65.
- At age 45, the chance of suffering a disability is reduced to only 21 percent.

- A person disabled for 90 days will probably go on to be disabled for at least 4 years.

Despite these statistics, very few people have adequate protection against long-term disability. They may purchase life insurance for their family's protection, but they have largely neglected their own income protection, even though the odds of a young or middle-aged person becoming disabled are far greater than the odds of dying. Tables 11-2 and 11-3 depict the relation of age to disability and the duration of the disability according to age.

TABLE 11-2
Number of People Who Will Be Disabled for at Least 90 Days Before Age 65

At Age	
30	24% — 1 out of 4
35	23% — 3 out of 13
40	22% — 2 out of 9
45	21% — 1 out of 5
50	18% — 2 out of 11
55	11% — 1 out of 9
60	9% — 1 out of 11

Source: *Transactions, Society of Actuaries 1981 Reports*, p. 265. Reprinted with permission.
(Editor's note: This is the last major study of these disability outcomes, partially because the relationships have not changed, and the study is expensive and time consuming.

TABLE 11-3
Average Duration of Disability That Lasts Over 90 Days

Age	Duration
Under 40	4 years
40–44	4 years, 4 months
45–49	4 years, 7 months
50–54	4 years, 6 months
55–59	3 years, 6 months
60–64	1 year, 9 months

Source: *Transactions, Society of Actuaries 1981 Reports*, p. 265. Reprinted with permission.

Table 11-4 illustrates someone's total income potential from his or her current age to age 65 for a number of income levels and ages. The table does not take into account any increases in salary that would change the projected figure at age 65. Even a 25-year-old currently earning $2,000 a month has the potential to earn nearly $1 million by the time he or she reaches 65.

These figures make a dramatic statement about the need for disability income insurance since the risk of disability is greater than the risk of death during most of people's working lives. Fortunately, there is a product to protect against these risks—disability income insurance.

TABLE 11-4
Possible Earnings to Age 65

Age	$2,000	$3,000	$4,000	$5,000	$6,000	$7,000	$8,000	$9,000	$10,000
25	960,000	1,440,000	1,920,000	2,400,000	2,880,000	3,360,000	3,840,000	4,320,000	4,800,000
26	936,000	1,404,000	1,872,000	2,340,000	2,808,000	3,276,000	3,744,000	4,212,000	4,680,000
27	912,000	1,368,000	1,824,000	2,280,000	2,736,000	3,192,000	3,648,000	4,104,000	4,560,000
28	888,000	1,332,000	1,776,000	2,220,000	2,664,000	3,108,000	3,552,000	3,996,000	4,440,000
29	864,000	1,296,000	1,728,000	2,160,000	2,529,000	3,024,000	3,456,000	3,888,000	4,320,000
30	840,000	1,260,000	1,680,000	2,100,000	2,520,000	2,940,000	3,360,000	3,780,000	4,200,000
31	816,000	1,224,000	1,632,000	2,040,000	2,448,000	2,856,000	3,264,000	3,672,000	4,080,000
32	792,000	1,188,000	1,584,000	1,980,000	2,376,000	2,772,000	3,168,000	3,564,000	3,960,000
33	768,000	1,152,000	1,536,000	1,920,000	2,304,000	2,688,000	3,072,000	3,456,000	3,840,000
34	744,000	1,116,000	1,488,000	1,860,000	2,232,000	2,604,000	2,976,000	3,348,000	3,720,000
35	720,000	1,080,000	1,440,000	1,800,000	2,160,000	2,520,000	2,880,000	3,240,000	3,600,000
36	696,000	1,044,000	1,392,000	1,740,000	2,088,000	2,436,000	2,748,000	3,132,000	3,480,000
37	672,000	1,008,000	1,344,000	1,680,000	2,016,000	2,352,000	2,688,000	3,024,000	3,360,000
38	648,000	972,000	1,296,000	1,620,000	1,944,000	2,268,000	2,592,000	2,916,000	3,240,000
39	624,000	936,000	1,248,000	1,560,000	1,872,000	2,184,000	2,496,000	2,808,000	3,120,000
40	600,000	900,000	1,200,000	1,500,000	1,800,000	2,100,000	2,400,000	2,700,000	3,000,000
41	576,000	864,000	1,152,000	1,440,000	1,728,000	2,016,000	2,304,000	2,592,000	2,880,000
42	552,000	828,000	1,104,000	1,380,000	1,656,000	1,932,000	2,208,000	2,484,000	2,760,000
43	528,000	792,000	1,056,000	1,320,000	1,584,000	1,848,000	2,112,000	2,376,000	2,640,000
44	504,000	756,000	1,008,000	1,260,000	1,512,000	1,764,000	2,016,000	2,268,000	2,560,000
45	480,000	720,000	960,000	1,200,000	1,440,000	1,680,000	1,920,000	2,160,000	2,400,000
46	456,000	684,000	912,000	1,140,000	1,368,000	1,596,000	1,824,000	2,052,000	2,280,000
47	432,000	648,000	864,000	1,080,000	1,296,000	1,512,000	1,728,000	1,944,000	2,160,000
48	408,000	612,000	816,000	1,020,000	1,224,000	1,428,000	1,632,000	1,836,000	2,040,000
49	384,000	576,000	768,000	960,000	1,152,000	1,344,000	1,536,000	1,728,000	1,920,000
50	360,000	540,000	720,000	900,000	1,080,000	1,260,000	1,440,000	1,620,000	1,800,000
51	336,000	504,000	672,000	840,000	1,008,000	1,176,000	1,344,000	1,512,000	1,680,000
52	312,000	468,000	624,000	780,000	936,000	1,092,000	1,248,000	1,404,000	1,560,000
53	288,000	432,000	576,000	720,000	864,000	1,008,000	1,152,000	1,296,000	1,440,000
54	264,000	396,000	528,000	660,000	792,000	924,000	1,056,000	1,188,000	1,320,000

Source: Based on a person's current monthly income

Understanding the Needs of the Insured

Disability income protection is usually offered through either group or individual plans. Group coverage defines exactly what is covered and is typically offered by an employer or association.

Individuals

Income producers need to protect their incomes in the event of disability. The temptation is to rely on government programs such as Social Security Disability Income (SSDI), but the availability of disability benefits through these programs is highly restricted. In order to qualify for benefits, the disability must prevent the worker from engaging in any substantially gainful employment and must also be expected to result in death or be expected to last at least 12 months. Benefits do not begin until the sixth full calendar month of disability. Even more alarming, however, is the report that as many as 70 percent of the disability claims submitted to Social Security have been denied, and benefits have been terminated for many hundreds of recipients.

When an income earner dies, there is generally a reduction in the surviving family's expenses if the deceased incurred no large medical expenses. If an income earner is disabled, it is likely that the family's expenses will increase. Not only is the individual still living and generating the normal amounts of expenses, there may be additional medical and rehabilitation expenses associated with the disability. The unfortunate fact is that a person who was once a source of income and support for a family can quickly becomes a financial burden. Not only is income lost, but other assets usually become sources of income replacement, and families may have to sell valuable property and assets below the fair market value. The family lifestyle is often irrevocably altered.

When disability strikes and personal finances are strained, it is frequently thought of as a "living death" for the individual and the family. It is, however, a situation that planners can improve by offering disability income protection to their clients and prospects. Along with providing income replacement for clients at a critical time, advising a client on the optimal form of disability income protection offers an intangible benefit to the planner—peace of mind.

Business Owners

Disability income protection usually interests business owners once they realize the potential financial implications of a personal disability. If the owner is directly involved with running the day-to-day operation of a business, a disability could close the business down completely. Even when the owner can still provide guidance to other employees in the business, it may prove difficult or impossible to keep the operation successful for an extended period of time.

Most business owners reinvest a considerable portion of their income in their businesses. A long-term disability will stop this infusion of cash, leading to serious cash shortages and a weakened financial position. These problems are especially severe to sole proprietorships and partnerships, yet they can be equally damaging to closely held corporations.

In most closely held corporations, a few key shareholders control and operate the business. If one of these individuals is disabled, serious management and operational problems can result. Medical expenses and income continuation difficulties can create serious cash problems for the individual and the business. Beyond this, as in a sole proprietorship or partnership, the other employees may worry about the viability of the firm and their continued employment.

On the other hand, the employees of a business are frequently indispensable to its profitable operation. The loss of a key employee through disability or death can seriously jeopardize the firm's success. As a result, disability income protection can provide practical protection against the problems associated with serious illness or injury to the owners and key employees of businesses. Whether the protection is provided by personal or group plans, disability income insurance should be a high priority. Many products offered in our market place protect the business owner beyond personal coverage. Alternative disability insurance protections include disability buy-out, overhead expense, and key employee protection.

Self-Employed Professionals

While other businesses may be able to use employees to keep operating, self-employed professionals often have nothing to sell beyond their own services and, if disabled, have no way to continue their income. Professionals have substantial investments in their practices or businesses. Beyond the obvious money expended for office equipment and general overhead expenses, professionals have typically invested in advanced, specialized educations and, often, in long periods of apprenticeship at relatively low pay. Professionals also expend a significant amount of time in growing their businesses or practices to the point where financial security is provided. It is during these periods of high income that their investment of both time and money is repaid.

Attorneys, CPAs, physicians, consultants, architects, dentists, engineers, and veterinarians are all usually at substantial risk from the impact of disability on their income earning capacities. At the foundation of a professional person's financial security should be adequate disability income protection.

Understanding the Tax Implications of Various Benefit Plans

Medical and Disability Benefits

Internal Revenue Sections 104 through 106 deals with a variety of benefits that may be received tax free by individuals on account of injuries or sickness. Such benefits include

- medical expense reimbursement plans
- disability policies
- workers' compensation acts
- certain damages
- government disability programs

Medical expense reimbursements from accident and health insurance plans are excluded from gross income to the extent the taxpayer has not claimed a medical expense deduction for the underlying medical costs as an itemized deduction (Schedule A of Form 1040).

Example: Mr. Apple had $10,000 of deductible medical expenses last year. In itemizing his deductions, he deducted a net medical expense of $2,000 (the excess expense after subtracting 7.5 percent of adjusted gross income). This year, he received a medical reimbursement check for $7,500 covering some of the costs incurred last year. Mr. Apple must include $2,000 of the reimbursement as income this year (representing the tax benefit he derived on last year's return). The balance of the reimbursement, $5,500, is excluded from gross income.

A disability policy or income replacement policy protects the insured against a financial loss that may occur if the individual is incapacitated and unable to work. If the taxpayer purchases the policy with after-tax dollars, the entire proceeds from the policy are excluded from gross income.

Example: Tom Hanes missed 12 weeks of work after falling two stories from a building in June. Because of the multiple fractures he suffered, he was unable to work in any capacity until September. As a result, Tom received $8,000 from a disability policy he had purchased several years ago. All of the policy proceeds are tax free because Tom had personally purchased the policy.

Amounts received by an employee under Social Security or workers' compensation as compensation for physical injury or sickness are excluded from gross income. In addition, workers' compensation acts extend to the survivors of a deceased employee and allow the recipients to exclude any benefits received on behalf of the deceased employee.

Government disability payments are also excluded from gross income if the payments (that is, pension, annuity, or similar allowance) are received for the personal physical injuries or sickness of the taxpayer. These awards are tax exempt if attributable to active service in the armed forces of any country, or in the Coast Guard and Geodetic Survey or Public Health Service, or as a disability annuity payable under the Foreign Service Act of 1980.

In addition, the law provides an exclusion for amounts received by an individual as disability income attributable to injuries incurred as a direct result of a terrorist attack. The attack must have occurred while the individual was an employee of the United States and engaged in performing official duties outside of the United States.

Damages

Certain damages may also be excluded from gross income. The exclusion applies to financial awards for damages received because of personal physical injury or sickness. The exclusion is limited to nonpunitive damages. Section 104 prohibits the exclusion of punitive damages. However, an exception to this rule exists for wrongful death cases. If under a state law in effect on September 13, 1995, the only damages awarded in a wrongful death action are punitive damages, then the wrongful death award is excluded from gross income.

Nonpunitive damages for personal injury are currently excludible from gross income only if they are paid on account of a physical injury or sickness. Financial awards related to emotional distress are generally not excludible under current law. The exclusion would apply only if the emotional distress award is attributed to a physical injury or sickness or represents reimbursement for medical expenses arising from the emotional distress. This same logic now applies to the taxation of financial awards for loss of employment, age and gender discrimination, and civil rights violations. The key test for excludibility is physical injury or sickness. Without this requirement, these awards are included in gross income. The exclusion extends to both court awards and settlement agreements received outside of litigation.

Employer-Provided Accident and Health Plans

Employers often contribute to the cost of an employee's accident and health care insurance. The plan will often make payments directly to the employee or health care provider. Under certain conditions, benefits received from the employer-sponsored plan may be excluded from the employee's gross income. IRC Section 105 addresses amounts received under accident and health plans. Employer contributions to accident and health plans are covered under Section 106.

In general, the tax treatment of amounts received under accident and health plans depends on why benefits are paid, who pays the premiums, and how the benefits are computed.

Although Section 104 permits the tax-free receipt of a disability or income replacement policy's proceeds, there is one catch. The exclusion from gross income results from the taxpayer's purchasing of the policy with after-tax dollars. Section 104 is therefore generally addressing self-purchased disability and income replacement policies. However, if the taxpayer's employer pays the premiums on a disability or income replacement policy as a tax-free fringe benefit to the employee, the tax issue regarding policy proceeds changes. Section 105 requires the employee to include the proceeds received from employer-purchased disability and income replacement policies in gross income, unless the employer allows the employee to elect to pay tax currently on the policy premiums paid by the employer.

If the employer and employee share the premium costs of a disability or income replacement policy, only part of the policy's proceeds are excluded from gross income.

The exclusion from gross income is proportional to the employee's after-tax contribution of the policy's premium.

Example:　　　　The ABC Corporation maintains a disability plan. The plan provides for regular wages to employees missing work because of personal injury or sickness. The corporation requires that all employees participate in the premium cost of the policy. Employees are required to contribute 35 percent of the policy's premium cost through after-tax payroll deductions. The balance is paid by the employer and is not taxable to the employees.

　　　　Johnson, an employee, suffered a personal injury during the year. As a result, Johnson missed 6 weeks of work. During his absence, Johnson received $3,000 in disability proceeds under the corporation's plan. Johnson must include $1,950 of the proceeds in gross income. The balance, $1,050, is excluded from gross income. The exclusion (35 percent of $3,000) is proportional to Johnson's premium payments.

As illustrated, the general rule is to tax amounts received for personal injuries or sickness under accident and health plans to employees where the employer pays for the cost of the plan. However, there are two significant exceptions to this general rule:

- amounts expended for medical care
- payments unrelated to absence from work

The first exception excludes from gross income amounts received as reimbursements from an accident or health plan for the medical care of the taxpayer, his or her spouse, or dependents. These benefits are excludible if an insurance company provides the accident and health insurance benefits. However, it should be noted that comprehensive nondiscrimination tests are applied to self-funded (uninsured) medical reimbursement plans.

Example: Sicck Corporation provides all employees with health care insurance. Amy, a Sicck Corporation employee, receives a $500 reimbursement for medical bills incurred during the year. The reimbursement is excluded from gross income even though Sicck Corporation paid the health care insurance premiums.

The second exception excludes payments unrelated to absence from work. If a taxpayer, a spouse, or a dependent incurs an injury that results in permanent disfigurement, loss or loss of using a body part, or loss of a bodily function, then the amounts received under the employer's accident or health care plan are excluded from gross income. For example, benefits paid for the loss of an arm, leg, or other bodily function are tax exempt. In addition, amounts received under an accident policy based on the nature of the injury are tax free. However, as previously stated, no exclusion is permitted if the length of time an employee is absent is a factor in determining the amount of the payment (that is, disability income proceeds).

Example: The Reading Railroad Corporation maintains an accident plan that provides payments for certain injuries. The plan provides for a $15,000 payment in the event an employee loses a limb. John, an employee who lost a leg, receives $15,000 from the corporation's plan. The $15,000 payment is excludible from John's gross income.

Ruling Railroad Corporation's plan also provides for payments of $400 weekly to each employee missing work on account of an injury. The corporation's plan covers employees for a maximum period of 26 weeks, regardless of the employee's injury. John received the maximum benefit ($10,400) under the plan. The entire amount received by John is included in gross income (disability income).

Qualified long-term care insurance is treated as accident or health insurance under Sections 104 through 106 (the related deduction rules appear under Section 213). As a medical expense reimbursement, long-term care reimbursements are excluded from gross income, subject to certain restrictions. For 2007, the exclusion for benefits paid from qualified long-term care insurance contracts is $260 a day per covered individual, as adjusted for inflation. Amounts in excess of the daily exclusion are also excluded from gross income to the extent that actual long-term care expenses exceed the daily benefit and are not otherwise reimbursed. In an employer-provided long-term care insurance plan, amounts received are treated in generally the same way as amounts received for medical care.

An employee's gross income does not include premiums paid by an employer for accident or health care insurance coverage for the employee, the employee's spouse, and the employee's dependents. Section 106 addresses contributions by employers to accident and health plans. This section specifically excludes contributions made by an employer to an accident or health plan to provide compensation, through insurance or otherwise, directly to an employee for personal injuries or sickness. This exclusion applies to both insured and self-funded (uninsured) plans regardless of the number of employees. However, if an employee is indemnified beyond the medical costs incurred under the accident and health insurance plan, the excess reimbursement represents taxable income to the employee.

Contributions continuing after an employee's death or retirement are also excluded under the statute.

In general, the employer may claim a tax deduction for premiums paid for accident and health care coverage for employees.

Self-Funded Medical Reimbursement Plans

self-funded medical reimbursement plan

The tax situation may be different than the above if an employer provides medical expense benefits through a self-funded plan (referred to in Section 105 of the Internal Revenue Code as a self-insured medical reimbursement plan) under which employers either (1) pay the providers of medical care directly or (2) reimburse employees for their medical expenses. If a *self-funded medical reimbursement plan* meets certain nondiscrimination requirements for highly compensated employees, the employer can deduct benefit payments as they are made, and the employee will have no taxable income. If a plan is discriminatory, the employer will still receive an income tax deduction. However, all or a portion of the benefits received by "highly compensated individuals," but not by other employees, will be treated as taxable income. A highly compensated individual is (1) one of the five highest-paid officers of the firm, (2) a shareholder who owns more than 10 percent of the firm's stock, or (3) one of the highest-paid 25 percent of the firm's employees. There are no nondiscrimination rules if a plan is not self-funded and provides benefits through an insurance contract, Blue Cross–Blue Shield plan, HMO, or PPO.

GIFTS, INHERITANCES, AND OTHER WINDFALLS

General Tax Rules

The value of money or property received as a gift, bequest, devise, or inheritance is generally excluded from gross income under IRC Section 102. However, the income from the property received is taxable. If income from property is assigned, the donor of the income is taxable, because income is taxed to the property owner. However, if the donor permanently disposes of the income-producing property, the income generated from the property is taxed to the recipient.

A gift can be defined as any voluntary transfer of property by one person to another that is not made as compensation and in return for which no consideration is given. If there is valuable consideration in money or money's worth for the transfer of the property, the transaction is not treated as a gift—it is a sale. A gift is defined as a gratuitous transfer of property. To be considered a gift, the following elements are essential:

- a donor competent to make the gift
- a donor's clear and unmistakable intention to make the gift

- a donee capable of receiving the gift
- an irrevocable conveyance, assignment, or transfer sufficient to vest legal title to the property in the donee
- a donor's relinquishment of dominion and control of the property by delivery to the donee

In order to have a valid gift for federal income tax purposes, the donor must have acted out of a "detached and disinterested" generosity in transferring the property. Gifts are normally made out of "affection, respect, admiration, charity, or like impulses."[1] Valid gifts have *no strings attached.*

Questions regarding gift or compensation normally arise as to payments where there is a past or present employment relationship. For federal income tax law purposes, a voluntary transfer without compensation is not necessarily a gift. It is not a gift if there is a legal or moral obligation for the transfer or if the donor expects to receive a benefit from the "gift." However, the mere absence of a legal or moral obligation for the transfer does not necessarily qualify the transfer as a gift. As previously stated, a transfer is a gift if it is made from detached or disinterested generosity. Ultimately, the question of gift or compensation is resolved by reviewing the donor's dominant reason for making the transfer.

Example 1:	Ms. Adams hires Julie to baby-sit her two young children while she goes shopping. Upon returning, Ms. Adams gives Julie $20 for minding the children. Julie has $20 of taxable income. She has given consideration (rendered services) in return for the amount received.
Example 2:	Michael is a tax accountant for a CPA firm. During tax season, he works 300 hours of overtime. The firm's policy is to compensate all employees at time and a half for all overtime hours up to a maximum of 250 hours of overtime. During his post-tax season review, the firm announces to Michael that in recognition of his outstanding work ethic and overtime contributions, the firm will make a gift to him of $2,500.
	Because of the employer-employee relationship, Michael has taxable income. The "gift" has been made to Michael in recognition of his work ethic and overtime hours. The IRS will treat the $2,500 payment as compensation for past services rendered and not as a gift.

As illustrated, amounts transferred from an employer to an employee will not generally be treated as gifts.

Income From Gifts

Section 102 of the Code does not apply to the income generated from excludible property or to a gift of income. For example, if a father gifts a mutual fund investment to his daughter, the value of the mutual fund is not taxable to her. However, any dividends or capital gains earned on that fund subsequent to the gift would be taxable to her.

Gifts of Income

Similar to the concept of income from gifts is that of gifts of income. Neither income from gifts nor gifts of income are excludible from gross income. If payments under the terms of a gift are to be made at intervals, the payments are taxable to the donee to the extent they are made out of income.

Example:	A father establishes a trust for his daughter. The daughter is given a life interest in the trust. She is not permitted to invade the principal of the trust. On an annual basis, she receives the income from the trust. The annual income from the trust is not a gift and is taxable to the daughter upon receipt.

However, a bequest of a specific sum of money or property is excluded, even if it is paid out of income. This treatment applies only if the bequest is paid or credited all at once or in not more than three installments. If the bequest is paid in more than three installments, it is taxable to the recipient to the extent it is actually paid from the income generated.

Example:	A decedent's will directs that a trustee will pay her husband $40,000 a year for 5 years. The husband is scheduled to receive the $40,000 regardless of how much income is earned on the trust's assets. Since payments extend for more than 3 years, the husband will be taxed annually on the amount he receives to the extent of income earned on the trust's assets. If trust earnings are $50,000 and $45,000 during the first 2 years, the husband will be taxed on the full $40,000 he receives each year. However, if in years

3 through 5, the trust's earnings dip to $35,000, $31,000, and $28,500, respectively, the outcome is different. Since the trustee is required to distribute $40,000 annually to the husband, he or she will be forced to invade principal to make the payments. As a result, the husband will only be taxed to the extent of the trust's income—$35,000, $31,000, and $28,500 in years 3, 4, and 5, respectively.

Inheritances

The rules pertaining to gifts also extend to inheritances. The value of property acquired by inheritance is tax free to the recipient. However, income earned on that property subsequent to the transfer is taxable to the recipient.

Although the exclusion rules are similar for gifts and inheritances, the basis rules are significantly different. The recipient's basis in inherited property is generally the fair market value of the property at the decedent's death. As a result, appreciation of the property prior to the decedent's death escapes federal income taxation. In contrast, a donee's basis in property acquired by gift is generally the donor's basis in the property at the time of the gift.

Other Windfalls

As previously illustrated, Section 102(a) allows taxpayers to exclude gifts from income. However, amounts transferred from an employer to an employee in the form of cash or other property is generally taxable. Although employers are prohibited from disguising compensation as a nontaxable gift, a de minimis exception exists under a qualified award program. Qualifying awards are deductible by the employer and nontaxable to the employee if the amount does not exceed statutory limits. Under these limitations, the property's cost cannot exceed $400 per employee annually for a length of service award and safety achievement or $1,600 annually for all qualified plan awards, including both lengths of service and safety achievement awards.

In addition, lottery recipients are often confused about the status of their awards. Lottery winnings are treated in the same way as any game show winnings and are therefore taxable. However, upon winning the lottery, the winner is often faced with an unusual dilemma. Winners typically have the option of receiving an annuity or a lump sum payment. A basic understanding of the "present value of an ordinary annuity" is required by the financial planner.

In a nutshell, the present value of an annuity is the single sum required to be invested today by compounding interest to yield a required stream of payments over a period of time. Stated another way, the present value of an ordinary annuity is the present value of a series of equal payments to be withdrawn at equal intervals.

Example: Charlene McNulty has just won a state lottery totaling $4,000,000. The lottery promises a payout of $200,000 annually over the next 20 years. As an alternative, the lottery offers a lump-sum payment of $1,700,000. How will the state fund the extended payout? Lottery officials will calculate that an investment of $1,702,712 invested today at 10 percent will enable them to withdraw $200,000 a year for 20 years to pay the recipient the $4,000,000 (using present value of an ordinary annuity tables). In either scenario, the proceeds are taxable to the winning recipient. The winner will need to gauge income and lifestyle needs, projected income tax brackets, and estate planning desires before finalizing his or her decision.

ESTATE PLANNING FOR THE ELDERLY AND INCAPACITATED

Another area of financial planning that deserves special attention is the unique aspects of estate planning for elderly and incapacitated individuals. Although the proper emphasis of an estate plan is usually the distribution of property to the estate owner's heirs with the least tax liability, often the preservation of assets during lifetime is of far greater importance to the client than after-death issues. Preparing for the future financial and long-term care needs of the elderly, ill, and incapacitated presents some estate planning challenges. For instance, an estate plan that is oriented primarily toward passing property to the next generation becomes irrelevant if the estate is practically depleted by the cost of long-term care. On the other hand, retention of assets can prevent an estate owner from meeting Medicaid eligibility requirements. A comprehensive estate plan must address the implications of the client's potential need for long-term care.

One possible solution to achieving estate asset preservation goals and meeting long-term care needs is long-term care insurance (LTCI). For the owners of large estates, money expended to pay LTCI premiums escapes estate taxation. While it is established that long-term care costs may be deductible from the gross estate, there is no assurance that, without LTCI, lengthy long-term care will not exhaust or greatly diminish the assets in an estate.

Retaining Control With Trusts and Durable Powers of Attorney

Trust arrangements and durable powers of attorney are two devices that allow a client to have continued asset management despite incompetency. The trustee manages the trust property in accordance with the settlor's directions as established in the trust terms. For example, the settlor can grant the trustee the power to distribute income or principal at regular, preestablished intervals or at the trustee's discretion should the settlor later become incapacitated. Keep in mind, however, that trusts are used specifically for asset management; trustees cannot make personal health care decisions for an incompetent.

Durable powers of attorney can provide guidance for the personal care and financial decisions resulting from a client's incapacity.

Special-Needs Trust (SNT)

special-needs trusts

Special-needs trusts are property management devices used to protect the assets of individuals who anticipate long-term disability situations in the future. Often the subjects of special-needs trusts are children. Ethical considerations abound in discussions of special-needs trusts because they entail arranging beneficiaries' financial interests to avail the beneficiaries of government assistance programs such as Medicaid, Supplemental Security Income (SSI), In-Home Medical Care Services, and so forth. In other words, an individual's private assets are put in a special-needs trust in order to keep those assets from being reached by the government for reimbursement. Insulation of the beneficiaries' assets are accomplished by having language in the document prohibiting trust principal from being used in substitution for governmental benefits. A few states view such trusts as against public policy and deny them legal recognition.

The basic forms of special-needs trusts include the following:

- Family SNT—the most widely used SNT; frequently used as an estate planning tool for incapacitated persons
- Third-party SNT—established by nonfamily or interested parties on behalf of an incapacitated person
- Settlement SNT—funded with personal injury lawsuit damages received by the incapacitated individual from a court decision
- Pooled SNT—funded with assets (including the disabled individual's personal assets) that are pooled with numerous other sources to increase investment results. Each state has a nonprofit organization established to achieve investment benefits.

Elder Law Durable Power of Attorney

In many instances, financial advisers and estate planners recommend that individuals have a financial plan in place in the event of later incompetency. A durable power of attorney may be a valuable addition to an estate owner's financial plans, especially in later years of life. There are some unique qualities that may pertain to a durable power of attorney for an elderly person—qualities and requirements to which an elder law attorney must be especially sensitive. Powers of attorney that are specifically for elderly clients are called elder law durable powers of attorney. Many of the reasons for such specificity involve the capacity of the elder client. Perhaps what drives an elderly client to execute a durable power of attorney is that the principal is aware of the beginning or intermediate signs of one or more forms of impairment and therefore anticipates greater disability as time passes. Given the appropriate powers, the attorney-in-fact may expedite the principal's Medicaid eligibility, arrange for in-home or nursing home care, hires necessary health care personnel, employ companions, and so forth.

If the elderly client seeking the power of attorney displays signs of incompetency or the drafter has reservations about the client's mental capacity, the elder law attorney's choices are more limited. One solution may be to, with the client's consent, get a written opinion about the client's competency from the client's doctor(s), family, and/or other close acquaintances before proceeding to draft the document. If this fails, the attorney will have to work within the framework of prior instruments and arrangements. The choice of the most appropriate agent(s) for elderly individuals is crucial. Protection from financial and personal abuse is paramount. In many cases, it is recommended that more than one agent be appointed with the requirement that one must approve the other's decisions or that the agents must be in agreement before decisions are made. Because the elderly client's children and/or spouse are often the agents under the power, having more than one caring family member has obvious built-in safeguards. On the other hand, having multiple agents (co-agents/co-attorneys-in-fact) may be cumbersome and result in more difficulty in reaching an agreement. If a spouse or other close family member is not particularly financially minded, a workable solution may be to appoint an independent financial agent along with one or more close family members as co-agents to achieve financial acumen balanced with personal knowledge. Careful drafting is, of course, necessary because a document with multiple agents should contain provisions for dispute resolution, hierarchy in decision making, and so forth. The issues that may be addressed in elder law durable powers of attorney are practically infinite, depending on the principal's particular circumstances. As an example, an important and common issue to resolve before a durable power of attorney becomes effective is whether the elderly principal wishes to remain in his or her home with caregivers during the remaining years of life. Clearly, elder law durable powers of attorney must be drafted with extreme care.

Sometimes a client resists executing a durable power of attorney because of the perception that it is an admission of the inability to manage his or her own affairs. In such a situation, a springing power of attorney may be advisable. Because a springing power of attorney does not become operative until the time of the principal's incapacity, what constitutes incapacity for the particular principal should be carefully delineated in the document.

The combination of a trust and durable power of attorney allows the creator to indirectly maintain control of personal and financial matters when physical or mental limitations prevent one from managing matters directly. An elderly client can retain personal dignity. A trust and durable power of attorney drafted with incapacity provisions may serve to avoid conservatorship or guardianship proceedings. Compared with a trust or durable power of attorney, these two court-supervised alternatives are expensive and time consuming, and they may undermine a person's self-esteem. Executing a trust or durable power of attorney, however, does not guarantee that the client will be completely protected from the appointment of a conservator or guardian. No matter how carefully the instruments are drafted, it is possible for court proceedings to result from a challenge to the estate owner's trust or durable power of attorney. For example, a disgruntled heir may claim that the client lacked capacity or was unfairly influenced by another at the time the document was executed and may seek to have it set aside.

Guardianship and Conservatorship

Judicial guardianship and conservatorship are more complicated, time-consuming, costly, and restrictive solutions to incompetency compared with the relatively simple agency relationship created by a durable power of attorney. A power of attorney reflects a voluntary, consensual agreement in which an individual (the principal) arranges for an agent (the attorney-in-fact) or named guardian to attend to the principal's personal care and property if the principal becomes incapacitated. Although one agent may be named to care for the principal, usually a relative or trusted friend becomes responsible for the care of the person while a bank or other entity oversees the property. In the absence of a durable power of attorney, a court proceeding may be held to establish incompetency to manage one's affairs. After hearing evidence of incompetency, a court may appoint a guardian or conservator to act on behalf of the disabled party, called a *ward*. The process is generally an unpleasant one that, in the end, results in substantial loss of a ward's liberties. In some cases, the term *guardian* pertains specifically to care of the person and the term *conservator* to

ward
guardian
conservator

management of the property. Sometimes these terms are used interchangeably. The scope of the court-appointed guardian's powers to act for the ward may be broad or limited. Usually, however, the guardian has responsibility for the ward personally and the ward's property. It is the court supervision of the guardianship relationship that proves costly, time consuming, and trying.

In addition to a durable power of attorney, other methods used to avoid judicial guardianship include joint ownership of property, advance medical directives, and trusts. When property is titled in more than one name, another party is already in place to manage the property, bank accounts, and so forth. As previously discussed, advance medical directives and living wills provide for health decision making prior to disability.

Guardianship may also be circumvented with trusts. A primary benefit of a revocable living trust is that the trustee manages the trust property according to trust terms stated by the grantor. The trustee continues to administer the assets during the grantor's incapacity. Another type of trust used in planning for **standby trust** incompetency is a *standby trust*. A standby trust often works in tandem with a durable or springing power of attorney. The trust is unfunded until such time as the grantor becomes incapacitated and an attorney-in-fact funds the trust with assets of the grantor for the trustee to manage.

The planner should take reasonable precautions to determine that the client is competent at the time documents are executed. To ascertain an elderly client's mental competency, the planner should establish that the client has knowledge of his or her property, recognizes the purposes of meeting with the planner with regard to the property, and understands the arrangements to be undertaken. Documentation supporting the client's apparent capacity can be placed in the client's file. Trusts and medical durable powers of attorney provide the estate planner and the estate owner with a broad scope of permissible powers and the necessary flexibility to fashion incapacity contingency plans.

Considerations Concerning Medical Assistance Programs

Another planning consideration is the possibility that the elderly client will inherit money or property from a family member's estate or receive death proceeds as the named beneficiary of a decedent's insurance policy. Since there is limited time to deal with the consequences of an unexpected increase in an elderly person's estate, such funds may cause greater estate tax liability than anticipated. In addition, if the recipient of the proceeds or inheritance is a Medicaid applicant, the property would be considered a Medicaid-available resource. Medicaid is a federal program that may help with payments for long-term care.

Although Medicare is often thought of as being a federal system to which qualifying individuals are entitled (because they had wages withheld and paid into the system), Medicaid is different. Taxpayers are not necessarily entitled to Medicaid. States obtain financial assistance from the federal government by administering their medical assistance programs in accordance with federal Medicaid rules. Certain levels of wealth or income determine whether or not a person qualifies to receive Medicaid assistance. The limits imposed on an applicant's assets and income is determined by the particular state.

Medicaid has sometimes been described as a welfare health care program. If an applicant or the spouse of an applicant is determined to have sufficient wealth to pay for health care, Medicaid will not pay for it. To be eligible for Medicaid benefits an applicant must be in relative poverty as determined under the Medicaid rules. Following changes in the Medicaid laws after the enactment of the Omnibus Budget Reconciliation Act of 1993 (OBRA '93), applicants may be denied Medicaid benefits if they or their spouses (1) have access to income in excess of a state's established maximum amounts, (2) have available assets in excess of permissible state-determined amounts, or (3) have made transfers of assets to other individuals within either 36 months or 60 months (depending on the nature of the particular transfer) prior to the date of application for benefits. (OBRA '93, 13611 and 13612, Pub. L.No. 103–66, 107 Stat. 312, 622–629 (August 10, 1993)). Under the Deficit Reduction Act of 2005 (DRA), the look-back period becomes 60 months for all gratuitous transfers made after January 2005. *(Note that there are ethical issues related to planning for eligibility for Medicaid.)*

Older persons who make lifetime gifts to reduce their taxable estates based on estate planning advice may delay eligibility for Medicaid assistance if the gifts occur within either a 36- or 60-month look-back period. If a client does not make gratuitous transfers within the appropriate time period before applying for Medicaid, transfers prior to that period will not cause disqualification. A properly drafted supplemental trust, also called a *Craven trust*, may be used, however, to provide supplemental maintenance for a nongrantor beneficiary without triggering the beneficiary's loss of governmental assistance benefits. Note also that an applicant's disclaimer of unexpected inheritance or insurance death proceeds to avoid being disqualified for Medicaid eligibility is likely to be unsuccessful because the particular state may consider the disclaimer to be a transfer for Medicaid eligibility purposes.

Due to the complexities and recent changes in the Medicaid laws, the prudent financial and/or estate planner should be well versed in Medicaid eligibility planning and other considerations specific to elderly or incapacitated clients.

> **FOCUS ON ETHICS**
> **When Confidentiality Becomes an Issue**
>
> Charlie is an estate planner who just acquired a new client, Fred Rice. Fred recently became a widower. After meeting with Fred several times to discuss his estate objectives, Charlie began to question his client's mental competency. Not only does Fred seem to change his intentions each time they meet, he also appears to be ambivalent about the children he wishes to include or omit as estate beneficiaries. Exacerbating what Charlie believes is already a disturbing situation is an additional complication. Though he at times seems uncertain about how to leave his estate, Fred has occasionally stated that he wants to leave the largest part of it to his oldest daughter, Kate, who is known to be a notorious substance abuser. Fred appears to be completely unaware of his daughter's addiction.
> What should Charlie do?

ESTATE PLANNING FOR MARRIED COUPLES

Financial and estate planners may have to take special considerations into account when planning for married couples. As previously indicated, U.S. law favors the marital status and treats a married couple as a single economic unit (for example, the unlimited marital gift and estate tax deduction and joint income tax returns). But a planner should be aware that the interests of a husband and wife may not be identical and may even be conflicting. Thus, one planner may not be able to fairly address the needs of both parties. In other words, just because a married couple seeks joint representation, the planner should not automatically conclude that the parties share identical objectives. Spousal estate planning and property disposition goals may be especially divergent and complicated when one or both have children from previous marriages. Other areas of potential conflict may be the existence of one or both spouses' community property, the subjection of marital or separate property to the claims of one spouse's creditors, reciprocal wills, the tax consequences of gift splitting, and the control or lack of control a surviving spouse will have over property after the first spouse's death.

Clearly, a financial or estate planner for a couple must ascertain whether the interests of both spouses are the same or adverse. If both spouses are in agreement and appear to be comfortable using the same planner, joint representation of both parties should not be an ethical or practical problem. However, if there seems to be marital conflict, the planner should recommend that each spouse seek separate estate planning advice. When a married couple with differing estate planning goals still want joint advice, all existing and potential conflicts should be disclosed, and the planner should obtain a written waiver or agreement from both parties concerning their joint representation for the planner's and the clients' protection. The agreement can establish some ground rules concerning the disclosure policy of each party's plan, documents, and joint and separate meetings. Addressing areas of potential conflict at the outset reduces the likelihood of problems for all parties. In keeping with current ethical concerns, some states require planners to send married couples a detailed joint representation letter outlining potential conflicts and to obtain the signatures of both parties before providing joint estate planning representation.

Separation and Divorce

Estate considerations also arise for separation and divorce. In this situation, it is advisable, if possible, for each spouse to have an attorney or other professional adviser review the estate plans of both persons. This allows both individuals to plan more effectively for the benefit of any children from the union. Both former spouses should also execute new wills, even if their intentions upon death remain the same.

Frequently, an irrevocable life insurance trust is used in divorce situations to provide for a surviving spouse and children. Often a trust is set up and the trustee purchases a policy on the life of the wealthier spouse, naming the surviving former spouse or children as beneficiaries. This arrangement can provide for the surviving beneficiaries' financial needs and, as long as the decedent former spouse did not hold any incidents of ownership in the policy or name the estate as beneficiary, the life insurance proceeds avoid inclusion in the insured-decedent's estate.

For gift tax purposes, divorcing spouses who enter into a written agreement addressing their marital and property rights may transfer marital or property rights to each other pursuant to the agreement free of federal gift taxation. Transfers of property between divorcing spouses that are incident to the divorce are not subject to federal gift taxation because the transfers and giving up of marital rights are treated as being made for full and adequate consideration in money or money's worth. The divorce, however, must occur with a 3-year period that revolves around the timing of the property settlement agreement for the transfer to avoid gift tax.

ESTATE PLANNING FOR SINGLES

Widows, widowers, single parents, and confirmed singles over the age of 35 comprise almost 30 percent of the U.S. population, according to the Census Bureau. This group is reported to hold approximately the same percentage of the country's wealth. Estate planning for singles may present some unique, nonroutine planning situations that do not typically arise with married clients. There are often different psychological factors for single and married clients.

For instance, some single clients, if they feel alone and vulnerable, may be less trusting. Therefore, more effort on the planner's part may be required to build rapport and establish trust. Single parents may be very dependent on child support payments to supplement income. Widows and widowers may be trying to live on monthly Social Security checks and small pension payments.

Older single people—but particularly widows and widowers—need to know or feel that they can act independently. Many fear becoming dependent on their children and other family members. They want to be able to take care of themselves for as long as possible. Older singles may gain a sense of independence, security, and confidence by knowing they have any or all of the following: certain investments, a living trust to manage their affairs if they become disabled, a durable power of attorney, a living will, an emergency or funeral fund, disability insurance, and long-term care insurance. A consolidated written list of accounts and their values can also provide a source of comfort to singles.

The financial or estate planner needs to recognize when planning for singles that their estate planning objectives and needs are likely to be somewhat different from the goals of married couples and two-parent family households. He or she must plan differently for single clients who are financially responsible for minor children than for those clients whose adult children are attempting to manage their finances or clients whose family members are asking for loans. The individual who is left financially strapped as a result of divorce has dissimilar concerns from the widow or widower who inherited substantial assets but is overwhelmed by the responsibility and complexity of the inheritance. Although planning for singles has some aspects in common (such as loss of both the marital deduction and gift splitting), the adviser must approach and analyze each situation individually and not according to a group stereotype.

ESTATE PLANNING INVOLVING NONTRADITIONAL LIVING ARRANGEMENTS

As illustrated earlier in the chapter, modern society has become more receptive to nontraditional living arrangements. Prevailing attitudes today encourage the acceptance of living styles that once were socially impermissible. The dissolution of nearly half of all marriages and a weariness of litigating domestic issues has probably contributed to this tolerance.

When advising married couples, financial and estate planners have ample state statutory and case law for guidance. However, with the exception of the 26 states (including Washington, D.C.) that recognize common-law marriages[*] and court decisions addressing palimony claims, there is no legal point of

---

[*] 2001 World Almanac, p. 745.

reference for individuals who live together outside of marriage. Simply living together is not sufficient to constitute a common-law marriage in those states that do recognize a common-law arrangement. A common-law couple must also publicly represent themselves as husband and wife and meet specific living requirements. Palimony lawsuits, on the other hand, are grounded on contractual claims for support after relationships have terminated. It is discrimination law rather than marital law that provides guidance for some other aspects of nontraditional living arrangements. Many of these cases arise from claims of different treatment due to sexual preference.

Just as the parties to a valid marriage can enter into agreements that delineate property ownership, rights, duties, expectations, obligations, and so forth in antenuptial or postnuptial contracts, unmarried persons who live together can also enter into cohabitation agreements. Such agreements can give structure to the living arrangements and may reduce the likelihood of palimony litigation if the relationship later dissolves.

Financial and estate planners are sailing in relatively uncharted waters when planning for clients who are living together outside of marriage. As with married clients, a planner should at the very least suggest separate, independent planners for each of the partners to protect their rights and also to protect the planner from conflicts of interest and claims of malpractice. The planner has to factor into any estate plan for couples living together outside of marriage the fact that such relationships are more easily terminated by the parties than marriages that are recognized under state law.

The presence of children adds to the complexity of estate planning for clients living in nontraditional arrangements. One of the partners may be the biological, custodial parent of children from a previous marriage or relationship. A nonbiological partner, however, may have formed a personal attachment to one or more of the children and may seek custody or visitation rights or may otherwise want to provide for them. Grandparents and other senior generation members may also be relevant in estate plans. Adoptions, stepchildren, half-siblings, surrogate births, artificial insemination, and in vitro fertilization all make the planning process even more confusing and intricate. Typical methods that may be used to plan for children of a previous relationship include annual gift tax exclusion gifts, trusts for the children under the Uniform Transfers (or Gifts) to Minors Act, testamentary trusts, life insurance, and Social Security benefits.

Negative family reactions and hostility add yet another layer of problems to estate planning for unmarried couples, especially same-gender couples. To deter anticipated will contests or other actions, some couples have resorted to adoption by one of the adult partners of the other as his or her legal child.

Nonmarried and same-sex couples may also have to contend with being denied visitation when a partner is in the hospital. Furthermore, a blood relative is more likely to be asked about a patient's medical wishes than a domestic partner. The solution to both of these issues is a health care power of attorney (HCPOA) or a health care representative appointment (HCRA). If the patient-partner is unable to communicate his or her wishes, a living will used in conjunction with an HCPOA or HCRA that nominates the healthy partner as agent should protect the partner's wishes, including access to the patient-partner in the hospital.

Currently, few states are recognized as being progressive, proactive, and responsive to nontraditional living arrangement issues. Vermont provides for civil unions that are practically indistinguishable from marriage. Hawaii has a "reciprocal beneficiaries" law with limited rights. New Jersey offers limited domestic partnership benefits. California allows same-sex partners to register as domestic partners for the purpose of obtaining certain legal rights held by married couples, including the right to inherit a partner's property, adopt a partner's child, and participate in health care privileges. (Under California law, the rights and duties of marriage to persons registered as domestic partners are allowed starting in 2005.) Massachusetts is, at the time of this writing, the only state to permit and grant full legal marital recognition to marriage between same-gender, Massachusetts-resident couples. Keep in mind, however, that despite the Full Faith and Credit Clause under the U.S. Constitution, which requires each state to give full effect to the laws of other states, there is an exception if giving effect to another state's law(s) violates a state's public policy.

A somewhat new document is also gaining acceptance and legal recognition in California, some municipalities, and places of private employment. This instrument may be referred to, for instance, as a cohabitation agreement, affidavit/contract of commitment, declaration of domestic partnership, domestic agreement, and similar terms. These documents, with relevant registration, may grant employees in nontraditional relationships benefits, like health care coverage and leave to care for an ailing partner, that typically were reserved for traditional married employees. Two additional considerations concerning these agreements are lack of confidentiality and the potential for joint financial responsibility.

Addressing Estate Planning Concerns of Nonmarital Partners

The unavailability of the unlimited marital gift and estate tax deduction is the greatest tax planning hurdle to overcome in estate planning issues involving couples who are not married. Keep in mind that a nontraditional family can be any family or household in which there are at least two or more unrelated people, or, if there are related parties in the household, at least one person is related nonlineally, such as a brother or sister. Another variation of a nontraditional family is one with related family members where at least one lineal generational level is absent. An example is grandparents who maintain a household for grandchildren, and the grandchildren's parents are not present. Other tax perspectives are necessary because tax matters cannot be postponed as readily without the marital deduction option. There are, however, several common estate planning methods used for nonmarital partners.

Joint Tenancy With Right of Survivorship

Titling property as joint tenants with right of survivorship is one way of providing for a partner. At death, the property passes directly to the surviving party to the relationship.

Although holding property in joint tenancy with right of survivorship provides a certain sense of security for same-gender or other unmarried parties, individuals should be aware of some considerations with respect to this form of ownership. They are

- It may be possible for one of the unmarried parties to sever a joint tenancy.
- With bank accounts and certain other assets, either partner may be able to make withdrawals or obtain the property irrespective of his or her percentage of contribution to the account.
- The creation of a joint tenancy may cause gift tax liability.
- The joint-tenancy property may be reachable by the creditors of both partners.

Gifting

Outright transfers of property utilizing the annual exclusion, or the donor's applicable credit amount if the transfer exceeds the annual exclusion amount, avoid gift tax liability. (Of course, gift splitting is not an option in nonmarital situations.)

Testamentary Bequests

Provisions may also be made under a client's will for a partner with whom the client lives. (Clearly, federal and state marital deductions cannot be used by unmarried couples.) Will provisions, however, do not become irrevocable until death and could then be vulnerable to will contests by the decedent's lineal heirs. Challenges to a will are especially likely from the decedent's children from a marriage. Therefore, partners who desire to provide for each other under a will need to be aware that family members, even those who appeared to accept their deceased relative's partner prior to death, may contest the will after the death of their family member. In this case, a revocable trust may prove more dependable for making sure property passes according to the partners' wishes. If the surviving partner receives less than what was promised or expected under his or her partner's will, an election against the will is not available. If the decedent dies without a valid will, the survivor will not receive anything, since state intestacy statutes are based solely on blood relationships. Also, if either of the life partners wishes the other partner to be executor, the will should specifically nominate the partner because a court will often, in the absence of a specific nomination, be more inclined to appoint a sibling, parent, or child rather than the unrelated partner. Figure 11-1 illustrates the intestate distribution scheme.

FIGURE 11-1
Common Distribution Scheme of Intestate Succession

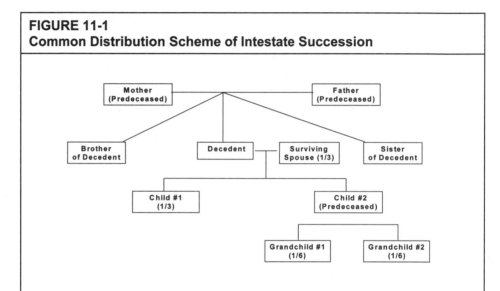

Surviving spouse takes 1/3; remaining 2/3 goes to children, or 1/3 to each. Child #2 predeceased decedent, so Child #2's share is divided equally, or 1/6 each, to each grandchild. If no children survived decedent, remaining 2/3 would pass to parents (1/3 each). If parents predeceased decedent, remaining 2/3 would go to their lineal descendants (brother and sister of decedent would receive 1/3 each). If no brothers or sisters of decedent survived, surviving spouse would get the rest. If there were no lineal descendants (including cousins), property would escheat to the state.

Revocable Trusts

An unmarried partner may use a living or a revocable trust arrangement to provide for the other party to the relationship by naming the partner as beneficiary. At the death of the grantor partner, the trust becomes irrevocable and the beneficiary partner receives the property or the income from the property according to the terms of the trust. The trust document may provide for alternates and may name a successor beneficiary in case the specific relationship is not sustained until the grantor's death.

Life Insurance and Retirement Plans

Life insurance and retirement plans may name the partner as beneficiary, thereby providing the partner with a sense of security during lifetime and with funds at the insured's and/or plan participant's death. If same-gender partners are concerned about listing their partner as the beneficiary of benefits their employer provides, naming a trust with the partner as trust beneficiary may be a possible solution. Also be aware that retirement benefits may not be made available to a surviving unmarried partner the way they are to a surviving spouse. Life insurance on the life of the pension participant may be considered to supplant the loss of retirement benefits when the retiree partner dies.

Because a domestic partner generally does not have an insurable interest in the insured partner's life, the purchase of a life insurance policy on the partner's life may prove difficult. An irrevocable life insurance trust or ILIT, however, may be used to overcome the insurability-requirement obstacle and achieve the partners' goals. With an ILIT, the trust is the policyowner and the partner is the trust beneficiary. For grantor-partners concerned about the irrevocability element of an ILIT and a potential for the relationship to fail in the future, the trust may be drafted to contain provisions directing the policy proceeds to someone other than an estranged partner under specified circumstances.

GRITs

Another way an individual could transfer property to his or her partner is with a grantor retained income trust (GRIT). Although Chapter 14 of the Internal Revenue Code (Sections 2701–2704) restricts tax benefits for GRITs between related parties, they can be a useful estate planning device for nontraditional couples. With a GRIT the grantor-partner retains a value in the assets that is based on the terms of the trust. The values of the grantor's retained interest and the remainderman-partner's interests are determined under the Section 7520 rate at the time the GRIT is created.

Martin, a grantor-partner, establishes a trust and funds it with $1 million. The funds are to be held in the trust for 10 years before the underlying property passes to his partner, Michael. Assume that the value of Martin's retained income interest is approximately $695,000 and that Martin's taxable gift to Michael, as remainderman, is valued at $305,000 (the difference between $1 million and the $695,000 value of the retained interest). Martin has achieved his goal of passing the property to his partner but with less gift tax for Martin compared with the tax payable on an immediate gift of the entire $1 million.

Court Decisions Involving Nontraditional Living Arrangements

A few notes of interest in this area include the following court decisions. A judicial ruling in Ontario, Canada, recently recognized the legal status of same-gender marriages. Other provinces in Canada are likely to follow this Ontario ruling. Keep in mind, however, that the United States does not have to recognize the laws from other countries. Also, the 1996 Defense of Marriage Act allows states to disregard same-sex marriages recognized under the laws of other states.

In the United States, one state's highest court recently ruled that an unmarried woman could make a claim for the loss of companionship that resulted from her male partner's car-accident-related injuries. Because the language used in rendering the decision was gender neutral, some practitioners believe the court may rule similarly for same-gender couples. (*Loyoza v. Sanchez*, 66 P.3d 948 (N.M.2003))

Finally, in a recent state appellate court case again in the United States, a former domestic partner was held liable for the financial support of children born during the relationship. (*L.S.K. v. H.A.N.*, 813 A.2d 872; 2002 Pa. Super. Lexis 3806)

The issues and cases mentioned above serve to highlight the increasing demand for the courts and legislatures to address the uncertainties and legal ramifications of nontraditional living arrangements.

Planning for individuals living in nontraditional circumstances can present an estate planning challenge. The planner must be diligent and thorough to obtain all the pertinent facts from the client(s). Finally, the planner must be alert to new laws and court decisions affecting parties living together outside of marriage. Unfortunately, this legislative uncertainty is not limited to estate dispositions, but impacts all our lifetime planning for special circumstances.

CHAPTER ELEVEN REVIEW

Key Terms and Concepts
Key Terms and Concepts are explained in the glossary.

alimony	special-needs trust
separate maintenance payments	ward
special school	guardian
eligible child	conservator
self-funded medical reimbursement plan	standby trust

Review Questions

The answers to the review questions are in the supplement. The self-test questions and the answers to them are also in the supplement and on The American College Online.

11-1.   Describe how the tax credit for children is phased out for certain upper-income taxpayers. [11-1]

11-2.   a.   In what postseparation year will the payer of an "excess alimony payment" be required to include the excess in income? [11-1]
   b.   How is the excess alimony payment determined? [11-1]

11-3.   Explain the federal tax consequences of transferring a life insurance policy pursuant to a separation agreement or divorce decree. [11-1]

11-4.   Explain how the allowable amount of the adoption credit is phased out for certain upper-income taxpayers. [11-2]

11-5.   Describe the allowable credit for adoption expenses for:
   a.   an eligible child who is not a special needs child [11-3]
   b.   a child with special needs [11-3]

11-6.   a.   Who is a "qualifying individual" for purposes of the dependent-care credit? [11-3]
   b.   What is the maximum amount of qualifying expenses available to a working taxpayer who is responsible for one qualifying individual? [11-3]

11-7.   Discuss the need for disability income insurance. [11-4]

11-8.   What are some of the special estate planning issues that may arise when planning for:
   a.   the elderly [11-6]
   b.   married couples [11-6]

11-9.   Explain what a standby trust is. [11-6, 11-8]

11-10.   Explain why it may be important for nonmarried couples to execute health care documents naming each other as agent or proxy. [11-8]

NOTE

1. *Placko v. Comm'r.,* 74 T.C. 452 (1980).

Appendix A

The Selling/Planning Process

The Selling/Planning Process

The eight-step selling/planning process encompasses the six-step financial planning process (FPP). As shown below, steps 3 through 8 of the selling/planning process comprise the six-step FPP. In conjunction with the sale of financial products, financial advisors should utilize the FPP when working with their clients.

1. Identify the Prospect
   - Marketing
   - Prospecting methods
   - Preapproach

2. Approach the Prospect
   - Telephone
   - Face-to-face

3. Meet the Prospect **(Step 1 of the FPP: Establish and Define the Advisor-Client Relationship)**
   - Establish a relationship
   - Introduce the type of work you do
   - Gain acceptance to proceed to the information-gathering step

4. Establish Goals and Gather Information **(Step 2 of the FPP: Determine Goals and Gather Data)**
   - Determine current situation (fact finder)
   - Establish goals
   - Prioritize goals
   - Acknowledge the need
   - Gain acceptance to work together to achieve the goals

5. Analyze the Information **(Step 3 of the FPP: Analyze and Evaluate the Data)**
   - Analyze the weakness(es) in the client's plan
   - Create a proposed plan for the situation

6. Develop and Present the Plan **(Step 4 of the FPP: Develop and Present a Plan)**
   - Propose the plan

- Handle objections, concerns, and misunderstandings

7. Implement the Plan **(Step 5 of the FPP: Implement the Plan)**
    - Ask for the sale
    - Complete necessary paperwork
    - Complete any necessary underwriting (if insurance product)
    - Deliver any policies, documents, etc.

8. Service the Plan **(Step 6 of the FPP: Monitor the Plan)**
    - Provide any requested service
    - Monitor the plan with annual or regular reviews
    - Cross sell opportunities and referrals

Appendix B

CFP® Certificant Disclosure Form

Sample CFP Certificant Disclosure Form (Form FPE) for Use in Financial Planning Engagements[*]

The following sample disclosure form *(filled in with sample answers)* is for use by CFP® certificants in complying with the CFP Board's *Code of Ethics and Professional Responsibility (Code of Ethics)* disclosure requirements for financial planning engagements. The form provides for certain disclosures to clients (or prospective clients) as required by the CFP Board's *Code of Ethics*, with corresponding Rules in the *Code of Ethics* referenced in parentheses (see chapter 3 for a discussion of the CFP Board's Code of Ethics). The client acknowledgments at the end of the disclosure form are not required by the CFP Board's *Code of Ethics*, but CFP certificants may wish to use them for their own purposes. Please note in Part II, section E of the form, a CFP certificant shall not hold out as a fee-only financial planning practitioner if the CFP certificant receives commissions or other forms of economic benefit from related parties. CFP certificants may use this form, SEC Form ADV Part II, or a form of their own design or choosing as long as the required *Code of Ethics* disclosures are included in whatever form is used by the CFP certificant. Compliance with the disclosure requirements of the *Code of Ethics* is accomplished only when all matetial information relevant to the professional relationship has been disclosed to the client (or prospective client).

For Use in Financial Planning Engagements

This disclosure form gives information about the CFP® certificant(s) and his/her/their business. This information has not been reviewed, approved or verified by CFP Board or by any governmental or self-regulatory authority. CFP Board does not warrant the specific qualifications of individuals certified to use its marks, nor does it warrant the correctness of advice or opinions provided.

PART   I.   GENERAL INFORMATION
(Code reference - Rule 401)

    A.   Business affiliation:

    B.   Address:

    C.   Telephone number:

    D.   Information required by all laws applicable to the relationship (that is, if the CFP certificant is a registered investment adviser, the disclosure document required by laws applicable to such registration):

PART   II.   MATERIAL INFORMATION RELEVANT TO THE PROFESSIONAL RELATIONSHIP
(Written disclosures required to be provided <u>prior to</u> the engagement)
(Code reference - Rule 402)

    A.   Basic philosophy of the CFP certificant (or firm) in working with clients:

    Our approach to personal financial planning is to obtain from you significant financial and other information including your attitudes, goals and objectives; to analyze the information obtained in order to develop alternatives for your consideration; to educate you about the implications of selecting a particular alternative; to implement the alternative selected by you; and to periodically update the plan adopted. It is our goal to become your chief financial advisor and to coordinate the efforts of your other advisors in your best interests. We want you to be educated about your own financial affairs and to take an active role in managing them.

    B.   Philosophy, theory and/or principles of financial planning which will be utilized:

    Our philosophy of financial planning is to gather adequate reliable information about a client's personal financial situation; to determine the client's goals and objectives, time horizon, and risk tolerance; to analyze all of the foregoing information in an objective manner and to develop recommendations for our clients based upon this thorough analysis and in the interest of rendering disinterested advice. In a personal financial planning engagement, we endeavor to consistently act in the interest of our client and to place his or her interest ahead of our own. Moreover, we believe that a client should be both informed and proactively involved in his or her personal financial affairs. Accordingly, we believe in holding frequent meetings with our clients to educate them about the financial planning process and their own financial situation.

C. **Attached to this disclosure form, or summarized in the space provided below, are resumes of principals and employees of the CFP® certificant's firm who are expected to provide financial planning services:**

   1. **Educational background:**

      John Doe:
      > *Bachelor of Science degree in accounting from Hofstra University, 1971. Master of Business Administration degree in Financial Services from Golden Gate University, 1975.*

   2. **Professional/employment history:**

      John Doe:
      > *Was employed as a stockbroker for DEF Brokerage for nearly ten years before becoming a partner in Comprehensive Financial Planning Services, Inc., in 1986 (see attached resume).*

   3. **Professional certifications and licenses held:**

      John Doe:
      > *CERTIFIED FINANCIAL PLANNER™ practitioner*
      > *NASD Series 7 (General Securities) license - 1974*
      > *Life and Health Insurance licenses - 1978, State of Arkansas*

D. **Description of the financial planning services to be provided by the CFP certificant:**

   Example 1:
   This engagement is limited in scope to retirement planning only. Other types of personal financial planning services will not be performed by us, unless they directly affect your retirement plan, and you give us your express permission prior to performing such additional services.

   Example 2:
   You have expressed interest in asset management services. These services include:

- *Analysis of your current financial condition, goals and objectives, and development of a personal financial plan.*
- *Design of an investment portfolio appropriate to your individual circumstances, needs, goals, risk tolerance, investment experience and time horizon.*
- *Quarterly written reports on the status of your investment portfolio.*
- *Two meetings each year to review and update your objectives and financial status and provide an evaluation of your investment portfolio.*
- *Ongoing monitoring of your investment portfolio.*
- *Recommendations involving investment repositioning and current opportunities for new investments.*
- *Availability of our professional staff to answer questions.*

E.   Conflict(s) of interest and source(s) of compensation:

1.   Conflict(s) of interest:

Example 1:
John Doe represents Larry Peters, your business partner.

Example 2:
My broker/dealer permits me to sell only those securities products which it has approved.

2.   Source(s) of compensation:

Example 1: Fees from clients

Example 2: Commissions from third parties

3.   Contingencies or other aspects material to the certificant's compensation:

I will not receive a commission unless you purchase the financial products recommended by me.

F.   Agency or employment relationships:

1.   Material agency or employment relationships with third parties.
Life & Health Insurance Broker for DEF Insurance Company

2.   Compensation resulting from such agency or employment relationships:
50% commissions on first year life insurance premiums and 0.25% commission upon annual renewal.

G.   **Other material information relevant to the professional relationship:**
John Doe is licensed only for the sale of mutual funds and variable annuities.

PART III.   ADDITIONAL NOTIFICATION

A.   **As a client or prospective client, you have the right to ask me, as a CFP®
certificant, at any time for information about my compensation related to the
services I provide you. I will communicate the requested information in
reasonable detail as it relates to our financial planning engagement, including
compensation derived from implementation. This disclosure of compensation:**

1.   **May be expressed as an approximate dollar amount or percentage or as a
range of dollar amounts or percentages.**
2.   **Shall be made at a time and to the extent that the requested information
can be reasonably ascertained.**
3.   **Will be based on reasonable assumptions, with estimates clearly identified.**
4.   **Will be updated in a timely manner if actual compensation significantly
differs from any estimates.**
(Code reference - Rules 402 and 403)

B.   **As a CFP certificant's personal financial planning client, you have the right to
receive annually my current SEC Form ADV Part II or the current revision
of the disclosure you received when our relationship began. (Code reference
- Rule 404)**

I hereby acknowledge receipt of this required disclosure.

_____/_____   _____/_____
Client's Signature   Date   Client's Signature   Date

Appendix C

Topic List for CFP® Certification Examinations

CERTIFIED FINANCIAL PLANNER
BOARD OF STANDARDS, INC.

TOPIC LIST FOR CFP® CERTIFICATION EXAMINATION

The following topics, based on the 2004 Job Analysis Study, are the basis for the CFP® Certification Examinations. Each exam question will be linked to one of the following topics, in the approximate percentages indicated following the general headings. Questions will pertain to all levels in Bloom's taxonomy with an emphasis on the higher cognitive levels. Questions often will be asked in the context of the financial planning process and presented in an integrative format.

In addition to being used for the CFP® Certification Examination, this list indicates topic coverage requirements to fulfill the pre-certification educational requirement. Continuing education (CE) programs and materials that address these topics will be eligible for CFP Board CE credit.

(References to sections (§) in this list refer to sections of the Internal Revenue Code)

First Test Date: November 2006

GENERAL PRINCIPLES OF FINANCIAL PLANNING (11%)

1. Financial planning process
   A. Purpose, benefits, and components
   B. Steps
      1) Establishing client-planner relationships
      2) Gathering client data and determining goals and expectations
      3) Determining the client's financial status by analyzing and evaluating general financial status, special needs, insurance and risk management, investments, taxation, employee benefits, retirement, and/or estate planning
      4) Developing and presenting the financial plan
      5) Implementing the financial plan
      6) Monitoring the financial plan
   C. Responsibilities
      1) Financial planner
      2) Client
      3) Other advisors

2. CFP Board's *Code of Ethics and Professional Responsibility* and *Disciplinary Rules and Procedures*
   A. *Code of Ethics and Professional Responsibility*
      1) Preamble and applicability
      2) Composition and scope
      3) Compliance
      4) Terminology
      5) Principles
         a) Principle 1 – Integrity
         b) Principle 2 – Objectivity
         c) Principle 3 – Competence
         d) Principle 4 – Fairness
         e) Principle 5 – Confidentiality
         f) Principle 6 – Professionalism
         g) Principle 7 – Diligence
      6) Rules
   B. *Disciplinary Rules and Procedures*

3. CFP Board's *Financial Planning Practice Standards*
   A) Purpose and applicability
   B) Content of each series (use most current *Practice Standards*, as posted on CFP Board's Web site at www.CFP.net)
   C. Enforcement through *Disciplinary Rules and Procedures*

4. Financial statements
   A. Personal
      1) Statement of financial position
      2) Statement of cash flow
   B. Business
      1) Balance sheet
      2) Income statement
      3) Statement of cash flows
      4) *Pro forma* statements

5. Cash flow management
   A. Budgeting
   B. Emergency fund planning
   C. Debt management ratios
      1) Consumer debt
      2) Housing costs
      3) Total debt
   D. Savings strategies

6. Financing strategies
   A. Long-term vs. short-term debt
   B. Secured vs. unsecured debt
   C. Buy vs. lease/rent
   D. Mortgage financing
      1) Conventional vs. adjustable-rate mortgage (ARM)
      2) Home equity loan and line of credit
      3) Refinancing cost-benefit analysis
      4) Reverse mortgage

7. Function, purpose, and regulation of financial institutions
   A. Banks
   B. Credit unions
   C. Brokerage companies
   D. Insurance companies
   E. Mutual fund companies
   F. Trust companies

8. Education planning
   A. Funding
      1) Needs analysis
      2) Tax credits/adjustments/deductions
      3) Funding strategies
      4) Ownership of assets
      5) Vehicles
         a) Qualified tuition programs (§529 plans)
         b) Coverdell Education Savings Accounts
         c) Uniform Transfers to Minors Act (UTMA) and Uniform Gifts to Minors Act (UGMA) accounts
         d) Savings bonds
   B. Financial aid

9. Financial planning for special circumstances
   A. Divorce
   B. Disability
   C. Terminal illness
   D. Non-traditional families
   E. Job change and job loss
   F. Dependents with special needs
   G. Monetary windfalls

10. Economic concepts
    A. Supply and demand
    B. Fiscal policy
    C. Monetary policy
    D. Economic indicators
    E. Business cycles
    F. Inflation, deflation, and stagflation
    G. Yield curve

11. Time value of money concepts and calculations
    A. Present value
    B. Future value
    C. Ordinary annuity and annuity due
    D. Net present value (NPV)
    E. Internal rate of return (IRR)
    F. Uneven cash flows
    G. Serial payments

12. Financial services regulations and requirements
    A. Registration and licensing
    B. Reporting
    C. Compliance
    D. State securities and insurance laws

13. Business law
    A. Contracts
    B. Agency
    C. Fiduciary liability

14. Consumer protection laws
    A. Bankruptcy
    B. Fair credit reporting laws
    C. Privacy policies
    D. Identity theft protection

INSURANCE PLANNING AND RISK MANAGEMENT (14%)

15. Principles of risk and insurance
    A. Definitions
    B. Concepts
       1) Peril
       2) Hazard
       3) Law of large numbers
       4) Adverse selection
       5) Insurable risks
       6) Self-insurance
    C. Risk management process

D. Response to risk
   1) Risk control
      a) Risk avoidance
      b) Risk diversification
      c) Risk reduction
   2) Risk financing
      a) Risk retention
      b) Risk transfer
E. Legal aspects of insurance
   1) Principle of indemnity
   2) Insurable interest
   3) Contract requirements
   4) Contract characteristics
   5) Policy ownership
   6) Designation of beneficiary

16. Analysis and evaluation of risk exposures
    A. Personal
       1) Death
       2) Disability
       3) Poor health
       4) Unemployment
       5) Superannuation
    B. Property
       1) Real
       2) Personal
       3) Auto
    C. Liability
       1) Negligence
       2) Intentional torts
       3) Strict liability
    D. Business-related

17. Property, casualty and liability insurance
    A. Individual
       1) Homeowners insurance
       2) Auto insurance
       3) Umbrella liability insurance
    B. Business
       1) Commercial property insurance
       2) Commercial liability insurance
          a) Auto liability
          b) Umbrella liability
          c) Professional liability
          d) Directors and officers liability
          e) Workers' compensation and employers liability

18. Health insurance and health care cost management (individual)
    A. Hospital, surgical, and physicians' expense insurance
    B. Major medical insurance and calculation of benefits
    C. Continuance and portability
    D. Medicare
    E. Taxation of premiums and benefits

19. Disability income insurance (individual)
    A. Definitions of disability
    B. Benefit period

C. Elimination period
D. Benefit amount
E. Provisions
F. Taxation of premiums and ber

20. Long-term care insurance (indiv
    A. Eligibility
    B. Services covered
    C. Medicare limitations
    D. Benefit period
    E. Elimination period
    F. Benefit amount
    G. Provisions
    H. Taxation of premiums and ber

21. Life insurance (individual)
    A. Concepts and personal uses
    B. Policy types
    C. Contractual provisions
    D. Dividend options
    E. Nonforfeiture options
    F. Settlement options
    G. Illustrations
    H. Policy replacement
    I. Viatical and life settlements

22. Income taxation of life insuranc
    A. Dividends
    B. Withdrawals and loans
    C. Death benefits
    D. Modified endowment contrac (MECs)
    E. Transfer-for-value
    F. §1035 exchanges

23. Business uses of insurance
    A. Buy-sell agreements
    B. Key employee life insurance
    C. Split-dollar life insurance
    D. Business overhead expense insurance

24. Insurance needs analysis
    A. Life insurance
    B. Disability income insurance
    C. Long-term care insurance
    D. Health insurance
    E. Property insurance
    F. Liability insurance

25. Insurance policy and company selection
    A. Purpose of coverage
    B. Duration of coverage
    C. Participating or non-participati
    D. Cost-benefit analysis
    E. Company selection
       1) Industry ratings
       2) Underwriting

2

nuities
Types
Uses
Taxation

LOYEE BENEFITS
NING (8%)

roup life insurance
Types and basic provisions
1) Group term
2) Group permanent
3) Dependent coverage
Income tax implications
Employee benefit analysis and
application
Conversion analysis
Carve-out plans

roup disability insurance
Types and basic provisions
1) Short-term coverage
2) Long-term coverage
Definitions of disability
Income tax implications
Employee benefit analysis and
application
Integration with other income

roup medical insurance
Types and basic provisions
1) Traditional indemnity
2) Managed care plans
   a) Preferred provider
      organization (PPO)
   b) Health maintenance
      organization (HMO)
   c) Point-of-service (POS)
Income tax implications
Employee benefit analysis and
application
COBRA/HIPAA provisions
Continuation
Savings accounts
1) Health savings account (HSA)
2) Archer medical savings account
   (MSA)
3) Health reimbursement
   arrangement (HRA)

ther employee benefits
§125 cafeteria plans and flexible
spending accounts (FSAs)
Fringe benefits
Voluntary employees' beneficiary
association (VEBA)
Prepaid legal services
Group long-term care insurance
Dental insurance
Vision insurance

31) Employee stock options
   A. Basic provisions
      1) Company restrictions
      2) Transferability
      3) Exercise price
      4) Vesting
      5) Expiration
      6) Cashless exercise
   B. Incentive stock options (ISOs)
      1) Income tax implications
         (regular, AMT, basis)
         a) Upon grant
         b) Upon exercise
         c) Upon sale
      2) Holding period requirements
      3) Disqualifying dispositions
      4) Planning opportunities and
         strategies
   C. Non-qualified stock options
      (NSOs)
      1) Income tax implications
         (regular, AMT, basis)
         a) Upon grant
         b) Upon exercise
         c) Upon sale
      2) Gifting opportunities
         a) Unvested/vested
         b) Exercised/unexercised
         c) Gift tax valuation
         d) Payment of gift tax
      3) Planning opportunities and
         strategies
      4) Employee benefits analysis and
         application
   D. Planning strategies for employees
      with both incentive stock options
      and non-qualified stock options
   E. Election to include in gross income
      in the year of transfer (§83(b)
      election)

32. Stock plans
   A. Types and basic provisions
      1) Restricted stock
      2) Phantom stock
      3) Stock appreciation rights
         (SARs)
      4) Employee stock purchase plan
         (ESPP)
   B. Income tax implications
   C. Employee benefit analysis and
      application
   D. Election to include in gross
      income in the year of transfer
      (§83(b) election)

33. Non-qualified deferred
    compensation
   A. Basic provisions and differences
      from qualified plans
   B. Types of plans and applications
      1) Salary reduction plans

   2) Salary continuation plans
   3) Rabbi trusts
   4) Secular trusts
   C. Income tax implications
      1) Constructive receipt
      2) Substantial risk of forfeiture
      3) Economic benefit doctrine
   D. Funding methods
   E. Strategies

INVESTMENT PLANNING
(19%)

34. Characteristics, uses and taxation
    of investment vehicles
   A. Cash and equivalents
      1) Certificates of deposit
      2) Money market funds
      3) Treasury bills
      4) Commercial paper
      5) Banker's acceptances
      6) Eurodollars
   B. Individual bonds
      1) U.S. Government bonds and
         agency securities
         a) Treasury notes and bonds
         b) Treasury STRIPS

         c) Treasury inflation-
            protection securities
            (TIPS)
         d) Series EE, HH, and I bonds
         e) Mortgage-backed
            securities
      2) Zero-coupon bonds
      3) Municipal bonds
         a) General obligation
         b) Revenue
      4) Corporate bonds
         a) Mortgage bond
         b) Debenture
         c) Investment grade
         d) High-yield
         e) Convertible
         f) Callable
      5) Foreign bonds
   C. Promissory notes
   D. Individual stocks
      1) Common
      2) Preferred
      3) American depositary receipts
         (ADRs)
   E. Pooled and managed
      investments
      1) Exchange-traded funds
         (ETFs)
      2) Unit investment trusts
      3) Mutual funds
      4) Closed-end investment
         companies

3

CERTIFIED FINANCIAL PLANNER | **CFP**

5) Index securities
6) Hedge funds
7) Limited partnerships
8) Privately managed accounts
9) Separately managed
accounts
F. Guaranteed investment
contracts (GICs)
G. Real Estate
1) Investor-managed
2) Real estate investment trusts
(REITs)
3) Real estate limited
partnerships (RELPs)
4) Real estate mortgage
investment conduits (REMICs)
H. Alternative investments
1) Derivatives
a) Puts
b) Calls
c) Long-term Equity
AnticiPation Securities
(LEAPS®)
d) Futures
e) Warrants and rights
2) Tangible assets
a) Collectibles
b) Natural resources
c) Precious metals

35. Types of investment risk
A. Systematic/market/
nondiversifiable
B. Purchasing power
C. Interest rate
D. Unsystematic/nonmarket/
diversifiable
E. Business
F. Financial
G. Liquidity and marketability
H. Reinvestment
I. Political (sovereign)
J. Exchange rate
K. Tax
L. Investment manager

36. Quantitative investment concepts
A. Distribution of returns
1) Normal distribution
2) Lognormal distribution
3) Skewness
4) Kurtosis
B. Correlation coefficient
C. Coefficient of determination (R²)
D. Coefficient of variation
E. Standard deviation
F. Beta
G. Covariance
H. Semivariance

37. Measures of investment returns
A. Simple vs. compound return

B. Geometric average vs. arithmetic
average return
C. Time-weighted vs. dollar-
weighted return
D. Real (inflation-adjusted) vs.
nominal return
E. Total return
F. Risk-adjusted return
G. Holding period return
H. Internal rate of return (IRR)
I. Yield-to-maturity
J. Yield-to-call
K. Current yield
L. Taxable equivalent yield (TEY)

38. Bond and stock valuation concepts
A. Bond duration and convexity
B. Capitalized earnings
C. Dividend growth models
D. Ratio analysis
1) Price/earnings
2) Price/free cash flow
3) Price/sales
4) Price/earnings ÷ growth (PEG)
E. Book value

39. Investment theory
A. Modern portfolio theory (MPT)
1) Capital market line (CML)
a) Mean-variance optimization
b) Efficient frontier
2) Security market line (SML)
B. Efficient market hypothesis (EMH)
1) Strong form
2) Semi-strong form
3) Weak form
4) Anomalies
C. Behavioral finance

40. Portfolio development and analysis
A. Fundamental analysis
1) Top-down analysis
2) Bottom-up analysis
3) Ratio analysis
a) Liquidity ratios
b) Activity ratios
c) Profitability ratios
d) Debt ratios
B. Technical analysis
1) Charting
2) Sentiment indicators
3) Flow of funds indicators
4) Market structure indicators
C. Investment policy statements
D. Appropriate benchmarks
E. Probability analysis, including
Monte Carlo
F. Tax efficiency
1) Turnover
2) Timing of capital gains and
losses

3) Wash sale rule
4) Qualified dividends
5) Tax-free income
G. Performance measures
1) Sharpe ratio
2) Treynor ratio
3) Jensen ratio
4) Information ratio

41. Investment strategies
A. Market timing
B. Passive investing (indexing)
C. Buy and hold
D. Portfolio immunization
E. Swaps and collars
F. Formula investing
1) Dollar cost averaging
2) Dividend reinvestment pla
(DRIPs)
3) Bond ladders, bullets, and
barbells
G. Use of leverage (margin)
H. Short selling
I. Hedging and option strategies

42. Asset allocation and portfolio
diversification
A. Strategic asset allocation
1) Application of client lifecy
analysis
2) Client risk tolerance
measurement and
application
3) Asset class definition and
correlation
B. Rebalancing
C. Tactical asset allocation
D. Control of volatility
E. Strategies for dealing with
concentrated portfolios

43. Asset pricing models
A. Capital asset pricing model
(CAPM)
B. Arbitrage pricing theory (APT)
C. Black-Scholes option valuation
model
D. Binomial option pricing

INCOME TAX PLANNING
(14%)

44. Income tax law fundamentals
A. Types of authority
1) Primary
2) Secondary
B. Research sources

4

2) Charitable and beneficiary gifting objectives
3) Medical costs, including long-term care needs analysis
4) Other (trust and foundation funding, education funding, etc.)
D. Straight-line returns vs. probability analysis
E. Pure annuity vs. capital preservation
F. Alternatives to compensate for projected cash-flow shortfalls

60. Social Security (Old Age, Survivor, and Disability Insurance, OASDI)
A. Paying into the system
B. Eligibility and benefit
1) Retirement
2) Disability
3) Survivor
4) Family limitations
C. How benefits are calculated
D. Working after retirement
E. Taxation of benefits

61. Types of retirement plans
A. Characteristics
1) Qualified plans
2) Non-qualified plans
B. Types and basic provisions of qualified plans
1) Defined contribution
a) Money purchase
b) Target benefit
c) Profit sharing
1) 401(k) plan
2) Safe harbor 401(k) plan
3) Age-based plan
4) Stock bonus plan
5) Employee stock ownership plan (ESOP)
6) New comparability plan
7) Thrift plan
2) Defined benefit
a) Traditional
b) Cash balance
c) 412(i) plan

62. Qualified plan rules and options
A. Nondiscrimination and eligibility requirements
1) Age and service requirements
2) Coverage requirements
3) Minimum participation
4) Highly compensated employee (HCE)
5) Permitted vesting schedules
6) ADP/ACP testing
7) Controlled group

B. Integration with Social Security/disparity limits
1) Defined benefit plans
2) Defined contribution plans
C. Factors affecting contributions or benefits
1) Deduction limit (§404(c))
2) Defined contribution limits
3) Defined benefit limit
4) Annual compensation limit
5) Definition of compensation
6) Multiple plans
7) Special rules for self-employed (non-corporations)
D. Top-heavy plans
1) Definition
2) Key employee
3) Vesting
4) Effects on contributions or benefits
E. Loans from qualified plans

63. Other tax-advantaged retirement plans
A. Types and basic provisions
1) Traditional IRA
2) Roth IRA, including conversion analysis
3) SEP
4) SIMPLE
5) §403(b) plans
6) §457 plans
7) Keogh (HR-10) plans

64. Regulatory considerations
A. Employee Retirement Income Security Act (ERISA)
B. Department of Labor (DOL) regulations
C. Fiduciary liability issues
D. Prohibited transactions
E. Reporting requirements

65. Key factors affecting plan selection for businesses
A. Owner's personal objectives
1) Tax considerations
2) Capital needs at retirement
3) Capital needs at death
B. Business' objectives
1) Tax considerations
2) Administrative cost
3) Cash flow situation and outlook
4) Employee demographics
5) Comparison of defined contribution and defined benefit plan alternatives

66. Investment considerations for retirement plans
A. Suitability

B. Time horizon
C. Diversification
D. Fiduciary considerations
E. Unrelated business taxable in (UBTI)
F. Life insurance
G. Appropriate assets for tax-advantaged vs. taxable accounts

67. Distribution rules, alternatives, and taxation
A. Premature distributions
1) Penalties
2) Exceptions to penalties
3) Substantially equal payments (§72(t))
B. Election of distribution optio
1) Lump sum distributions
2) Annuity options
3) Rollover
4) Direct transfer
C. Required minimum distributions
1) Rules
2) Calculations
3) Penalties
D. Beneficiary considerations/ Stretch IRAs
E. Qualified domestic relations order (QDRO)
F. Taxation of distributions
1) Tax management techniqu
2) Net unrealized appreciatio (NUA)

ESTATE PLANNING (15%)

68. Characteristics and consequence of property titling
A. Community property vs. non-community property
B. Sole ownership
C. Joint tenancy with right of survivorship (JTWROS)
D. Tenancy by the entirety
E. Tenancy in common
F. Trust ownership

69. Methods of property transfer at death
A. Transfers through the probate process
1) Testamentary distribution
2) Intestate succession
3) Advantages and disadvantages of probate
4) Assets subject to probate estate
5) Probate avoidance strategie

6

7

CERTIFIED FINANCIAL PLANNER™ | CFP®

84. Intra-family and other business transfer techniques
   A. Characteristics
   B. Techniques
      1) Buy-sell agreement
      2) Installment note
      3) Self-canceling installment note (SCIN)
      4) Private annuity
      5) Transfers in trust
      6) Intra-family loan
      7) Bargain sale
      8) Gift or sale leaseback
      9) Intentionally defective grantor trust
      10) Family limited partnership (FLP) or limited liability company (LLC)
   C. Federal income, gift, estate, and generation-skipping transfer tax implications

85) Generation-skipping transfer tax (GSTT)
   A. Identify transfers subject to the GSTT
      1) Direct skips
      2) Taxable distributions
      3) Taxable terminations
   B. Exemptions and exclusions from the GSTT
      1) The GSTT exemption
      2) Qualifying annual exclusion gifts and direct transfers

86. Fiduciaries
   A. Types of fiduciaries
      1) Executor/Personal representative
      2) Trustee
      3) Guardian
   B. Duties of fiduciaries
   C. Breach of fiduciary duties

87. Income in respect of a decedent (IRD)
   A. Assets qualifying as IRD
   B. Calculation for IRD deduction
   C. Income tax treatment

88. Postmortem estate planning techniques
   A. Alternate valuation date
   B. Qualified disclaimer
   C. Deferral of estate tax (§6166)
   D. Corporate stock redemption (§303)
   E. Special use valuation (§2032A)

89. Estate planning for non-traditional relationships
   A. Children of another relationship
   B. Cohabitation
   C. Adoption
   D. Same-sex relationships

ADDENDUM

The following topics are an addendum to the *Topic List for CFP® Certification Examination*. Although individuals taking the CFP® Certification Examination will not be tested directly over these topics, CFP Board registered programs are strongly encouraged to teach them in their curricula) Continuing education (CE) programs and materials that address these topics will be eligible for CFP Board CE credit.

1. Client and planner attitudes, values, biases and behavioral characteristics and the impact on financial planning
   A. Cultural
   B. Family (e.g. biological; non-traditional)
   C. Emotional
   D. Life cycle and age
   E. Client's level of knowledge, experience, and expertise
   F. Risk tolerance
   G. Values-driven planning

2. Principles of communication and counseling
   A. Types of structured communication
      1) Interviewing
      2) Counseling
      3) Advising
   B. Essentials in financial counseling
      1) Establishing structure
      2) Creating rapport
      3) Recognizing resistance
   C. Characteristics of effective counselors
      1) Unconditional positive regard
      2) Accurate empathy
      3) Genuineness and self-awareness
   D. Nonverbal behaviors
      1) Body positions, movements, and gestures
      2) Facial expressions and eye contact
      3) Voice tone and pitch
      4) Interpreting the meaning of nonverbal behaviors
   E. Attending and listening skills
      1) Physical attending
      2) Active listening
      3) Responding during active listening; leading response
   F. Effective use of questions
      1) Appropriate types of questions
      2) Ineffective and counterproductive questioning techniques

8

CFP. | CERTIFIED FINANCIAL PLANNER™ | CFP®

Appendix D

Survey of Financial Risk Tolerance

Client Name/ID _____

FINANCIAL

PLANNING

Survey of Financial Risk Tolerance

Introduction

The Survey of Financial Risk Tolerance (hereinafter referred to as the Survey) is a 40-item questionnaire that takes approximately 15 to 20 minutes to complete. Each individual question on the Survey is based on one of the approaches to assessing risk tolerance discussed in chapter 4.

The Survey relies on direct measures of risk tolerance as well as proxy measures of this characteristic. Please understand, however, that this questionnaire, like all others, is meant to complement rather than serve as a substitute for a more comprehensive assessment (as described in chapter 4). Always be sure to compare the impressions you gain using this questionnaire with other more objective evidence. For instance, one section of the questionnaire asks the client to indicate his or her preference for various investment vehicles. You should determine whether the expressed preferences match the client's actual portfolio of past and current investments.

Remember too that other factors besides the person's characteristic level of risk tolerance can influence the amount of risk he or she may be willing to take. As noted in chapter 4, research suggests that people treat money differently depending on how it was acquired. Generally money that was easily earned, especially if acquired through a windfall (other than by an inheritance from a beloved relative), is more apt to be exposed to risk than money that was earned through hard labor. Likewise, since investments are likely to vary in their value and returns more sharply in the short run than in the long run, the client's investment horizon is a critical consideration. If a client is able to adopt a long-term horizon, there may be a correspondingly greater willingness to take a risk.

The financial advisor therefore needs to determine the suitability of the assessment procedure for the particular client and the client's unique situation. The Survey is intended only as a tool to assist the advisor in assessing a client's attitudes toward risk taking as part of a comprehensive review of appropriate investment choices. The Survey is not intended to substitute for the advisor's professional judgment of the client's level of risk tolerance and financial ability to sustain a loss.

How the Survey Can Be Used

There are two ways to use the Survey in the financial planning process, and both ways are described below.

As an Interview Discussion Aid

It is possible to use the Survey as a list of questions to ask the client during the course of a face-to-face interview, allowing the client to respond in his or her own words. For example, "How do you react to unexpected bad financial news?" can be answered by the client in a variety of ways. The answer, of course, needs to be analyzed by the financial advisor for the degree of risk aversion it conveys. This procedure imposes minimal restraints on the client's answers and allows the advisor to explore in depth through further questioning the reasons underlying them. But the costs are the amount of time it takes to ask the number of questions necessary to get a feel for the pattern of the client's answers and the potential for ambiguity in the answers.

As an Information-Gathering Device

The second way to use the Survey is to have the client complete the Survey by answering the questions. The advisor will then be able to obtain some sense of the client's risk tolerance by examining his or her answers to see if they follow a consistent pattern. This is possible because, with the exception of question 32, the answers for each question are arranged on a continuum, reflecting a progression from risk-averse to risk-tolerant behaviors. The use of standardized options provides a uniform basis for interpreting the client's responses. The more risk-taking options the client selects, the more risk taking he or she is likely to be.

The Importance of Risk Tolerance Questionnaires

Although understanding the risk tolerance of a client is so critically important to proper investment and financial planning, there is no simple formula, tool, or technique that allows an advisor to identify the client's financial risk tolerance and then relate it to an investment portfolio. The fact that measurement of financial risk tolerance is not perfect, however, does not mean it cannot or should not be done. For this reason, The American College developed the Survey of Financial Risk Tolerance. While the Survey can be used to assist financial advisors in assessing their clients' attitudes toward risk taking, its purpose in being included in this book is to show just how important risk tolerance questionnaires are to the financial planning process.

Most financial advisors use risk tolerance questionnaires that are designed to be used with specific financial planning software. Moreover, many large financial services companies have developed their own risk tolerance questionnaires to satisfy compliance departments, and they fully expect their advisor-representatives to use them. Therefore, even though other questionnaires are available and even required, the real value of The College's Survey lies in providing an example of the types of questions that advisors need to ask in their assessment of clients' risk tolerances.

Whether engaged in single purpose, multiple-purpose, or comprehensive financial planning, a financial advisor should make the use of a risk tolerance questionnaire a top priority in data gathering (for step 2 of the financial planning process). The type of information provided by a risk tolerance questionnaire is necessary in order for an advisor to develop a financial and/or investment plan (in step 4 of the financial planning process) for his or her client. When the questionnaire has been completed and analyzed (in step 3 of the financial planning process), it provides the advisor with information that can help in assessing the client's risk tolerance. In other words, this type of information is intended to complement and reinforce the advisor's judgment about the client's level of risk tolerance.

Financial advisors are under a legal and an ethical obligation to help clients make investment choices that are suitable for their particular circumstances. Determining suitability requires consideration of the client's goals (as determined in step 2 of the financial planning process), his or her ability to sustain a financial loss, and his or her psychological attitudes toward risk taking. Developing a suitable financial and/or investment plan for the client should lead to a lasting and profitable relationship with the client. Not only will the client be happy, but the advisor will come away with a sense of personal satisfaction and professional pride from having fulfilled the client's expectations.

Client Name/ID_____

Survey of Financial Risk Tolerance

Directions: Please answer all questions by circling the number in front of the answer that indicates your response.

1. **Do you experience "anxiety" or "thrill" when awaiting the outcome of an important investment decision?**

   1   Always anxiety
   2   Most frequently anxiety
   3   Neither anxiety nor thrill
   4   Most frequently thrill
   5   Always thrill

2. **How do you react to unexpected bad financial news?**

   1   Always overreact
   2   Frequently overreact
   3   Rarely overreact
   4   Almost never overreact
   5   Never overreact

3. **Assume you're an executive. Your company offers you two ways of collecting your bonus: either the cash equivalent of 6 months' salary or a stock option with a 50-50 chance of either doubling in value or becoming worthless in the next year. Which would you take?**

   1   Definitely the cash
   2   Probably the cash
   3   Not sure
   4   Probably the stock option
   5   Definitely the stock option

4. **Once you have made an investment decision, how sure do you usually feel that your choice was the correct one?**

   1   Very unsure
   2   Somewhat unsure
   3   Somewhat sure
   4   Very sure

5. **Which of the following investment portfolios do you find most appealing?**

   1   60 percent in low-risk
       30 percent in medium-risk
       10 percent in high-risk investments

   2   30 percent in low-risk
       40 percent in medium-risk
       30 percent in high-risk investments

   3   10 percent in low-risk
       50 percent in medium-risk
       40 percent in high-risk investments

6. **When you think of the word risk in an investment context, which of the following words comes to mind first?**

   1   Danger
   2   Uncertainty
   3   Opportunity
   4   Thrill

7. **How often have you invested a large sum in a risky investment primarily for the "thrill" of seeing whether it went up or down in value?**

   1   Never
   2   Very rarely
   3   Somewhat rarely
   4   Somewhat frequently
   5   Very frequently

8. **How easily do you adapt to unfavorable financial changes in your life?**

   1   Very uneasily
   2   Somewhat uneasily
   3   Somewhat easily
   4   Very easily

Survey of Financial Risk Tolerance

9. You are considering an investment that amounts to 25 percent of the funds you have allocated for investment purposes. The expected return on this investment is about twice the return you would get by placing the money into a savings account at your local bank. However, this investment, unlike a bank account, is not protected against loss of the principal. What would the chance of loss have to be in order for you to make this investment?

   1   Zero
   2   Very improbable
   3   Low chance
   4   Even chance

10. Compared with other investors, how sophisticated are you about investing money?

    1   Very unsophisticated
    2   Somewhat unsophisticated
    3   Somewhat sophisticated
    4   Very sophisticated

11. If your friends were interviewed, how would *they* describe *your* evaluation of financial risks?

    1   Severely overestimates the risks
    2   Somewhat overestimates the risks
    3   Estimates the risks correctly
    4   Somewhat underestimates the risks
    5   Severely underestimates the risks

12. You are faced with a choice between (a) greater job security with a small pay raise and (b) a high pay raise but less job security. Which would you select?

    1   Definitely greater job security
    2   Probably greater job security
    3   Not sure
    4   Probably higher pay raise
    5   Definitely higher pay raise

13. An investment decision involves the possibility of making an amount of money as well as the possibility of losing all or some portion of the funds invested. Some people focus more on the possibility of making money, whereas others focus more on the possibility of losing money as a result of the decision. When making an important investment decision, what dominates your thinking?

    1   The potential loss, by far
    2   The potential loss, somewhat more
    3   The potential gain, somewhat more
    4   The potential gain, by far

14. In the past what have been the outcomes of your high-risk investment decisions?

    1   Almost always unfavorable
    2   Usually unfavorable
    3   Equal mix of favorable and unfavorable outcomes
    4   Usually favorable
    5   Almost always favorable

15. How long does it take you to make an important financial decision?

    1   Very long time
    2   Long time
    3   Average amount of time
    4   Short time
    5   Very short time

16. Compared with other people you know, how would you rate your ability to tolerate the stress associated with important financial matters?

    1   Very low
    2   Low
    3   Average
    4   High
    5   Very high

Survey of Financial Risk Tolerance

17. **Some people view financial losses as personal failures. Others consider these same consequences as merely setbacks. How do you tend to view these issues?**

    1   Almost always as personal failures
    2   Mainly as personal failures
    3   Sometimes as personal failures and sometimes as merely setbacks
    4   Mainly as just setbacks
    5   Almost always as just setbacks

18. **If you were to become unemployed, which of the following would you be most likely to do?**

    1   Definitely take the first job offered, even if it was not exactly what I was looking for
    2   Probably take the first job offered, even if it was not exactly what I was looking for
    3   Not sure
    4   Probably hold out for the kind of job I really wanted
    5   Definitely hold out for the kind of job I really wanted

19. **What is your general outlook on the eventual outcome of your financial decisions after you make them?**

    1   Very pessimistic
    2   Somewhat pessimistic
    3   Somewhere in the middle
    4   Somewhat optimistic
    5   Very optimistic

20. **Which of the following comes closest to your ideal employment compensation structure involving some mix of *salary* and *commissions*?**

    1   Entirely salary
    2   Primarily salary
    3   Equal mix of salary and commissions
    4   Primarily commissions
    5   Entirely commissions

21. **What degree of risk have you assumed on your investments in the past?**

    1   Very small
    2   Small
    3   Medium
    4   Large
    5   Very large

22. **Do you consider yourself reflective or impulsive when making investment decisions?**

    1   Very reflective
    2   Somewhat reflective
    3   Neither reflective nor impulsive
    4   Somewhat impulsive
    5   Very impulsive

23. **You are applying for a mortgage. The interest rates have been coming down over the last several months, and there's a possibility that they may drop another percentage point in the next month. However, the possibility also exists that the rates will start climbing again. It's unclear which of the two possibilities is more likely since economists disagree in their forecasts. You have the option of locking in on the current interest rate or letting it float. If you lock in, you will get the current rate, even if interest rates go up. If the rates go down, though, you'll have to settle at the higher rate. What would you do?**

    1   Definitely lock in
    2   Probably lock in
    3   Probably let it float
    4   Definitely let it float

Survey of Financial Risk Tolerance

24. **Assume you are a contestant on a TV game show. After winning a prize that's equivalent to one year's salary, you are offered the option of walking away with this prize money or taking a chance on either doubling it or losing it all. What are the odds of success that you would require before agreeing to accept this gamble?**

    1　Would not take the bet no matter what the odds
    2　9 in 10
    3　8 in 10
    4　7 in 10
    5　6 in 10
    6　5 in 10
    7　4 in 10
    8　3 in 10
    9　2 in 10
    10　1 in 10

25. **Have you ever borrowed money in order to make an investment (other than a home-mortgage loan)?**

    1　No
    2　Yes

26. **How much confidence do you have in your ability to make money?**

    1　Very low confidence
    2　Low confidence
    3　Average level of confidence
    4　High confidence
    5　Very high confidence

27. **Compared with other people you know, how much time do you spend reading about financial and investment matters?**

    1　Much less than most
    2　Somewhat less than most
    3　About the same
    4　Somewhat more than most
    5　Much more than most

28. **Suppose that 5 years ago you bought stock issued by a company highly recommended by your financial advisor. That same year the company experienced a severe decline in sales due to poor management. The price of the stock dropped drastically, and you sold your shares at a substantial loss. The company is now restructured under new management, and most analysts expect its stock to produce better-than-average returns. Given your bad experience with this stock in the past, how likely are you now to purchase shares of this stock?**

    1　Definitely would not buy
    2　Probably would not buy
    3　Not sure
    4　Probably would buy
    5　Definitely would buy

29. **Is it more important to be protected from inflation or to be assured of the safety of your principal?**

    1　Much more important to be assured of the safety of principal
    2　Somewhat more important to be assured of the safety of principal
    3　Somewhat more important to be protected from inflation
    4　Much more important to be protected from inflation

30. **What percent of your funds are you willing to place in investments that are of above-average risk?**

    1　0 percent
    2　1–9 percent
    3　10–19 percent
    4　20–29 percent
    5　30–39 percent
    6　40–49 percent
    7　50–59 percent
    8　60–69 percent
    9　70–79 percent
    10　80–89 percent
    11　90–99 percent
    12　100 percent

Survey of Financial Risk Tolerance

31. In some instances you are faced with a choice between (a) earning a certain amount of money for sure and (b) taking a risk and earning either a larger amount of money or nothing at all.

    For example, consider an investment choice between a certain gain of $50 and an 80 percent chance of earning $100. If you take the certain choice, you will get $50 for sure (no more, no less). On the other hand, if you take the 80 percent probability of earning $100, you also stand a 20 percent chance of earning nothing at all.

    For the choices shown below please indicate whether you would take the sure gain or some probability of earning twice as much (or nothing at all). Be sure to select one option for each pair, A through F.

Pair A: 1   A certain gain of $10,000
            2   80 percent probability of gaining $20,000 (with a corresponding 20 percent chance of earning nothing)

Pair B: 1   A certain gain of $10,000
            2   50 percent probability of gaining $20,000 (with a corresponding 50 percent chance of earning nothing)

Pair C: 1   A certain gain of $30,000
            2   80 percent probability of gaining $60,000 (with a corresponding 20 percent chance of earning nothing)

Pair D: 1   A certain gain of $30,000
            2   50 percent probability of gaining $60,000 (with a corresponding 50 percent chance of earning nothing)

Pair E: 1   A certain gain of $50,000
            2   80 percent probability of gaining $100,000 (with a corresponding 20 percent chance of earning nothing)

Pair F: 1   A certain gain of $50,000
            2   50 percent probability of gaining $100,000 (with a corresponding 50 percent chance of earning nothing)

32. How likely is it that you would be willing to place one-fourth of your net wealth into each of the following classes of investments?

LOW RISK

		Very Unlikely	Somewhat Unlikely	Not Sure	Somewhat Likely	Very Likely
(a)	90-day U.S. Treasury bill	1	2	3	4	5
(b)	Deposit account (savings, CD)	1	2	3	4	5
(c)	Money market fund	1	2	3	4	5
(d)	U.S. government bond	1	2	3	4	5
(e)	Municipal bond	1	2	3	4	5
(f)	Corporate bond	1	2	3	4	5
(g)	Blue-chip common stock	1	2	3	4	5
(h)	Convertible security	1	2	3	4	5
(i)	Aggressive-growth common stock	1	2	3	4	5
(j)	Venture capital	1	2	3	4	5
(k)	Limited-partnership unit	1	2	3	4	5
(l)	Junk bond	1	2	3	4	5
(m)	Options/commodities	1	2	3	4	5

HIGH RISK

33. Diversification is typically the soundest investment strategy. However, suppose an eccentric uncle left you an inheritance of $75,000, stipulating in his will that you invest *all* the money in only *one* of the following investments. Which one would you select?

    1   Savings account
    2   Mutual fund (moderate growth)
    3   Blue-chip common stock
    4   Limited partnership
    5   Naked option/commodities futures contract

Survey of Financial Risk Tolerance

34. **Investments can go up and down in value. What is the maximum drop in the value of your total investment portfolio that you could tolerate before feeling uncomfortable?**

   1   0 percent
   2   1–9 percent
   3   10–19 percent
   4   20–29 percent
   5   30–39 percent
   6   40–49 percent
   7   50–59 percent
   8   60–69 percent
   9   70–79 percent
   10 80–89 percent
   11 90–99 percent
   12 100 percent

35. **A long-lost relative dies and leaves you her house. The house is in disrepair but is located in a neighborhood that's being rehabilitated. As is, the house would probably sell for about $75,000, but if you were to spend about $25,000 on renovations, the selling price would be approximately $150,000. However, there's some talk about constructing a major highway next to the house, which would lower its value considerably. What would you do?**

   1   Sell it as is.
   2   Keep it as is, but rent it out.
   3   Take out a $25,000 mortgage for the necessary renovations.

36. **You are offered an investment in which you stand an even chance of either losing half of your personal net worth or making a certain amount of money. What's the lowest return you would need in order to make such an investment?**

   1   I would not make the investment no matter what the rate of return.
   2   Quadruple my net worth
   3   Triple my net worth
   4   Double my net worth
   5   Less than double my net worth

37. **What types of changes have you made in your investment portfolio in the past?**

   1   Always toward less risky investments
   2   Mostly toward less risky investments
   3   No changes or changes with no clear direction
   4   Mostly toward more risky investments
   5   Always toward more risky investments

38. **How often have you used "short selling" or "margin buying" in stock market investments?**

   1   Never
   2   Seldom
   3   Frequently
   4   Very frequently

39. **Suppose you are the beneficiary of a $100,000 life insurance policy from a beloved relative. You are considering various investment possibilities, including some of very high risk. How much of this money could you lose *forever* without feeling that you were betraying your relative's motive for leaving you this sum?**

   1   $0
   2   $1,000–$9,000
   3   $10,000–$19,000
   4   $20,000–$29,000
   5   $30,000–$39,000
   6   $40,000–$49,000
   7   $50,000–$59,000
   8   $60,000–$69,000
   9   $70,000–$79,000
   10 $80,000–$89,000
   11 $90,000–$100,000

40. **How do you rate your willingness to take investment risks in comparison with the general population?**

   1   Extremely low risk taker
   2   Very low risk taker
   3   Low risk taker
   4   Average risk taker
   5   High risk taker
   6   Very high risk taker
   7   Extremely high risk taker

Client Name/ID _____

Demographic Data Form

The following information will allow your risk-tolerance score to be classified by relevant demographic categories. Please be assured that this information, like your responses to the risk-tolerance questions, will remain confidential. Circle the number in front of the answer that indicates your response.

1. Sex   1   Male
            2   Female

2. Age _____

3. Marital status

    1   Single
    2   Married
    3   Divorced
    4   Widowed

4. Number of dependents, including yourself

    _____

5. Highest education level

    1   Less than high school
    2   High school
    3   Some college
    4   Bachelor's degree
    5   Master's degree
    6   Law degree
    7   Doctorate

6. Occupation

    1   An employee of a private company or business, or an individual working for wages, salary, or commissions
    2   A government employee (federal, state, county, or local)
    3   Self-employed in your own business, professional practice, or farm
    4   Retired

7. If you are an employee, how many years have you been with the same employer? _____

8. Approximate income, before taxes, from all sources. Please indicate your own income *and* total household income.

	a. Your income	b. Household income
Under $50,000	1	1
$50,000 to $99,000	2	2
$100,000 to $149,000	3	3
$150,000 to $199,000	4	4
$200,000 to $249,000	5	5
$250,000 to $500,000	6	6
Over $500,000	7	7

9. Which category describes your approximate net wealth?

    1   Under $250,000
    2    $250,000 to $499,000
    3    $500,000 to $999,000
    4    $1,000,000 to $2,499,000
    5    $2,500,000 to $5,000,000
    6   Over $5,000,000

10. Which of the following investments do you presently own? (Circle all that apply.)

    1   Life insurance
    2   Savings account or CDs
    3   Money market funds
    4   Bonds
    5   Stocks
    6   Real estate (other than primary residence)
    7   Options or futures
    8   Other (list)

    _____
    _____
    _____

Client Name/ID _____

Survey of Financial Risk Tolerance   **Answer Sheet**

Directions: *The client has answered the questions on the Survey and the Demographic Data Form by circling a number corresponding to his or her answer. Transfer these numbers to the appropriate spaces in the Answer columns.*

Survey Answers--

Question Number	Answer	Question Number	Answer	Question Number	Answer	Question Number	Answer
1.	____	16.	____	31. Pair A	____	32. j	____
2.	____	17.	____	31. Pair B	____	32. k	____
3.	____	18.	____	31. Pair C	____	32. 1	____
4.	____	19.	____	31. Pair D	____	32. m	____
5.	____	20.	____	31. Pair E	____	33.	____
6.	____	21.	____	31. Pair F	____	34.	____
7.	____	22.	____	32. a	____	35.	____
8.	____	23.	____	32. b	____	36.	____
9.	____	24.	____	32. c	____	37.	____
10.	____	25.	____	32. d	____	38.	____
11.	____	26.	____	32. e	____	39.	____
12.	____	27.	____	32. f	____	40.	____
13.	____	28.	____	32. g	____		
14.	____	29.	____	32. h	____		
15.	____	30.	____	32. i	____		

To assist the advisor in interpreting the client's answers to the Survey questions, remember that, except for question 32, the answers for each question are arranged on a continuum, reflecting a progression from risk-averse (a low number) to risk-tolerant (a high number) behaviors. Therefore, the higher the total score on all questions, except question 32, the more risk tolerant the client is likely to be. The range of possible total scores is from 44 (very risk averse) to 213 (very risk tolerant). Question 32 is excluded from the scoring because it needs to be assessed apart from the other questions.

Demographic Data---

Question Number	Answer	Question Number	Answer	
1.	____	10. List all numbers circled in numerical order.		List other investments below.
2.	____			_____
3.	____			_____
4.	____		____	_____
5.	____		____	_____
6.	____		____	_____
7.	____		____	_____
8a.	____		____	_____
8b.	____		____	_____
9.	____		____	_____

Appendix E

Comprehensive Financial Planning
Fact Finder

Comprehensive Financial Planning
Fact Finder

Client's Name _____

Spouse's Name _____

Date Compiled _____

The information collected and maintained in this document will be held in the utmost confidentiality. It will not be shared except as may be required by law or as may be authorized in writing by the client.

_____
(Client's Signature)

_____
(Spouse's Signature)

_____
(Advisor's Signature)

THE
AMERICAN
COLLEGE
THE LEADER IN FINANCIAL SERVICES EDUCATION

CONTENTS

PERSONAL DATA

Client's name	
Spouse's name	
Home address	
Mailing address (if different from home address)	
Business address	Client: Spouse:

Phone numbers	Home: Cell: Business:
	            Client Client
	            Spouse Spouse

E-mail address(es)	Home: Business:
	  Client Client
	  Spouse Spouse

Other Advisors

	* ✓	Name	Address	Phone
Attorney personal				
business				
Accountant personal				
business				
Trust officer				
Other bank officer				
Life insurance agent				
Property and liability insurance agent				
Investment advisor (securities broker)				
Primary financial advisor				

* Please check the names of those with whom we can share information about your financial affairs.

Notes

PERSONAL DATA (continued)

Client and Spouse*

	Date of Birth	Social Security Number	Occupation	Amount of Support by Client/Spouse	Health Problems/ Special Needs
Client[1]					
Spouse[1]					

1. If not U.S. citizen, indicate nationality.

Children[2]/Grandchildren

2. Indicate whether by prior marriage, adopted or stepchild.

Client's Parents, Siblings

Spouse's Parents, Siblings

* If possible, obtain addresses, phone numbers, and Social Security numbers of family members, especially those who are, or may become, beneficiaries, executors, guardians, etc.

Notes

PERSONAL DATA (continued)

Marital status	Check appropriate status: ☐ Married ☐ Divorced ☐ Widowed Date: ☐ Never married
	Any former marriages? ☐ Yes ☐ No If yes, to whom? Client: Spouse:

	Client:
	  Are you paying alimony? ☐ Yes ☐ No If yes, amount:
	  Are you paying child support? ☐ Yes ☐ No If yes, amount:
	  Is your spouse paying alimony? ☐ Yes ☐ No If yes, amount:
	  Is your spouse paying child support? ☐ Yes ☐ No If yes, amount:

Nuptial agreements	Does a prenuptial or postnuptial agreement exist? ☐ Yes ☐ No If yes, describe briefly.
Wills	Do you have a will? ☐ Yes ☐ No Date of will:
	Does your spouse have a will? ☐ Yes ☐ No Date of will:
Estate plan	Do you have a basic estate plan? ☐ Yes ☐ No If yes, describe briefly.
Executor nominations	Who has been named as executor in your will? in your spouse's will? Name: Name: Address: Address: Phone: Phone:
Guardian nominations	Have guardians been named for your children? ☐ Yes ☐ No If yes, who? Name: Address: Phone:
Trust/trustee nominations	Have you created grantor, insurance, or testamentary trusts? ☐ Yes ☐ No If yes, who is the trustee?
	Who are the beneficiaries?
	Has your spouse created grantor, insurance, or testamentary trusts? ☐ Yes ☐ No If yes, who is the trustee?
	Who are the beneficiaries?
Custodianships	Have you or your spouse ever made a gift under the Uniform Gifts to Minors Act or Uniform Transfer to Minors Act? ☐ Yes ☐ No If yes, in which state?
	Who is the custodian?
	Who are the donees?
Trust beneficiary	Are you or any members of your immediate family beneficiaries of a trust? ☐ Yes ☐ No If yes, who? Amount expected:
Gifts/inheritances	Do you or your spouse expect to receive gifts/inheritances? ☐ Yes ☐ No If yes, who? How much? From whom? When?
Education	What is the level of your education?
	What is the level of your spouse's education?
Military or government service benefits	Are you or your spouse eligible for any benefits deriving from military or government service? ☐ Yes ☐ No If yes, explain.

Notes

FINANCIAL OBJECTIVES

Rank from 1 to 9 the importance of being able to do the following:

_____   Maintain/expand standard of living/family income.

_____   Enjoy a comfortable retirement/retirement planning.

_____   Take care of self and family during a period of long-term disability.

_____   Invest and accumulate wealth/investment planning.

_____   Reduce income tax burden/income tax planning.

_____   Provide college educations for children.

_____   Take care of family in the event of my death/insurance planning.

_____   Develop an estate distribution plan/estate planning.

_____   Other important financial planning goals. Specify:

Do you have a formal monthly budget?	☐ Yes ☐ No	If yes, indicate amount:
How much do you save/invest annually?	In what form?	Why?
How much do you think you should be able to save/invest annually?		For what purpose?

FACTORS AFFECTING YOUR FINANCIAL PLAN

Have you or your spouse ever made substantial gifts to family members or to tax-exempt beneficiaries?   ☐ Yes ☐ No
If yes, give details.

What special bequests do you or your spouse intend to make (including charitable bequests)?

Are you dissatisfied with your previous saving/investment results?   ☐ Yes ☐ No Explain.

Are there any savings/investments you feel committed to (for past performance, family, or social reasons)? ☐ Yes   ☐ No
If yes, explain.

Is your spouse good at handling money? ☐ Yes   ☐ No

If you die, would your spouse be able to manage family finances? ☐ Yes   ☐ No

At what age would you like to retire?   At what age would your spouse like to retire?

Tax considerations aside, in what manner would you (or your spouse) want your estate(s) distributed? Explain.

What do you think financial planning should do for you?

Notes

OBJECTIVES REQUIRING ADDITIONAL INCOME/CAPITAL

Do your children attend public or private schools?	
If private, annual cost: (elementary)	(secondary)

Do you plan for your children to attend private schools later? ☐ Yes ☐ No

If yes, when?

Education Fund

Name of Child	Age	No. Years until College	Estimated 4-Year Cost		Estimated Graduate School Costs	Capital Allocated	Monthly Income Allocated
			If Private	**If Public**			

Support for Family Member(s)

Name	Age	Relation	Estimated Cost	Estimated Period of Funding	Capital Allocated	Monthly Income Allocated

Other Objectives

Objective	Target Date	Estimated Cost	Estimated Period of Funding	Capital Allocated	Monthly Income Allocated

Notes

SOURCES OF INCOME

Annual Income

	Client	Spouse*	Dependents*
Wages, salary, bonus, etc.			
Income as business owner (self-employment)			
Real estate rental			
Dividends			
Investments (public stock, mutual funds, etc.)			
Close corporation stock			
Interest			
Investments (bonds, money market funds, T-bills, etc.)			
Savings accounts, certificates of deposit			
Loans, notes			
Trust income			
Life insurance settlement options			
Child support/alimony			
Annuities			
Other sources (specify)			
Other sources (specify)			
Other sources (specify)			
Total annual income			

*If spouse or dependents are employed, give details here.

Income Tax Last year

Federal			
State			
Local			
Total income tax paid last year			
Estimated quarterly tax this year			

Future Annual Income Estimate

Next year			
Three years			
Five years			
How often do you expect a salary increase or bonus?			
On average, how much of a salary increase or bonus do you expect annually?			
Has your total annual income fluctuated significantly during the past three years?			

CASH FLOW STATEMENT

Annual Income

	Current Yr. 20____	Projections for Subsequent Years				
		Assumptions	20____	20____	20____	20____
Wages, salary, bonus, etc.: Client						
Wages, salary, bonus, etc.: Spouse						
Income as business owner (self-employment)						
Real estate rental						
Dividends—investments						
Dividends—close corporation stock						
Interest on bonds: Taxable						
Interest on bonds: Tax exempt						
Interest on savings accts., CDs						
Interest on loans, notes, etc.						
Trust income						
Life insurance settlement options						
Annuities						
Child support/alimony						
Other sources (specify)						
Total annual income						

Fixed Expenses

Housing (mortgage/rent)						
Utilities and telephone						
Food, groceries, etc.						
Clothing and cleaning						
Income and Social Security taxes						
Property taxes						
Transportation (auto/commuting)						
Medical/dental/drugs/health insurance						
Debt repayment						
House upkeep/repairs/maintenance						
Life, property and liability insurance						
Child support/alimony						
Current education expenses						
Total fixed expenses						

Discretionary Expenses

Vacations/travel/etc.						
Recreation/entertainment						
Contributions/gifts						
Household furnishings						
Education fund						
Savings/investments						
Other (specify)						
Total discretionary expenses						
Total annual expenses						
Net cash flow (total annual income minus total annual expenses)						

INVENTORY OF ASSETS

Cash, Near-Cash Equivalents

Items	No. Units or Shares	Date Acquired	Amount, Cost, or Other Basis	Market Value and Titled Owners					
				Client	Spouse	Joint (survivor rights)	Joint (no survivor rights)	Community Property	Other*
Checking accounts/cash									
Savings accounts									
Money-market funds									
Treasury bills									
Commercial paper									
Short-term CDs									
Cash value, life insurance									
Accum. dividends, life insurance									
Savings bonds									
Other (specify)									
Subtotal									

U.S. Govt., Municipal, Corporate Bonds, and Bond Funds: Issuer, Maturity, Call Dates

Subtotal									

Preferred Stock: Issuer, Maturity, Call Dates

Subtotal									

Common Stock: Issuer, Listed (L), Unlisted (U), Nonmarketable (NM)

Subtotal									

Warrants and Options: Issuer, Expiration Date

Subtotal									

Mutual Funds and Type: Growth (G), Income (I), Balanced (B), Indexed (IX), Speculative (S)

Subtotal									

*Life estate, leasehold or term interest, future interest, tenancy in common, powers, children, custodial accounts, trusts, etc.

INVENTORY OF ASSETS (continued)

Cash, Near-Cash Equivalents

Annual Yield		Amount Available for Liquidity	Amount of Indebt-edness	Location, Description, Client's Reasons for Holding Asset, etc.	Items
%	$				
					Checking accounts/cash
					Savings accounts
					Money-market funds
					Treasury bills
					Commercial paper
					Short-term CDs
					Cash value, life insurance
					Accum. dividends, life insurance
					Savings bonds
					Other (specify)
					Subtotal

U.S. Govt., Municipal, Corporate Bonds, and Bond Funds: Issuer, Maturity, Call Dates

					Subtotal

Preferred Stock: Issuer, Maturity, Call Dates

					Subtotal

Common Stock: Issuer, Listed (L), Unlisted (U), Nonmarketable (NM)

					Subtotal

Warrants and Options: Issuer, Expiration Date

					Subtotal

Mutual Funds and Type: Growth (G), Income (I), Balanced (B), Indexed (IX), Speculative (S)

					Subtotal

INVENTORY OF ASSETS (continued)

Real Estate

Items	No. Units or Shares	Date Acquired	Amount, Cost, or Other Basis	Market Value and Titled Owners					
				Client	Spouse	Joint (survivor rights)	Joint (no survivor rights)	Community Property	Other*
Personal residence									
Seasonal residence									
Investment (residential)									
Investment (commercial)									
Land									
Other (specify)									
Subtotal									

Long-Term, Nonmarketable Assets

Long-term CDs									
Vested retirement benefits									
Life insurance cash values									
Annuities (fixed/indexed/variable)									
HR-10 plan (Keogh)									
IRAs (Roth/traditional)									
Mortgages owned									
Land contracts									
Limited partnership units									
Other (specify)									
Subtotal									

Personal Assets

Household furnishings									
Automobile(s)									
Recreational vehicles									
Boats									
Jewelry/furs									
Collections (art, coins, etc.)									
Hobby equipment									
Other (specify)									
Subtotal									

Miscellaneous Assets

Interest(s) in trust(s)									
Receivables									
Patents, copyrights, royalties									
Other (specify)									
Subtotal									
Totals of all columns									

*Life estate, leasehold or term interest, future interest, tenancy in common, powers, children, custodial accounts, trusts, etc.

INVENTORY OF ASSETS (continued)

Real Estate

Annual Yield		Amount Available for Liquidity	Amount of Indebt-edness	Location, Description, Client's Reasons for Holding Asset, etc.	Items
%	$				
					Personal residence
					Seasonal residence
					Investment (residential)
					Investment (commercial)
					Land
					Other (specify)
					Subtotal

Long-Term, Nonmarketable Assets

					Long-term CDs
					Vested retirement benefits
					Life insurance cash values
					Annuities (fixed/indexed/variable)
					HR-10 plan (Keogh)
					IRAs (Roth/traditional)
					Mortgages owned
					Land contracts
					Limited partnership units
					Other (specify)
					Subtotal

Personal Assets

					Household furnishings
					Automobile(s)
					Recreational vehicles
					Boats
					Jewelry/furs
					Collections (art, coins, etc.)
					Hobby equipment
					Other (specify)
					Subtotal

Miscellaneous Assets

					Interest(s) in trust(s)
					Receivables
					Patents, copyrights, royalties
					Other (specify)
					Subtotal
					Totals of all columns

BUSINESS INTEREST

General Information

Full legal name	Phone
Address	
Business now operates as ☐ proprietorship ☐ partnership ☐ corporation ☐ S corporation ☐ other (specify)	
When does the fiscal year end?	
What accounting method is used?	
What is the principal business activity?	
In what year did this business begin operation?	

If it began other than as a corporation, what was the date of incorporation?	State of incorporation?	
Classes of stock	No. authorized shares	No. outstanding shares

What is your function in the business?
Do you have an employment contract?

Present Owners*

		Insurability Problem?		Form of Business		
				Corporation		Partnership
		Yes	No			
(A)	_Client_	☐	☐	owns _____ % common _____ % preferred		_____ % _____
(B)	_____	☐	☐	owns _____ % common _____ % preferred		_____ % _____
(C)	_____	☐	☐	owns _____ % common _____ % preferred		_____ % _____
(D)	_____	☐	☐	owns _____ % common _____ % preferred		_____ % _____
(E)	_____	☐	☐	owns _____ % common _____ % preferred		_____ % _____

* Indicate relationship to client by blood or marriage.

Key Employees (other than present owners)

	Insurability Problem			Insurability Problem	
	Yes	No		Yes	No
_____	☐	☐	_____	☐	☐
_____	☐	☐	_____	☐	☐
_____	☐	☐	_____	☐	☐
_____	☐	☐	_____	☐	☐

BUSINESS INTEREST (continued)

Disposition of Business Interest

Do you want your business interest retained or sold if you
retire? ☐ retained ☐ sold   become disabled? ☐ retained ☐ sold   die? ☐ retained ☐ sold

IF RETAINED
Who will own your interest and how will the person(s) acquire it?

Who will replace you in your job?

IF SOLD
Who will buy your interest?

How is purchase price to be determined?

What is the funding arrangement?

Do you have a buy-sell agreement?   ☐ Yes ☐ No

If yes, is it a cross-purchase, entity-purchase, or "wait-and-see" type of agreement?

Where is it located?

Valuation of Business Interest

Estimate the lowest price for which the entire business might be sold as a going concern today.

What is the lowest price you would accept for your interest today?

If you were not an owner, what is your estimate of the highest price you would pay today for the entire business as a going concern?

What is the highest price you would pay today to buy the interest of your coowners?

Has an impartial valuation of the business been made? ☐ Yes ☐ No If yes, when?
What valuation method was used?   What value was established?

What is the average business indebtedness?
Estimate the highest it has ever been.   Estimate the lowest it has ever been.

Are there patents, special processes, or leased equipment/real property used by, but not owned by, the business?
☐ Yes ☐ No If yes, who owns what, and under what terms is each used or leased?

What are the prospects for growth, sale, merger, or going public?

Survivor Control (letters in parentheses refer to owners named on page 14)

IF (A) DIES	IF (B) DIES	IF (C) DIES	IF (D) DIES	IF (E) DIES
B wants _____% control	A wants _____%	A wants _____%	A wants _____%	A wants _____%
C wants _____% control	C wants _____%	B wants _____%	B wants _____%	B wants _____%
D wants _____% control	D wants _____%	D wants _____%	C wants _____%	C wants _____%
E wants _____% control	E wants _____%	E wants _____%	E wants _____%	D wants _____%
__ wants _____% control	__ wants _____%	__ wants _____%	__ wants _____%	__ wants _____%

EMPLOYEE CENSUS DATA*

	Sex	Marital Status	Name			Date of Birth			Date Employed†			Full-time‡	Hourly	Salaried	Earnings		Member of Collective Bargaining Unit?	Occupation or Job Title
			Last	First	M.I.	Month	Day	Year	Month	Day	Year				Annual Salary or Wage	Additional Compensation		
1																		
2																		
3																		
4																		
5																		
6																		
7																		
8																		
9																		
10																		
11																		
12																		
13																		
14																		
15																		
16																		
17																		
18																		
19																		
20																		
21																		
22																		
23																		
24																		
25																		

*It is suggested that the client request this data directly from the bookkeeper or other appropriate person.
†The date of its incorporation is also the date of employment of former proprietors or partners of a business.
‡A full-time employee is one who works 1,000 or more hours per year.

INVENTORY OF LIABILITIES

Outstanding Obligations of Client or Spouse	Original Amount	Maximum Credit Available	Present Balance	Monthly/ Annual Repayment	Effective Interest Rate	Payments Remaining/ Maturity Date	Secured?	Insured?
Retail charge accounts								
Credit cards								
Family/personal loans								
Securities margin loans								
Investment liabilities								
Bank loans								
Life insurance policy loans								
Income tax liability								
Federal								
State								
Local								
Property taxes								
Mortgage(s)								
Lease(s)								
Family member support								
Child support/alimony								
Other (specify)								
Total								

Are there any other liabilities your estate might be called on to pay?   ☐ Yes ☐ No If yes, explain.

Do you foresee any future liabilities (business expansion, new home, etc.)?   ☐ Yes ☐ No If yes, explain.

INDIVIDUALLY OWNED INSURANCE*

Life Insurance

Item	Policy 1	Policy 2	Policy 3
Policy number			
Name of insurance company			
Issue age			
Insured			
Owner of policy			
Type of policy			
Annual premium			
Net annual outlay by client			
Current cash value			
Extra benefits (for example, waiver of premium, accidental death, etc.)			
Amount of base policy			
Dividends (value & option)			
Term rider(s)			
Loan outstanding			
Net amount payable at death			
Primary beneficiary and settlement option elected			
Secondary beneficiary and settlement option elected			

Long-Term Care Insurance

Item	Policy 1	Policy 2	Policy 3
Policy number			
Name of insurance company			
Issue age			
Insured			
Owner of policy			
Type of policy (Qualified/Nonqualified)			
Annual premium			
Inflation protection			
Nonforfeiture benefit			
Third party notification Name:			
Issued prior to January 1, 1997	☐ Yes ☐ No	☐ Yes ☐ No	☐ Yes ☐ No
Level of care			
Term rider(s)			
Elimination period (days)			
Maximum duration (years)			
Restoration	☐ Yes ☐ No	☐ Yes ☐ No	☐ Yes ☐ No
Spousal coverage	☐ Yes ☐ No	☐ Yes ☐ No	☐ Yes ☐ No
Maximum benefit day/cumulative			

*Policies and most recent policy anniversary premium notices should be examined for the information recorded on this page.

INDIVIDUALLY OWNED INSURANCE* (continued)

Medical/Dental Insurance

Item	Policy 1	Policy 2	Policy 3	Policy 4
Type of policy				
Policy number				
Name of insurance company or other provider				
Insured				
Annual cost to client				
Type of continuance or renewal provision				
Deductible				
Percentage participation				
Stop-loss limit				
Inside limits				
Overall maximum				

Disability Income Insurance

Item	Policy 1	Policy 2	Policy 3	Policy 4
Policy number				
Name of insurance company or other provider				
Insured				
Annual cost to client				
Type of continuance or renewal provision				
Definition of disability				
Monthly disability income				
Accident				
Sickness				
Partial disability provision				
Waiting period				
Accident				
Sickness				
Benefit period				
Accident				
Sickness				

*Policies should be examined for the information recorded on this page.

INDIVIDUALLY OWNED INSURANCE* (continued)

Homeowners Insurance

Item	Principal Residence	Seasonal Residence	Other Property
Policy number			
Name of insurance company			
Address of property			
HO form # (or other type of policy)			
Coverage on dwelling			
Replacement cost of dwelling			
Replacement cost of contents			
Liability limits			
Endorsements			
Deductibles			
Annual cost			

Automobile Insurance

Item	Auto #1	Auto #2	Auto #3 (or other vehicles, trailers)
Policy number			
Name of insurance company			
Automobile make/year			
Liability limits			
No-fault/medical benefits			
Uninsured motorist			
Collision/deductible			
Comprehensive/deductible			
Annual cost			

Other Property/Liability Insurance

Item	Policy 1	Policy 2	Policy 3
Type of policy			
Policy number			
Name of insurance company			
Property covered			
Limits			
Annual cost			

Umbrella Liability Insurance

Item	Policy
Policy number	
Name of insurance company	
Liability limits	
Retention	
Annual cost	

*Policies should be examined for the information recorded on this page.

EMPLOYMENT-RELATED BENEFITS CHECKLIST

Name and address of client's employer _____

Name and address of spouse's employer _____

Who can provide detailed information on employee benefits for you and your spouse?

Client	*Spouse*
Name _____	Name _____
Title _____	Title _____
Department _____	Department _____
Phone _____	Phone _____

	Benefit now provided for client?		Benefit now provided for spouse?		Information/Comments
Life and Health Insurance	Yes	No	Yes	No	
Death benefits	☐	☐	☐	☐	_____
Accidental death/dismemberment	☐	☐	☐	☐	_____
Travel accident	☐	☐	☐	☐	_____
Medical expense benefits	☐	☐	☐	☐	_____
Short-term disability income (sick pay)	☐	☐	☐	☐	_____
Long-term disability income	☐	☐	☐	☐	_____
Retirement Benefits/ Deferred Compensation*					
Qualified pension plan	☐	☐	☐	☐	_____
Qualified profit-sharing plan	☐	☐	☐	☐	_____
Nonqualified deferred-compensation plan	☐	☐	☐	☐	_____
Salary reduction plan [§401(k)]	☐	☐	☐	☐	_____
Simplified employee pension (SEP)	☐	☐	☐	☐	_____
Stock bonus plan	☐	☐	☐	☐	_____
Employee stock-ownership plan (ESOP)	☐	☐	☐	☐	_____
Employee stock-purchase plan	☐	☐	☐	☐	_____
Incentive stock-option plan [§422]	☐	☐	☐	☐	_____
Restricted stock plan [§83(b)]	☐	☐	☐	☐	_____
Phantom stock plan [§83(a)]	☐	☐	☐	☐	_____
Tax-deferred annuity plan [§403(b)]	☐	☐	☐	☐	_____
Salary continuation after death	☐	☐	☐	☐	_____
Other (specify)	☐	☐	☐	☐	_____
Miscellaneous Benefits					
Excess medical reimbursement plan	☐	☐	☐	☐	_____
Split-dollar life insurance	☐	☐	☐	☐	_____
Auto/homeowners insurance	☐	☐	☐	☐	_____
Legal expense	☐	☐	☐	☐	_____
Company car	☐	☐	☐	☐	_____
Education reimbursement	☐	☐	☐	☐	_____
Club membership	☐	☐	☐	☐	_____
Other (specify)	☐	☐	☐	☐	_____

*Describe appropriate benefits on page 22.

EMPLOYMENT-RELATED
RETIREMENT BENEFITS/DEFERRED COMPENSATION

Type	Employee's Annual Contribution	Benefits to Client			Benefits to Survivors			
		Lump-sum Pmts.	Monthly Income		Beneficiary	Lump-sum Pmts.	Monthly Income	
			Amount	Beginning/ Ending			Amount	Beginning/ Ending
Qualified pension plan								
Qualified profit-sharing plan								
Nonqualified deferred-compensation plan								
Salary reduction plan [§401(k)]								
Stock bonus plan								
Employee stock-ownership plan (ESOP)								
Employee stock-purchase plan								
Incentive stock-option plan [§422]								
Restricted stock plan [§83(b)]								
Phantom stock plan [§83(a)]								
Tax-deferred annuity plan [§403(b)]								
Salary continuation after death								
Other (specify)								
Other (specify)								

Explain and describe pertinent details for planning purposes here (for example, anticipated benefits not yet in place; client's views on relevance, need, and feasibility of these benefits; problems associated with implementing benefits; etc.).

Social Security Benefits

What are the estimated retirement benefits (in current dollars)?
Client only: Client and spouse:
What are the estimated disability benefits the client is eligible for if disabled today?
Client only: Client and spouse:
What are the estimated survivor's benefits payable to the client's family if death should occur today?

RISK/RETURN PROFILE

On a scale from 0 to 5, with 5 representing a strong preference and 0 representing an aversion, indicate your preference for the following instruments of savings and investment by circling the appropriate number.

Savings account	0	1	2	3	4	5
Money-market fund	0	1	2	3	4	5
U.S. government bond	0	1	2	3	4	5
Corporate bond	0	1	2	3	4	5
Mutual fund (growth)	0	1	2	3	4	5
Common stock (growth)	0	1	2	3	4	5
Mutual fund (income)	0	1	2	3	4	5
Municipal bond	0	1	2	3	4	5
Real estate (direct ownership)	0	1	2	3	4	5
Variable annuity	0	1	2	3	4	5
Limited partnership unit (real estate, oil and gas, cattle, equipment leasing)	0	1	2	3	4	5
Commodities, gold, collectibles	0	1	2	3	4	5

On a scale from 0 to 5, circle the number to the right of each of the items below that most accurately reflects your own financial concerns; 5 indicates a very strong concern and 0 indicates no concern.

Liquidity	0	1	2	3	4	5
Safety of principal	0	1	2	3	4	5
Capital appreciation	0	1	2	3	4	5
Current income	0	1	2	3	4	5
Inflation protection	0	1	2	3	4	5
Future income	0	1	2	3	4	5
Tax reduction/deferral	0	1	2	3	4	5

Advisor's comments and observations

INCOME AND LUMP-SUM NEEDS FOR DISABILITY, RETIREMENT, AND DEATH

	Client	Spouse/ Children
Disability Income Needs Monthly income needed in current dollars	$ _____	$ _____
Retirement Income Needs Monthly income needed in current dollars	$ _____	$ _____
Survivors' Income Needs* Monthly income needed in current dollars for surviving family members during the following periods after death:		
Adjustment period (adjustment of standard of living in a transitional period, as needed)	$ _____	$ _____
Until youngest child is self-supporting (number of years _____)	$ _____	$ _____
After youngest child is self-supporting	$ _____	$ _____
Survivors' Lump-sum Needs* Last expenses (final illness and funeral)	$ _____	$ _____
Emergency fund	$ _____	$ _____
Mortgage cancellation fund (if appropriate)	$ _____	$ _____
Notes and loans payable	$ _____	$ _____
Accrued taxes (income, real estate, etc., if not withheld)	$ _____	$ _____
Children's education (if not already funded)	$ _____	$ _____
Estate settlement costs and taxes (if not provided by liquidity)	$ _____	$ _____
Other (specify)	$ _____	$ _____
Total lump-sum needs in current dollars	$ _____	$ _____

* Some survivors' needs may be met by either periodic income or lump-sum payments or by some combination of the two approaches. Double counting in both categories should be avoided.

Notes

AUTHORIZATION FOR INFORMATION

TO: _____

_____

_____

Please provide any information that is in your possession and that is asked for in connection with a survey of my/our financial affairs to _____

_____
(client's signature)

_____
(spouse's signature)

_____
(date)

TO: _____
(company)

Please provide any information that is in your possession and that is requested by _____

_____ concerning the following policies of which I am the owner:

_____   _____

_____   _____

_____   _____

_____
(policyowner's signature)

_____
(date)

[Page intentionally left blank]

RECEIPT FOR DOCUMENTS

Insurance Policies: Life, Long-Term Care, Medical/Dental, Disability Income, and Property/Liability

Company	Policy Number	☑	Company	Policy Number	☑
_____	_____	☐	_____	_____	☐
_____	_____	☐	_____	_____	☐
_____	_____	☐	_____	_____	☐
_____	_____	☐	_____	_____	☐
_____	_____	☐	_____	_____	☐

Original policies checked ☑ above have been received for review and analysis; they will be returned upon completion of analysis or client request.

_____
(advisor)

_____
(address)

_____
(phone)

_____
(date)

All original policies and documents checked in this receipt have been returned to me.

_____
(client)

_____
(date)

Personal/Family Documents (copies)	**Date**	**Business Documents (copies)**	**Date**
☐ Tax returns (3–5 years)	_____	☐ Tax returns (3–5 years)	_____
☐ Wills (client and spouse)	_____	☐ Financial statements (3–5 years)	_____
☐ Trust instruments	_____	☐ Deferred-compensation plan	_____
☐ Financial statements	_____	☐ HR-10 plan (Keogh)	_____
☐ Personal/family budgets	_____	☐ IRAs (Roth/traditional)	_____
☐ Sale/purchase contract	_____	☐ Simplified employee pension (SEP)	_____
☐ Current insurance offers	_____	☐ Pension/profit-sharing plan	_____
☐ Current investment offers	_____	☐ §401(k) or §403(b) plan	_____
☐ Deeds, mortgages, land contracts	_____	☐ Stock-option/purchase agreement	_____
☐ Guardian nominations	_____	☐ Buy-sell agreements	_____
☐ Leases (as lessor or lessee)	_____	☐ Employment agreement	_____
☐ Notices of awards, elections	_____	☐ Employee benefits booklet	_____
☐ Power of attorney/appointment	_____	☐ Articles of incorporation	_____
☐ Separation/divorce/nuptial	_____	☐ Merger/acquisition agreement	_____
☐ Patents/copyrights/royalties	_____	☐ Partnership agreement	_____
☐ Employee benefits statement	_____	☐ Company patents	_____
☐ Other (specify)	_____	☐ Equipment leasing agreement(s)	_____
☐ Other (specify)	_____	☐ Other (specify)	_____

[Page intentionally left blank]

OBSERVATIONS FROM PLANNING SESSIONS

As soon after planning sessions as possible the financial advisor should record observations and impressions about the client in terms of the following:

Personal interests (sports, hobbies, music, etc.) _____

_____

_____

Civic-mindedness _____

_____

Financial sophistication _____

_____

College ties _____

_____

Condition of health _____

_____

_____

Financial risk-taking propensity _____

_____

Investment decisions client has made and why _____

_____

_____

Observations and impressions

[Page intentionally left blank]

TAX-PLANNING CHECKLIST*

Individual Planning

	At Present Yes	No	Advisable Yes	No
1. Does the client itemize rather than utilize the standard deduction?	☐	☐	☐	☐
2. Are all personal and dependency exemptions being taken (children, parents, foster children, etc.)? [§§151, 152]	☐	☐	☐	☐
3. Are maximum deductions for all expenses related to the production of income being taken?	☐	☐	☐	☐
4. a. Is optimum utilization being made of retirement plans for tax advantage?	☐	☐	☐	☐
b. Has the appropriate type of plan or plans been chosen?	☐	☐	☐	☐
5. Are contributions to charitable and other tax-exempt organizations being used as fully as the client is disposed to use them? [§170]	☐	☐	☐	☐
6. Are the client's real property investments being fully used for tax advantages?	☐	☐	☐	☐
7. Is the impact of the alternative minimum tax being considered for transactions involving tax-preference items? [§55]	☐	☐	☐	☐
8. Are income and deductions being directed to specific years to avoid drastic fluctuation by				
a. accelerating income	☐	☐	☐	☐
b. postponing deductions	☐	☐	☐	☐
c. postponing income	☐	☐	☐	☐
d. accelerating deductions	☐	☐	☐	☐
e. avoiding constructive receipt	☐	☐	☐	☐
9. To reduce estate taxes				
a. Have incidents of life insurance ownership been assigned?	☐	☐	☐	☐
b. Is a life insurance trust being used? [§§2035, 2042]	☐	☐	☐	☐
10. Have installment sales of investments or property been arranged to minimize tax? [§453]	☐	☐	☐	☐
11. Is investment in tax-exempt instruments being used?	☐	☐	☐	☐
12. Is income being shifted to lower-bracket taxpayers through outright gifts or other lifetime transfers such as family partnerships or irrevocable trusts?	☐	☐	☐	☐
13. Is a qualified minors [§2503(c)] trust being used effectively for income shifting or other tax advantage?	☐	☐	☐	☐
14. Have gifts been made under the Uniform Gifts to Minors Act (UGMA) or the Uniform Transfers to Minors Act (UTMA)?	☐	☐	☐	☐
15. Are gift/sale leasebacks being used?	☐	☐	☐	☐

*All code section references are to the Internal Revenue Code of 1986 as amended.

TAX-PLANNING CHECKLIST (continued)

Individual Planning (continued)

		At Present Yes	No	Advisable Yes	No
16.	Have alternative distribution methods for qualified plans been analyzed for tax consequences?	☐	☐	☐	☐
17.	Are capital-loss offsets being used to reduce total income subject to tax?	☐	☐	☐	☐
18.	Are qualified plan distributions, rollovers to another qualified plan, or IRAs advisable for the client in the near future?	☐	☐	☐	☐
19.	Are contributions to a new or existing IRA advisable if				
	a. the client can make deductible contributions?	☐	☐	☐	☐
	b. the client can make only nondeductible contributions?	☐	☐	☐	☐
20.	Have like-kind exchanges of property been compared with sale and repurchase and utilized when more advantageous? [§1031]	☐	☐	☐	☐
21.	Is the client paying substantial amounts of nondeductible loan interest that should be consolidated under deductible home equity loans? [§163]	☐	☐	☐	☐
22.	Have returns of capital on investment been distinguished from taxable income? (For example, has the client's basis in the investment been ascertained and any special tax treatment to which that investment is entitled determined?)	☐	☐	☐	☐
23.	Is the client suited for tax-advantaged investments?	☐	☐	☐	☐
24.	Indicate any situation unique to this client that does not appear above.				

TAX-PLANNING CHECKLIST (continued)

Business Planning

	At Present Yes	No	Advisable Yes	No
1. Are maximum allowable deductions for all expenses being taken?	☐	☐	☐	☐
2. Are expiring carryovers of credits, net operating losses, and charitable contributions being effectively used through timing of income and deductions? [§§39, 170, 172]	☐	☐	☐	☐
3. a. Is optimum use being made of retirement plans for tax advantage?	☐	☐	☐	☐
b. Has the appropriate type of plan or plans been chosen?	☐	☐	☐	☐
4. Are contributions to charitable and other tax-exempt organizations being used as fully as the client is disposed to use them? [§§170, 501]	☐	☐	☐	☐
5. a. Is the form of client's business or investment being fully utilized to maximize personal deductions and credits (for example, corporation, partnership, trust, S corp.)?	☐	☐	☐	☐
b. Are the business's investments being fully used to maximize deductions and credits to the shareholder(s)?	☐	☐	☐	☐
6. Are income and deductions being directed to specific years to avoid drastic fluctuation by				
a. accelerating income	☐	☐	☐	☐
b. postponing deductions	☐	☐	☐	☐
c. postponing income	☐	☐	☐	☐
d. accelerating deductions	☐	☐	☐	☐
e. avoiding constructive receipt	☐	☐	☐	☐
7. Is the full range of deductible employment fringe benefits being explored and used within the client's limits?	☐	☐	☐	☐
8. Are gift/sale leasebacks appropriate for this client?	☐	☐	☐	☐
9. Have alternative distribution methods for qualified plans been analyzed for tax consequences?	☐	☐	☐	☐
10. Is sale-or-exchange treatment preferable for redemption of equity in a closely held corporation? [§§301, 302, 303, 318]	☐	☐	☐	☐
11. Have nonqualified retirement or deferred-compensation plans been considered? [§83]	☐	☐	☐	☐
12. Are stock options possible and advantageous? [§422]	☐	☐	☐	☐
13. Have simplified employee pensions (SEPs) been compared with other forms of deferred compensation?	☐	☐	☐	☐
14. Are qualified plans designed for maximum employee advantage during employment as well as at retirement? (For example, do they permit loans and rollovers from other plans, etc.?)	☐	☐	☐	☐

TAX-PLANNING CHECKLIST (continued)

Business Planning (continued)

		At Present		Advisable	
		Yes	No	Yes	No
15.	a. Have buy-sell plans to take effect at death been developed and formalized by legal agreements?	☐	☐	☐	☐
	b. If yes, have they been appropriately funded?	☐	☐	☐	☐
16.	Have lifetime transfer methods been considered to facilitate the orderly continuation of the business, for example, in case of disability?	☐	☐	☐	☐
17.	Are employment contracts being used effectively to support the reasonableness of executive compensation?	☐	☐	☐	☐
18.	Indicate any situation unique to this client that does not appear above.				

TAX-PLANNING CHECKLIST (continued)

Estate Planning

		At Present		Advisable	
		Yes	No	Yes	No
1.	Have the client and spouse considered electing not to fully use the marital deduction if such an election is tax advantageous to their cumulative estates? [§2056]	☐	☐	☐	☐
2.	Have life insurance policies been properly positioned to minimize estate taxes?	☐	☐	☐	☐
3.	Does the estate appear to have sufficient liquidity to fund postmortem expenses and estate/inheritance tax liabilities?	☐	☐	☐	☐
4.	Has optimum use been made of generation-skipping transfer exemptions? [§§2601–2664]	☐	☐	☐	☐
5.	Have testamentary charitable dispositions and their advantages been explored? [§2055]	☐	☐	☐	☐
6.	a. Are lifetime gifting programs being used to shift ownership of assets from the client's estate? [§§2503(b), 2503(c)]	☐	☐	☐	☐
	b. Have gifts been made under the Uniform Gifts to Minors Act (UGMA) or the Uniform Transfers to Minors Act (UTMA)?	☐	☐	☐	☐
7.	a. Is the client's will current?	☐	☐	☐	☐
	b. Does the will dispose of estate assets in accordance with the client's wishes?	☐	☐	☐	☐
8.	Has the value of each estate asset been explored in order to obtain an estimate of potential estate tax liability?	☐	☐	☐	☐
9.	Has it been determined that the client can qualify for estate tax deferral? [§6166]	☐	☐	☐	☐
10.	If the client qualifies for the requisite percentage of ownership in a corporation, can §303 be utilized to assure sale-or-exchange treatment for stock redeemed to pay administration expenses and estate taxes?	☐	☐	☐	☐
11.	Have the client's personal planning objectives, feelings, and thoughts been given equal weight with tax planning?	☐	☐	☐	☐
12.	Has an existing estate plan been evaluated as to the impact of the current applicable credit amount, marital deduction, and gift tax exclusion? [§§2010, 2056, 2503, 2523]	☐	☐	☐	☐
13.	Has the impact of state death taxes on the client's estate been evaluated?	☐	☐	☐	☐
14.	Has consideration been given to the potential consequence of certain transfers made within 3 years of death? [§2035]	☐	☐	☐	☐
15.	Have rules on valuation of certain property (for example, family farms and real property used in a closely held business) been considered? [§2032A]	☐	☐	☐	☐
16.	a. Does the client have any reversionary interests or hold any powers of appointment?	☐	☐	☐	☐
	b. If so, have they been examined for their potential tax impact? [§§2037, 2041]	☐	☐	☐	☐
17.	a. Does the client have an incapacity plan in place?	☐	☐	☐	☐
	b. Does the client have a durable power of attorney?	☐	☐	☐	☐
	c. Has consideration been given to appropriate health care and advance medical directive documents?	☐	☐	☐	☐
18.	Indicate any situation unique to this client that does not appear above.				

[Page intentionally left blank]

FINANCIAL POSITION STATEMENT

Assets

Cash, Near-Cash Equivalents	Current Value	Projections for Subsequent Years			
		Assumptions	20____	20____	20____
Checking accounts/cash					
Savings accounts					
Money-market funds					
Treasury bills					
Commercial paper					
Short-term CDs					
Life insurance/annuity cash values					
Life insurance, accumulated dividends					
Savings bonds					
Other (specify)					
Subtotal					

Other Financial Assets					
U.S. government bonds					
Municipal bonds					
Corporate bonds					
Preferred stock					
Common stock					
Nonmarketable securities					
Warrants and options					
Mutual funds					
Investment real estate (residential/commercial)					
Long-term CDs					
Vested retirement benefits					
Annuities (fixed/indexed/variable)					
HR-10 plan (Keogh)					
IRAs (Roth/traditional)					
Mortgages owned					
Land contracts					
Limited partnership units					
Interest(s) in trust(s)					
Receivables					
Patents, copyrights, royalties					
Value of business interest (from page 15)					
Other (specify)					
Subtotal					

FINANCIAL POSITION STATEMENT (continued)

Assets (continued)

Personal Assets	Current Value	Projections for Subsequent Years			
		Assumptions	20___	20___	20___
Personal residence					
Seasonal residence					
Automobile(s)					
Recreation vehicles					
Household furnishings					
Boats					
Jewelry/furs					
Collections (art, coins, etc.)					
Hobby equipment					
Other (specify)					
Subtotal					
Total assets					

Liabilities

Charge accts./credit cards					
Family/personal loans					
Margin/bank/life ins. loans					
Income taxes (fed., state, local)					
Property taxes					
Investment liabilities					
Mortgage(s)					
Lease(s)					
Child support					
Alimony					
Other (specify)					
Other (specify)					
Other (specify)					
Total Liabilities					

Net Worth

Total assets minus total liabilities					

INCOME AND LUMP-SUM RESOURCES FOR DISABILITY, RETIREMENT*, AND DEATH

Sources of Funds	For Disability			For Retirement			For Death		
	Lump-sum Pmts.	Monthly Income		Lump-sum Pmts.	Monthly Income		Lump-sum Pmts.	Monthly Income	
		Amount	Begin-ning/ Ending		Amount	Begin-ning/ Ending		Amount	Begin-ning/ Ending
Continuing income†									
Income of spouse									
Social Security benefits‡									
Qualified pension plan									
Qualified profit-sharing plan									
HR-10 plan (Keogh)									
IRAs (Roth/traditional)									
Nonqualified deferred compensation									
Salary reduction plan [§401(k)]									
Tax-deferred annuity plan [§403(b)]									
Other retirement benefits*									
Group life insurance									
Personal life insurance									
Annuities (fixed, indexed, variable)									
Group short-term disability income									
Group long-term disability income									
Personal disability income insurance									
Asset liquidation									
Proceeds of sale of business interest									
Other (specify)									
Other (specify)									
Other (specify)									
Totals									

*See page 22 of the Fact Finder for a complete listing of Employment-Related Retirement Benefits/Deferred Compensation.
†Be sure to adjust for income sources from page 8 of the Fact Finder that will terminate or decrease if client or spouse dies, retires, or is disabled.
‡See the bottom of page 22.

[Page intentionally left blank]

CHECKLIST FOR FINANCIAL PLANNING REVIEW

Change in	Has Occurred	Is Expected		Has Occurred	Is Expected
1. Marital status			Purchase, spouse owned	☐	☐
Marriage	☐	☐	Purchase, dependent owned	☐	☐
Separation	☐	☐	Transfer to joint ownership	☐	☐
Divorce	☐	☐	Transfer to client	☐	☐
Remarriage	☐	☐	Transfer to spouse	☐	☐
			Transfer to dependent	☐	☐
2. Number of dependents			Transfer to trustee	☐	☐
Increase	☐	☐			
Decrease	☐	☐	**10. Liabilities**		
			Leases executed	☐	☐
3. Health status			Mortgage increase	☐	☐
Client	☐	☐	Lawsuit against	☐	☐
Spouse	☐	☐	Judgment against	☐	☐
Dependent	☐	☐	Unsecured borrowing	☐	☐
			Cosigning of notes	☐	☐
4. Residence	☐	☐			
			11. Business ownership		
5. Occupation			New business formation	☐	☐
Client	☐	☐	Interest purchase	☐	☐
Spouse	☐	☐	Sale of interest	☐	☐
Dependent	☐	☐	Transfer of interest	☐	☐
			Reorganization among owners	☐	☐
6. Family financial status			Liquidation	☐	☐
Borrowing	☐	☐	Change of carrier	☐	☐
Lending	☐	☐	Termination or lapse	☐	☐
Gifts over $1,000 received	☐	☐	Surrender	☐	☐
Gifts over $1,000 made	☐	☐			
Purchase of property	☐	☐	**12. Legal document status**		
Sale of property	☐	☐	Change in last will	☐	☐
Investments	☐	☐	Change in trust	☐	☐
Inheritance	☐	☐	Buy-sell agreement	☐	☐
Deferred income	☐	☐	Agreement to defer income	☐	☐
Pension plan	☐	☐	Advance medical directives	☐	☐
Tax-deferred annuity	☐	☐	Powers of attorney	☐	☐
Dependent's income	☐	☐	Nuptial agreements	☐	☐
7. Sources of income			**13. Insurance status**		
As employee	☐	☐	Life insurance	☐	☐
From self-employment	☐	☐	Health insurance	☐	☐
From tax-exempt employer	☐	☐	Long-term care insurance	☐	☐
From investments	☐	☐	Disability income insurance	☐	☐
Inventions, patents, copyrights	☐	☐	Annuities	☐	☐
Hobbies, avocations	☐	☐	Group insurance	☐	☐
			Other employer plan	☐	☐
8. Income tax status			Property insurance	☐	☐
From single to joint return	☐	☐	Liability insurance	☐	☐
From joint to single return	☐	☐	Change of plan	☐	☐
Capital gains	☐	☐			
Capital losses	☐	☐	**14. Attitudes toward others**		
Charitable contributions	☐	☐	In family	☐	☐
Unreimbursed casualty loss	☐	☐	In business	☐	☐
Sick pay received	☐	☐	In accepting professional advice	☐	☐
Unreimbursed medical expenses					
Tax-impact investment(s)	☐	☐	**15. Interest in**		
	☐	☐	Idea previously discussed	☐	☐
9. Property ownership			Plans seen or heard about	☐	☐
Purchase in joint ownership					
Purchase, n client owned					

[Page intentionally left blank]

Appendix F

Time Value of Money Tables

Appendix F
Time Value of Money Tables

TABLE F.1
FUTURE VALUE OF A SINGLE SUM FACTORS
FVSS Factor = $(1 + i)^n$ where i = rate and n = periods

i =	0.5%	1%	1.5%	2%	2.5%	3%	3.5%	4%	4.5%	5%
n = 1	1.0050	1.0100	1.0150	1.0200	1.0250	1.0300	1.0350	1.0400	1.0450	1.0500
2	1.0100	1.0201	1.0302	1.0404	1.0506	1.0609	1.0712	1.0816	1.0920	1.1025
3	1.0151	1.0303	1.0457	1.0612	1.0769	1.0927	1.1087	1.1249	1.1412	1.1576
4	1.0202	1.0406	1.0614	1.0824	1.1038	1.1255	1.1475	1.1699	1.1925	1.2155
5	1.0253	1.0510	1.0773	1.1041	1.1314	1.1593	1.1877	1.2167	1.2462	1.2763
6	1.0304	1.0615	1.0934	1.1262	1.1597	1.1941	1.2293	1.2653	1.3023	1.3401
7	1.0355	1.0721	1.1098	1.1487	1.1887	1.2299	1.2723	1.3159	1.3609	1.4071
8	1.0407	1.0829	1.1265	1.1717	1.2184	1.2668	1.3168	1.3686	1.4221	1.4775
9	1.0459	1.0937	1.1434	1.1951	1.2489	1.3048	1.3629	1.4233	1.4861	1.5513
10	1.0511	1.1046	1.1605	1.2190	1.2801	1.3439	1.4106	1.4802	1.5530	1.6289
11	1.0564	1.1157	1.1779	1.2434	1.3121	1.3842	1.4600	1.5395	1.6229	1.7103
12	1.0617	1.1268	1.1956	1.2682	1.3449	1.4258	1.5111	1.6010	1.6959	1.7959
13	1.0670	1.1381	1.2136	1.2936	1.3785	1.4685	1.5640	1.6651	1.7722	1.8856
14	1.0723	1.1495	1.2318	1.3195	1.4130	1.5126	1.6187	1.7317	1.8519	1.9799
15	1.0777	1.1610	1.2502	1.3459	1.4483	1.5580	1.6753	1.8009	1.9353	2.0789
16	1.0831	1.1726	1.2690	1.3728	1.4845	1.6047	1.7340	1.8730	2.0224	2.1829
17	1.0885	1.1843	1.2880	1.4002	1.5216	1.6528	1.7947	1.9479	2.1134	2.2920
18	1.0939	1.1961	1.3073	1.4282	1.5597	1.7024	1.8575	2.0258	2.2085	2.4066
19	1.0994	1.2081	1.3270	1.4568	1.5987	1.7535	1.9225	2.1068	2.3079	2.5270
20	1.1049	1.2202	1.3469	1.4859	1.6386	1.8061	1.9898	2.1911	2.4117	2.6533
21	1.1104	1.2324	1.3671	1.5157	1.6796	1.8603	2.0594	2.2788	2.5202	2.7860
22	1.1160	1.2447	1.3876	1.5460	1.7216	1.9161	2.1315	2.3699	2.6337	2.9253
23	1.1216	1.2572	1.4084	1.5769	1.7646	1.9736	2.2061	2.4647	2.7522	3.0715
24	1.1272	1.2697	1.4295	1.6084	1.8087	2.0328	2.2833	2.5633	2.8760	3.2251
25	1.1328	1.2824	1.4509	1.6406	1.8539	2.0938	2.3632	2.6658	3.0054	3.3864
26	1.1385	1.2953	1.4727	1.6734	1.9003	2.1566	2.4460	2.7725	3.1407	3.5557
27	1.1442	1.3082	1.4948	1.7069	1.9478	2.2213	2.5316	2.8834	3.2820	3.7335
28	1.1499	1.3213	1.5172	1.7410	1.9965	2.2879	2.6202	2.9987	3.4297	3.9201
29	1.1556	1.3345	1.5400	1.7758	2.0464	2.3566	2.7119	3.1187	3.5840	4.1161
30	1.1614	1.3478	1.5631	1.8114	2.0976	2.4273	2.8068	3.2434	3.7453	4.3219
35	1.1907	1.4166	1.6839	1.9999	2.3732	2.8139	3.3336	3.9461	4.6673	5.5160
40	1.2208	1.4889	1.8140	2.2080	2.6851	3.2620	3.9593	4.8010	5.8164	7.0400
45	1.2516	1.5648	1.9542	2.4379	3.0379	3.7816	4.7024	5.8412	7.2482	8.9850
50	1.2832	1.6446	2.1052	2.6916	3.4371	4.3839	5.5849	7.1067	9.0326	11.4674

TABLE F.1 (CONTINUED)
FUTURE VALUE OF A SINGLE SUM FACTORS
FVSS Factor = $(1 + i)^n$ where i = rate and n = periods

i =	5.5%	6%	6.5%	7%	7.5%	8%	8.5%	9%	9.5%	10%
n = 1	1.0550	1.0600	1.0650	1.0700	1.0750	1.0800	1.0850	1.0900	1.0950	1.1000
2	1.1130	1.1236	1.1342	1.1449	1.1556	1.1664	1.1772	1.1881	1.1990	1.2100
3	1.1742	1.1910	1.2079	1.2250	1.2423	1.2597	1.2773	1.2950	1.3129	1.3310
4	1.2388	1.2625	1.2865	1.3108	1.3355	1.3605	1.3859	1.4116	1.4377	1.4641
5	1.3070	1.3382	1.3701	1.4026	1.4356	1.4693	1.5037	1.5386	1.5742	1.6105
6	1.3788	1.4185	1.4591	1.5007	1.5433	1.5869	1.6315	1.6771	1.7238	1.7716
7	1.4547	1.5036	1.5540	1.6058	1.6590	1.7138	1.7701	1.8280	1.8876	1.9487
8	1.5347	1.5938	1.6550	1.7182	1.7835	1.8509	1.9206	1.9926	2.0669	2.1436
9	1.6191	1.6895	1.7626	1.8385	1.9172	1.9990	2.0839	2.1719	2.2632	2.3579
10	1.7081	1.7908	1.8771	1.9672	2.0610	2.1589	2.2610	2.3674	2.4782	2.5937
11	1.8021	1.8983	1.9992	2.1049	2.2156	2.3316	2.4532	2.5804	2.7137	2.8531
12	1.9012	2.0122	2.1291	2.2522	2.3818	2.5182	2.6617	2.8127	2.9715	3.1384
13	2.0058	2.1329	2.2675	2.4098	2.5604	2.7196	2.8879	3.0658	3.2537	3.4523
14	2.1161	2.2609	2.4149	2.5785	2.7524	2.9372	3.1334	3.3417	3.5629	3.7975
15	2.2325	2.3966	2.5718	2.7590	2.9589	3.1722	3.3997	3.6425	3.9013	4.1772
16	2.3553	2.5404	2.7390	2.9522	3.1808	3.4259	3.6887	3.9703	4.2719	4.5950
17	2.4848	2.6928	2.9170	3.1588	3.4194	3.7000	4.0023	4.3276	4.6778	5.0545
18	2.6215	2.8543	3.1067	3.3799	3.6758	3.9960	4.3425	4.7171	5.1222	5.5599
19	2.7656	3.0256	3.3086	3.6165	3.9515	4.3157	4.7116	5.1417	5.6088	6.1159
20	2.9178	3.2071	3.5236	3.8697	4.2479	4.6610	5.1120	5.6044	6.1416	6.7275
21	3.0782	3.3996	3.7527	4.1406	4.5664	5.0338	5.5466	6.1088	6.7251	7.4002
22	3.2475	3.6035	3.9966	4.4304	4.9089	5.4365	6.0180	6.6586	7.3639	8.1403
23	3.4262	3.8197	4.2564	4.7405	5.2771	5.8715	6.5296	7.2579	8.0635	8.9543
24	3.6146	4.0489	4.5331	5.0724	5.6729	6.3412	7.0846	7.9111	8.8296	9.8497
25	3.8134	4.2919	4.8277	5.4274	6.0983	6.8485	7.6868	8.6231	9.6684	10.8347
26	4.0231	4.5494	5.1415	5.8074	6.5557	7.3964	8.3401	9.3992	10.5869	11.9182
27	4.2444	4.8223	5.4757	6.2139	7.0474	7.9881	9.0490	10.2451	11.5926	13.1100
28	4.4778	5.1117	5.8316	6.6488	7.5759	8.6271	9.8182	11.1671	12.6939	14.4210
29	4.7241	5.4184	6.2107	7.1143	8.1441	9.3173	10.6528	12.1722	13.8998	15.8631
30	4.9840	5.7435	6.6144	7.6123	8.7550	10.0627	11.5583	13.2677	15.2203	17.4494
35	6.5138	7.6861	9.0623	10.6766	12.5689	14.7853	17.3796	20.4140	23.9604	28.1024
40	8.5133	10.2857	12.4161	14.9745	18.0442	21.7245	26.1330	31.4094	37.7194	45.2593
45	11.1266	13.7646	17.0111	21.0025	25.9048	31.9204	39.2951	48.3273	59.3793	72.8905
50	14.5420	18.4202	23.3067	29.4570	37.1897	46.9016	59.0863	74.3575	93.4773	117.391

TABLE F.1 (CONTINUED)
FUTURE VALUE OF A SINGLE SUM FACTORS
FVSS Factor = $(1 + i)^n$ where i = rate and n = periods

i =	10.5%	11%	11.5%	12%	12.5%	13%	13.5%	14%	14.5%	15%
n = 1	1.1050	1.1100	1.1150	1.1200	1.1250	1.1300	1.1350	1.1400	1.1450	1.1500
2	1.2210	1.2321	1.2432	1.2544	1.2656	1.2769	1.2882	1.2996	1.3110	1.3225
3	1.3492	1.3676	1.3862	1.4049	1.4238	1.4429	1.4621	1.4815	1.5011	1.5209
4	1.4909	1.5181	1.5456	1.5735	1.6018	1.6305	1.6595	1.6890	1.7188	1.7490
5	1.6474	1.6851	1.7234	1.7623	1.8020	1.8424	1.8836	1.9254	1.9680	2.0114
6	1.8204	1.8704	1.9215	1.9738	2.0273	2.0820	2.1378	2.1950	2.2534	2.3131
7	2.0116	2.0762	2.1425	2.2107	2.2807	2.3526	2.4264	2.5023	2.5801	2.6600
8	2.2228	2.3045	2.3889	2.4760	2.5658	2.6584	2.7540	2.8526	2.9542	3.0590
9	2.4562	2.5580	2.6636	2.7731	2.8865	3.0040	3.1258	3.2519	3.3826	3.5179
10	2.7141	2.8394	2.9699	3.1058	3.2473	3.3946	3.5478	3.7072	3.8731	4.0456
11	2.9991	3.1518	3.3115	3.4785	3.6532	3.8359	4.0267	4.2262	4.4347	4.6524
12	3.3140	3.4985	3.6923	3.8960	4.1099	4.3345	4.5704	4.8179	5.0777	5.3503
13	3.6619	3.8833	4.1169	4.3635	4.6236	4.8980	5.1874	5.4924	5.8140	6.1528
14	4.0464	4.3104	4.5904	4.8871	5.2016	5.5348	5.8877	6.2613	6.6570	7.0757
15	4.4713	4.7846	5.1183	5.4736	5.8518	6.2543	6.6825	7.1379	7.6222	8.1371
16	4.9408	5.3109	5.7069	6.1304	6.5833	7.0673	7.5846	8.1372	8.7275	9.3576
17	5.4596	5.8951	6.3632	6.8660	7.4062	7.9861	8.6085	9.2765	9.9929	10.7613
18	6.0328	6.5436	7.0949	7.6900	8.3319	9.0243	9.7707	10.5752	11.4419	12.3755
19	6.6663	7.2633	7.9108	8.6128	9.3734	10.1974	11.0897	12.0557	13.1010	14.2318
20	7.3662	8.0623	8.8206	9.6463	10.5451	11.5231	12.5869	13.7435	15.0006	16.3665
21	8.1397	8.9492	9.8350	10.8038	11.8632	13.0211	14.2861	15.6676	17.1757	18.8215
22	8.9944	9.9336	10.9660	12.1003	13.3461	14.7138	16.2147	17.8610	19.6662	21.6447
23	9.9388	11.0263	12.2271	13.5523	15.0144	16.6266	18.4037	20.3616	22.5178	24.8915
24	10.9823	12.2392	13.6332	15.1786	16.8912	18.7881	20.8882	23.2122	25.7829	28.6252
25	12.1355	13.5855	15.2010	17.0001	19.0026	21.2305	23.7081	26.4619	29.5214	32.9190
26	13.4097	15.0799	16.9491	19.0401	21.3779	23.9905	26.9087	30.1666	33.8020	37.8568
27	14.8177	16.7386	18.8982	21.3249	24.0502	27.1093	30.5414	34.3899	38.7033	43.5353
28	16.3736	18.5799	21.0715	23.8839	27.0564	30.6335	34.6644	39.2045	44.3153	50.0656
29	18.0928	20.6237	23.4948	26.7499	30.4385	34.6158	39.3441	44.6931	50.7410	57.5755
30	19.9926	22.8923	26.1967	29.9599	34.2433	39.1159	44.6556	50.9502	58.0985	66.2118
35	32.9367	38.5749	45.1461	52.7996	61.7075	72.0685	84.1115	98.1002	114.338	133.176
40	54.2614	65.0009	77.8027	93.0510	111.199	132.782	158.429	188.884	225.019	267.864
45	89.3928	109.530	134.082	163.988	200.384	244.641	298.410	363.679	442.840	538.769
50	147.270	184.565	231.070	289.002	361.099	450.736	562.073	700.233	871.514	1083.66

TABLE F.1 (CONTINUED)
FUTURE VALUE OF A SINGLE SUM FACTORS
FVSS Factor = $(1 + i)^n$ where i = rate and n = periods

i =	16%	17%	18%	19%	20%	22%	24%	26%	28%	30%
n = 1	1.1600	1.1700	1.1800	1.1900	1.2000	1.2200	1.2400	1.2600	1.2800	1.3000
2	1.3456	1.3689	1.3924	1.4161	1.4400	1.4884	1.5376	1.5876	1.6384	1.6900
3	1.5609	1.6016	1.6430	1.6852	1.7280	1.8158	1.9066	2.0004	2.0972	2.1970
4	1.8106	1.8739	1.9388	2.0053	2.0736	2.2153	2.3642	2.5205	2.6844	2.8561
5	2.1003	2.1924	2.2878	2.3864	2.4883	2.7027	2.9316	3.1758	3.4360	3.7129
6	2.4364	2.5652	2.6996	2.8398	2.9860	3.2973	3.6352	4.0015	4.3980	4.8268
7	2.8262	3.0012	3.1855	3.3793	3.5832	4.0227	4.5077	5.0419	5.6295	6.2749
8	3.2784	3.5115	3.7589	4.0214	4.2998	4.9077	5.5895	6.3528	7.2058	8.1573
9	3.8030	4.1084	4.4355	4.7854	5.1598	5.9874	6.9310	8.0045	9.2234	10.6045
10	4.4114	4.8068	5.2338	5.6947	6.1917	7.3046	8.5944	10.0857	11.8059	13.7858
11	5.1173	5.6240	6.1759	6.7767	7.4301	8.9117	10.6571	12.7080	15.1116	17.9216
12	5.9360	6.5801	7.2876	8.0642	8.9161	10.8722	13.2148	16.0120	19.3428	23.2981
13	6.8858	7.6987	8.5994	9.5964	10.6993	13.2641	16.3863	20.1752	24.7588	30.2875
14	7.9875	9.0075	10.1472	11.4198	12.8392	16.1822	20.3191	25.4207	31.6913	39.3738
15	9.2655	10.5387	11.9737	13.5895	15.4070	19.7423	25.1956	32.0301	40.5648	51.1859
16	10.7480	12.3303	14.1290	16.1715	18.4884	24.0856	31.2426	40.3579	51.9230	66.5417
17	12.4677	14.4265	16.6722	19.2441	22.1861	29.3844	38.7408	50.8510	66.4614	86.5042
18	14.4625	16.8790	19.6733	22.9005	26.6233	35.8490	48.0386	64.0722	85.0706	112.455
19	16.7765	19.7484	23.2144	27.2516	31.9480	43.7358	59.5679	80.7310	108.890	146.192
20	19.4608	23.1056	27.3930	32.4294	38.3376	53.3576	73.8641	101.721	139.380	190.050
21	22.5745	27.0336	32.3238	38.5910	46.0051	65.0963	91.5915	128.169	178.406	247.065
22	26.1864	31.6293	38.1421	45.9233	55.2061	79.4175	113.574	161.492	228.360	321.184
23	30.3762	37.0062	45.0076	54.6487	66.2474	96.8894	140.831	203.480	292.300	417.539
24	35.2364	43.2973	53.1090	65.0320	79.4968	118.205	174.631	256.385	374.144	542.801
25	40.8742	50.6578	62.6686	77.3881	95.3962	144.210	216.542	323.045	478.905	705.641
26	47.4141	59.2697	73.9490	92.0918	114.475	175.936	268.512	407.037	612.998	917.333
27	55.0004	69.3455	87.2598	109.589	137.371	214.642	332.955	512.867	784.638	1192.53
28	63.8004	81.1342	102.967	130.411	164.845	261.864	412.864	646.212	1004.34	1550.29
29	74.0085	94.9271	121.501	155.189	197.814	319.474	511.952	814.228	1285.55	2015.38
30	85.8499	111.065	143.371	184.675	237.376	389.758	634.820	1025.93	1645.50	2620.00
35	180.314	243.503	327.997	440.701	590.668	1053.40	1861.05	3258.14	5653.91	9727.86
40	378.721	533.869	750.378	1051.67	1469.77	2847.04	5455.91	10347.2	19426.7	36118.9
45	795.444	1170.48	1716.68	2509.65	3657.26	7694.71	15994.7	32860.5	66749.6	134106.8
50	1670.70	2566.22	3927.36	5988.91	9100.44	20796.6	46890.4	104358.4	229349.9	497929.2

TABLE F.2
PRESENT VALUE OF A SINGLE SUM FACTORS
PVSS FACTOR = $1/(1 + i)^n$ where i = rate and n = periods

i =	0.5%	1%	1.5%	2%	2.5%	3%	3.5%	4%	4.5%	5%
n = 1	0.9950	0.9901	0.9852	0.9804	0.9756	0.9709	0.9662	0.9615	0.9569	0.9524
2	0.9901	0.9803	0.9707	0.9612	0.9518	0.9426	0.9335	0.9246	0.9157	0.9070
3	0.9851	0.9706	0.9563	0.9423	0.9286	0.9151	0.9019	0.8890	0.8763	0.8638
4	0.9802	0.9610	0.9422	0.9238	0.9060	0.8885	0.8714	0.8548	0.8386	0.8227
5	0.9754	0.9515	0.9283	0.9057	0.8839	0.8626	0.8420	0.8219	0.8025	0.7835
6	0.9705	0.9420	0.9145	0.8880	0.8623	0.8375	0.8135	0.7903	0.7679	0.7462
7	0.9657	0.9327	0.9010	0.8706	0.8413	0.8131	0.7860	0.7599	0.7348	0.7107
8	0.9609	0.9235	0.8877	0.8535	0.8207	0.7894	0.7594	0.7307	0.7032	0.6768
9	0.9561	0.9143	0.8746	0.8368	0.8007	0.7664	0.7337	0.7026	0.6729	0.6446
10	0.9513	0.9053	0.8617	0.8203	0.7812	0.7441	0.7089	0.6756	0.6439	0.6139
11	0.9466	0.8963	0.8489	0.8043	0.7621	0.7224	0.6849	0.6496	0.6162	0.5847
12	0.9419	0.8874	0.8364	0.7885	0.7436	0.7014	0.6618	0.6246	0.5897	0.5568
13	0.9372	0.8787	0.8240	0.7730	0.7254	0.6810	0.6394	0.6006	0.5643	0.5303
14	0.9326	0.8700	0.8118	0.7579	0.7077	0.6611	0.6178	0.5775	0.5400	0.5051
15	0.9279	0.8613	0.7999	0.7430	0.6905	0.6419	0.5969	0.5553	0.5167	0.4810
16	0.9233	0.8528	0.7880	0.7284	0.6736	0.6232	0.5767	0.5339	0.4945	0.4581
17	0.9187	0.8444	0.7764	0.7142	0.6572	0.6050	0.5572	0.5134	0.4732	0.4363
18	0.9141	0.8360	0.7649	0.7002	0.6412	0.5874	0.5384	0.4936	0.4528	0.4155
19	0.9096	0.8277	0.7536	0.6864	0.6255	0.5703	0.5202	0.4746	0.4333	0.3957
20	0.9051	0.8195	0.7425	0.6730	0.6103	0.5537	0.5026	0.4564	0.4146	0.3769
21	0.9006	0.8114	0.7315	0.6598	0.5954	0.5375	0.4856	0.4388	0.3968	0.3589
22	0.8961	0.8034	0.7207	0.6468	0.5809	0.5219	0.4692	0.4220	0.3797	0.3418
23	0.8916	0.7954	0.7100	0.6342	0.5667	0.5067	0.4533	0.4057	0.3634	0.3256
24	0.8872	0.7876	0.6995	0.6217	0.5529	0.4919	0.4380	0.3901	0.3477	0.3101
25	0.8828	0.7798	0.6892	0.6095	0.5394	0.4776	0.4231	0.3751	0.3327	0.2953
26	0.8784	0.7720	0.6790	0.5976	0.5262	0.4637	0.4088	0.3607	0.3184	0.2812
27	0.8740	0.7644	0.6690	0.5859	0.5134	0.4502	0.3950	0.3468	0.3047	0.2678
28	0.8697	0.7568	0.6591	0.5744	0.5009	0.4371	0.3817	0.3335	0.2916	0.2551
29	0.8653	0.7493	0.6494	0.5631	0.4887	0.4243	0.3687	0.3207	0.2790	0.2429
30	0.8610	0.7419	0.6398	0.5521	0.4767	0.4120	0.3563	0.3083	0.2670	0.2314
35	0.8398	0.7059	0.5939	0.5000	0.4214	0.3554	0.3000	0.2534	0.2143	0.1813
40	0.8191	0.6717	0.5513	0.4529	0.3724	0.3066	0.2526	0.2083	0.1719	0.1420
45	0.7990	0.6391	0.5117	0.4102	0.3292	0.2644	0.2127	0.1712	0.1380	0.1113
50	0.7793	0.6080	0.4750	0.3715	0.2909	0.2281	0.1791	0.1407	0.1107	0.0872

TABLE F.2 (CONTINUED)
PRESENT VALUE OF A SINGLE SUM FACTORS
PVSS FACTOR = $1/(1 + i)^n$ where i = rate and n = periods

i =	5.5%	6%	6.5%	7%	7.5%	8%	8.5%	9%	9.5%	10%
n = 1	0.9479	0.9434	0.9390	0.9346	0.9302	0.9259	0.9217	0.9174	0.9132	0.9091
2	0.8985	0.8900	0.8817	0.8734	0.8653	0.8573	0.8495	0.8417	0.8340	0.8264
3	0.8516	0.8396	0.8278	0.8163	0.8050	0.7938	0.7829	0.7722	0.7617	0.7513
4	0.8072	0.7921	0.7773	0.7629	0.7488	0.7350	0.7216	0.7084	0.6956	0.6830
5	0.7651	0.7473	0.7299	0.7130	0.6966	0.6806	0.6650	0.6499	0.6352	0.6209
6	0.7252	0.7050	0.6853	0.6663	0.6480	0.6302	0.6129	0.5963	0.5801	0.5645
7	0.6874	0.6651	0.6435	0.6227	0.6028	0.5835	0.5649	0.5470	0.5298	0.5132
8	0.6516	0.6274	0.6042	0.5820	0.5607	0.5403	0.5207	0.5019	0.4838	0.4665
9	0.6176	0.5919	0.5674	0.5439	0.5216	0.5002	0.4799	0.4604	0.4418	0.4241
10	0.5854	0.5584	0.5327	0.5083	0.4852	0.4632	0.4423	0.4224	0.4035	0.3855
11	0.5549	0.5268	0.5002	0.4751	0.4513	0.4289	0.4076	0.3875	0.3685	0.3505
12	0.5260	0.4970	0.4697	0.4440	0.4199	0.3971	0.3757	0.3555	0.3365	0.3186
13	0.4986	0.4688	0.4410	0.4150	0.3906	0.3677	0.3463	0.3262	0.3073	0.2897
14	0.4726	0.4423	0.4141	0.3878	0.3633	0.3405	0.3191	0.2992	0.2807	0.2633
15	0.4479	0.4173	0.3888	0.3624	0.3380	0.3152	0.2941	0.2745	0.2563	0.2394
16	0.4246	0.3936	0.3651	0.3387	0.3144	0.2919	0.2711	0.2519	0.2341	0.2176
17	0.4024	0.3714	0.3428	0.3166	0.2925	0.2703	0.2499	0.2311	0.2138	0.1978
18	0.3815	0.3503	0.3219	0.2959	0.2720	0.2502	0.2303	0.2120	0.1952	0.1799
19	0.3616	0.3305	0.3022	0.2765	0.2531	0.2317	0.2122	0.1945	0.1783	0.1635
20	0.3427	0.3118	0.2838	0.2584	0.2354	0.2145	0.1956	0.1784	0.1628	0.1486
21	0.3249	0.2942	0.2665	0.2415	0.2190	0.1987	0.1803	0.1637	0.1487	0.1351
22	0.3079	0.2775	0.2502	0.2257	0.2037	0.1839	0.1662	0.1502	0.1358	0.1228
23	0.2919	0.2618	0.2349	0.2109	0.1895	0.1703	0.1531	0.1378	0.1240	0.1117
24	0.2767	0.2470	0.2206	0.1971	0.1763	0.1577	0.1412	0.1264	0.1133	0.1015
25	0.2622	0.2330	0.2071	0.1842	0.1640	0.1460	0.1301	0.1160	0.1034	0.0923
26	0.2486	0.2198	0.1945	0.1722	0.1525	0.1352	0.1199	0.1064	0.0945	0.0839
27	0.2356	0.2074	0.1826	0.1609	0.1419	0.1252	0.1105	0.0976	0.0863	0.0763
28	0.2233	0.1956	0.1715	0.1504	0.1320	0.1159	0.1019	0.0895	0.0788	0.0693
29	0.2117	0.1846	0.1610	0.1406	0.1228	0.1073	0.0939	0.0822	0.0719	0.0630
30	0.2006	0.1741	0.1512	0.1314	0.1142	0.0994	0.0865	0.0754	0.0657	0.0573
35	0.1535	0.1301	0.1103	0.0937	0.0796	0.0676	0.0575	0.0490	0.0417	0.0356
40	0.1175	0.0972	0.0805	0.0668	0.0554	0.0460	0.0383	0.0318	0.0265	0.0221
45	0.0899	0.0727	0.0588	0.0476	0.0386	0.0313	0.0254	0.0207	0.0168	0.0137
50	0.0688	0.0543	0.0429	0.0339	0.0269	0.0213	0.0169	0.0134	0.0107	0.0085

TABLE F.2 (CONTINUED)
PRESENT VALUE OF A SINGLE SUM FACTORS
PVSS FACTOR = $1/(1 + i)^n$　where i = rate and n = periods

i =	10.5%	11%	11.5%	12%	12.5%	13%	13.5%	14%	14.5%	15%
n = 1	0.9050	0.9009	0.8969	0.8929	0.8889	0.8850	0.8811	0.8772	0.8734	0.8696
2	0.8190	0.8116	0.8044	0.7972	0.7901	0.7831	0.7763	0.7695	0.7628	0.7561
3	0.7412	0.7312	0.7214	0.7118	0.7023	0.6931	0.6839	0.6750	0.6662	0.6575
4	0.6707	0.6587	0.6470	0.6355	0.6243	0.6133	0.6026	0.5921	0.5818	0.5718
5	0.6070	0.5935	0.5803	0.5674	0.5549	0.5428	0.5309	0.5194	0.5081	0.4972
6	0.5493	0.5346	0.5204	0.5066	0.4933	0.4803	0.4678	0.4556	0.4438	0.4323
7	0.4971	0.4817	0.4667	0.4523	0.4385	0.4251	0.4121	0.3996	0.3876	0.3759
8	0.4499	0.4339	0.4186	0.4039	0.3897	0.3762	0.3631	0.3506	0.3385	0.3269
9	0.4071	0.3909	0.3754	0.3606	0.3464	0.3329	0.3199	0.3075	0.2956	0.2843
10	0.3684	0.3522	0.3367	0.3220	0.3079	0.2946	0.2819	0.2697	0.2582	0.2472
11	0.3334	0.3173	0.3020	0.2875	0.2737	0.2607	0.2483	0.2366	0.2255	0.2149
12	0.3018	0.2858	0.2708	0.2567	0.2433	0.2307	0.2188	0.2076	0.1969	0.1869
13	0.2731	0.2575	0.2429	0.2292	0.2163	0.2042	0.1928	0.1821	0.1720	0.1625
14	0.2471	0.2320	0.2178	0.2046	0.1922	0.1807	0.1698	0.1597	0.1502	0.1413
15	0.2236	0.2090	0.1954	0.1827	0.1709	0.1599	0.1496	0.1401	0.1312	0.1229
16	0.2024	0.1883	0.1752	0.1631	0.1519	0.1415	0.1318	0.1229	0.1146	0.1069
17	0.1832	0.1696	0.1572	0.1456	0.1350	0.1252	0.1162	0.1078	0.1001	0.0929
18	0.1658	0.1528	0.1409	0.1300	0.1200	0.1108	0.1023	0.0946	0.0874	0.0808
19	0.1500	0.1377	0.1264	0.1161	0.1067	0.0981	0.0902	0.0829	0.0763	0.0703
20	0.1358	0.1240	0.1134	0.1037	0.0948	0.0868	0.0794	0.0728	0.0667	0.0611
21	0.1229	0.1117	0.1017	0.0926	0.0843	0.0768	0.0700	0.0638	0.0582	0.0531
22	0.1112	0.1007	0.0912	0.0826	0.0749	0.0680	0.0617	0.0560	0.0508	0.0462
23	0.1006	0.0907	0.0818	0.0738	0.0666	0.0601	0.0543	0.0491	0.0444	0.0402
24	0.0911	0.0817	0.0734	0.0659	0.0592	0.0532	0.0479	0.0431	0.0388	0.0349
25	0.0824	0.0736	0.0658	0.0588	0.0526	0.0471	0.0422	0.0378	0.0339	0.0304
26	0.0746	0.0663	0.0590	0.0525	0.0468	0.0417	0.0372	0.0331	0.0296	0.0264
27	0.0675	0.0597	0.0529	0.0469	0.0416	0.0369	0.0327	0.0291	0.0258	0.0230
28	0.0611	0.0538	0.0475	0.0419	0.0370	0.0326	0.0288	0.0255	0.0226	0.0200
29	0.0553	0.0485	0.0426	0.0374	0.0329	0.0289	0.0254	0.0224	0.0197	0.0174
30	0.0500	0.0437	0.0382	0.0334	0.0292	0.0256	0.0224	0.0196	0.0172	0.0151
35	0.0304	0.0259	0.0222	0.0189	0.0162	0.0139	0.0119	0.0102	0.0087	0.0075
40	0.0184	0.0154	0.0129	0.0107	0.0090	0.0075	0.0063	0.0053	0.0044	0.0037
45	0.0112	0.0091	0.0075	0.0061	0.0050	0.0041	0.0034	0.0027	0.0023	0.0019
50	0.0068	0.0054	0.0043	0.0035	0.0028	0.0022	0.0018	0.0014	0.0011	0.0009

TABLE F.2 (CONTINUED)
PRESENT VALUE OF A SINGLE SUM FACTORS
PVSS FACTOR = $1/(1 + i)^n$ where i = rate and n = periods

i =	16%	17%	18%	19%	20%	22%	24%	26%	28%	30%
n = 1	0.8621	0.8547	0.8475	0.8403	0.8333	0.8197	0.8065	0.7937	0.7813	0.7692
2	0.7432	0.7305	0.7182	0.7062	0.6944	0.6719	0.6504	0.6299	0.6104	0.5917
3	0.6407	0.6244	0.6086	0.5934	0.5787	0.5507	0.5245	0.4999	0.4768	0.4552
4	0.5523	0.5337	0.5158	0.4987	0.4823	0.4514	0.4230	0.3968	0.3725	0.3501
5	0.4761	0.4561	0.4371	0.4190	0.4019	0.3700	0.3411	0.3149	0.2910	0.2693
6	0.4104	0.3898	0.3704	0.3521	0.3349	0.3033	0.2751	0.2499	0.2274	0.2072
7	0.3538	0.3332	0.3139	0.2959	0.2791	0.2486	0.2218	0.1983	0.1776	0.1594
8	0.3050	0.2848	0.2660	0.2487	0.2326	0.2038	0.1789	0.1574	0.1388	0.1226
9	0.2630	0.2434	0.2255	0.2090	0.1938	0.1670	0.1443	0.1249	0.1084	0.0943
10	0.2267	0.2080	0.1911	0.1756	0.1615	0.1369	0.1164	0.0992	0.0847	0.0725
11	0.1954	0.1778	0.1619	0.1476	0.1346	0.1122	0.0938	0.0787	0.0662	0.0558
12	0.1685	0.1520	0.1372	0.1240	0.1122	0.0920	0.0757	0.0625	0.0517	0.0429
13	0.1452	0.1299	0.1163	0.1042	0.0935	0.0754	0.0610	0.0496	0.0404	0.0330
14	0.1252	0.1110	0.0985	0.0876	0.0779	0.0618	0.0492	0.0393	0.0316	0.0254
15	0.1079	0.0949	0.0835	0.0736	0.0649	0.0507	0.0397	0.0312	0.0247	0.0195
16	0.0930	0.0811	0.0708	0.0618	0.0541	0.0415	0.0320	0.0248	0.0193	0.0150
17	0.0802	0.0693	0.0600	0.0520	0.0451	0.0340	0.0258	0.0197	0.0150	0.0116
18	0.0691	0.0592	0.0508	0.0437	0.0376	0.0279	0.0208	0.0156	0.0118	0.0089
19	0.0596	0.0506	0.0431	0.0367	0.0313	0.0229	0.0168	0.0124	0.0092	0.0068
20	0.0514	0.0433	0.0365	0.0308	0.0261	0.0187	0.0135	0.0098	0.0072	0.0053
21	0.0443	0.0370	0.0309	0.0259	0.0217	0.0154	0.0109	0.0078	0.0056	0.0040
22	0.0382	0.0316	0.0262	0.0218	0.0181	0.0126	0.0088	0.0062	0.0044	0.0031
23	0.0329	0.0270	0.0222	0.0183	0.0151	0.0103	0.0071	0.0049	0.0034	0.0024
24	0.0284	0.0231	0.0188	0.0154	0.0126	0.0085	0.0057	0.0039	0.0027	0.0018
25	0.0245	0.0197	0.0160	0.0129	0.0105	0.0069	0.0046	0.0031	0.0021	0.0014
26	0.0211	0.0169	0.0135	0.0109	0.0087	0.0057	0.0037	0.0025	0.0016	0.0011
27	0.0182	0.0144	0.0115	0.0091	0.0073	0.0047	0.0030	0.0019	0.0013	0.0008
28	0.0157	0.0123	0.0097	0.0077	0.0061	0.0038	0.0024	0.0015	0.0010	0.0006
29	0.0135	0.0105	0.0082	0.0064	0.0051	0.0031	0.0020	0.0012	0.0008	0.0005
30	0.0116	0.0090	0.0070	0.0054	0.0042	0.0026	0.0016	0.0010	0.0006	0.0004
35	0.0055	0.0041	0.0030	0.0023	0.0017	0.0009	0.0005	0.0003	0.0002	0.0001
40	0.0026	0.0019	0.0013	0.0010	0.0007	0.0004	0.0002	0.0001	<0.0001	<0.0001
45	0.0013	0.0009	0.0006	0.0004	0.0003	0.0001	0.0001	<0.0001	<0.0001	<0.0001
50	0.0006	0.0004	0.0003	0.0002	0.0001	<0.0001	<0.0001	<0.0001	<0.0001	<0.0001

TABLE F.3
FUTURE VALUE OF AN ANNUITY FACTORS
FVA Factor = $((1 + i)^n - 1)/i$ where i = rate and n = periods

i =	0.5%	1%	1.5%	2%	2.5%	3%	3.5%	4%	4.5%	5%
n = 1	1.0000	1.0000	1.0000	1.0000	1.0000	1.0000	1.0000	1.0000	1.0000	1.0000
2	2.0050	2.0100	2.0150	2.0200	2.0250	2.0300	2.0350	2.0400	2.0450	2.0500
3	3.0150	3.0301	3.0452	3.0604	3.0756	3.0909	3.1062	3.1216	3.1370	3.1525
4	4.0301	4.0604	4.0909	4.1216	4.1525	4.1836	4.2149	4.2465	4.2782	4.3101
5	5.0503	5.1010	5.1523	5.2040	5.2563	5.3091	5.3625	5.4163	5.4707	5.5256
6	6.0755	6.1520	6.2296	6.3081	6.3877	6.4684	6.5502	6.6330	6.7169	6.8019
7	7.1059	7.2135	7.3230	7.4343	7.5474	7.6625	7.7794	7.8983	8.0192	8.1420
8	8.1414	8.2857	8.4328	8.5830	8.7361	8.8923	9.0517	9.2142	9.3800	9.5491
9	9.1821	9.3685	9.5593	9.7546	9.9545	10.1591	10.3685	10.5828	10.8021	11.0266
10	10.2280	10.4622	10.7027	10.9497	11.2034	11.4639	11.7314	12.0061	12.2882	12.5779
11	11.2792	11.5668	11.8633	12.1687	12.4835	12.8078	13.1420	13.4864	13.8412	14.2068
12	12.3356	12.6825	13.0412	13.4121	13.7956	14.1920	14.6020	15.0258	15.4640	15.9171
13	13.3972	13.8093	14.2368	14.6803	15.1404	15.6178	16.1130	16.6268	17.1599	17.7130
14	14.4642	14.9474	15.4504	15.9739	16.5190	17.0863	17.6770	18.2919	18.9321	19.5986
15	15.5365	16.0969	16.6821	17.2934	17.9319	18.5989	19.2957	20.0236	20.7841	21.5786
16	16.6142	17.2579	17.9324	18.6393	19.3802	20.1569	20.9710	21.8245	22.7193	23.6575
17	17.6973	18.4304	19.2014	20.0121	20.8647	21.7616	22.7050	23.6975	24.7417	25.8404
18	18.7858	19.6147	20.4894	21.4123	22.3863	23.4144	24.4997	25.6454	26.8551	28.1324
19	19.8797	20.8109	21.7967	22.8406	23.9460	25.1169	26.3572	27.6712	29.0636	30.5390
20	20.9791	22.0190	23.1237	24.2974	25.5447	26.8704	28.2797	29.7781	31.3714	33.0660
21	22.0840	23.2392	24.4705	25.7833	27.1833	28.6765	30.2695	31.9692	33.7831	35.7193
22	23.1944	24.4716	25.8376	27.2990	28.8629	30.5368	32.3289	34.2480	36.3034	38.5052
23	24.3104	25.7163	27.2251	28.8450	30.5844	32.4529	34.4604	36.6179	38.9370	41.4305
24	25.4320	26.9735	28.6335	30.4219	32.3490	34.4265	36.6665	39.0826	41.6892	44.5020
25	26.5591	28.2432	30.0630	32.0303	34.1578	36.4593	38.9499	41.6459	44.5652	47.7271
26	27.6919	29.5256	31.5140	33.6709	36.0117	38.5530	41.3131	44.3117	47.5706	51.1135
27	28.8304	30.8209	32.9867	35.3443	37.9120	40.7096	43.7591	47.0842	50.7113	54.6691
28	29.9745	32.1291	34.4815	37.0512	39.8598	42.9309	46.2906	49.9676	53.9933	58.4026
29	31.1244	33.4504	35.9987	38.7922	41.8563	45.2189	48.9108	52.9663	57.4230	62.3227
30	32.2800	34.7849	37.5387	40.5681	43.9027	47.5754	51.6227	56.0849	61.0071	66.4388
35	38.1454	41.6603	45.5921	49.9945	54.9282	60.4621	66.6740	73.6522	81.4966	90.3203
40	44.1588	48.8864	54.2679	60.4020	67.4026	75.4013	84.5503	95.0255	107.030	120.800
45	50.3242	56.4811	63.6142	71.8927	81.5161	92.7199	105.782	121.029	138.850	159.700
50	56.6452	64.4632	73.6828	84.5794	97.4843	112.797	130.998	152.667	178.503	209.348

TABLE F.3 (CONTINUED)
FUTURE VALUE OF AN ANNUITY FACTORS
FVA Factor = $((1 + i)^n - 1)/i$ where i = rate and n = periods

i =	5.5%	6%	6.5%	7%	7.5%	8%	8.5%	9%	9.5%	10%
n = 1	1.0000	1.0000	1.0000	1.0000	1.0000	1.0000	1.0000	1.0000	1.0000	1.0000
2	2.0550	2.0600	2.0650	2.0700	2.0750	2.0800	2.0850	2.0900	2.0950	2.1000
3	3.1680	3.1836	3.1992	3.2149	3.2306	3.2464	3.2622	3.2781	3.2940	3.3100
4	4.3423	4.3746	4.4072	4.4399	4.4729	4.5061	4.5395	4.5731	4.6070	4.6410
5	5.5811	5.6371	5.6936	5.7507	5.8084	5.8666	5.9254	5.9847	6.0446	6.1051
6	6.8881	6.9753	7.0637	7.1533	7.2440	7.3359	7.4290	7.5233	7.6189	7.7156
7	8.2669	8.3938	8.5229	8.6540	8.7873	8.9228	9.0605	9.2004	9.3426	9.4872
8	9.7216	9.8975	10.0769	10.2598	10.4464	10.6366	10.8306	11.0285	11.2302	11.4359
9	11.2563	11.4913	11.7319	11.9780	12.2298	12.4876	12.7512	13.0210	13.2971	13.5795
10	12.8754	13.1808	13.4944	13.8164	14.1471	14.4866	14.8351	15.1929	15.5603	15.9374
11	14.5835	14.9716	15.3716	15.7836	16.2081	16.6455	17.0961	17.5603	18.0385	18.5312
12	16.3856	16.8699	17.3707	17.8885	18.4237	18.9771	19.5492	20.1407	20.7522	21.3843
13	18.2868	18.8821	19.4998	20.1406	20.8055	21.4953	22.2109	22.9534	23.7236	24.5227
14	20.2926	21.0151	21.7673	22.5505	23.3659	24.2149	25.0989	26.0192	26.9774	27.9750
15	22.4087	23.2760	24.1822	25.1290	26.1184	27.1521	28.2323	29.3609	30.5402	31.7725
16	24.6411	25.6725	26.7540	27.8881	29.0772	30.3243	31.6320	33.0034	34.4416	35.9497
17	26.9964	28.2129	29.4930	30.8402	32.2580	33.7502	35.3207	36.9737	38.7135	40.5447
18	29.4812	30.9057	32.4101	33.9990	35.6774	37.4502	39.3230	41.3013	43.3913	45.5992
19	32.1027	33.7600	35.5167	37.3790	39.3532	41.4463	43.6654	46.0185	48.5135	51.1591
20	34.8683	36.7856	38.8253	40.9955	43.3047	45.7620	48.3770	51.1601	54.1222	57.2750
21	37.7861	39.9927	42.3490	44.8652	47.5525	50.4229	53.4891	56.7645	60.2638	64.0025
22	40.8643	43.3923	46.1016	49.0057	52.1190	55.4568	59.0356	62.8733	66.9889	71.4027
23	44.1118	46.9958	50.0982	53.4361	57.0279	60.8933	65.0537	69.5319	74.3529	79.5430
24	47.5380	50.8156	54.3546	58.1767	62.3050	66.7648	71.5832	76.7898	82.4164	88.4973
25	51.1526	54.8645	58.8877	63.2490	67.9779	73.1059	78.6678	84.7009	91.2459	98.3471
26	54.9660	59.1564	63.7154	68.6765	74.0762	79.9544	86.3546	93.3240	100.914	109.182
27	58.9891	63.7058	68.8569	74.4838	80.6319	87.3508	94.6947	102.723	111.501	121.100
28	63.2335	68.5281	74.3326	80.6977	87.6793	95.3388	103.744	112.968	123.094	134.210
29	67.7114	73.6398	80.1642	87.3465	95.2553	103.966	113.562	124.135	135.788	148.631
30	72.4355	79.0582	86.3749	94.4608	103.399	113.283	124.215	136.308	149.688	164.494
35	100.251	111.435	124.035	138.237	154.252	172.317	192.702	215.711	241.688	271.024
40	136.606	154.762	175.632	199.635	227.257	259.057	295.683	337.882	386.520	442.593
45	184.119	212.744	246.325	285.749	332.065	386.506	450.530	525.859	614.519	718.905
50	246.217	290.336	343.180	406.529	482.530	573.770	683.368	815.084	973.445	1163.91

TABLE F.3 (CONTINUED)
FUTURE VALUE OF AN ANNUITY FACTORS
FVA Factor = $((1 + i)^n - 1)/i$ where i = rate and n = periods

i =	10.5%	11%	11.5%	12%	12.5%	13%	13.5%	14%	14.5%	15%
n = 1	1.0000	1.0000	1.0000	1.0000	1.0000	1.0000	1.0000	1.0000	1.0000	1.0000
2	2.1050	2.1100	2.1150	2.1200	2.1250	2.1300	2.1350	2.1400	2.1450	2.1500
3	3.3260	3.3421	3.3582	3.3744	3.3906	3.4069	3.4232	3.4396	3.4560	3.4725
4	4.6753	4.7097	4.7444	4.7793	4.8145	4.8498	4.8854	4.9211	4.9571	4.9934
5	6.1662	6.2278	6.2900	6.3528	6.4163	6.4803	6.5449	6.6101	6.6759	6.7424
6	7.8136	7.9129	8.0134	8.1152	8.2183	8.3227	8.4284	8.5355	8.6439	8.7537
7	9.6340	9.7833	9.9349	10.0890	10.2456	10.4047	10.5663	10.7305	10.8973	11.0668
8	11.6456	11.8594	12.0774	12.2997	12.5263	12.7573	12.9927	13.2328	13.4774	13.7268
9	13.8684	14.1640	14.4663	14.7757	15.0921	15.4157	15.7468	16.0853	16.4317	16.7858
10	16.3246	16.7220	17.1300	17.5487	17.9786	18.4197	18.8726	19.3373	19.8142	20.3037
11	19.0387	19.5614	20.0999	20.6546	21.2259	21.8143	22.4204	23.0445	23.6873	24.3493
12	22.0377	22.7132	23.4114	24.1331	24.8791	25.6502	26.4471	27.2707	28.1220	29.0017
13	25.3517	26.2116	27.1037	28.0291	28.9890	29.9847	31.0175	32.0887	33.1997	34.3519
14	29.0136	30.0949	31.2207	32.3926	33.6126	34.8827	36.2048	37.5811	39.0136	40.5047
15	33.0600	34.4054	35.8110	37.2797	38.8142	40.4175	42.0925	43.8424	45.6706	47.5804
16	37.5313	39.1899	40.9293	42.7533	44.6660	46.6717	48.7750	50.9804	53.2928	55.7175
17	42.4721	44.5008	46.6362	48.8837	51.2493	53.7391	56.3596	59.1176	62.0203	65.0751
18	47.9317	50.3959	52.9993	55.7497	58.6554	61.7251	64.9681	68.3941	72.0132	75.8364
19	53.9645	56.9395	60.0942	63.4397	66.9873	70.7494	74.7388	78.9692	83.4551	88.2118
20	60.6308	64.2028	68.0051	72.0524	76.3608	80.9468	85.8286	91.0249	96.5561	102.444
21	67.9970	72.2651	76.8257	81.6987	86.9058	92.4699	98.4154	104.768	111.557	118.810
22	76.1367	81.2143	86.6606	92.5026	98.7691	105.491	112.701	120.436	128.732	137.632
23	85.1311	91.1479	97.6266	104.603	112.115	120.205	128.916	138.297	148.399	159.276
24	95.0699	102.174	109.854	118.155	127.130	136.831	147.320	158.659	170.917	184.168
25	106.052	114.413	123.487	133.334	144.021	155.620	168.208	181.871	196.699	212.793
26	118.188	127.999	138.688	150.334	163.023	176.850	191.916	208.333	226.221	245.712
27	131.597	143.079	155.637	169.374	184.401	200.841	218.825	238.499	260.023	283.569
28	146.415	159.817	174.535	190.699	208.452	227.950	249.366	272.889	298.726	327.104
29	162.789	178.397	195.607	214.583	235.508	258.583	284.031	312.094	343.041	377.170
30	180.881	199.021	219.101	241.333	265.946	293.199	323.375	356.787	393.782	434.745
35	304.159	341.590	383.879	431.663	485.660	546.681	615.640	693.573	781.644	881.170
40	507.252	581.826	667.850	767.091	881.592	1013.70	1166.14	1342.03	1544.96	1779.09
45	841.836	986.639	1157.23	1358.23	1595.07	1874.16	2203.04	2590.56	3047.17	3585.13
50	1393.05	1668.77	2000.61	2400.02	2880.79	3459.51	4156.10	4994.52	6003.54	7217.72

TABLE F.3 (CONTINUED)
FUTURE VALUE OF AN ANNUITY FACTORS
FVA Factor = $((1 + i)^n - 1)/i$ where i = rate and n = periods

i =	16%	17%	18%	19%	20%	22%	24%	26%	28%	30%
n = 1	1.0000	1.0000	1.0000	1.0000	1.0000	1.0000	1.0000	1.0000	1.0000	1.0000
2	2.1600	2.1700	2.1800	2.1900	2.2000	2.2200	2.2400	2.2600	2.2800	2.3000
3	3.5056	3.5389	3.5724	3.6061	3.6400	3.7084	3.7776	3.8476	3.9184	3.9900
4	5.0665	5.1405	5.2154	5.2913	5.3680	5.5242	5.6842	5.8480	6.0156	6.1870
5	6.8771	7.0144	7.1542	7.2966	7.4416	7.7396	8.0484	8.3684	8.6999	9.0431
6	8.9775	9.2068	9.4420	9.6830	9.9299	10.4423	10.9801	11.5442	12.1359	12.7560
7	11.4139	11.7720	12.1415	12.5227	12.9159	13.7396	14.6153	15.5458	16.5339	17.5828
8	14.2401	14.7733	15.3270	15.9020	16.4991	17.7623	19.1229	20.5876	22.1634	23.8577
9	17.5185	18.2847	19.0859	19.9234	20.7989	22.6700	24.7125	26.9404	29.3692	32.0150
10	21.3215	22.3931	23.5213	24.7089	25.9587	28.6574	31.6434	34.9449	38.5926	42.6195
11	25.7329	27.1999	28.7551	30.4035	32.1504	35.9620	40.2379	45.0306	50.3985	56.4053
12	30.8502	32.8239	34.9311	37.1802	39.5805	44.8737	50.8950	57.7386	65.5100	74.3270
13	36.7862	39.4040	42.2187	45.2445	48.4966	55.7459	64.1097	73.7506	84.8529	97.6250
14	43.6720	47.1027	50.8180	54.8409	59.1959	69.0100	80.4961	93.9258	109.612	127.913
15	51.6595	56.1101	60.9653	66.2607	72.0351	85.1922	100.815	119.347	141.303	167.286
16	60.9250	66.6488	72.9390	79.8502	87.4421	104.935	126.011	151.377	181.868	218.472
17	71.6730	78.9792	87.0680	96.0218	105.931	129.020	157.253	191.735	233.791	285.014
18	84.1407	93.4056	103.740	115.266	128.117	158.405	195.994	242.585	300.252	371.518
19	98.6032	110.285	123.414	138.166	154.740	194.254	244.033	306.658	385.323	483.973
20	115.380	130.033	146.628	165.418	186.688	237.989	303.601	387.389	494.213	630.165
21	134.841	153.139	174.021	197.847	225.026	291.347	377.465	489.110	633.593	820.215
22	157.415	180.172	206.345	236.438	271.031	356.443	469.056	617.278	811.999	1067.28
23	183.601	211.801	244.487	282.362	326.237	435.861	582.630	778.771	1040.36	1388.46
24	213.978	248.808	289.494	337.010	392.484	532.750	723.461	982.251	1332.66	1806.00
25	249.214	292.105	342.603	402.042	471.981	650.955	898.092	1238.64	1706.80	2348.80
26	290.088	342.763	405.272	479.431	567.377	795.165	1114.63	1561.68	2185.71	3054.44
27	337.502	402.032	479.221	571.522	681.853	971.102	1383.15	1968.72	2798.71	3971.78
28	392.503	471.378	566.481	681.112	819.223	1185.74	1716.10	2481.59	3583.34	5164.31
29	456.303	552.512	669.447	811.523	984.068	1447.61	2128.96	3127.80	4587.68	6714.60
30	530.312	647.439	790.948	966.712	1181.88	1767.08	2640.92	3942.03	5873.23	8729.99
35	1120.71	1426.49	1816.65	2314.21	2948.34	4783.64	7750.23	12527.4	20189.0	32422.9
40	2360.76	3134.52	4163.21	5529.83	7343.86	12936.5	22728.8	39793.0	69377.5	120393
45	4965.27	6879.29	9531.58	13203.4	18281.3	34971.4	66640.4	126383	238388	447019
50	10435.6	15089.5	21813.1	31515.3	45497.2	94525.3	195373	401374	819103	1659761

TABLE F.4
PRESENT VALUE OF AN ANNUITY FACTORS
PVA Factor = $(1 - (1/(1 + i)^n))/i$ where i = rate and n = periods

i =	0.5%	1%	1.5%	2%	2.5%	3%	3.5%	4%	4.5%	5%
n = 1	0.9950	0.9901	0.9852	0.9804	0.9756	0.9709	0.9662	0.9615	0.9569	0.9524
2	1.9851	1.9704	1.9559	1.9416	1.9274	1.9135	1.8997	1.8861	1.8727	1.8594
3	2.9702	2.9410	2.9122	2.8839	2.8560	2.8286	2.8016	2.7751	2.7490	2.7232
4	3.9505	3.9020	3.8544	3.8077	3.7620	3.7171	3.6731	3.6299	3.5875	3.5460
5	4.9259	4.8534	4.7826	4.7135	4.6458	4.5797	4.5151	4.4518	4.3900	4.3295
6	5.8964	5.7955	5.6972	5.6014	5.5081	5.4172	5.3286	5.2421	5.1579	5.0757
7	6.8621	6.7282	6.5982	6.4720	6.3494	6.2303	6.1145	6.0021	5.8927	5.7864
8	7.8230	7.6517	7.4859	7.3255	7.1701	7.0197	6.8740	6.7327	6.5959	6.4632
9	8.7791	8.5660	8.3605	8.1622	7.9709	7.7861	7.6077	7.4353	7.2688	7.1078
10	9.7304	9.4713	9.2222	8.9826	8.7521	8.5302	8.3166	8.1109	7.9127	7.7217
11	10.6770	10.3676	10.0711	9.7868	9.5142	9.2526	9.0016	8.7605	8.5289	8.3064
12	11.6189	11.2551	10.9075	10.5753	10.2578	9.9540	9.6633	9.3851	9.1186	8.8633
13	12.5562	12.1337	11.7315	11.3484	10.9832	10.6350	10.3027	9.9856	9.6829	9.3936
14	13.4887	13.0037	12.5434	12.1062	11.6909	11.2961	10.9205	10.5631	10.2228	9.8986
15	14.4166	13.8651	13.3432	12.8493	12.3814	11.9379	11.5174	11.1184	10.7395	10.3797
16	15.3399	14.7179	14.1313	13.5777	13.0550	12.5611	12.0941	11.6523	11.2340	10.8378
17	16.2586	15.5623	14.9076	14.2919	13.7122	13.1661	12.6513	12.1657	11.7072	11.2741
18	17.1728	16.3983	15.6726	14.9920	14.3534	13.7535	13.1897	12.6593	12.1600	11.6896
19	18.0824	17.2260	16.4262	15.6785	14.9789	14.3238	13.7098	13.1339	12.5933	12.0853
20	18.9874	18.0456	17.1686	16.3514	15.5892	14.8775	14.2124	13.5903	13.0079	12.4622
21	19.8880	18.8570	17.9001	17.0112	16.1845	15.4150	14.6980	14.0292	13.4047	12.8212
22	20.7841	19.6604	18.6208	17.6580	16.7654	15.9369	15.1671	14.4511	13.7844	13.1630
23	21.6757	20.4558	19.3309	18.2922	17.3321	16.4436	15.6204	14.8568	14.1478	13.4886
24	22.5629	21.2434	20.0304	18.9139	17.8850	16.9355	16.0584	15.2470	14.4955	13.7986
25	23.4456	22.0232	20.7196	19.5235	18.4244	17.4131	16.4815	15.6221	14.8282	14.0939
26	24.3240	22.7952	21.3986	20.1210	18.9506	17.8768	16.8904	15.9828	15.1466	14.3752
27	25.1980	23.5596	22.0676	20.7069	19.4640	18.3270	17.2854	16.3296	15.4513	14.6430
28	26.0677	24.3164	22.7267	21.2813	19.9649	18.7641	17.6670	16.6631	15.7429	14.8981
29	26.9330	25.0658	23.3761	21.8444	20.4535	19.1885	18.0358	16.9837	16.0219	15.1411
30	27.7941	25.8077	24.0158	22.3965	20.9303	19.6004	18.3920	17.2920	16.2889	15.3725
35	32.0354	29.4086	27.0756	24.9986	23.1452	21.4872	20.0007	18.6646	17.4610	16.3742
40	36.1722	32.8347	29.9158	27.3555	25.1028	23.1148	21.3551	19.7928	18.4016	17.1591
45	40.2072	36.0945	32.5523	29.4902	26.8330	24.5187	22.4955	20.7200	19.1563	17.7741
50	44.1428	39.1961	34.9997	31.4236	28.3623	25.7298	23.4556	21.4822	19.7620	18.2559

TABLE F.4 (CONTINUED)
PRESENT VALUE OF AN ANNUITY FACTORS
PVA Factor = $(1 - (1/(1 + i)^n))/i$ where i = rate and n = periods

i =	5.5%	6%	6.5%	7%	7.5%	8%	8.5%	9%	9.5%	10%
n = 1	0.9479	0.9434	0.9390	0.9346	0.9302	0.9259	0.9217	0.9174	0.9132	0.9091
2	1.8463	1.8334	1.8206	1.8080	1.7956	1.7833	1.7711	1.7591	1.7473	1.7355
3	2.6979	2.6730	2.6485	2.6243	2.6005	2.5771	2.5540	2.5313	2.5089	2.4869
4	3.5052	3.4651	3.4258	3.3872	3.3493	3.3121	3.2756	3.2397	3.2045	3.1699
5	4.2703	4.2124	4.1557	4.1002	4.0459	3.9927	3.9406	3.8897	3.8397	3.7908
6	4.9955	4.9173	4.8410	4.7665	4.6938	4.6229	4.5536	4.4859	4.4198	4.3553
7	5.6830	5.5824	5.4845	5.3893	5.2966	5.2064	5.1185	5.0330	4.9496	4.8684
8	6.3346	6.2098	6.0888	5.9713	5.8573	5.7466	5.6392	5.5348	5.4334	5.3349
9	6.9522	6.8017	6.6561	6.5152	6.3789	6.2469	6.1191	5.9952	5.8753	5.7590
10	7.5376	7.3601	7.1888	7.0236	6.8641	6.7101	6.5613	6.4177	6.2788	6.1446
11	8.0925	7.8869	7.6890	7.4987	7.3154	7.1390	6.9690	6.8052	6.6473	6.4951
12	8.6185	8.3838	8.1587	7.9427	7.7353	7.5361	7.3447	7.1607	6.9838	6.8137
13	9.1171	8.8527	8.5997	8.3577	8.1258	7.9038	7.6910	7.4869	7.2912	7.1034
14	9.5896	9.2950	9.0138	8.7455	8.4892	8.2442	8.0101	7.7862	7.5719	7.3667
15	10.0376	9.7122	9.4027	9.1079	8.8271	8.5595	8.3042	8.0607	7.8282	7.6061
16	10.4622	10.1059	9.7678	9.4466	9.1415	8.8514	8.5753	8.3126	8.0623	7.8237
17	10.8646	10.4773	10.1106	9.7632	9.4340	9.1216	8.8252	8.5436	8.2760	8.0216
18	11.2461	10.8276	10.4325	10.0591	9.7060	9.3719	9.0555	8.7556	8.4713	8.2014
19	11.6077	11.1581	10.7347	10.3356	9.9591	9.6036	9.2677	8.9501	8.6496	8.3649
20	11.9504	11.4699	11.0185	10.5940	10.1945	9.8181	9.4633	9.1285	8.8124	8.5136
21	12.2752	11.7641	11.2850	10.8355	10.4135	10.0168	9.6436	9.2922	8.9611	8.6487
22	12.5832	12.0416	11.5352	11.0612	10.6172	10.2007	9.8098	9.4424	9.0969	8.7715
23	12.8750	12.3034	11.7701	11.2722	10.8067	10.3711	9.9629	9.5802	9.2209	8.8832
24	13.1517	12.5504	11.9907	11.4693	10.9830	10.5288	10.1041	9.7066	9.3341	8.9847
25	13.4139	12.7834	12.1979	11.6536	11.1469	10.6748	10.2342	9.8226	9.4376	9.0770
26	13.6625	13.0032	12.3924	11.8258	11.2995	10.8100	10.3541	9.9290	9.5320	9.1609
27	13.8981	13.2105	12.5750	11.9867	11.4414	10.9352	10.4646	10.0266	9.6183	9.2372
28	14.1214	13.4062	12.7465	12.1371	11.5734	11.0511	10.5665	10.1161	9.6971	9.3066
29	14.3331	13.5907	12.9075	12.2777	11.6962	11.1584	10.6603	10.1983	9.7690	9.3696
30	14.5337	13.7648	13.0587	12.4090	11.8104	11.2578	10.7468	10.2737	9.8347	9.4269
35	15.3906	14.4982	13.6870	12.9477	12.2725	11.6546	11.0878	10.5668	10.0870	9.6442
40	16.0461	15.0463	14.1455	13.3317	12.5944	11.9246	11.3145	10.7574	10.2472	9.7791
45	16.5477	15.4558	14.4802	13.6055	12.8186	12.1084	11.4653	10.8812	10.3490	9.8628
50	16.9315	15.7619	14.7245	13.8007	12.9748	12.2335	11.5656	10.9617	10.4137	9.9148

TABLE F.4 (CONTINUED)
PRESENT VALUE OF AN ANNUITY FACTORS
PVA Factor = $(1 - (1/(1 + i)^n))/i$ where i = rate and n = periods

i =	10.5%	11%	11.5%	12%	12.5%	13%	13.5%	14%	14.5%	15%
n = 1	0.9050	0.9009	0.8969	0.8929	0.8889	0.8850	0.8811	0.8772	0.8734	0.8696
2	1.7240	1.7125	1.7012	1.6901	1.6790	1.6681	1.6573	1.6467	1.6361	1.6257
3	2.4651	2.4437	2.4226	2.4018	2.3813	2.3612	2.3413	2.3216	2.3023	2.2832
4	3.1359	3.1024	3.0696	3.0373	3.0056	2.9745	2.9438	2.9137	2.8841	2.8550
5	3.7429	3.6959	3.6499	3.6048	3.5606	3.5172	3.4747	3.4331	3.3922	3.3522
6	4.2922	4.2305	4.1703	4.1114	4.0538	3.9975	3.9425	3.8887	3.8360	3.7845
7	4.7893	4.7122	4.6370	4.5638	4.4923	4.4226	4.3546	4.2883	4.2236	4.1604
8	5.2392	5.1461	5.0556	4.9676	4.8820	4.7988	4.7177	4.6389	4.5621	4.4873
9	5.6463	5.5370	5.4311	5.3282	5.2285	5.1317	5.0377	4.9464	4.8577	4.7716
10	6.0148	5.8892	5.7678	5.6502	5.5364	5.4262	5.3195	5.2161	5.1159	5.0188
11	6.3482	6.2065	6.0697	5.9377	5.8102	5.6869	5.5679	5.4527	5.3414	5.2337
12	6.6500	6.4924	6.3406	6.1944	6.0535	5.9176	5.7867	5.6603	5.5383	5.4206
13	6.9230	6.7499	6.5835	6.4235	6.2698	6.1218	5.9794	5.8424	5.7103	5.5831
14	7.1702	6.9819	6.8013	6.6282	6.4620	6.3025	6.1493	6.0021	5.8606	5.7245
15	7.3938	7.1909	6.9967	6.8109	6.6329	6.4624	6.2989	6.1422	5.9918	5.8474
16	7.5962	7.3792	7.1719	6.9740	6.7848	6.6039	6.4308	6.2651	6.1063	5.9542
17	7.7794	7.5488	7.3291	7.1196	6.9198	6.7291	6.5469	6.3729	6.2064	6.0472
18	7.9451	7.7016	7.4700	7.2497	7.0398	6.8399	6.6493	6.4674	6.2938	6.1280
19	8.0952	7.8393	7.5964	7.3658	7.1465	6.9380	6.7395	6.5504	6.3701	6.1982
20	8.2309	7.9633	7.7098	7.4694	7.2414	7.0248	6.8189	6.6231	6.4368	6.2593
21	8.3538	8.0751	7.8115	7.5620	7.3256	7.1016	6.8889	6.6870	6.4950	6.3125
22	8.4649	8.1757	7.9027	7.6446	7.4006	7.1695	6.9506	6.7429	6.5459	6.3587
23	8.5656	8.2664	7.9845	7.7184	7.4672	7.2297	7.0049	6.7921	6.5903	6.3988
24	8.6566	8.3481	8.0578	7.7843	7.5264	7.2829	7.0528	6.8351	6.6291	6.4338
25	8.7390	8.4217	8.1236	7.8431	7.5790	7.3300	7.0950	6.8729	6.6629	6.4641
26	8.8136	8.4881	8.1826	7.8957	7.6258	7.3717	7.1321	6.9061	6.6925	6.4906
27	8.8811	8.5478	8.2355	7.9426	7.6674	7.4086	7.1649	6.9352	6.7184	6.5135
28	8.9422	8.6016	8.2830	7.9844	7.7043	7.4412	7.1937	6.9607	6.7409	6.5335
29	8.9974	8.6501	8.3255	8.0218	7.7372	7.4701	7.2191	6.9830	6.7606	6.5509
30	9.0474	8.6938	8.3637	8.0552	7.7664	7.4957	7.2415	7.0027	6.7778	6.5660
35	9.2347	8.8552	8.5030	8.1755	7.8704	7.5856	7.3193	7.0700	6.8362	6.6166
40	9.3483	8.9511	8.5839	8.2438	7.9281	7.6344	7.3607	7.1050	6.8659	6.6418
45	9.4173	9.0079	8.6308	8.2825	7.9601	7.6609	7.3826	7.1232	6.8810	6.6543
50	9.4591	9.0417	8.6580	8.3045	7.9778	7.6752	7.3942	7.1327	6.8886	6.6605

TABLE F.4 (CONTINUED)
PRESENT VALUE OF AN ANNUITY FACTORS
PVA Factor = $(1 - (1/(1 + i)^n))/i$ where i = rate and n = periods

i =	16%	17%	18%	19%	20%	22%	24%	26%	28%	30%
n = 1	0.8621	0.8547	0.8475	0.8403	0.8333	0.8197	0.8065	0.7937	0.7813	0.7692
2	1.6052	1.5852	1.5656	1.5465	1.5278	1.4915	1.4568	1.4235	1.3916	1.3609
3	2.2459	2.2096	2.1743	2.1399	2.1065	2.0422	1.9813	1.9234	1.8684	1.8161
4	2.7982	2.7432	2.6901	2.6386	2.5887	2.4936	2.4043	2.3202	2.2410	2.1662
5	3.2743	3.1993	3.1272	3.0576	2.9906	2.8636	2.7454	2.6351	2.5320	2.4356
6	3.6847	3.5892	3.4976	3.4098	3.3255	3.1669	3.0205	2.8850	2.7594	2.6427
7	4.0386	3.9224	3.8115	3.7057	3.6046	3.4155	3.2423	3.0833	2.9370	2.8021
8	4.3436	4.2072	4.0776	3.9544	3.8372	3.6193	3.4212	3.2407	3.0758	2.9247
9	4.6065	4.4506	4.3030	4.1633	4.0310	3.7863	3.5655	3.3657	3.1842	3.0190
10	4.8332	4.6586	4.4941	4.3389	4.1925	3.9232	3.6819	3.4648	3.2689	3.0915
11	5.0286	4.8364	4.6560	4.4865	4.3271	4.0354	3.7757	3.5435	3.3351	3.1473
12	5.1971	4.9884	4.7932	4.6105	4.4392	4.1274	3.8514	3.6059	3.3868	3.1903
13	5.3423	5.1183	4.9095	4.7147	4.5327	4.2028	3.9124	3.6555	3.4272	3.2233
14	5.4675	5.2293	5.0081	4.8023	4.6106	4.2646	3.9616	3.6949	3.4587	3.2487
15	5.5755	5.3242	5.0916	4.8759	4.6755	4.3152	4.0013	3.7261	3.4834	3.2682
16	5.6685	5.4053	5.1624	4.9377	4.7296	4.3567	4.0333	3.7509	3.5026	3.2832
17	5.7487	5.4746	5.2223	4.9897	4.7746	4.3908	4.0591	3.7705	3.5177	3.2948
18	5.8178	5.5339	5.2732	5.0333	4.8122	4.4187	4.0799	3.7861	3.5294	3.3037
19	5.8775	5.5845	5.3162	5.0700	4.8435	4.4415	4.0967	3.7985	3.5386	3.3105
20	5.9288	5.6278	5.3527	5.1009	4.8696	4.4603	4.1103	3.8083	3.5458	3.3158
21	5.9731	5.6648	5.3837	5.1268	4.8913	4.4756	4.1212	3.8161	3.5514	3.3198
22	6.0113	5.6964	5.4099	5.1486	4.9094	4.4882	4.1300	3.8223	3.5558	3.3230
23	6.0442	5.7234	5.4321	5.1668	4.9245	4.4985	4.1371	3.8273	3.5592	3.3254
24	6.0726	5.7465	5.4509	5.1822	4.9371	4.5070	4.1428	3.8312	3.5619	3.3272
25	6.0971	5.7662	5.4669	5.1951	4.9476	4.5139	4.1474	3.8342	3.5640	3.3286
26	6.1182	5.7831	5.4804	5.2060	4.9563	4.5196	4.1511	3.8367	3.5656	3.3297
27	6.1364	5.7975	5.4919	5.2151	4.9636	4.5243	4.1542	3.8387	3.5669	3.3305
28	6.1520	5.8099	5.5016	5.2228	4.9697	4.5281	4.1566	3.8402	3.5679	3.3312
29	6.1656	5.8204	5.5098	5.2292	4.9747	4.5312	4.1585	3.8414	3.5687	3.3317
30	6.1772	5.8294	5.5168	5.2347	4.9789	4.5338	4.1601	3.8424	3.5693	3.3321
35	6.2153	5.8582	5.5386	5.2512	4.9915	4.5411	4.1644	3.8450	3.5708	3.3330
40	6.2335	5.8713	5.5482	5.2582	4.9966	4.5439	4.1659	3.8458	3.5712	3.3332
45	6.2421	5.8773	5.5523	5.2611	4.9986	4.5449	4.1664	3.8460	3.5714	3.3333
50	6.2463	5.8801	5.5541	5.2623	4.9995	4.5452	4.1666	3.8461	3.5714	3.3333

Appendix G

Recognizing Time-Value-of-Money Problems

Recognizing Time-Value-of-Money Problems

When financial advisors make mistakes in TVM calculations, it is usually because they fail to recognize the structure of the problem. A typical error is trying to solve a present value of an annuity problem as if it is a future value of an annuity problem. For example, calculating monthly payments on a loan has a present value of an annuity structure even though the unknown value (the monthly payment) occurs in the future.

The following table shows many different types of TVM problems according to the values that are known and the value that is being sought. Recognizing the structure of a TVM problem helps the experienced advisor to "guesstimate" an answer. However, even a novice can often detect an error in calculations by understanding basic concepts.

For example, consider the calculation of loan payments for a $24,000 loan to be paid with 24 equal monthly payments at a rate of 12 percent. One should recognize immediately that the payments must exceed $1,000 per month since the sum of the payments (24 x $1,000) must exceed the loan value or else the lender earns no interest. Someone who mistakenly treats this problem as an FVA problem rather than a PVA problem will calculate a monthly payment of $889.76, which is clearly unreasonable. The actual answer is $1,129.76.

RECOGNIZING TIME-VALUE-OF-MONEY PROBLEMS

Problem No.	Known Values	Value Sought	Problem	Time Line
1.	PVSS, i, n	FVSS	If you invest $150 today and earn 8 percent compounded annually, what will it be worth in 6 years?	
2.	FVSS, i, n	PVSS	How much do you need to invest today to accumulate $5,000 in 5 years, if you can earn 10 percent annually?	
3.	PVSS, FVSS, n	i	If 6 years ago you invested $8,000 and it has grown to $20,000, what rate of return have you earned?	
4.	PVSS, FVSS, i	n	If you invest $500 today at 10 percent annually, how many years will it take to grow to $800?	
5.	PMT, i, n	FVA	If you invest $100 at year-end for each of the next 5 years, how much will you have at the end of the fifth year if you earn 8 percent annually?	
6.	FVA, i, n	PMT	If 6 years from now you need to have $10,000 and can earn 9 percent annually, what size year-end annual payments will accomplish your goal?	

RECOGNIZING TIME-VALUE-OF-MONEY PROBLEMS (cont'd)

Problem No.	Formula Format	Formula Solution (Use Appendix F Factor Tables)	HP-10BII Keystrokes
1.	$FVSS = PVSS \times (1 + i)^n$	FV = \$150 $\times$ 1.08^6 = \$150 $\times$ 1.5869 = \$238.04	▭, C ALL; 150, +/–, PV; 8, I/YR; 6, N; FV Answer: \$238.03
2.	$PVSS = FVSS \times \left[\dfrac{1}{(1 + i)^n} \right]$	PV = \$5,000 $\times$ $\dfrac{1}{1.10^5}$ = \$5,000 $\times$ 0.6209 = \$3104.50	▭, C ALL; 5000, FV; 10, I/YR; 5, N; PV Answer: \$3,104.61
3.			▭, C ALL; 8000, +/–, PV; 20000, FV; 6, N; I/YR Answer: 16.50%
4.			▭, C ALL; 500, +/–, PV; 800, FV; 10, I/YR; N Answer: 4.93 years
5.	$FVA = PMT \times \left[\dfrac{(1 + i)^n - 1}{i} \right]$	FVA = \$100 $\times$ $\left[\dfrac{1.08^5 - 1}{.08} \right]$ = \$100 $\times$ 5.8666 = \$586.66	▭, C ALL; ▭, BEG/END (if BEGIN displayed); 100, +/–, PMT; 8, I/YR; 5, N; FV Answer: \$586.66
6.	$PMT = FVA \div \left[\dfrac{(1+i)^n - 1}{i} \right]$	PMT = \$10,000 $\div$ $\left[\dfrac{1.09^6 - 1}{.09} \right]$ = \$10,000 $\div$ 7.5233 = \$1,329.20	▭, C ALL; ▭, BEG/END (if BEGIN displayed); 10000, FV; 9, I/YR; 6, N; PMT Answer: \$1,329.20

RECOGNIZING TIME-VALUE-OF-MONEY PROBLEMS

Problem No.	Known Values	Value Sought	Problem	Time Line
7.	FVA, PMT, n	i	You need to accumulate $1,000 in 5 years. If you can afford to invest $150 at the end of each year, what rate of return will be required to reach your goal?	
8.	FVA, PMT, i	n	Evelyn will begin receiving payments of $2,000 per year beginning one year from now. If she invests the money at a 12 percent return, how long will it take for her to accumulate $15,000?	
9.	PMT, i, n	PVA	If you can afford to make loan payments of $100 at the end of each of the next 5 years, how much can you borrow today if the interest rate is 10 percent?	
10.	PVA, i, n	PMT	If you can borrow $20,000 today at a rate of 7 percent for 6 years, how much will your annual payments be?	
11.	PVA, PMT, n	i	A $50,000 business loan requires payments of $12,000 per year for 5 years. What is the interest rate on the loan?	

RECOGNIZING TIME-VALUE-OF-MONEY PROBLEMS (cont'd)

Problem No.	Formula Format	Formula Solution (Use Appendix F Factor Tables)	HP-10BII Keystrokes
7.			▭, C ALL; ▭, BEG/END (if BEGIN displayed); 150, +/−, PMT; 1000, FV; 5, N; I/YR Answer: 14.43%
8.			▭, C ALL; ▭, BEG/END (if BEGIN displayed); 2000, +/−, PMT; 15000, FV; 12, I/YR; N Answer: 5.66 years
9.	$PVA = PMT \times \left[\dfrac{1 - \dfrac{1}{(1+i)^n}}{i} \right]$	$PVA = \$100 \times \left[\dfrac{1 - \dfrac{1}{1.10^5}}{.10} \right]$ $= \$100 \times 3.7908$ $= \$379.08$	▭, C ALL; ▭, BEG/END (if BEGIN displayed); 100, +/−, PMT; 10, I/YR; 5, N; PV Answer: $379.08
10.	$PMT = PVA \div \left[\dfrac{1 - \dfrac{1}{(1+i)^n}}{i} \right]$	$PMT = \$20,000 \div \left[\dfrac{1 - \dfrac{1}{1.07^6}}{.07} \right]$ $= \$20,000 \div 4.7665$ $= \$4,195.95$	▭, C ALL; ▭, BEG/END (if BEGIN displayed); 20000, PV; 7, I/YR; 6, N; PMT Answer: $4,195.92
11.			▭, C ALL; ▭, BEG/END (if BEGIN displayed); 50000, PV; 12000, +/−, PMT; 5, N; I/YR Answer: 6.40%

RECOGNIZING TIME-VALUE-OF-MONEY PROBLEMS

Problem No.	Known Values	Value Sought	Problem	Time Line
12.	PVA, PMT, i	n	Jack needs to borrow $10,000 and can make payments of $2,000 per year. If the interest rate is 11 percent, how long will it take to pay off the loan?	$10,000 i=11% 1 2 3 4 n=? $2,000 $2,000 $2,000 $2,000 $2,000 x
13.	PMT, i, n	FVAD	If you invest $100 at the beginning of each of the next 5 years starting today, how much will it be worth at the end of 5 years at a rate of 8 percent?	FVAD? i=8% 1 2 3 4 5 $100 $100 $100 $100 $100
14.	FVAD, i, n	PMT	If you want to accumulate $10,000 in 6 years and want to make equal payments at the beginning of each of those years, how large must the payments be if the rate is 6 percent?	$10,000 i=6% 1 2 3 4 5 6 PMT? PMT? PMT? PMT? PMT? PMT?
15.	FVAD, PMT, n	i	You plan to invest $1,000 at the beginning of each of the next 4 years. If you want to accumulate $6,000 by the end of the fourth year, what rate must you earn?	$6,000 i=? 1 2 3 4 $1,000 $1,000 $1,000 $1,000
16.	FVAD, PMT, i	n	Fran is starting a savings program. She will deposit $1,000 annually with the first payment made today. If she earns 10 percent, how long will it take to accumulate $7,000?	$7,000 i=10% 1 2 3 n=? $1,000 $1,000 $1,000 $1,000 $1,000 x

RECOGNIZING TIME-VALUE-OF-MONEY PROBLEMS (cont'd)			
Problem No.	Formula Format	Formula Solution (Use Appendix F Factor Tables)	HP-10BII Keystrokes
12.			▭, C ALL; ▭, BEG/END (if BEGIN displayed); 10000, PV; 2000, +/–, PMT; 11, I/YR; N Answer: 7.65 years
13.	$FVAD = PMT \times$ $$\left[\frac{(1+i)^n - 1}{i}\right] \times (1+i)$$	$FVAD = \$100 \times$ $$\left[\frac{1.08^5 - 1}{.08}\right] \times 1.08$$ $= \$100 \times 5.8666 \times 1.08$ $= \$633.59$	▭, C ALL; ▭, BEG/END (if BEGIN not displayed); 100, +/–, PMT; 8, I/YR; 5, N; FV Answer: \$633.59
14.	$PMT = FVAD \div$ $$\left[\left[\frac{(1+i)^n - 1}{i}\right] \times (1+i)\right]$$	$PMT = \$10,000 \div$ $$\left[\left[\frac{1.06^6 - 1}{.06}\right] \times 1.06\right]$$ $= \$10,000 \div (6.9753 \times 1.06)$ $= \$1353.18$	▭, C ALL; ▭, BEG/END (if BEGIN not displayed); 10000, FV; 6, N; 6, I/YR; PMT Answer: \$1,352.48
15.			▭, C ALL; ▭, BEG/END (if BEGIN not displayed); 1000, +/–, PMT; 6000, FV; 4, N; I/YR Answer: 16.90%
16.			▭, C ALL; ▭, BEG/END (if BEGIN not displayed); 1000, +/–, PMT; 7000, FV; 10, I/YR; N Answer: 5.17 years

RECOGNIZING TIME-VALUE-OF-MONEY PROBLEMS

Problem No.	Known Values	Value Sought	Problem	Time Line
17.	PMT, i, n	PVAD	A manufacturer offers you six payments of $800 per year for rights to your invention. Using a 7 percent discount rate with the first payment due immediately, how much cash would you accept right now in lieu of the annual payments?	$800 $800 $800 $800 $800 $800 i=7% 1 2 3 4 5 6 PVAD?
18.	PVAD, i, n	PMT	A prospect says she will buy your business for $100,000, but wants to pay in five equal annual installments. If the first payment is made today and you require a 12 percent return for financing the sale, what will the payments be?	$100,000 i=12% 1 2 3 4 5 PMT? PMT? PMT? PMT? PMT?
19.	PVAD, PMT, n	i	Sally is offered $8,000 for her invention. As an alternative, she can receive six annual payments of $1,500 with the first payment made today. If she accepts the annual payments, what is the implied interest rate?	$1,500 $1,500 $1,500 $1,500 $1,500 $1,500 i=? 1 2 3 4 5 6 $8,000
20.	PVAD, PMT, i	n	Gary is offered $10,000 for his financial planning practice. Instead he asks for $2,500 per year for the rest of his life, with the first payment due today. How long would Gary have to live for the annual payments to equate to a 12 percent rate of return?	$2,500 $2,500 $2,500 $2,500 $2,500 x i=12% 1 2 3 n=? $10,000

RECOGNIZING TIME-VALUE-OF-MONEY PROBLEMS (cont'd)

Problem No.	Formula Format	Formula Solution (Use Appendix F Factor Tables)	HP-10BII Keystrokes
17.	$PVAD = PMT \times$ $$\left[\dfrac{1 - \dfrac{1}{(1+i)^n}}{i}\right] \times (1+i)$$	$PVAD = \$800 \times$ $$\left[\dfrac{1 - \dfrac{1}{1.07^6}}{.07}\right] \times 1.07$$ $= \$800 \times 4.7665 \times 1.07$ $= \$4,080.12$	▭, C ALL; ▭, BEG/END (if BEGIN not displayed); 800, PMT; 6, N; 7, I/YR; PV Answer: \$4,080.16
18.	$PMT = PVAD \div$ $$\left[\left[\dfrac{1 - \dfrac{1}{(1+i)^n}}{i}\right] \times (1+i)\right]$$	$PVAD = \$100,000 \div$ $$\left[\left[\dfrac{1 - \dfrac{1}{1.12^5}}{.12}\right] \times 1.12\right]$$ $= \$100,000 \div [3.6048 \times 1.12]$ $= \$24,752.48$	▭, C ALL; ▭, BEG/END (if BEGIN not displayed); 100000, +/–, PV; 12, I/YR; 5, N; PMT Answer: \$24,768.73
19.			▭, C ALL; ▭, BEG/END (if BEGIN not displayed); 8000, +/–, PV; 1500, PMT; 6, N; I/YR Answer: 4.97%
20.			▭, C ALL; ▭, BEG/END (if BEGIN not displayed); 10000, +/–, PV; 2500, PMT; 12, I/YR; N Answer: 4.94 years

Appendix H

Keystrokes for Solving Selected TVM Problems Using the HP-10BII Calculator

Note: The individual keystroke sequences in this appendix are separated by semicolons.

1. Preliminary "housekeeping" and miscellaneous chores
   a. Turning the machine on or off
      ON; ⬛, OFF
   b. Clearing a problem or data from memory
      ⬛, C ALL
   c. Setting number of decimal places to be displayed
      ⬛, DISP, desired number
   d. Clearing display screen of an incorrect or unwanted number or error message
      C
   e. Eliminating last keystroke before entering
      ←
   f. Setting number of payment periods/compounding periods per year to one if both are the same
      1, ⬛, P/YR, C; to check current setting, press ⬛ and hold down C ALL key
   g. Setting the calculator for payments at beginning of period or end of period
      ⬛, BEG/END; screen will display BEGIN or nothing; to change setting, press ⬛ and BEG/END again
   h. Raising a number to a power base
      number, ⬛, y^x, exponent, =
2. Future value of a single sum problems
   a. Finding FVSS
      amount of present value, +/–, PV; number of periods, N; periodic interest rate, I/YR; FV
   b. Finding N (number of periods)
      amount of present value, +/–, PV; amount of future value, FV; periodic interest rate, I/YR; N
   c. Finding I/YR (periodic interest rate)
      amount of present value, +/–, PV; amount of future value, FV; number of periods, N; I/YR
3. Present value of a single sum problems
   a. Finding PVSS
      amount of future value, FV; number of periods, N; periodic interest rate, I/YR; PV
   b. Finding N (number of periods)
      see 2.b., above
   c. Finding I/YR (periodic interest rate)
      see 2.c., above

4. Future value of an annuity problems
   a. Finding FVA

      set the calculator for end-of-period payments (see 1.g., above); set the calculator for one payment/compounding period per year, if both are the same (see 1.f., above); amount of one payment, +/−, PMT; periodic interest rate, I/YR; number of payments, N; FV

   b. Finding N (number of payments)

      set the calculator for end-of-period payments (see 1.g., above); set the calculator for one payment/compounding period per year, if both are the same (see 1.f., above); amount of one payment, +/−, PMT; periodic interest rate, I/YR; amount of future value, FV; N

   c. Finding I/YR (periodic interest rate)

      set the calculator for end-of-period payments (see 1.g., above); set the calculator for one payment/compounding period per year, if both are the same (see 1.f., above); amount of one payment, +/−, PMT; number of payments, N; amount of future value, FV; I/YR

5. Future value of an annuity due problems
   a. Finding FVAD

      set the calculator for beginning-of-period payments (see 1.g., above); set the calculator for one payment/compounding period per year, if both are the same (see 1.f., above); amount of one payment, +/−, PMT; periodic interest rate, I/YR; number of payments, N; FV

   b. Finding N (number of payments)

      set the calculator for beginning-of-period payments (see 1.g., above); set the calculator for one payment/compounding period per year, if both are the same (see 1.f., above); amount of one payment, +/−, PMT; periodic interest rate, I/YR; amount of future value, FV; N

   c. Finding I/YR (periodic interest rate)

      set the calculator for beginning-of-period payments (see 1.g., above); set the calculator for one payment/compounding period per year, if both are the same (see 1.f., above); amount of one payment, +/−, PMT; number of payments, N; amount of future value, FV; I/YR

6. Sinking fund problems
   a. Finding sinking fund payment

      set the calculator for beginning-of-period or end-of-period payments, as appropriate (see 1.g., above); set the calculator for one payment/compounding period per year, if both are the same (see 1.f., above); target amount of sinking fund, FV; periodic interest rate, I/YR; number of payments, N; PMT

b. Finding N (number of payments)

set the calculator for beginning-of-period or end-of-period payments, as appropriate (see 1.g., above); set the calculator for one payment/compounding period per year, if both are the same (see 1.f., above); target amount of sinking fund, FV; periodic interest rate, I/YR; amount of one payment, +/–, PMT; N

c. Finding I/YR (periodic interest rate)

set the calculator for beginning-of-period or end-of-period payments, as appropriate (see 1.g., above); set the calculator for one payment/compounding period per year, if both are the same (see 1.f., above); target amount of sinking fund, FV; number of payments, N; amount of one payment, +/–, PMT; I/YR

7. Present value of an annuity problems

a. Finding PVA

set the calculator for end-of-period payments (see 1.g., above); set the calculator for one payment/compounding period per year, if both are the same (see 1.f., above); amount of one payment, PMT; periodic interest rate, I/YR; number of payments, N; PV

b. Finding N (number of payments)

set the calculator for end-of-period payments (see 1.g., above); set the calculator for one payment/compounding period per year, if both are the same (see 1.f., above); amount of one payment, PMT; periodic interest rate, I/YR; amount of present value, +/–, PV; N

c. Finding I/YR (periodic interest rate)

set the calculator for end-of-period payments (see 1.g., above); set the calculator for one payment/compounding period per year, if both are the same (see 1.f., above); amount of one payment, PMT; number of payments, N; amount of present value, +/–, PV; I/Y

8. Present value of an annuity due problems

a. Finding PVAD

set the calculator for beginning-of-period payments (see 1.g., above); set the calculator for one payment/compounding period per year, if both are the same (see 1.f., above); amount of one payment, PMT; periodic interest rate, I/YR; number of payments, N; PV

      b.   Finding N (number of payments)

set the calculator for beginning-of-period payments (see 1.g., above); set the calculator for one payment/compounding period per year, if both are the same (see 1.f., above); amount of one payment, PMT; periodic interest rate, I/YR; amount of present value, +/−, PV; N

      c.   Finding I/YR (periodic interest rate)

set the calculator for beginning-of-period payments (see 1.g., above); set the calculator for one payment/compounding period per year, if both are the same (see 1.f., above); amount of one payment, PMT; number of payments, N; amount of present value, +/−, PV; I/YR

9.   Debt service/capital-sum-liquidation problems

      a.   Finding the payment

set the calculator for beginning-of-period or end-of-period payments, as appropriate (see 1.g., above); set the calculator for one payment/compounding period per year, if both are the same (see 1.f., above); beginning amount of loan or capital sum, PV; periodic interest rate, I/YR; number of payments, N; PMT

      b.   Finding N (number of payments)

set the calculator for beginning-of-period or end-of-period payments, as appropriate (see 1.g., above); set the calculator for one payment/compounding period per year, if both are the same (see 1.f., above); beginning amount of loan or capital sum, PV; periodic interest rate, I/YR; amount of one payment, +/−, PMT; N

      c.   Finding I/YR (periodic interest rate)

set the calculator for beginning-of-period or end-of-period payments, as appropriate (see 1.g., above); set the calculator for one payment/compounding period per year, if both are the same (see 1.f., above); beginning amount of loan or capital sum, PV; number of payments, N; amount of one payment, +/−, PMT; I/YR

      d.   Creating an amortization schedule

set the calculator for end-of-period payments, (see 1.g., above); set the calculator for one payment/compounding period per year, if both are the same (see 1.f., above); number of payments, N; periodic interest rate, I/YR; original amount of the loan, PV; PMT (to see amount of each payment); 1, INPUT, ▭, AMORT (1–1 displayed); = (to see principal paid in the first amortization period); = (to see interest paid in the first amortization period); = (to see the unpaid balance at the end of the first amortization period); 2, INPUT, ▭, AMORT (2–2 displayed); = (to see principal paid in the second amortization period); = (to see interest paid in the second amortization period); = (to see the unpaid balance at the end of the second amortization period); 3, INPUT, ▭, AMORT (3–3 displayed); and so on through the loan's final amortization period.

10. Present value of uneven cash flows problems
    a. Cash flows at end of year:
        0, CFj; amount of first cash flow, CFj, (number of times it occurs if more than once, ▭, Nj,); amount of second cash flow, CFj, (number of times it occurs if more than once, ▭, Nj,); amount of third cash flow, and so on through entire sequence; then interest rate, I/YR; ▭, NPV
    b. Cash flows at beginning of year
        amount of first cash flow, CFj; amount of second cash flow, CFj, (number of times it occurs if more than once, ▭, Nj,); amount of third cash flow, and so on through entire sequence; then interest rate, I/YR; ▭, NPV
    c. Cash flows that grow by a constant percentage, with first payment made immediately
        set calculator for beginning-of-period payments; amount of first cash flow, PMT; 1 plus interest rate, ÷, 1 plus growth rate, −, 1, x, 100, =, I/YR; number of payments, N; PV
    d. Cash flows that grow by a constant percentage, with first payment made after one period
        (take answer found in 10.c., above and without reentering all the information, enter) PV; ÷, 1 plus interest rate, =
11. Future value of uneven cash flows problems
    a. Generally
        compute present value as in 10.a. or b., above; then +/−, PV; number of periods, N; FV
    b. Special case: deposits growing by a constant percentage
        Compute present value as in 10.c. or d., above; then interest rate, I/YR; 0, PMT; FV
12. Net present value problems (Editor's Note: Each cash flow should be entered as a positive or negative amount, as appropriate.)
        use procedure in 10.a. or b., above, but press +/− key after any cash flows that are outflows
13. Internal rate of return problems
        set calculator for 4 decimal precision (see 1.c., above); same as NPV except for last two keystroke sequences; instead of interest rate, I/YR; ▭, NPV; press ▭, IRR/YR

14. Conversion of nominal interest rate to effective interest rate problems

set caluclator for 4 decimal precision (see 1.c., above); nominal interest rate, ▭, NOM%; number of compounding or discounting times per year, ▭, P/YR; ▭, EFF%; then 1, ▭, P/YR, C to restore setting to one payment/compounding period per year

Appendix I

Table of Effective Interest Rates

TABLE I
Effective Annual Interest Rates

Nominal Rate	Compounding Frequency					
	Semi-Annually	Quarterly	Monthly	Weekly	Daily (365 days)	Continuous
0.25%	0.2502%	0.2502%	0.2503%	0.2503%	0.2503%	0.2503%
0.50%	0.5006%	0.5009%	0.5011%	0.5012%	0.5012%	0.5013%
0.75%	0.7514%	0.7521%	0.7526%	0.7528%	0.7528%	0.7528%
1.00%	1.0025%	1.0038%	1.0046%	1.0049%	1.0050%	1.0050%
1.25%	1.2539%	1.2559%	1.2572%	1.2577%	1.2578%	1.2578%
1.50%	1.5056%	1.5085%	1.5104%	1.5111%	1.5113%	1.5113%
1.75%	1.7577%	1.7615%	1.7641%	1.7651%	1.7654%	1.7654%
2.00%	2.0100%	2.0151%	2.0184%	2.0197%	2.0201%	2.0201%
2.25%	2.2627%	2.2691%	2.2733%	2.2750%	2.2754%	2.2755%
2.50%	2.5156%	2.5235%	2.5288%	2.5309%	2.5314%	2.5315%
2.75%	2.7689%	2.7785%	2.7849%	2.7874%	2.7881%	2.7882%
3.00%	3.0225%	3.0339%	3.0416%	3.0446%	3.0453%	3.0455%
3.25%	3.2764%	3.2898%	3.2989%	3.3023%	3.3032%	3.3034%
3.50%	3.5306%	3.5462%	3.5567%	3.5608%	3.5618%	3.5620%
3.75%	3.7852%	3.8031%	3.8151%	3.8198%	3.8210%	3.8212%
4.00%	4.0400%	4.0604%	4.0742%	4.0795%	4.0808%	4.0811%
4.25%	4.2952%	4.3182%	4.3338%	4.3398%	4.3413%	4.3416%
4.50%	4.5506%	4.5765%	4.5940%	4.6008%	4.6025%	4.6028%
4.75%	4.8064%	4.8353%	4.8548%	4.8623%	4.8643%	4.8646%
5.00%	5.0625%	5.0945%	5.1162%	5.1246%	5.1267%	5.1271%
5.25%	5.3189%	5.3543%	5.3782%	5.3875%	5.3899%	5.3903%
5.50%	5.5756%	5.6145%	5.6408%	5.6510%	5.6536%	5.6541%
5.75%	5.8327%	5.8752%	5.9040%	5.9152%	5.9180%	5.9185%
6.00%	6.0900%	6.1364%	6.1678%	6.1800%	6.1831%	6.1837%
6.25%	6.3477%	6.3980%	6.4322%	6.4455%	6.4489%	6.4494%
6.50%	6.6056%	6.6602%	6.6972%	6.7116%	6.7153%	6.7159%
6.75%	6.8639%	6.9228%	6.9628%	6.9783%	6.9824%	6.9830%
7.00%	7.1225%	7.1859%	7.2290%	7.2458%	7.2501%	7.2508%
7.25%	7.3814%	7.4495%	7.4958%	7.5139%	7.5185%	7.5193%
7.50%	7.6406%	7.7136%	7.7633%	7.7826%	7.7876%	7.7884%
7.75%	7.9002%	7.9782%	8.0313%	8.0520%	8.0573%	8.0582%
8.00%	8.1600%	8.2432%	8.3000%	8.3220%	8.3278%	8.3287%
8.25%	8.4202%	8.5088%	8.5692%	8.5928%	8.5989%	8.5999%
8.50%	8.6806%	8.7748%	8.8391%	8.8642%	8.8706%	8.8717%
8.75%	8.9414%	9.0413%	9.1096%	9.1362%	9.1431%	9.1442%
9.00%	9.2025%	9.3083%	9.3807%	9.4089%	9.4162%	9.4174%
9.25%	9.4639%	9.5758%	9.6524%	9.6823%	9.6900%	9.6913%
9.50%	9.7256%	9.8438%	9.9248%	9.9564%	9.9645%	9.9659%
9.75%	9.9877%	10.1123%	10.1977%	10.2311%	10.2397%	10.2411%
10.00%	10.2500%	10.3813%	10.4713%	10.5065%	10.5156%	10.5171%

TABLE I (CONTINUED)
Effective Annual Interest Rates

Nominal Rate	Compounding Frequency					
	Semi-Annually	Quarterly	Monthly	Weekly	Daily (365 days)	Continuous
10.25%	10.5127%	10.6508%	10.7455%	10.7826%	10.7921%	10.7937%
10.50%	10.7756%	10.9207%	11.0203%	11.0593%	11.0694%	11.0711%
10.75%	11.0389%	11.1912%	11.2958%	11.3367%	11.3473%	11.3491%
11.00%	11.3025%	11.4621%	11.5719%	11.6148%	11.6260%	11.6278%
11.25%	11.5664%	11.7336%	11.8486%	11.8936%	11.9053%	11.9072%
11.50%	11.8306%	12.0055%	12.1259%	12.1731%	12.1853%	12.1873%
11.75%	12.0952%	12.2779%	12.4039%	12.4533%	12.4660%	12.4682%
12.00%	12.3600%	12.5509%	12.6825%	12.7341%	12.7475%	12.7497%
12.25%	12.6252%	12.8243%	12.9617%	13.0156%	13.0296%	13.0319%
12.50%	12.8906%	13.0982%	13.2416%	13.2978%	13.3124%	13.3148%
12.75%	13.1564%	13.3727%	13.5221%	13.5808%	13.5960%	13.5985%
13.00%	13.4225%	13.6476%	13.8032%	13.8644%	13.8802%	13.8828%
13.25%	13.6889%	13.9230%	14.0850%	14.1487%	14.1652%	14.1679%
13.50%	13.9556%	14.1989%	14.3674%	14.4337%	14.4508%	14.4537%
13.75%	14.2227%	14.4754%	14.6505%	14.7194%	14.7372%	14.7402%
14.00%	14.4900%	14.7523%	14.9342%	15.0057%	15.0243%	15.0274%
14.25%	14.7577%	15.0297%	15.2185%	15.2928%	15.3121%	15.3153%
14.50%	15.0256%	15.3077%	15.5035%	15.5806%	15.6006%	15.6040%
14.75%	15.2939%	15.5861%	15.7892%	15.8691%	15.8899%	15.8933%
15.00%	15.5625%	15.8650%	16.0755%	16.1583%	16.1798%	16.1834%
15.25%	15.8314%	16.1445%	16.3624%	16.4483%	16.4705%	16.4742%
15.50%	16.1006%	16.4244%	16.6500%	16.7389%	16.7620%	16.7658%
15.75%	16.3702%	16.7049%	16.9382%	17.0302%	17.0541%	17.0581%
16.00%	16.6400%	16.9859%	17.2271%	17.3223%	17.3470%	17.3511%
16.25%	16.9102%	17.2673%	17.5166%	17.6150%	17.6406%	17.6448%
16.50%	17.1806%	17.5493%	17.8068%	17.9085%	17.9349%	17.9393%
16.75%	17.4514%	17.8318%	18.0977%	18.2027%	18.2300%	18.2345%
17.00%	17.7225%	18.1148%	18.3892%	18.4976%	18.5258%	18.5305%
17.25%	17.9939%	18.3983%	18.6813%	18.7933%	18.8223%	18.8272%
17.50%	18.2656%	18.6823%	18.9742%	19.0896%	19.1196%	19.1246%
17.75%	18.5377%	18.9668%	19.2677%	19.3867%	19.4177%	19.4228%
18.00%	18.8100%	19.2519%	19.5618%	19.6845%	19.7164%	19.7217%
18.25%	19.0827%	19.5374%	19.8566%	19.9831%	20.0159%	20.0214%
18.50%	19.3556%	19.8235%	20.1521%	20.2823%	20.3162%	20.3218%
18.75%	19.6289%	20.1100%	20.4483%	20.5824%	20.6172%	20.6230%
19.00%	19.9025%	20.3971%	20.7451%	20.8831%	20.9190%	20.9250%
19.25%	20.1764%	20.6847%	21.0426%	21.1846%	21.2215%	21.2277%
19.50%	20.4506%	20.9728%	21.3408%	21.4868%	21.5248%	21.5311%
19.75%	20.7252%	21.2615%	21.6396%	21.7897%	21.8288%	21.8353%
20.00%	21.0000%	21.5506%	21.9391%	22.0934%	22.1336%	22.1403%

Appendix J

Certified Financial Planner
Advisory Opinions

Certified Financial Planner Advisory Opinions[1]

Editor's Note: CFP candidates should be familiar with Advisory Opinions issued by the Board of Professional Review of the Certified Financial Planner Board of Standards. Advisory Opinions are intended to clarify the Board's position and serve as a guide to both CFP professionals and their clients. Advisory Opinion 2001-1 relates to loans between CFP Board designees and their clients. Advisory Opinion 2003-1 describes appropriate use of the term "fee only." In addition to formal Advisory Opinions, a letter from the then-Chairman of the CFP Board of Standards provides guidance concerning the definition of the term "client."

ADVISORY OPINION 2001-1

Loans between CFP Board designees and their clients should be avoided in the client-planner relationship.

Background

The Board of Professional Review (the "BOPR") has generally viewed loans between CFP Board designees and their clients unfavorably and, in the majority of cases, to be a violation of the Code of Ethics and Professional Responsibility (the "Code"). Since the Code does not have a rule that specifically prohibits such transactions, however, the BOPR has addressed the issue under various rules, depending upon the facts and circumstances of the case being examined.

Due to an increase in the number of disciplinary cases that involve the issue of loans between a CFP Board designee and his or her client, the BOPR is issuing this advisory opinion to clarify its position and to serve as a guide to both CFP Board designees and their clients.

Issue

Whether a loan between a CFP Board designee and his or her client(s) violates the Code of Ethics and Professional Responsibility.

Analysis

Cases involving a loan between a CFP Board designee and a client involve an investigation of whether that CFP Board designee has violated the Code. The BOPR has evaluated these cases under a number of rules, including, but not limited to, Rules 201, 202, 401, 402, 606, 607 and 703. To determine which, if any, rules have been violated, the BOPR considers:

- whether the designee is a financial planning practitioner (as defined by the Code).
- whether the client is a family member or a financial institution. The degree to which CFP Board designee is related to the client is relevant. (The rationale for considering the type of relationship is discussed later in this opinion.)
- whether the terms and conditions of the loan are fair and reasonable to the client.

While any and/or all of the rules mentioned above, and others, may apply in a particular case, this advisory opinion focuses on two rules which are implicated in the majority of "loan" cases and are, therefore, most frequently cited by the BOPR: Rules 202 and 607.

Rule 202. Rule 202 of the Code requires financial planning practitioners to act in the best interest of their clients. Accordingly, this rule applies to CFP Board designees who are acting as financial planning practitioners, defined in the Code as:

[A] person who is capable and qualified to offer objective, integrated, and comprehensive financial advice to or for the benefit of clients to help them achieve their financial objectives and who engages in financial planning using the financial planning process in working with clients.

Borrowing From a Client

In cases involving a loan between a financial planning practitioner and a client, where the client is the lender and the practitioner is the borrower, the BOPR presumes that the practitioner is not acting in the best interest of the client.

BOPR Recognizes Exceptions

There are two exceptions to this presumption:

(1) when the client is a family member
(2) when the client is a financial institution acting in its normal course of business activity

The BOPR recognizes that borrowing and/or lending of funds between family members is a common, generally accepted, practice. Likewise, financial institutions are in the business of borrowing and lending funds and, as such, often provide loans to individuals, regardless of whether they are CFP Board designees. In both instances, loans between these groups can fall outside the scope of the planner-client relationship.

In either of the two situations described above, while the BOPR does not presume that the planner's borrowing of funds is a violation of Rule 202, it may still find that the transaction was not in the client's best interests if the financial planning practitioner is unable to establish that:

- the terms and conditions of the loan were clearly and objectively disclosed to the client, taking into consideration the client's level of sophistication
- the terms and conditions of the transaction were fair and reasonable under the circumstances
- the client fully understood (a) the terms and conditions of the transaction and (b) the impact of the transaction on his/her financial situation.

Lending to a Client

In the more rare case where a financial planning practitioner lends funds to a client, the BOPR will presume that the practitioner is not acting in the best interest of the client, as a client who borrows funds from his or her planner is likely to be inhibited from ending the planner-client relationship, regardless of whether the client's financial planning needs are being met. Even if the financial planning practitioner can demonstrate that a particular loan to a client did not inhibit the client from ending the relationship, the transaction will still be presumed to be a violation of Rule 202 if (a) the loan was used as an enticement for the client to make a financial decision, including, but not limited to, purchasing a financial product, or (b) the loan had a below market interest rate and could be considered a form of rebate.

The exception to this presumption is when the client is a family member. Even if the client is a family member, however, the BOPR may still find that the transaction was not in the client's best interest if the financial planning practitioner is unable to establish that (a) the terms and conditions of the loan were clearly and objectively disclosed to the client, taking into consideration the client's level of sophistication, (b) the terms and conditions of the transaction were fair and reasonable under the circumstances, and (c) the client fully understood the terms and conditions of the transaction and the impact the transaction may have on his/her financial situation.

Rule 607. Rule 607 prohibits a CFP Board designee from engaging "in any conduct which reflects adversely on his or her integrity or fitness as a CFP Board designee, upon the marks, or upon the profession."

As defined in the Code, CFP Board designees include individuals who are currently certified, candidates for certification, and individuals who have any entitlement, either direct or indirect, to use the CFP certification marks. Accordingly, this rule has been interpreted to apply to all CFP Board designees regardless of whether they are practitioners, including candidates for certification, and individuals who have the right to renew their CFP™ certification without re-taking CFP Board's CFP™ Certification Examination.

Whether the Client Is the Borrower or Lender

The BOPR interprets Rule 607 broadly, finding conduct which gives the "appearance of impropriety" to be a violation of the rule. Accordingly, the BOPR has taken the position that most loans between a CFP Board designee and a client give the appearance of impropriety and, therefore, reflect negatively on the integrity of the designee, the CFP marks and the financial planning profession.

BOPR Recognizes Exceptions

The same two exceptions discussed under Rule 202 (i.e., loans between a planner and a family member or loans between a planner and a financial institution) apply under Rule 607 when the planner is the borrower. In cases where the client is the borrower, only the family member exception applies. Even if one of the exceptions applies, the BOPR may still find that the transaction violates Rule 607 if CFP Board designee fails to establish that:

- the terms and conditions of the loan were clearly and objectively disclosed to the client
- the terms and conditions of the transaction were fair and reasonable under the circumstances
- the client fully understood (a) the terms and conditions of the transaction and (b) the impact of the transaction on his/her financial situation

Summary

The BOPR urges all CFP Board designees to avoid the practice of borrowing from or lending to clients. This advisory opinion focuses on the two most frequently cited rules (Rules 202 and 607) in cases involving loans between CFP Board designees and their clients. CFP Board designees should remember, however, that the BOPR may find such transactions to be in violation of other rules in the Code, as well.

ADVISORY OPINION 2003-1

CFP Board designees must avoid possible misrepresentation when using the term "fee-only."

Background

The Board of Professional Review ("BOPR") views misrepresentation of compensation arrangements to be a violation of the *Code of Ethics and Professional Responsibility (Code of Ethics)*. The *Code of Ethics* defines the term "fee-only" as denoting "a method of compensation in which compensation is received solely from a client with neither the personal financial planning practitioner nor any related party receiving compensation which is contingent upon the purchase or sale of any financial product." BOPR Advisory Opinions 97-1 and 97-2 allowed for a designee to use the term "fee-only" to describe the compensation received from a specific client, even if other methods of compensation were used with other clients, and to offer "fee-only" services to a client, even if the designee also received commissions from the same client or other clients for other services. In light of recent regulatory trends regarding the misrepresentation of methods of compensation, media focus on the issue, and the perceptions of the general public, the BOPR has redefined the appropriate use of the term "fee-only."

The purpose of this Advisory Opinion is to reduce confusion on the part of CFP Board designees, their clients and the public, and to maintain consistency with other organizations' use of the term "fee-only." Thus, the Board of Governors withdrew Advisory Opinions 97-1 and 97-2 in January 2002 and the *Code of Ethics* definition can no longer be considered an accurate reflection of the BOPR's position on this issue.

Issue

When may a CFP Board designee use the term "fee-only" to describe the designee as an individual, the designee's practice or the designee's services?

Analysis

A fee arrangement exists when the CFP Board designee is compensated solely by the client, or another party operating exclusively on behalf of the client, for professional services provided. The BOPR has defined types of compensation arrangements. The following qualify as fees:

- *Hourly, fixed or flat fees*
- *Percentage fees*, which are based on some aspect of the client's financial profile, such as assets under management or earned income
- *Performance-based fees*, which are tied to the profitability of the client's invested assets

There are other compensation arrangements under which a CFP Board designee could be compensated for working with a client. In some of these arrangements, the designee may be paid by a third party for the recommending, referring or selling of a product and/or service. These arrangements, including, but not limited to the following, shall not be interpreted as fees under the *Code of Ethics*:

- *Commission*, generated from a product or service. In addition to traditional commissions, this includes 12(b)1 fees, trailing commissions, surrender charges, and contingent deferred sales charges, even if used to reduce or offset other fees.
- *Referral compensation*, providing compensation or other economic benefits to the CFP Board designee for recommending, introducing or referring a product or service provided by another person or entity, even if used to reduce or offset other fees.

Use of the Term "Fee-Only"

In order for a CFP Board designee to describe his or her compensation as "fee-only," all compensation from all clients must be derived solely from fees. Minimal exceptions may be allowed provided the compensation is inconsequential and independent of the purchase of any product or service. Likewise, when using terms including, but not limited to, "fee-only services" and "fee-only firm," the same requirements apply.

Potential Rule Violations

Cases involving misrepresentation of compensation arrangements or failure to disclose compensation arrangements warrant investigation of whether that CFP Board designee has violated the *Code of Ethics*. The rules implicated in this analysis include, but are not limited to, Rules 101(a) and (b), 102, 201, 202, 401, 402, 606, 607 and 702. The BOPR must consider whether the CFP Board designee is a financial planning practitioner (as defined by the *Code of Ethics*) in determining which, if any, rules have been violated. While any and/or all of the rules mentioned above may apply in a particular case, this advisory opinion focuses on three rules that would most often be implicated in a case involving misrepresentation of and/or failure to disclose compensation arrangements: Rules 101(a) and (b), 401 and 402.

Rule 401

Rule 401 of the *Code of Ethics* requires CFP Board designees to disclose to the client material information relative to the professional relationship, including compensation structure. The BOPR urges that disclosures under Rule 401 be clear, straightforward and unambiguous so as to be easily understood by all parties. In cases involving CFP Board designees who represent themselves as "fee-only" to a client but accept compensation not defined as fees by the BOPR from that relationship or other client relationships, the BOPR presumes that the CFP Board designee has failed to disclose material information relative to the professional relationship.

Rule 402

Rule 402 requires CFP Board designees in a financial planning engagement to make timely written disclosure of all material information relative to the professional relationship, in all circumstances and prior to the relationship, including sources of compensation. Adherence to the provisions of Rule 402 by CFP Board designees in financial planning engagements allows the public to make informed decisions about whether to use the professional services of the CFP Board designee. Rule 402(a) is violated when the CFP Board designee in a financial planning engagement, in the disclosure provided to the client, represents himself or herself as "fee-only" when, in fact, that designee accepts compensation not defined as fees by the BOPR in that relationship or other client relationships.

Rule 101(a) and (b)

Rule 101(a) and (b) prohibits CFP Board designees from soliciting clients through false or misleading advertisements and/or promotional activities. The use of the term "fee-only" must be used carefully and only when the CFP Board designee derives all compensation from all clients solely from fees. The BOPR presumes advertisements and/or promotional activities to be false or misleading when they contain the term "fee-only" and the CFP Board designee advertising or promoting his or her services accepts compensation not defined as fees from that client relationship or any other client relationships.

Summary

The public regards compensation structure as important information when choosing a financial planning professional. The *Code of Ethics* requires CFP Board designees to act with integrity and fairness toward the public in all activities. The appropriate use of the term "fee-only" in all public discourse provides a key opportunity for CFP Board designees to demonstrate professionalism by avoiding casual use of the term. The BOPR advises CFP Board designees to avoid using the term "fee-only" except when all compensation from all clients is derived solely from fees. CFP Board designees should also avoid the use of other terms designed to induce the public into a distorted belief that the designee receives "fee-only" compensation when in fact the designee receives commissions, referral compensation, or any other form of compensation not defined as fees by the BOPR.

DEFINITION OF CLIENT

Definition of Client Letter to CFP Licensees
December 22, 1998

Dear CFP Licensee:

CFP Board of Governors members and the staff of CFP Board are deeply appreciative of the comments and suggestions many of you have provided regarding the definition of the term "client," as used in the Code of Ethics and Professional Responsibility. As you may remember, the current definition has been in effect since 1996. However, in the discussions related to the promulgation of Practice Standards, some licensees raised concerns regarding the definition of client. During the ensuing months the Board invited feedback from licensees and representatives of the Institute of Certified Financial Planners and the International Association for Financial Planning. The Board had extensive discussions regarding the issues raised through fax and e-mail, in committee meetings and at its September Board meeting.

Based on these discussions, a careful reading of submitted letters and e-mail (all members of CFP Board of Governors received every one of the comments sent to CFP Board), as well as information prepared by the Board's legal staff and provided by outside counsel and consultants, the Board proposed, and on September 25 issued for comment, the following modified definition of client:

"Client" denotes a person, persons or entity who engages a practitioner and for whom professional services are rendered. For purposes of this definition, a practitioner is engaged when an individual, based upon the relevant facts and circumstances, reasonably relies upon information or services provided by that practitioner. Where the services of the practitioner are provided to an entity (corporation, trust, partnership, estate, etc.), the client is the entity acting through its legally authorized representative.

During the comment period that ended December 1, we received numerous responses. As before, all responses were provided to each member of the Board of Governors. After thoughtful consideration and much discussion, CFP Board of Governors has adopted the definition of client noted above, effective January 1, 1999.

Having done so, we recognize that the decision will be of concern to some of our caring and committed licensees. Based on a review of the comments we have received and our discussion with those licensees who have requested modifications to the definition as adopted, we believe that the primary concerns are related to the following issues:

1. CFP Board's definition of client does not include the concept of "mutual agreement."
2. The definition does not require compensation.
3. The Board's definition does not provide a "bright line" standard for determining the point of engagement, and there is no requirement for an agreement to be in writing.

Because we value the opinions of all licensees and consider the licensee community one of our most important stakeholders, I would like to share with you the thought process behind the Board's decisions with respect to these issues.

Mutual Agreement

Established legal principles hold physicians, lawyers, and virtually all professionals responsible for professional conduct, even when that conduct occurs outside of a contractual relationship. Since CFP licensees are professionals who possess superior information and knowledge about their areas of expertise, this same obligation accrues to them. It is for this reason that CFP Board decided to define the term "client" to include more than those individuals with whom a CFP licensee has a mutual agreement or a compensation arrangement. The Board's intent is to use the term "client" to clearly reflect the degree of liability to which licensees, as professionals, can already be legally held by the courts or judicial entities. These principles say that when respected professionals provide professional advice on which an individual reasonably relies, the professional can be held responsible for damages that the individual suffers as a result of his or her reliance. [A general discussion of this underlying general concept, including its history, can be found at Williston, A Treatise on the Law of Contracts, § 8.1-8.6. (4th ed. 1992.)]

This concept is called "reasonable reliance." The standard of reasonable reliance calls for professionals to adjust their level of advice to the context of the situation and seeks to determine if the advice relied upon was appropriate to the situation, regardless of contract law or the exchange of consideration or compensation. By defining the term "client" in this broader sense, the Board of Governors is seeking to provide a practical definition that recognizes potential action that may arise in the courts or in organizations outside CFP Board's authority. In summary, based on established legal principles, CFP licensees, as professionals, may still owe an obligation to people outside their contractual engagements.

Compensation

In many of the comments received from CFP licensees, the receipt of compensation was suggested as a required condition for the determination of the existence of a contractual relationship between the planner and the client. In the real world, however, and as discussed above, contracts can be implied from the circumstances whether or not any compensation has been exchanged. Further, I'm sure all our licensees would agree that a CFP practitioner should be no less professional when no compensation is received as in pro bono or charitable work. Since, based upon well-established legal precedent, the receipt of compensation is immaterial to the issue of whether or not a contract or a duty exists between the practitioner and the consumer, and since professionals are held to a professional standard for conduct occurring both within and outside a contractual relationship, the Board concluded that compensation should not be an element of the definition of client.

Bright Line, Written Agreements

While we understand the desire of licensees to know when they may be responsible for advice rendered, due to legal realities, CFP Board is unable to provide that certainty. Valid, enforceable oral contracts and agreements are concluded each and every day without any written documentation. In the event of dispute, courts, arbitrators and regulators look to the specific circumstances of the proposed agreement to see if either party reasonably relied upon those circumstances to understand that a duty was owed from one to the other (generally from the professional to the consumer). It was of concern to the Board that a more restrictive or bright line definition could actually create a false sense of security among licensees who felt that certain relationships carried no liability when the courts or arbitrators might rule otherwise.

Reasonable Reliance

While this concept has been discussed in the remarks above, it is significant enough to repeat here. The concept of reasonable reliance is a well-recognized principle in equity, an area of law influenced by principles of ethics and fairness, rather than contract law (the branch of law dealing with formal agreements between parties). If, taken in the context of the specific facts and circumstances of a professional relationship, proposed or otherwise, a consumer has properly come to understand that she was entitled to rely upon the information which the practitioner had given to her, then the practitioner is responsible for the consequences of having provided that information. Thus, the concept of reasonable reliance does not allow for a specific rule that addresses all possible conditions and issues. It is in this concept, and others like it, that the judicial system attempts to weigh competing values and to "do justice." Similarly, arbitrators and regulators follow this method so as to be in harmony with the courts. This is an important reality, which is a product of established legal precedent. The Board neither believes we can, nor we should, attempt to set ourselves apart from such precedents and commonly accepted professional standards. [The concept of reasonable (or justifiable) reliance is discussed in various legal authorities, including Prosser and Keeton on the Law of Torts (5th ed. 1984) § 108; Restatement of Contracts § 90 comment b.]

Managing Expectations

The Board believes that it has, by the adoption of the amended definition of client, provided CFP licensees increased flexibility in deciding the best way to manage specific situations. Some professions restrict giving advice outside a contractual relationship. However, CFP Board's amended definition of client does not inhibit your ability to determine your own work style (including the decision to reduce agreements to writing), leaving you free to draw on your own experience to guide your behavior. Implicit in this freedom, of course, is the recognition of the necessity to comply with the mandates and requirements of all applicable federal and state laws and regulations, as well as the responsibility to act in a professionally responsible manner in all professional services and activities.

Recognizing this responsibility, CFP licensees can make their own decisions as to the professional activities with which they are comfortable and take steps to manage other people's expectations, which could include:

- Using written disclaimers and/or agreements in all cases related to providing professional financial planning advice. Limiting advice only to contractual situations.

- Being cautious when offering general advice at social gatherings, Internet chat rooms, talk shows, "hot lines" or "financial makeovers." (Consider qualifying or disclaiming the advice given in such situations.)
- Using disclaimers in seminar literature and in informational or educational articles written for newspapers and magazines.

In addition, the practice standards can help you with managing others' expectations. For example, as noted above, one of the concerns raised in the comments we received was the idea that mutuality should be present in an engagement with a client. Although the courts do not require mutuality for someone to have relied on a professional's advice, licensees can use the first practice standard (100-1: Defining the Scope of the Engagement) to help clarify the expectation regarding the services an individual is requesting. Please be assured, however, that the definition of client does not determine when practice standards should be used. The practice standards, which are based on the six-step financial planning process, clearly state that they are to be used only when providing financial planning services.

Well, that's the story about the "why." Unfortunately, some licensees seem concerned that the problems they perceived in the definition of "client" are a result of the definition's having been crafted by individuals who do not understand the complexities and realities of everyday practice. That perception is inaccurate and generally springs from a lack of knowledge about the Board and its composition. So now I'd like to conclude with a comment about the "who." I recognize that for some licensees, CFP Board is something of an unknown entity. We very much wish it otherwise and encourage you to read CFP Board Report, a newsletter written for CFP licensees, and to frequently visit the home page at www.CFP-Board.org. Still, recognizing reality, I think it would be useful to review something about the individuals who collectively made this decision.

The ultimate responsibility for making decisions regarding the practice standards and the Code of Ethics and Professional Responsibility rests with the Board of Governors. The Board of Governors is composed of 20 members. CFP Board President Bob Goss serves as a non-voting member. Currently, 17 members are CFP licensees, 15 of the licensees are in everyday practice and 10 members have their own practices. Four members are in senior management in national and international financial services firms. Two members are public representatives, including a judge, and two are academics with a focus on financial planning. I hope by including this brief resume about the Board's members, I've addressed any fears that these members do not understand the nature of the problems you face when making decisions that so directly affect your life. In fact, most of us do face the same problems every day.

The Board of Governors delegates some activities to the sub-boards and standing committees of the Board of Governors. The Board of Professional Review (nine voting members, each a current or past practitioner of substantial experience) has been charged with enforcing the Code of Ethics (including the existing definition of client) for several years. The Board of Practice Standards consists of nine practitioners averaging over 10 years experience. These practitioners were selected from a list of nominees recommended by the IAFP and the ICFP. The Board of Practice Standards, naturally, used the existing definition of client in crafting its recommendations on practice standards to the Board of Governors. The work of these two sub-boards and of additional committees and task forces was significant and helpful in assisting the Board of Governors in reaching a final decision. It is the Board of Governors, however, that bears the responsibility for setting policy.

Finally, I'd like to reiterate that the members of the Board and staff are extremely grateful to those of you who submitted what were obviously well thought out comments, not only in the last two months but also in prior comments that caused us to respond with the changes we made. Your efforts reflect much concern for our profession. Although some licensees may not agree with the decisions of the Board, we hope that the explanation in this letter and the enclosed question and answer sheet will address some of your questions and concerns. If not, we encourage those of you who have additional questions to email us at mail@CFP-Board.org or call us at 1-800-487-1497.

Yours truly,

Harold R. Evensky, CFP
Chair, Board of Governors

Questions and Answers About the Definition of Client

Does "reasonably relies upon" exclude advice given in a casual conversation? What should I say in a social situation to protect myself? If I comment on the stock market casually, am I liable?

Opinions given in casual settings, particularly if they are very specific or not qualified, may be the kind of opinions that the recipient fairly believes he can act upon. To protect yourself, always be cautious when offering general advice in casual conversations with individuals. Consider qualifying or disclaiming any advice you give in such situations.

I want to know when someone is relying on my advice. How can I be sure?

Unfortunately, no one can always know when someone is actually relying on his or her advice, but actual reliance is not the standard. Rather it is one of reasonableness. Although you cannot always know what in hindsight will be considered reasonable reliance, you can ask yourself the question: Would the average person in the same situation be apt to take action based on what I have said? When you look at it this way, you can see how qualifying and disclaiming language can help to protect you. It is less likely that someone will act upon your opinion if you expressly tell him or her that the opinion is based on incomplete information and that they should contact someone professionally before taking any action. Another step you can take to manage other people's expectations is to consider limiting your advice to contractual situations, where both the client and practitioner are in agreement that an engagement has taken place.

Why can't a standard of mutual agreement or compensation be used to determine when someone is a client?

In most cases, mutuality or compensation will be present. However, case law involving physicians, lawyers, and other professionals has established that those who give unqualified, erroneous advice, even outside a contractual relationship (where no mutuality of agreement or mutuality of obligation is evident) can be held responsible for this advice if it damages others and the circumstances under which the individual relied on their advice were reasonable. This is a legal concept known as "reasonable reliance." The standard of reasonable reliance calls for professionals to adjust their level of advice to the context of the situation and seeks to determine if the advice relied upon was appropriate to the situation, regardless of contract law or the exchange of consideration or compensation.

Why is it that CPAs have no client relationship without a signed contract? What about the SEC's definition of investment advisor, which states that compensation must be received?

Even without a signed contract, CPAs can still be held accountable in a court of law for their advice. The SEC's definition is not intended to define a client, but rather specifies the requirements for classifying someone as an investment advisor under federal statutes.

Could I be considered to have a client even though I'm not giving financial planning advice?

Yes. CFP Board's Code of Ethics recognizes a potential client relationship for purposes of ethics and other professional responsibilities beyond the scope of financial planning advice, which requires the use of the practice standards. However, if you are not providing financial planning advice, the practice standards would not apply.

What do I do on a radio talk show or a call-in "hot line"? Are the individuals listening to me my clients? What about in an open forum or speaking to the general public?

Perhaps. Depending upon the way in which financial information is given, individuals might reasonably conclude that they could act upon your "advice." Consider using such disclaimers in your explanations as "Because I don't have a full picture of your financial situation, I can only give you general advice." Close your conversations by suggesting they contact a financial planner (or you) directly after the show.

What about when I'm teaching a seminar or participating in an Internet chat room?

Again, when preparing to give a seminar, consider using disclaimers in seminar literature. Be cautious about what you promise in your advertisements. Internet chat rooms also require a good deal of caution. Could the individual reasonably rely on the information he or she receives from you? Use disclaimers over the Internet as well.

What about someone reading my article/newsletter? With no reciprocity on my part to agree to be engaged, should I assume they're a client?

Again, "client" describes any individual who could potentially be affected by a professional's advice and to whom a CFP practitioner, therefore, owes a professional responsibility. These individuals include not only those with whom licensees have a mutually agreed upon engagement, but also others who may, because of licensee's expertise and knowledge, reasonably rely and act upon his or her opinions. Consider using disclaimers in all written material, such as "Figures quoted subject to change" or "To determine what specific action to take given your personal financial situation, contact."

Am I entitled to express an opinion without being subject to liability?

Of course. However, it is because of the respect that professionals such as CFP practitioners command and the trust they engender that the courts require the added responsibility of reasonable reliance. Therefore, use caution about the settings in which you give your financial opinion.

What should I do when I have a pro bono client?

As with any client, CFP practitioners should use the first practice standard (100-1: Defining the Scope of the Engagement) to understand an individual's expectation regarding the services he or she is requesting. CFP practitioners should clarify the nature of the financial planning services that are to be provided at no cost to the client.

What about the person relying on information I extend in a complimentary or exploratory interview?

Explain up front the nature of your services and what you will need from the prospect in order to perform those services. Then, consider distinguishing for the prospect the difference between the complimentary information you are giving (the imparting of facts or data) versus the financial advice you could give him as a client (your opinion of what could or should be done about an issue, based on an understanding of a client's situation). Consider promotional literature that describes the nature of that first complimentary interview.

Why did the Board ignore contract law? The AICPA requires a contractual obligation as a determinant of client. Why didn't the Board adopt the same concept?

Contract law was not ignored. This broader definition of the term client is based on equity law—a system of jurisprudence. This concept is influenced by principles of ethics and fairness, rather than contract law, the branch of law dealing with formal agreements between parties, and takes into account the way in which the courts are most likely to impose liability. Unlike the AICPA definition, which refers to an individual's engagement of a member for the performance of professional services, the term "client" as used in the Code of Ethics encompasses all the possible individuals who might be affected by a CFP practitioner's professional advice. These people include individuals who have mutually agreed to work with us as financial planners as well as others who, in certain circumstances, might reasonably act upon our statements.

When do the practice standards apply?

If financial planning services are being undertaken, then practice standards apply. Use Practice Standard 100-1 (Determining the Scope of the Engagement) to clarify the individual's expectations of the engagement. If an individual only wants you to execute a transaction, such as the sale of stock, and you confine your services to non-planning activities, then it's not financial planning and practice standards do not apply.

How might the amended definition of client be applied under the practice standards?

Beginning January 1, 1999, the first three practice standards become effective for all CFP licensees. Accordingly, CFP Board may then receive complaints that CFP licensees have not followed the practice standards. CFP Board will only entertain complaints alleging practice standards violations if they originated from a licensee or a person with whom the CFP licensee has or has had a contractual relationship, either expressed or implied. Upon receipt of such a complaint, CFP Board will conduct an investigation, as outlined in CFP Board's Disciplinary Rules and Procedures. Under those procedures, the Board of Professional Review will interpret and apply the definition of client, including reasonable reliance, in a manner similar to how the judicial system might apply these same practice standards.

Appendix K

Examination Information for Broker-Dealers, Transfer Agents, Clearing Agencies, Investment Advisers, and Investment Companies

EXAMINATION INFORMATION FOR BROKER-DEALERS, TRANSFER AGENTS, CLEARING AGENCIES, INVESTMENT ADVISERS, AND INVESTMENT COMPANIES.

This brochure, prepared by the staff of the Securities and Exchange Commission (SEC or Commission), provides information about examinations conducted by the SEC examination staff, including the examination process and the methods employed by the staff for resolving problems found during examinations. This information, provided to firms under examination, should help you to better understand the Commission's objectives in this area.

I. <u>PURPOSE OF EXAMINATIONS</u>

The Securities Exchange Act of 1934, the Investment Advisers Act of 1940, and the Investment Company Act of 1940 authorize the SEC to conduct examinations of firms that are registered with the SEC, including registered broker-dealers, transfer agents, clearing agencies, investment advisers, and investment companies. These statutes also authorize the SEC, by rule, to require registered firms to maintain certain books and records. The purpose of SEC examinations is to protect investors. Thus, during examinations, the SEC staff will seek to determine whether the firm is: conducting its activities in accordance with the federal securities laws and rules adopted under these laws (including, where applicable, the rules of self-regulatory organizations subject to the SEC's oversight); adhering to the disclosures it has made to investors; and implementing supervisory systems and/or compliance policies and procedures that are reasonably designed to ensure that the firm's operations are in compliance with the law. The SEC staff appreciates your cooperation with the examination process.

II. <u>THE EXAMINATION PROCESS</u>

Examinations are conducted by professional examination staff from the SEC's 11 regional offices, and its headquarters office in Washington, DC. The Office of Compliance Inspections and Examinations, located in Washington, DC, is responsible for the SEC's overall examination program.

Firms may be selected for examination for any number of reasons, including for a routine examination, because of an investor complaint, or in connection with a review of a particular compliance risk area. The reason why firms have been selected for examination is non-public information, and typically will not be shared with the firm under examination.

Examinations may be conducted on an announced or unannounced basis. When the examination is announced, the staff will send the firm a letter notifying it of the examination and containing a request list that identifies certain information or documents that SEC examiners will review as part of the examination. In some instances, the examiners may request that certain of the information and documents be provided in an electronic format. The request list may ask that the information and documents: (1) be delivered to the SEC's offices by a specified date; (2) be made available for review at the firm's offices on a specified date; or (3) some combination of the two.

Please communicate promptly with the examiners if you have any questions about the documents and information requested. In all cases, producing requested information and documents in a timely manner will facilitate the efficient completion of the examination.

As part of our pre-examination planning process, we actively work to ensure that our regulatory efforts are not duplicative. If you have any concerns in this regard, please contact the examiners responsible for the examination.

The examiners will provide the firm with SEC Form 1661, "*Supplemental Information for Regulated Entities Directed to Supply Information Other Than Pursuant to a Commission Subpoena,*" which provides information concerning the possible uses of information provided to the SEC (this form can also be accessed at www.sec.gov/about/forms/sec1661.pdf.) Upon request, the examiners will also provide the name and telephone number of their supervisor.

In many examinations, the examiners will visit the firm to conduct examination work on-site. Upon arrival, the examiners will identify themselves and present their SEC identifications. The examiners may conduct an initial interview. During this initial interview, the examiners will ask a series of questions about the firm and the activities to be examined. This information assists examiners in understanding the firm and its operations, and often assists examiners in determining the scope of the examination. The examiners may also ask for a walk-through of the firm's offices to gain an overall understanding of the firm's organization, flow of work, and control environment. Some examinations may be completed through the examiners' review of records in the SEC's offices along with telephonic or other interviews, as needed.

If the examination is unannounced, as soon as the examiners arrive they will provide the firm with an information or document request list and conduct an initial interview. During the initial interview, the examiners will go over the information or document request list to ensure that you understand the information and documents requested.

Following this initial phase of the examination, the examiners will review the information and documents provided by the firm. During this review, the examiners may make supplemental requests for additional information and documents. They may also request meetings with firm employees to discuss the firm's operations and the information and documents provided. These meetings help the examiners gain a better understanding of the firm's activities and compliance processes. The examiners may also request relevant information and documents from third parties that, for example, perform work for, or in conjunction with, the firm or where the third party activity may have a material impact on the firm.

On the last day of the on-site visit, the examiners will typically conduct an "exit interview" during which they will discuss the status of the examination and any outstanding information and document requests and, if appropriate, the issues identified during the examination to that point.
During an exit interview, the firm will be given an opportunity to discuss any of the issues that the examiners found and provide additional relevant information, including with respect to any actions that the firm has taken or plans to take to address the issues.

The examiners will then return to the SEC offices. In many cases, the examiners will perform additional analyses of the information or data obtained during the examination. This may include contacting the firm to ask clarifying questions or to request additional information or documents. In formulating the findings of the examination, the examiners may consult with other staff within the SEC, including supervisory staff and staff in relevant offices and divisions, to ensure that the findings are consistent with Commission rules, regulations, and interpretations.

If work performed subsequent to completion of the on-site portion of the examination identifies issues in addition to those discussed during the exit interview conducted on the last day of the on-site visit, the examiners will contact the firm, usually by telephone, to discuss these additional findings. During this discussion, which may constitute a "final exit interview," the firm will be given an opportunity to discuss any of the issues that the examiners found and provide additional relevant information, including with respect to any actions that the firm has taken or plans to take to address the issues identified.

III. <u>COMPLETING AN EXAMINATION</u>

After the completion of the on-site portion of the examination, the examiners will normally complete the examination within 120 days. If the examiners are unable to complete their work within that time, on or about the 120th day they will contact the firm to discuss the status of the examination and the likely schedule for completing the examination and for providing a final exit interview.

When an examination has been completed, the firm will be sent a written notification. This notification will generally take one of two forms: (1) the examination staff may send the firm a letter indicating that the examination has concluded without findings (often referred to as a *"nofurther action letter"*); or (2) the examination staff may send the firm a letter that describes the issues identified, asks the firm to undertake corrective action and to provide the staff with a written response outlining those actions, and possibly requests a conference at the SEC's office (often referred to as a *"deficiency letter"*). If serious problems are found, in addition to sending the firm a deficiency letter, the examination staff may refer the problems to the Commission's Division of Enforcement, or to a self-regulatory organization, state regulatory agency, or other regulator for possible action. Notwithstanding the above, on occasion (usually in the context of certain exigent circumstances) problems may be referred to the Division of Enforcement without an exit interview or a deficiency letter.

As described above, a written notification that the examination has concluded will generally be sent to the firm no later than 120 days following the end of the fieldwork phase of the examination. The firm will be asked to respond in writing to any issues identified in a deficiency letter, including any steps that it has taken or will take to address the problems and to ensure that they do not reoccur. This response will generally be due within 30 days of the date of the deficiency letter.

Providing a timely and complete response to a deficiency letter will facilitate the examination staff's review of your response. In particular, please be sure to address all of the issues identified by the examiners. If the examiners have comments on your response, they will generally either provide them to you within 60 days, or contact you toward the end of that period to discuss their schedule for providing them to you. If the examiners have no further comments after receiving your response to a deficiency letter, they will send no further communication and the examination will be closed.

* * *

If you have any questions, comments, complaints, or concerns during an examination or after it is completed, please raise them with the examiners or with the examiners' supervisors in the respective regional office or headquarters office. Most questions and issues can be resolved by discussing them with members of the examination team. You may also communicate comments, complaints, or concerns through the *Examination Hotline*, (202) 551-EXAM. The *Hotline* is staffed by senior-level attorneys in the Office of Compliance Inspections and Examinations in Washington, DC, who will follow-up on any matter brought to their attention. When you speak with staff on the *Examination Hotline*, you may identify yourself or request anonymity.

Glossary

absolute risk tolerance • an individual's willingness to incur financial risk in absolute (such as dollar) terms; typically gauged by the amount of wealth one allocates to risky assets

accurate empathy • a bonding that occurs when the financial advisor's sense of the client's world fits the client's self-image; it gives clients the sense that the advisor is in touch with them

active listening • the act of putting together a speaker's words and nonverbal behaviors to get the essence of the communication being sent. With active listening, one becomes involved in the inner world of another person while, at the same time, maintaining one's own identity and responding meaningfully to the person's messages.

advising • one form of structured communication. It is defined as an expert (advisor) giving specific guidance or suggestions to a client who in turn may use this knowledge to help reach a decision.

alimony or separate maintenance payments • an allowance for support made under court order to a divorced person by the former spouse. When separated the payments are called alimony; when divorced they are called maintenance payments.

altruism • an unselfish regard for the welfare of others

amortization schedule • a tool used in connection with installment loans. It shows how much of a debt service payment is used to pay interest and how much is being applied to reduce the principal of a loan.

annual percentage rate (APR) • the periodic interest rate multiplied by the number of periods in a year. For example, a daily rate is multiplied by 365, a monthly rate by 12, a quarterly rate by 4, and so on.

annuity • a finite stream of equal payments made at the end of each of a number of consecutive periods

annuity due • a series of equal payments made at the beginning of each of a number of consecutive periods

asset allocation • how the portfolio is divided between different types of investments. For example, it may be divided between stocks, bonds, money market securities, and cash.

assets under management • defined in Section 203(A) of the Investment Advisers Act of 1940 as the securities portfolios with respect to which an investment adviser provides continuous and regular supervisory or management services

attorney-in-fact • a person who holds power of attorney and is legally empowered to transact business and execute documents on behalf of another person

availability bias • a bias that alters the perception of risk. Events that are easy to imagine or recall (such as those that receive heavy media coverage) tend to be judged as more probable than they actually are; events that are dull or abstract are judged as less probable than they actually are.

baby-boom generation • the generation of people born between 1946 and 1964

back ratio • the percentage of gross monthly income allocated to housing expenses plus consumer debt payments. Mortgage lenders typically have an underwriting standard of 36 percent, but they may be more willing to be flexible on the back ratio than they would be on the front ratio.

back-end ratio • *See* back ratio.

balance sheet • a financial report that shows the status of an individual's assets, liabilities, and net worth on a given date. The balance sheet is a listing of the items that make up the two sides of the basic accounting equation, which states that assets equal (or balance) liabilities plus net worth. Also called the financial position statement. *See* financial position statement.

Bank for International Settlements (BIS) • an international organization that fosters international monetary and financial cooperation and serves as a bank for central banks.

Bank Holding Company Act of 1956 • requires Federal Reserve Board approval for the establishment of a bank holding company. It also prohibited bank holding companies headquartered in one state from acquiring a bank in another state.

Banking Act of 1933 (Glass-Steagall Act) • created the Federal Deposit Insurance Corporation (FDIC) as a temporary agency to insure deposits and limited the ability of banks to underwrite securities to those issued by governmental bodies. It permitted statewide branching for national banks if allowed by governing state law.

bounded rationality • the manner in which human beings behave because of the limits on their rationality. People's choices in financial matters are shaped not only by knowledge and rational thinking but also by values and emotions.

brochure rule (SEC Rule 204-3) • an SEC rule requiring all registered investment advisers to deliver a written disclosure statement to each existing and prospective client

budgeting • the process of creating and following an explicit plan for spending and investing the resources available to the client, which works via the establishment of a working budget model followed by a comparison of actual and expected results. It provides a means of financial self-evaluation and a guideline to measure actual performance.

business standard • a test set forth by SEC Release No. IA-770 to determine if the Investment Advisers Act of 1940 applies to a financial services professional; it concerns whether or not the practitioner is presented to the public as being "in the business" of providing advice about securities

cash flow analysis • the process of gathering cash flow information, presenting the data in an organized format (the cash flow statement), and identifying strengths, weaknesses, and important patterns. Also called income and expense analysis.

cash flow management • the budget planning and control process. It consists of three components—cash flow analysis, cash flow planning, and budgeting.

cash flow planning • identifying courses of action that help optimize net cash flow. Net cash flow is the difference between income and expenses. A positive net cash flow is available for any use whether for consumption, investment, or gifting, although the primary benefit of net cash flow for most financial planning situations is to provide a source of investable funds.

cash flow statement • a statement that summarizes a client's financial activities over a specified period of time by comparing cash inflows and cash outflows, and indicating whether the net cash flow for the period is positive or negative. The cash flow statement contains three basic classifications—income, expenses, and net cash flow—that are related in an equation, which states that income minus expenses equals net cash flow. *See also* income statement.

CFP Board designees • denotes current certificants, candidates for certification, and individuals who have any entitlement, direct or indirect, to the CFP certification marks

choice shift • a phenomenon seen when studying the difference between individual and group reactions to risk. A group decision is usually more extreme than a decision favored by most members of the group when they are polled individually, before group discussion. The shift is typically toward more risky action, although it may sometimes be toward a more cautious one.

clarifying response • a type of understanding response associated with active listening that enhances communication. There are two forms of clarifying response. In the first, the listener attempts to restate or clarify what the speaker has had difficulty in expressing clearly. In the second, the listener asks the speaker to clarify what he or she means.

client • in determining whether an investment adviser must register with the SEC or the state, a client is any natural person, and (1) any minor child of the natural person, (2) any relative, spouse, or relative of the spouse of the natural person who has the same principal residence, (3) all accounts of which the natural person and/or the persons referred to above are the only primary beneficiaries, and (4) all trusts of which the natural person and/or the persons referred to above are the only primary beneficiaries

client-focused selling • a sales philosophy that rejects high pressure, hard sell methods and instead emphasizes finding solutions that help clients achieve their financial goals

closed-ended question • a type of question that solicits singular facts or a yes or no response

compensation test • a test set forth by SEC Release No. IA-770 to determine if the Investment Advisers Act of 1940 applies to a financial advisor. A practitioner who charges a fee for investment advice or receives a commission on the sale of a securities product meets this test; in fact, it is almost impossible for a financial advisor not to meet this test in today's environment.

Competitive Equality Banking Act of 1987 • established new standards for expedited funds availability and recapitalized the Federal Savings & Loan Insurance Company (FSLIC). It expanded FDIC authority for open bank assistance transactions including bridge banks.

complex annuity • an annuity in which the frequency of payments and the frequency of compounding or discounting are different. For example, a series of 12 monthly deposits that are credited with interest daily is a complex annuity.

complex annuity due • an annuity due in which the frequency of payments and the frequency of compounding or discounting are different. For example, a series of eight quarterly deposits that are credited with interest monthly is a complex annuity due.

compound interest • interest computed by applying the interest rate to the sum of the original principal and the interest credited to it in earlier time periods

compounding • the process by which money today (present value) grows over time to a larger amount (future value)

comprehensive approach • the approach to financial planning that occurs when an advisor uses the financial planning process to develop a comprehensive financial plan that solves a client's financial problems. The plan considers all aspects of a client's financial position, which typically includes financial problems from all the major planning areas. In addition, the plan usually encompasses several integrated and coordinated planning strategies that can be used to help solve the client's problems and achieve his or her goals.

conservator • an individual appointed by the court to manage the property of someone declared incompetent (may be used interchangeably with the term *guardian*)

Consumer Credit Reporting Reform Act • strengthened the provisions of the Fair Credit Reporting Act

Consumer Leasing Act • designed to protect individuals in consumer-leasing transactions by requiring clear disclosure of key terms of the leasing arrangement and all costs

consumer price index (CPI) • the index that measures the change in consumer prices as determined by a monthly survey of the U.S. Bureau of Labor Statistics. It measures change in consumer purchasing power due to price inflation (deflation). It is also referred to as the cost-of-living index.

continuing response • a type of understanding response associated with active listening. It is a relatively unobtrusive response that encourages a speaker to continue talking. Examples include "uh-huh," "mmmm," "then?," "and . . . ?". They communicate to the speaker: "Go on, I'm with you."

continuous compounding • the process of compounding interest an infinite number of times per year rather than at discrete time intervals. It represents the upper limit of the total interest credited to a sum for a particular stated or nominal annual interest rate.

conversion of interest earnings into principal • occurs when interest is credited to a sum and begins to earn interest on itself

cost of attendance (COA) • a specific amount for each individual college that includes tuition and fees, on-campus room and board, and allowances for books, supplies, transportation, loan fees, and certain other costs

counseling • one form of structured communication. It provides assistance to clients as they explore their present situations, begin to understand where they are in relation to where they want to be, and act to get from where they are to where they want to be. It evolves over a period of time, and an interpersonal relationship often develops between the counselor (advisor) and client.

Credit Repair Organizations Act • prohibits a variety of false and misleading statements as well as fraud by credit repair organizations (CROs)

debt burden ratio • also known as the front ratio or front-end ratio. It compares a client's total monthly consumer credit payments (excluding mortgage payments) with the amount of his or her monthly take-home pay.

debt service problem • a type of financial problem that involves calculation of the periodic level payment required to pay off a loan at a specific interest rate in a specific period of time

debt service ratio • calculated by dividing total annual loan payments (that is, mortgage and consumer debt payments) by gross income. The ratio (which also can be calculated on a monthly basis) indicates the percentage of the client's income required to cover existing loan payments. *See also* back ratio.

deferred annuity • a series of consecutive, equal, periodic payments that will begin more than one period from the present

denial of risk • the tendency of some individuals to engage in risky behaviors on a voluntary basis, seemingly failing to appreciate the true level of danger in the situation. They may know the statistical odds but refuse to believe that these odds apply to them personally.

Depository Institution Act of 1982 (Garn-St. Germain) • expanded FDIC powers to assist troubled banks. It established the Net Worth Certificate program and expanded the powers of thrift institutions.

Depository Institutions Deregulation and Monetary Control Act of 1980 • established "NOW Accounts" and began the phaseout of interest rate ceilings on deposits. It established the Depository Institutions Deregulation Committee, granted new powers to thrift institutions, and raised the deposit insurance ceiling to $100,000.

directive interview • a type of structured communication in which the interviewer (advisor) directs and controls the pace and content to be covered; it is a formalized, structured form of interaction. Its advantages are that it can be brief and that it provides measurable data; its disadvantages are that it is often inflexible and does not allow the interviewee (client) to choose topics for discussion.

discounting • the process by which money due in the future (future value) is reduced over time to a smaller amount today (present value)

disintermediation • when depositors stop using financial intermediaries like banks and thrifts and invest on their own to capture higher yields

effective annual interest rate (EAR) • the annual interest rate that produces in one compounding the same amount of interest as does the nominal annual rate with its compounding frequency

either/or question • a relatively ineffective type of question in which the client's answer is limited to only two options

Electronic Fund Transfer Act • places limits on the extent to which a consumer can be held liable for the unauthorized use of an ATM or debit card

eligible child • a person either under the age of 18 or older if physically or mentally incapable of self-care

Employee Retirement Income Security Act of 1974 (ERISA) • a federal law that sets minimum standards for pension plans in private industry. ERISA also established the Pension Benefit Guaranty Corporation.

Equal Credit Opportunity Act • states that an individual cannot be denied credit based on his or her race, sex, marital status, religion, age, national origin, or receipt of public assistance. In addition, in applying for credit, individuals have the right to have reliable public assistance payments considered in the same manner as other income. Finally, if credit is denied, the applicant has a legal right to know why.

expected family contribution (EFC) • the total amount that a student and student's family are expected to contribute annually for college education before becoming eligible for financial aid. The amount is calculated by adding together the expected student contribution (ESC) and the expected parent contribution (EPC).

expected parent contribution (EPC) • the total amount that a student's parents are expected to contribute annually for college education before becoming eligible for financial aid

expected student contribution (ESC) • the total amount that a student is expected to contribute annually for college education before becoming eligible for financial aid

explanatory response • a type of leading response in which the advisor explains something to the client in a simple, concise, and comprehensible way

fact-finder form • a form that needs to be completed by a financial advisor engaged in financial planning for a client. It typically includes both quantitative and qualitative information that the advisor needs in order to develop a financial plan for the client.

FAFSA (Free Application for Federal Student Aid) • the application used to qualify college students for financial aid

Fair and Accurate Credit Transaction Act • allows consumers to get one free copy of their credit report annually from each consumer-reporting agency

Fair Credit and Charge Card Disclosure Act • requires creditors to include certain information in preapproved credit offers and credit card statements

Fair Credit Billing Act • establishes acceptable procedures when disputes arise in connection with billing errors on open-end (revolving) credit accounts

Fair Credit Reporting Act • helps to ensure that consumer-reporting agencies (credit bureaus) furnish correct and complete information to lenders and other businesses to use when evaluating an individual's credit application

Fair Debt Collection Practices Act • requires that debt collectors treat debtors fairly and prohibits certain methods of debt collection

familiarity bias • an inclination or prejudice that alters people's perception of risk. Risks that are familiar are feared less than those that are unfamiliar; this helps explain why people overreact to unexpected news.

Federal Deposit Insurance Corporation Improvement Act of 1991 • greatly increased the power and authority of the FDIC. Its major provisions recapitalized the Bank Insurance Fund and allowed the FDIC to strengthen the fund by borrowing from the Treasury.

Federal Loan Consolidation Programs • available under both the Direct and FFEL loan programs. A borrower's (student or parent) college loans are repaid and a new consolidation loan is created. Stafford loans, PLUS loans, and Federal Perkins Loans, as well as certain Health and Human Services/Health Professionals Loans, are eligible for consolidation. While loans can be consolidated after the student has left school under both the Direct and FFEL programs, the Direct program also permits students to consolidate their loans while still in school.

Federal Pell grant • a federal grant for undergraduate students who qualify under the needs-analysis formula; available in amounts of up to $4,050 per year (2004–2005)

Federal Perkins loans • loans of up to $4,000 per year ($20,000 cumulative) for students who show exceptional need. The program is administered by colleges but uses federal funds; interest is only 5 percent, and payments can be spread over 10 years after the student leaves school.

Federal Supplemental Education Opportunity Grant (FSEOG) • a federal grant available in amounts of up to $4,000 per year for college students who show exceptional need

fiduciary • a person who holds another's trust or confidence. A financial advisor engaged in financial planning is a fiduciary who owes the client an affirmative duty of utmost good faith and full and fair disclosure of all the material facts.

financial assets • assets that consist of cash and cash equivalents (or liquid assets) and other financial (or investment) assets. Cash and cash equivalents are liquid in the sense that they are either already cash or can be converted into cash relatively quickly with little or no loss in value. Other financial assets represent a variety of assets with wide-ranging degrees of risk in which clients may invest in an effort to earn a return. *See also* nonfinancial assets.

Financial Institutions Reform, Recovery, and Enforcement Act of 1989 (FIRREA) • abolished the Federal Savings & Loan Insurance Corporation (FSLIC), and gave the FDIC the responsibility of insuring the deposits of thrift institutions in its place. FIRREA also abolished the Federal Home Loan Bank Board. Finally, FIRREA created the Resolution Trust Corporation (RTC) as a temporary agency of the government.

financial life cycle • the five distinct phases in an individual's financial life or career. The five phases are (1) early career, (2) career development, (3) peak accumulation, (4) preretirement, and (5) retirement. Together the five phases span a person's entire financial life. Starting at a relatively young age, a career-minded person typically will pass through four phases en route to phase 5 and his or her retirement.

financial plan • a plan designed to carry a client from his or her present financial position to the attainment of financial goals. Since no two clients are alike, the plan must be designed for the individual, with all the advisor's recommended strategies tailored to each particular client's needs, abilities, and financial goals.

financial planning • a process that focuses on ascertaining a client's financial goals and then developing a plan to help the client achieve those goals

financial planning process • a six-step process that financial advisors must follow when they are engaged in financial planning. The steps are (1) establish and define the advisor-client relationship, (2) determine goals and gather data, (3) analyze and evaluate the data, (4) develop and present a plan, (5) implement the plan, and (6) monitor the plan.

financial planning pyramid • a widely accepted approach for developing a comprehensive financial plan over time. It prioritizes financial goals by categorizing them into three levels. Level 1 goals provide protection against uncertainties, level 2 goals focus on growing investments, and level 3 goals address retirement and estate concerns.

financial position statement • an organized list of the components of an individual's or family's wealth at a specified time. It reflects the results of past financial activities and covers three basic classifications: assets, liabilities, and net worth. *See also* balance sheet.

financial risk tolerance • a client's psychological attitude toward his or her willingness to expose financial assets to the possibility of loss for the chance to achieve greater financial gain. It is measured along a continuum with indivuduals who are very risk tolerant at one end and those who are very risk averse at the other.

Fisher effect • describes the dilutive effect of inflation on nominal interest rates to arrive at a real rate of return

Form ADV • the SEC form that a financial advisor must complete and file to become a registered investment adviser

framing • the way in which a question is structured with regard to the issue being evaluated. For example, the same objective facts can be described either in terms of the probability of gaining or the probability of losing.

front ratio • the percentage of gross monthly income allocated to housing expenses, specifically PITI—principal, interest, taxes, and insurance. Mortgage lenders typically have an underwriting standard of 28 percent or less for the front ratio.

front-end ratio • *See* front ratio.

future value of an annuity (FVA) • the amount to which an annuity would accumulate by the end of its term if the payments earned a specific rate of return during the entire time period

future value of an annuity due (FVAD) • the amount to which an annuity due would accumulate by the end of its term if the payments earned a specific rate of return during the entire time period

future value of a single sum (FVSS) • an amount determined by compounding a present value at a particular interest rate for a particular length of time

FVA factor • used in determining the future value of an annuity. The FVA factor is $\left[\dfrac{(1+i)^n - 1}{i} \right]$, where i is the periodic interest rate expressed as a decimal and n is the number of time periods. *See also* appendix F, table F.3.

FVA formula • a formula, FVA = periodic payment x $\left[\dfrac{(1+i)^n - 1}{i} \right]$, where FVA is the future value of an annuity, periodic payment is the amount of each payment, i is the periodic interest rate expressed as a decimal, and n is the number of periods over which the annuity is paid

FVAD formula • a formula, FVAD = periodic payment x $\left[\dfrac{(1+i)^n - 1}{i} \right]$ x $(1 + i)$, where FVAD is the future value of an annuity due, periodic payment is the amount of each payment, i is the periodic interest rate expressed as a decimal, and n is the number of periods over which the annuity due is paid

FVSS factor • used in determining the future value of a single sum. The FVSS factor is $(1 + i)^n$, where i is the periodic interest rate expressed as a decimal and n is the number of periods during which compounding occurs. *See also* appendix F, table F.1.

FVSS formula • a basic formula, FVSS = PVSS x $(1 + i)^n$, where FVSS is the future value of a single sum, PVSS is the present value of a single sum, i is the periodic interest rate expressed as a decimal, and n is the number of periods during which compounding occurs

genuineness • a quality necessary to be an effective advisor. Financial advisors who are genuine are aware of themselves and their feelings, thoughts, values, and attitudes; always express themselves openly and honestly; do not play roles; communicate expressively without concealing anything; and are consistent (do not think or feel one thing but say another).

Gramm-Leach-Bliley Act of 1999 • repeals the last vestiges of the Glass-Steagall Act of 1933. It modifies portions of the Bank Holding Company Act to allow affiliations between banks and insurance underwriters. While preserving the authority of states to regulate insurance, the act prohibits state actions that have the effect of preventing bank-affiliated firms from selling insurance on an equal basis with other insurance agents.

grouped cash flows • a cash flow sequence that has some consecutive payments of the same amount and arithmetic sign (positive or negative)

guardian • an individual whom the court has appointed to handle the personal care of someone declared incompetent (may be used interchangeably with the term *conservator*)

Home Ownership and Equity Protection Act (HOEPA) • amended the Truth-in-Lending Act and established requirements for certain mortgage loans with high rates and/or high fees. A number of features were banned from high-rate, high-fee loans including nearly all balloon payments, negative amortization, default interest rates higher than predefault interest rates, and most prepayment penalties.

Hope Scholarship Tax Credit • an education tax credit of up to $1,500 per student per year for tuition and related expenses incurred during the first 2 years of post-secondary education; the credit equals 100 percent of the first $1,000 of tuition and fees, and 50 percent of the next $1,000 of tuition and fees. The credit may be reduced based on modified adjusted gross income.

Indentity Theft and Assumption Deterrence Act • made the theft of identity information a crime and established restitution provisions for individual victims

illusion of control bias • an inclination or prejudice that alters people's perception of risk. People tend to underestimate the risk involved in events under their control, such as driving a car, relative to activities in which control is given to someone else, such as flying as a passenger in a plane.

income statement • summary of the various income and expense items of an individual or company during an accounting period, which is typically one year. *See also* cash flow statement.

insider trading • the buying or selling of a security, in breach of a fiduciary duty or other relationship of trust and confidence, while in possession of material, nonpublic information about the security. Insider trading violations can also include tipping such information, securities trading by the person tipped, and securities trading by those who misappropriate such information.

Insider Trading Sanction Act of 1984 • a law that, among other things, gives the SEC the authority to seek the imposition of civil penalties against insider-trading violations for as much as three times the profit gained (or loss avoided) as a result of the unlawful purchase or sale of securities

Insider Trading and Securities Fraud Enforcement Act of 1988 • a legal mandate that says investment advisers must have written policies and procedures that reduce the likelihood of insider trading and securities fraud. The SEC was authorized to award bounty to informants with the bounty coming from money paid as penalties under the act.

interest • the cost of using money. It quantifies the opportunity cost incurred by waiting to receive money or by giving up the opportunity to delay payment.

internal rate of return (IRR) • the interest rate that equates the present value of the stream of cash inflows to the present value of the stream of cash outflows

International Money Laundering Abatement and Financial Anti-Terrorism Act of 2001• designed to prevent terrorists and others from anonymously using the U.S. financial system to move funds obtained from or destined for illegal activity

interpretive response • a type of leading response in which the advisor cuts to the heart of the matter, "translating" what the client has said

interviewing • one form of structured communication. It can be defined as a process of communication, most often between two people, with a predetermined and specific purpose, usually involving the asking and answering of questions designed to gather meaningful information.

investment adviser representative • defined in the SEC's Rule 203-3(a) as a supervised person of an investment adviser if clients who are natural persons represent more than 10 percent of the clients of the supervised person. In 1998, SEC Release No. IA-1733 changed this, specifying that a supervised person can have the greater of five natural-person clients or the number of natural-person clients permitted under the 10 percent allowance without being subject to state qualification requirements.

Investment Advisers Act of 1940 • the statutory body of law that controls the regulation of investment advisers. With certain exceptions, it requires that firms or sole practitioners compensated for advising others about securities investments register with the SEC and conform to regulations designed to protect investors. Since the act was amended in 1996, generally only advisers who have at least $25 million of assets under management or who advise a registered investment company must register with the SEC.

Investment Advisers Supervision Coordination Act of 1996 • a law that primarily concerns the regulation of investment advisers by the SEC or state authorities based on the level of assets under an adviser's management; as a result, investment advisers need to register with either the SEC or state authorities, but not both

Investment Company Act of 1940 • regulates the organization of companies including mutual funds that engage primarily in investing, reinvesting, and trading in securities, and whose own securities are offered to the investing public. The focus of the act is on disclosure to the investing public of information about the fund and its investment objectives, as well as on investment company structure and operations.

leading question • a question that steers the client toward a conclusion that the advisor, not the client, has already formulated. These types of questions are considered ineffective, dishonest, and manipulative.

leading response • a type of response in which the financial advisor takes the lead (to a certain extent) and deviates somewhat from the client's preceding responses

life-cycle financial planning • a financial planning process that is ongoing and occurs throughout a client's financial life. The advisor who monitors this type of planning is practicing life-cycle financial planning.

Lifetime Learning Tax Credit • an education tax credit of up to $2,000 calculated as 20 percent of the first $10,000 of tuition and related expenses paid for all eligible students. The credit may be reduced based on modified adjusted gross income.

liquidity • the ability to quickly convert an asset to cash with little or no uncertainty as to value

loan-to-value (LTV) • the ratio of debt to the lower of appraised value or market price. A lender sets maximum loan-to-value limits and establishes other loan underwriting standards as part of its decision to extend credit. First mortgages typically require private mortgage insurance if the loan-to-value is greater than 80 percent.

loss aversion • the characteristic of seeking to limit the size of the potential loss rather than seeking to minimize the variability of the potential returns

marketability • the ease of (buying or) selling an asset for its market value

May Day 1975 • the day the stock market officially moved away from a fixed commission structure for broker commissions

McCarran-Ferguson Act of 1945 • stated that regulation of insurance would remain with the states provided the states actually regulated the insurance companies operating in their state

monetary policy • the process of controlling the amount of money in the economy by controlling the amount of reserves in the banking system. The Federal Reserve Board controls this process though open market operations where it adds or subtracts reserves from the system and by establishing a targeted Federal Funds Rate and Discount Rate. The FED also establishes reserve requirements for depository institutions and margin rates for brokerage accounts.

multiple-purpose approach • the approach to financial planning that occurs when an advisor follows the financial planning process to develop a plan that solves two or more financial problems for a client. The plan may focus on solving several problems from one of the major planning areas, or it may focus on problems from two or three major planning areas.

national de minimis standard • a part of the Investment Advisers Supervision Coordination Act that relieves some investment advisers from some regulatory burden; investment advisers may not be required to register in any state unless the adviser has a place of business in the state or, during the preceding 12-month period, has had more than five clients who are residents of the state

National Securities Market Improvement Act of 1996 • delineated the requirements for the SEC and state registration of investment advisers based primarily on the level of assets under management. It also established a national de minimis standard for state registration of investment advisers.

net cash flow • the difference between income and expenses. A positive net cash flow is available for any use, whether for consumption, investment, or gifting. However, in most financial planning situations, the primary benefit of a positive net cash flow is to provide a source of investable funds.

net present value (NPV) • the present value of a stream of cash inflows minus the present value of a stream of cash outflows, with both present values calculated on the basis of an appropriate rate of interest

nominal rate of return • the stated rate of interest not adjusted for compounding

nondirective interview • a type of structured communication that allows both the interviewer (advisor) and interviewee (client) to discuss a wider range of subject matters; the interviewee (client) usually controls the pacing and purpose of the interview. Its advantages are that there is greater flexibility and more in-depth responses than with a directive interview, and a closer relationship between the interviewer (advisor) and interviewee (client) is established. Its disadvantages are that it consumes more time than a directive interview, and it often provides data that are difficult to measure objectively.

nonfinancial (personal) assets • assets bought primarily for the creature comforts they provide. They include such things as the client's primary residence, his or her vehicles, and other tangible (personal) assets like clothes, household furnishings, antiques, and hobby equipment. Nonfinancial assets also include the client's net equity in nonresidential real estate and in privately held businesses.

nonverbal behaviors • nonlinguistic actions that make up a large part of communication. From the two main sources of nonverbal behaviors, the body and the voice, come seven important types of nonverbal signs of meaning: body position, body movement, gestures, facial expressions, eye contact, voice tone, and voice pitch.

norms • standards of measurement, such as average, that allow comparison of an individual to a representative group. For instance, using a normed measure of risk tolerance, it is possible to see whether the client is more or less risk tolerant than people in general or to compare the client to other people of the same age and sex.

Office of Compliance Inspections and Examinations (OCIE) • the part of the SEC that administers the Compliance Examination Program through its field offices

open access • the lack of barriers to entry or use

open-ended question • a type of question that encourages expansive responses especially when soliciting opinions, thoughts, ideas, values, and feelings

opportunity cost • the implied cost of undertaking a financial action. It is usually represented as the rate that could have been earned by investing in the best alternative activity with the same resources.

Parent Loans for Undergraduate Students (PLUS loans) • a loan available through the Direct Loan Program and the Family Federal Education Loan Program. This type of loan is not based on need, but the borrower cannot have a bad credit record; it must be repaid within 10 years.

perceived risk • an interpretation of the riskiness of a situation, which is not necessarily the same as the objective riskiness. A person's experiences and inclinations toward risk taking as well as the circumstances of a particular situation affect the interpretation of riskiness.

performance (incentive) fees • fees charged by an investment adviser based on capital appreciation of all or any portion of a client's funds; it is permitted only in certain situations. Also called an incentive fee.

perpetuity • an infinite stream of equal periodic payments

physical attending • using one's body to communicate. The five basic attributes associated with physical attending are to (1) face the other person squarely, (2) adopt an open posture, (3) lean toward the other person, (4) maintain good eye contact, and (5) be relaxed while attending.

prepaid tuition plan • a type of Section 529 plan that allows tuition costs to be locked in years before enrollment

present value of an annuity (PVA) • the present value of a series of equal periodic payments made at the end of each period and discounted at an appropriate rate

present value of an annuity due (PVAD) • the present value of a series of equal periodic payments made at the beginning of each period and discounted at an appropriate rate

present value of a single sum (PVSS) • an amount determined by discounting a future value at a particular interest rate for a particular length of time

prime interest rate • the short-term interest rate banks charge their most creditworthy commercial customers. It is a key interest rate because loans to less creditworthy customers are often tied to the prime rate.

pro forma • projected. Pro forma financial statements represent the advisor's best estimate of how the statements will look at a future point in time.

professional • a person engaged in a field that requires specialized knowledge not generally understood by the public, a threshold entrance requirement, a sense of altruism, and a code of ethics

PVA factor • used in determining the present value of an annuity. The PVA

factor is $\left[\dfrac{1 - \dfrac{1}{(1 + i)^n}}{i} \right]$, where i is the periodic interest rate expressed as a

decimal and n is the number of time periods. *See also* appendix F, table F.4.

PVA formula • a formula, PVA = periodic payment x $\left[\dfrac{1 - \dfrac{1}{(1 + i)^n}}{i} \right]$, where

PVA is the present value of an annuity, periodic payment is the amount of each payment, i is the periodic interest rate expressed as a decimal, and n is the number of periods over which the annuity is paid

PVAD formula • a formula, PVAD = periodic payment

x $\left[\dfrac{1 - \dfrac{1}{(1 + i)^n}}{i} \right]$ x $(1 + i)$, where PVAD is the present value of an annuity due,

periodic payment is the amount of each payment, i is the periodic interest rate expressed as a decimal, and n is the number of periods over which the annuity due is paid

PVSS factor • used in determining the present value of a single sum. The PVSS factor is $1/(1 + i)^n$, where i is the periodic interest rate expressed as a decimal and n is the number of periods over which discounting occurs. *See also* appendix F, table F.2.

PVSS formula • a basic formula, PVSS = FVSS x $\left[\dfrac{1}{(1 + i)^n} \right]$, where PVSS is

the present value of a single sum, FVSS is the future value of a single sum, i is the periodic interest rate expressed as a decimal, and n is the number of periods during which discounting occurs

qualified tuition program (QTP) • *See* Section 529 plan.

question bombardment • a faulty questioning technique in which the advisor asks two or more questions without giving the client a chance to respond

rapport • a relationship marked by harmony or accord. Rapport between a financial advisor and client can be aided by the advisor's friendly, interested concern; an unhurried, leisurely pace; an accepting, nonjudgmental attitude; attentive, active listening; and an egalitarian relationship.

reassuring response • a type of leading response that is intended to reassure or encourage the client. Although reassuring responses can make the client feel better and enhance rapport with the advisor, they do not address the underlying situation.

reflection-of-feeling response • a type of understanding response associated with active listening. It enhances communication and shows an understanding of the speaker's experience by responding to the speaker's feelings. By paraphrasing the speaker's feelings, the listener enables the speaker to get in closer touch with those feelings. This, in turn, facilitates the working through of the speaker's problem.

registered investment adviser (RIA) • an investment adviser who has registered with either the SEC or the appropriate state agency as an investment adviser

relative risk tolerance • an individual's relative willingness to incur financial risk, typically measured by the proportion of one's wealth allocated to risky assets

resistance • in an advisor-client relationship, behavior by the client being counseled that impedes the counseling process. It is often expressed as overt or covert hostility toward the advisor.

restatement-of-content response • a type of understanding response associated with active listening. The listener (the advisor) enhances communication by paraphrasing what the speaker (the client) has just said. It encourages the speaker to delve more deeply into the situation because he or she feels the listener is "on the same wavelength."

Riegle-Neal Interstate Banking and Branching Efficiency Act of 1994 • permits adequately capitalized and managed bank holding companies to acquire banks in any state one year after enactment. It specifies limits and requires evaluations by the Federal Reserve before acquisitions can be approved.

risk • the variability of outcomes in situations in which (1) the various consequences of each alternative are known, and (2) their exact probabilities can be specified

risk averters (risk rejecters) • individuals who are relatively unwilling to incur financial risk

risk-free rate • the rate of return that can be achieved by investing in an alternative that has no risk. The usual surrogate for the risk-free rate is the short-term Treasury bill rate, although even Treasury bills are subject to inflation risk.

risk indifferent • a willingness to make an investment based on its expected return without regard to its risk

risk premium • the increment of return required above the risk-free rate that an investor demands to reward him or her for accepting risk. The amount of the risk premium is directly related to the amount of risk undertaken and is typically added to the short-term Treasury bill rate to calculate the required rate of return for the investment.

Risk/Return Investment Pyramid • used to graphically show the trade-off of risk against return. Investment media are arranged in a pyramid with the most conservative, least risky, and generally lowest-yielding media forming the broad base of the pyramid. The investment media become progressively riskier as they approach the apex where commodities are located. Toward the apex there is typically a corresponding and commensurate potential for higher return.

risk seekers (risk-tolerant individuals) • individuals who are willing to incur a high degree of financial risk

Roth IRA • a type of individual retirement account in which after-tax contributions are required, but earnings and distributions after age 59½ are not taxed. Roth IRAs also have other characteristics that make them more beneficial than traditional IRAs for many people.

Rule of 72 • a quick method of estimating how long it will take for an amount to double in value at various compound interest rates. In this method, the number 72 is divided by the applicable interest rate expressed as a whole number. The quotient is the approximate number of periods until the amount doubles.

safety of principal • often a goal for conservative investors, it speaks to the probability of loss in an investment and as such is an assessment of risk

sandwiched generation • another name for the baby-boom generation. Many of its members are faced with financing their children's education and aiding their parents while trying to save for their own retirement.

Sarbanes-Oxley Act of 2002 • mandated a number of reforms to enhance corporate responsibility and financial disclosures and also combat corporate and accounting fraud; created the Public Company Accounting Oversight Board (PCAOB)

SEC Release No. IA-770 • a 1981 pronouncement from the Securities and Exchange Commission that sets forth three separate tests (advice or analyses about securities, business standard, and compensation test) to determine whether the Investment Advisers Act of 1940 applies to a financial advisor's activities

SEC Release No. IA-1092 • a 1987 pronouncement from the Securities and Exchange Commission that reaffirmed the three-prong approach set forth in IA-770 and clarified certain antifraud and full disclosure provisions of the Investment Advisers Act of 1940

SEC Release No. IA-1633 • a pronouncement from the Securities and Exchange Commission that specifies final rules relating to the Investment Adviser Supervision and Coordination Act of 1997. It specifies how to determine an investment adviser's assets under management, which is the determining factor in whether the adviser must register with the SEC or the state.

SEC Release No. IA-2091 • a ruling from the SEC that allows investment advisers operating principally on the Internet, with no connection to a particular state for operations, to be SEC registered rather than state registered

SEC Release No. IA-2204 • a ruling from the SEC requiring registered investment advisers to name a compliance officer, write and implement compliance procedures, and review compliance annually. In the case of an investment company, the chief compliance officer will report directly to the fund's board.

SEC Release No. IA-2256 • a ruling from the SEC that requires registered investment advisers to adopt and follow a code of ethics. The codes of ethics must set forth standards of conduct expected of advisory personnel and address conflicts that arise from personal trading by advisory personnel. Among other things, the rule requires advisers' supervised persons to report their personal securities transactions, including transactions in any mutual fund managed by the adviser.

Section 529 plans • a tax-advantaged approach to funding higher education expenses; also called a qualified tuition program (QTP). Types of plans include prepaid tuition programs and savings plans.

Section 529 savings plan • a tax-advantaged approach to funding higher education expenses; investment returns are tax advantaged when used for qualified education expenses but there is no guarantee that the returns will keep pace with college cost increases

secured debt • a loan that has an asset as collateral. The lender has a security interest in the asset and that security interest provides a method of recouping all or part of the outstanding loan balance if the borrower defaults on the loan agreement.

Securities Act of 1933 • referred to as the "truth-in-securities" law. Its two basic objectives are to require that investors receive financial and other significant information concerning securities being offered for public sale and to prohibit deceit, misrepresentations, and other fraud in the sale of securities.

Securities Exchange Act of 1934 • created the Securities and Exchange Commission. The act empowers the SEC with broad authority over all aspects of the securities industry. This authority includes the power to register, regulate, and oversee securities firms, transfer agents, and clearing agencies as well as self-regulatory organizations (SROs).

security • as used in interpreting the Investment Advisers Act of 1940, one of many financial instruments including stocks, bonds, certificates of deposit, commercial paper, limited partnerships, variable annuity products, investment contracts, and numerous others

self-awareness • in an advisor-client relationship, the advisor's relative under-standing of his or her own value systems. This gives the advisor a better chance of avoiding the imposition of his or her values onto clients.

self-funded medical reimbursement plan • an employer-funded medical plan in which employers either pay the providers of medical care directly or reimburse employees for their medical expenses

self-regulatory organization (SRO) • a national securities exchange, registered securities association, or registered clearing agency that is authorized by the Securities Exchange Act of 1934 to regulate the conduct and activities of its members, subject to oversight by a specific government regulatory agency. For example, the National Association of Securities Dealers (NASD) and the New York Stock Exchange (NYSE) are SROs with SEC oversight.

separate maintenance payments • *See* alimony.

simple annuity • an annuity in which the frequency of payments and the frequency of compounding or discounting are identical

simple annuity due • an annuity due in which the frequency of payments and the frequency of compounding or discounting are identical

simple interest • interest computed by applying the interest rate to only the original principal sum

single-purpose approach • the approach to financial planning that occurs when an advisor follows the financial planning process to develop a plan that solves a single financial problem for a client. The plan may be as simple as selling a single financial product or service to the client in order to solve the problem.

sinking fund • a fund where a target amount is achieved by contributing a series of equal payments. In a sinking fund problem, the target amount, the number of payments, and the compound interest rate are known while the size of the payments must be determined.

social styles • predictable patterns of behavior that people display and that can be observed. The American population is evenly divided among four social styles: driver, expressive, amiable, and analytical. Appropriate responses to the characteristics of each social style indicate how an advisor can best establish rapport with a client who has that style.

special-needs trust • property management devices used to protect assets of individuals who anticipate long-term disability situations in the future

special school • an institution that offers education and/or training directed toward helping a student compensate for or overcome a handicap in anticipation of attending a regular school or developing a routine lifestyle

Stafford loan • this type of loan is the major source of education borrowing from the federal government; such loans are available directly from the federal government through the Direct Loan Program, or through Family Federal Education Loan Programs from participating banks, credit unions, and other lenders. This type of loan may be subsidized (for students with financial need) or unsubsidized (available even to those with no need under the aid formula), and must be repaid within 10 years.

Standard & Poor's 500 Index • a broad-based measurement of changes in stock-market conditions based on the average performance of 500 widely held common stocks

standby trust • a trust that remains unfunded until such time as the grantor becomes incapacitated at which point an attorney-in-fact funds the trust with the grantor's assets for the trustee to manage

student aid report (SAR) • a report that is sent out by the Department of Education after it processes a free application for student aid (FAFSA). It provides an electronic version of the results for schools listed on the FAFSA. Schools use the SAR's Expected Family Contribution number to determine if a student will receive federal financial aid.

suggestive response • a type of leading response in which the advisor gives advice to the client in the form of a suggestion or several suggestions about which the client has the final decision

summarization response • a type of understanding response associated with active listening that enhances communication. Summaries can focus and capsulize a series of scattered ideas to present a clear perspective. Summarization permits both the speaker and listener to gauge the accuracy with which messages have been sent and received.

supervised person • defined in Section 202(a)(25) of the Investment Advisers Act of 1940 as a partner, officer, director (or other person occupying a similar status or performing similar functions), or employee of an investment adviser, or other person who provides investment advice on behalf of the investment adviser and is subject to the supervision and control of the investment adviser

thrill seeker • the personality type most likely to be consistently risk seeking in all aspects of life, including financial matters

time value of money • the concept that a specific amount of money received (paid) in a specific time period has a different value than the same amount received (paid) in a different time period

true/false question • a closed-ended question in which the client's response must indicate whether the question is true or false

Trust Indenture Act of 1939 • applies to debt securities such as bonds, debentures, and notes offered for public sale. Even though such securities may be registered under the Securities Act, they may not be offered for sale to the public unless a formal agreement between the issuer of bonds and the bondholder, known as the trust indenture, conforms to the standards of the act.

Truth-in-Lending Act • designed to protect consumers in credit transactions by requiring clear disclosure of key terms of the lending arrangement and all costs

uncertainty • a situation in which the possible outcomes and/or their associated probabilities of occurrence are unknown

unconditional positive regard • an attitude of valuing the client or being able to express appreciation of the client as a unique and worthwhile person

ungrouped cash flows • cash flow sequences that include no consecutive payments of the same amount and arithmetic sign (positive or negative)

unpacking effect • the finding that the perceived likelihood of an event is influenced by how specifically it is described. The more specific the description of the event, the more the event is judged as likely to occur.

unsecured debt • a loan that has no collateral or assets backing the loan agreement. The lender, short of available legal remedies, relies on the borrower's promise to repay the loan.

ward • an individual whom the court has determined to be incompetent or mentally disabled

why question • a question that should generally be avoided because asking "why" tends to question the client's motivation or lack of it, and thus creates a certain defensiveness. Why questions carry with them a connotation of implied disapproval, forcing the client to justify or defend his or her thoughts, ideas, or actions.

Index

THE AMERICAN COLLEGE
ALUMNI
ASSOCIATION

Your Bridge to a Lifetime of Professional Achievement

We encourage you to take advantage of knowing more about The Alumni Association. Together we can create a stronger community and explore new opportunities for professional success.

Call us at (610) 526-1200

e-mail: russell.figueira@theamericancollege.edu